The Wrongful Convictions Reader

D1319447

The Wrongful Convictions Reader

Edited by

Russell D. Covey
PROFESSOR OF LAW
GEORGIA STATE UNIVERSITY COLLEGE OF LAW

Valena E. Beety
PROFESSOR OF LAW
DIRECTOR OF THE WEST VIRGINIA INNOCENCE PROJECT
WEST VIRGINIA UNIVERSITY COLLEGE OF LAW

CAROLINA ACADEMIC PRESS
Durham, North Carolina

Copyright © 2019
Carolina Academic Press, LLC
All Rights Reserved

Library of Congress Cataloging-in-Publication Data

Names: Covey, Russell D., editor. | Beety, Valena E., editor.
Title: The Wrongful Convictions Reader / edited by Russell D. Covey and
Valena E. Beety.
Description: Durham, North Carolina : Carolina Academic Press, LLC, 2018.
Identifiers: LCCN 2018030260 | ISBN 9781531006327 (alk. paper)
Subjects: LCSH: Judicial error--United States. | Criminal justice,
Administration of--Corrupt practices--United States. | Criminal investigation--
Corrupt practices--United States. | Forensic sciences--United States.
Classification: LCC KF9756 .W765 2018 | DDC 345.73/0122--dc23
LC record available at https://lccn.loc.gov/2018030260

e-ISBN 978-1-5310-0633-4

Cover Art:
John Thompson from *Resurrected: The Innocence Portraits*
© Daniel Bolick • www.danielbolick.com

Carolina Academic Press
700 Kent Street
Durham, North Carolina 27701
Telephone (919) 489-7486
Fax (919) 493-5668
www.cap-press.com

Printed in the United States of America
2020 Printing

To Noah and Reuben — may justice always guide you — and to all wrongfully convicted men and women, who have paid the price on our behalf.

— R.D.C.

To my wife Jenn for her light and love; to my students for their fire and tenacity; and to my clients for their brave and kind hearts. You have taught me how we each create our own freedom.

— V.E.B.

Summary of Contents

Contents

Preface

This volume is intended primarily as a teaching tool for law students, undergraduate and graduate students, lawyers, judges, and those interested in educating themselves (or teaching others) about the current state of knowledge regarding wrongful convictions. This includes what we do and do not know about their prevalence, what causes them to occur, what might be done to limit their number, and how we should think about balancing the costs of preventing them with the costs of maintaining an effective criminal justice system.

The book represents some of the most important work in the field of wrongful convictions studies of the past three decades. Contributions were selected not only to inform readers about the current state-of-the-art, but also to give readers a sense of the historical progress of innocence scholarship and the innocence movement, and to expose readers to the sometimes heated debates that were its byproduct. Participants in those debates include countless scholars and researchers, reporters, prosecutors, forensic scientists, advocates for the innocent, judges, and Supreme Court justices. We are deeply grateful for the willingness of the numerous contributing authors, journals, and news media to allow us to collect and publish their path-breaking work in this volume. Needless to say, this is but the tip of a large and ever-growing iceberg of research, scholarship, adjudication, and reporting dealing with the phenomena of wrongful convictions. A great amount of important work was necessarily omitted from this volume due to the inevitable space constraints.

Acknowledgments

We acknowledge with great appreciation the following authors, journals, magazines, newspapers, and publishers who have so graciously permitted us to reproduce excerpts of their work in this reader. Because this book is intended primarily as a teaching tool, citations and footnotes have in most cases been omitted for purposes of readability, and in some instances material has been reordered from the original. Textual alterations, omissions and deletions have been indicated. Those wishing to use these works for purposes of scholarship should consult the original sources.

Artist Dan Bolick painted and sketched exonerated men and women for his series, "Resurrected: The Innocence Portraits." He graciously permitted us to use his portrait of John Thompson, or JT, for the cover of the *Reader*. John Thompson passed away on October 4, 2017; he had spent 18 years in prison for a crime he did not commit, 14 of those years on death row, before he was exonerated. He established Resurrection After Exoneration (RAE) as a home for new exonerees, called out widely for prosecutor reform, and his civil case resulted in one of the most infamous U.S. Supreme Court decisions on prosecutorial misconduct: *Connick v. Thompson*, 563 U.S. 51 (2011). Thank you to JT, and to all wrongfully convicted men and women, for their will to fight and their pursuit of justice.

Finally, special thanks go to Kelly Parker and Christopher Maidona, West Virginia University College of Law, Class of 2018, whose research and technical assistance were critical to completing this reader. We wish you the best in your careers.

James R. Acker, The Flipside Injustice of Wrongful Convictions: When the Guilty Go Free, 76 Alb. L. Rev. 1629, 1629–31 (2013). Reprinted with permission.

Michelle Alexander, The New Jim Crow: Mass Incarceration in the Age of Colorblindness, 175–76, 184 The New Press (2012). Reprinted with permission.

Hugo Adam Bedau and Michael L. Radelet, Miscarriages of Justice in Potentially Capital Cases, 40 Stan. L. Rev. 21, 39–47 (1987). Reprinted with permission.

Valena E. Beety, Changing the Culture of Disclosure and Forensics, 73 Wash. & Lee L. Rev. Online 580, 581–82 (2017). Reprinted with permission.

Stephanos Bibas, Harmonizing Substantive-Criminal-Law Values and Criminal Procedure: The Case of Alford and Nolo Contendere Pleas, 88 Cornell L. Rev. 1361, 1382–87 (2003). Reprinted with permission.

John H. Blume and Rebecca K. Helm, The Unexonerated: Factually Innocent Defendants Who Plead Guilty, 100 Cornell L. Rev. 157, 158–61 (2014). Reprinted with permission.

Alafair S. Burke, Improving Prosecutorial Decision Making: Some Lessons of Cognitive Science, 47 Wm & Mary L. Rev. 1587, 1588–613 (2006). Reprinted with permission.

Stephen B. Bright, Counsel for the Poor: The Death Sentence Not for the Worst Crime but for the Worst Lawyer, 103 Yale L.J. 1835, 1841–62 (1994). Reprinted with permission.

Justin Brooks & Alexander Simpson, Blood Sugar Sex Magik: A Review of Postconviction DNA Testing Statutes and Legislative Recommendations, 59 Drake L. Rev. 799, 804–24 (2011). Reprinted with permission.

Carrie L. Buist, Emily Lenning, Queer Criminology: New Directions in Critical Criminology, 76–77, Routledge, Taylor & Francis Group (2016). Reprinted with permission.

John Butler, U.S. Initiatives to Strengthen Forensic Science & International Standards in Forensic DNA, 18 Forensic Sci. Int. Genet. 4–20 (Sept. 2015). Reprinted with permission.

I. Bennett Capers, Cross Dressing and the Criminal, 20 Yale J.L. & Human. 1, 8–10, 18–19, 21 (2008). Reprinted with permission.

Tucker Carrington, Mississippi Innocence: The Convictions and Exonerations of Levon Brooks and Kennedy Brewer and the Failure of the American Promise, 28 Geo. J. Legal Ethics 123, 123–75 (2015). Reprinted with permission.

Jessica Blank and Erik Jensen, The Exonerated 42 (Faber & Faber) (2004). Reprinted with permission.

Paul G. Cassell, Can We Protect the Innocent Without Freeing the Guilty? Thoughts on Innocence Reforms that Avoid Harmful Tradeoffs, in Twenty Five Years of Innocence Exonerations (Cambridge Univ. Press) (2017). Reprinted with permission.

Mike Celizic, She sent him to jail for rape; now they're friends: DNA evidence exonerated him; today they're co-authors fighting for justice, TODAY (updated 3/10/2009).

Jessica Gabel Cino, Tackling Technical Debt: Managing Advances in DNA Technology that Outpace the Evolution of Law, 54 Am. Crim. L. Rev. 373, 377–82 (2017). Reprinted with permission.

Steven E. Clark, Costs and benefits of eyewitness identification reform: Psychological science and public policy. Perspectives on Psychological Science, 7, 238–259 (2012). Reprinted with permission.

Simon Cole, Forensic Science and Wrongful Convictions: From Exposer to Contributor to Corrector, 46 New Eng. L. Rev. 711, 712–19 (2012). Reprinted with permission.

Russell D. Covey, Abolishing Jailhouse Snitch Testimony, 49 Wake Forest L. Rev. 1375, 1375–1429 (2014). Reprinted with permission.

Russell D. Covey, Police Misconduct as a Cause of Wrongful Convictions, 90 Wash. U. L. Rev. 1133, 1137–61 (2013). Reprinted with permission.

Deborah Denno, Concocting Criminal Intent, 105 Georgetown L. J. 323, 349, 341–43 (2017). Reprinted with permission.

Lucian E. Dervan, Bargained Justice: Plea-Bargaining's Innocence Problem and the Brady Safety-Valve, 2012 Utah L. Rev. 51, 84–86 (2012). Reprinted with permission.

Lucian E. Dervan & Vanessa A. Edkins, Ph.D., The Innocent Defendant's Dilemma: An Innovative Empirical Study of Plea Bargaining's Innocence Problem, 103 J. Crim. L. & Criminology 1, 2–4 (2013). Reprinted with permission.

Dr. Rachel Dioso-Villa, Scientific and Legal Developments in Fire and Arson Investigation Expertise in Texas v. Willingham, 14 Minn. J.L. Sci. & Tech. 817, 817–48 (2013). Reprinted with permission.

James M. Doyle, Orwell's Elephant and the Etiology of Wrongful Convictions, 79 Alb. L. Rev. 895, 897–98 (2016). Reprinted with permission.

Tigran W. Eldred, Prescriptions for Ethical Blindness: Improving Advocacy for Indigent Defendants in Criminal Cases, 65 Rutgers L. Rev. 333, 344–51 (2013). Reprinted with permission.

David Feige, The Dark Side of Innocence, The New York Times Magazine (June 15, 2003). Reprinted with permission of the author and the New York Times Magazine.

Keith A. Findley, Innocence Protection in the Appellate Process, 93 Marq. L. Rev. 591, 601–08 (2009). Reprinted with permission.

Keith Findley and Michael S. Scott, The Multiple Dimensions of Tunnel Vision in Criminal Cases, 2006 Wis. L. Rev. 291, 291–397. Reprinted with permission.

Alison Flowers, Exoneree Diaries: The Fight for Innocence, Independence, and Identity, p. 21–22 (Haymarket Books, 2016). Reprinted with permission.

Eric M. Freedman, Earl Washington's Ordeal, 29 Hofstra L. Rev. 1089, 1090–1112 (2001). Reprinted with permission.

Henry J. Friendly, Is Innocence Irrelevant? Collateral Attack on Criminal Judgments, 38 U. Chi. L. Rev. 142, 142–144 (1970). Reprinted with permission of the University of Chicago Law Review.

Brandon L. Garrett, The Substance of False Confessions, 62 Stan. L. Rev. 1051, 1052–1118 (2010). Reprinted with permission.

Brandon L. Garrett, Judging Innocence, 108 Colum. L. Rev. 55, 56–116 (2008). Reprinted with permission.

Mark Godsey, Blind Injustice: A Former Prosecutor Exposes the Psychology and Politics of Wrongful Convictions. (c) 2017 by Mark Godsey. Published by the University of California Press. Reprinted with permission.

Jon B. Gould & Richard A. Leo, One Hundred Years Later: Wrongful Convictions after a Century of Research, 100 J. Crim. L. & Criminology 825, 827–32 (2010). Reprinted with permission.

Jon B. Gould, Julia Carrano, Richard A. Leo, and Katie Hail-Jares, Predicting Erroneous Convictions, 99 Iowa L. Rev. 471, 475–77, 494–502 (2014). Reprinted with permission.

Bruce A. Green, Access to Criminal Justice: Where Are the Prosecutors? 3 Tex. A&M L. Rev. 515, 522–531 (2016). Reprinted with permission.

Lisa Kern Griffin, State Incentives, Plea Bargaining Regulation, and the Failed Market for Indigent Defense, Law & Contemp. Probs., 2017, at 83, 88–90. Reprinted with permission.

Samuel R. Gross, Kristen Jacoby, Daniel J. Matheson, Nicholas Montgomery, Sujata Patil, Exonerations In The United States 1989 Through 2003, 95 J. Crim. L. & Criminology 523, 523–54 (2005). Reprinted with permission.

Samuel R. Gross, Pretrial Incentives, Post-Conviction Review, and Sorting Criminal Prosecutions by Guilt or Innocence, 56 N.Y.L. Sch. L. Rev. 1009, 1022–24 (2012). Reprinted with permission.

Emily Hughes, Innocence Unmodified, 89 N.C. L. Rev. 1083, 1084–85 (2011). Reprinted with permission.

The Innocence Project: Access to Post-Conviction DNA Testing. Reprinted with permission.

Peter A. Joy, The Relationship Between Prosecutorial Misconduct And Wrongful Convictions: Shaping Remedies for a Broken System, 2006 Wis. L. Rev. 399, 399–427. Reprinted with permission.

Saul M. Kassin, Steven A. Drizin, Steven A. Drizin, Thomas Grisso, Gisli H. Gudjonsson, Richard A. Leo, Allison D. Redlich, Police-Induced Confessions: Risk Factors and Recommendations, 34 Law & Hum. Behav. 3, 6–18 (2010). Reprinted with permission.

Jonathan J. Koehler, Error and Exaggeration in the Presentation of DNA Evidence at Trial, 34 Jurimetrics J. 21, 21–35 (1994). Reprinted with permission.

Jonathan J. Koehler, Fingerprint Error Rates and Proficiency Tests: What They Are and Why They Matter, 59 Hastings L.J. 1077, 1077–1100 (2008). Reprinted with permission.

Courtney Lance and Nikki Pope, Pruno, Ramen, and a Side of Hope: Stories of Surviving Wrongful Conviction. (Post Hill Press 2015). Reprinted with permission.

Larry Laudan, The Elementary Epistemic Arithmetic of Criminal Justice, 5 Episteme 282, 282–94 (2008). Reprinted with permission.

Jennifer E. Laurin, Remapping the Path Forward: Toward a Systemic View of Forensic Science Reform and Oversight, 91 Texas L. Rev. 1051, 1076–79 (2013). Reprinted with permission.

John Lentini; Michael Bowers, Forensic Science Reform: Protecting the Innocent; Confronting Inaccuracy in Fire Cause Determinations 66 (Edited by Wendy Koen, Michael Bowers, (Elsevier, Inc. 2017)). Reprinted with permission.

Richard A. Leo, Steven A. Drizin, Peter J. Neufeld, Bradley R. Hall, Amy Vatner, Bringing Reliability Back In: False Confessions and Legal Safeguards in the Twenty-First Century, 2006 Wis. L. Rev. 479, 479–86 (2006). Reprinted with permission.

Andrea Lewis, Sara Sommervold, Death, but is it Murder? The Role of Stereotypes and Cultural Perceptions in the Wrongful Convictions of Women, 78 Alb. L. Rev. 1035, 1035 (2015). Reprinted with permission.

Ian F. Haney Lopez, White By Law: The Legal Construction of Race 111, 118–19 (New York University Press 1996). Reprinted with permission.

Kara MacKillop and Neil Vidmar, Decision-Making in the Dark: How Pre-Trial Errors Change the Narrative in Criminal Jury Trials, 90 Chi.-Kent L. Rev. 957, 970–72 (2015). Reprinted with permission.

Joshua Marquis, The Innocent and the Shammed, The New York Times, January 26, 2006. Reprinted with permission of the author and the New York Times.

Larry May and Nancy Viner, Actual Innocence and Manifest Injustice, 49 St. Louis U. L.J. 481, 482 (2005). Reprinted with permission.

Jacqueline McMurtrie, The Unindicted Co-Ejaculator and Necrophilia: Addressing Prosecutors' Logic-Defying Responses to Exculpatory DNA Results, 105 J. Crim. L. & Criminology 853, 854–58 (2015). Reprinted with permission.

Jacqueline McMurtrie, Strange Bedfellows: Can Insurers Play A Role in Advancing Gideon's Promise?, 45 Hofstra L. Rev. 391, 395–97 (2016). Reprinted with permission.

Daniel Medwed, Innocentrism, U. of Ill. L. Rev. 1549, 1560–63, 1566–70 (2008). Reprinted with permission.

Daniel S. Medwed, The Innocent Prisoner's Dilemma: Consequences of Failing to Admit Guilt at Parole Hearings, 93 Iowa L. Rev. 491, 493–541 (2008). Reprinted with permission.

Vanessa Meterko, Strengths and Limitations of Forensic Science: What DNA Exonerations Have Taught Us and Where to Go from Here, 119 W. Va. L. Rev. 639, 639, 640–646 (2016). Reprinted with permission.

Jennifer L. Mnookin, The Courts, The NAS, and the Future of Forensic Science, 75 Brook. L. Rev. 1209–27, 1230–32 (2010). Reprinted with permission.

Joey Mogul, Queer (In)Justice: The Criminalization of LGBT People in the United States XI–XII, 12, 23–24, 69–70, 73 (Beacon Press 2012). Reprinted with permission of the author and Beacon Press.

Timothy E. Moore, Shaping Eyewitness and Alibi Testimony with Coercive Interview Practices, Champion, October 2014, at 34, 34–35. Reprinted with permission of the author and The Champion.

Robert P. Mosteller, The Special Threat of Informants to the Innocent Who Are Not Innocents: Producing "First Drafts," Recording Incentives, and Taking a Fresh Look at the Evidence, 6 Ohio St. J. Crim. L. 519, 554–57 (2009). Reprinted with permission.

Erin Murphy, The Art in the Science of DNA: A Layperson's Guide to the Subjectivity Inherent in Forensic DNA Typing, 58 Emory L.J. 489, 492–96 (2008). Reprinted with permission.

Sherry Nakhaeizadeh, Iteil E. Dror, and Ruth M. Morgan, The Emergence of Cognitive Bias in Forensic Science and Criminal Investigation, 4 Brit. J. Am. Legal Stud. 527, 534–42 (2015). Reprinted with permission.

Alexandra Natapoff, Beyond Unreliable: How Snitches Contribute to Wrongful Convictions, 37 Golden Gate U. L. Rev. 107, 107–12 (2006). Reprinted with permission.

David Oshinsky, Worse Than Slavery: Parchman Farm And The Ordeal Of Jim Crow Justice, 56–57, 63, 71, (Free Press, 1996). Copyright © 1996 by David Oshinsky. Reprinted with permission of the Free Press, a division of Simon & Schuster, Inc.

Michael Leo Owens & Elizabeth Griffiths, Uneven Reparations for Wrongful Convictions: Examining the State Politics of Statutory Compensation Legislation, 75 Alb. L. Rev. 1283, 1283–1305 (2012). Reprinted with permission.

Todd E. Pettys, Killing Roger Coleman: Habeas, Finality, and the Innocence Gap, 48 Wm. & Mary L. Rev. 2313, 2313–2363 (2007). Reprinted with permission.

Caitlin Plummer and Imran Syed, "Shifted Science" Revisited: Percolation Delays and the Persistence of Wrongful Convictions Based on Outdated Science, 64 Clev. St. L. Rev. 483, 483–518 (2016). Reprinted with permission.

Eve Brensike Primus, Defense Counsel and Public Defense, In Academy For Justice, A Report on Scholarship and Criminal Justice Reform (Erik Luna ed., 2017). Reprinted with permission.

Jed Rakoff, Why Innocent People Plead Guilty, The New York Review of Books, November 20, 2014. Reprinted with permission of the New York Review of Books.

L. Song Richardson, Systemic Triage: Implicit Racial Bias In The Criminal Courtroom, 126 Yale L.J. 862, 882 (2017). Reprinted with permission.

Michael Risinger and Lesley C. Risinger, Miscarriages of Justice: A Theoretical and Practical Overview, 7 J. Marshall L.J. 373, 389–404 (2014). Reprinted with permission.

D. Michael Risinger, Innocents Convicted: An Empirically Justified Factual Wrongful Conviction Rate, 97 J. Crim. L. & Criminology 761, 761–800 (2007). Reprinted with permission.

Jennifer Roberts, Why Misdemeanors Matter: Defining Effective Advocacy in the Lower Criminal Courts, 45 U.C. Davis L. Rev. 277 (2011). Reprinted with permission.

Jessica A. Roth, Informant Witnesses and the Risk of Wrongful Convictions, 53 Am. Crim. L. Rev. 737, 743–44 (2016). Reprinted with permission.

Meghan J. Ryan & John Adams, Cultivating Judgment on the Tools of Wrongful Conviction, 68 SMU L. Rev. 1073, 1096–99 (2015). Reprinted with permission.

Michael J. Saks, Jonathan J. Koehler, The Coming Paradigm Shift in Forensic Identification Science, Vol. 309, Issue 5736, pp. 892–895. Reprinted with permission of the authors and Science.

Boaz Sangero and Mordechai Halpert, Why a Conviction Should Not Be Based on a Single Piece of Evidence: A Proposal for Reform, 48 Jurimetrics J. 43, 44–45 (2007). Reprinted with permission.

Barry Scheck, Peter Neufeld and Jim Dwyer, Actual Innocence: Five Days to Execution, and Other Dispatches from the Wrongly Convicted, copyright © 2000 by Barry Scheck, Peter Neufeld and Jim Dwyer. Used by permission of Doubleday, an imprint of the Knopf Doubleday Publishing Group, a division of Penguin Random House LLC. All rights reserved.

David S. Schwartz & Chelsey B. Metcalf, Disfavored Treatment of Third-Party Guilt Evidence, 2016 Wis. L. Rev. 337, 338–39 (2016).

Dan Simon, Criminal Law at the Crossroads: Turn to Accuracy, 87 S. Cal. L. Rev. 421, 437–39 (2014). Reprinted with permission.

Chris Smith, Central Park Revisited, Oct. 21, 2002, New York Magazine. Reprinted with permission of New York Magazine.

Abbe Smith, In Praise of the Guilty Project: A Criminal Defense Lawyer's Growing Anxiety About Innocence Projects, 13 U. Pa. J. L. & Soc. Change 315, 323–26 (2010). Reprinted with permission.

Douglas Starr, The Interview: Do Police Interrogation Techniques Produce False Confessions? The New Yorker, Dec. 9 2013. Reprinted with permission of The New Yorker.

Nancy K. Steblay, Scientific Advances in Eyewitness Identification Evidence, 41 Wm. Mitchell L. Rev. 1090, 1102–11 (2015). Reprinted with permission.

Carol S. Steiker and Jorden Steiker, The Seduction of Innocence: The Attraction and Limitations of the Focus on Innocence in Capital Punishment Law and Advocacy, 95 J. Crim. L. & Criminology 587, 619–21 (2005). Reprinted with permission.

Bryan Stevenson, Just Mercy: A Story of Justice and Redemption, 23–24, 58–60 Random House (2014). Reprinted with permission of Random House.

Sandra Guerra Thompson and Nicole Bremner Cásarez, Building the Infrastructure for "Justice Through Science": The Texas Model, 119 W. Va. L. Rev. 711, 711–748 (2016). Reprinted with permission.

William C. Thompson, Beyond Bad Apples: Analyzing the Role of Forensic Science in Wrongful Convictions, 37 Sw. L. Rev. 1027, 1028–30 (2008). Reprinted with permission.

William C. Thompson and Edward L. Schumann, The Prosecutor's Fallacy and the Defense Attorney's Fallacy, 11 Law & Human Behavior 167 (1987). Reprinted with permission.

Deborah Tuerkheimer, Science-Dependent Prosecution and the Problem of Epistemic Contingency: A Study of Shaken Baby Syndrome, 62 Alabama L. Rev. 513, 513–69 (2011). Reprinted with permission.

Gary L. Wells, Eyewitness Identification: Systemic Reforms, 2006 Wis. L. Rev. 615, 615–20 (2006). Reprinted with permission.

Elizabeth Webster, Jody Miller, Gendering and Racing Wrongful Conviction: Intersectionality, "Normal Crimes," and Women's Experiences of Miscarriage of Justice, 78 Alb. L. Rev. 973, 1000–1007, 1030–31 (2015). Reprinted with permission.

Molly J. Walker Wilson, Defense Attorney Bias and the Rush to the Plea, 65 U. Kan. L. Rev. 271, 273–76 (2016). Reprinted with permission.

Jordan Blair Woods, LGBT Identity and Crime, 105 California Law Review 667, 674, 681, 684 (2017). Reprinted with permission.

American Bar Association, Section of Criminal Justice, Report to the House of Delegates Recommendation (2005).

American Bar Association, Resolution Against Coercive Alford Pleas (2017).

Swedish Agency for Health Tech. Assessment & Assessment of Social Services, Traumatic Shaking: The Role of the Triad in Medical Investigations of Suspected Traumatic Shaking—A Systematic Review (2016).

National Research Council, Strengthening Forensic Science in the United States: A Path Forward, National Academy of Sciences (2009).

President's Council of Advisors on Science & Technology, An Addendum to the PCAST Report on Forensic Science in Criminal Courts (2017).

Introduction

This is a very smart book. It serves as the best introduction yet to the impact of the innocence movement and the systematic study of wrongful convictions.

When the Innocence Project began twenty-six years ago as a clinical program at the Benjamin N. Cardozo School of Law it featured a seminar on "Wrongful Convictions: Causes and Remedies," as well as a docket of post-conviction cases involving clients from across the country trying to prove their innocence and vacate their convictions. From the beginning, the innocence movement was deliberately organized through law school programs, combining interdisciplinary scholarship with litigation strategies, an agenda of legislative reforms, and advocacy through the media. As I write this introduction, there is an Innocence Network that consists of 56 organizations within the United States, most of them affiliated with law schools, and 11 international organizations. There have been 358 post-conviction DNA exonerations (in 47% of those cases the person who committed the crime has been identified) and, according to the National Registry of Exonerations, 2,252 United States exonerations since 1989, involving DNA and non-DNA evidence.

The success of the innocence movement is always best understood through the experiences of the exonerees and their families, not just the good case law established in courts, the laws passed by legislatures, or the reforms implemented by criminal justice stakeholders. But the intellectual foundation of the enterprise, the unstinting struggle to understand in all its dimensions why the innocent are convicted and what can be done to prevent miscarriages of justice, is what generates energy, shapes the narrative, and assures long-term sustainability of what we believe is an international human rights movement. This book is a wonderful contribution to that effort.

Professors Covey and Beety make wise selections from a rich, interdisciplinary literature that demonstrate how dramatically the examination of wrongful convictions has influenced experimental psychology (excellent chapters on false confessions and eyewitness identification research) and forensic science (a chapter on reform efforts to bring sound scientific and statistical standards to the field as a whole and a chapter on exposés of "junk science" in the fields of arson investigation and the complex area of Shaken Baby Syndrome/Abusive Head Trauma). In Chapter 7 they astutely introduce the problem of prosecutorial misconduct from the perspective of cognitive bias and "tunnel vision," an emphasis that avoids ad hominem attack and ineluctably points to ways criminal investigations can be improved. This sets the stage for subsequent chapters on "Police and Prosecutorial Misconduct," "Informants and Snitches," and "Incompetent Lawyering and the Tilted Playing Field" that pull no punches. The overarching focus on a scientific approach to criminal justice reform, a core value of the innocence movement, continually invites the faculty and students to engage with controversial and potentially polarizing issues in a rigorous and objective fashion.

Accordingly, Covey and Beety include chapters on "The Innocence 'Myth' and the Costs of Preventing Wrongful Convictions," and "Reconsidering Innocence: Rethinking Causes and Addressing Consequences," that fairly and appropriately feature criticisms of the innocence movement and the dangers of focusing too much on wrongful convictions from prosecutors (Josh Marquis), capital lawyers (Carol and Jordan Steiker), public defenders (Abbe Smith and David Feige), and a long time leader of the movement (Daniel Medwed). They are equally careful at the beginning of the book to include readings that explore how "exoneration," "innocence," and "miscarriage of justice" have been defined over time in the literature (Chapter 2 "Defining Innocence and Miscarriages of Justice") and to establish the limitations of what we know about the extent of wrongful convictions and what "causes" them (Chapter 3 "Overview of the Causes of Wrongful Convictions").

The authors do not neglect the heartland issues for a traditional legal curriculum with thoughtful readings in Chapter 13 "Guilty Pleas, Pretrial Procedure, and Innocence," excepts from the key Supreme Court "innocence" cases in Chapter 14, and realistic assessments about the severe limitations created by the "harmless error" doctrine, the demands of "finality," and the strictures of federal habeas law in Chapter 15, "Appellate and Post-Conviction Review of Innocence: An Assessment." In Chapter 16, "Intersections: Race, Gender, Sexual Orientation and Innocence," powerful readings are assembled addressing the most pressing issues of the day that ought to be part of every law school curriculum.

In short, this casebook lays out a stimulating course of study that ought to be exciting for students in many graduate schools to take, not just law students, and a pleasure to teach.

Barry Scheck
Co-Founder of the Innocence Project
Professor, Benjamin N. Cardozo School of Law

The Wrongful Convictions Reader

Chapter One

Prologue to Wrongful Convictions

A. Readings

Eric M. Freedman, *Earl Washington's Ordeal*

29 Hofstra L. Rev. 1089, 1090–1112 (2001)

On June 4, 1982, Rebecca Lynn Williams, returning home at noontime with her two young children to her apartment in the town of Culpeper, Virginia, was raped and stabbed. She could do no more than identify her assailant as a black man acting alone, and died a few hours later. At trial, the officer who responded to the call testified, "I asked her if she knew who her attacker was. She replied, no. I asked her then if the attacker was black or white and she replied, black. I then asked her if there was more than one and she replied, no." Similarly, Ms. Williams' husband testified, "I asked her, you know, who did it, and the only thing she replied to me was, a black man, and that was about it."

Almost a year later, on May 21, 1983, Earl Washington, "a black man, aged 22 at the time, with a general I.Q. in the range of 69, that of a child in the 10.3 year age group," was arrested on unrelated charges by the police in Warrenton, in Fauquier County, Virginia.

Those charges arose as follows. After Mr. Washington had spent a number of hours drinking heavily with family members, a dispute arose. Mr. Washington broke into a nearby house for the purpose of stealing a pistol that he knew to be there, and was surprised by the householder, Mrs. Hazel Weeks. He hit her over the head with a chair, and returned to the gathering. As he entered the house with the gun at his side, it accidentally discharged, hitting his brother, Robert, in the foot. Mr. Washington fled into the woods, where the police found him a few hours later.

While in police custody, Mr. Washington "confessed" to five different crimes. In four of the cases, the "confession" proved to be so inconsistent with the crime it purported to describe that it was simply rejected by the Commonwealth as the unreliable product of Mr. Washington's acquiescence to the officers. In the fifth case—which resulted in the capital murder conviction and sentence—the statement had to be reshaped through four rehearsal sessions before reaching a form the authorities considered usable.

Confession #1: The questioning began on the morning of May 21, 1993, when law enforcement officers of Fauquier County secured from Mr. Washington a waiver of his Miranda rights. They began by discussing the Weeks case and ultimately obtained a "confession." According to a vivid account contained in this document, Mr. Washington had attempted to rape Mrs. Weeks. But Mrs. Weeks testified to the contrary at the preliminary hearing, and the Commonwealth dropped the charge of attempted rape. Thereafter, Mr. Washington pleaded guilty to statutory burglary and malicious wounding, and was sentenced to consecutive fifteen-year prison terms. But on the morning of May 21, 1983, all of this lay in the future.

Confession #2: Having obtained Mr. Washington's "confession" to the Weeks crime, the police turned the conversation to an attempted rape that had occurred on Waterloo Road. Mr. Washington confessed to this too, but the charge was dismissed. Mr. Washington's "confession" was inconsistent with important facts in that case.

Confession #3: Next, the police obtained Mr. Washington's "confession" to a breaking and entering on Winchester Street. He was never charged with this crime. The victim saw him in a line-up and stated that he was not the assailant.

Confession #4: Mr. Washington then "confessed" to the rape of another woman. He was charged with this crime, but the charge was dismissed by the Commonwealth. The victim's description of the attacker was inconsistent with Mr. Washington and she had previously identified someone else as the assailant.

Confession #5: At this point in the interrogation, according to handwritten police notes given to—but never used by—counsel who represented Mr. Washington in his capital case,

> Because I felt that he was still hiding something, being nervous, and due to the nature of his crimes that he was already charged with and would be charged with, we decided to ask him about the murder which occurred in Culpeper in 1982.
>
> … Earl didn't look at us, but was still very nervous. Asked Earl if he knew anything about it. Earl sat there and didn't reply just as he did in the other cases prior to admitting them. At this time I asked Earl—"EARL DID YOU KILL THAT GIRL IN CULPEPER?" Earl sat there silent for about five seconds and then shook his head yes and started crying.

The entire interrogation that followed consisted of the officers asking Mr. Washington a series of leading questions about the crime and obtaining affirmative responses. This process eventually ceased, as the police notes frankly acknowledge, because the police had exhausted their store of information about the crime. Thus, for example, the Fauquier County officers did not know that Ms. Williams had been raped, and Mr. Washington did not supply any such information.

At this point, the Fauquier police called the Culpeper police and invited them to participate in the questioning. The following morning, May 22, 1983, Mr. Washington first had another session with the Fauquier authorities at which, according to the officers' notes, "[h]e went through the story (as on 05/21/83) again." Then two officers from Culpeper, following oral Miranda warnings, began to interrogate Mr. Washington. No contemporaneous records of this second interrogation have ever been produced, and it was apparently not recorded.

However, the interrogating officer later described the session in court. He testified that Mr. Washington initially wrongly identified Ms. Williams as having been black, and only corrected the statement on being re-asked the question. This pattern was common throughout the interrogation: "I asked him to describe this woman. He had problems with describing."

Thus, in addition to not knowing the race of Ms. Williams, when asked non-leading questions:

- He had described the victim as "short." She was 5'8" tall.

- He had said that he stabbed the victim "once or twice." She had been stabbed 38 times.

- He had said he saw no one else in the apartment. Two of the victim's young children were present.

After approximately an hour of review of the facts, according to the police testimony, the officers informed Mr. Washington that they would ask him the same questions once more, this time reducing the conversation to writing. They did so, and the resulting document was admitted at trial as his "confession."

During the afternoon of May 22, 1983, while Mr. Washington's statement of that day was being typed up for his signature, officers drove him to numerous apartment buildings in Culpeper in an effort to get him to identify the scene of the crime. Three times they drove into the apartment complex where the crime had actually occurred. On the third occasion, when asked to point out the scene of the crime, Mr. Washington "pointed to an apartment on the exact opposite end from where the Williams girl was killed. At that time I pointed to the Williams apartment and asked him directly, is that the one?" This question obtained an affirmative response.

Similarly, the police officers had Mr. Washington identify as his own a shirt of unknown provenance that was found at the apartment and given to them by family members six weeks after the crime. During the guilt phase of the trial, the only evidence offered by the prosecution to link Mr. Washington to the crime consisted of his statements (including his identification of the shirt).

Defense counsel failed to obtain or offer available evidence that:

- The Commonwealth's own serologic analysis of the seminal fluid found on the blanket where the crime took place showed that it could not have come from Mr. Washington.

- According to the same serological methodology the semen type was consistent with the Commonwealth's first suspect, James Pendleton.

- The hairs found in the pocket of the shirt found at the crime scene were consistent in part with that suspect's facial hair, but were not compared to Mr. Washington's hairs. When the state crime laboratory pointed out this inconsistency to the Culpeper police and requested additional Washington hairs for comparison, the police refused.

Defense counsel also failed to show that Mr. Washington was wholly incapable of understanding Miranda warnings, or that the process of suggestion by which the police officers had obtained the "confession" dovetailed precisely with his adaptive strategy for living in the normal world, which consisted of attempting to please his interlocutors by telling them what they wanted to hear. Instead, defense counsel put Mr. Washington on the stand, perhaps intending that this mentally challenged individual—who cannot name the colors of the American flag or state the function of a thermometer—testify that, although he had signed the confession, its contents were false. In any event, what he did testify was that he had never made the confession.

Defense counsel then made a closing argument which simply asked the jury to give Mr. Washington his day in court, without, however, discussing one iota of the evidence the jury had heard.

Not surprisingly, Mr. Washington was convicted.

At the punishment phase, the Commonwealth relied solely on the aggravating circumstance that the defendant's "conduct in committing the offense was outrageously or wantonly vile, horrible or inhuman." It called as a witness, without objection by defense counsel, Helen T. Richards, the victim's mother. The exclusive subject of her testimony was the traumatic psychological effect of the murder upon two of the victim's young children. After describing this, and the special psychiatric care that the two were receiving, Mrs. Richards continued:

> [T]hey have a telephone that is just used for talking to their mama in heaven and this is the way they talk about their problems. They sit down on the phone and they take turns talking to mama in heaven, to let her know how things are going, especially if they're very, very upset or something has upset them, and they sit down ... it's a little ... it's just a regular telephone, a little black phone, and they sit down and they dial and they talk to their mama. It's not an easy thing to work with children that are emotionally disturbed like this. They're beautiful children.

Defense counsel's jury argument at the punishment phase took up in its entirety twenty-seven lines in the record. After the prosecutor had graphically and repeatedly described the thirty-eight stab wounds to fourteen vital organs and the "pool of blood" in which the victim lay, defense counsel advised the jury that "this is Earl Washington's day in Court and you must do him justice." He gave no reason why the jury should not impose the death penalty. As to the factors the jury should consider, he submitted:

> there is really, not really, in the course of human experience, any particular standard that governs us all with respect to punishment, so each of you, each of you must search within yourself to consider the crime and consider the gentleman whom you have found to be its perpetrator and look at him and look at the crime and determine what punishment is just for him. His life is in your hands.

Not surprisingly, the jury sentenced Mr. Washington to death. The direct appeal was handled by the trial lawyer. Not surprisingly, it was summarily denied.

On the reasonable assumption that certiorari would not be granted at this stage, the next step would be the filing of a state habeas corpus petition, which, among other things, was and is a statutory prerequisite to the filing of a federal habeas corpus petition. Virginia, however, did not provide for the appointment of counsel at this phase, and the trial lawyer's motion for that relief was denied.

Thus, in August, 1985, when Mr. Washington — facing an execution date of September 5 — was moved to Virginia's Death House, he had no legal representation. Meanwhile, his fellow prisoner Joseph Giarratano had been attempting to bring Mr. Washington's plight to anyone who would listen, including the local District Judge and Marie M. Deans, director of the Virginia Coalition on Jails and Prisons. Mr. Giarratano and Ms. Deans (who had been frantically but unsuccessfully soliciting law firms around the country to volunteer for the case) raised the matter with Martha Geer. Ms. Geer, then a junior associate at Paul, Weiss, Rifkind, Wharton, & Garrison of New York City, was in Virginia to prepare the lawsuit that eventually became Murray v. Giarratano. She brought the matter to the attention of her superiors at Paul, Weiss and Jay Topkis, a senior partner in that firm who had repeatedly arranged for it to donate its resources to death penalty cases, agreed that it could undertake to save Mr. Washington's life.

A team of lawyers from Paul, Weiss under my direction as senior associate managed, after a virtually sleepless week, to file a 1600-page petition for state habeas corpus, along with several applications for ancillary relief. One of these, an application for a stay of execution, was granted by the circuit judge, thereby forestalling the execution nine days before it was scheduled to take place.

As planned, Paul, Weiss then sought volunteer lawyers to take its place. As a result, Peter C. Huber, and then Robert T. Hall, assumed primary responsibility for Mr. Washington's representation. At this stage, Mr. Hall discovered the exculpatory semen stain evidence — which, having been appropriately turned over by the government, lay unappreciated in the files of the former defense counsel.

Notwithstanding this evidence (and a great deal more) of ineffective performance by counsel, the state habeas corpus petition raising this and other claims was denied without a hearing. The Virginia Supreme Court denied review. Mr. Hall then filed a federal habeas corpus petition. This, too, was denied without a hearing.

Having by this time become a law professor, I undertook the appeal of this decision, which succeeded to the extent of a remand for an evidentiary hearing. On remand, Gerald T. Zerkin joined the legal team, and the two sides presented a good deal of testimony, from the trial attorneys and from experts, concerning the exculpatory evidence. Eventually, the district court issued an opinion stating that defense counsel had made a conscious decision, for tactical reasons, not to offer the exculpatory evidence.

That finding was so utterly without evidentiary support that the government did not even attempt to defend it on oral argument of the resulting appeal, on which I again represented Mr. Washington. Rather, the government urged the theory that a divided Fourth Circuit panel eventually accepted: that defense counsel's performance had indeed been ineffective, but the error was non-prejudicial in light of the overwhelming weight of the evidence against Mr. Washington, namely his confessions.

Since that case-specific ruling was hardly one likely to result in a grant of certiorari, the legal system at this point had given its final sanction to Mr. Washington's execution, which in ordinary course would be likely to occur within a few months. During this period, a conversation during a chance encounter on a Richmond street between Mr. Zerkin and an attorney for the government resulted in an agreement that DNA tests (which had by now become available) should be performed on samples recovered from the vaginal vault of the victim. At this point, Barry C. Scheck and Peter Neufeld volunteered their DNA expertise, and Barry Weinstein of the Virginia Resource Center joined the legal team to help in compiling a pardon petition to Governor L. Douglas Wilder.

That petition, filed on December 20, 1993, included the DNA test results as reported by the Virginia Division of Forensic Science. For the single genetic marker examined, Mr. Washington had DNA type 1.2, 4; Ms. and Clifford Williams were both of DNA type 4,4; the DNA type of the sperm found in Ms. Williams body was 1.1, 1.2, 4. Thus, the testing showed that the sperm contained a genetic characteristic (a 1.1 allele) that could not belong to any of these individuals.

It was the view of Mr. Washington's counsel—one that the Attorney General initially shared—that at this point there was simply no case remaining against Mr. Washington. Counsel accordingly urged Governor Wilder to recognize his innocence through the grant of a full pardon. But the Governor refused to do so. Instead, on January 14, 1994, hours before the expiration of his term, he commuted Mr. Washington's sentence to life imprisonment with the right of parole.

In the aftermath of this "political half-loaf" various government officials advanced imaginative theories to justify Governor Wilder's failure to release Mr. Washington. For instance, if some hitherto-unmentioned person (one with a 1.1 allele) had joined with Mr. Washington in raping Ms. Williams, then this might provide an explanation for the test results. That hypothesis, however, was entirely inconsistent with the known facts. Not only did the Commonwealth's case at trial rest on Mr. Washington's "confession," which made no mention of any such third person, but, as recounted above, Ms. Williams stated specifically to two people (her husband and a police officer) that she had been raped by only one man.

Moreover, this scenario was as implausible scientifically as it was forensically. The 4 allele found by the testing was probably a result of an incomplete separation of the male and female contributions to the mixture, and thus a contamination from the victim's own genetic material. In that case, the true genotype of the sperm would be 1.1, 1.2. If so, Mr. Washington could not possibly have been involved—the sample would not only contain a 1.1 allele (which concededly could not be his), but would also fail to contain a 4 allele (which it would necessarily need to contain if he were the donor).

But Mr. Washington had no judicial avenue by which to press his claims. The time limit in Virginia for the reopening of a criminal case on the basis of newly discovered evidence was (and is) twenty-one days, and the prospects in federal court were less than favorable. Thus, despite one abortive effort to gain him legislative relief, Mr. Washington languished in prison.

After many painful years, Mr. Scheck was able to inform the rest of the legal team that advances in DNA technology might be able to unlock the door to Mr. Washington's cell. The invention of the Short Tandem Repeater (STR) test, which sampled many more genetic markers than the single marker tested in 1993, could lay to rest all scenarios, no matter how fanciful, that implicated Mr. Washington.

But without a judicial avenue available, the only recourse was to the governor. Accordingly, beginning in early 2000, counsel requested Governor James S. Gilmore, III to order additional testing. Since the governor was not legally obligated to act, and had political reasons to avoid doing so for as long as possible, months went by with no reply, until eventually the Virginia press began demanding to know why. In May, Peter Neufeld, Bob Hall and Jerry Zerkin met with Gilmore's counsel. Neufeld explained the new science and communicated that without a legal remedy, Mr. Washington's only avenue for obtaining gubernatorial action was through the press. On June 1, 2000, the governor announced that he was ordering the testing. His spokeswoman said it should be completed in a few weeks. With no results received after three months, the national press intensified its coverage. Counsel filed a pardon petition on September 7. On October 2, 2000, the governor announced that he was issuing a full pardon on the capital charges. Of critical importance to Mr. Washington's proof of innocence, not only did the new round of DNA testing completely eliminate him as a contributor to either the vaginal swab or the blanket stains, but it also identified the source of semen on the blanket. The state compared the DNA profile from the blanket to the Virginia DNA database of convicted offenders and obtained a match to a prisoner serving time for rape who had been at liberty at the time of the Williams murder.

However, notwithstanding counsel's request, the governor took no action to commute the non-capital sentence for the burglary and malicious wounding of Hazel Weeks, even though Mr. Washington would have been paroled on those charges long before if he had not been wrongly convicted of the capital charges. As a result, Mr. Washington remained in prison until his mandatory release date of February 12, 2001.

Tucker Carrington, *Mississippi Innocence: The Convictions and Exonerations of Levon Brooks and Kennedy Brewer and the Failure of the American Promise*
28 Geo. J. Legal Ethics 123, 123–75 (2015)

Prologue

The early spring day of March 25, 1995, dawned beautiful and fair in central east Mississippi. By noon, the temperature outside edged toward seventy degrees. The unseasonably warm weather was the last thing on Kennedy Brewer's mind though.

Locked up in a cramped jail cell on the second floor of the county courthouse, he passed the time trying to ignore the things he could just barely get his mind around: the four years he had already spent behind bars waiting for a trial, his conviction for murder the day before, even the ill-fitting suit his lawyers had given him to wear. He prayed on the one thing he could not get his mind around: the fact that just down the hallway twelve jurors were deciding whether he should spend the rest of his life in prison for his crimes, or die for them.

Likely as not, Brewer was on a fast track to execution. The day before, the same jury had convicted him of the abduction, sexual assault, and murder of three-year-old Christine Jackson, his girlfriend's daughter. For the most part, Brewer's trial had been relatively uncomplicated and presented few thorny legal issues. From beginning to end it lasted just shy of two weeks. The prosecution's evidence was overwhelming. Brewer admitted to having been alone at home—a low-slung, mustard-colored clapboard house set a few feet off a rural gravel road—with the little girl in the hours immediately preceding her disappearance. Although he had always maintained that he had no idea what had happened to Christine—he claimed to have been sound asleep when she disappeared—he could offer no explanation about how someone could have gained entry into the house, much less access to the lone living space.

Then there were the bite marks—some nineteen in total—spread across her body. They matched precisely molds that law enforcement investigators had made of Brewer's teeth. According to the medical personnel who performed the autopsy and analysis, there were many more, but at a certain point it seemed fruitless to continue counting.

The second part of the trial—the penalty phase—had likewise been brief and not seriously contested. The facts of the case—a brutal sexual assault, manual strangling and the disposal of Jackson's corpse in a creek, combined with whatever kind of savagery it took to cover her tiny body with bite marks—were by their very nature heinous, atrocious and cruel: the factors that the State was obligated to prove in order to distinguish Brewer's crime from less egregious murders and earn a death sentence.

To make matters worse, there had been talk that this might not have been Brewer's first victim. Eighteen months earlier, another three-year-old girl had been raped and murdered only a few miles from Brewer's house. Like Christine Jackson, the first victim, Courtney Smith, had been sexually assaulted, manually strangled, and dumped into a small body of water. Law enforcement had arrested another local man for that crime—Levon Brooks—and he had been convicted and sentenced to a term of life imprisonment. However, the almost identical *modus operandi* in both cases led some to believe that Brewer was responsible for both homicides.

Brewer's defense attorneys also had little to present to the jury in the way of mitigation evidence—evidence that Brewer was deserving of something less than death. He showed no remorse, nor signs of mental retardation or other history of physical or mental illness. As for a childhood of abuse and neglect—frequently present in the lives of capital murder defendants and sometimes illustrative of vitiated culpability—there was none. In short, everything pointed to the seemingly inescapable conclusion that Brewer was a dissociative child killer who was eligible for the ultimate criminal sanction.

Brewer passed the early afternoon in his cell. Shortly before 2:00 p.m. those lingering in the courtroom heard a knock from the door leading to the jury deliberation room. The clerk walked to the door, cracked it slightly, and received a folded piece of paper. She read it quickly and then looked up. The jury had reached a unanimous decision. After sheriff's deputies ushered Brewer from his cell and back to his seat beside his lawyers, Judge Lee J. Howard returned to the bench and the clerk opened the rear door. The jurors filed in. They were solemn, their eyes averted from the defendant and his attorneys. Many had measured and drawn looks on their faces.

Judge Howard confirmed that they had in fact reached a unanimous verdict and then had the foreperson hand the verdict form to the deputy clerk so that it could be read into the record.

"We, the jury," the clerk read, "find that the defendant should suffer the penalty of death."

As the clerk's voice died away, Judge Howard ordered Brewer to enter the well of the courtroom. Brewer dutifully obeyed. Bracketed by security personnel, he slowly stepped forward toward the bench.

"Mr. Brewer," Judge Howard said, "the jury of citizens of Lowndes County, Mississippi, has found you guilty of the crime of capital murder ... The jury has returned that verdict in open court. That verdict was that you should suffer death. Do you have anything you desire to say to the Court before sentence is imposed?"

"No," Mr. Brewer responded softly.

> I am by law required at this time to set a date for your execution.... I hereby direct that the sheriff immediately take custody of your body and immediately transport you to the maximum security unit of the Mississippi Department of Corrections at Parchman, Mississippi. You are to there remain in custody until May the twelfth of nineteen ninety-five, at which time you will be removed to a place where you shall suffer death by lethal injection. May God have mercy on your soul.

Guards ushered Brewer from court. With the jurors' work done, Judge Howard thanked them for their service and then formally dismissed them. It had been difficult work. The crime had been horrifying. Then there had been the trial, with its ineffably sad moments: the testimony about Christine, Brewer's mother's plea to spare her son's life....

But there did seem to be something hopeful—if that was the right word—about the trial's end. What with their work done, and seemingly done well, and several hours still remaining in the lovely spring afternoon, it did not seem unreasonable to perceive some promise of a new and better season. As the jurors gathered their belongings— some speaking quietly together, others choosing to remain alone with their thoughts— they walked down the short flight of stairs and out into the daylight.

Brewer, meanwhile, was already *en route* to Parchman Penitentiary, where he was fitted with a red jumpsuit and led to a small cell—number 285—in the heart of Maximum Security Unit 32, popularly known as "Death Row." He faced a bleak future of once-a-week showers, one hour per day of solitary recreation, and a looming execution date. Levon Brooks, Courtney Smith's convicted killer, was also housed in Parchman, across the prison grounds in a separate unit, finishing year four of his life sentence. According to actuarial tables for incarcerated prisoners, Brooks would age in prison twice as quickly as he would have on the outside, and be dead in approximately thirty years.

And that would have been that. Except for one thing: Kennedy Brewer and Levon Brooks were both innocent.

* * *

The Murders

On a hot Sunday morning in May, a little over a year and a half after Courtney Smith's abduction and murder, Annie Brewer, Kennedy Brewer's seventy-three-year-old mother, was at home in the small black community of Pilgrim's Rest, about eight miles from Brooksville, "'fixin' to go to church," she recalls, when her telephone rang. She answered to the voice of one of her daughters. "Christine is missing," her daughter said. Christine was not actually Annie Brewer's granddaughter—Kennedy Brewer and his girlfriend, Gloria Jackson, did have a child between them—but Annie Brewer treated Christine like her own. For several months, Gloria and Kennedy and the two children had been living together in a rental property a couple of miles away from Annie Brewer's place. Gloria had a history of mental health issues, and social services had visited their home on several occasions after neighbors reported seeing the children unattended, dirty, and unfed. Of the two, Kennedy Brewer was the better parent, but at nineteen and underemployed, most of his efforts consisted of occasionally bringing the children to his mother's and sisters' houses to get them fed and bathed.

When Annie Brewer heard the news, she threw down her broom and jumped in her car. By the time she arrived at the house, dozens of neighbors had already formed a search party. They had searched through the house. People were beginning to fan out across the nearby fields and cow pastures. Others hiked down toward Horse Hunter Creek, a small stream that meanders southeast through the low-lying pastureland. Shortly after the sheriff's department arrived, so did volunteers with tracking dogs. The dogs used Christine's clothing for a scent, but the unseasonable heat and dry weather made the trail difficult for them to track. After it grew dark, the searchers decided to quit and regroup the following morning.

The next day a new dog team of three dogs—all bloodhounds—arrived and began searching north of the bridge that crosses over the creek. They worked south, toward the pastures and away from the houses. As the dogs made their way down the creek bed and in and out of the thick brush, they came to a pool of water. One of the dogs reacted—"pawing the water" as her handler described it—and when searchers looked they saw a small opening in the brush on the other side of the creek. Clearly visible on the opposite bank was a slip mark. By then, though, the dogs were tired and it was getting dark again, so the searchers called off the search for a second day.

The next morning a helicopter from the Meridian Mississippi Naval Base joined the search. The pilot picked up a sheriff's deputy and a couple members of the dog team near Macon and then flew to the scene. They followed the creek north to Pilgrim's Rest and tracked south to the pool that had excited the dogs the day before. Someone on the helicopter spotted something in the water but couldn't tell what it was. As they lowered into position over the pool, the rotors "just boiled that water right up," one deputy sheriff who was inside the helicopter said, and Christine's body floated to the top.

* * *

[A] state-designated pathologist, Dr. Steven T. Hayne, ... performed the autopsy. *** Dr. Hayne noticed a number of abrasions on the front lateral and posterior surfaces of Christine's arm, forearm, hand and fingers. They were small—from between three-eighths of an inch to about five-eighths of an inch. He suspected that they were bite marks and reached out to a friendly colleague and frequent collaborator, a clinical dentist in Hattiesburg, Mississippi named Michael, who was also a forensic odontologist—a bitemark identification expert.... [D]ental impressions were taken of Brewer's teeth. The models were compared to the wounds on Christine's body. According to [forensic ondontologist Dr. Michael] West, there were nineteen areas on Christine's body that matched the bite pattern. Brewer was indicted, and ... the veteran district attorney, Forrest Allgood, announced that he would be seeking the death penalty.

* * *

"The Extra Mile"

For much of Southern history, black victims of crime and black perpetrators did not arouse much interest from law enforcement. As the [Jackson] *Clarion Ledger* reported in 1904: "We had the usual number of [Negro] killings during the week just closed. Aside from the dozen or so reported in the press, several homicides occurred which the county correspondents did not deem sufficient to be chronicled in the dispatches." But when the call came in to the Noxubee County sheriff's department to report Courtney Smith's disappearance, it was a different era.

* * *

Dr. West arrived at the Rankin County morgue to meet with Hayne the day after Hayne had conducted his autopsy. As Dr. Hayne would later explain in his trial testimony, his determination to associate the forensic odontologist, Dr. West, was based not only on his own suspicions about the marks, but on West's impeccable credentials. West had recently been named researcher of the year by the American Academy of Forensic Sciences. Not only did he have a thriving clinical dental practice in Hattiesburg, but he was also engaged in ground-breaking forensic bite-mark research that used alternative sources of light to reveal bite injuries that would otherwise remain invisible during routine post-mortem examinations.... [West and Hayne would proceed to testify in both the Levon Brooks and the Kennedy Brewer cases.]

West began his examination of Hayne's initial findings by comparing the unique features present in the marks on Christine Jackson's body to the unique class and individual characteristics that he could identify in each of the separate suspects. Class characteristics, as West described his experiences with them in his forensic research, were characteristics found in a certain specific group of objects. He often analogized by comparing a box of flat head screwdrivers to a box of Philips-head screwdrivers: though each of the Philips-head screwdrivers may be different sizes, they all display the same class characteristic—a Philips-head shape—which distinguishes them from flat head screwdrivers. According to West, these same class differentiations are observable in individuals' dentition—in the arch, the shape of the jaw, overbites, underbites, and so forth. Even an individual tooth, he explained, may sometimes exhibit class characteristics.

Individual characteristics, on the other hand, West explained, usually occur from "random wear and tear"—things like chipped or broken teeth. Though these individual characteristics are not always obvious, even small cracks or other imperfections can create visible differences on the biting surface. West also considered additional factors: the relative positioning of the biter and the person being bitten—in this case Christine—the likely reaction of each during a violent struggle, or the elasticity, or lack of it, in the skin at the site of the bite.

His analysis revealed that five of the nineteen bites were "very good bite marks;" the remaining ranged from "fair to average or—or poor." All of them, though, West concluded, matched Brewer. On May 14th, just over ten days after Christine had disappeared, West wrote a letter to Noxubee County law enforcement that summarized his findings: the "bite marks found on the body of Christine Jackson were indeed and without doubt inflicted by Kennedy Brewer."

* * * [West had given similar testimony in Brooks' earlier trial that the bite-marks found on Courtney Smith's body matched Levon Brooks' dentition.]

There is nothing to indicate that the juries were anything other than fair. Brooks's jury deliberated for several days, and after convicting him returned with a life sentence. Brewer's verdicts were returned more quickly. The evidence, especially the forensic work that discovered and then corroborated the matching bite marks, was overwhelming. The verdicts in both cases were a foregone conclusion.

"I Don't Want That to Happen to Me"

Brooks's appeal was written and filed by one of his trial attorneys. The only issue of merit involved West's testimony. Having grown weary of what it viewed as baseless challenges to bite mark evidence, the State Supreme Court not only affirmed Brooks's conviction but also took the time to "state affirmatively that bite-mark identification evidence is admissible in Mississippi."

For all intents and purposes, Levon Brooks's fight was over. The Sixth Amendment right to counsel does not provide a lawyer for post-conviction claims, so any challenge would have to be drafted by Brooks himself. That kind of legal training is beyond the ability of most attorneys. Levon Brooks didn't even try. Instead, he settled in to serve his life sentence. He honed his self-taught artistic skills and drafted homemade greeting cards that he sold or traded to fellow inmates and dwelled on his mother's parting advice: "You go on up there and do right, and the Lord will bring you home."

[Meanwhile,] after Brewer's appeal was filed, the Mississippi Supreme Court finally found "no error in the trial of this matter that necessitates a reversal or any other ground upon which Brewer is entitled to relief from the conviction or the sentence of death by lethal injection." Brewer appealed to the United States Supreme Court, which, presumably because it found no error, declined to hear it. Two days after the Supreme Court denied his appeal, Mississippi sought permission to re-schedule Brewer's execution date.

Brewer wrote to his lawyer. "[C]ould you send me about $60.00 to get me a type writer[?]" he asked. "[W]hat I am doing is fixing to get involve in learning the law because I just can't spend my life in prison for nothing that's why I try to learn more and about the law each day." His lawyer never sent him one, so Brewer pulled out a clean piece of lined notebook paper and wrote a letter. He addressed it to an organization that he had heard about in the back of a magazine. "Dear Mrs. Greene," he began in careful script, "how are you today? I know you probably don't know me but the reason am writing is can you ... help me out concerning my case ... I really, really, really would highly appreciated."

Four days later, Brewer's letter arrived at the Innocence Project in New York.

The Truth

In the fall of 2007, along with several other attorneys, I represented Levon Brooks and Kennedy Brewer in the effort to free them. I was at the time — and still am — the director of the Mississippi Innocence Project. Our offices and legal clinic are housed at the University of Mississippi's Law School in Oxford, Mississippi. Brooks was our first client. I have since worked closely with both men, not only on their criminal cases, but also on the kinds of issues — legal and otherwise — that the wrongfully imprisoned typically face upon their return to free society. During the course of my representation, I have spent significant time with them and their families — as well as with many others who were involved to one extent or another in their cases.

I wanted to understand what happened to them, and why.[1] * * *

On the night that Courtney Smith was abducted and murdered, Levon Brooks was at work. He was a jack-of-all-trades at the Santa Barbara nightclub, a sort of modern-day Mississippi juke joint east of Brooksville. (During the day Brooks worked as a custodian at a local public school.) Soon after Brooks arrived at the Santa Barbara that evening for his shift, the club filled quickly. He knew almost everyone there. He recognized friends and the faces of regulars. Virtually every patron who came to the club that night had contact with him. Some handed him their cover charge at the door. In the small hours of the morning just before the club closed, remaining cus-

---

1. Editor's note: This section was moved from the introduction to enhance the readability of the condensed excerpt.

tomers—and there would have been a lot of them—would have waited around for Brooks to begin in his favorite task: cooking up fried fish dinners. It was close to the perfect alibi.

And so, when Forrest Allgood completed his opening statement in Brooks's trial, it was Brooks's lawyers' turn to answer, their first opportunity to let the jury know how and why their client was factually innocent. But they did nothing. They did not stand. They did not say anything to the jury. The moment no doubt passed quickly; defense counsel's decision not to respond takes up just over a line of the trial transcript. But the effect was devastating. The message to the jury could not have been any clearer: Brooks's lawyers said nothing because they had nothing to say. It was the functional equivalent of endorsing Allgood's opening statement. If a criminal trial is an exercise in granting a defendant his day in court, Levon Brooks had just watched his come and go in a matter of seconds. * * *

Of course what should have concerned everyone ... was the forensic fraud being perpetrated in the case. That type of fraud has a long tradition in Mississippi, and its courts have been willing participants when it comes to admitting it into evidence. For years, forensic fraud was often used to whitewash civil rights abuses. In some instances, the fraud was of morbid interest, as in the official medical reports about the death of Robert Johnson, the fabled Mississippi Delta bluesman. Johnson was most likely poisoned by strychnine or lye by a jealous husband at a juke-joint near Greenwood, Mississippi, in 1938. His death was reputedly horrible and protracted. He vomited for hours, bled from his mouth and crawled around on the floor howling like a dog. He died about three days later. The coroner's report listed the cause of death as "No doctor."

At other times, particularly during the Civil Rights movement, the death investigation system was almost exclusively controlled by small-town, elected county officials, frequently county coroners—who formed a mostly hidden but murderously powerful good old boy network. Issues of public health, including criminal culpability in suspicious deaths, were frequently sacrificed to advance broader efforts to maintain racial codes. In 1955, three shotgun blasts to the head killed Reverend George Lee, a black Baptist minister who had the temerity to found a local NAACP chapter in rural Humphreys County, Mississippi. At the all-white inquest into Lee's death, the coroner determined that the mortal injuries were indeed sustained in an unfortunate car accident, but that the shotgun blasts were merely the sound of blown tires. As for the lead pellets removed from Lee's head? The inquest's report explained that they were merely tooth fillings. The coroner concurred with the findings, and the official cause of death was listed as "unknown." No criminal investigation was ever opened, and the case remains unsolved to this day.

By the time of Brooks's and Brewer's trials, Dr. Steven Hayne, the forensic pathologist, had secured for himself through a series of orchestrated maneuvers a virtual monopoly on the State's autopsy needs. As a result, the State medical examiner office was essentially vacant, and so Hayne could operate with no official oversight. Among the public health disasters that occurred was that Hayne and West, the forensic odontologist, formalized their business relationship. Hayne performed autopsies in bulk with West's help, and West, with Hayne supplying him a steady stream of bodies, was able to practice his unique brand of forensic wound identification. The two also cultivated their favorite customer base: law enforcement. They took out ads in law enforcement trade journals touting their services. According to one ad, retaining their services would "achieve higher conviction rates" by using a novel forensic investigation tool—alternative light imaging—that involved using ultraviolet light to enhance wound markings. "[I]t could become a valuable asset to your department, too," they claimed.

* * *

The hazards that flowed from Hayne's assembly line body farm were well-known dirty secrets among those who had observed his work: corpses lined up like cordwood on the loading dock; forensic reports claiming that organs had been observed and weighed but that in reality had never been removed. But prosecutors and more than a few plaintiffs' lawyers were willing to overlook these issues because Hayne was the only game in town and an effective co-conspirator in winning a conviction or attaining a lucrative judgment in a wrongful death case. Remarkably, courts also accepted Hayne's testimony despite his grandiose claims and documented mistakes. Even worse, he was accepted as an expert despite the fact that he had failed to obtain a license from the American Board of Pathology—the field's premier peer-governed association. He had sat for—but failed—the Board's exam; or, in Hayne's version, decided not to finish it. * * *

Dr. West's claims were similarly suspect.... In 1991, someone stabbed Kim Ancona to death at the bar in Phoenix, Arizona, where she worked as a cocktail waitress. Ray Krone was arrested for the crime because witnesses claimed that Ancona closed up the bar that evening with a man named "Ray," and also because Ancona had a bite mark on her breast that resembled Krone's odd tooth structure. Krone had been involved in a traumatic car accident as a child that required extensive reconstructive surgery. Dubbed the "Snaggletooth Killer," he was convicted and sentenced to death based almost entirely on the testimony of a forensic odontologist who claimed that "the teeth of Ray Krone did cause the injuries on the body of Kimberly Ancona to a reasonable medical certainty. This represents the highest order of confidence that no other person caused the bite mark injuries." A decade later, DNA tests—from trace amounts of saliva on Ancona's tank top left by the biter—excluded Krone, and he was exonerated.

One of Krone's appellate lawyers was so disturbed by the self-assuredness of the bite mark expert relative to the field's lack of scientific bona fides that he decided to conduct an external blind proficiency test of his own. Wanting to find an odontologist who was unfamiliar with the case, he looked east of the Mississippi—and happened upon West. Using the photographs of Ancona's injuries, as well as dental molds from a "suspect" who had no connection whatsoever to the case, the lawyer sent material to West for an opinion about the existence, or non-existence, of a match between the molds and the injuries. He paid West a $750 retainer for his services and told him that the evidence was from a three year-old murder case of a college student from Idaho that had gone unsolved because of a lack of evidence against the prime suspect.

West quickly produced a videotaped report that demonstrated in detail how the "suspect's" dentition lined up with the injuries on Ancona's breast. He confidently claimed that the teeth conformed to the wounds and that the "odds of that happening if these weren't the teeth that created this bite would be almost astronomical. I feel very confident that there are enough points of unique individual characteristics in this study model to say that these teeth inflicted this bite mark." When informed of this type of gross error, any legitimate forensic scientist would have tried to figure out where his methodologies and analysis had gone wrong. West remained undaunted by the setback. In fact, if anything, he seemed emboldened. So were those in need of his expert services. * * *

Neither law enforcement nor Forrest Allgood had any reservations about continuing to use West in Brewer's case investigation or trial, though. In fact, Allgood questioned West for the jury on the previous years' professional difficulties. The two of them chalked it up to West being a scientist ahead of his time, surrounded by professional jealousy. "Much has been made of our use of Dr. West in ... [the Brewer trial]," Allgood has recently explained. "Dr. West was, at the time, one of the foremost names in forensic odontology ... He enjoyed an international reputation and was lecturing in London and China.... It was not 'junk' science."

Mississippi courts welcomed West's testimony. Brooks's lawyers' efforts to bar it in his case testimony were tepid, at best. Not only did they fail to raise much in the way of a substantive objection, they acted reflexively and hired a forensic odontologist of their own. To make matters worse, their expert was firmly in the professional sway of West. He agreed with West's findings that of the approximately one dozen tooth molds that had been taken from the suspects in Courtney's death, all could be excluded save one: Levon Brooks's. He also agreed that Brooks's dentition matched — although he was only willing to say that the match was consistent with Brooks's dentition, not "indeed and without doubt," as West claimed. He did add that the marks on the body may not have been bite marks at all — that they could have been made by "gravel or — or fingernails or — or I don't know, any number of things."

Given how much Brooks's expert actually buttressed the State's case, Allgood's cross-examination was more like the direct examination of a corroborating expert. In response to his claim that the marks could have been caused by any number of items, Allgood asked him if, "However, ... [he] nonetheless found that there were consistencies with these marks with the teeth of Levon Brooks, is that correct?" he asked Brooks's witness. The following conversation ensued:

"Yes," the expert answered.

"Now, Doctor, what is the — just — just out of the sake of clarifying, what is the nearest animal that has teeth like a human being?"

"Well I suppose an ape," he said.

"We don't have many of those running loose in — in the United States, is that correct?" Allgood asked. At which point, the expert finally located within himself a modicum of professional discretion.

"I could make a joke," he said, "but I won't."

With that answer, Brooks's lawyers rested their case.

* * *

In most cases of wrongful conviction, particularly those that occurred prior to the advent of sophisticated DNA technology, the real perpetrator is extraordinarily difficult — often impossible — to identify. There is no physical evidence or witnesses that offer a different version of events than the one that the prosecution adopts. But [Brewer]'s case was different.

Not long before Courtney Smith was abducted, there had been another similar incident in Noxubee County — involving a nighttime home invasion and attempted sexual assault. The perpetrator had broken into an elderly woman's house not far from Courtney's home and attempted to assault her. He was arrested. His name was Justin Albert Johnson. Among the things that witnesses reported seeing the night Courtney was abducted was a certain car parked near the pond where her body was eventually discovered. The car belonged to Johnson. Deputies interviewed him. His explanations for how his car could have been there were enigmatic, to say the least. Johnson told the deputies that if "someone say they saw my car over there, I can't say they didn't see it, but I am saying I wasn't over there. I know I wasn't over there."

"Have you ever been arrested?" one of the interviewing officers asked.

"Yes," he said, and then offered that it had been for a sex offense — breaking into an elderly woman's house and attempting to sexually assault her. Shortly after Johnson provided blood and hair samples, though, Hayne's and West's findings implicated Brooks, and Johnson was dropped as a suspect.

By the time Brooks went to trial, Johnson had been involved in another incident. On June 18, 1991, Verlinda Monroe had fallen asleep with her clothes on in her bedroom in Crawford, Mississippi.... Monroe was in her twenties and lived in the house with her brother, who worked at Bryan Foods, a nearby chicken processing plant. At about two in the morning, Monroe woke up because she felt something on her stomach. When she opened her eyes she could see a figure standing over top of her. She screamed and the individual ran off and out of the back door. Monroe's brother, who was asleep in the next room, woke up and turned on the lights. He saw a figure heading out the back door and gave chase but couldn't catch him. Monroe noticed that her pants had been unbuttoned and zipped down and that she had scratches in her pubic area. Though her brother was not able to catch the intruder he did get a glimpse of his face. He recognized him as a co-worker from Bryan Foods. It was Justin Johnson. Johnson was arrested that same day and charged with sexual assault, a felony that, unlike the earlier incident that had reduced to a non-serious misdemeanor charge, exposed him to serious jail time. Johnson was able to make bail and was released while he waited for the grand jury to return an indictment.

Johnson was a plausible alternate suspect and critical to Brooks's defense theory. He was also affirmative evidence of law enforcement's rush to judgment. Police and prosecutors had traded a known sex offender whose car was in the area of the pond the night Courtney disappeared and who could provide no reasonable explanation of why it—and he—had been there for two quacks peddling their pseudo-science. But there was a problem: Brooks's attorney had also been appointed by the court to represent Johnson in his two sex assault cases.

This type of conflict of interest is not uncommon, especially in smaller jurisdictions where the usual suspects are appointed to represent indigent defendants charged with crimes. Brooks's and Johnson's attorney was required to provide both of them a professional standard of care that included a duty of loyalty and confidentiality that he could not possibly provide to both. That the conflict of interest existed was obvious—Brooks's lawyer recognized that it "had jumped out of the book at … [him]." What escaped him, and everyone else, was how it should be handled.

Instead of keeping the conflict confidential—which was especially critical in his ongoing representation of Johnson—Brooks's lawyer informed Brooks in a letter that he represented both Brooks and Johnson, and then sent copies of the letter to the prosecutor and to the judge. The import of the conflict—that Johnson was a central part of Brooks's defense—never occurred to him and, as it turned out, to anyone else either. Instead of correcting Brooks's lawyer's professional and ethical gaffes, the trial judge turned to Brooks—in open court and minutes before his trial commenced—and asked if Brooks had had a chance to read the letter. Brooks said that he had. His attorneys told the court that they had each spoken with Brooks and fully explained the ramifications of the conflict. Leaving aside the fact that Brooks's attorneys were the last people that should have been discussing the substance of their conflict with him, precisely what they had discussed was never articulated. Instead, the following colloquy took place between Brooks and the court:

Court: You understand what … [your lawyer] has brought out, that he has represented some of these individuals [Johnson], is that correct?

Brooks: Yes, sir.

Court: And you understand that he—do you have any objection to him continuing the work as your co-counsel with … [your other attorney] in this case?

Brooks: No, sir.

Court: And you feel that he's looking out for your best interest and he's protecting your rights here today?

Brooks: Yes, sir.

Court: And you know what you're doing?

Brooks: Yes, sir.

Brewer's lawyers' challenge to West's testimony was more spirited than Brooks's lawyers, but it met with the same result: West was allowed to testify. Brewer's case—like Brooks's—would have also been aided by evidence that someone else had the motive, opportunity and ability to commit the offense. And like Brooks's case, Brewer's attorneys did not have to look far. Police reports provided to Brewer's lawyers included reports listing Justin Johnson as a suspect. His inclusion made intuitive sense. He lived a stone's throw from Brewer's house. At the time of Christine's murder he had not yet pleaded guilty to the sexual assault in the trailer. He was out on bail.

After his detention as a suspect in Brewer's case, Johnson underwent a medical examination to check for lacerations or bruising—presumably because anyone who had cut through the thick brush to deposit Christine's body in the creek would have minor cuts and scrapes. Of all the examined suspects, including Brewer, Johnson was the only one who had any sort of noticeable wounds. A nurse who observed his arms noted superficial scratches. When asked the cause, Johnson explained that they were "self-inflicted." Law enforcement never followed-up. Though the report was in the pre-trial discovery provided to defense counsel, Brewer's lawyers didn't either.

During the penalty phase of Brewer's trial, his lawyers called his mother, Annie Brewer, as a witness. She begged the jury to spare her son's life: "Please, please, sir, and please, ma'am, don't put the death penalty on Kenny. Please. I'm askin', please. Please, don't." When Allgood cross-examined her on her plea, he asked her whether there had been "any three year old girls sexually assaulted, killed and dumped in creeks in Noxubee County" since her son had been locked up. She had to agree that there hadn't been.

What she had no way of knowing, but that Allgood and law enforcement did, was that Justin Albert Johnson, with Levon Brooks's lawyer standing beside him, had pleaded guilty shortly after Christine Jackson's murder to the sexual assault of Verlinda Monroe in her trailer in Crawford. He could not have assaulted any more Noxubee victims even had he wanted to—he was serving a sentence at Parchman Penitentiary. But he had been out when Christine was murdered. And had anyone bothered to look at the court jackets kept as a public record in the clerk's office, they would have discovered something else of interest: receipts for the hospital's examinations in both the Brooks case and Brewer cases. They had one name in common: Justin Albert Johnson.

* * *

After Innocence Project lawyers asked that DNA from Brewer's case be tested, the request was granted, and in the late fall of 2007, Noxubee County law enforcement sent several boxes of physical evidence to a lab in California. The evidence included material from Brooks's case, too, because Brewer's lawyers were of the mind that the true perpetrator had likely committed both crimes. The lab began its testing on the semen from Brewer's case and quickly identified a single profile—a profile that did not match Brewer. That wasn't enough for Allgood, however. Because he remained convinced of Brewer's involvement, it was imperative that the source be identified, if at all possible.

The cheek swabs taken from the suspects in Brewer's case were still testable. So the lab went to work on those. After locating useable DNA, he began his analyses. "Part of my role in the investigations is to take the data and go through and analyze it and inter-compare the samples," he explains. "And so, I'm sitting at my computer and I'm going through this data — and, can I use a four-letter word? — I'm sitting at my computer and I'm going 'Holy Shit!' we've identified the sperm source. It's Justin Johnson."

When Brewer's attorneys were notified of the results, they kept the news from All-good and Noxubee law enforcement, both of whom had a vested interest in defending the integrity of their investigations and prosecutions, and turned instead to the Mississippi Attorney General's office for help. Investigators traveled from their offices in Jackson to Pilgrim's Rest and turned left about a half mile after passing Kennedy and Gloria Jackson's old house. Less than a quarter mile later they pulled up beside a small, dark green cottage. Some of the agents covered the rear of the house while two others knocked on the front door. Justin Johnson answered. After being confronted with the DNA test results and placed under arrest, he agreed to return with the investigators to the crime scenes.

At Brewer's old house, he showed them how he had walked up to the bedroom window, quietly opened it and reached in and taken Christine, sexually assaulted her, strangled and thrown her, still alive, into the creek. He admitted driving his car to Brooksville and parking near the pond. He described walking to Courtney's house, through the unlocked door, past the sleeping figure of Courtney's uncle, and into the bedroom. He had acted alone, he said. He didn't know Levon Brooks or Kennedy Brewer. He didn't bite either girl.

Discovering the quantity and quality of evidence necessary to exonerate someone typically takes years, at best. Given the age of many potential wrongful-conviction cases and the vagaries of physical evidence — mainly its storage and degradation — the death or disappearance of witnesses, their diminishing memories, combined with procedural difficulties that arise in a post-conviction setting that values finality, each exoneration is in its own way a minor miracle. In Brooks's and Brewer's cases, however, the dispositive results of the DNA testing along with Johnson's unequivocal confessions forced the State to drop any opposition and the cases moved to a conclusion rapidly. * * *

Epilogue

Brewer was exonerated in Noxubee County Circuit Court in February, 2008. Levon Brooks a few weeks later — in early March. Together, the two had spent almost thirty years imprisoned for crimes that they did not commit. * * *

Of all the people who were involved, the one who has the most at stake — his life — is the only one who has come clean. When law enforcement officers surrounded

Justin Johnson's house in early February of 2008, he identified himself and admitted to being the perpetrator in both cases.

For that, Forrest Allgood has announced, he will seek the death penalty.

B. Legal Materials, Exercises, and Media

1. *Exercise*: The National Registry of Exonerations "collects, analyzes and disseminates information about all known exonerations of innocent criminal defendants in the United States, from 1989 to the present." The Registry publishes the stories of exonerees and provides searchable statistical data online about their individual cases.

    Go to the National Registry of Exonerations online at http://www.law.umich.edu/special/exoneration/Pages/about.aspx.

    Under Using the Registry, go to Browse Cases and look up an exoneree and his or her story. What were the contributing factors to your exoneree's wrongful conviction?

2. *Reflective Essay*: Why would anyone accuse or prosecute an innocent man? Hannah Arendt, a political theorist, notes in her book *Eichmann in Jerusalem: A Report on the Banality of Evil*:

    > Might the problem of good and evil, our faculty for telling right from wrong, be connected with our faculty of thought? ... Could the activity of thinking, as such, the habit of examining whatever happens to come to pass or attract attention, regardless of results or specific contents, could this activity be among the conditions that make men abstain from evil-doing or even actually "condition" them against it? ... Do the inability to think and a disastrous failure of what we commonly call conscience coincide?

    What do you think? Do wrongful convictions occur simply from a lack of thought? Why or why not? Explain your answer in a one-page reflective essay.

3. *Recommended Viewing*: *Mississippi Innocence* documents the wrongful convictions of Kenny Brewer and Levon Brooks in Noxubee County, Mississippi. Watch a clip about the forensic evidence used to convict Kenny Brewer at https://vimeo.com/21777255, from 5:24–10:12. For more on the film, visit https://mississippiinnocencefilm.com.

    Levon Brooks passed away at the age of 58 on January 24, 2018. Just months before his death, the U.S. Court of Appeals for the Fifth Circuit denied his legal claims against Stephen Hayne and Michael West for their fraudulent forensic testimony at his trial. The Court found that although Hayne and West may have been grossly negligent, they did not intentionally fabricate their testimony and they acted as agents of the state, protected from legal accountability by qualified immunity. *Brooks v. Hayne*, 860 F.3d 819 (5th Cir. 2017).

For more on Levon's life and death, read this in memoriam by Radley Balko in *The Washington Post*, https://www.washingtonpost.com/news/the-watch/wp/2018/01/26/levon-brooks-a-mississippi-man-wrongly-convicted-by-bad-forensics-dies-at-58/?utm_term=.30b1f599f5f5.

4. *Recommended Viewing*: George Stinney became the youngest person executed in the United States when South Carolina executed him in 1944. Stinney, a 14-year-old African-American boy, was convicted of killing two white girls after a trial that lasted three hours, and a jury deliberation of only 10 minutes. In 2014 he was exonerated. Watch a four-minute clip on Stinney's case and its role in history at CNN, http://www.cnn.com/videos/crime/2014/12/18/erin-dnt-mattingly-george-stinney-exonerated.cnn.

5. *Additional Readings*: Many notable books share the experiences of exonerees and their wrongful convictions. To name only a few, we suggest *Chasing Justice: My Story of Freeing Myself After Two Decades on Death Row for a Crime I Didn't Commit* by Kerry Max Cook, *The Innocent Man* by John Grisham, and *Actual Innocence: When Justice Goes Wrong and How to Make It Right* by Barry Scheck, Peter Neufeld, and Jim Dwyer.

Chapter Two

Defining Innocence and Miscarriages of Justice

The present case requires us to further amplify the meaning of "actual innocence".... A prototypical example of "actual innocence" in a colloquial sense is the case where the State has convicted the wrong person of the crime. Such claims are of course regularly made on motions for new trial after conviction in both state and federal courts, and quite regularly denied because the evidence adduced in support of them fails to meet the rigorous standards for granting such motions. But in rare instances it may turn out later, for example, that another person has credibly confessed to the crime, and it is evident that the law has made a mistake.

—*Sawyer v. Whitley*, 505 U.S. 333, 340–41 (1992)

A. Readings

Larry May and Nancy Viner,
Actual Innocence and Manifest Injustice

49 St. Louis U. L.J. 481, 482, 497 (2005)

One of the most disturbing aspects of the contemporary death penalty jurisprudence in the United States is the reluctance of courts to examine claims of actual innocence of those who are scheduled for execution.... It may seem odd to those who do not know this debate that there is even a controversy here. Surely, on common-sense grounds it is odd that anyone would argue in favor of executing the innocent, as seems to have been the position of the Attorney General of Missouri in the *Amrine* case.[2] To motivate consideration of this issue, it is important first to note that the term "legally innocent" could merely be a technical term for someone who has not been convicted by a court of law. Used in this way, there are no cases of "actual innocence" on appeal because either one has indeed been convicted in which case one is not now innocent, or one has not been convicted, in which case one is indeed innocent, but then one is not in need of appeal because one would not be on death row. If a person is "legally innocent," in this technical sense, then no one

---

2. State *ex rel.* Amrine v. Roper, 102 S.W.3d 541, 543 (Mo. 2003) (en banc).

would argue that this person should be executed. But the controversy concerns what is sometimes called "factual innocence," roughly synonymous for "did not commit the act that one is accused of having committed." There is a way to make sense of this dispute by distinguishing between being "legally innocent" and being "factually innocent," where the latter status does not turn on what a trial court has decided. Those who argue against appellate review of actual innocence cases often argue that it is inefficient or unfair to the families of victims not to allow finality in these emotionally charged cases where "legal innocence" has been disproved. [Here], we will be exclusively concerned with actual innocence cases concerning factual innocence. * * * If claims of actual innocence, especially in capital cases, are not claims that fall under habeas review, it is unclear what complaints would ever properly fall under habeas review. Contrary to what the assistant attorney general argued in the *Amrine* case, and consistent with a long line of theorists who have considered this issue, everything possible should be done to make sure that the state does not execute the innocent.

Hugo Adam Bedau and Michael L. Radelet, *Miscarriages of Justice in Potentially Capital Cases*
40 STAN. L. REV. 21, 39–47 (1987)

The primary aim of this article is to reach a better understanding of the miscarriages of justice in capital or potentially capital cases that have occurred in the United States during this century. To this end, we undertook as our main task the construction, on uniform principles, of a catalogue of cases in which such grave errors occurred.

* * *

The Concept of a Miscarriage of Justice

"Miscarriage of justice" is a concept open to various definitions and applications. Because it has no standard or preferred use, we need to explain as precisely as possible how we define and use the concept....

A. Criminal Intent

Some years ago, Charles Black argued that the death penalty, no matter how it is actually administered, inherently encounters the possibility of mistake in its application. He pointed out that "[i]f we resume use of the death penalty"—as, indeed, the nation has subsequently done—"we will be killing some people by mistake...." As Black observed, the "range of possible 'mistake' is much broader than [is usually supposed]." He identified three sorts of error—mistake of law and two types of mistake of fact. Black bifurcated the latter category into what he called mistake of "gross physical facts" and mistake of "psychological facts." As the term is used in this article, miscarriage of justice excludes Black's "mistake of law" and "psychological" errors.... If person A is convicted of killing person B, and A did in fact kill B, then A is not a victim of a miscarriage of justice, even though it is later discovered that A was insane, acted in self-defense, or had some other legally valid excuse or justification.

Consider the following case in this light. In 1907, on a picket line outside a restaurant in Nevada, Morrie R. Preston shot and killed the restaurant owner, who had approached Preston with a gun. Preston was convicted of second-degree murder and sentenced to twenty-five years in prison. Seven years later, however, the parole board released Preston, conceding that the testimony of a star witness had been perjured and that Preston had acted in self-defense. If we accept as correct the judgment on which the parole board based its decision, then the error in originally convicting Preston involved what Black has called "the psychological facts." The conviction rested on imputing to the defendant a "psychological" condition—namely, an intention to kill another, or the mens rea of murder—that he did not have. Although a comprehensive discussion of the topic of miscarriage of justice in capital cases would, ideally, include consideration of such errors, we decided to exclude all such cases. One reason is that our limited resources fell far short of what would be needed to investigate the many cases of this sort that undoubtedly await systematic inquiry. Another and more fundamental reason, relating to the criteria for "due process," will be explained below.

Killing in self-defense is, of course, only one of several subcategories of homicide in which the mens rea of murder is absent. The defendant may in fact have been incapable of forming criminal intent, even though the trial court erroneously found otherwise. For example, in the 1976 Arizona case of Joe Cota Morales,[3] the defendant was convicted of first-degree murder and sentenced to death. On appeal, the conviction was reversed because the trial judge had erred in instructing the jury to exclude from its consideration the effect of the defendant's intoxication on his ability to form criminal intent. At retrial, Morales was acquitted. The original conviction was no doubt a miscarriage of justice; nevertheless, we did not include this case and others like it.

In some excluded cases, the factual situation is much more complex. One such case is the 1921 shoot-out in Centralia, Washington, between local I.W.W. union members and parading American Legionnaires. A somewhat similar shoot-out took place in 1929 between striking workers and the police in the mill town of Gastonia, North Carolina. On each occasion, the victims were shot and killed by persons unknown. Nonetheless, the police arrested several workers, juries convicted them of murder (and in the Gastonia case, sentenced several to death), and later events vindicated the defendants. The violations of due process in each case were massive and incontestable. But whether the defendants, rather than some of the others associated with them, fired the fatal shots was never established; furthermore, whoever did shoot probably did so in self-defense in the face of provocative and life-threatening behavior by the authorities. If this is the correct interpretation of the events, then exclusion of these cases from our catalogue is appropriate.

Consider also the 1976 Nebraska case of Erwin Simants.[4] He was convicted on six counts of first-degree murder and sentenced to death. On appeal, the convictions were overturned on the technicality that the sheriff had improperly visited the se-

---

3. State v. Morales, 587 P.2d 236 (Ariz. 1978).
4. Simants v. State, 277 N.W.2d 217 (Neb. 1979).

questered jurors. But at retrial Simants was acquitted on the ground of insanity. Simants' conviction was without doubt another miscarriage of justice in a capital case, but not the type with which we are concerned. Finally, consider the 1975 Maryland case of Sylvester Morris, which we also exclude. Morris was convicted of first-degree murder and sentenced to life imprisonment. After losing his appeals in the state courts, Morris sought a federal writ of habeas corpus, and was granted a new trial because the judge had improperly instructed the jury that the burden was on the accused to prove that the killing was (as Morris claimed) accidental. At retrial, Morris was acquitted after the state failed to convince the trial court that the killing was not accidental. The above cases illustrate several kinds of grave errors that appellate courts have identified and rectified. Not in dispute in any of the foregoing is "the gross physical fact" as to who killed the victim. Preston, Morales, Simants, and Morris pleaded not guilty, and on the facts before us, none was legally guilty as charged. Yet there is little doubt that each defendant killed the person of whose murder he was convicted. Nonetheless, these cases and the many others like them are excluded from our catalogue of miscarriages of justice, because they embody primarily what we will call "due process" errors, rather than the more fundamental error of convicting the wrong person.

B. The Criminal Act

In light of the foregoing discussion, it might appear that all miscarriages of justice, as the term is used in this article, must involve a conviction of the wrong person and not merely the conviction of someone unfairly tried. This is not quite correct, because it is also necessary in some cases to reject the presupposition that someone is guilty of the crime in question. Miscarriages also arise whenever the criminal act resulting in conviction was never committed.

The California case of Antonio Rivera and Merla Walpole illustrates this point. In 1974, they were convicted in San Bernardino of the murder of their infant daughter. Nearly two years after their conviction, however, the young girl was found alive in San Francisco. Her parents had abandoned her there in 1965, distraught by their poverty and inability to care for the sick child. In this case, there was no homicide even if there was a crime of child abandonment. Rivera and Walpole were not the wrong persons to convict of the alleged homicide: No one should have been convicted of homicide because no homicide occurred. Accordingly, to establish that a miscarriage of justice has occurred, it is sufficient for our purposes to show that someone has been convicted of a potentially capital crime when no such crime actually occurred.

C. Accomplices

We also do not consider a defendant innocent simply because he can demonstrate that, in a case of homicide, it was not he but a codefendant who fired the fatal shot. For example, in 1941 Edward Kiernan was convicted of first-degree murder in the killing by his accomplices of a Sing Sing prison guard and a police officer during an escape attempt. His conviction was vacated in 1961 on the ground that his confession was coerced. Evidence submitted at trial showed that, at the time of the killings, Kiernan was outside the prison walls, ready with a car to help the escaping prisoners. Because no evidence exists that Kiernan killed, tried to kill, or intended to kill anyone, and there is no dispute as to the cause or the location of the killings, it is arguable that he should be regarded as guilty of the murders. But because the law does not nullify Kiernan's culpability merely because he was not the triggerman, we do not treat him as innocent.

Another example, even more unusual, is the case of David Almeida in Pennsylvania in 1947. Almeida and his co-defendants were engaged in the armed robbery of a supermarket. A police officer was killed while attempting to apprehend them. Later evidence proved that the fatal bullet was not fired by Almeida, or even by one of his co-felons, but by another police officer. Nevertheless, Almeida was convicted of murder and sentenced to death. On appeal, his conviction was overturned. Although his conviction was in error, we do not regard him as innocent under our criteria. Of course, for other purposes, such as those of concern to Black and many other critics of the death penalty, cases such as Kiernan's and Almeida's may be quite legitimately counted as miscarriages of justice in capital cases.

D. Conviction Averted

We could also have cast our net more inclusively than we did by including several other kinds of cases, such as those in which a conviction was fortuitously averted. There are many potentially capital cases of this sort. One frequently cited is the 1924 Connecticut case of Harold Israel. Israel confessed to murder, and a ballistics expert testified at trial that Israel's gun was the murder weapon. Homer S. Cummings, the prosecuting attorney (later Attorney General of the United States), nevertheless decided to drop the prosecution after discovering that the witness was unreliable and that the defendant's confession was coerced. It was later said of this case that "[w]ithout question, Israel would have hanged if it had not been for the conscientiousness of the Connecticut prosecutor." In a 1934 Massachusetts case, Louis Berrett and Clement Molway were identified by eight eyewitnesses as the men who killed a theater employee. Just prior to the final arguments at their trial, the actual killers confessed. The jury foreman was later quoted as saying, "This trial has taught me one thing. Before it I was a firm believer in capital punishment. I'm not now." In 1962 in Idaho, Gerald Anderson confessed to the murders of two neighbors. Anderson was in jail for ten months, although his confession was the only evidence against him. It later became evident that the confession had been obtained by coercion. Meanwhile, another man confessed and was tried and convicted of the crimes. The 1964 New York case of George Whitmore, Jr., received considerable publicity. Whitmore, a semi-literate youth, confessed under coercion to three murders and was convicted of an assault and attempted rape in a fourth case. A 1965 trial on one of the homicide charges ended in a hung jury, and his conviction for the assault was reversed on appeal. He was retried twice and reconvicted on the assault charge. Eventually, another person was arrested and convicted for the two murders. In 1973, when new evidence conclusively established Whitmore's innocence, the third assault conviction was reversed and the charges dropped.

One of the most widely publicized recent cases of this sort occurred in Georgia. In 1977, five young black men—"the Dawson Five"—were arrested and charged with the murder of a white man and threatened with the death penalty. The sole evidence against the five youths was an allegedly coerced confession by one of them. Under considerable pressure from local and national publicity, the prosecution dropped any interest in the death sentence and eventually dropped the indictments as well. No one else confessed or was arrested, but the five Dawson youths have been widely regarded as entirely innocent.

On the facts before us, Israel, Berrett and Molway, Anderson, Whitmore, and the Dawson Five were undoubtedly innocent. In each case someone else was guilty and in some of these cases, the guilty person was eventually found. But in each case the criminal process was interrupted before any of the most fateful official steps ending in death—sentence, denial of clemency, execution—ever took place. All these steps were mooted because the crucial first step, conviction, was fortunately averted.

We exclude all such cases. Our chief reason for doing so is that when a trial is interrupted (whether because of new-found evidence that the defendant is innocent or for other reasons), the criminal justice system is arguably shown to have been nearly as effective as it could be. No conceivable system of criminal justice can be expected to arrest, indict, and try only the guilty; some risk of error must always be embraced at the decision points of whether to arrest the suspect, try the accused, and convict the defendant. Accordingly, when one of the innocent is tried but not convicted (or, as in the Anderson case, not even brought to trial), no fundamental flaw in the system is revealed that could be easily remedied by any plausible alternative system.

It is, of course, useful in the broad context to recognize that many such cases of incipient error do occur. No doubt the risk of executing the innocent grows as the risks of arresting, indicting, and trying the innocent also rise. The Israel case and others more recent prove that these latter risks continue to be greater than zero. But the risk that really matters is the risk of erroneous conviction. It is also true that the risk of convicting the innocent is increased so long as due process errors are committed and uncorrected. But involuntary confessions, perjured testimony, "planted" circumstantial evidence, and other errors and mistakes are irrelevant for the purposes of our study except when they play a role in securing the conviction of an innocent defendant.

E. Operational Definition

[W]e [thus] use the term "miscarriage of justice" to refer only to those cases in which: (a) The defendant was convicted of homicide or sentenced to death for rape; and (b) when either (i) no such crime actually occurred, or (ii) the defendant was legally and physically uninvolved in the crime. We have three main reasons for adopting these relatively strict criteria.

First, we are primarily concerned with wrong-person mistakes—the conviction and execution of the factually "innocent"—and not with the erroneous conviction of those who are legally innocent (as in cases of killing in self-defense). Second, in holding to the narrower criteria, we are continuing in the tradition pioneered by Borchard. For him, "convicting the innocent" meant convicting the wrong person, someone not involved in the crime (if, indeed, the crime even occurred). The errors he documented did not include convicting the right person for the wrong reasons or by unfair means or with violations of constitutional due process. Nor did they include convicting a mere accessory or an accomplice to a crime committed by a co-felon. If we can show—as, indeed, we can—that the number of erroneous convictions is substantial in potentially capital cases in which the central (even if not the only) error was convicting the wholly innocent, that will suffice to reinforce an important lesson: Our criminal justice system is fallible and the gravest possible errors in its administration can be documented.

Finally, and most importantly, if the concept of miscarriage of justice in capital cases is extended to include all those cases in which errors and mistakes accompany the arrest, trial, conviction, or sentencing of someone who indeed is involved in the crime (whether or not the error or mistake is negligent, rather than deliberate), then it is unclear whether any capital case can be regarded as free of mistake. A central thesis of the modern critique of capital punishment, which our research supports, is that mistake in death penalty cases, once mistake is taken in its broadest sense, is "not [one of those] fringe-problems, susceptible to being mopped up by minor refinements in concept and technique." Rather, it is "ineradicable in the administration of the death penalty." Moreover, it has been aggravated by the complex structure of contemporary capital punishment statutory and constitutional law and by the way its daily use in trial and appellate courts gives rise to errors narrowly describable as "mistake of law." The problem of adequately defining a capital crime—a crime in which the guilty defendant "deserves" the death penalty—is not new; it is virtually as old as the history of the death penalty itself. The issue is also much more general than our discussion so far indicates. Attempts to solve it began most conspicuously in this country at the end of the eighteenth century with the enactment of statutes defining a special class of homicide cases suitable for the death penalty and designated as "first-degree murder." Critics have long indicated the difficulties in defining and applying the distinction between "degrees" of murder, as well as in other attempts to carve out by statute a class of crimes appropriately punished by death. The result of these and other related difficulties is that "[t]he concept of mistake fades out as the standard"—that is, the standard distinguishing the legally permissible from the legally impermissible procedures at each stage of the criminal process—"grows more and more vague and unintelligible." No empirical research, such as ours, could hope to investigate all the kinds of "mistakes" that occur, once it is granted that the very concept of a mistake has become blurred beyond recognition. We reduce this problem, if we do not entirely avoid it, by excluding all cases in which, so far as we can tell, the errors do not include the conviction of a person both legally and factually innocent.

D. Michael Risinger and Lesley C. Risinger,
Miscarriages of Justice: A Theoretical and Practical Overview
7 J. Marshall L.J. 373, 389–404 (2014)

Conviction on the Wrong Theory and Miscarriage of Justice

[A] recurring category of cases presenting vexing issues involves conviction based on an account of a crime later shown by strong evidence to be untenable and false. This presents a problem because we are now moving away from assuming circumstances that affirmatively establish the factual innocence of the convicted person. That person may still be guilty of the charged crime, but they were convicted on a clearly false premise. This kind of scenario raises two linked questions: How far ought the state be able to go in proposing alternate scenarios of guilt to overcome the collapse of the factual account upon which the conviction was based; and, if a retrial is in fact ordered and is practically impossible, what is the status of the defendant? Has he been "exonerated?" We will delay the consideration of the second question until after an exploration of the first question.

A series of examples may help to clarify these problems. We will give what appears to us to be the easiest first, and proceed from there. Assume that a person is charged with the homicide of a forty-year old female drug addict that took place on a public street in an urban high-crime neighborhood sometime between 5:30 and 5:45 a.m. on a very cold late January morning. Assume further that, when investigating the crime, after many unproductive leads, the police found a person, another local with a bad drug problem, who swears that he saw the defendant commit the crime. Assume that on the testimony of this sole eyewitness, with virtually no other evidence save the fact that the defendant was a young male who lived in the general neighborhood and had been a street dealer of drugs (like many others in the general neighborhood), the defendant is convicted of the murder. Finally, assume that ten years later, post-conviction counsel have found virtually certain proof that the sole prosecution witness identifying the defendant as the perpetrator of the murder was ten miles away when the murder occurred. It would be ludicrous to allow the prosecution to defend this conviction on the basis that the complete destruction of the sole witness against the defendant did not establish that the defendant did not in fact commit the murder, although this is an analytically true proposition. And of course this is not inconsistent with current practice. Assuming that the evidence qualifies as "newly discovered," the standard is generally whether the new information might or would likely have caused the jury to have a reasonable doubt about guilt. Any formulation of such a standard is clearly met here, most particularly because the evidence now available would at least arguably be insufficient to submit the case to a jury at all.

Now vary the hypothetical to include weak evidence of motive—credible evidence admitted at trial that defendant had had an altercation over a drug deal with the deceased two weeks before the murder, and the defendant had slapped the deceased, a drug addict who was a customer of the defendant's from time to time, as she was of numerous others in the surrounding blocks. Again, it would seem inappropriate to let the prosecution argue that the evidence failed to show innocence and thus the conviction should be left untouched on finality grounds, since the evidence left on the trial record would by itself be insufficient to sustain a verdict of guilt virtually everywhere.

Next, assume that along with the weak evidence of motive just given, there was a second eyewitness who in pretrial statements to various people gave many variations about where they were and what they had actually seen at the time of the murder, both in pre-trial statements and under cross examination, but had never withdrawn during cross the statement made on direct that they had seen the murder from a distance of some fifty yards under poor lighting conditions, but that they recognized defendant, whom they knew from the street, as the murderer by his build, gait, and face, even though he was wearing a dark stocking cap and nondescript coat (a dark-colored ski jacket). Here, even without the perjury of the discredited witness, the evidence remaining would have been arguably sufficient to sustain a conviction, given the extremity of the American position that juries are free to believe weakly warranted identification testimony. However, even against that background, the prosecution should not be able to avoid a new trial by arguing that the defendant still may be guilty, and that the jury might have so found him. The key word is "might." The truth is that the jury did not find him guilty on that record, and we have no idea if that jury would have found him guilty on the single weak identification remaining. And further, the issue arguably ought not to be merely whether the jury would have found him guilty in the absence of the perjury of the now-discredited witness, but whether, at the original trial, they would have found him guilty if the perjurious witness had testified and been exposed by the introduction of the newly discovered evidence.

Now consider another variation. In this variation you must assume that the testimony of the second witness was much more positive and detailed, and much less subject to impeaching circumstances brought out on cross-examination at trial. Should that make a difference in the propriety of the prosecution's being able to argue that no new trial is required? We fail to see how. What the prosecution is arguing is essentially harmless error, although it may be packaged in such a way as to place "the burden" on the defendant to establish that it was not harmless. But for the reasons given in the previous hypothetical, it would seem that virtual certainty concerning guilt based on the other evidence in the case should be the only thing that prevents a new trial in such a case.

Now let us shift the hypothetical to present a recurring problem of a slightly different kind. Let us go back to the "single witness" version of the hypothetical, that is, the case that the defendant was the perpetrator, based solely on the evidence of the single eyewitness. This eyewitness tells a story that is very explicit in its details — the defendant approached the victim with a gun in his hand, there was a short interchange of words, which the witness did not hear clearly, then the defendant raised his hand and shot the victim in the head. The witness testifies that he saw the gun in defendant's hand, saw the muzzle flash, and saw the victim drop to the ground as the defendant simultaneously bolted and ran off. Now once again, assume that ten years after the conviction, post-conviction counsel has obtained evidence from a re-examination of the autopsy records, the body, and the crime scene evidence, that establishes beyond any rational doubt that the victim was shot while lying on the ground. Should the prosecution be able to defend the conviction and avoid a new trial under these circumstances by asserting a new factual account completely different from the one presented at trial, according to which the defendant required the victim to lie down before the shooting, and characterizing the details of the sole witness's testimony as "mere errors of perception or interpretation not going to the ultimate issue of guilt"? Whether the prosecution should be allowed to defend a conviction by arguing a factual theory of the case that was not presented to the convicting jury, because the factual theory presented to the convicting jury has been rendered untenable by new evidence, is an important question. It is a question to which we supply a simple answer — the prosecution should not be allowed to do this. While the original conviction may have been tenable on the evidence then before the jury, to sustain it when the operative factual theory of the case must be changed because the original factual theory is no longer consistent with the now-known facts, is to turn the original conviction into a miscarriage of justice, not because the convicted person is clearly innocent, but because he is not clearly guilty enough for the continued recognition of the conviction to be just. It is, in the term used in such cases in England and Wales, unsafe, and perhaps better described as radically unsafe.

Variations on this theme regularly occur in the DNA exoneration context. The defendant is tried on the theory that he was a lone perpetrator in a rape-murder. After trial, DNA testing establishes that the defendant is not the source of the semen found in the victim and on the sheets on the bed where she was found. The prosecution, in order to defend the conviction, alleges now that the rape-murder was committed by the defendant and a second person, who was the source of the semen.[5] This kind of reimagining has even happened when the crime was rape, the victim survived, and had said that the crime was committed by a single perpetrator. Some of the alternative scenarios suggested by prosecutors in such cases have gone beyond the merely implausible to the truly bizarre. Courts, too, have been known to indulge in unfounded speculation about alternate theories of guilt in order to maintain a conviction. When, if ever, should such a fundamental change in the factual theory of the crime be allowed to have any weight in the decision to grant a new trial? As we have already indicated, we have a simple, categorical answer to this question, which is "never."

However, explaining why such a simple and general conclusion is proper requires some explication. First, the operative notion here is "fundamental change in factual theory." We are not saying that every statement by a witness, even a sole witness, shown to be factually in error automatically requires a new trial. Were the witness shown to be wrong about the exact time of the shooting by 15 minutes, that would

---

5. This issue is discussed in greater detail in Chapter 11. See Jacqueline McMurtrie, The Unindicted Co-Ejaculator and Necrophilia: Addressing Prosecutors' Logic-Defying Responses to Exculpatory DNA Results, 105 J. Crim. L. & Criminology 853 (2015).

not require a new trial unless that 15 minutes made some other difference. The factual circumstances we have in mind that constitute the fundamental "factual theory of the case" are the operative details that describe the way the crime was committed and the defendant's actions in committing it. This will obviously present some cases where reasonable people might differ. If the witness testified that the defendant hit the victim with a club he held in his right hand, and after trial it was established by some means that the victim was struck by a club held in the perpetrator's left hand, this switch might or might not be enough to trigger the principle we are proposing. It would depend on the context. One large factor is the type of error, and whether the nature of the erroneous testimony fundamentally undermines all the testimony given by the witness by raising a profound distrust of all of the witness' testimony. Remembering the wrong hand might not present such a case. Supposedly remembering a detailed scene in which the defendant was shot while upright after a certain kind of interaction, when in fact the defendant was shot execution-style while lying on the ground, would clearly be such a case. Because there are borderline cases does not mean that the general rule should not be adopted as the default rule and beginning point for analysis.

* * *

Here we are getting into the issue of exactly how much weight to give to notions of finality in criminal trials. On this issue we agree with Judge Henry Friendly, that when the issues raised involve a substantial likelihood of actual innocence, the state has no legitimate interest in finality.[6] Finality in criminal cases serves a number of claimed purposes. The primary purposes are said to be the protection of the state's resources from being depleted through constantly having to revisit the same conviction over and over post-trial, and the protection of the law's reputation for being able to reliably and accurately solve and punish crime. We will deal with the latter asserted justification first.

The law, especially the criminal law, does sometimes adopt practices that appear to be directed more towards maintaining a mythic appearance of accuracy than towards accuracy itself. For instance, the way in which the defendant's allocution in connection with a guilty plea is later taken as a more reliable indicator of factual guilt than any rational observer ought to credit, is one such practice. This is because the law, and those who administer it, are very interested in maintaining that convictions are highly accurate factually, whether arrived at through trial or through plea. Of course the whole area is burdened with many inconsistencies and incoherencies. If we really credited the epistemic strength of the allocution, we would not allow a guilty plea to be withdrawn once made, but every jurisdiction allows for such withdrawal under many circumstances before the plea attains finality. An allocution is no more than a coerced confession arrived at as a necessary part of a bargain in regard to the risks entailed in the charges brought. Like coerced confessions generally, it is likely to be accurate in the same percentage of cases where the investigatory system

---

6. See infra, Chapter 15.

has in fact brought the actually guilty party to the bar, and vice versa. In other words, it is likely simply to mirror base rates of innocence and guilt resulting from our investigatory practices. And what are those base rates? We simply do not know with any specificity, although we like to think that our investigatory practices are of sufficient diagnosticity that the factually guilty are charged much more than the factually innocent. There is good news and bad news on that front from recent studies attempting to derive rates of factual innocence from an examination of concluded cases. From these studies it seems clear that somewhere between 85% and 97% of the persons in the reference classes studied were factually guilty. While it is impossible to generalize from these results to an actual innocence rate in all classes of felony, it seems fair to say that the factual diagnosticity of the criminal justice system is better than it might be, but by no means so good that miscarriages of justice do not occur with disturbing frequency. Indeed, they occur with such frequency that a respectable system must institutionalize procedures to seek them out, and to correct them when found. If we can identify a set of cases that is likely to contain more innocents than truly guilty persons, any argument for finality applied to such a set would constitute an argument for fundamental injustice.

But how are we to isolate any such sets of cases from the vast mass of convictions, given that the substantial majority of the guilty will be attempting to raise whatever issues they can, regardless of truth, in order to obtain a hope of release, and also to attempt to mimic the claims of the truly innocent when they can? This is the "haystack" problem that bedevils and threatens to crush judges. But there is a solution that will allow a subset rich in factually innocent persons to be pulled from the haystack and be given the serious and careful consideration they deserve.

This solution is to privilege filings raising serious issues of actual innocence that are filed by lawyers acting as "innocence lawyers," and which reflect substantial investments of resources in reinvestigation of the underlying conviction. By privilege we do not mean "grant relief uncritically." What we do mean is that such filings should be freed from procedural obstacles based on the "need" for finality, and be given serious consideration involving appropriate reflective evaluation (meaning, among other things, time) by the judge to whom the case is assigned, even if this means some docket relief in regard to the judge's other more routine duties. The best way to do this is for each state to establish a true innocence commission, and apply these principles at least to the product of that commission. However, as of now, only one state, North Carolina, has such an innocence commission. Absent such a commission, the second best solution is to apply the same criteria to such filings by innocence organizations, or by those performing the same function by acting as "innocence lawyers" in the particular case.

We have invoked an unfamiliar term and an unfamiliar role: "innocence lawyer." In a recent book chapter, we have gone into the meaning, justification for, and implications of such a role post-conviction (as distinguished most particularly from "criminal defense lawyer"). We will not attempt to reproduce all that we said there, but the main point is that one serving as an innocence lawyer post-conviction is obliged to attempt to identify among the convicted those with substantial claims to factual innocence (including those whose verdicts are radically unsafe), and to expend the resources necessary to reinvestigate those cases and, when that reinvestigation supports and reinforces the initial evaluation that there is a miscarriage of justice in regard to factual guilt, marshal and present that evidence in persuasive detail. In the average non-DNA case of this kind, the expenditure of time and effort required is truly monumental. The best estimates of what is required in investigator and lawyer time and other resources runs from 350,000 to 500,000 dollars per case, and often involves four or five thousand lawyer hours, most of which will be uncompensated to any significant extent. Needless to say, two things are true of such filings—there will never be a huge number of them for the system to deal with (they themselves will never constitute a haystack), and they will at a minimum constitute a set of cases where one would be surprised if at least the majority of those filed did not involve persons who were not actually innocent. In this regard, one thing that separates the innocence lawyer function from the criminal defense function is the signal that the innocence lawyer gives, must give, and must be allowed to give. Criminal defense lawyers by tradition and often by rule are not supposed to communicate personal opinions concerning the guilt or innocence of their clients. The essence of the innocence lawyer function is exactly that communication—that signal that warrants to the courts the seriousness of the claim and the high likelihood of the claim's substantive merit. The oldest innocence organization in the United States, Centurion Ministries, takes its name and its motto from one translation of the words of the centurion at the foot of the cross of Christ, "Surely, this one is innocent." Our less specific and less poetic expansion is "surely this set of cases is so rich in actual innocents that each case should be dealt with carefully on all the evidence."

But what about the risk of freeing the actually guilty? Does freeing a guilty person not also count as a miscarriage of justice? The answer to this question is undoubtedly yes, but we must remember two things. First, as we have noted previously, some miscarriages are more serious than others, and our entire legal tradition is committed to the proposition that convicting (or not exonerating) an innocent person is worse— in fact much worse—than acquitting (or freeing) a guilty person. Second, what we have proposed does not present any greater risk of freeing the actually guilty than any other arrangement that actually takes the responsibility to identify and consider substantively those with significant claims of factual innocence. Each case will still be judicially evaluated and determined based on a rational assessment of the evidence at hand. Proper judicial evaluation will presumably work to check whatever enthusiasms may infect this or that filing, and insure that the factually guilty will not be released willy-nilly just because an innocence organization has made a filing on their behalf. What we propose will lead neither to haystacks of cases, nor to the irresponsible throwing open of the prison gates. It will, on the other hand, fulfill the obligation of a system of justice to recognize the inevitable miscarriage of the trial process that will convict a not-insignificant number of the factually innocent, and the concomitant responsibility to embrace effective approaches to finding and correcting those miscarriages.

Emily Hughes, *Innocence Unmodified*

89 N.C. L. Rev. 1083, 1084–85 (2011)

The Innocence Movement has participated in deconstructing the concept of innocence into "actual" and "legal" innocence. By focusing attention on people who were not involved in the crime for which they were convicted, the Innocence Movement has helped hundreds of wrongly convicted people obtain freedom. At the same time, however, focusing on actual innocence minimizes other reasons for wrongful convictions. It overlooks the fact that a person can be wrongly convicted even if he actually committed the charged crime—such as someone whose constitutional rights were violated in the process of being convicted. [We] need to reclaim an understanding of innocence unmodified by qualifiers such as "actual" or "legal" in order to safeguard the fundamental constitutional rights that protect us all.

The media and legal scholars often use the terms "actually innocent" and "factually innocent" to describe a person who had nothing to do with a crime: he is not actually the person who committed the crime; the facts show that somebody else did it. Similarly, the Supreme Court uses the terms "actual innocence" and "factual innocence" interchangeably. Seldom do people focus on other kinds of wrongful convictions, such as wrongful convictions stemming from violations of constitutional rights. This strong focus on the wrongful convictions of people who had nothing to do with their charged crimes dilutes the spectrum of other reasons why people are wrongly convicted. One downside of the focus on actual innocence is that courts, scholars, attorneys, and the media overlook the wrongful convictions of people who have purely constitutional claims without accompanying claims of actual innocence.

For example, on one end of the innocence spectrum, a person may be considered actually innocent of a crime because he was not there and had nothing to do with it. When DNA evidence exists in such a case, it may be useful for exonerating this kind of actually innocent person because the DNA evidence does not match the DNA of the wrongly convicted person. Another kind of actual innocence includes people who did not commit the crime and whose innocence cannot be proven through DNA testing. Such people might have been wrongly convicted because an eyewitness mistakenly identified them, because the true culprit framed them, or because the prosecution withheld exculpatory evidence. To prove innocence in these non-DNA cases, defendants may show that witnesses have recanted their previous testimony or that additional evidence has surfaced. When taken as a whole, this new evidence may illuminate the defendant's innocence. At the other end of the innocence spectrum are people who did commit a crime but are nonetheless wrongly convicted and thus legally innocent. Maybe the defendant did not understand the nature of the charge against him, thus rendering his plea involuntary. Maybe the police coerced a confession and relied on that coerced confession to obtain the conviction. Or maybe a defendant pled guilty to a greater offense than his actions warranted, such as second-degree murder instead of manslaughter. Because such people did engage in conduct that could be considered criminal, they are not actually innocent in the way the media, courts, and Congress usually employ that phrase. Nonetheless, they are wrongly convicted — legally innocent — of the crime because their constitutional rights were violated to obtain the conviction. In this way, legal innocence could be said to constitute the other end of the innocence spectrum.

Legal scholars have observed that the premium on factual innocence has created a "supercategory of innocence, elevating factual innocence over the other categories." After identifying this "supercategory of innocence," Margaret Raymond observed that "the [I]nnocence [M]ovement may have unintended consequences for the criminal justice system." Similarly, Carol Steiker and Jordan Steiker have discussed one danger of focusing on actual innocence: "Americans can empathize with the harms that they fear could happen to themselves, rather than those that happen only to 'bad people.'" They also observe that "[l]urking behind innocence's appeal ... might be indifference if not hostility to other types of injustice."[7] This focus on actual innocence has diluted the core conception of innocence, and at least two dangers have emerged as a result. One danger is the creation of an "us" versus "them" mentality, whereby the public identifies with the actually innocent "good" people and vilifies other wrongly convicted "bad" people who have been convicted in violation of their constitutional rights. This polarization runs the risk of reinforcing the public's hostility to other types of wrongful convictions, such as wrongful convictions derived from violations of constitutional rights without actual innocence.

A second danger is that pitting actual innocence against legal innocence dilutes what innocence means.... Agreeing to take (or to keep) clients such as these — with wrongful conviction claims based on a deprivation of fundamental constitutional protections rather than on what is commonly referred to as "actual" innocence — would be one step toward reclaiming an unmodified vision of innocence. But mere caseload expansion would be meaningless without first developing a more fundamental change in thinking and language.

Daniel S. Medwed, *Innocentrism*
2008 U. ILL. L. REV. 1549, 1560–63 (2008)

The saga of Bruce Dallas Goodman illustrates the dilemma of ascertaining what qualifies as an exoneration based on actual innocence. Goodman was convicted of murder based on the death of Sherry Ann Fales Williams, whose corpse was discovered the morning of November 30, 1984, near Interstate 15 north of Beaver, Utah. Investigators retrieved several items of physical evidence from the crime scene, including a partially smoked cigarette later found to have been smoked by a type "A" secretor. Moreover, tests performed on the rape kit revealed that Williams had engaged in sexual intercourse with a type "A" secretor during the previous twenty-four to thirty-six hours. The testimony at Goodman's trial indicated that 32 percent of the general

---

7. See infra, Chapter 17, Carol S. Steiker and Jorden Steiker, The Seduction of Innocence: The Attraction and Limitations of the Focus on Innocence in Capital Punishment Law and Advocacy, 95 J. Crim. L. & Criminology 587 (2005).

population can be classified as type "A" secretors, that is, people who secrete "A" antigens into their bodily fluids. More precise methods of testing biological evidence—most notably, DNA testing—were still in their infancy at the time of the Williams murder.

Goodman, an "A" secretor and Williams's former lover, became the chief suspect. At trial, Goodman claimed to have left Nevada for California before November 30 without Williams, who had expressed a wish to return to her estranged husband. Two defense witnesses verified Goodman's alibi that he was in California at the time of Williams's death. The prosecution, however, presented evidence from a witness who worked at a casino in Mesquite, Nevada, and who testified that a couple fitting the description of Goodman and Williams were embroiled in a heated argument at that location early in the morning of November 30. A Utah state trial judge found Goodman guilty of murder in the second degree in 1986, and the Utah Supreme Court conceded that "[w]ithout question this was a close case" but nonetheless affirmed Goodman's conviction on appeal.

After many years of incarceration, Goodman obtained help from the Rocky Mountain Innocence Center (RMIC), a nonprofit organization that investigates and litigates post-conviction claims of innocence by inmates in Nevada, Utah, and Wyoming. RMIC petitioned the state crime lab for access to the evidence in the hope of subjecting the remaining biological specimens from the Williams murder to DNA testing. After RMIC received the evidence and submitted it for testing, the results proved that none of the existing samples could be attributed to Goodman. The DNA evidence instead clarified that the evidence derived from two other, unidentified people.

These new findings clashed directly with the prosecution's theory of the case, which from the outset had revolved around the assumption that Goodman had killed Williams by himself. Instead of admitting error and accepting Goodman's innocence, the prosecution crafted a new theory—that Goodman was but one of several perpetrators who participated in the Williams murder that morning and that the DNA evidence did not conclusively exclude him as a perpetrator.

Faced with the prosecutors' new theory, RMIC pondered its next step and, in particular, considered two distinct post-conviction avenues: Utah's Post-Conviction DNA Testing Statute or its state habeas corpus remedy. Pursuing relief through the DNA statute would allow a judge to dismiss the conviction with prejudice if Goodman could prove his actual innocence by clear and convincing DNA evidence. The state habeas corpus procedure, in turn, gives courts the power to set aside convictions when presented with evidence of previously unknown constitutional violations or newly discovered evidence that undermines confidence in the propriety of the verdict. Unlike the Post-Conviction DNA Testing Statute, the state habeas corpus procedure permits a subsequent retrial on the charges. In the end, given the prosecution's intransigence and after weighing the benefits of the respective options, RMIC agreed to file a state habeas corpus petition to vacate Goodman's conviction as opposed to striving to prove its client's innocence through the state Post-Conviction DNA Testing statute. As part of this agreement, the prosecution vowed not to contest the habeas petition or seek a retrial on the grounds that the DNA evidence, while short of proving actual innocence, did create reasonable doubt about the conviction. Goodman was released from prison in November 2004 but not completely cleared of the crime through any official declaration of innocence.

Should Goodman's case "count" as one involving actual innocence? The Innocence Project in New York lists Bruce Dallas Goodman as one of the innocent inmates freed through post-conviction DNA testing. Cassell, Marquis, and McAdams, I suspect, might dispute this characterization. I imagine it is theoretically possible that Goodman acted with two or more unknown assailants in killing Williams, as the post-conviction prosecutors claimed, but there is no evidence whatsoever to support that version of the incident. In determining whether to classify a post-conviction reversal as a case of actual innocence, should the mere possibility of guilt, without concrete evidence, override overwhelming evidence of innocence and render that case ineligible for such classification? In my view, the answer is no; otherwise, virtually every case would come up lacking and this would run counter to the actual evidence from these matters, not to mention common sense. Defining "exoneration" necessarily involves a value judgment along a spectrum of degrees of likely innocence. Granted, attempts at classifying a case as one of actual innocence should aim as close to certainty as possible—requiring absolute proof, though, would be profoundly unrealistic.

James R. Acker, *The Flipside Injustice of Wrongful Convictions: When the Guilty Go Free*
76 ALB. L. REV. 1629, 1629–31 (2013)

Wrongful convictions entail profound social costs in addition to the hardships borne by the unfortunate individuals who are erroneously adjudged guilty. When innocents are convicted, the guilty go free. Offenders thus remain capable of committing new crimes and exposing untold numbers of additional citizens to continuing risk of victimization. Public confidence in the administration of the criminal law suffers when justice miscarries.... With the exception of the actual offenders, everyone benefits, and no one loses when innocent parties are spared conviction and when the actual perpetrators of crimes are brought to justice.

* * *

When the wrong person is convicted of a crime, the true offender remains at large, free to commit additional offenses. The actual perpetrators of crimes were identified in nearly half (149/307, or 48.5%) of the DNA-exoneration cases reported by the Innocence Project through February 2013. These true offenders are known to have committed at least 123 additional violent crimes, including 32 murders and 68 rapes, following the arrest of the eventual exonerees who were erroneously prosecuted and convicted. Had they been apprehended in a timely fashion, rather than the innocent persons accused in their place, their future victims would have been spared death, injury, and the related pernicious consequences of criminal violence.

An exhaustive analysis completed by the Better Government Association and the Center on Wrongful Convictions of eighty-five exonerations in Illinois between 1989 and 2010, documented the crimes committed by actual offenders while innocent parties were instead punished. "[W]hile 85 people were wrongfully incarcerated, the actual perpetrators were on a collective crime spree that included 14 murders, 11 sexual assaults, 10 kidnappings and at least 62 other felonies." The study noted that the true criminals remained unknown in many of the exoneration cases, involving wrongful conviction for thirty-five murders, eleven rapes, and two rape-murders. The ninety-seven offenses known to have claimed new victims thus undoubtedly comprised "just a fraction of the total number of crimes committed by the actual perpetrators."

B. Legal Materials, Exercises, and Media

1. *Inside an Innocence Organization, Recommended Listening*: Marissa Boyers Bluestine was the Legal Director and then Executive Director of the Pennsylvania Innocence Project from 2009–2019. In her interview with David Harris on the Criminal (In)Justice Podcast, Bluestine discusses innocence, how her project defines innocence, and the inner-workings of her innocence project. Listen to her interview at http://www.criminalinjusticepodcast.com/blog/2016/5/16/50-establishing-innocence-after-a-guilty-verdict?rq=bluestine (11:25–21:50).

2. *Reflective Essay on Defining Innocence*: How do *you* define innocence and is there a difference between being innocent and being wrongfully convicted? Is there a difference between moral innocence and legal innocence?

3. *Reflective Essay on Labels and Power*: The philosopher Michel Foucault once said "Whoever determines what can be talked about, determines what can be known." The power to direct a discussion coincides with the power to create labels and reinforce them. Are incarcerated people labeled in ways that make them outsiders and keep wrongful convictions unknown?

Chapter Three

Overview of the Causes of Wrongful Convictions

Table 3.1 Exonerations by Crime and Contributing Factors (1989–2012)*

	Mistaken Witness Identification	Perjury or False Accusation	False Confession	False or Misleading Forensic Evidence	Official Misconduct
Homicide (416)	27%	64%	25%	23%	56%
Sexual Assault (203)	80%	23%	8%	37%	18%
Child Sex Abuse (102)	26%	74%	7%	21%	35%
Robbery (47)	81%	17%	2%	6%	26%
Other Violent Crimes (47)	51%	43%	15%	17%	40%
Non-Violent Crimes (58)	19%	52%	3%	3%	55%
ALL CASES (873)	43%	51%	15%	24%	42%

* Table included in Samuel R. Gross & Michael Shaffer, Exonerations in the United States, 1989–2012: Report by the National Registry of Exonerations 40 (2012), http://www.law.umich.edu/special/exoneration/Documents/exonerations.us.1989.2012.full.report.pdf [http://perma.cc/2VDH-H77A].

A. Readings

Samuel R. Gross, Kristen Jacoby, Daniel J. Matheson, Nicholas Montgomery, and Sujata Patil, *Exonerations in the United States 1989 through 2003*

95 J. Crim. L. & Criminology 523, 523–54 (2005)

On August 14, 1989, the Cook County Circuit Court in Chicago, Illinois, vacated Gary Dotson's 1979 rape conviction and dismissed the charges. Mr. Dotson—who had spent ten years in and out of prison and on parole for this conviction—was not the first innocent prisoner to be exonerated and released in America. But his case was a breakthrough nonetheless: he was the first who was cleared by DNA identification technology. It was the beginning of a revolution in the American criminal justice system. Until then, exonerations of falsely convicted defendants were seen as aberrational. Since 1989, these once-rare events have become disturbingly commonplace.

This is a report on a study of exonerations in the United States from 1989 through 2003. We discuss all exonerations that we have been able to locate that occurred in that fifteen-year period, and that resulted from investigations into the particular cases of the exonerated individuals. Overall, we found 340 exonerations, 327 men and 13 women; 144 of them were cleared by DNA evidence, 196 by other means. With a handful of exceptions, they had been in prison for years. More than half had served terms of ten years or more; 80% had been imprisoned for at least five years. As a group, they had spent more than 3400 years in prison for crimes for which they should never have been convicted—an average of more than ten years each.

As we use the term, "exoneration" is an official act declaring a defendant not guilty of a crime for which he or she had previously been convicted. The exonerations we have studied occurred in four ways: (1) In forty-two cases governors (or other appropriate executive officers) issued pardons based on evidence of the defendants' innocence. (2) In 263 cases criminal charges were dismissed by courts after new evidence of innocence emerged, such as DNA. (3) In thirty-one cases the defendants were acquitted at a retrial on the basis of evidence that they had no role in the crimes for which they were originally convicted. (4) In four cases, states posthumously acknowledged the innocence of defendants who had already died in prison: Frank Lee Smith, exonerated in Florida in 2000; Louis Greco and Henry Tameleo, exonerated in Massachusetts in 2002; and John Jeffers, exonerated in Indiana in 2002.

This is the most comprehensive compilation of exonerations available, but it is not exhaustive. The criminal justice system in the United States is notoriously fragmented—it is administered by fifty separate states (plus the federal government and the District of Columbia) and by more than 3000 separate counties, with thousands of administratively separate trial courts and prosecuting authorities. There is no national registry of exonerations, or any simple way to tell from official records which dismissals, pardons, etc., are based on innocence. As a result, we learned about many of the cases in our database from media reports. But the media inevitably miss some cases—and we, no doubt, have missed some cases that were reported.

In the great majority of these cases there was, at the end of the day, no dispute about the innocence of the exonerated defendants. This is not surprising. Our legal system places great weight on the finality of criminal convictions. Courts and prosecutors are exceedingly reluctant to reverse judgments or reconsider closed cases; when they do—and it's rare—it's usually because of a compelling showing of error. Even so, some state officials continue to express doubts about the innocence of exonerated defendants, sometimes in the face of extraordinary evidence. Two brief examples:

- When Charles Fain was exonerated by DNA in Idaho in 2001, after eighteen years on death row for a rape murder, the original prosecutor in the case said, "It doesn't really change my opinion that much that Fain's guilty."

- On December 8, 1995, at the request of the prosecution, the DuPage County, Illinois, Circuit Court dismissed all charges against Alejandro Hernandez, who had spent eleven and one-half years in prison for an abduction, rape and murder in which he had no role. By that time DNA tests and a confession had established that the real criminal was an imprisoned serial rapist and murderer by the name of Brian Dugan; a police officer who provided crucial evidence had admitted to perjury; and Hernandez's co-defendant, Rolando Cruz, was acquitted by a judge who was harshly critical of the investigation and prosecution of the case. Nonetheless, when Hernandez was released, the prosecutor said: "The action I have taken today is neither a vindication nor an acquittal of the defendant."

Needless to say, we are in no position to reach an independent judgment on the factual innocence of each defendant in our data. That is not our purpose in this report. Instead, we look at overall patterns in the exonerations that have accumulated in the past fifteen years and hope to learn something about the causes of false convictions, and about the operation of our criminal justice system in general. It is possible that a few of the hundreds of exonerated defendants we have studied were involved in the crimes for which they were convicted, despite our efforts to exclude such cases. On the other hand, it is certain—this is the clearest implication of our study—that many defendants who are not on this list, no doubt thousands, have been falsely convicted of serious crimes but have not been exonerated.

I. Exonerations Over Time

The rate of exonerations has increased sharply over the fifteen-year period of this study, from an average of twelve a year from 1989 through 1994, to an average of forty-two a year since 2000. The highest yearly total was forty-four, in 2002 and again in 2003.

The number of DNA exonerations has increased across this period, from one or two a year in 1989 to 1991, to an average of six a year from 1992 through 1995, to an average of twenty a year since 2000. Non-DNA exonerations were less rare initially, and remained relatively stable through the 1990s, averaging about ten a year. Their numbers have increased rapidly in the last several years, averaging twenty-three a year since 2000.

This rapid increase in reported exonerations probably reflects the combined effects of three interrelated trends. First, the growing availability and sophistication of DNA identification technology has, of course, produced an increase in DNA exonerations over time. Second, the singular importance of the DNA revolution has made exonerations increasingly newsworthy; as a result, we are probably aware of a higher proportion of the exonerations that occurred in 2003 than in 1989. And third, this increase in attention has in turn led to a substantial increase in the number of false convictions that in fact do come to light and end in exonerations, by DNA or other means. More resources are devoted to the problem—there are now, for example, forty-one Innocence Projects in thirty-one states—and judges, prosecutors, defense lawyers, and police officers have all become more aware of the danger of false convictions.

Table 3.2 Exonerations by Crime and Basis

Crime	Number of Exonerations	DNA	Other
Murder	205 (60%)	39	166
Death Sentences	74 (22%)	13	61
Other Murder Cases	131 (39%)	26	105
Rape	121 (36%)	105	16
Other Crimes of Violence	11 (3%	0	11
Drug and Property Crime	3 (1%)	0	3
TOTAL*	340 (101%)	144	196

* The total adds up to 101% because of rounding error.

II. The Crimes for Which Exonerated Defendants Were Convicted

Ninety-six percent of the known exonerations of individual defendants since 1989 were either for murder — 60% (205/345) — or for rape or sexual assault — 36% (121/340). Most of the remaining fourteen cases were crimes of violence — six robberies, two attempted murders, a kidnapping and an assault — plus a larceny, a gun possession case and two drug cases. See Table 3.2.

This highly skewed distribution tells us a great deal about the relationship between exonerations — those erroneous convictions that are discovered and remedied, at least in part — and the larger group of all false convictions, the vast majority of which are never discovered. We consider that relationship by examining the two major categories of crimes for which exonerations are comparatively common.

III. The Relationship Between Known Exonerations and All False Convictions

1. Why Do So Many Exonerations Involve Rape?

At the end of 2001, about 118,000 prisoners in state prisons were serving sentences for rape and sexual assault, less than 10% of the total prison population. There were also over 155,000 prisoners who had been convicted of robbery, nearly 119,000 who were in prison for assault, more than 27,000 for other violent felonies, and over 600,000 for property, drug and public order offenses. Why are 90% of the exonerations for non-homicidal crimes concentrated among the rape cases?

The comparison between rape and robbery is particularly telling. Robbery and rape are both crimes of violence in which the perpetrator is often a stranger to the victim. As a result, robberies and rapes alike are susceptible to the well-known dangers of eyewitness misidentification. In fact, there is every reason to believe that misidentifications in robberies outnumber those in rapes, by a lot:

(1) Robberies are more numerous than rapes. In 2002, for example, the FBI estimates that 95,136 forcible rapes and 420,637 robberies were reported to

police departments in the United States, leading to 20,126 arrests for rape and 77,342 arrests for robbery.

(2) Eyewitness misidentification is almost entirely restricted to crimes committed by strangers, which includes about three quarters of robberies, but only a third of rapes.

(3) The nature of the crime of rape is such that the victim usually spends a considerable amount of time in close physical proximity to the criminal; robberies are frequently quick, and may involve less immediate physical contact.

In 1987, a detailed study analyzed all known cases of eyewitness misidentification in the United States from 1900 through 1983, 136 in all. That study found that misidentifications in robberies outnumbered those in rapes by more than two to one; in fact, robberies accounted for more than half of all known cases of proven misidentifications. The pattern in our study could hardly be more different. We have 121 exonerations in rape cases; in 88% of them (107/121) the defendant was the victim of eyewitness misidentification. But we have only six robbery exonerations, all of which include eyewitness misidentifications. What changed? The answer is obvious: DNA. In 1987, the first DNA exoneration in the country was two years in the future. Since 1989, however, 87% of exonerated rape defendants were cleared by DNA evidence. Only 19% of murder exonerations included DNA evidence (and none of the other non-rape exonerations), and all but a couple of those murders also included rape as well.

The implication is clear. If we had a technique for detecting false convictions in robberies that was comparable to DNA identification for rapes, robbery exonerations would greatly outnumber rape exonerations, and the total number of falsely convicted defendants who were exonerated would be several times what we report. And even among rape cases, DNA is only useful if testable samples of biological evidence were preserved and can be found, which is not always true.

In short, the clearest and most important lesson from the recent spike in rape exonerations is that the false convictions that come to light are the tip of an iceberg. Beneath the surface there are other undetected miscarriages of justice in rape cases without testable DNA, and a much larger group of undetected false convictions in robberies and other serious crimes of violence for which DNA identification is useless.

2. Why Are Exonerations Heavily Concentrated Among Murder Cases, and Especially Among Capital Murders?

What about exonerations that are not based on DNA? In 2001, about 13% of state prisoners were serving sentences for murder or non-negligent manslaughter, but 85% of non-DNA exonerations (166/196) are found among this group. For prisoners under sentence of death the contrast is even more stark. The death-row population in America peaked in 2001, at about a quarter of 1% of the American prison population—and yet seventy-four exonerations in the past fifteen years, 22% of the total, were drawn from this tiny sliver of the prison population. What accounts for this enormous over-representation of murder defendants, and especially death-row inmates, among those who are exonerated?

There are only two possible explanations:

> One possibility is that false convictions are not more likely to occur in murder and death penalty cases, but only more likely to be discovered because of the comparatively high level of attention that is devoted to reviewing those cases after conviction. This is no doubt true, at least in part. Because of the seriousness of their consequences, murder convictions—and especially death sentences—are reviewed more carefully than other criminal convictions. In 1999, for example, Dennis Fritz was exonerated by DNA evidence and released from a life sentence for a rape murder he did not commit. But he was exonerated as a by-product of an intensive investigation that led to the exoneration of his co-defendant, Ron Williamson, who had been sentenced to death. If Williamson had not been sentenced to death, Fritz would probably be in prison to this day.

But could this be the entire explanation? Could it be that false convictions in capital cases really are no more common than in other cases? If that were the whole story it would mean that if we reviewed prison sentences with the same level of care that we devote to death sentences, there would have been over 29,000 non-death row exonerations in the past fifteen years rather than the 266 that have in fact occurred—including more than 3,700 exonerations in non-capital murder cases alone. This is a shocking prospect.

On the other hand, if this first explanation is not the whole story, that inescapably means that false convictions are more likely to occur in murder cases, and much more likely in death penalty cases, than in other criminal prosecutions. There are several reasons (apart from the evidence presented here) to believe that this too is almost certainly true: the extraordinary pressure to secure convictions for heinous crimes; the difficulty of investigating many homicides because, by definition, the victims are unavailable; extreme incentives for the real killers to frame innocent fall guys when they are facing the possibility of execution. Whatever the causes, this is a terrible prospect: that we are most likely to convict innocent defendants in those cases in which their very lives are at stake.

Considering the huge discrepancies between the exoneration rates for death sentences, for other murder convictions, and for criminal convictions generally, the truth is probably a combination of these two appalling possibilities: We are both much more likely to convict innocent defendants of murder—and especially capital murder—than of other crimes, and a large number of false convictions in non-capital cases are never discovered because nobody ever seriously investigates the possibility of error.

3. What Are We Missing Entirely?

We have only counted individual defendants who were exonerated—those whose convictions were nullified by official acts by governors, courts or prosecutors because of compelling evidence that they were not guilty of crimes for which they had been convicted. Several categories of falsely convicted defendants are entirely missing from this count.

(a) Mass Exonerations

Our data include only defendants who were exonerated because of evidence of innocence that focused on their individual cases. We have not included data from mass exonerations of innocent defendants who were falsely convicted as a result of large scale patterns of police perjury and corruption....[8]

(b) Comparatively Light Sentences

With a handful of exceptions, everyone on our list of exonerees was sentenced to death or to a long term of imprisonment. Ninety-three percent were sentenced to ten years in prison or more; 77% were sentenced to at least twenty-five years; more than half were sentenced to life imprisonment or to death. This is a highly atypical group. Most criminal defendants are convicted (if at all) of misdemeanors; and of those who are convicted of felonies, most are sentenced to probation or to months in jail rather than to years in prison.

Exonerations are the end products of a lot of work, usually over a long period. The average time from conviction to exoneration is more than eleven years. A falsely convicted defendant who has served his time for burglary and been released has little incentive to invest years of his life keeping the case alive in the hope of clearing his name—and if he wanted to, he'd probably have a hard time finding anybody to help. Our data reflect this: nobody, it seems, seriously pursues exonerations for defendants who are falsely convicted of shoplifting, misdemeanor assault, drug possession, or routine felonies—auto thefts or run-of-the-mill burglaries—and sentenced to probation, a $2000 fine, or even six months in the county jail or eighteen months in state prison.

But obviously such errors occur. It is well known, for example, that many defendants who can't afford bail plead guilty in return for short sentences, often probation and credit for time served, rather than stay in jail for months and then go to trial and risk much more severe punishment if convicted. This is one facet of a system in which about 90% of defendants who are convicted plead guilty rather than go to trial. Some defendants who accept these deals are innocent, possibly in numbers that dwarf false convictions in the less common but more serious violent felonies, but they are almost never exonerated—at least not in individual cases.

Only twenty of the exonerees in our database pled guilty, less than six percent of the total: fifteen innocent murder defendants and four innocent rape defendants who took deals that included long prison terms in order to avoid the risk of life imprisonment or the death penalty, and one innocent defendant pled guilty to gun possession to avoid life imprisonment as a habitual criminal. By contrast, thirty-one of the thirty-nine Tulia defendants pled guilty to drug offenses they did not commit, as did the majority of the 100 or more exonerated defendants in the Rampart scandal in Los Angeles. Most of the Rampart and Tulia defendants had been released by the time they were exonerated, two to four years after conviction. They were exonerated because the false convictions in their cases were produced by systematic programs of

---

8. Some of these cases are discussed, infra, in Chapter 13.

police perjury that were uncovered as part of large-scale investigations. If these same defendants had been falsely convicted of the same crimes by mistake—or even because of unsystematic acts of deliberate dishonesty—we would never have known.

(c) Innocent Defendants Who Have Not Been Exonerated

(i) Pending cases

Some falsely convicted defendants have not been exonerated—at least not yet—because government officials are dragging their feet. On March 12, 2003, for example, Josiah Sutton was released from prison in Texas after DNA tests cleared him of a rape conviction for which he had served four and one-half years of a twenty-five-year sentence. Over a year later, Sutton remained free on bail, with his case theoretically pending, because the Houston District Attorney, who agrees that Sutton should be pardoned, won't say that the pardon should be "based on innocence"—apparently because that classification would subject the state to liability for Sutton's wrongful imprisonment. Although there was no doubt that Sutton was falsely convicted, he was not exonerated by the end of 2003 and is not included in this study.

(ii) Pleas of guilty or no contest

Sometimes a defendant who has protested his innocence for years, and who had obtained a reversal of his conviction, accepts an offer from the state to plead guilty to a lesser crime and go free immediately, rather than stay in jail and risk a re-trial that could result in another false conviction. For example, in 1978 Curtis McGhee was convicted of murder in Council Bluffs, Iowa, on the basis of a confession from a supposed accomplice. In February, 2003, the Iowa Supreme Court reversed the convictions because the police had concealed the fact that they had questioned another suspect who was seen near the scene of the crime, and who failed a polygraph test. By then the confessor, and all other key prosecution witnesses, had recanted their testimony. McGhee was offered a deal: plead guilty to second degree murder and go free; he decided to play it safe, took the deal, and was released. We have not included McGhee in our data, nor any other defendant who pled guilty in order to be released, regardless of the evidence of the defendant's innocence. We are examining exonerations, and the final official act in such a case is not an exoneration but a conviction, however nominal or misleading. (We have included McGhee's co-defendant, Terry Harrington, who refused to take a similar deal, and got a dismissal after the state's star witness at the original trial recanted once more.)

(iii) Inexplicable failures to exonerate

In some cases there is no rational explanation for the fact that an innocent defendant has not been exonerated. There is no doubt, for example, that Victoria Banks was falsely convicted of manslaughter in 2001. She is a mentally retarded woman who confessed to killing her newborn baby; but there is no physical evidence that the baby ever existed, and medical tests confirm that she had a tubal ligation that was intact throughout the relevant period, making pregnancy impossible. But Ms. Banks—who confessed to her imaginary crime and pled guilty to manslaughter after being charged with capital murder—does not dispute her guilt, and the state of Alabama, to its shame, continues to imprison this mentally deficient and delusional woman for manslaughter as well as unrelated charges. One of her two co-defendants—who is also mentally retarded—was exonerated and released in 2003 after three and half years in prison; a second retarded co-defendant had her sentence reduced and was released in 2002.

(iv) The childcare sex abuse and satanic ritual cases

Finally, in one major set of false conviction cases the patterns of injustice are so complex and murky that we can hardly ever say that specific defendants were "exonerated," even though there is no doubt that most were falsely convicted. We're referring here to the epidemic of child sex abuse prosecutions that swept across the country in the late 1980s and early 1990s, focusing especially on childcare centers, and frequently including allegations of bizarre satanic rituals.

In almost all of the exoneration cases that we consider in this report there is no question that the murder, rape or other crime did occur. The problem is that someone other than the defendant did it. In these mass child molestation prosecutions the identity of the perpetrators is not an issue. The question, rather, is: Did the crimes really happen at all?

In many of these child-molestation cases, the accusations were bizarre if not impossible on their face. Some children at the Little Rascals Day Care Center in Edenton, North Carolina, for example, said that they had seen babies killed at the daycare center, children taken out on boats and thrown overboard to feed sharks, and children taken to outer space in a hot air balloon. In Kern County, California, children described mass orgies with as many as fourteen adults who forced groups of children to inhale eighteen-inch lines of cocaine or heroin, gave them injections with syringes that left large bruises, and hung the children from hooks as the adults repeatedly sodomized them. Needless to say, no physical evidence ever corroborated any of these unlikely claims. In other cases, the accusations were merely implausible, and appear to be have been generated by over-eager prosecutors and therapists who demanded that the young children they examined tell them that they had been molested, and would not take No for an answer.

Overall, more than 150 defendants were initially charged in at least ten major child sex abuse and satanic ritual prosecutions across the country, from 1984 to 1995, and at least seventy-two were convicted. It is clear that the great majority were totally innocent; almost all were eventually released by one means or another before they completed their terms. It is possible, however, that some of these defendants did commit some acts of sexual molestation, incidents that later grew into implausible and impossible allegations as the children were interviewed repeatedly by prosecutors and therapists. We have included only one of these cases in our database, a case in which we know that all of the supposed victims now say that they were never molested in the first place—that the crime never occurred. Otherwise, none of the wrongfully convicted victims of this terrible episode in American legal history are included on this list because they have not been officially exonerated.

Table 3.3 **Exonerations by State**

Rank	State	Number of Exonerations
1	Illinois	54
2	New York	35
3	Texas	28
4	California	27
5	Louisiana	17
6	Massachusetts	16
7	Florida	15
8	Pennsylvania	13
9	Oklahoma	11
10	Missouri	10

IV. Exonerations by State

The exonerations we found occurred in thirty-eight states and the District of Columbia, but the top four states—Illinois, New York, Texas and California—account for more than 40% of the total (144 of 340), and the top ten (those four plus Florida, Massachusetts, Louisiana, Pennsylvania, Oklahoma and Missouri) include two thirds (226/340). See Table 3.3.

This ranking corresponds in part to the sizes of state populations. The five most populous states—California, Texas, New York, Florida and Illinois, in that order—include five of the seven with the largest numbers of recent exonerations. These numbers may also be influenced by the use of the death penalty; all but two of the top ten states have—or, in the case of Illinois, recently had—large death row populations. It is also probably no coincidence that the two leading exoneration states, Illinois and New York, are home to the two largest and best established organizations in the United States that work to identify false convictions and obtain exonerations—The Center on Wrongful Convictions at Northwestern University Law School in Chicago, and The Innocence Project at Cardozo Law School in New York City; that these two states were the first to authorize post-conviction DNA testing for inmates; and that both include major metropolitan media markets in which the issue of wrongful conviction has received extensive coverage.

V. Some of the Causes of the False Convictions

One way to think of false convictions is as a species of accidents. Like many accidents, they are caused by a mix of carelessness, misconduct, and bad luck. We don't claim to be able to describe with any precision the causal mechanisms that produce these tragic errors, but even with the limited information at our disposal, some basic patterns are apparent.

1. Rapes and Murders: Mistakes Versus Lies

The most common cause of wrongful convictions is eyewitness misidentification. This is not news. It was first shown in 1932 by Professor Edwin Borchard in his classic book Convicting the Innocent, and it is apparent again in our data: In 64% of these exonerations (219/340), at least one eyewitness misidentified the defendant. The pattern, however, is heavily lopsided. Almost 90% of the rape cases (107/121), but only half of the homicides (102/205), included at least one eyewitness misidentification.

The gap in the frequency of misidentification reflects a fundamental difference between police investigations of rapes and of homicides. In a non-homicidal rape there is always a surviving witness—the victim—and she is usually able to attempt to identify the criminal. As a result, almost all the false rape convictions that led to exonerations involved mistakes that occurred in that identification process. A murder, on the other hand, frequently leaves no surviving eyewitness, which forces the police to search for other types of evidence—evidence that is usually more difficult to obtain than eyewitness identifications.

Because the stakes in murder cases are so high, the police invest far more resources in investigating them than they devote to other crimes of violence. This is as it should be. The main effect is that the clearance rate for murders is higher than for other crimes—killers are more likely than rapists to be caught and brought to justice. These same high stakes, however, can also produce false evidence. The real perpetrator is at far greater risk, and far more motivated to frame an innocent person to deflect attention, for a murder than for a rape—particularly if he might be sentenced to death. Co-defendants, accomplices, jailhouse snitches and other police informants, can all hope for substantial rewards if they provide critical evidence in a murder case—even false evidence—especially if the police are desperate for leads. The police themselves may be tempted to cut corners and falsify evidence to convict a person they believe committed a terrible murder.

In 71% of the rape exonerations the victims and all other eyewitnesses who testified were strangers to the falsely convicted defendant. By contrast, 85% of exonerated murder defendants knew the victim, or at least one supposed eyewitness, before the crime. The central problem in most rape investigations that go wrong is the mistaken identification of a defendant who is otherwise unknown to those involved. The common problem in the investigations of the murder cases we studied is deliberately false evidence implicating an innocent defendant with a known relationship to the victim or the lying witness.

An eyewitness misidentification by a stranger is easy to spot, once you know that the person identified is innocent. Detecting a deliberate lie is harder; there may be no simple way to tell if a statement was false, and if so whether the falsehood was intentional. As a result, our information on perjury understates the extent of the

Table 3.4 Causes of False Convictions for Exonerations in Murder and Rape Cases*

	Murder (205)	Rape (121)
Eyewitness Misidentification	50%	88%
Reported Perjury	56%	25%
False Confession	20%	7%

* The columns add up to more than 100% because some false convictions had multiple causes.

problem. Even so, known perjury is a surprisingly common feature of the trials that led to the convictions of these exonerated defendants.

In at least sixty of the 340 exonerations, the defendant was deliberately falsely accused at trial by someone who claimed to have witnessed the crime: a supposed victim, participant, or eyewitness. About a quarter of these false accusations (14/60) occurred in rape cases; in each, the false accuser was a complaining witness who lied about the occurrence of the crime. Almost three-quarters of the exonerated defendants who were falsely accused were convicted of murder (44/60). In two cases the false accusers were surviving victims; most of the rest were (or claimed to be) participants in the crimes. In other words, deliberate false accusations were a major cause of misidentification in murder exonerations. In 43% of the murder exonerations in which the defendant was misidentified by one or more eyewitnesses (44/102), we also have information that at least one of those witnesses misidentified the defendant deliberately.

In five of the exonerations that we have studied there are reports of perjury by police officers. In an additional twenty-four we have similar information on perjury by forensic scientists testifying for the government. In at least seventeen exoneration cases the real criminal lied under oath to get the defendant convicted; in at least ninety-seven cases a civilian witness who did not claim to be directly involved in the crime committed perjury—usually a jailhouse snitch or another witness who stood to gain from the false testimony.

Overall, in 43% of all exonerations (146/340) at least one sort of perjury is reported—including 56% of murder exonerations (114/205), and 25% of rape exonerations (30/121). See Table 3.4.

* * *

VI. Race

1. Race and Rape

Over two-thirds of the exonerated defendants we studied were minorities, 55% African Americans and 13% Hispanics. Sadly, this is not altogether surprising; blacks and Hispanics comprise about 62% of all American prisoners. But only part of this pattern can be explained by the pervasive over representation of minorities in general,

Table 3.5 Race of Exonerated Defendants, by Crime

	Murder(193)	Rape (107)	All Cases (311)
White	34%	28%	32%
Black	50%	64%	55%
Hispanic	16%	7%	13%
Other	1%	0%	1%
TOTAL*	101%	99%	101%

* The totals may not add up to 100% because of rounding error.

and African Americans in particular, among those arrested and imprisoned for serious crimes.

At of the end of 2002, 35% of state prisoners serving sentences for murder were white, 48% were black and 17% were Hispanic. The proportions of exonerations in murder cases are very similar: 34% whites, 50% Blacks and 16% Hispanics.

For rape, however, the story is different. A majority of rape prisoners in 2002 were white, 58%; only 29% were black; and 13% were Hispanic. But for rape exonerations the proportions are reversed: almost two thirds of the defendants are black, 64%; only 28% are white; and 7% are Hispanic. See Table 3.5.

Why are blacks so greatly over-represented among those defendants who were falsely convicted of rape and then exonerated, mostly by DNA? The key is probably the race of the victims. We know the race of the victim for 75% of the sixty-nine rape exonerations with black defendants, and in 75% of those cases the victim was white. (We see a similar pattern, on a smaller scale for Hispanic exonerees: we know the race of the victim for seven of the eight who were falsely convicted of rape, and in four of those cases the victim was white.) Most women who are raped are victimized by members of their own racial or ethnic groups. Inter-racial rape is uncommon, and rapes of white women by black men in particular account for well under 10% of all rapes. But among rape exonerations for which we know the race of both parties, almost exactly half (39/80) involve a black man who was falsely convicted of raping a white woman.

There are many possible explanations for this disturbing pattern. Of all the problems that plague the American system of criminal justice, few are as incendiary as the relationship between race and rape. Nobody would be surprised to find that bias and discrimination continue to play a role in rape prosecutions. Still, the most obvious explanation for this racial disparity is probably also the most powerful: the perils of cross-racial identification. Virtually all of the inter-racial rape convictions in our data were based, at least in part, on eyewitness misidentifications, and one of the strongest findings of systematic studies of eyewitness evidence is that white Americans are much more likely to mistake one black person for another than to do the same for members of their own race.

Table 3.6 Juvenile Exonerations by Race and Crime

	Juvenile Murder Exonerations (23)	Juvenile Rape Exonerations (7)	All Juv. Exonerations (32)
White	13%	0%	9%
Black	78%	86%	78%
Hispanic	9%	14%	13%
TOTAL	100%	100%	100%

2. Race and Age

The juveniles on our list of exonerated defendants are overwhelmingly members of minority groups. Over ninety percent of exonerated defendants who were under eighteen at the time of arrest were black or Hispanic. There are virtually no non-Hispanic white juveniles among the exonerated defendants we have studied—three out of 340, less than 1% of the total. See Table 3.6.

As we have seen, minorities, and African Americans in particular, are over-represented among all exonerations, especially the rape cases. Even so, white defendants account for 34% of all murder exonerations and 28% of all rape exonerations—but only 1% of juvenile murder exonerations, and not a single juvenile rape exoneration. A majority of the teenagers arrested for these two crimes are white—62% of juvenile rape arrests in 2002, and 46% of juvenile murder arrests—and yet white juveniles are all but entirely absent from our list of exonerees. Why?

In part, this disparity reflects general racial patterns in juvenile justice in America. Many juveniles who are arrested are not prosecuted at all but returned to the custody of their parents or guardians for less formal discipline; among those who are prosecuted, only a small fraction are treated as adults and punished accordingly. The juvenile exonerees in our data are all drawn from the small group of juvenile suspects who are prosecuted as adults and sentenced to long terms in prison—or, in three cases, to death. Race plays a major role at each stage of the sorting process that produces this rarified group.

For example, although only 27% of all juveniles arrested in the United States in 1990, 1992 and 1994 were black, a Department of Justice study found that 41% of defendants in juvenile courts in those three years were black, and 67% of juveniles prosecuted as adults were black. In other words, white teenagers who are arrested by the police are less likely than blacks to be prosecuted in juvenile court, and much less likely to be prosecuted in felony court as adults.

All but one of the juvenile exonerees in our database were convicted, as adults, of rape or murder. For these two extremely serious crimes, the racial winnowing of juvenile offenders is severe. In 1990–94, 59% of murder defendants in juvenile court were white and 36% were black; but among juvenile murder defendants who were tried as adults the proportions were more than reversed: 69% were black and only 25% were white. For rape, the proportion of blacks went from 44% of juveniles arrested, to 53% of those prosecuted for rape in juvenile court, to 72% of juvenile rape defendants prosecuted as adults. There are, no doubt, false convictions among the cases that remain in juvenile court, and a substantial proportion of them may involve white defendants. Like other false convictions with comparatively light sentences, these are errors that are unlikely to ever be corrected by formal exoneration. None appear in this database.

Even so, 25% of juvenile murder defendants prosecuted in adult courts in the early 1990s were white, as were 28% of juvenile rape defendants—but only 9% of juvenile exonerees. The disparity could be due to chance; the number of cases is not large. It could also be due to systematic racial differences in the process of investigation. Black juvenile rape defendants, like all black rape defendants, face a special danger of cross-racial misidentification. In many of the juvenile murder exonerations (and in some of the rapes) the primary evidence against the defendant was a false confession. Eight-five percent of the juvenile exonerees who falsely confessed were African American (11/13). It may be that police officers are more likely to use coercive interrogation tactics on black juveniles than on white juveniles—that would explain the high proportion of blacks among the innocent juveniles who falsely confessed—but there is no way to tell directly from these data.

The broad picture, however, is no mystery. We have a dual system of juvenile justice in this country, one track for white adolescents, a separate and unequal one for black adolescents. The sharp racial differences in exonerations of falsely convicted juvenile defendants are just one manifestation of that racial divide.

Summary and Conclusion

We can't come close to estimating the number of false convictions that occur in the United States, but the accumulating mass of exonerations gives us a glimpse of what we're missing. We have located 340 exonerations from 1989 through 2003, not counting hundreds of additional exonerated defendants in the Tulia and Rampart scandals and other mass exonerations, or more than seventy convicted child-care sex abuse defendants. Almost all the individual exonerations that we know about are clustered in two crimes, rape and murder. They are surrounded by widening circles of categories of cases with false convictions that have not been detected: rape convictions that have not been reexamined with DNA evidence; robberies, for which DNA identification is useless; murder cases that are ignored because the defendants were not sentenced to death; assault and drug convictions that are forgotten entirely. Any plausible guess at the total number of miscarriages of justice in America in the last fifteen years must be in the thousands, perhaps tens of thousands.

We can see some clear patterns in those false convictions that have come to light: who was convicted, and why. For rape the dominant problem is eyewitness misidentification—and cross-racial misidentification in particular, which accounts for the extraordinary number of false rape convictions with black defendants and white victims. For murder, the leading cause of the false convictions we know about is perjury—including perjury by supposed participants or eyewitnesses to the crime who knew the innocent defendants in advance. False confessions also played a large role in the murder convictions that led to exonerations, primarily among two particularly vulnerable groups of innocent defendants: juveniles, and those who are mentally retarded or mentally ill. Almost all the juvenile exonerees who falsely confessed are African American. In fact, one of our most startling findings is that over 90% of all exonerated juvenile defendants are black or Hispanic, an extreme disparity that, sadly, is of a piece with racial disparities in our juvenile justice system in general.

The death penalty runs through this story as a major theme. Death sentences provide a window on the underlying rate of false convictions, one of two such windows. Rapes are vastly over represented among exonerations because DNA identification enables us to detect errors in rape convictions that were obtained before that technology became available. Death sentences are over represented—by an even greater margin—in part because we work hard to detect and correct errors in judgments that could lead to the execution of innocent defendants. That poses a terrible question: How many additional hundreds or thousands of false convictions would we have discovered if we had worked just as hard to find them among non-capital murders, or among non-homicidal felonies?

The extraordinary rate of exoneration of death-sentenced defendants also raises deep questions about the accuracy of our system for determining guilt in capital cases. Exonerations from death row are more than twenty-five times more frequent than exonerations for other prisoners convicted of murder, and more than 100 times more frequent than for all imprisoned felons. This huge discrepancy must mean that false convictions are more likely for death sentences than for all murder cases, and much likely than among felony convictions generally—an unavoidable and extremely disturbing conclusion.

Finally, the frequency of exonerations from death row is a chilling reminder of the consequences of these false convictions. If we managed to identify and release 75% of innocent death-row inmates before they were put to death, then we also executed twenty-five innocent defendants from 1989 through 2003. If, somehow, we have caught 90% of false capital convictions, than we only executed eight innocent defendants in that fifteen-year period. Is it conceivable that a system that produces all these horrendous errors in the first place could also detect and correct 90% of those errors, after the fact? And considering the number of mistakes in capital trials, even an unlikely 90% exoneration rate would be disturbingly low.

Worse yet, the high rate of death-row exoneration is limited to defendants who have been sentenced to death. Approximately half of all defendants who are convicted at capital trials are sentenced to life imprisonment instead; and of those who are sentenced to death most are resentenced to life imprisonment at some point in the process of review; about 40% have their convictions or sentences reversed on their first appeal, and most of them are ultimately resentenced to life. In other words, the bulk of defendants at capital trials are subject to the frightening risk of error that plagues capital prosecutions—they are as likely as other capital defendants to be convicted of murders they did not commit—but they get little or none of the special care that is devoted to re-examining death sentences after conviction. In all likelihood, the great majority of innocent defendants who are convicted of capital murder are neither executed nor exonerated but sentenced to prison for life, and then forgotten.

Brandon L. Garrett, *Judging Innocence*
108 Colum. L. Rev. 55, 56–93 (2008)

Postconviction DNA testing changed the landscape of criminal justice in the United States. Actors in the criminal system long doubted whether courts ever wrongly convicted people; for example, Judge Learned Hand famously called "the ghost of the innocent man convicted ... an unreal dream." With the benefit of DNA testing, we now know our courts have convicted innocent people and have even sentenced some to death. This has happened, as Justice Souter recently noted, "in numbers never imagined before the development of DNA tests." Since 1989, when postconviction DNA testing was first performed, people have been exonerated by postconviction DNA testing in the United States.

Exoneration cases have altered the ways judges, lawyers, legislators, the public, and scholars perceive the criminal system's accuracy. Courts now debate the legal significance of these exonerations, with the U.S. Supreme Court in the last term engaging in its first "empirical argument" on the subject. Lawyers, journalists, and others have established an "innocence network" of projects, including clinics at dozens of law schools, all designed to locate more innocence cases. Public distrust of the criminal justice system has increased as a result of exonerations. Popular television shows, books, movies, and plays have dramatized the stories of exonerations. States have declared moratoria on executions, citing examples of wrongful convictions. Moreover, forty-three states and the District of Columbia have passed legislation providing access to post-conviction DNA testing. Six states have created innocence commissions designed to investigate possible innocence cases, and others have enacted reforms aimed at improving the accuracy of criminal investigations and trials. In 2000, Congress passed the DNA Analysis Backlog Elimination Act to grant the states additional funding for DNA analysis, and then in 2004 passed the Innocence Protection Act to encourage postconviction DNA testing. Social scientists have begun to study the causes of wrongful convictions, and legal scholars are beginning to reassess our constitutional criminal procedure's efficacy in light of exonerations.

Despite the attention now devoted to the problem of wrongful convictions, no one has studied how postconviction DNA exonerees fared in our criminal system. This Article presents the results of an empirical study that examines how our criminal system handled, from start to finish, the cases of the first 200 persons exonerated by postconviction DNA testing in the United States.

* * *

Table 3.7: DNA Exonerees' Convictions and Capital Sentences

Conviction	Number of Cases
Rape	141
Murder	12
Rape-Murder	44
Other	3

II. Results: From Trial to Exoneration

A. Criminal Trials

[A]lmost all of the 200 exonerees were convicted of rape and murder, typically based on eyewitness identifications, forensic evidence, informant testimony, or confessions. Yet very few raised, much less received relief on, claims relating to these pieces of factual evidence, many of which we now know were unreliable or false.

1. Rape and Murder Convictions. — The 200 exonerees were charged and convicted chiefly of rape (71%), murder (6%), or both murder and rape (22%). This is not surprising; rape cases in particular often have relevant biological material for DNA testing. Fourteen were sentenced to death. Fifty were sentenced to life in prison. The table above depicts this distribution.

These 200 exonerees do not reflect the typical criminal convicts in that very few suspects are charged with rape or murder and even fewer are convicted. According to the Bureau of Justice Statistics (BJS), only 0.7% of felony defendants are convicted of murder and only 0.8% are convicted of rape.

Only nine of the exonerees pleaded guilty. Presumably, some refused to accept guilty pleas because they knew they were innocent, although in these serious murder and rape cases prosecutors may not have offered plea bargains that were palatable to an innocent defendant. The members of the innocence group are thus very different from typical criminal defendants. All but the nine who pleaded guilty in the innocence group (96%) were convicted at criminal trials. In contrast, 68% of murder convictions and 84% of felony rape convictions were obtained through plea bargaining.

Murder and rape cases are differently situated. BJS statistics show that while 16% of rape convictions were based on a trial verdict, 32% of murder convictions were based on a trial verdict. Several additional features distinguish rape from murder convictions. Rape cases typically involve a victim identification and perhaps biological evidence from a rape kit. In the time before DNA testing could be performed, one would expect many stranger rape cases to plea bargain on the strength of the victim's identification, with more equivocal cases, perhaps often involving non-strangers and issues of consent, going to trial. In contrast, in murder cases, if the victim was the only witness, law enforcement may face great difficulties identifying the perpetrator. Again, the more equivocal cases may go to trial, rather than result in convictions based on guilty pleas. However, given the seriousness of a murder case, police have

Table 3.8: Evidence Supporting DNA Exonerees' Convictions

Type of Evidence	Percentage whose convictions were supported by type of evidence (Number)[a]	
	(of all 200 cases)	(of the 133 cases with written decisions)
Eyewitness Identification	79 (158)	78 (104)
Forensic Evidence	57 (113)	58 (77)
Informant Testimony	18 (35)	23 (30)
Confession	16 (31)	15 (20)

[a] In the tables that follow, "N" stands for "Number."

far greater incentives to invest in their investigation and prosecution. These reasons may explain why there is a higher conviction rate for felony defendants charged with murder than for those charged with felony rape, despite fewer guilty pleas in murder cases; in felony rape cases there are more dismissals, acquittals, and misdemeanor convictions.

2. Trial Evidence Supporting Wrongful Convictions. — Due to DNA testing, we know now that at least some of the evidence introduced at trial against these 200 exonerees was false or misleading. Eyewitnesses were incorrect or misled by police suggestion, a confession was false, if not coerced, or expert testimony on hair or blood evidence was wrong or not probative. In this Part, I examine data regarding evidence supporting these wrongful convictions, including the interaction of multiple types of evidence. For example, one can assess how often the victim's testimony alone supported the conviction (in 26% of cases), or how many exonerees were sentenced to death based only on blood serology and a jailhouse informant. This assessment will provide a more complete picture of what evidence supported trial convictions of innocent defendants. The table above examines the main types of evidence that supported wrongful convictions.

The sections that follow will discuss these sources of evidence in turn: eyewitness identifications, forensic evidence, informant testimony, and confessions. The first column in Table 3.8 describes the percentage of the 200 exonerees whose convictions were supported by a particular type of evidence, analyzing only evidence introduced at trial. The second column in Table 3.8 describes the same phenomenon, but narrows the pool of exonerees to the 133 exonerees whose convictions were supported by a particular type of evidence and who also received written decisions during their appeals or postconviction proceedings. These data relate to Table 3.9, which analyzes how many of those with written decisions asserted claims during appellate or postconviction proceedings to challenge particular types of evidence.

Table 3.9 demonstrates that, with the exception of defendants in cases relying on confessions, fewer than half of the defendants brought constitutional claims chal-

Table 3.9: Factual Claims Brought by Exonerees

Type of Evidence	Percentage of those in Table 3.8, Col. 3, who brought a constitutional claim directly challenging the type of evidence (N)	Percentage who had their claim granted (N)[a]	Percentage who brought any claim to challenge evidence (N)	Percentage who brought any claim to challenge type of evidence and had that claim granted (N)[a]
Eyewitness Identification	28 (29)	0 (0)	45 (47)	4 (4)
Forensic Evidence	0 (0)	0 (0)	32 (25)	8 (6)
Informant Testimony	3 (1)	3 (1)	40 (12)	3 (1)
Confession	50 (10)	0 (0)	65 (13)	0 (0)

[a] These columns include only cases in which the court granted a vacatur of the conviction and where that reversal was affirmed on appeal.

lenging the types of evidence supporting their wrongful convictions. In part this is because few such constitutional claims exist. Nor did many who brought such claims succeed. The two columns on the right address how exonerees not only raised constitutional claims directly challenging particular evidence, but also raised additional factual challenges using other less direct constitutional claims or state law claims. For example, rather than bring a claim that a confession was involuntary, one might indirectly assert a claim that the attorney was ineffective for failing to challenge the confession. Furthermore, state law may provide broader avenues for attacking the reliability of factual evidence at trial. Even including those claims, significant percentages of those exonerees falsely convicted based on a given type of factual evidence never challenged it.

Thirty-four percent of those with written decisions—forty-five exonerees—challenged none of the above categories of facts that supported their convictions during their appeals and postconviction proceedings. Plausible explanations include the possibilities that those exonerees had no legal contention that could provide relief, that they uncovered no new facts to support a claim, that their claims were defaulted at trial, or that they litigated without effective or resourceful counsel.

a. Eyewitness Misidentifications.—The overwhelming number of convictions of the innocent involved eyewitness identification—158 of 200 cases (79%). Though fewer than a third of rape cases involve assaults by strangers, almost all of these innocence cases involved identifications by strangers; only eight involved incorrect acquaintance identifications. In 135 cases (68%), the victim provided identification testimony, while in thirty-three cases (17%), a non-victim eyewitness provided testimony (in some cases along with the victim). In fifty-six cases (28%), the victim's identification testimony was the central evidence supporting the conviction.

The high proportion of cases involving eyewitness identifications should be no surprise, for the prosecution of stranger rape cases will typically be predicated on the victim's identification. It would be difficult to go forward, obviously, if the victim does not identify the perpetrator (at least absent DNA evidence). For that reason, of 141 rape cases, 125 involved victim identifications (89%). Indeed, 126 of the 158 eyewitness identifications were in rape cases.

* * *

A total of forty-seven exonerees brought some kind of claim attacking the eyewitness identifications, or 45% of those with written decisions identified by eyewitnesses. Few raised constitutional claims challenging the reliability of these eyewitness identifications. Twenty-nine of the exonerees raised suggestive eyewitness identification claims during their appeals or postconviction proceedings; such claims allege that the police improperly indicated to the eyewitness who their suspect was. In other words, 28% of the 104 exonerees who had written decisions and who were convicted based on eyewitnesses' testimonies brought these claims. None of the claims regarding suggestive eyewitness identifications were granted. Four exonerees brought claims asserting their right, established by *United States v. Wade*,[9] to have counsel present at a postarrest lineup; none of the claims were granted. Thus, thirty-one, or 30% of those exonerees with written decisions, brought constitutional claims attacking their identifications. Sixteen additional exonerees brought state law claims (9) or used other constitutional claims to indirectly challenge the identification, such as ineffective assistance of counsel claims (5), newly discovered evidence of innocence claims (4), or challenges to jury instructions (2). (Two brought multiple claims.)

* * *

The results in these innocence cases show that most exonerees had no successful basis for challenging what we now know to be incorrect eyewitness identifications. Courts denied relief on all suggestive eyewitness identification claims, even in instances where we know in retrospect that the eyewitness was not "reliable," but instead was in error. Moreover, only four exonerees succeeded in bringing indirect challenges to the eyewitness identification.

b. Faulty Forensic Evidence.— Forensic evidence was the second leading type of evidence supporting these erroneous convictions. In many cases, little more than flimsy forensic evidence supported the conviction. Some had more than one type introduced. One hundred and thirteen cases (57%) involved introduction of forensic evidence at trial, with serological analysis of blood or semen the most common (79 cases), followed by expert comparison of hair evidence (43 cases), soil comparison (5 cases), DNA tests (3 cases), bite mark evidence (3 cases), fingerprint evidence (2

---

9. 388 U.S. 218 (1967).

cases), dog scent identification (2 cases), spectrographic voice evidence (1 case), shoe prints (1 case), and fiber comparison (1 case).

The forensic evidence was often fairly central to the prosecution's case even though it may have been known to have limited probative power at the time of trial. For example, exonerations in cases involving serology may not show misconduct, but rather either the limitations of old-fashioned serology as compared with more advanced DNA testing technology or unintentional error in conducting such testing. Serological testing sorts individuals into just a handful of different blood types, typically using the A, B, and H antigens, each shared by high percentages of the population; for example, approximately 40% of the population possesses only the H antigen, making them the O type. In contrast, DNA testing can provide random match probabilities greater than all humans who have ever lived (for example, one in 100 trillion).

Despite its relative lack of probative power, serological evidence was often all that law enforcement could use at the time of the investigation. In this group of cases, which chiefly consist of rape convictions in the pre-DNA era, serological evidence was the most common type of forensic evidence introduced at trial, and it typically involved analysis of materials from a rape kit prepared after an assault. Serological evidence was usually not the only evidence at trial—though in one case the serological evidence was the central evidence at trial and in another case serology and hair evidence were the central evidence at trial. In forty-six of the exonerees' cases (23%), there was an eyewitness identification added to the serological evidence. In four cases, the serology was added to a confession. In three more it was added to alleged self-inculpatory remarks. In two cases, the serological evidence was added to informant testimony. Thus, despite its typical lack of probative power, serological evidence often bolstered other evidence at trial.

Many, and perhaps most, cases, however, appear to have involved not merely use of evidence with limited probative value, but the improper use of then-existing forensic science. To a surprising extent, the forensic testimony at trial was improper based on science at the time. A preliminary review of serological testimony during these exonerees' trials disclosed that more than half involved improper testimony by forensic examiners.

The second most common type of evidence in these cases, visual hair comparison testimony, is notoriously unreliable. Absent any data regarding probabilities that hair or fiber may match visually, experts can make only a subjective assessment whether two hairs or two fibers are "consistent" and share similarities. Forty-three cases (22%) involved false visual hair or fiber comparison. Hair evidence was used in forty-two cases. In some cases that visual hair comparison evidence was particularly central to the prosecution's case. Calvin Scott spent twenty years behind bars based largely on hair comparison evidence alone, in a case where the victim did not get a good look at her attacker and could not identify Scott. In eleven cases, visual hair comparison testimony was added to eyewitness testimony as evidence of identity. In five cases, hair comparison testimony and an informant were presented at trial.

Just as with the serological cases, a preliminary review suggests that microscopic hair comparison testimony at trial often distorted or misstated the forensic evidence to inflate its probative significance. Errors were due not merely to the underlying unreliability of visual hair comparison, but were at a minimum compounded by improper and misleading testimony regarding comparisons conducted. Most commonly, state experts mischaracterized their results by purporting to "match" hairs or constructing the probability of such a match, rather than merely visually comparing hairs and either observing certain similarities or excluding any common source.... Bite mark evidence, also notoriously unreliable, was relied on in three cases, in one providing the only evidence of guilt in a capital case.

The forensic evidence was rarely challenged with any success on appeal or post-conviction, though six exonerees obtained reversals based on challenges to forensic evidence at trial. None of the 113 persons who were convicted based on forensic evidence raised a fabrication of evidence claim under the Due Process Clause. However, some exonerees raised state evidence law claims (15), ineffective assistance claims (11), or prosecutorial misconduct claims (2) to challenge the forensic evidence introduced at trial. These figures represent a total of twenty-five exonerees, or 32% of the seventy-seven cases with written decisions involving convictions based on forensic evidence. One reason for the dearth of challenges to forensic evidence may be that indigent defendants could not afford to hire a forensic expert. Indigent defendants frequently fail to receive funding for such independent experts. Thus, until the DNA testing was done, these exonerees may simply have been unable to show that the forensic evidence at trial was false or unreliable.

c. False Informant Testimony. — In thirty-five cases (18%), an informant, jailhouse informant, or cooperating alleged co-perpetrator provided false testimony. In twenty-three of those cases it was a jailhouse informant. The Supreme Court has approved the use of informants so long as proper discovery is provided regarding the relationship between the informant and the defendant. Police use such informants frequently, though "jailhouse informants are considered among the least reliable witnesses in the criminal justice system." These DNA exonerations provide cases in point. Since DNA testing proved these people innocent, we know now that they likely did not "confess" to jailhouse informants. We also know they likely could not have told these informants anything nonpublic about how the crimes happened, since they did not commit the crimes. Instead, we know that these informants often lied, which should not be surprising given their great incentives to cooperate with law enforcement (though any preferential treatment must be disclosed to the jury).

Twelve of thirty-five, or 34%, of those convicted based on informant testimony brought claims to challenge it. No exoneree raised fabrication claims under the Due Process Clause regarding jailhouse informant testimony, probably because they could not locate any evidence to prove that the informants testified falsely. Two brought Massiah claims that they were denied the right to have counsel present during an interrogation by a government informant. Verneal Jimerson brought the only fabrication claim regarding a codefendant, and he received a reversal on it. In

Jimerson's case, police concealed that they obtained the testimony of codefendant Paula Gray by offering her inducements. Gray's testimony is now known to be false: She was a juvenile, mentally retarded, innocent, and also wrongly convicted along with three others in what became known as the Ford Heights Four case. Nine additional exonerees who were convicted based on informant testimony brought a range of indirect claims challenging this testimony, such as Brady claims (4), state evidence law claims (3), Strickland claims (2), and one claim regarding the jury instruction.

* * *

[J]ailhouse informants testified in almost half of the false capital convictions, [yet none of the exonerees] brought claims that jailhouse informant testimony was fabricated. This fact is unsurprising, since it would be very difficult for one to obtain evidence to show fabrication. In addition, despite the dangers of lying and unreliable informants illustrated by these cases, most states have not enacted any protections requiring review of informant testimony. Illinois, after experiencing heightened numbers of exonerations, is now the only state to require that trial courts conduct reliability hearings to evaluate jailhouse informants in capital cases. The Oklahoma Criminal Appellate Court requires enhanced disclosure regarding informant testimony, but so far, other states have not followed suit, though some have adopted instructions cautioning the jury regarding the reliability of informants.

d. False Confessions.—In thirty-one cases (16%), a false confession was introduced at trial. As noted below, this excludes cases in which the exoneree had allegedly made self-inculpatory remarks but not a confession to a crime of which he was convicted. This also excludes eleven cases in which a codefendant falsely confessed. Seven of those who confessed were sentenced to death (half of the fourteen capital cases). Eleven of those who falsely confessed were mentally retarded (35%), but nevertheless the confession was introduced at trial and led to a wrongful conviction. Twelve of those who confessed were juveniles (39%), five of whom were also mentally retarded; there were twenty-two juveniles amongst the exonerees (five in the "Central Park Jogger" case). In eighteen false confession cases, the defendant was either mentally retarded or under eighteen at the time of the offense, or both.

The confessions were particularly powerful at trial, perhaps in part because in some cases law enforcement supplied false facts to bolster false confessions. Furthermore, in most cases, having obtained a confession, the State relied on little else to convict. In seven cases, the confession was the central evidence of guilt. In nine more cases, the confession was accompanied by only one other type of evidence (a jailhouse snitch, an eyewitness, or blood or hair evidence).

* * *

To deter law enforcement coercion that would violate the Fifth Amendment right against self-incrimination as incorporated against the states, the Supreme Court enacted Miranda protections that require police to give warnings before beginning an interrogation. The Court also requires the trial court to exclude involuntary confessions from the trial. Courts must assess the voluntariness of confessions flexibly, based on "the totality of all the surrounding circumstances," including any coercion applied and the "characteristics of the accused."

Persons who falsely confessed did not always raise constitutional claims challenging their confessions, at least as reported in written decisions. Seven of the twenty exonerees who confessed falsely and had written decisions (35%) raised Fifth Amendment claims that their confessions were involuntary. Three more (15%) alleged that their confessions were obtained in violation of Miranda. Thus, ten of twenty (50%) raised constitutional claims directly challenging their confessions. None who brought claims regarding Miranda or coercion received any relief. Three others raised state law claims or indirect constitutional claims, increasing the number of those who raised constitutional claims to 65%. One of these three received a reversal on an ineffective assistance claim. The others, though they falsely confessed and were intimately familiar with what had gone wrong, may have had no evidence to prove coercion under the Court's deferential voluntariness test, which examines the circumstances surrounding the examination.

There is no constitutional claim that offers relief from a false confession, as opposed to a confession secured because of coercion or lack of capacity. The exoneree could raise a fabrication claim under the Due Process Clause if police officers told the suspect what to say, but then falsely testified at trial that the suspect volunteered non-public information about the crime that only the perpetrator could know. No exoneree brought such a claim during appeals or postconviction proceedings. Without a recording of the interrogation and before obtaining DNA testing, these exonerees likely had no way to prove fabrication by law enforcement.

In thirteen cases the exoneree allegedly made self-inculpatory statements but not a full confession to the crime of which he or she was convicted. Five such exonerees brought coerced confession claims regarding their self-inculpatory statements to police. None of these alleged voluntary statements, as reported by police or witnesses, were successfully challenged on appeal or postconviction, likely because a claim of coercion would be difficult to make for a statement that was putatively volunteered.

3. False Capital Convictions. — False capital convictions are of particular salience to the administration of the death penalty. The Supreme Court has recently noted that "a disturbing number of inmates on death row have been exonerated," and polls suggest that DNA exonerations may explain lagging public support for the death penalty. The study by James Liebman, Jeff Fagan, and Valerie West examining error rates in all capital cases from 1973 to 1995 found not only that the vast majority of all capital cases are reversed on appeal or postconviction, but also that 7% of those whose sentences were overturned later obtained a determination on retrial that they were not guilty of the capital crime.[10]

---

10. James Liebman, Jeffrey Fagan & Valerie West, A Broken System; Error Rates In Capital Cases, 1973–1995 (2000).

Fourteen of the 200 members of the innocence group had been convicted of capital crimes. Many more capital prisoners have been released from death row based on non-DNA evidence of innocence; capital cases usually involve murders, while only a small percentage are rape-murders for which biological evidence is available to test.

Many capital convictions of the innocent were predicated on surprisingly weak evidence, perhaps because they involved difficult stranger homicide cases that tended not to have had any witnesses. As a result, these capital trials typically involved few types of evidence. Two of the cases involved death sentences resting on a single type of evidence—Ray Krone based on a mere bite mark comparison and Frank Smith based on eyewitness identifications by non-victims. Another troubling capital case, that of Charles Fain, involved only a jailhouse informant and hair evidence. Three more capital cases involved eyewitness evidence together with an informant or jailhouse informant.

Six capital cases (43%) involved jailhouse informants. In Ron Williamson's case, the actual perpetrator was a witness testifying for the State at trial. Other studies of non-DNA cases confirm that perjury by prosecution witnesses is a leading cause of erroneous capital convictions.

In seven capital cases the defendant falsely confessed; three of the seven involved mentally retarded persons. (In its Atkins decision, the Court noted that one such case existed; there have actually been several.) In each of the cases involving a false confession, some other evidence supported the conviction.

These data suggest that erroneous death sentences can flow from unreliable evidence ranging from jailhouse informants to unreliable forensic and eyewitness evidence. These false capital convictions already have spurred action by lawmakers. The Illinois legislature, for example, has enacted a statute barring death sentences based solely on uncorroborated eyewitness or informant testimony.

In conclusion, a few categories of evidence introduced at trial commonly supported wrongful convictions of the innocent: eyewitness identifications, forensic evidence, informant testimony, and confessions. Few exonerees raised claims relating to those types of evidence and even fewer succeeded in obtaining reversals on appeal or during postconviction proceedings. This was true even in erroneous capital convictions, which were often premised on particularly flimsy informant evidence. These findings ... suggest the reluctance or inability of defendants to raise resource-intensive factual challenges during appeals and postconviction proceedings, and the reluctance or inability of courts to grant relief on claims relating to facts.

Jon B. Gould and Richard A. Leo, *One Hundred Years Later: Wrongful Convictions After a Century of Research*

100 J. Crim. L. & Criminology 825, 827–32 (2010)

A Short History of Research on Wrongful Convictions

In 1913, Edwin Borchard's article opened the eyes of American observers to the scourge of wrongful convictions by describing European approaches to righting the wrongs of erroneous convictions. Twenty years later, his book, Convicting the Innocent: Sixty-Five Actual Errors of Criminal Justice, created a stir when it identified sixty-five cases in which an innocent person had been convicted. Borchard also classified the likely "sources of error including erroneous eyewitness testimony, false confessions, faulty circumstantial evidence, and prosecutorial excesses." Yet, for the next fifty years, research on wrongful convictions was sporadic. "Typically, one big-picture book or major article [was] published every decade or so on the subject of miscarriages of justice," many of which "followed a familiar structure." Authors would assert the importance of clearing the innocent; they would describe cases in which an innocent defendant had been convicted; and they would close by proposing reforms to prevent future errors. Among those who followed in this literary path were Erle Stanley Gardner, creator of the fictional defense lawyer Perry Mason, and Judge Jerome Frank, who collaborated with his daughter Barbara on the book, Not Guilty.

"Until the late 1980s, it might have seemed bizarre, if not incoherent, to suggest that the study of miscarriages of justice constituted a field or area of academic study, rather than merely a series of unrelated and relatively infrequent articles and books." However, in 1987, Hugo Bedau and Michael Radelet published their groundbreaking study in the Stanford Law Review, claiming that 350 individuals had been wrongly convicted in potentially capital cases over much of the twentieth century.[11] In addition to describing the facts of these cases, Bedau and Radelet systematically analyzed the sources of these errors and the methods by which the mistakes had been discovered. Their work led to a florescence of research on wrongful convictions, inspiring others to research and write about the sources and consequences of wrongful convictions, as well as to re-analyze and extend their findings. All the while, they have continued to collect, analyze, and publish data about wrongful conviction cases.

Bedau and Radelet's article was followed in the 1990s by a series of books on the subject.... Yet, for the attention these books may have received, everything paled in the face of the revolution that arrived in the 1990s when DNA testing became feasible and affordable in many cases. Once limited to such imperfect techniques as serology testing or hair comparison analysis, law enforcement officials found that they could test biological evidence for common genetic links between perpetrators and potential suspects, permitting results that were infinitely more accurate. Innocent defendants also recognized the potential of DNA testing to clear them even after conviction if

---

11. See supra, Chapter 2.

biological evidence from the crime scene had been retained. In what appeared to be an avalanche of cases over the next decade, advocates have managed to exonerate over 250 innocent persons of crimes they had not committed, including several defendants who had been on death row. Even more individuals have been exonerated in this period in cases not involving DNA testing.

These cases rightly drew media attention to the frailties of the criminal justice system and, perhaps more importantly, revealed serious problems in everyday police work. In 1996, the National Institute of Justice released a report noting that in "every year since 1989, in about 25 percent of the sexual assault cases referred to the FBI ... the primary suspect has been excluded by DNA testing." Put another way, among rape cases referred to the FBI for DNA testing, law enforcement officers had been wrong one out of every four times in naming an initial suspect.

The advent of DNA testing not only generated more attention for, and research about, wrongful convictions, but it also seemed to have pushed academicians from "pure" research to research/advocacy. Here, the influence of Barry Scheck and Peter Neufeld cannot be underestimated. Two former legal aid attorneys, the pair founded the Innocence Project in 1992 at the Benjamin N. Cardozo School of Law. Today, the Innocence Project (IP) is a non-profit legal clinic that "handles cases where post-conviction DNA testing of evidence can yield conclusive proof of innocence. As a clinic, students handle the case work while supervised by a team of attorneys and clinic staff." The IP has led successful efforts to exonerate hundreds of innocent defendants. It also has spawned the creation of regional innocence projects and legal clinics at law schools around the country. Among the most famous is Northwestern University's Center on Wrongful Conviction and Medill Innocence Project, at which law and journalism professors, along with their students and professional journalists, were the catalysts for a statewide investigation into wrongful convictions in Illinois. In an unprecedented move in 2000, then-Governor George Ryan commuted all death sentences and imposed a moratorium on further executions until a special commission and the General Assembly addressed the several problems in investigations and prosecutions that had led to more convicted murderers released from prison upon questions of their guilt than actually executed over a twenty-two-year period.

Illinois is not alone; North Carolina, Virginia, and California have also seen innocence commissions, modeled in many ways on the Criminal Case Review Commission (CCRC) in the United Kingdom and the Royal Commissions of Inquiry in Canada. The Royal Commissions have been available for over a century, with national and provincial governments permitted to conduct independent, nongovernment-affiliated investigations regarding the conduct of public businesses or the fair administration of justice. Two of the most famous examples of the commissions were those investigating the exonerations of Guy Paul Morin and Thomas Sophonow. More recently, the U.K. established the CCRV in 1997. The CCRV has jurisdiction over criminal cases from any Magistrates' or Crown Court in England, Wales, and Northern Ireland "to review possible miscarriages of justice and decide if they should be referred to an appeal court."

[R]esearch has been instrumental in assisting innocence or related government commissions to establish "best practices" to prevent wrongful convictions, whether in the United States or abroad.... Indeed, in many ways, we have reached the point where researchers are now performing a dual function with regard to wrongful convictions; on one level scholars are conducting research for its intrinsic insight into the functioning of the criminal justice system; on another level, researchers have become instruments of reform, working alongside policymakers to implement the lessons their research uncovers. That alone is a significant step in the near-century of inquiry, one that Borchard hardly may have expected when he first published his article....

B. Legal Materials, Exercises, and Media

1. *First DNA Exoneree from Death Row:*

    In the 1980s, DNA was a brand new thing. Kirk made himself an expert, in the obsessive way only a man in prison can. He got hopeful. "But they said the physical evidence from my case was gone. It was lost. No one knew where it was. In the end they said it had been inadvertently destroyed. I was locked up, and now it felt like they had thrown away the key. But one day my lawyer was at the courthouse, and he knew one of the bailiffs, because he was there a lot, and the guy asked, 'What are you looking for?' And my lawyer said, 'the Hamilton evidence from the Bloodsworth case.' And the guy said, 'Oh, that's in the judge's closet. In a paper bag in a cardboard box.' And it was. Just dumped in there. They recovered half a cell from it. Which is very damn small in the scheme of things. And the DNA proved I didn't do it."

    — excerpt from *Anatomy of Innocence: Testimonies of the Wrongfully Convicted,* edited by Laura Caldwell and Leslie Klinger, sharing death row exoneree Kirk Bloodsworth's story

2. *First DNA Exoneree from Death Row, Recommended Listening:* Kirk Bloodsworth, a former marine from Maryland, was the first person on death row to be exonerated by DNA evidence. His story also contains other hallmarks of wrongful conviction, including mistaken eyewitness identification and ineffective assistance of defense counsel. Listen to Kirk Bloodsworth describe his wrongful conviction on Season 1, Episode 7, Sentenced to Death, Exonerated by DNA: The Wrongful Conviction of Kirk Bloodsworth, of *Wrongful Conviction with Jason Flom* (5:00–10:00, mistaken eyewitness identification) (13:30–16:10, ineffective assistance of counsel) (23:10–28:20, DNA evidence and exoneration): https://art19.com/shows/wrongful-conviction-with-jason-flom.

3. *Exercise, Motion for DNA Testing:* In teams, prepare to orally argue a Motion for DNA Testing, each person taking a side.

Motion for DNA Testing (Jason Crowe/Regina Parker)

Oral Argument

On April 30, 1989, Ms. Regina Parker was sexually assaulted in her home in Kokomo, Indiana. According to Ms. Parker and her trial testimony, she was asleep on the couch in the living room when someone knocked at the front door and then opened the unlocked door and entered the house. Ms. Parker recognized the man as her cousin, Jason Crowe, whom she had known since he was a child. Allegedly, Mr. Crowe pulled out a gun and threatened Ms. Parker, and then vaginally sexually assaulted her on the couch. When Mr. Crowe agreed to allow Ms. Parker to go use the bathroom, Ms. Parker kicked Mr. Crowe and ran out the door. She went to her neighbor's house and called the police; when the police arrived, the man who had raped Ms. Parker was gone.

Ms. Parker went to the hospital, where doctors performed a rape kit on her. Her house was never searched for hair, fibers, or fingerprints. Ms. Parker was the only witness to see the intruder. Mr. Crowe was arrested and charged based on Ms. Parker's identification; he voluntarily gave blood and hair for DNA testing. Mr. Crowe is mentally handicapped. He lived with his parents, but everyone was asleep in the house at the time of the assault, so he did not have a strong alibi. Mr. Crowe made statements to the police of his innocence at the time of the investigation.

On February 24, 1990, Jason Crowe was convicted of rape and burglary of a dwelling place. He was sentenced to life with parole. His conviction rested solely on eyewitness testimony of the victim, and microscopic hair analysis. Microscopic hair analysis was completed matching a foreign hair found in the rape kit with the defendant's hair; an expert at trial said from analyzing the color of the two hairs, their length, their diameter, and the thickness and color of their cuticles that he matched the hair to Mr. Crowe, within a reasonable degree of certainty. Although DNA evidence was collected as part of the rape kit, preserved, and tested by the State using RFLP, the testing was inconclusive because the sample size was not large enough.

Mr. Crowe appealed his conviction, arguing his sentence should have been limited to twenty years because he was not mentally competent to make an informed decision to accept or reject a plea bargain of twenty years offered him. Mr. Crowe was 16 at the time of the assault, 17 at the time of his conviction. The Indiana Supreme Court affirmed the conviction. Mr. Crowe never filed a petition for habeas relief, nor for DNA testing.

Mr. Crowe now seeks to submit the rape kit to new and complete Y-STR DNA testing, which requires a fraction of the sample to produce a result, and was not available in Indiana at the time of his trial. The Indiana Crime Lab has the rape kit and has properly stored it for the past twenty years. Ever since the original testing was ordered by the State and completed by the Indiana Crime Lab, the evidence has been solely in the hands of the Indiana Crime Lab. Mr. Crowe submitted a motion for DNA Testing to the original trial court, and the court has ordered a hearing for both sides to argue the motion. The State has not responded in writing to Mr.

Crowe's motion, and likely will not. The motion was served on both the State and the Indiana Crime Lab.

Mr. Crowe is currently in the psychiatric ward within his prison. He has visions, and when you visit with him he'll have conversations with the Lord in your presence. He has been housed in the psychiatric ward of the prison since 2005. Mr. Crowe continues to maintain that he did not sexually assault his cousin, Regina Parker, and verified the Motion for DNA Testing.

Argue as either Mr. Crowe's defense counsel petitioning for DNA testing, or as the State challenging the DNA testing.

Reminders: Make sure to satisfy the requirements of Indiana Code s. 35-38-7 (Post-Conviction DNA Testing and Analysis).

Chapter Four

The Innocence "Myth" and the Costs of Preventing Wrongful Convictions

Joshua Marquis,[*] *The Innocent and the Shammed*

The New York Times, January 26, 2006

As the words scroll across a darkened TV screen, we hear an authoritative voice announce that every year an alarming number of people in this country "are wrongfully convicted." Millions of Americans who watched these promotions in recent weeks knew they were pitches for the new ABC television drama "In Justice." But if they'd been listening from the next room, they might easily have thought from the somber tone that it was a tease for the nightly news or "20/20."

"In Justice" has received dismal reviews. But that hasn't stopped its premise from permeating the conventional wisdom: that our prisons are chock-full of doe-eyed innocents who have been framed by venal prosecutors and corrupt police officers with the help of grossly incompetent public defenders. It is a misconception that has run through our popular culture from "Perry Mason" to the novels of Scott Turow to the recent hit play "The Exonerated."

It was also seen on the front pages in recent weeks, in reporting about Roger Coleman, who was executed in Virginia in 1992 for rape and murder. DNA testing at the time had placed him within one-fifth of a percent of possible suspects, leading to widespread claims that he was innocent. The governor, L. Douglas Wilder, said he would consider commuting Mr. Coleman's sentence if he passed a lie detector test. He failed and was executed.

For more than a decade opponents of the death penalty have held up the Coleman case as the example that would prove that America executed an innocent man. Yet on Jan. 12 the Canadian laboratory that had been sent the last remaining DNA sample in the case announced the results of more advanced testing: it put the odds of Mr. Coleman not being the killer at less than 1 in 19 million. Still, while Mr. Coleman's face graced the cover of Time magazine at the height of the controversy, it is unlikely you will see him on the cover again marking his rightful conviction.

---

[*] Joshua Marquis is the district attorney of Clatsop County in Oregon and on the Board of Directors for the National District Attorneys Association.

Americans love the underdog. Thousands of law students aspire to be Atticus Finch, the famous fictional lawyer from "To Kill A Mockingbird." But this can go too far: one of the jurors who acquitted the actor Robert Blake of murder last year cited the TV program "CSI" as the basis of her knowledge of what good police work should be. And if we take a deep breath and examine the state of American justice, a very different picture will emerge.

To start, only 14 Americans who were once on death row have been exonerated by DNA evidence alone. The hordes of Americans wrongfully convicted exist primarily on Planet Hollywood. In the Winter 2005 Journal of Criminal Law and Criminology, a group led by Samuel Gross, a law professor at the University of Michigan, published an exhaustive study of exonerations around the country from 1989 to 2003 in cases ranging from robbery to capital murder. They were able to document only 340 inmates who were eventually freed. (They counted cases where defendants were retried after an initial conviction and subsequently found not guilty as "exonerations.") Yet, despite the relatively small number his research came up with, Mr. Gross says he is certain that far more innocents languish undiscovered in prison.

So, let's give the professor the benefit of the doubt: let's assume that he understated the number of innocents by roughly a factor of 10, that instead of 340 there were 4,000 people in prison who weren't involved in the crime in any way. During that same 15 years, there were more than 15 million felony convictions across the country. That would make the error rate .027 percent — or, to put it another way, a success rate of 99.973 percent.

Most industries would like to claim such a record of efficiency. And while, of course, people's lives are far more important than widgets, we have an entire appeals court system intended to intervene in those few cases where the innocent are in jeopardy.

It is understandable that journalists focus on the rare case in which an innocent man or woman is sent to prison — because, as all reporters know, how many planes landed safely today has never been news. The larger issue is whether those who influence the culture, like an enormous television network, have a moral responsibility to keep the facts straight regardless of their thirst for drama. "In Justice" may soon find itself on the canceled list, but several million people will still have watched it, and they are likely to have the impression that wrongfully convicted death row inmates are the virtual rule.

The words "innocent" and "exonerated" carry tremendous emotional and political weight. But these terms have been tortured beyond recognition — not just by defense lawyers, but by the disseminators of entertainment under the guise of social conscience.

"The Exonerated" played for several years Off Broadway with a Who's Who of stage and screen stars portraying six supposedly innocent people who were once on death row. The play, originally subsidized by George Soros, the liberal billionaire philanthropist, now tours college campuses and was made into a television movie by Court TV.

The script never mentions that two of the play's six characters (Sonia Jacobs and Kerry Cook) were not exonerated, but were let out of prison after a combined 36 years behind bars when they agreed to plea bargains. A third (Robert Hayes) was unavailable to do publicity tours because he is in prison, having pleaded guilty to another homicide almost identical to the one of which he was acquitted.

American justice is a work in progress, and those of us charged with administering it are well aware that it needs constant improvement. But nothing is gained by deluding the public into believing that the police and prosecutors are trying to send innocent people to prison. Any experienced defense lawyer will concede that he would starve if he accepted only "innocent" clients. Americans should be far more worried about the wrongfully freed than the wrongfully convicted.

Kansas v. Marsh
548 U.S. 163 (2006)

Editor's note: *Marsh was convicted of capital murder and a penalty-phase hearing was conducted to determine if Marsh would receive the death penalty. Kansas law provides that if a unanimous jury finds that aggravating circumstances are not outweighed by mitigating circumstances, the death penalty shall be imposed. The jury sentenced Marsh to death. Marsh appealed his sentence, claiming the Kansas provision was unconstitutional. Marsh argued that the Constitution requires juries to be instructed that they may not recommend a death sentence unless they affirmatively find that the aggravating circumstances outweigh the mitigating circumstances. A majority of the Court rejected that claim and upheld the death sentence.*

In a dissenting opinion, Justice Souter made the following points:

In Kansas, when a jury applies the State's own standards of relative culpability and cannot decide that a defendant is among the most culpable, the state law says that equivocal evidence is good enough and the defendant must die. A law that requires execution when the case for aggravation has failed to convince the sentencing jury is morally absurd, and the Court's holding that the Constitution tolerates this moral irrationality defies decades of precedent aimed at eliminating freakish capital sentencing in the United States.

III

That precedent, demanding reasoned moral judgment, developed in response to facts that could not be ignored, the kaleidoscope of life and death verdicts that made no sense in fact or morality in the random sentencing before *Furman*[12] was decided in 1972. Today, a new body of fact must be accounted for in deciding what, in practical terms, the Eighth Amendment guarantees should tolerate, for the period starting in 1989 has seen repeated exonerations of convicts under death sentences, in numbers never imagined before the development of DNA tests. We cannot face up to these facts and still hold that the guarantee of morally justifiable sentencing is hollow

---

12. Furman v. Georgia, 408 U.S. 238 (1972).

enough to allow maximizing death sentences, by requiring them when juries fail to find the worst degree of culpability: when, by a State's own standards and a State's own characterization, the case for death is "doubtful."

A few numbers from a growing literature will give a sense of the reality that must be addressed. When the Governor of Illinois imposed a moratorium on executions in 2000, 13 prisoners under death sentences had been released since 1977 after a number of them were shown to be innocent, as described in a report which used their examples to illustrate a theme common to all 13, of "relatively little solid evidence connecting the charged defendants to the crimes."[13] During the same period, 12 condemned convicts had been executed. Subsequently the Governor determined that 4 more death row inmates were innocent. Illinois had thus wrongly convicted and condemned even more capital defendants than it had executed, but it may well not have been otherwise unique; one recent study reports that between 1989 and 2003, 74 American prisoners condemned to death were exonerated, Gross, Jacoby, Matheson, Montgomery, & Patil, *Exonerations in the United States 1989 Through 2003*, 95 J.Crim. L. & C. 523, 531 (2006) (hereinafter Gross), many of them cleared by DNA evidence. Another report states that "more than 110" death row prisoners have been released since 1973 upon findings that they were innocent of the crimes charged, and "[h]undreds of additional wrongful convictions in potentially capital cases have been documented over the past century."[14] Most of these wrongful convictions and sentences resulted from eyewitness misidentification, false confession, and (most frequently) perjury, and the total shows that among all prosecutions homicide cases suffer an unusually high incidence of false conviction, probably owing to the combined difficulty of investigating without help from the victim, intense pressure to get convictions in homicide cases, and the corresponding incentive for the guilty to frame the innocent.

We are thus in a period of new empirical argument about how "death is different," *Gregg*, 428 U.S., at 188: not only would these false verdicts defy correction after the fatal moment, the Illinois experience shows them to be remarkable in number, and they are probably disproportionately high in capital cases. While it is far too soon for any generalization about the soundness of capital sentencing across the country, the cautionary lesson of recent experience addresses the tie-breaking potential of the Kansas statute: the same risks of falsity that infect proof of guilt raise questions about sentences, when the circumstances of the crime are aggravating factors and bear on predictions of future dangerousness.

In the face of evidence of the hazards of capital prosecution, maintaining a sentencing system mandating death when the sentencer finds the evidence pro and con to be in equipoise is obtuse by any moral or social measure. And unless application of the Eighth Amendment no longer calls for reasoned moral judgment in substance as well as form, the Kansas law is unconstitutional.

---

13. State of Illinois, G. Ryan, Governor, Report of the Governor's Commission on Capital Punishment: Recommendations Only 7 (Apr.2002) (hereinafter Report).

14. Lanier & Acker, Capital Punishment, the Moratorium Movement, and Empirical Questions, 10 Psychology, Public Policy & Law 577, 593 (2004).

Justice SCALIA, concurring in the majority opinion.

I join the opinion of the Court. I write separately to clarify briefly the import of my joinder, and to respond at somewhat greater length … to Justice SOUTER's claims about risks inherent in capital punishment.

I

Part III of the Court's opinion — which makes plain why *Walton v. Arizona*, 497 U.S. 639 (1990), controls this case — would be sufficient to reverse the judgment below. I nonetheless join Part IV as well, which describes why Kansas's death penalty statute easily satisfies even a capital jurisprudence as incoherent as ours has become. In doing so, I do not endorse that incoherence, but adhere to my previous statement that "I will not … vote to uphold an Eighth Amendment claim that the sentencer's discretion has been unlawfully restricted."

* * *

III

Finally, I must say a few words (indeed, more than a few) in response to Part III of Justice SOUTER's dissent. This contains the disclaimer that the dissenters are not (*yet*) ready to "generaliz[e] about the soundness of capital sentencing across the country," but that is in fact precisely what they do. The dissent essentially argues that capital punishment is such an undesirable institution — it results in the condemnation of such a large number of innocents — that any legal rule which eliminates its pronouncement, including the one favored by the dissenters in the present case, should be embraced.

* * *

It should be noted at the outset that the dissent does not discuss a single case — not one — in which it is clear that a person was executed for a crime he did not commit. If such an event had occurred in recent years, we would not have to hunt for it; the innocent's name would be shouted from the rooftops by the abolition lobby. The dissent makes much of the new-found capacity of DNA testing to establish innocence. But in every case of an executed defendant of which I am aware, that technology has *confirmed* guilt.

* * *

Another of the dissent's leading authorities on exoneration of the innocent is Gross, Jacoby, Matheson, Montgomery, & Patil, *Exonerations in the United States 1989 Through 2003*, 95 J.Crim. L. & C. 523 (2006) (hereinafter Gross). The dissent quotes that study's self-congratulatory "criteria" of exoneration — seemingly so rigorous that no one could doubt the study's reliability. But in fact that article, like the others cited, is notable not for its rigorous investigation and analysis, but for the fervor of its belief that the American justice system is condemning the innocent "in numbers," as the dissent puts it, "never imagined before the development of DNA tests." Among the article's list of 74 "exonerees" is Jay Smith of Pennsylvania. Smith — a school principal — earned three death sentences for slaying one of his teachers and her two young children.[15] His retrial for triple murder was barred on double jeopardy grounds because of prosecutorial misconduct during the first trial. But Smith could not leave well enough alone. He had the gall to sue, under 42 U.S.C. § 1983, for false imprisonment. The Court of Appeals for the Third Circuit affirmed the jury verdict for the defendants, observing along the way that "our confidence in Smith's convictions is not diminished in the least. We remain firmly convinced of the integrity of those guilty verdicts."

* * *

Of course, even with its distorted concept of what constitutes "exoneration," the claims of the Gross article are fairly modest: Between 1989 and 2003, the authors identify 340 "exonerations" *nationwide*—not just for capital cases, mind you, nor even just for murder convictions, but for various felonies. Joshua Marquis, a district attorney in Oregon, recently responded to this article as follows:

> [L]et's give the professor the benefit of the doubt: let's assume that he understated the number of innocents by roughly a factor of 10, that instead of 340 there were 4,000 people in prison who weren't involved in the crime in any way. During that same 15 years, there were more than 15 million felony convictions across the country. That would make the error rate .027 percent—or, to put it another way, a success rate of 99.973 percent.

The dissent's suggestion that capital defendants are *especially* liable to suffer from the lack of 100% perfection in our criminal justice system is implausible. Capital cases are given especially close scrutiny at every level, which is why in most cases many years elapse before the sentence is executed. And of course capital cases receive special attention in the application of executive clemency. Indeed, one of the arguments made by abolitionists is that the process of finally completing all the appeals and reexaminations of capital sentences is so lengthy, and thus so expensive for the State, that the game is not worth the candle. The proof of the pudding, of course, is that as far as anyone can determine (and many are looking), *none* of cases included in the .027% error rate for American verdicts involved a capital defendant erroneously executed.

Since 1976 there have been approximately a half million murders in the United States. In that time, 7,000 murderers have been sentenced to death; about 950 of them have been executed; and about 3,700 inmates are currently on death row.[16] As a consequence of the sensitivity of the criminal justice system to the due-process rights of defendants sentenced to death, almost two-thirds of all death sentences are overturned. "Virtually none" of these reversals, however, are attributable to a defendant's "'actual innocence.'" Most are based on legal errors that have little or nothing to do with guilt. The studies cited by the dissent demonstrate nothing more.

Like other human institutions, courts and juries are not perfect. One cannot have a system of criminal punishment without accepting the possibility that someone will

---

15. See Smith v. Holtz, 210 F.3d 186, 188 (C.A.3 2000).
16. See Marquis, *The Myth of Innocence*, 95 J. Crim. L. & C. 501, 518 (2006).

be punished mistakenly. That is a truism, not a revelation. But with regard to the punishment of death in the current American system, that possibility has been reduced to an insignificant minimum. This explains why those ideologically driven to ferret out and proclaim a mistaken modern execution have not a single verifiable case to point to, whereas it is easy as pie to identify plainly guilty murderers who have been set free. The American people have determined that the good to be derived from capital punishment—in deterrence, and perhaps most of all in the meting out of condign justice for horrible crimes—outweighs the risk of error. It is no proper part of the business of this Court, or of its Justices, to second-guess that judgment, much less to impugn it before the world, and less still to frustrate it by imposing judicially invented obstacles to its execution.

D. Michael Risinger, *Innocents Convicted: An Empirically Justified Factual Wrongful Conviction Rate*

97 J. CRIM. L. & CRIMINOLOGY 761, 761–800 (2007)

That would make the error rate [in felony convictions] .027 percent—or, to put it another way, a success rate of 99.973 percent.

—Justice Antonin Scalia, concurring in *Kansas v. Marsh*,
June 26, 2006 (quoting Joshua Marquis)

I. Introduction

The news about the astounding accuracy of felony convictions in the United States, delivered by Justice Scalia and Joshua Marquis in the passage set out epigrammatically above, would be cause for rejoicing if it were true. Imagine. Only 27 factually wrong felony convictions out of every 100,000! Unfortunately, it is not true, as the empirical data analyzed in ... this article show.... But first, some historical context:

II. Paleyites and Romillists

People who think about the problem of wrongful conviction often fall into two camps, which we might label Paleyites and Romillists. Paleyites, whom I have named after the early exponent of this position, the 18th-century proto-utilitarian the Rev. William Paley, believe that, even though it is wrong to convict an innocent person, such convictions not only are inevitable in a human system, but represent the necessary social price of maintaining sufficient criminal law enforcement to provide an appropriate level of security for the public in general. Hence, one should not be moved by the prospect of wrongful conviction to take actions that would reduce such convictions, no matter how common, at the cost of reducing convictions of the guilty to a dysfunctional level. Paleyites tend to be conservative, in the sense that any changes to current ways of conducting the criminal justice process, proposed for their supposed effect on protecting the innocent, will be presumed so counterproductive in their effect on convicting the guilty that they will be opposed.

Romillists, whom I have named after the early 19th-century reformist Sir Samuel Romilly, have such a horror of convicting the innocent that they are willing to propose many changes to whatever system exists, on the ground that such changes in our way of criminal law enforcement will better protect the innocent. In so doing, it may be that some of the proposals might make the conviction of the truly guilty more difficult, perhaps significantly so. Whatever the actual effect, the Paleyites can be counted on to find the potential effect abhorrent, and to label the proponents "soft-headed sentimentalists" or some similar characterization, while the Romillists in turn will label the Paleyites hard-hearted troglodytes, indifferent to the plight of the convicted innocent, with knee jerk opposition to reform.

What neither side has a good handle on, however, is the magnitude of the problem of factually wrongful conviction and wrongful acquittal. Partly this is due to the inherent difficulty of establishing the ground truth of factual guilt or innocence better than the trials (or plea bargains) that resulted originally in acquittals or convictions. But, at least with regard to convictions, it is also partly due to the fact the legal system is structured to operate as if it were controlled by Paleyites, whatever the personal beliefs of individual participants. This is the result of rather extreme doctrines intended to uphold the integrity and finality of the results of criminal trials. Nevertheless, both post-conviction legal doctrines and those who administer them, prosecutors and judges alike, resist new evidence of innocence to such a degree that it often passes the bounds of rationality. And what but the word "concealment," albeit in the name of protecting the public legitimacy of the system, can explain the efforts undertaken to oppose DNA testing in regard to those already executed, where such DNA testing would conclusively establish guilt or innocence in fact.

Traditionally, a certain stripe of Paleyite has also denied that wrongful convictions happen at all, or, that if they happen, they happen so rarely that worrying about them is like worrying about being struck by a meteorite. The reasons assigned for this assumed near-perfection in regard to false-positive error have generally been the numerous layers of filtration involved in the pre-trial system, and the general fairness of the adversary trial itself, with its formal requirement that the prosecution prove guilt beyond a reasonable doubt.

Such a position is very difficult to take in the era of DNA exonerations. Difficult— but not impossible. As one can see from the epigram at the beginning of this Article, Paleyites such as Justice Scalia and Joshua Marquis still speculate about, and embrace, ludicrously low wrongful conviction rates. However, such speculation has become both obsolete and untenable, since, as I propose to demonstrate, the data and the elementary statistical tools necessary to arrive at a reliable minimum rate of factually wrongful conviction, at least in a certain significant subset of cases, are actually in hand. And from this specific minimum innocence rate other inferences may defensibly be drawn about the problem of factually wrongful conviction. Once Paleyites and Romillists are forced to agree on at least a partial description of the problem of factually wrongful conviction, they can then proceed to develop and set out informed normative responses to the empirical reality.

III. An Empirically Justified Factual Wrongful Conviction Rate: The Case of Capital Rape Murders in the 1980s

In order to derive a minimum factual wrongful conviction rate (a factual innocence rate), we must, of course, have a numerator and a denominator. The denominator would represent a certain reference set of convictions, and the numerator would represent the number of factually wrongful convictions in the reference set. We might look for our numerator in the number of exonerations that have taken place over a certain period of time, whether based on DNA evidence or not. I have chosen, however, to include only DNA exonerations as part of a numerator, in order to avoid the epistemic problems that could arise in regard to any rationally debatable exonerations, since it is easiest to establish DNA exonerations as being close to indisputable cases of factually wrongful conviction.

So let us look for our numerator somewhere in the statistical pool provided by the DNA exonerations, and then define the boundaries of the universe of cases these exonerations represent, in order to find a denominator and establish a minimum rate of factual innocence for that universe of cases. Then we can examine the question of what the DNA cases can tell us in general about rates of wrongful conviction and factual innocence.

To obtain a proper sample of DNA exonerations to work with, one must understand that the cases in which DNA exonerations occur are by definition not a random sample of all cases of criminal conviction. Virtually all such exonerations occur in cases of serious felony, often capital felony, in which a trial resulted in a conviction. The DNA exonerations can usefully be divided into four groups: capital cases, non-capital homicide cases, non-capital rape/sexual assault cases, and others. The most obvious group to examine in searching for a denominator is the capital cases. This group consists of an externally defined set of capital cases of finite and known number in the United States during the period of time since the reestablishment of the death penalty in 1976 from which such exonerations are drawn. These would be specifically the capital sentences imposed from the date of the first such conviction that finally culminated in a DNA exoneration, to the date of the latest trial of the case finally culminating in the capital DNA exoneration, roughly 1977 to 1999. There are fourteen capital-case DNA exonerations so far in cases tried from 1977 to 1999. During that same period of time, 5968 capital sentences were imposed. These figures give an absolute minimum factual error rate for capital sentences imposed during that period of .23%.

Whether the imposition of a death sentence on a factually innocent person two or three times out of every thousand impositions of capital punishment is too high a rate is a heavy question of morality and policy. But of course this percentage does not represent the actual rate of factually wrongful conviction. In fact, it is clearly grossly understated, because we are using the wrong denominator. The choice of the right denominator is what makes it empirically defensible to derive a factual innocence rate from the DNA exonerations. We must therefore carefully define the boundaries of the universe of cases represented by the group of DNA exonerations chosen.

The DNA exonerations can only occur in the subset of capital convictions in which it is reasonable to believe that bodily sources of DNA might have been left in such a way as to provide the basis for including or excluding a defendant as the possible perpetrator. Generally, in capital case exonerations, this has meant what can be called "rape-murders," generally homicides where the victim is raped, then killed. In fact, thirteen of the fourteen DNA exonerations in capital cases involved rape-murders.

Looking at these thirteen cases, two important points emerge about the window that the DNA exonerations open on the problem of wrongful conviction rates in general. First, that window is closing. As DNA technology has become more sensitive, more accurate, and more generally available and understood, the number of cases in which such testing is not done for the original trial shrinks. This is, of course, a great net benefit for the criminal justice system. Those who are guilty in the relatively small percentage of cases where DNA evidence is available will be convicted with much greater confidence, and those who can be exonerated by DNA will be exonerated before or at trial. But it is extremely important to remember that the conditions that cause wrongful conviction in non-DNA cases—the vast majority of cases—remain unaffected by this development. We must use the post-conviction DNA exonerations wisely to throw light on the more general problem. Second, the closing window has statistical implications for our study. Our choice of denominator must be chosen with care, both with respect to the kind of defendants we are examining and with respect to the time period chosen for examination.

The twelve trials of the thirteen capital rape-murder defendants that resulted in their factually wrongful convictions took place between 1979 and 1996. Two of the twelve trials are clearly outliers—the 1979 trial of Dennis Williams took place three years before the next later trial, and the first trial of Ray Krone (1992) occurred three years after the next earlier trial. The Williams case was unusually early for usable DNA evidence to have been preserved and discovered, but this prescience is perhaps accounted for by the fact that the state in that case was still looking to prosecute a co-defendant, which they did not manage to do until 1985 (Verneal Jimerson, also later exonerated by DNA). The Ray Krone case in 1992/1996 is remarkably belated for DNA not to have been utilized originally. At any rate, it seems clear that it is neither required nor justified statistically to retain these two outlier examples in the numerator set. So for purposes of looking at the wrongful conviction rate, we will limit ourselves to the eleven cases that were tried from 1982 to 1989 inclusive. In addition, we will reduce the number by half an exoneration, in order to give some cushion against the criticism that it is not beyond every doubt that every person exonerated by DNA was factually innocent. As noted earlier, there are the Paleyites of the world, such as Joshua Marquis, who will claim that these exonerations are not sufficiently absolute because it is possible to imagine (usually exceedingly unlikely) scenarios in which this or that exoneree might still be guilty. Nevertheless, even the most aggressive of these Paleyites would probably not argue that such exercises in creative imagination mean that none of the DNA exonerees is factually innocent. If we give an exceedingly generous probability of one in twenty to the factual guilt of an apparently exonerated defendant, then a statistical exclusion of one-half an exoneration covers it.

So we start with a numerator of 10.5. What, then, is the denominator? If we choose all death penalties imposed from 1982 to 1989 inclusive, we get a denominator of 2235. That denominator would yield a minimum factual innocence rate of .47%, or nearly five in a thousand (and more than double the figure arrived at when we used all capital DNA exonerations and all death sentences).

But that denominator is still understating the factual innocence rate, because it is still incorrect. The number of all death penalties imposed from 1982 to 1989 inclusive includes all sorts of capital cases that were not rape-murders. The proper denominator is the number of capital rape-murder cases. An analysis of a sample of 406 capital convictions imposed in the period 1982–1989 inclusive indicates that only 21.45% of capital sentences involve a rape-murder. Thus, the proper denominator is 479, and thus the factual innocence rate for capital rape-murder convictions in the period 1982–1989 inclusive is at least 2.2%.

We have not finished yet with our denominator, however. It is still overstated. DNA exonerations can only occur in those rape-murder cases where usable DNA connected to the perpetrator is found to be available when requested for testing. The universe represented by the DNA exonerations, therefore, is defined by that condition. In what percentage of cases involving trials in the reference period is that condition present?

So far as I know, there is only one organization in the country, governmental or non-governmental, with records of sufficient experience to give a defensible answer to this question: the Innocence Project at Cardozo Law School. Established by Barry Scheck and Peter Neufeld in 1992, the Innocence Project has concentrated from the beginning on the exoneration of the convicted innocent through DNA. As the undisputed leader in pursuing that goal, there is little doubt that it has records of more requests for DNA evidence in more cases than any other entity. In the summer of 2006 I contacted the Innocence Project and asked them to use their records to determine in what percentage of cases tried during the reference time period for which requests for the discovery of DNA evidence had been made in which it was subsequently established that, either because it was never collected, because it was discarded or destroyed, or because it was degraded, no usable DNA survived. The Innocence Project itself has dealt with a limited number of capital cases, since those cases usually have other sources of post-conviction representation. However, the Innocence Project has dealt with many non-capital rape-murders, and even more non-murder rapes, and there seems no reason to believe that the percentage of cases in which no usable DNA survived would be significantly different for either of those categories than that in capital rape-murders.

By a lucky coincidence, at the same time that I contacted them, the Innocence Project had just begun a comprehensive file review in order to collect various data across cases, therefore isolating the data on "no usable DNA" in regard to their cases in the reference period was not too burdensome, and they graciously agreed to do it. The results were that 77 of the 212 cases tried during the reference time period for which the Innocence Project made requests for DNA testing did not yield usable DNA, a rate of 36.3%. In that set of 212, there were 15 rape-murders, of which 5 (33.3%) yielded no usable DNA. Although the rape-murder set is smaller, I have elected to use the 33.3% rate in an abundance of caution, since it is lower than the rate associated with total number of cases for which requests were made.

The denominator of 479 for the number of capital rape-murder convictions in the reference period, which we previously derived, must therefore be reduced by 33.3% to account for cases with no usable DNA available for testing, thereby yielding a denominator of 319. Using 10.5 as the numerator, as previously explained, and 319 as the denominator yields a true minimum innocence rate for rape-murder from 1982–1989 inclusive of (pace Joshua Marquis and Justice Scalia) 3.3%.

So there we have it. A conservative minimum factual innocence rate, derived from a real, not insignificant, set of serious criminal convictions, and capital convictions to boot. The question immediately comes to mind: What can this specific rate tell us about wrongful conviction rates in general?

Before addressing this important question, however, we must examine one more issue in regard to our initial reference set: capital rape-murder convictions in the 1980s. We have derived a minimum factual innocence rate. What, if anything, can be said about the maximum factual innocence rate? We have a floor. What can we say about a ceiling?

As it turns out, I think we can say some closely defensible things. We start off being reasonably sure that there are around 319 capital rape-murder cases (more or less) with potentially usable DNA evidence during that period. We also know that many of these cases have had the DNA requested and analyzed. We do not know how many cases exactly, because there is no central database of such information, but capital cases generally attract post-conviction aid from anti-death penalty advocates. Among those 319 cases, to be sure, there are a few that are so clear on factual guilt that DNA analysis might not be requested. For instance, Charles McDowell broke into a house in his own neighborhood and attacked the maid, who was alone in the house at the time. Because of the victim's screams, a neighbor who knew him confronted him as he was leaving the premises covered in blood. He stabbed the neighbor, but police were called by other neighbors. The police followed the blood trail, and within a short period of time, found him hiding in some bushes at the other end of the blood trail. There was semen on the victim's panties, but DNA evidence was not likely to help the defense.[17]

However, most cases are not so clear as the McDowell case with regard to factual guilt independent of DNA. Thus, DNA exclusion is the greatest post-conviction hope, and would generally be worth requesting. It would be quite surprising, perhaps even shocking, if capital post-conviction counsel had failed to request DNA testing in any-

---

17. See People v. McDowell, 763 P.2d 1269, 1271–72 (Cal. 1988).

thing close to half the 319 capital rape-murder cases in the reference set. Additionally, even in these cases, it is likely that the requests, if not universally made, would be skewed toward being made in the otherwise more factually questionable cases. So I believe we can conclude without much doubt that the ceiling is not double the floor (which would give a maximum ceiling figure for actual innocence of 6.4%), but is in fact substantially less. I believe it is fair to put a reasonable maximum under these circumstances at around 5%.

Thus, we have an empirical minimum of 3.3% and a fairly generous likely maximum of 5% for factually wrongful convictions in capital rape-murders in the 1980s.

IV. Implications of a 3–5% Factual Wrongful Conviction Rate for Both Paleyites and Romillists

These figures are guaranteed not to make many people happy. Whatever the depth (or shallowness) of one's emotional or moral response to a 3–5% factual innocence error rate in a significant set of real-world capital cases, it is hard to characterize it as de minimis, or to fairly say that it represents a "remote" possibility of conviction of the innocent. Paleyites often depend on the tenability of such assertions either to make themselves feel better, or to convince the general mass of people that there is no systemic problem of wrongful conviction to be considered, or both. When real data carefully derived destroy the tenability of such claims, one can depend on the Joshua Marquises and the Justice Scalias not to be happy with that result.

In addition, Paleyites will find little to comfort them regarding claims that such exonerations are demonstrations of "the system working," or that reversals through the ordinary appellate process take care of the problem of wrongful conviction. In general, over two-thirds of all capital convictions are reversed, and more than half of defendants who initially receive capital sentences are ultimately removed from death row (although fewer than four in one thousand are acquitted on re-trial). However, of the eleven rape-murder exonerations in our numerator set, while five were the subject of reversals prior to the DNA evidence being developed, only one (or perhaps two, depending on how you count Verneal Jimerson) got off of death row as a result. Kirk Bloodsworth (who even Joshua Marquis concedes was factually innocent) was retried and again convicted, but sentenced "only" to life without possibility of parole. Verneal Jimerson was awaiting retrial when the DNA results came in. The other nine would all have been executed if DNA testing had not been invented. Thus, the results of procedural reversals do not appear to track actual innocence very well.

On the other hand, some Romillists may also find themselves unhappy. We can usefully divide modern Romillists between anti-death penalty advocates and Innocence Network activists (I count myself at least an honorary member of the latter). The anti-death penalty people whose opposition is based upon a general pro-life moral position ("the state should not meet one murder with another," etc.) are often only indirectly or supplementarily concerned with innocence. Some believe that emphasis on execution of the innocent might get in the way of global abolition of the death penalty for the cases of the obviously (factually) guilty. Many, however, will use innocence data as a tool, and to that end, they would like the innocence rate to be as high as possible, high enough perhaps for a 10% error rate to be a credible claim (thus apparently meeting the Blackstone ratio threshold, a rhetorically attractive point to reach for purposes of persuasion). Real data moving that claim from more tenable to less tenable are unlikely to be welcomed.

On the other hand, Innocence Network people (those whose main horror is the conviction of the factually innocent in any context, capital or non-capital) are likely to be more conflicted. Some may regard the wrongful conviction figure as about what they suspected. Some may view empirical indications that the system works more accurately than their worst fears as good news, though they may have a queasy feeling that a 3–5% rate of conviction of the factually innocent is not high enough or dramatic enough to engage the conscience of the average citizen, or of the average politician, or the average judge. I will try to address these concerns later. But for now, I can only say to all sides, the facts seem to be the facts.

V. The Factual Error Rate for Capital Rape-Murders in the 1980s: Generalizing to Other Crimes and Other Times

I have just said that the facts seem to be the facts. Certainly for the actual reference set—that is, capital rape-murder convictions in the 1980s—the minimum figure has a strong claim to factual status, and the somewhat softer reasons for the upper limit seem pretty reasonable also. But can we generalize this rate (or rate range) to other sets of criminal convictions?

This question, of course, is a variation on the question raised earlier in the text, and deferred: What can this rate tell us about factual wrongful conviction rates in general? But one should not confuse the question of "wrongful conviction rates in general" with the question of a "general wrongful conviction rate." The vastly understated Scalia/Marquis rate was a claimed "general wrongful conviction rate," that is, an average wrongful conviction rate for all felonies.

It seems likely to be quite common for people who begin pondering the question of wrongful conviction to ask themselves questions like, "What do you suppose the number of factually wrongful convictions per thousand convictions is generally?" or similar questions. There are two reasons why we should resist the temptation to expend much effort in pondering such a general average factual wrongful conviction rate: first, we are unlikely to ever be able to derive it very specifically, and, second, it would not tell us anything very important if we knew it. Both facts are largely the product of a common reality, which is also intimately involved in the issue of what the capital rape-murder data from the 1980s can tell us about other crimes and other times: the universe of criminal convictions is almost certainly heavily substructured in regard to factual innocence rates.

In order to make clear what substructuring means and why it is important, we must spend a little time going back to basics. Human knowledge is easiest to gain in regard to universes of objects that are all the same relative to the inquiry of interest. When one deals with such fungible entities and conditions, then what is known locally will also be true globally, and what is true globally will also be true locally. This eliminates the hard issues of sampling bias, of statistical inference, of "external validity" (reasoning from data about parts of a universe to conclusions about other parts of the universe or the universe as a whole), and of deduction (reasoning from general data or propositions about the universe to conclusions about subsets or individuals within the universe). These conditions are most closely approached in classical physics and chemistry. They are clearly not commonly applicable to most biological or social phenomena, like the distribution of eye color, or, almost certainly, the distribution of factual innocence rates among different types of criminal convictions.

Let us stay with the case of the distribution of eye color in humans. If you knew that brown was the most common eye color in humans, and you were dropped from Mars into a randomly selected place on the planet and asked to guess the eye color of the first human you would encounter, you would rationally guess brown. However, if you happened to be dropped in Copenhagen, brown would perhaps not be the best statistical bet (if you only knew). In your position, however, you have neither more particularized or localized information, nor any affirmative reason to believe the general statistic does not hold true everywhere. But let us assume that before being dropped onto Earth, you are told that the distribution of eye color is not even, but, for want of a better technical term, "lumpy"; that is, that there are a significant number of subsets of places where the distribution is substantially higher or substantially lower than the distribution for the Earth's population as a whole. In making your bet, you would still bet "brown," but you would now have affirmative reason to wish you had more particularized information about the structure of the subset distribution (the "substructuring" of the general universe). In fact, unless there is good reason to rule out substructuring, more particularized information is always preferable to more general information, even if both reflect the same probability number.

Now suppose before you are dropped, you are told that there is not only significant substructuring in the distribution of eye color, but that it is so distributed that few if any of the subsets have distributions near the average for the whole universe. Now when you bet, you may still bet "brown" as the best bet on what is known, but you will pretty well know that the average figure (which is the only one you know) is unlikely to represent what is, in some sense, your "real" chance of being right. This situation seems very likely in regard to rates of wrongful conviction for various kinds of crimes in various contexts. So just as one cannot jump from a 3–5% factual wrongful conviction rate in capital rape-murders in the 1980s to a general factual wrongful conviction rate for crimes (the average figure may be more or less, and getting data to derive such an average figure reliably would be daunting), it is also true that one could not reliably reason from a known low average rate (if one were available) to the conclusion that the rate was similarly low for every kind of case. There still might be, and probably would be, contexts and kinds of crime in which the rate of factual innocence was higher, perhaps shockingly so, and it would seem incumbent upon us to develop more particularized information to discover those islands of trouble, rather than salve our consciences with the average number, even if we had one.

So we will eschew speaking in terms of any global rate of wrongful conviction. But that does not prevent us from making some reasonably powerful claims regarding generalization of the capital rape-murder factual innocence rate established above to other crimes, and other times.

First, in regard to other capital murder prosecutions resulting in the imposition of the death penalty, there seems to be no strong reason to believe that the rate was (or is) significantly lower. Most, if not all, of the same forces would seem to be at work (death-qualified juries, horrendous facts, differences in resources between prosecution and defense). Richard A. Rosen has recently written that DNA exonerations should be viewed as providing "a random audit" of convictions because they vary from other convictions only by the fortuitous circumstance of the presence of testable DNA. While this argument becomes weaker as the conviction sets become more differentiated, it is fairly robust with regard to capital convictions generally, or at least those in which perpetrator identity is the main contestable issue.

Second, regarding non-homicide, pre-DNA rape cases (or at least the stranger-on-stranger cases that are most troubling with respect to wrongful identification analogous to rape-murder cases), it is true that in such cases there is often victim testimony of identification, but given the vagaries of eyewitness identification, it is not clear which way this cuts. Heavy jury reliance on such identifications might actually raise the factual wrongful conviction rate, depending on what the rate of mistaken identifications in such circumstances is. There are no good data on this issue directly, but there is reason to suspect that the rate could be high, indeed, higher than the three or four percent innocence rate in the reference set under some conditions. Fortunately, DNA technology has greatly reduced the problem in regard to stranger rapes (but not in regard to murders and other crimes heavily dependent on eyewitness identification).

This brings us to those non-capitally sentenced murders wherein the main issue is perpetrator identity. If the factual wrongful conviction rate in capital non-rape murders seems likely to be about the same as in capital rape-murders, can we generalize this rate to analogous non-capital murders?

* * *

We can hope, at least, that capitally sentenced cases would be the cases in which juries would regard themselves as especially obligated to be sure of guilt, given the jury's role in the imposition of the death sentence itself. If this is the case, it seems reasonable to suspect that the factual innocence rate in other "analogous" murder cases might be at least as high, if not higher, than in capitally sentenced cases. On the other hand, capital juries are "death-qualified," which may give them a lower decision threshold on the issue of guilt.

In addition, many more of the non-capital murder convictions are the result of pleas. Pleas would, perhaps, be expected to represent fewer unsafe convictions than verdicts—except that many non-capital murder convictions are obtained through guilty pleas negotiated in the shadow of a potential death sentence, a reality which, to some degree, could be expected to undermine the reliability of these pleas. We also know that some of these pleas took place in cases later resulting in exoneration by DNA. All in all, there seems to be no good reason for believing that the factual innocence rate for non-capitally sentenced murder convictions properly "analogous" to capital murder, when the central issue is the identity of the defendant as the perpetrator, are substantially lower than the capital rape-murder innocence rate in the 1980s established earlier in this article. It would seem incumbent on those who claim otherwise to proffer substantial particular reasons for the claimed differences, rather than simply invoking general problems of extension and external validity.

What is true for capital cases in general and for non-capital "analogous" murders, however, may not necessarily be very persuasively true for other kinds of crime. I suspect that the wrongful conviction rate for many kinds of crimes of interpersonal violence (robbery, for example) might be at least as high, while the rate for white collar crimes may be much lower. But without more study, we cannot really know for sure.

VI. Why Should We Care About Factually Wrongful Convictions, and What (If Anything) Are We Morally Obliged to Do About Them?

* * *

So what should be our response to factually wrongful convictions? All are bad, some are worse, but what should we do about them? An absolutist might say that we should never convict anyone without absolute proof of guilt. On reflection, however, such an absolutist would have to admit that this position would require convicting no one, since we live in a world of probabilities and imperfect knowledge. Human systems cannot eliminate all risk of error and still function, though it is important to note that this does not mean that we cannot get significantly better and still be functional. It depends on the definition of "functional," and the costs that attach to this conception of functionality.

Here the Blackstone ratio, or some version of it, comes into play. You will recall that the Blackstone ratio is the name for Blackstone's version of the moral assertion "it is better that ___ guilty men go free than that one innocent person be convicted." The number Blackstone chose was ten, though Alexander Volokh has rather amusingly shown that various thinkers over the centuries have put the number at various places between one and a thousand. In general, it is fair to say that the ratio image is meant as a general declaration that, for any given crime, the relative disvalue of a wrongful acquittal is less, perhaps significantly less, than the disvalue of a wrongful conviction. This ratio was not conceived of by statisticians, and it was never meant, nor should it be used, in my opinion, to announce the acceptability of a system of criminal justice so long as no more than ten percent of those convicted are innocent. In fact, it would seem that if we knew that ten percent of the prison population were factually innocent, we should believe that our efforts at accurate apprehension and conviction, with their various layers of investigatory and trial filtering, had suffered a significant failure. Even the 3–5% rate for capital rape-murder cases in the 1980s, generalized to the entire prison population, would be shockingly high in the eyes of many. After all, there is nothing inherent in a 10% failure rate, or a 1% failure rate, that makes a system prima facie successful. If one in every hundred commercial airplane flights (never mind one in ten) crashed before arrival at its destination, no one would regard this statistic as an indicator of the success of commercial aviation (nor would most people elect to fly).

* * *

Perhaps in some contexts, a 3.3% factual wrongful conviction rate wouldn't be so horrible—if there were nothing that could be done about it.

And here is where I believe the moral rubber meets the road for every citizen, and especially every police officer, prosecutor, judge, or legislator. Even if we might not be horrified at a 3.3% factual wrongful conviction rate in the abstract, I believe we would all admit that if we could identify the wrongfully convicted cost-free, we would be morally obliged to release them. And if there were reforms that could be made to the system that would better filter out the innocent initially, with no associated cost, we would be obliged to make those reforms. Beyond this, I take it we would also be morally obliged to take such actions if the costs were not prohibitive. How are we to approach the question of what constitutes a prohibitive cost? I will set aside issues of monetary cost, not because they might not be relevant under some circumstances, but because monetary costs and other social costs, primarily reduced efficiency in punishing the guilty, are incommensurate, and thus not easily discussed together. Instead, I will concentrate on actions that do not empty the prisons, but instead exonerate one factually innocent person at the cost of the release of, or failure to convict, some number of the guilty.

Here the perceptive reader will hear an echo of the Blackstone ratio, but not a ratio to be used as an image to attempt to norm judges and jurors to a high decision threshold for individual cases. Rather, it is to be used as an approach to taking reformatory actions that will improve the performance of a system-in-being at the margins.

* * *

Hence I offer what I will call the Reform Ratio:

Any wrongful conviction that can be corrected or avoided without allowing more than one or two perpetrators of similar crimes to escape ought to be corrected or avoided; in addition, system alterations (reforms, if you will) that there is good reason to believe will accomplish this ought to be embraced.

You will note that in setting out the first principle, I have been very conservative in my "Reform Ratio." For reforms working a marginal saving in wrongful convictions, I only propose utilizing them when an innocent saved by the reform is counterbalanced by no more than one or two wrongful acquittals or reversals. However, in my second principle, I have placed a rather low standard of proof concerning the effects of reform onto the proponents, and a correspondingly high standard of proof for those opposing such reform. Reforms that are undertaken that have counterproductive effects can be undone when these effects become apparent in the implementation. But reforms that are never undertaken based on remotely likely and conjectural effects invoked by opponents who simply are satisfied with the current way of doing things (because it generates conviction rates they like, at costs they are currently perfectly happy with, since the costs don't fall on them) are simply never undertaken.

There are many reforms currently proposed that arguably fit the above criteria. Some of these proposals, indeed, would seem to be what one might refer to as cost-free proposals, presenting no risk of losing any defensible convictions of the guilty. The best examples, to my mind, are the calls for blind testing protocols in forensic science practice, and for similar masking procedures in the administration of line-ups and photo-spreads. There is no rational argument that can establish a way in which the criminal justice system loses any relevant, reliable, or otherwise defensible information concerning guilt by the adoption of such changes. Yet the calls for the former reforms have fallen on deaf ears, and for the latter reforms have been met by adoption in but a small number of jurisdictions, and stiff resistance in the majority (even though the experiences in adopting jurisdictions confirm the workability of such blind identification procedures).

I do not intend to attempt a complete listing of reforms which would appear to meet the obligations of the "reform ratio," though there is, in my opinion, a remarkable catalogue of them. Only the inertia or hostility of the main players in our criminal justice system has prevented such proposals from being seriously considered and widely implemented. Perhaps faced with hard numbers, and a reground moral lens, they can be persuaded to approach such reforms more positively.

Larry Laudan, *The Elementary Epistemic Arithmetic of Criminal Justice*
5 Episteme 282–94 (2008)

In the epic battle between those who hold that we should convict more of the bad guys and those who think we should convict fewer of the good ones, each side exhibits the classic symptom of the ideologue: a mighty indifference to the empirical data. The one camp firmly believes that false convictions are as rare as hen's teeth, which they are not, and that convictions massively deter crime, which may or may not be true. The other camp believes that the costs of false acquittals are trivial compared to the costs of false convictions, thereby justifying its opposition to putting any meaningful controls on the frequency of false acquittals. The trouble here is that the social and human costs of false acquittals are not trivial in comparison with the costs of false convictions. This second camp likewise denies that there is any important causal relation between the rate of conviction and the rate of violent crime, even when this particular inverse relation is one of the few robust conclusions to emerge from criminology. In short, both camps are in data denial. We have ample evidence that false convictions are commonplace, an injustice that should neither be dismissed nor downplayed. But we also have impressive evidence that false acquittals have a dramatic, deleterious effect on the crime rate, chiefly by failing to incapacitate serial offenders.

It goes without saying that data denial is a worrisome thing. But my plea today is not so much that we need to take the data more seriously than we have—true as that is—but, rather, that we need to be a lot more savvy and careful than we have been about the conceptual tools we use for embedding those data in our discussions about crime, punishment, and the rules of trial. To that end ... I want to present some home truths about how the justice system can, and does, work. My preferred idiom will be garden-variety arithmetic and, where necessary, plain English; my aim will be to show that we have fastened on the wrong measures and the wrong quantitative ideals for thinking about the problems of error in the law.

* * *

If, as honest fallibilists must, we once accept that mistakes—including this particularly egregious form of mistake—are inevitable in human affairs, then the issue becomes not a matter of wholly eliminating such errors from the repertoire of criminal justice but rather one of framing a coherent answer to the question: what is an *acceptable* level of false convictions? One-in-ten? One in a hundred? Should we share the obvious shock of our colleague Professor Sam Gross and his fellow researchers at discovering, at the end of a lengthy study of exonerations over a decade and a half, that: "Any plausible guess at the total number of miscarriages of justice in America in the last fifteen years must be in the thousands, perhaps tens of thousands."[18] Should we be appalled to discover that, out of more than fifteen million criminal convictions in this period, perhaps 10,000 or more of them were false convictions?

Even if Prof. Gross's worst fears are realized, the justice system makes a mistake less than once in every thousand convictions. Is there *any* other form of human deliberation in which errors are so rare? I know no epistemologist or experimental psychologist or statistician who would not regard this figure, if true, as anything less than an astonishingly successful cognitive achievement. Even if there were 100,000 false convictions in the fifteen years covered by Gross's study—instead of the 340 that he actually found—this would still represent an error rate of less than one percent. Would a type-I error rate as "high" as that really be unacceptable? Almost no one wants to give that question a straight answer. Partly, the reluctance stems ... from a recognition that any answer greater than zero would appear to (and, indeed, would) acquiesce in and condone committing the occasional grave injustice. But mostly, it derives not so much from such squeamishness as from an unresolved perplexity about how we might go about rationally deciding what an acceptable number would be. Muddling on, or blithely suggesting that we must do the best we can to keep false convictions to a minimum, is neither very informative nor very ameliorative, since literally "doing the best we can to protect the innocent" ... exacts a higher price in lost convictions of the guilty than any reasonable person should be prepared to pay.

In this paper, I will eventually propose a politically incorrect answer to this morally delicate question. But our route from here to there must take us along a pair of detours that have, in my view, profoundly muddied the waters and thus muddled our thinking about the problem of false convictions. I begin by reminding us all that

---

18. Gross, 2005, 551.

legal scholars have generally fastened on one of two ratios for exploring this matter. They have either settled on the Blackstone ratio (given by N_{FA}/N_{FC}),[19] which they want to keep high, or they have focused on the false conviction rate (given by N_{FC}/N_C),[20] which they want to keep low. In the first section of my remarks, I will try to explain why these foci are misleading and have stymied our arriving at any convincing answer to the question: How many false convictions are acceptable? In the second, more constructive and controversial, part of the paper, I will suggest what the answer to that question ought to be.

Blackstone and Other Misleading Ratios

a) Blackstone and the Mystic Order-of-Magnitude Cult

It has become an almost unquestioned article of faith in Anglo-Saxon legal circles that justice fails to be served if there are fewer than ten false acquittals for every false conviction at trial. Serious scholars have attempted, notably without success, to devise ways of defining the standard of proof so that it will guarantee that the error ratio in real trials will reproduce this ratio. Never mind that ... one can show that *no* standard of proof can be guaranteed to produce *any* particular ratio of errors, since the actual error ratio in any random run of trials will inevitably reflect the uncontrollable vagaries of genuine guilt and innocence among those defendants brought to trial.

What I want to challenge here is the notion that we should adopt *as a regulative ideal* the thesis that an important indicator that a justice system is indeed just is whether it is acquitting around ten guilty defendants at trial for every innocent one convicted.

What work does a BR=10 do for us? At a minimum, it guarantees that, in a representative run of 100 criminal trials, there would be no more than 9 false convictions. That is all well and good; still, Blackstone does sanction up to 9 false convictions and since 9 false convictions in every 100 trials would generally be regarded as wholly unacceptable, especially among those left nauseous by the thought of even one of them, we perhaps need to rethink what we are doing. Aside from noting that adherence to BR=10 does not maintain the frequency of false convictions within acceptable limits, there are even more unseemly consequences. In the scenario just described, for instance, at least 90 false acquittals would be required by the BR, leaving at best the possibility that one verdict out of 100 was correct. So, the BR permits more false convictions than are acceptable and—thanks to that promiscuity—countenances obscenely high levels of general error. At least in this scenario, we are doing nothing whatever to control errors in general and precious little to control erroneous convictions in particular. Virtually every innocent defendant is convicted and virtually every guilty defendant is acquitted. Still, the BR=10 rule has been scrupulously observed.

---

19. *Ed. Note*: That is, the number of False Acquittals divided by the number of False Convictions.
20. *Ed. Note*: The number of False Convictions divided by the number of Convictions.

Take a less extreme scenario. Suppose that there are 50 convictions in a sequence of 100 trials, 5 of which are false. Blackstone would clearly require fifty false acquittals. So, *every* acquittal would have to be false, meaning fifty guilty felons would go free and 45 guilty felons were convicted. The risk that an innocent defendant runs of being convicted under this scenario is 100%, twice the risk that a felon runs of being convicted. In its way, this scenario is nearly as perverse as the previous one. Yet this, too, is Blackstone-compliant.

If we contemplate more reasonable scenarios, the problem is not that the BR=10 intuition leads to unacceptable results, but that it produces no results at all. Suppose that, as a general rule, 75% of defendants on trial are convicted and that some 5% of those convictions are false. (These figures are probably a good first approximation to the state of affairs in US courts today.) In this case, roughly 4 innocent defendants will be convicted in every 100 trials. Blackstone obviously requires this to be balanced against roughly 40 false acquittals. But there are only 25 acquittals to be had, even if we implausibly suppose that every acquitted defendant is guilty. In short, the BR=10 rule cannot in principle be satisfied in American courts, given highly plausible assumptions about how American trials work.

* * *

Well then, is this a judgment we are prepared to endorse? Are we, on the strength of a number (ten) produced by a conjurer's trick—a number which has never been justified by an even cursory examination of the respective costs of false convictions and false acquittals—prepared to label as unjust every legal system that fails to yield ten false acquittals for every false conviction? The question, of course, is rhetorical. But the answer has to include an acknowledgement that the Blackstone ratio is not *the* (nor even *a*) key part of what any legal system should aspire to satisfy. It permits a prodigious harvest of both sorts of error; it requires the deliberate erroneous acquittal of vast numbers of guilty defendants (given plausible assumptions about the de facto frequency of false convictions): and it never had any but the shallowest justification. The wonder is that this piece of drivel has driven legal theorizing for so long. The most charitable view of it was that its early proponents supposed that false convictions were indeed rare and that the false acquittals necessary to counterbalance them could be had without acquitting almost every guilty defendant.

b) The False Conviction Rate

When legal scholars are not holding forth on how thoroughly the awfulness of a false conviction swamps the egregiousness of a false acquittal (and that point is the central message of virtually every discussion of the Blackstone ratio since the eighteenth century), they are voicing alarm at the size of another ratio, namely, the rate of false convictions. Understood as the proportion of convictions at trial that involve innocent defendants, the false conviction rate—especially in capital cases—has attracted much attention in the last three-quarters of a century. It typically involves scholars using ex- oneration studies or judge-jury agreement studies to estimate how many of those con- victed of felonies have been materially innocent. While different studies have arrived at different estimates, it is reasonable to infer that an upper-bound on the rate of false convictions in cases that go to trial is about five percent, although the actual value is probably modestly less than this. Upon acknowledging this point, there is generally much ritual wringing-of-hands, accompanied by a firm resolve to devise strategies to bring this ratio down to acceptable levels (supposing that one knew what those were).

I do not for a minute wish to underestimate or to understate the quantitative magnitude of the rate of false convictions. I'm disposed to concede that they occur far more often than many, perhaps most, commentators believe and still more often than most consider acceptable. In particular, I believe that 5% is probably a good (if mildly on the high side) stab at the current value of this ratio in American criminal trials. But I am reluctant, at least for the moment, to join the army of hand-wringers. My reluctance stems, not from a callous indifference to false convictions, but from a hunch that fixating on the *rate* of false convictions obscures what should be our genuine concern. More concretely, I intend now to argue that the focus on the rate of false convictions as either an intellectual or a moral problem has been blown out of all proportion to its real significance, which *may* be vanishingly small. While every one of those false convictions represents a grievous injustice, a preoccupation with the *rate* of false convictions is, I submit, a decidedly unilluminating way to pose the question.

To explain why, I will first remind you that we could have a very low rate of false convictions and yet many false convictions, just as we could have a very high *rate* of false convictions with few false convictions. This is because there are three factors that principally determine how many false convictions occur in any system of criminal justice: the number of trials, the proportion of those trials that result in convictions, and the proportion of those convictions that are false (this latter is what I have been calling the false conviction rate). There is a very simple relation that obtains between these four values:

$$N_{FC} = N_{trials} \times (N_{convictions}/N_{trials}) \times (N_{FC}/N_{convictions})$$

This equation makes clear that the total number of false convictions in any system (during, say, one year) is the product of how many trials there are, the conviction rate per trial and the false conviction rate that obtained in those trials. So, if we want to keep the frequency—as opposed to the rate—of false convictions very low, there are at least these three distinct options for doing so: staging fewer trials, lowering the conviction rate or lowering the false conviction rate. This formula also shows that a system with a high false conviction rate can be made to produce as few false convictions as we like, provided we jigger with the conviction rate and/or the number of trials suitably. The general point here is that a 'high' false conviction rate by itself tells us nothing about how many innocent people are being skewered by the system. Neither does a high conviction rate.

If we wish to know how much damage the system is doing (and that is surely an essential preliminary to figuring out whether the current level of damage is acceptable), we have to focus on the question: *How many innocents in the general population are being falsely convicted?* The pertinent question is not: What proportion of the convicted are innocent? But rather: What proportion of the innocent (in the general population) are convicted? Provided the latter ratio is "acceptably low" (and we will shortly figure out how to define that), we can and should be benignly indifferent to the rate of false convictions at trial. Return briefly to the worry voiced by Professor Gross: what if upwards of ten thousand Americans have been falsely convicted in the last fifteen years? That comes to 667 false convictions per year, meaning that the annual risk an average American runs of being falsely convicted of some crime or other is less than 0.0003%. This risk is the same as the odds of a man my age dying within the next 90 minutes or the odds that you will choke to death this year on something you have eaten. We don't fret very much about those dangers. Why, then, the abiding preoccupation with false convictions?

c) Shielding the Innocent

An analogous argument applies to a third ratio that one might be tempted to explore: the proportion of those innocents committed for trial who are acquitted ($N_{\text{innocents acquitted}}/N_{\text{innocents tried}}$). This seems a promising relation. After all, a natural way of voicing one's concern about protecting the innocent is to say that we want to insure that most innocent persons who go to trial are acquitted. Therefore, one might think that we want this ratio—basically the ratio of true acquittals to innocents at risk by trial—to be as large as we can make it. But this suffers from precisely the same defects as the rate of false convictions. If prosecutors take many innocent defendants to trial, and even if the vast majority of them are acquitted, it may still be true that many innocents are being falsely convicted. Similarly, if we dramatically increase the number of trials, even a regime with a very high ratio of true acquittals to innocent defendants can lead to as many false convictions as the current system or more. The general point can be put this way:

$$N_{FC} = N_{\text{trials}} \times (N_{\text{innocents tried}}/N_{\text{trials}}) \times (N_{FC}/N_{\text{innocents tried}})$$

This equality shows that the proportion of innocents convicted among those on trial could be very high even while the overall number of false convictions would still be very low, provided that either the proportion of innocents tried was low and/or the number of trials was low. Likewise, we could get large numbers of innocents convicted even if the ratio of innocents acquitted to innocents tried was quite low, provided that there were a vast number of trials. So this ratio of innocents acquitted to innocents convicted, like the false conviction rate, fails to get us to the nub of the issue, which is how to keep a cap on the number of innocents (in the general population) who are falsely convicted.

The point, then, is that we should not be aiming to maximize or otherwise to settle in advance the value of the ratio of false acquittals to false convictions. Nor should we make it our primary target to minimize the rate of false convictions or to maximize the proportion of innocent defendants who win acquittals. What we *should* be aiming to do is to keep the probability that a random innocent citizen will be convicted within acceptable limits. This doesn't yet tell us what those limits are but it does identify the ratio that must concern us. It gives us, in short, the right numerator and denominator, without yet telling us what the value of their ratio should be.

The Real Ratios at Stake

So, then, how might we go about the task of deciding when too many innocent people are being convicted? Put in this bald fashion, the problem eludes solution, for whatever number we pick looks about as arbitrary as the ten in Blackstone's ratio. What we need is a reasonable benchmark against which we can argue for fixing this value at one point rather than another.

There is one ready to hand, if we are willing to use it. To see what it is, we simply have to put together information that we already know or can easily enough assemble.

For starters, we know (as we have seen) that the number of innocents convicted depends upon the number of trials, the number of convictions, and the rate of false convictions.

We thus know that reducing either the number of convictions or the rate of false conviction would reduce the numbers of false convictions below current rates. So, we aren't in the dark about how to reduce false convictions, if that is what we were bent on doing: tinker with the rules of trial so as to reduce either the proportion of persons convicted and/or the rate of false convictions. Or, simpler still, cut the frequency of trials by half. But such maneuvers fail to address our key question: what would an *acceptable* level of false convictions be? This tactic assumes that we have already settled that too many innocent persons are being falsely convicted and proceeds to drive that number downwards. But, one has to ask, how do we know that we should be aiming to *reduce* this number instead of increasing it? Suppose that the number of those falsely convicted is well below what a rational person would regard as acceptable? And, even if it is now too high, how low must it go before our consciences are clear?

Throw in a third thing that we know, and the outlines of the solution to our enigma begin to appear. We know that most of the steps that we might take to reduce either the false conviction rate or the conviction rate are likely to have a predictable, deleterious effect: to wit, they will increase, perhaps dramatically, the number of false acquittals. Each of those is an injustice in its own right but the more salient point is that the average truly guilty felon who is falsely acquitted will return to the streets, and commit a certain number, n, of felonies each year. Those n crimes per year would have been prevented had the felon gotten his just deserts. The evidence against him, in the trial in which he was acquitted, was powerful enough to persuade the police to arrest him, a grand jury or prosecutor to indict him, and a judge to agree that there was a powerful prima facie case against him. Indeed, if the case actually went to a jury, the judge in question had likewise ascertained that one could believe beyond a reasonable doubt that the prosecutor's case was solid. Still, he was acquitted and falsely so. Had the rules of trial, including the standard of proof, been less acquittal-prone than they are, it is likely that he would have been convicted, incarcerated, and thus incapacitated from committing crimes for the duration of his time in prison.

So, if we want to know what is an acceptable upper bound on the number of false convictions that a compassionate society would accept, we have to balance the costs of a false conviction against the costs of a false acquittal. There is no free lunch, and *almost* everything that we might do to reduce the level of false convictions will raise, perhaps dramatically, the rate of false acquittals and thereby the frequency of serious crime.

Let's begin with some of the data we already know. The recent spate of exoneration studies puts us in a position to say that the lifetime risk of being falsely convicted of a serious crime is less than one-tenth of one percent. By contrast, data from the BJS suggest that the lifetime risk of being a victim of a serious crime is about 83%. In short, the average American is at least 90,000% more likely to be seriously victimized than falsely convicted of a serious crime. (I should add that, because I have interpreted the figures very unfavorably with respect to my own hypothesis, the more likely ratio of these risks is about 8,000:1, in which case one is 800,000% more likely to be a crime victim than the victim of a false conviction.) This is an impressive contrast in magnitude between two dreadful risks. But it is not yet the most salient ratio.

Much more germane to our discussion would be the ratio of being the victim of a serious crime committed by someone who was falsely acquitted and the risk of being falsely convicted. This is the salient proportion for it is the one that should be driving decisions about how defendant-friendly the rules of trial should be. But how can we figure that out, since we don't know how often the legal system falsely acquits defendants? We likewise need to know how often such acquitted but guilty defendants are likely to commit grave crimes.

Let's tackle the second question first. Statistics from both the US and the UK peg that number somewhere between 12 and 15 per year per felon. For purposes of our discussion, and so as not to skew the figures in favor of my analysis, and as a kind of sop to Lord Blackstone's memory, let us adopt conservatively a value for n of ten. Of those 10 felonies per year, something like 1.3 will — on average — be serious, violent crimes. We likewise know that the average sentenced felon will spend about six years in prison. So, for any given false acquittal for a serious crime, we can anticipate eight crimes that would have been prevented had the legal system not decided to let the guilty felon out of its clutches, either by explicit acquittal or by a dropping or dismissal of charges against him. Of those eight serious crimes, 0.2 will be a homicide, 0.4 will be rapes and 7.4 will be armed robbery or aggravated assault. [I here wholly ignore the effects of deterrence, if any. Adding those in would make the case for reducing false acquittals stronger but empirically more precarious.] So, we have a rough and ready but plausible measure of the gravity of a false acquittal.

But we still don't know how often false acquittals occur. We could try to guestimate that figure but for the purposes of my analysis here, we don't actually need it. This is because we can pose the problem in the following way: The standard of proof and the rules of trial should be set at that point where the ratio of *procedurally* preventable crimes to *procedurally* preventable false convictions approaches a value of one or, to be more precise, where the product of the ratio of the number of preventable crimes times the social cost of those crimes approaches to the product of the value of preventable false convictions times their social cost. That is rather a mouthful so let me express it a bit more elegantly as:

$$\text{NFC} \times \text{Cost}_{FC} \approx \text{N}_{FA} \times (\text{N}_{\text{crimes unprevented}}/\text{N}_{FA}) \times \text{Cost}_{\text{crime unprevented}}$$

which reduces to

$$\text{N}_{FC} \times \text{Cost}_{FC} \approx \text{N}_{\text{crimes unprevented}} \times \text{Cost}_{\text{crime unprevented}}$$

Supposing, just for the sake of illustration, that the costs of a false conviction for a violent crime and the costs of an unprevented but preventable violent crime are nearly the same, we could say that we should be looking for a justice system (and more specifically a standard of proof) capable of producing this ratio of outcomes:

$$\text{N}_{FC}/\text{N}_{\text{crimes unprevented}} \approx 1$$

In other words, so long as the typical felon who is falsely convicted is likely to commit at least one serious crime during the time when he would otherwise have been incarcerated (and the actual number is vastly greater than one), it is simply false to say that securing one fewer erroneous conviction in every hundred is desirable, even if it brings one additional false acquittal in its wake. And, returning full circle to my opening remarks, the Blackstonian intuition that it would be worthwhile reducing the false conviction rate by one — even if that brought *ten* false acquittals in its wake — makes for a completely muddled political morality.

* * *

I submit that this is the ratio that should be driving our inquiries, for this ratio is unique in telling us whether the expected utilities embodied in the social contract are being respected by the present rules of trial. Moreover ... we are already in a position to assess and to reject the pleas of those numerous distributionist voices who are calling for an overhaul in existing rules of trial so as to reduce still further the risk of false conviction by resorting to remedies that will increase still further the risk of being victimized by someone who was falsely acquitted.

To conclude: Almost 40 years ago, Lawrence Tribe wrote a famous essay [in which] he inveighed against taking quantification too seriously in the law.[21] I have tried to suggest that quantification has important, even indispensable, uses in assessing the workings of any legal system. But quantification is only as good as the perspicacity we bring to the decision about which parameters to focus on and is only as robust as the clarity with which we work out how those parameters play off against one another. As Yogi Berra (had he known anything about the law) might have put it: Legal epistemology is ninety per cent quantitative. The other half is qualitative.

---

21. Laurence H. Tribe, *Trial by Mathematics: Precision and Ritual in the Legal Process*, 84 HARV. L. REV. 1329 (1971).

Chapter Five

Eyewitness Misidentifications

Eyewitness misidentification is the greatest contributing factor to wrongful convictions proven by DNA testing, playing a role in more than 70% of convictions overturned through DNA testing nationwide.

Innocence Project Website—
Causes of Wrongful Convictions

A. Case Study

Mike Celizic, *She Sent Him to Jail for Rape; Now They're Friends*

Today Contributor, March 10, 2009

In 1984, Jennifer Thompson was 22 and a student at Elon College in North Carolina when a man broke into her house during the night and raped her. As he assaulted her, she memorized his face, his voice, everything she could about him. She intended to survive, and when it was over, she wanted to put him in prison for what he did.

After the rapist assaulted her, she offered to make him a drink, and when he agreed, she fled the house, wrapped only in a blanket. A couple living next door let her into their house and called police. After being treated for her injuries, Thompson-Cannino helped police draw a composite sketch of her attacker.

'100 percent certain'

Her description seemed to fit Cotton, who was the same age as the victim. He had had several minor scrapes with the law, and several years earlier, when he was 16, he had sneaked into his girlfriend's bedroom through a window and was caught snuggling with the girl by her mother. The mother called police, and Cotton was charged with several offenses, including breaking and entering and sexual assault. The charges were eventually all dismissed, but Cotton's name and mug shot were now on file.

Investigators showed Thompson-Cannino a number of photos of possible suspects. She now knows that her mind was trying to find the person in the group who most closely resembled the sketch she had helped the police artist draw.

"There's six photographs in front of me, so consciously I'm trying to figure out the person in the photographic lineup that most closely resembles the sketch, as opposed to the actual attacker," she told Vieira.

Figure 5.1

She picked Cotton. Later, police put him in a physical lineup and she picked him again. "It was 100 percent certain," she said.

During many of those years in prison, Cotton actually knew who the real rapist was. His name was Bobby Poole, and he landed in the same prison as Cotton. The two bore a striking physical resemblance to one another, and to the police sketch of Thompson-Cannino's attacker.

The fragility of memory

Cotton even asked Poole if he raped Thompson-Cannino. Poole denied it, but one of Poole's friends told Cotton the man confessed to him. Cotton used that information to win a retrial, but Thompson-Cannino's memory by now had firmly replaced her rapist's face with that of Cotton. When she saw both Poole and Cotton in the same courtroom, she again identified Cotton as her rapist with absolute certainty.

"That's just the way memory works," Thompson-Cannino now knows. "Memory takes certain visuals. In my case, after doing a composite sketch, that was the last visual I had in my memory, and it's very subconscious."

The second trial came three years after the first, and during that time, Thompson-Cannino's memory cemented Cotton's image as that of her attacker.

"Now three years have gone by and Ronald Cotton was the rapist. Period," she told Vieira. "That's how memory works. It's so fragile. It's so easily contaminated."

The years in prison were a nightmare, Cotton told Vieira. "I just had to keep myself together, which wasn't easy at all. I was missing my family, my loved ones. I took it day to day and hoped that true justice would prevail and open a door for me."

Cotton's break came in 1995 when he was watching the O.J. Simpson trial on television. Attorneys and investigators kept talking about DNA evidence, something he had never heard of before. He contacted his attorneys, who were able to recover one tiny sample of sperm from the rape kit that had been used to treat Thompson-Cannino 11 years earlier.

Figure 5.2

There was enough DNA in the sample to prove Cotton was innocent and Poole was guilty. And just like that, Cotton was a free man.

A new life

"It was like a dream come true. I couldn't believe it," Cotton told Vieira. "The warden of the penitentiary called me in his office and told me I was going home tomorrow. I told him, 'Please don't pull my leg, it's already long enough.' But it was true. I finally went home to be with my family and loved ones."

Cotton began the difficult task of beginning a new life. He got some money in compensation from the state of North Carolina, but he also worked two jobs to get himself back on his feet. He married and today is the father of a 10-year-old daughter.

As for Thompson-Cannino, she was torn apart by the revelation that her dead-certain testimony had imprisoned an innocent man.

"I was devastated, I really was," she told Vieira. "One of the things that is really important is that I never felt any shame being a rape victim. I knew that I had been innocent that night. I now felt this debilitating guilt and shame over 11 years of a man's life [that] was just gone."

She lived with her mental torment for two years before finally reaching out to Cotton. When they met, she told him if she atoned every day for the rest of her life, it would not be enough to make up for the years Cotton had lost.

Her fears that he would want revenge were unfounded, and he quickly allayed her guilt. Cotton simply told her he had forgiven her long ago; it wasn't her fault.

Today, when they travel together to give speeches, people sometimes assume they're a couple and ask them how they met. It is, they reply, a long story.

B. Readings

Table 5.1 *Standard 3 (Witness Response) × 2 (Culprit Present Versus Absent) Results From an Eyewitness Identification Experiment*[22]

Culprit presence	Identification of suspect	Identification of filler	No identification
Culprit present (suspect guilty)	Accurate identification	Filler error Type I	Incorrect rejection
	46.1%	21.2%	32.7%
Culprit absent (suspect innocent)	Mistaken identification	Filler error Type II	Correct rejection
	13.4%	34.5%	52.0%

Gary L. Wells, *Eyewitness Identification: Systemic Reforms*
2006 Wis. L. Rev. 615, 615–20 (2006)

The vagaries of eyewitness identification are well known; the annals of criminal law are rife with instances of mistaken identification.

—Justice William S. Brennan

It has long been conjectured that eyewitness identification evidence is a major cause of the conviction of innocent persons. Although the empirical foundations for Justice Brennan's claim were not in place in the 1960s, by the 1980s there were substantial analyses showing that mistaken eyewitness identification was the major source of wrongful convictions. Even more compelling evidence has developed over the last decade based on post-conviction forensic DNA tests. Case analyses of people in the United States who were convicted of crimes that they did not commit (as revealed through later DNA tests) show that mistaken identifications account for more of these wrongful convictions than all other causes combined.

In the mid 1970s, experimental psychologists began conducting scientific experiments to examine the conditions under which eyewitness identification evidence is more reliable or less reliable. Using controlled research methods in which events (for example, staged crimes and video events) were created for unsuspecting people, eyewitness researchers began isolating variables that could help explain and perhaps

---

22. *Note:* These data are from Clark et al.'s (2008) quantitative summary of 94 eyewitness identification studies. Clark, S. E., Howell, R. T., & Davey, S. L. (2008). Regularities in eyewitness identification. *Law and Human Behavior, 32,* 187–218. http://dx.doi.org/10.1007/sl0979-006-9082-4.

control the phenomenon of eyewitness misidentification. This research has proven the general thesis that mistaken eyewitness identifications can be very common under certain conditions. A major line of this research has focused on "system variables," which are factors affecting the reliability of eyewitness identifications that the criminal justice system could (or should) control. Today, there is a vast body of knowledge in scientific psychology about improving the reliability of eyewitness identification evidence. Several recommendations that scientific psychologists have made for improving how lineups are conducted are particularly compelling. These advances in our understanding of how to improve eyewitness identification evidence have resulted in some jurisdictions making dramatic changes to the procedures used to collect and preserve eyewitness identification evidence.

* * *

I. Understanding Lineups and Relative Judgments

A. The Lineup

A typical police lineup in the United States is composed of six people, one is a suspect and the remainder are "fillers." A filler (sometimes called a stand-in, distractor, or foil) is a nonsuspect person in the lineup who is there merely to help make the process fair to the suspect. There are a number of variations on this: sometimes the lineup is a set of photographs (photo lineup), sometimes the lineup is live (live lineup).... Sometimes lineups contain more or less than six people, but six is the most common number. Sometimes a lineup contains more than one suspect, and some lineups have been composed totally of suspects, which is a very dangerous practice. The purpose of the lineup is to see if the eyewitness will identify the suspect as being the offender rather than identifying one of the known-innocent fillers.

B. Relative Judgments

Although the cognitive processes underlying human recognition memory are complex..., there is one underlying process that is both simple to understand and highly informative. Specifically, people have a tendency to select the person who looks most like the offender relative to the other members of the lineup. At first glance, this relative-judgment process would seem to be nonproblematic. In fact, however, the relative-judgment process is extremely problematic. The problem is made apparent by considering the fact that there is always someone who looks more like the offender than the remaining members of the lineup, even when the lineup does not include the offender. In these cases, eyewitnesses have a tendency to select that innocent person and confuse this relative-judgment process with recognition memory.

The relative-judgment problem is well-illustrated in an experiment in which a crime was staged 200 times for 200 separate witnesses. All of the witnesses were then shown one of two lineups. Every witness was warned that the offender might or might not be in the lineup. Half of the witnesses viewed a six-person lineup in which the offender was present. Of these 100 witnesses, 21% made no selection at all, 54% picked the offender, 13% picked a particular filler, and the remaining witnesses spread their choices across the other lineup members. The other half of the witnesses viewed a lineup in which the offender was removed and was not replaced. The critical question in this scenario is what happened to the 54% of witnesses who would have chosen the offender had he been present; did they shift to the no-choice category, thereby causing 75% to make no choice? No. Of these 100 witnesses, the no-choice rate increased to only 32% whereas the person who was previously picked only 13% of the time was now picked 38% of the time. In other words, even though all of the witnesses were warned that the offender might not be in the lineup, removing the offender from the lineup led witnesses to shift to the "next best choice," nearly tripling the jeopardy of that person. Controlled eyewitness experiments consistently show that the most difficult problem for eyewitnesses is recognizing the absence of the offender because, even when the offender is not in the lineup, there is still someone who looks most like the offender relative to other members of the lineup.

The majority of DNA exoneration cases represent instances in which the actual offender was not in the lineup. This is precisely what eyewitness researchers had predicted based on data from controlled experiments. Unfortunately, there are hundreds of circumstances under which police might unknowingly place an innocent suspect in a lineup. Sometimes police place an innocent suspect in a lineup because they received an anonymous but erroneous tip that the person was the offender; sometimes an innocent suspect is placed in a lineup merely because the person fits the general physical description and was in the vicinity of the crime; sometimes an innocent person came into possession of something linked to the crime; and sometimes one or more detectives places a suspect in a lineup based on a "hunch." Whatever the cause, it can never be presumed that the suspect is the offender; if police knew that, they would not need the lineup at all....

C. False Confidence

The confidence (or certainty) that an eyewitness expresses in his or her identification during a lineup is a powerful determinant of whether police, prosecutors, judges, and jurors will accept the identification as proof that the identified person is the actual offender. Controlled experiments, however, show that eyewitnesses can be both highly confident (even "positive") and yet totally mistaken in an eyewitness identification. Meta-analyses, which combine the results of a large number of controlled experiments, show that the correlation between confidence and accuracy in eyewitness identification is likely to be somewhere in the range of +.40, where +1.0 is a perfect correlation and 0.0 is no correlation at all. This means that a confident witness is more likely to be accurate than is a nonconfident witness. However, the +.40 correlation is far from perfect (+1.0), indicating that there are many confident witnesses who are inaccurate and many nonconfident witnesses who are accurate.

In practice, the problem with using eyewitness confidence to infer accuracy is even more problematic than the +.40 correlation suggests. Recent research shows that "feedback" to eyewitnesses who have made mistaken identifications can lead them to inflate their confidence dramatically. In these experiments, eyewitnesses who had made mistaken identifications were simply told, "Good, you identified the actual suspect" (confirming feedback) or were told nothing (a control condition). Later, they were asked a series of questions about their identifications, including how certain they were at the time that they had identified the actual gunman. In the control condition, 15% of these mistaken eyewitnesses said that they were positive or nearly positive that they identified the actual gunman. However, in the confirming feedback condition, 50% of the mistaken witnesses reported that they were positive or nearly positive. This research also showed that most eyewitnesses denied that the feedback influenced them and that those who denied being influenced were just as influenced as those who admitted that they might have been influenced.

The confidence of an eyewitness should be based on the witness's memory alone, not on feedback from the investigators. The case of Ronald Cotton, who was misidentified by Jennifer Thompson, illustrates this point. When Jennifer Thompson erroneously identified Ronald Cotton's photo from a photo lineup, the detectives turned and said to her, "We thought this might be the one." At trial, Thompson was absolutely positive that Ronald Cotton was the man who raped her. Like the eyewitnesses who received confirming feedback in the research experiments, there is no reason to think that she would be aware of the way this influenced her confidence.

In effect, the influence that feedback has on confidence shows the importance of establishing protocols for lineups that police should follow....

Nancy K. Steblay, *Scientific Advances in Eyewitness Identification Evidence*
41 Wm. Mitchell L. Rev. 1090, 1102–11 (2015)

The DNA exoneration cases deliver a specific lesson about eyewitness error that aligns well with a persistent scientific question. Namely, the lineups that produced identification errors did not include the real culprit. The police had a suspect, of course, but that suspect was not the perpetrator of the crime. Yet these well-intentioned eyewitnesses chose the innocent suspect and went on to accuse him in a courtroom. Clearly, the lineup member chosen could not have matched the witness's memory of the culprit and yet, these witnesses failed to claim "he's not there" or "I don't recognize any of these faces"—which would have been the correct answer to a lineup in which the culprit is not present.

And, there is more to the problem. It is not just the identification that can drive an investigation forward, convince a prosecutor to charge a case, or be compelling evidence at trial. That eyewitness must also be confident. Thus, the perplexing question for eyewitness scientists: Why does an eyewitness select a lineup member even in the absence of recognition memory? Furthermore, how can an eyewitness who has made a wrong identification be so confident? And a very important final question: Why did the witness specifically choose *the suspect* from the lineup if he or she is innocent?

Why Do Eyewitnesses Make Errors?

Consider the ideal eyewitness: All sensory systems operate optimally (including required eyewear and absence of ear-buds), in an attentive, calm, and non-intoxicated witness, within a situation that provides an unobstructed, well-illuminated view at a distance and for a duration of time that allows a reasonable study of the culprit and circumstances. The ideal witness will *attend to and perceive* all that transpires; *encode* this information completely, meaningfully, and accurately into memory; *retain* the information across time; and then *retrieve and report* it faithfully and fully when requested by investigators. This ideal witness has passed through four steps of a simple model akin to the operation of our memory system. Eyewitnesses perceive stimuli and subsequently encode, retain, and retrieve information and images. This simple example of the ideal witness is an appealing device for grasping the witness experience and for understanding all that can go wrong in the eyewitness account of a crime. Because, alas, this ideal witness does not exist. In the next paragraphs, witness vulnerability to error at each of these four stages is explored.

1. Estimator and System Variables

There is a useful forensic distinction to be made between the first two steps of the eyewitness memory experience (perception and encoding) and the final two steps (retention and retrieval). Even before law enforcement arrives on the scene, many factors will influence perception and encoding processes. Consider a distracted witness who only briefly views three strangers wearing dark glasses and hats under conditions of poor lighting at a substantial distance. Research supports common-sense assumptions that short crime duration, greater distance, poor illumination, offender disguises, and distractions from full attention will diminish the quality of eyewitness memory.

Research has also uncovered influences on memory that may not always be common knowledge. Three examples from the eyewitness literature illustrate this point. First, witness fear and stress are likely to diminish, rather than aid, the quality of memory, contrary to common wisdom. The human "fight or flight" physiological response to threat—that mobilizes energy for the physical action of fighting hard or running fast—is geared toward enhancing prospects of survival, not memory. While the gist of the frightening experience is not easily forgotten, details are often not encoded correctly, if at all.

A second well-documented phenomenon is the "weapon focus effect." Research shows that a weapon is likely to draw the attention of the witness, reducing time for attention directed to facial features. Lab studies indicate that presence (versus absence) of a weapon reduces accuracy of later lineup identifications.

A third example is that identification errors are significantly more likely when the event is "cross-race." Most people are much better at encoding facial details for members of their own race than other races. A meta-analysis of studies spanning thirty years and encompassing the laboratory experiences of nearly 5000 research participants found that witnesses were 1.40 times more likely to correctly identify a previously-seen face of their own race compared to a face of another race, and 1.56 times more likely to falsely identify an other-race face never seen before.

Unfortunately, the justice system cannot mandate whether the race of the victim is the same as the offender, whether or not the offender carries a weapon, the illumination of the offender's face, and additional critical factors. These many factors that diminish the quality of witness memory during perception and encoding are out of the control of law enforcement. Furthermore, the impact of these issues on any specific witness can only be estimated after the fact. Thus, these factors are referred to as "estimator variables."

Once law enforcement has arrived on the scene, however, investigators can potentially control subsequent influences on witness memory. Impact of these "system variables" can be adjusted by the legal system through better procedures. System variables have become the focus of lineup procedural recommendations. For example, best police practices require that witnesses be interviewed sooner rather than later, that witness interviews be documented immediately, and that co-witnesses be separated before they confer in order to avoid memory contamination. Some of these practices cannot always be achieved (e.g., multiple witnesses to a crime frequently share their impressions before police have a chance to interview them), but many can be applied with greater consistency.

2. Eyewitness Memory Vulnerabilities During Memory Retention and Retrieval

An eyewitness to a crime is placed in an undesirable and unusual circumstance. There is often a powerful self-imposed pressure, as well as a push from investigators, family, and/or the media, to generate a detailed and coherent narrative of what happened and who is responsible. Witnesses may second-guess their own version of events when hearing co-witness accounts or details from a case investigator or other sources. For example, the "John Doe" sought in a costly FBI manhunt following the Oklahoma bombing of 1995 is now believed to have been non-existent, although three eyewitnesses described Timothy McVeigh's "accomplice" at the time. The co-witnesses at a truck rental shop were apparently influenced by one employee who recalled confidently that Timothy McVeigh was with another man when he rented the truck used in the bombing. All three witnesses described the accomplice to investigators—after they first shared their recall with one another.

The human cognitive system is a marvelous structure for building one's knowledge base through learning and reasoning processes. At the same time, the memory and decision processes that work adequately for us most of the time may not work ideally for eyewitnesses. For example, an otherwise useful cognitive function that purges or updates old information in favor of new may present difficulties for the eyewitness.

It is not surprising that eyewitnesses forget both important and unimportant details as time goes by, as we all do. But, eyewitness memory also can err through commission, incorporating new information that may seemingly sharpen the experience or shape the narrative for the witness in ways that, even if factually correct, become no longer a veridical report of that eyewitness's original experience. This is illustrated in the manner in which we incorporate new information seamlessly into our cognitive system and in the way we can reason ourselves into an answer in the absence of requisite knowledge.

3. Incorporation of New Information

As has been cautioned now for decades, eyewitness memory is not like a play-back system that can be accessed for a clean, full version of a past event. Information encoded into memory at the time of a crime is not stored in pristine or immutable condition but is instead quite vulnerable to revision, contrary to a common assumption of an image "burned into memory." Memories are not so much "retrieved" as they are "reconstructed," often using current knowledge to understand the past event or to fill in a gap in the story in ways that make sense within a personal belief system. Furthermore, the content of new information is better remembered than the source of that information.

Thus, eyewitness veracity is dually cursed by the likelihood that original memory of the crime event will be tainted by new external information and that the witness will be unable to effectively parse information into what she knows now, versus what she knew at the time of the crime (a source monitoring error). An eyewitness may replace (or confuse) a perpetrator's face with another image — of an innocent lineup member, a police composite, or a face seen in a mug-shot or other post-event context. Nevertheless, the subsequent "memory" is often quite compelling to the eyewitness, investigators, and jury. A challenge for eyewitness researchers and the legal system is to assess the level of reconstruction that afflicts an eyewitness's memory report.

One of the most riveting and well-publicized DNA exoneration cases, the rape conviction of Ronald Cotton, includes a chain of identification tasks — a composite sketch, a photo lineup, a physical lineup, an in-court ID — during which the face of the rapist, Bobby Poole, was replaced in the victim's memory with that of innocent Ronald Cotton. With one hundred percent confidence at trial, victim Jennifer Thompson called the day of Cotton's conviction, "the happiest day of my life" but failed to recognize Poole when she finally was confronted with him.

In at least fourteen DNA-exoneration cases "the exoneree was the only person repeated in multiple viewings" by the same eyewitness. These cases have the common thread of mistaken identification by eyewitnesses who became increasingly but erroneously convinced of the culprit's identity across two or more identification tasks. Eyewitness research similarly demonstrates the problems for eyewitness identification of repeated identification tasks. Repeated identification tasks are not uncommon in practice. Yet, most jurisdictions have no written policies about identification practices.

4. Memory Strength and Reasoning Processes

Remember back to a past exam of multiple-choice items — a college exam, a written driver's test, the LSAT, or the SAT. For some items, a quick scan of the response options was enough to immediately recognize the answer. For other items, the correct answer did not jump out. Memory failed, so a secondary strategy was called up: eliminate unlikely options, try to find a decipherable cue in the question itself, or make a best guess. Helpful assistance from others might even have been attempted (another test-taker or the instructor).

In a similar manner, eyewitnesses are asked to report whether they recognize a suspect from a lineup. A witness may have an immediate recognition experience, a fast automatic positive identification (a "jump-out"). In the absence of immediate recognition—when memory for the culprit is not strong, culprit appearance has changed, or the culprit is not in the lineup—secondary processes will be prompted: slower, more effortful and deliberative modes of decision making. These psychological processes involve a continuum of judgment from automatic to deliberative. The witness using a deliberative process may be essentially attempting to find the suspect, a reasoning process that is quite different from immediate recognition. This difference in decision strategy has implications for the quality of evidence from a positive identification, and provides a basis for the procedural improvements recommended by scientists.

One common secondary strategy in our daily lives is to respond to a difficult question by answering an easier one, usually without noticing the change in tack. This strategy is often successful and rather effortless. For example, when we try to locate a vaguely-remembered server mid-meal in a restaurant (Was that the young man who took my order?), the answer to an alternative question may easily suffice (Which of these servers is *closest* to what I remember?). An error in this scenario has limited if any repercussions. This process of choosing the *closest* to memory is well-known in lineup literature. In this context, however, repercussions are very serious. *Relative judgment* is the comparison of lineup members to one another in order to select the one who looks *most like* the offender relative to the other lineup members. Relative judgment may work well if the culprit is in the lineup. However, the intuitive "correctness" of relative judgment for the witness produces a dangerous situation when police place an innocent suspect in a lineup, particularly one who resembles the true culprit. A witness who moves from an absolute (this is the guy!) to a relative (closest!) judgment strategy places an innocent suspect at risk.

Research indicates that a very difficult task for eyewitnesses is to recognize when the culprit is not in the lineup. This straightforward conceptualization of *relative judgment* as a secondary decision strategy is rich in its implications for lineup procedural revisions and has provided the basis for recommended new lineup procedures. For example, the sequential (one-at-a-time) lineup was developed as a means to reduce witness reliance on relative judgment when immediate recognition fails.

* * *

Ideally, lineup procedures should capture the original experience of the eyewitness (without external influence), should be fair to the suspect (avoiding suggestiveness), and should minimize procedural biases that may prompt witnesses with weak or no memory of the culprit to choose from the lineup. Procedural biases may operate as general-impairment or specific suspect. A general-impairment bias (or more simply, general bias) pushes a witness to make an identification, but the push is not necessarily directed toward the suspect. Specific suspect bias (or more simply, suspect bias) points the witness toward the suspect and away from the fillers, who are the known-innocent members of the lineup. For example, a biased lineup instruction ("Which of these is the person?") may prompt more identifications and thereby incur an increase in witness choosing but it does not explicitly implicate the suspect (a general-impairment bias). On the other hand, a poorly constructed lineup in which only the suspect bears resemblance to the witness's description of the culprit will likely prompt a witness to pick the suspect (a specific suspect bias). Similarly, repeated identification tasks involving the same witness and suspect produce specific bias against a suspect, because a suspect may stand out in a lineup when he or she has appeared in a prior identification context: a mug shot book, a show-up (presentation of the suspect alone), or an earlier lineup. The issue of specific suspect bias is quite relevant to jury considerations. A jury may hear a case in which encoding and retention conditions were clearly substandard (*e.g.*, a witness with a poor view who makes a cross-race identification long after the event). Yet, the jury may be minimally impressed by warnings about general-impairment concerns, because, after all, the witness still picked the defendant from a lineup. Suspect-bias variables, on the other hand, can provide an answer to the pressing question of why the witness picked this defendant if he or she is not guilty.

Scientific Recommendations for Lineup Procedure

The lineup procedural revisions recommended by scientists to increase the reliability of eyewitness evidence include components of lineup construction, lineup instructions to the witness, presentation of the lineup, and recording of lineup results.

A. Lineup Construction

The purpose of a lineup is for law enforcement to gather reliable evidence to test a suspicion that the suspect is indeed the perpetrator. Law enforcement presents a single suspect to the witnesses along with "fillers" (known innocents) of similar physical attributes. A witness's firm rejection of a lineup ("He's not there.") may prompt police to reevaluate their suspicion about the suspect. A filler selection can indicate a weak witness memory or that the filler looks more like the perpetrator than does the suspect. And, of course, a suspect identification offers incriminating evidence against the suspect.

Properly selected lineup fillers help to ensure that the lineup does not immediately suggest to the witness who the police think the suspect is (i.e., it avoids a suspect bias). When all fillers match the witness's description of the culprit and no lineup member stands out, the witness cannot use a simple process of elimination to arrive at the suspect. An eyewitness whose memory is weak should be dissuaded by the many unfamiliar faces in the lineup from falsely claiming recognition of the suspect.

Furthermore, suppose a witness with a poor memory nevertheless makes a lineup pick, perhaps using relative judgment. The risk to an innocent suspect is diminished if that risk is spread across lineup fillers. With a fairly-constructed lineup of six members, the likelihood that any one lineup member will be chosen by chance is one in six. Thus, the likelihood that an innocent suspect will be chosen by a witness who is simply guessing is one in six. A larger lineup can further reduce risk to an innocent suspect; for example, an eight-member lineup decreases the risk to an innocent suspect to one in eight. This rationale exposes the problem of a show-up, in which a single suspect is unprotected from a simple guess.

The recommendation that only one suspect be included in a lineup is based on this logic, which asserts that risk from an unreliable witness can and should be spread away from an innocent suspect. The extreme end of a contrary lineup construction strategy—an all-suspect lineup—can be seen in the Duke University lacrosse team rape case that came to attention in 2006. The witness, who described the multiple offenders as lacrosse team members, was shown a series of lineups with all team members, including one display with all forty-six lacrosse players. There were no fillers. Any witness pick would incriminate that selected team member— just as throwing a dart at the photos would have netted a suspect hit. In short, the procedures used were non-diagnostic for the guilt or innocence of the young men in the lineup. And, it is important to note that the absence of fillers in the lineups also meant that the witness's credibility could not be challenged; she could not make a "wrong" pick.

Police do not know if the suspect is the culprit when they build the lineup. Therefore, fair lineup construction requires a method of *fit-to-description* as a means to limit bias against a suspect who may be innocent. That is, all lineup members should match the description of the culprit provided by the eyewitness. Variability in lineup member appearance is allowed around the core verbal descriptors provided by the witness, a method that avoids both an impossible "clone" lineup and one that unfairly flags the suspect. A lineup constructed to increase physical similarity beyond the level of witness description provides no additional protection to the innocent suspect and can harm the eyewitness's ability to identify the perpetrator.

B. Lineup Instructions

One of the most intractable problems of eyewitness identification is that many witnesses will choose a lineup member when they in fact should have said "he's not there" or "I don't know." It appears that inherent pressure of a lineup scenario or the expectations that the perpetrators must be in the lineup prompts witnesses to make lineup selections even in the absence of clear recognition. Witnesses may shift to relative judgment—picking the lineup member closest to memory—a process that places an innocent suspect at risk. One means to reduce witness reliance on relative judgment, that is, to inhibit witnesses from picking from a lineup when they do not have sufficient memory strength, is to provide an instruction that (correctly) informs them that the culprit they saw may not be in the lineup. The recommendation is for an explicit instruction to the witness that the offender may or may not be in the lineup, thereby also allowing that "none of the above" may be the correct and reasonable response to the lineup. The *NIJ Guide* embraced this recommendation, and this cautionary instruction has become a noncontroversial policy reform in many U.S. jurisdictions.

This author recently evaluated sixteen experimental lab studies in a meta-analysis that specifically tested the presence versus absence of a *may-or-may-not* instruction. The instruction significantly reduced identification errors when the culprit was missing from the lineup, from seventy percent to forty-three percent, and a designated innocent suspect was picked by half as many witnesses (nineteen percent vs. forty percent). This instruction also led to a non-significant and small (five percent) loss of correct identifications. The research is clear: an instruction that specifically alerts the witness to the possibility that the true perpetrator may not be in the lineup significantly decreases erroneous witness picks from the lineup, compared to an instruction that suggests culprit presence in the array. The primary impact of the admonition is to inhibit choosing from witnesses who otherwise would make identification errors, an avoidance of a general bias.

C. Double-Blind Lineup Administration

A standard protective measure of experimental and clinical research design is a double-blind procedure, in which neither the research participant nor the experimenter knows whether the participant is in the treatment or control group. In medical research, double-blind procedure requires that neither the evaluating clinician nor the patient know whether the patient is receiving the treatment or a placebo. The purpose is that the double-blind procedure protects against the inadvertent impact of knowledge that could taint research results (how the clinician interacts with the patient, records patient information and evaluates clinical outcomes, and how the patient perceives and reports the experience). The double-blind procedure also protects the research against claims of influence or bias.

In lineup practice, most police already use a "single-blind" procedure. The eyewitness is not told who the suspect is in the lineup (i.e., police do not instruct the witness: "Here is a lineup of six guys. We think number three is the one who robbed you. What do you think?"). Of course, this would be highly suggestive and contradict the purpose of the lineup. The scientific recommendation is that lineup procedures should in fact be "double-blind" to keep both the eyewitness and lineup administrator unaware of which lineup member is the police suspect. The lineup administrator does not know which lineup member is the suspect, and furthermore, the witness is informed that the administrator does not know. This protocol avoids unintentional leaks of information from the lineup administrator regarding which lineup member is the suspect and which are mere fillers (a suspect bias) and cautions the witness that administrator comments or behaviors are not helpful clues to who the suspect is. As in clinical trials, double-blind procedure prompts recording clarity and integrity and protects against claims of administrator influence.

The recommendation for a double blind identification procedure was issued over two decades ago and has been long endorsed by eyewitness scientists. Identifications from lineups conducted by blind administrators have been found to be more diagnostic of suspect guilt than those conducted under a non-blind procedure. Exploration of the underlying conditions for witness vulnerability to influence has found that the impact from non-blind administrators is greatest when the lineup procedure is also affected by general bias factors of biased lineup instructions and simultaneous lineup format. Non-blind administrators behave differently toward witnesses. Yet, both witnesses and administrators may be unaware of administrator influence.

Beyond the worry of direct influence during the lineup procedure, there are additional negative effects of the non-blind lineup administration after the lineup decision is made. Research has established the impact of a non-blind lineup administrator on the written report of the lineup procedure and outcomes. An administrative reporting difference was documented in real field lineups. Analysis of eighty-seven lineups indicated that non-blind investigators administering simultaneous lineups were forty-four percent less likely to report verbatim witness comments (e.g., "That's him, I recognize the crooked teeth.") than were blind investigators administering sequential lineups. Non-blind administrators more frequently reported in third-person form (e.g., "The witness identified the suspect."), revealing an interpretation of the lineup outcome filtered through the lens of investigator knowledge. In this field comparison, blind status of the lineup was confounded with lineup format. Nevertheless, the take-away point is that a blind lineup administrator, by virtue of the lack of knowledge about the suspect, is unable to interject conclusions based on case information. In a similar manner, a blind lineup administrator cannot contaminate a witness's confidence with comments about the "correctness" of a witness's lineup selection, a problem that is discussed in a section below.

D. Sequential Lineup Presentation

A traditional identification procedure presents all lineup members at the same time (simultaneously). Yet, there is no logical or empirical basis to assume that a reliable witness's memory of the culprit can be improved with a side-by-side comparison of lineup members, nor is there a financial benefit of a simultaneous display. Also, there is a risk in the traditional procedure: simultaneous lineup presentation allows witnesses to engage in relative judgment, thereby prompting lineup picks (a general bias), but also increasing risk to an innocent suspect who looks most like the culprit (a suspect bias). The scientific recommendation for increasing the reliability of eyewitness identification evidence is to employ a sequential rather than simultaneous display of the lineup members. That is, all lineups, photographic or live, should be presented to the witness one member at a time and the witness should make a decision about each lineup member before moving to the next. A sizable amount of experimental literature has compared performance of eyewitnesses using the two lineup procedures (seventy-two studies). The most complete and recent review has revealed a common pattern: compared to the simultaneous procedure, a sequential procedure produces a large reduction in mistaken identifications (twenty-two percent) with some accompanying loss of correct identifications (eight percent). The loss of correct identifications is presumably due to the fact that witnesses could no longer employ relative judgment to find the suspect. A subsequent analysis of the same data by a different team of researchers concluded that the sequential procedure promotes a more conservative witness decision process ("the tendency of witnesses to choose from or reject a lineup"). It is likely this more conservative criterion is responsible for the higher overall accuracy rates with the sequential procedure.

Sequential and simultaneous lineup procedures were directly compared in a controlled, randomized field experiment sponsored by the American Judicature Society (AJS) involving almost 500 lineups, including both real witnesses and real crimes, ranging from fraud to murder, in four U.S. police jurisdictions. The lineups were randomly assigned to simultaneous versus sequential lineup procedures. Results were in concert with laboratory findings, in that sequential lineups generated significantly fewer (11.1%) filler identifications compared to simultaneous lineups (17.8%), with no loss of suspect identifications.

For police, the critical question is: "Is the identification a good predictor of the suspect's guilt?" Once a witness has made a positive identification from the lineup, the likelihood that this pick was a guilty rather than innocent person is better if the lineup was sequential versus simultaneous. In short, sequential lineup procedure produces identification evidence that is more probative. These results are now echoed with the AJS field data. While suspect identifications did not differ between sequential and simultaneous field lineups, forty-one percent of witness selections from simultaneous field lineups were filler picks compared to thirty-one percent of witness picks from sequential lineups. In this way, the sequential procedure increases the probative value of the identification evidence.

E. Witness Confidence Statements

As noted above, it is not only a positive identification of a suspect that presents strong evidence at trial, but also high witness confidence in that identification. The escalation of witness confidence between identification and court testimony can potentially be spurred by any number of external sources, including media reports of a suspect's previous crimes, police or attorney information about the status of the investigation, or new knowledge regarding co-witness statements. Thus, confidence at trial may be substantially higher than that at the identification. For this reason, best practice is to take a confidence statement in the witness's own words immediately at the time of the identification and before feedback about the correctness of that decision arrives from any source (as directed in the *NIJ Guide*).

This procedural recommendation is more nuanced than perhaps immediately appreciated. The thin slice of time immediately after the witness's identification is the first point of vulnerability for what can quickly become false witness confidence. A sizable body of research literature has revealed the astonishing power of a casual positive comment from a lineup administrator to affect eyewitness confidence. In the first study to examine this phenomenon, witness-participants viewed a security video and were asked to identify the offender from a lineup. The lineup did not include the offender, yet all witnesses made a selection. Immediately after these mistaken identifications, (false) confirming feedback was provided to a randomly-assigned group of witnesses: "Good. You identified the actual suspect." Witnesses assigned to the control group were told nothing about their identification accuracy. Confirming feedback significantly inflated witnesses' retrospective confidence reports compared to the control group. Furthermore, an extensive range of variables was inflated in conjunction with retrospective certainty, including witnesses' positive evaluation of their viewing experience for the crime. Yet, the witnesses believed that the feedback did not affect their perceptions.

The post-identification feedback effect is robust across studies and noteworthy for multiple reasons. First, witnesses whose decisions were confirmed became more certain of their identification both at the time of the feedback (perhaps not surprisingly) but also retrospectively for the time of the identification. Importantly, these witnesses typically have made identifications from culprit-absent lineups; hence, their distorted reports correspond to mistaken identifications of innocent suspects, a forensically-relevant scenario of critical importance. This dramatic effect is produced by a simple, casual, even seemingly helpful, comment from the lineup administrator.

Second, memory of the circumstances surrounding the identification task and the crime itself has been altered. After confirming feedback, witnesses recalled greater ease and speed of the identification and reported having had a better view of the perpetrator, having paid more attention, having had a better basis to make an identification, and having greater clarity of the offender's image in mind. These aspects of eyewitness experience are the very attributes that are likely to bolster eyewitness credibility in the eyes of investigators, prosecutors, and juries. In short, the identification evidence has been contaminated.

Additionally, witnesses who received confirming feedback showed elevation in broader subjective measures: belief that they possess good memory for strangers, greater trust in eyewitnesses with similar experiences, and an increased willingness to testify about their eyewitness experience. This combination—that jurors are especially willing to believe a confident witness and that lineup administrators can influence a witness's confidence—poses a serious problem for courtroom evidence. The confidence of the witness can be misaligned with accuracy, yet a witness who is truly convinced of the correctness of the testimony will not exude cues of deception or insincerity. Importantly, this post-identification feedback effect has been replicated with real eyewitnesses to crimes and with both incorrect and correct witness decisions.

How can this slip of a comment be inhibited, so as to prohibit false confidence? A recent study supports the most frequently offered advice to law enforcement as to how to avoid post-identification feedback effects: a blind lineup administrator who can secure the confidence rating from the witness at the time of the lineup.

Steven E. Clark, *Costs and Benefits of Eyewitness Identification Reform: Psychological Science and Public Policy*
7 Persp. on Psychol. Sci. 238–259 (2012)

The link between mistaken identification and wrongful convictions in the United States is empirically well-established. There is no doubt: Eyewitnesses make mistakes that send innocent people to prison (Gross, Jacoby, Matheson, Montgomery, & Patil, 2005).

Four decades of scientific psychological research have shown that the risk of such false identifications could be significantly reduced if the criminal justice system were to change the procedures it uses to obtain eyewitness identification evidence. This process of reform is already under way. The states of New Jersey, Wisconsin, North Carolina, Ohio, and West Virginia have passed legislation, or developed guidelines, to change the procedures used by law enforcement to obtain eyewitness identification evidence....

The reforms are directed at fundamental aspects of the identification process: How lineups are constructed, what witnesses are told and how they are instructed prior to the lineup, the way that the lineup is presented, and what police officers should and should not say and do during the identification procedure. Five specific recommendations are addressed in this article: (a) the witness should be instructed prior to the lineup that the perpetrator of the crime might not be present in the lineup; (b) the individuals in a lineup should be presented to the witness sequentially, rather than simultaneously; (c) the police officer or detective who conducts the lineup should not say or do anything that could influence the witness's decision; (d) the lineup should be composed in such a way that the suspect does not stand out; (e) the presentation of a single suspect, alone, in a procedure called a *one-person showup*, should be avoided in favor of full lineups that typically present the suspect along with a minimum of five fillers. These recommendations, which will be discussed in detail, are based on empirical data from laboratory experiments and are closely tied to fundamental issues regarding human memory, decision-making, and social influence.

The reform movement has also been driven by an assertion that the recommended procedures can reduce the false identification rate with little or no reduction in the correct identification rate (*e.g.*, Wells, Memon, & Penrod, 2006; Wells & Seelau, 1995; Wells et al., 1998). This view has not only been expressed by eyewitness research psychologists, but also by legal scholars (Findley, 2008; Garrett, 2008), and it is referred to here as the no-cost view. As will be shown, the no-cost view is convincingly contradicted by data. To the contrary, the data show (with one exception) a general trade-off pattern. Correct identifications of the guilty are lost as false identifications of the innocent are avoided. This trade-off makes policy decisions regarding the implementation of the recommended procedures more complicated.

* * *

The No-Cost View and Its Implications

The no-cost argument can be illustrated with what may be the most well-known and well-documented case of false identification in recent history. In 1984, Jennifer Thompson identified Ronald Cotton, not once, but three times, as the man who broke into her apartment and raped her. Cotton was convicted and sentenced to life plus 50 years in prison. But DNA evidence analyzed only after Cotton's conviction showed that Cotton did not rape Jennifer Thompson—Bobby Poole did (Thompson-Cannino, Cotton, & Torneo, 2009).

The Cotton case provides a useful model to illustrate and define the basic elements of the no-cost view. Consider if the investigation had led police to Poole, rather than Cotton, and Poole had been placed in the lineup shown to Jennifer Thompson. Using the standard terminology of the research literature, a lineup with Poole in it would be called a *perpetrator-present* lineup, and an identification of Poole would be referred to as a *correct identification*. Of course, the investigation led police to Cotton, and again, using the standard terminology of the research literature, a lineup with Cotton, instead of Poole, is called a *perpetrator-absent* lineup, and the identification of Cotton is referred to as a *false identification*.

The no-cost argument for eyewitness identification reform asserts that recommended identification procedures reduce the risk of a false identification of an innocent suspect such as Ronald Cotton, but have little or no effect on the likelihood of a correct identification of actual criminals such as Bobby Poole. Put another way, the recommended procedures would protect Ronald Cotton, without letting Bobby Poole get away.

This provides a compelling argument for reform, as it claims that recommended procedures provide substantial benefits with no costs. In the purest version of the no-cost view, eyewitness identification procedural reform offers a policy choice between dominating and dominated alternatives. Alternative A dominates Alternative B if A is superior to B on at least one dimension, and inferior to B on no dimensions. According to the no-cost view, recommended procedures dominate standard or nonrecommended procedures because they are superior on the dimension of false identification rate and no worse on the dimension of correct identification rate. Thus, the recommended procedure is obviously better, the nonrecommended procedure is a "noncontender," and the choice of the recommended procedure over the non-recommended procedure is a demonstrably correct decision. Failure to implement recommended procedures would be irrational.

This version of the no-cost view has been expressed many times over the last 30 years. More recently, for some reforms, the no-cost view has evolved into a weaker version. The weaker version acknowledges some losses of correct identifications associated with recommended procedures; however, those losses are described as uncertain (i.e., there *may* be a loss of correct identifications) and so small as to be functionally irrelevant.

The no-cost view has profound implications. Specifically, by denying or minimizing the trade-off between correct identifications lost and false identifications avoided, the no-cost view implies that policymakers need not confront the possibility that citizens within a society may have conflicting, but equally legitimate, values (Berlin, 1958, 1969). Thus, those who are primarily concerned with protecting the constitutional due-process rights of criminal defendants should embrace the recommended procedures because they lower the risk of false identification, and those who are primarily concerned with crime control and the conviction of the guilty should be satisfied in knowing that recommended procedures will not increase the risk that the truly guilty will escape justice. The no-cost view implies that there is no tension between due process and crime control models of criminal justice (Findley, 2008; see

Packer, 1964 for a broader discussion of due process and crime control models). Unfortunately, this view is contradicted by data presented in the next section.

Unbiased versus biased lineup instructions

Prior to a lineup or showup, the administrator (typically a police officer or detective) will instruct the witness regarding what is about to happen. Researchers have recommended that the instructions be unbiased with respect to the presence or absence of the perpetrator and unbiased with respect to the possible response options. Simply put, the recommendation is that the lineup administrator should warn the witness that the perpetrator may not be in the lineup and acknowledge that "the person I saw isn't there" is an acceptable response. Biased instructions explicitly state or imply that the perpetrator is in the lineup and that it is the witness's "job" to pick him out. According to the no-cost view, unbiased instructions decrease the risk of false identification with no change in the correct identification rate. This has been stated many times in the eyewitness identification literature—for example, by Steblay (1997), "biased instructions produced a moderate effect on accuracy in target-absent lineups ... but minimal effect in target-present lineups," and by Wells *et al.*'s (1998) summary of the Steblay meta-analysis:

> *A recent meta-analysis of instruction effects shows that the "might or might not be present" instruction has the effect of reducing identifications when the perpetrator is absent from the lineup while having no effect on identifying the perpetrator when the perpetrator is in the lineup.*

In 2005, Clark reexamined the Steblay (1997) meta-analysis and concluded that correct and false identifications both decreased with unbiased instructions. Additional data, published after 2005, have also shown decreases in correct and false identification rates, and the no-cost view has evolved accordingly but hesitatingly, noting that correct identification rates "might be slightly harmed" by unbiased instructions (Wells et al., 2006) and that biased instructions, "sometimes result in a higher proportion of culprit selections," (Brewer & Palmer, 2010). In a case recently decided by the New Jersey Supreme Court (State of New Jersey v. Larry R. Henderson, 2010), the claim was made that, "the loss in accurate identifications [due to unbiased instructions] pales in comparison to the drop in mistaken identifications," (Scheck, Edwards, & McNamara, 2010). In its opinion, the Court noted the effects of biased instructions on false identifications, but made no mention of the effects for correct identifications. Some recent reviews continue to claim that correct identifications are not affected by the "not there" warning (Fulero, 2009), and others focus only on the reduction of false identifications, without mention of the correct identification rates (Hope, 2010).

The average correct and false identification rates, comparing biased and unbiased instructions, are shown in the two leftmost columns of Table 2. False identification rates are lower with unbiased instructions (.09) than with biased instructions (.15); correct identification rates are also lower for unbiased instructions (.50) than with biased instructions (.59). Thus, the empirical results do not support the no-cost view.

Table 5.2 Analysis of Different Lineup Conditions Using Correct and False Identification Rates

Condition	CORRECT	FALSE
Lineup instructions (n = 23)		
Biased	0.59	0.15
Unbiased	0.5	0.09
Presentation format (n = 51)		
Simultaneous	0.54	0.15
Sequential	0.43	0.09
Lineup foil similarity (n = 18)		
Lower	0.67	0.31
Higher	0.59	0.16
Administrator influence (n = 11)		
More	0.58	0.21
Less	0.45	0.11
Showups vs. lineups (n − 15)		
Showup	0.41	0.18
Lineup	0.43	0.11

They also do not support the assertion that the loss of correct identifications pales in comparison to the reduction in false identifications.

Presentation format: Sequential versus simultaneous lineups

Wells (1984) hypothesized that false identifications are often a product of witnesses making relative judgments, specifically choosing, "the lineup member who most resembles the witness's memory (of the perpetrator) relative to other lineup members." To minimize witnesses' reliance on relative judgments, Lindsay and Wells (1985) proposed that lineup members be presented sequentially, such that witnesses must decide yes ("that's him") or no ("that's not him") for each lineup member as he or she is presented. Because the lineup members are not all presented together, the tendency to make comparisons between lineup members and to make identifications based on relative judgments should be minimized.

The first experiment that compared simultaneous and sequential lineups showed a substantial decrease in the false identification rate (from .43 to .17) and a much smaller decrease in the correct identification rate (from .58 to .50). Lindsay and Wells (1985) emphasized this asymmetry in the results, noting a "reduction of inaccurate identifications without loss of accurate identifications." This view has been echoed by others (e.g., American Bar Association, 2004; Devenport, Penrod, & Cutler, 1997; Lindsay et al., 1991).

A meta-analytic review by Steblay, Dysart, Fulero, and Lindsay (2001) reported a .15 decrease in correct identifications in sequential lineups in comparison with simultaneous lineups, contrary to the no-cost view. However, the loss of correct identifications continues to generate controversy. The .15 decrease in the correct identification rate was dismissed by the researchers who reported it. "Under the most realistic simulations of crimes and police procedures ... the differences between the correct identification rates for simultaneous and sequential lineups are likely to be small or non-existent" (p. 471). It is not clear, however, which studies were deemed to be most realistic.

More recent assessments have acknowledged the loss of correct identifications, and the controversy regarding the loss of correct identifications due to sequential lineup presentation appeared settled (Lindsay, Mansour, Beaudry, Leach, & Bertrand, 2009; Wells, 2006). However, Steblay, Dysart, and Wells (2011) have recently published an updated meta-analysis which reports only an 8% loss in correct identifications and suggests that a "better estimate" of the loss is 5% (p. 127). Although the cost is not zero, it appears quite small in comparison to the 22% reduction in errors in perpetrator-absent lineups reported by Steblay, Dysart, and Wells (2011). Their conclusion is not that there is zero cost in terms of lost correct identifications, but a 5%–8% loss in correct identifications certainly does appear pale in comparison to a 22% reduction in errors arising from perpetrator-absent lineups. However, these results require careful examination.

Most important, the 22% reduction in errors for perpetrator-absent lineups, reported by Steblay et al. in their abstract, refers to all identification errors: false identifications of the innocent suspect plus identifications of lineup foils. As noted earlier, the incorrect identification of a lineup foil is a very different kind of error than the false identification of an innocent suspect. The false identification of an innocent suspect can result in prosecution and false conviction. The identification of a foil, because it is a known error, almost never leads to prosecution of the identified person. Thus, the 22% decrease in "errors" provides the wrong comparison and greatly overestimates the reduction in false identifications.

The results of the present analysis show lower false identification rates for sequential lineups (.09) than for simultaneous lineups (.15) but also lower correct identification rates for sequential lineups (.43) than for simultaneous lineups (.54). Thus, the empirical results, showing roughly equivalent decreases in both correct and false identification rates, contradict the no-cost view.

* * *

Summary

With the exception of showup-lineup comparisons, identification procedures that reduce the risk of false identifications also reduce the probability of correct identifications. The decreases in correct identification rates are not trivial, ranging from .09 to .13, and in many cases they are numerically as large or larger than the decrease in false identification rates. Clearly, policy decisions about eyewitness identification procedures are not easy choices between dominating and dominated alternatives. Rather, they involve choices between alternatives with cost-benefit trade-offs. This raises the question as to how much cost in terms of lost correct identifications should policymakers accept in exchange for the benefit of a reduction in false identifications.

Timothy E. Moore et al., *Shaping Eyewitness and Alibi Testimony with Coercive Interview Practices*
THE CHAMPION 34, 35 (2014)

Eyewitness memory often plays a substantial role in solving the crime. The general belief is that a bystander eyewitness who is not motivated to distort the events will cooperate and describe what she saw. Sometimes, however, the eyewitness may be reluctant to say what she knows—or worse—may be motivated to deliberately deceive law enforcement in order to protect another person. Fred Inbau (a criminologist who specialized in developing interrogation techniques) and colleagues address this problem in the most recent edition of the Reid Technique manual: "Although a criminal investigator ordinarily will experience little difficulty obtaining information from witnesses to a crime or from persons in possession of information derived from some other source, there are instances when a witness or prospective informant will attempt to withhold whatever information is known concerning another's guilt." They go on to recommend steps that investigators can take to ensure the safety and increase the compliance of reluctant witnesses (e.g., promising confidentiality, providing a police guard to protect the witness). These steps are not always successful, in which case the authors state that "[w]hen all other methods have failed, the investigator should accuse the subject of committing the crime (or of being implicated in it in some way) and proceed with an interrogation as though the person was, in fact, considered to have involvement in the crime. A witness or other prospective informant, thus, faced with a false accusation, may be motivated to abandon his efforts to protect the offender or to maintain antisocial or anti-police attitudes." An alibi witness may be subjected to the same forces insofar as the alibi witness is an eyewitness. In other words, if the alibi witness is a friend of the suspect's and testifies that he was with the suspect at the time the crime was committed, the alibi witness is giving eyewitness testimony. While the alibi witness in this example may be unlikely to be subject to the errors of eyewitness identification (for he may know the suspect well), the alibi witness must rely on his memory about the suspect's whereabouts and actions at a specific time and location.

The research on eyewitness memory demonstrates that recall can be influenced by subtle post-event misleading information.... If the default position to take with an assumed "uncooperative" witness is to treat him as a suspect, then it would be expected that the full range of maximization and minimization tactics ... would (at least potentially) be visited on the witness. These tactics would include accusations and confrontations on the one hand and empathy, sympathy, and offers of morally justified excuses for having been uncooperative on the other. As noted earlier, innocent persons can be induced to falsely confess to murder. It should not be a surprise, therefore, that a witness could be persuaded, using the same tactics, to transform, invent, or retract an eyewitness account so that it conforms to the inferred wishes of the interviewer.

What are the investigative advantages of interrogating an eyewitness or alibi witness as if she was a suspect? The benefits are numerous and they all stem from the initial assumption of the target suspect's guilt. An eyewitness who claims that the perpetrator that she saw was *not* the suspect is either mistaken or lying. An eyewitness's testimony is compelling even when incorrect, so such an eyewitness would weaken the case against the suspect. A positive identification of the suspect as the perpetrator, however, would strengthen the case. Likewise, an alibi witness who is a friend or acquaintance of the suspect and claims to have been with him at the very moment the crime occurred represents an inconsistency that weakens the case against the suspect. Again, assuming the suspect's guilt, the alibi witness must be mistaken or deceptive. The case against the suspect can be salvaged if the alibi witness "recalls" that he was with the suspect just before and maybe even just after the crime but perhaps not for the few minutes surrounding the time the crime actually occurred. Alternatively, an interrogation that reduces the confidence of any of these witnesses will help sustain a belief in the suspect's culpability. At the very least, an eyewitness who initially says "it's not him" and then later says "it might be him" can be neutralized on the witness stand through exposure of the inconsistency should she choose to revert to her original testimony. Likewise, an alibi witness who makes contradictory assertions can be discredited on the witness stand. There may be much to gain from getting the witnesses to offer inculpatory statements or retract their exculpatory statements for the camera, no matter how strong-handed the tactics, for research on the impact of confessions shows that it is the confession itself that matters to jurors. The coerciveness of the procedures is not on their radar.

C. Current Law: Overview

Right to Counsel at Line-Ups

The Sixth Amendment of the U.S. Constitution guarantees a right to counsel for the accused. This right includes counsel at a post-indictment line-up. *U.S. v. Wade*, 388 U.S. 218, 236–39 (1967). In *United States v. Wade*, the Supreme Court identified a post-indictment line-up as a "critical stage" where the importance of the evidence and the risks of error necessitate access to an attorney for the defendant. If a suspect is denied an attorney, the identification can be suppressed. However, the right to counsel only attaches after criminal proceedings have begun, thus only for a post-indictment line-up. *Kirby v. Illinois*, 406 U.S. 682 (1972).

Suggestibility of Show-Ups and Line-Ups

If the procedure for an eyewitness identification is too suggestive to be reliable, the identification can be suppressed as a due process violation, regardless of whether the identification is pre or post-indictment. *Stovall v. Deno,* 388 U.S. 293, 301–02 (1967).

Eyewitness misidentification is an issue of reliability that can be mitigated by the role of police when interacting with eyewitnesses, and also by courts in identifying biased identifications pre-trial. The case law below addresses the role of the courts in confronting the reliability of an eyewitness identification.

The Supreme Court and Reliability

As the Supreme Court has famously stated, "reliability is the linchpin in determining the admissibility of identification testimony." *Manson v. Brathwaite,* 432 U.S. 98, 114 (1977). In *Manson,* the Supreme Court created a test to determine whether eyewitness identifications should be admitted as evidence, confirming five factors for reliability established in another case, *Neil v. Biggers,* 409 U.S. 188, 199–200 (1972). The factors—all self-reported by the witness—are:

- the opportunity of the witness to view the criminal at the time of the crime,
- the witness's degree of attention,
- the accuracy of the witness's prior description of the criminal,
- the level of certainty demonstrated by the witness at confrontation,
- and the length of time between the crime and the confrontation.

Neil v. Biggers, 409 U.S. 188, 199–200 (1972).

The Supreme Court provided a lenient standard for admitting this evidence, believing jurors capable of judging the accuracy and importance of identification testimony. The Court remained "content to rely upon the good sense and judgment of American juries," finding that "[j]uries are not so susceptible that they cannot measure intelligently the weight of identification testimony that has some questionable feature." *Manson v. Brathwaite,* 432 U.S. 98, 112, 116 (1977).

Since the *Manson* decision in 1977, over 2000 studies have been conducted on eyewitnesses, demonstrating that the *Manson* test's five factors are poor indicators of a witness's reliability. Nonetheless, the admissibility standard of *Manson* remains unchanged.

In *Perry v. New Hampshire,* the U.S. Supreme Court affirmed that the five *Manson* factors represented "the approach appropriately used to determine whether the Due Process Clause requires suppression of an eyewitness identification tainted by police arrangement." *Perry v. New Hampshire,* 132 S. Ct. 716, 721 (2012). The Court held that a pre-admission judicial ruling on the reliability of an eyewitness identification was only required where a suggestive pretrial identification had been arranged by law enforcement. Any harms of the identification could be negated by cross-examination, expert testimony on the problems with eyewitness identification, and jury instructions. Justice Sonia Sotomayor dissented, noting the substantial problems associated with misidentification, whether or not the identification had been organized by the police. In quoting New Jersey Supreme Court case *State v. Henderson,* Sotomayor wrote,

"The empirical evidence demonstrates that eyewitness misidentification is 'the single greatest cause of wrongful convictions in this country.'"

State Court Reliability Tests

State supreme courts, like the New Jersey Supreme Court, have moved to implement safeguards for ensuring the reliability of eyewitness identifications. In *State v. Henderson*, the New Jersey Supreme Court appointed a Special Master who interviewed seven experts, evaluated the current scientific evidence on eyewitnesses, and then presented the Supreme Court with 2000 transcript pages and reports on hundreds of scientific studies. *State v. Henderson*, 27 A.3d 872, 919–22 (N.J. 2011). The court incorporated this empirical evidence to find that the current admissibility standard was not in keeping with due process obligations under the New Jersey Constitution. It formulated a new test that allows the defendant to establish suggestiveness and for the State to then counter with the reliability of the eyewitness identification; the ultimate burden falls on the defendant to show a "substantial likelihood of irreparable misidentification." The court in Henderson specifically addressed estimator variables, such as visibility, age of the viewer, and lighting, and system variables, such as lineup procedures and police interaction. The court focused primarily on the system variables and changing police protocol because they are factors "within the control of the criminal justice system."

In *State v. Lawson*, the Supreme Court of Oregon changed its rules of evidence, requiring the State to establish the relevancy of an eyewitness identification if a defendant files a motion to exclude it. *State v. Lawson* 291 P.3d 673, 690–91 (Or. 2012). If the State meets its burden, the defendant must then show that the probative value of the identification is "substantially outweighed" by the prejudicial impact. The court has a range of remedial procedures for limiting the potentially prejudicial impact of eyewitness identification evidence, which include limiting witness testimony, permitting expert testimony explaining the science behind eyewitness identifications, or excluding the identification all together. The Oregon Supreme Court concluded that the Oregon Evidence Code was the proper way to determine admissibility of eyewitness evidence because the rules "articulate minimum standards of reliability intended to apply broadly to many types of evidence."

D. Legal Materials, Exercises, and Media

The police issued material witness warrants for seven teenagers who were at the club the night of the murder. The teens described "Shorty" and the shooter. As a group, they described the shooter as wearing a t-shirt (described as "white" and also as "black and white"), holding a gun in his hand, and wearing a gold medallion. The police should have questioned each eyewitness separately and not allowed them to influence each other as a group, reaching consensus on the shooter's description. Nevertheless, that's what they did. The eyewitnesses agreed that the shooter was a good-looking Puerto Rican man with a light goatee (one said a mustache that grew into a goatee), approximately five foot eleven and weighed about one-hundred and sixty-five pounds. Fernando Bermudez is Dominican and at the time of the shooting he was six foot two and weighed two hundred and twenty pounds. He had a thick, bushy mustache, no beard or goatee, and no acne.

"I want you to look at these photos here in front of you," the detective told the eyewitnesses, "and decide which one you think is responsible."

—excerpt from *Pruno, Ramen, and a Side of Hope: Stories of Surviving Wrongful Conviction*, by Courtney Lance and Nikki Pope, sharing exoneree Fernando Bermudez' story

1. *Eyewitness Misidentification, Recommended Listening:* Listen to Fernando Bermudez describe his wrongful conviction on Season 1, Episode 3, The Actual Innocence of Fernando Bermudez, of *Wrongful Conviction with Jason Flom*: https://art19.com/shows/wrongful-conviction-with-jason-flom.

2. Picking Cotton *and Recommended Viewing:* Jennifer Thompson and Ronald Cotton were the witness and the accused in perhaps the most well-known case of mistaken identification, which they recount in their book *Picking Cotton* (2009). As you read in the excerpted article above, Jennifer, a young, white college student, misidentified Ronald Cotton, an African-American man, as her rapist. As a result, Ronald Cotton spent years in prison before DNA evidence finally exonerated him.

Mistaken identification, such as Jennifer's, is the leading contributing factor in wrongful convictions. 60 Minutes reported on their case and also interviewed experts in eyewitness identifications—and authors in this chapter—Dr. Elizabeth Loftus and Dr. Gary Wells.

a. *Memory Test with Dr. Elizabeth Loftus:* Watch this 60 Minutes excerpt, "Manufacturing Memories," on memory tests and eyewitness identifications: https://www.youtube.com/watch?v=P3ldO66qrb0.

How did you do? Describe your experience in a few sentences.

b. *Line-Up Study with Dr. Gary Wells:* Watch this 60 Minutes excerpt, "How Accurate is Visual Memory," on line-ups and accurately identifying the perpetrator: https://www.youtube.com/watch?v=xtDt-THaH_o.

How did you do? Describe your experience in a few sentences.

c. *Review Questions:* Identify each of the following statements as either TRUE or FALSE regarding issues of eyewitness identification:

i. When the real perpetrator is not in the lineup, witnesses recognize this absence and don't choose anyone in the lineup.

ii. Eyewitness testimony is highly persuasive to jurors, even when someone is genuinely in error.

      iii. Recognition memory takes time, usually 5–10 minutes is common to determine the true perpetrator from a lineup.

      iv. Reinforcing language from law enforcement after a lineup, like "good, you picked the suspect", increases witness confidence in their selection.

      v. A memory can be altered by outside confirmation and information.

3. *Statutes and Law Enforcement Initiatives:*

    a. *Exercise, Read and Identify:* Fourteen state legislatures have adopted eyewitness identification procedures. West Virginia's statute, W.V. Code §§ 62-1E-1, -2, -3, is considered one of the more detailed statutes, like Ohio and North Carolina, and requires law enforcement use particular practices. Read West Virginia Code § 62-1E-1, § 62-1E-2, and § 62-1E-3, available at http://law.justia.com/codes/west-virginia/2014/chapter-62/article-1e/, and compare with Nevada Revised Statute § 171.1237, available at http://law.justia.com/codes/nevada/2013/chapter-171/statute-171.1237. In a paragraph, describe the similarities and differences.

    b. *Folder Shuffle Method, Recommended Viewing:* Leadership in law enforcement has taken the initiative in creating policies and procedures to govern the use of photo and live lineups, and show-ups. In 2009, the Commission on Accreditation for Law Enforcement Agencies (CALEA) issued Law Enforcement Accreditation Standards 42.2.11 and 42.2.12, which require that agencies have written directives for administering eyewitness identification procedures. In 2010, The International Association of Chiefs of Police (IACP) revised its model policy on eyewitness identification to take the latest research into account. In 2013, the Police Executive Research Forum (PERF) published the findings of its national survey on eyewitness identification police practices, concluding that most surveyed agencies lack written policies, and in 2013, the IACP and DOJ's Office of justice Programs released a report of the National Summit on Wrongful Convictions: Building a Systemic Approach to Prevent Wrongful Convictions. Among its 30 recommendations are best practices for eyewitness identification.

        The Wellesley Police Department in conjunction with the New England Innocence Project created a training video on the folder shuffle method—a recommended protocol for blind or blinded administration of a line-up by law enforcement: https://www.youtube.com/watch?v=i5a75NShfAc.

    c. *Review Questions:* Based on the readings, the *Folder Shuffle* video, and comparing the West Virginia and Nevada statutes, please provide a short answer for each of the following questions on best practices for law enforcement and line-ups.

      i. What are some proposed instructions to the eyewitness, and what is their purpose?

      ii. What is blind or blinded administration of a photo or live line-up?

      iii. What is a confidence statement?

      iv. What is the purpose of video-recording the identification procedure?

      v. Should the filler photos in the line-up match the suspect or the witness description of the perpetrator?

4. *Reflective Essay*: How do police protocols on eyewitness identifications intersect with race? Explain your answer in a one-page reflective essay.

5. *Cross-Racial Misidentifications, Recommended Listening:* According to the National Registry of Exonerations, "Assaults on white women by African-American men are a small minority of all sexual assaults in the United States, but they constitute half of sexual assaults with eyewitness misidentifications that led to exoneration. (The unreliability of cross-racial eyewitness identification also appears to have contributed to racial disparities in false convictions for other crimes, but to a lesser extent.)"

Listen to exoneree Cornelius Dupree describe his wrongful conviction due to a cross-racial misidentification on Season 2, Episode 12, We Are A Family: Stories From The 2017 Innocence Network Conference Part One, of *Wrongful Conviction with Jason Flom* (37:00–45:00): https://art19.com/shows/wrongful-conviction-with-jason-flom.

6. *Exercise, Read and Identify*: Read the transcript below of a real eyewitness identification:

    Q. Let me show you a few photographs if you don't care. Have you ever seen this guy before? {**picture one JIM BROWN**}
    A. Uh-uh {negative}

    Q. Or this guy? {**picture two, TITO LOPEZ**}
    A. No.

    Q. Does this vehicle look familiar? {**picture three**}
    A. Uh-uh {negative}

    Q. What about this guy here? {**picture four, MARTY WALKER**}
    A. No.

    Q. Did you know SANDRA COPPER?
    A. No.

    Q. Ever seen that guy before? {**picture five, JIM BROWN**}
    A. Uh-uh {negative} is that the same guy? He's been in trouble a lot?

    Q. He looks different in every picture doesn't he?
    A. I'm tellin' ya.

    Q. Yeah that is just him like a couple months apart.
    A. Wow.

    Q. Looks like two different people doesn't it?
    A. Heck yeah.

    Q. What about that gentleman? {**picture six, TIM SMITH**}

A. No.

Q. Or this guy? {**picture seven, ERIC SHAFFER JUNIOR**}

A. Uh-uh {negative}

Q. You said this guy had glasses on, it is possible that that's the guy that you saw? {**picture eight, ERIC SHAFFER SENIOR**}

A. Could be, I mean if you go back—if somebody went back to FBI Head-quarters and did a composite, and he had a big nose I can remember that too but I don't know.

Q. Yeah.

A. Side view I might be able to tell.

Q. Have you ever seen this lady here before? {**picture nine, HEIDI COPELAND**}

A. Uh-uh {negative}

Q. Is it possible that that could be the guy in the vehicle? {**picture ten, JIM BROWN**}

A. I was thinkin' he looked bigger but it could have been the way he was setting, like I said he was all laid back·with·his arm on the back of the seat.

Q. Just relaxed huh?

A. All I noticed was.... l know he was heavy, (inaudible) with me.

Q. Heavy set, glasses, driving back and forth from one spot to the other, wasn't in any way, shape or form trying to hide himself?

A. Uh-uh {negative}

Q. And if you don't recognize, believe me its fine, I just wanted to show you a couple pictures and ask you if it was possible, if it would be possible if it were this guy....

A. If any it would be this one {**picture of ERIC SHAFFER SR**} maybe that one {**picture ten, TITO LOPEZ**}
I doubt it though, this one looks more {**picture of ERIC SHAFFER SR**}.

Q. Okay.

A. I think, but seriously, I think if I seen the man's picture I'd be like...

Q. You would know right away that it was him....

A. Yeah.

Q .... because it really stuck out in your mind. That's another picture of that guy that had all the other {**picture eleven, BROWN**} see how....

A. Reminds me of those posters they have hanging this is a meth head and it shows the real pretty lady and it walks her down.... oh I am not saying he's on drugs, I don't know the guy but that's what it reminds me of.

Did the police officer follow best practices in interviewing the eyewitness to obtain the identification? Why or why not? Can you tell who the police suspect is?

7. *National Academy of Sciences Report on Eyewitness Identification:* In 2014, the National Academy of Sciences released their report *Identifying the Culprit: Assessing*

Eyewitness Identification. The Report contained the following recommendations: train law enforcement on vision and memory, implement double-blind lineup and photo array procedures, develop and use standardized witness instructions, document witness confidence judgments, and videotape the witness identification process. In the courtroom, the Report recommended: a judge make basic inquiries when eyewitness identification evidence is offered, judges make juries aware of prior identifications, experts on eyewitness memory and identifications be permitted, and jury instructions be given on eyewitness identifications.

Chapter Six

False Confessions

GARY: They used that vision statement for a *confession*.

And they wouldn't let me say anything besides how I would've done it. Anytime I tried to say anything else, they would just holler at me, and holler at me, and holler at me.

After I made the statement about my mom, I cried for about three minutes, and then I told them how I would have killed my father. And then I said—I *told* them—"This is just hypothetical. I have absolutely no memory of any of this."

The autopsies showed that everything I said in those statements was wrong. But nothing was written down, nothing was recorded. At the trial they said that I was never under arrest, I was free to go at any time, that I had voluntarily "chatted" with them for *twelve hours*, and then suddenly blurted out facts that only the killer would know.

—excerpt from *The Exonerated*, a play by Jessica Blank and Erik Jensen; recounting the false confession by exoneree Gary Gauger

A. Readings

Richard A. Leo, Steven A. Drizin, Peter J. Neufeld, Bradley R. Hall, and Amy Vatner, *Bringing Reliability Back In: False Confessions and Legal Safeguards in the Twenty-First Century*

2006 WIS. L. REV. 479, 479–86 (2006)

It was a crime that shocked the nation. In April 1989, a young woman was attacked while jogging in New York City's Central Park. She was dragged into a wooded area, beaten within an inch of her life, and raped. When her body was finally discovered, she had been beaten so severely that she had lost nearly 80 percent of her blood. Her identity was scrupulously guarded by authorities and the media. To most of the world, she was known only as the "Central Park Jogger."

Because the jogger's survival was very much in doubt, Manhattan North homicide detectives soon took over the investigation. They focused their attention on a large group of teenage boys who had been in the park that night creating mayhem. These boys had entered the park near 110th Street in Harlem and went on a rampage as they walked from north to south through the park, assaulting and attempting to rob bicyclists and joggers. Some of the boys finally ended up at the north end of the reservoir near Ninety-seventh Street where they hid and jumped several other joggers before fleeing at the sound of police sirens. Two of the boys, fifteen-year-olds Steven Lopez and Raymond Santana, did not flee and were taken into police custody. A third, fourteen-year-old Kevin Richardson, was apprehended after a short chase.

Lopez, Santana, and Richardson had been arrested and processed and were awaiting their release when officers at the Central Park Precinct were informed that a female jogger's body had been discovered in the park. This discovery led detectives to leap to the conclusion that the juveniles involved in the other assaults on joggers and bicyclists must have also assaulted the Central Park Jogger. Throughout the night and the next day, detectives interrogated Lopez, Santana, and Richardson and apprehended others whom they had named as accomplices. Antron McRay, age fifteen, was taken into custody at eleven o'clock the next morning, and Yusef Salaam, age fifteen, and Kharey Wise, age sixteen, were both brought in at ten o'clock that same night.

Ultimately, police obtained five confessions to the beating and rape of the Central Park Jogger. Four of the confessions—those of Wise, Santana, McCray, and Richardson—were captured on videotape by prosecutors. Although the confessions themselves were videotaped and most of the boys confessed on camera in the presence of their parents, the hours of interrogation preceding the confessions were not recorded. The fifth defendant, Salaam, only gave an oral confession because his mother arrived at the station and instructed him not to speak to police or prosecutors anymore without an attorney.

Precisely what happened before the confessions was a matter of great dispute both in pretrial motions and at trial. The boys and their parents claimed that the interrogations were highly coercive, alleging that officers slapped the boys, yelled and cursed at them, and called them liars. Several boys claimed they were told that they were being questioned as mere "witnesses" who would be released from custody if they confessed. At least one of the boys, Wise, claimed that police officers fed him details about the crime. The police officers denied using any coercive tactics, although one detective admitted that he lied to Salaam when he told him that his fingerprints would be found on the victim's jogging shorts. At the end of the pretrial hearing, which took nearly seven weeks, Judge Thomas Galligan found that the police detectives were more credible than the defense witnesses and ruled that the defendants' statements were voluntary, making them admissible at trial.

Based largely on these statements, all five defendants who confessed were convicted of participating in the rape of the Central Park Jogger and the assaults on several cyclists and other joggers. They were convicted despite the fact that DNA testing of semen, taken from a cervical swab of the jogger and found on a sock near where she was discovered, excluded all five boys as the source. All of the boys who went to trial were sentenced to between five and fifteen years in prison. Judge Galligan's decision to admit the confessions, and the boys' convictions and sentences, were later upheld on appeal.

In January 2002, nearly thirteen years after the attack on the jogger, a convict named Matias Reyes contacted authorities and informed them that he, acting alone, had raped the Central Park Jogger. Reyes was one of New York City's most notorious serial rapists. Between June 1989 and his apprehension in August of that year, Reyes terrorized the Upper East Side, raping four women, including a pregnant woman whom he killed after raping her in front of her children. In all of these attacks, Reyes acted alone. When Reyes's DNA matched DNA taken from semen recovered from the Central Park Jogger crime scene, the Manhattan District Attorney's Office (DA) launched a reinvestigation of the case.

The DA's office interviewed Reyes on several occasions. Reyes provided an accurate description of the assault and rape of the jogger. His story was rich in detail and included facts that none of the boys had mentioned. Unlike the boys, Reyes was clear about where the attack occurred, going so far as to draw a map of the area. Reyes described how he stalked the jogger at the 102nd Street traverse, how he was able to follow her because she was listening to a walkman, and how he picked up a stick off the road and struck her in the head. Reyes explained how the jogger had tried to run away after he dragged her off the road and how he caught, beat, and raped her in a second location. He told the investigators that he took her keys and planned to rob her apartment, but grew angry with her when she refused to tell him her address. Reyes also provided police with information that they did not know, admitting to a sexual assault of a second woman in the park just two days before the attack on the jogger. In his interviews with the DA's office and in an interview aired on national television, Reyes insisted that he did not know any of the boys who were convicted of the rape.

Reyes's emergence forced prosecutors to take a closer look at the boys' confessions. First, prosecutors noted that all of the boys minimized their involvement in the crime, a fact that added some weight to the defendants' claims at trial that they had been told they would be viewed as witnesses rather than perpetrators if they spoke about the crime. Second, when prosecutors compared the boys' confessions with each other, they found that the defendants' accounts differed on nearly "every major aspect of the crime—who initiated the attack, who knocked the victim down, who undressed her, who struck her, who held her, who raped her, what weapons were used in the course of the assault and when in the sequence of events the attack took place." Third, while some of what the defendants told authorities was consistent with the objectively known facts of the crime (for example, one defendant claimed the jogger wore a white shirt and a second claimed she was struck by a pipe, the kind of blunt object that could have caused her head injuries), most of the details in their statements were "not corroborated by, consistent with, or explanatory of objective, independent evidence," and some of what they said was just plain wrong. Significantly, none of the defendants correctly described where the attack on the jogger took place, a nonpublic piece of information that the true perpetrators surely would have known. All of the boys claimed the attack on the Central Park Jogger took place near the reservoir. Only Wise, in his second taped confession recorded after the police took him to the crime scene and prosecutors showed him crime scene photos, appeared to describe the crime scene.

In light of the credibility of Reyes's confession, the indisputable DNA link of Reyes to the crime, and the multiple problems with the boys' confessions, prosecutors conceded that the new evidence made it likely that the jury would have reached a different verdict. Accordingly, they supported the defendants' motions to vacate their convictions. On December 19, 2002, Judge Charles Tejada granted the motion and vacated all of the convictions of the original Central Park Jogger defendants.

In retrospect, perhaps it is not so surprising that all five Central Park Jogger defendants were erroneously convicted — in two separate jury trials — almost entirely on the basis of their confessions. Although the Central Park Jogger case remains one of the most staggering miscarriages of justice in modern history, it is not unique. There are now over 170 DNA exonerations of convictions, approximately 20 to 25 percent of which resulted in whole or in part from police-induced false confessions. Apart from the DNA exonerations, there are many more recently documented proven false confessions that have also led to wrongfully convicting the innocent. When courts fail to dismiss these false confession cases at the pretrial stage, the overwhelming majority of defendants will be wrongfully convicted. In a 1998 study of sixty false confessions, 73 percent of the false confessors whose cases went to trial were wrongly convicted; in a 2004 study of 125 false confessions, 81 percent of the false confessors whose cases went to trial were wrongfully convicted. These results are consistent with the findings of mock jury studies in experimental psychology literature.

Confessions are among the most powerful forms of evidence introduced in a court of law, even when they are contradicted by other case evidence and contain significant errors. This is because police, prosecutors, judges, jurors, and the media all tend to view confessions as self-authenticating and see them as dispositive evidence of guilt. Juries tend to discount the possibility of false confessions as unthinkable, if not impossible. False confessions are viewed as contrary to common sense, irrational, and self-destructive. Moreover, police-induced false confessions tend to be facially persuasive because police make sure the confessor includes "elective statements" such as crime scene details, expressions of remorse, the confessor's alleged motives for committing the offense, and acknowledgements of voluntariness.

Concerns with juror overreliance on confession evidence gave rise to a series of evolving rules designed to exclude unreliable confessions from being admitted at trial and prevent erroneous convictions. These doctrines, which developed both in the common law of evidence and under the Constitution, fell into two distinct sets of legal rules: the voluntariness rule and the corroboration rule. The voluntariness rule, which first developed at common law and is now a constitutional requirement, is premised in part on the idea that torture, threats of harm, promises of leniency, and other coercive police procedures used to obtain confessions could lead innocent suspects to confess. By barring interrogations that involved such tactics, courts sought to reduce the possibility of wrongful convictions based on false confessions. The corroboration rule, by contrast, requires that confessions must be corroborated by independent evidence to be admissible. This rule was implemented to serve three primary purposes: to prevent false confessions, to provide incentives to law enforcement to seek additional evidence, and to protect against jurors' tendency to view confession evidence uncritically (regardless of the circumstances under which a confession was given or the extent of corroboration).

Chris Smith, *Central Park Revisited*
New York Magazine, Oct. 21, 2002

New York in the spring of 1989 was a city of jangling nerves and rising fears. Crack was blighting whole families and neighborhoods. Violent-crime rates were rising for the third straight year, and homicides would set a record. On Wall Street, the mergers-and-acquisitions bubble was giving way to corporate scandals. A new buzzword, *underclass*, was emerging as the label for the seemingly intractable urban pathology spawned by poverty.

Race relations framed many of the media's big stories. The Reverend Al Sharpton was still loudly proclaiming that Tawana Brawley told the truth. Three white men convicted of chasing a 23-year-old black man, Michael Griffith, to his death on the Belt Parkway were beginning a contentious appeal.

And 1989 was a mayoral-election year. Ed Koch's shrillness was a central issue in a tight Democratic-primary campaign. His strongest rival, Manhattan borough president David Dinkins, was, not coincidentally, a black man with an anodyne personality. Racial tensions worsened in August, when 16-year-old Yusef Hawkins, a black kid lost in Bensonhurst, was attacked by racist white thugs, shot, and killed.

Beneath these volatile events churned the Central Park jogger case. The victim was white and middle-class and female, a promising young investment banker at Salomon Brothers with a Wellesley-Yale-Phi Beta Kappa pedigree. The suspects were black and Latino and male and much younger, some with dubious school records, some from fractured homes, all from Harlem. That the crime took place in Central Park, mythologized as the city's verdant, democratic refuge, played right into the theme of middle-class violation.

Almost from the moment the jogger was found, the Central Park case has existed as a vehicle for clashing worldviews: that held by the older, white, traditional-family-structure New York and that of the newer, nonwhite, poorer, marginalized New York. The furious reaction to the arrests and the trials illustrated how stark that cultural divide had become. And though the current legal breakthrough in the jogger case comes from the advent of cold, scientific DNA testing, the war for perceptions remains trapped in opposing views of the police: faith or mistrust.

* * *

The tabloids and TV news were predictably sensationalistic. But a presumption of guilt infected coverage everywhere: "A 28-year-old investment banker, jogging through Central Park, was attacked by a group of teenagers. They kicked and beat her in the head with a pipe and raped her. The teenagers, who were from East Harlem, were quickly arrested." That's from the *Times*, and it appeared on May 29, a little more than one month after the five were indicted.

* * *

Mike Sheehan, 54, one of the key detectives in the Central Park case, comes out of the city's tradition of street-savvy Irish cops. Michael Warren, 58, the lawyer who is trying to vindicate McCray, Richardson, and Santana, comes out of the sixties tradition of black radicalism. Both men, and the camps they represent, are tenacious in defending their sense of emotional innocence. "All this stuff about coercion really pisses me off," Sheehan says. "Do you honestly think that we—detectives with more than twenty years in, family men with pensions—would risk all of that so we could put words in the mouth of a 15-year-old kid? Absolutely not."

In Sheehan's account of the Central Park interrogations, the police officers never raised their voices, let alone their fists. The detectives were so concerned with proper procedure, Sheehan says, that they moved the suspects from the 20th to the 24th Precinct so that they would be videotaped according to regulations, in a designated "youth room." Coercion? Just the opposite, Sheehan says: When Santana spontaneously started describing the attack on the jogger, Sheehan says he told the boy to wait until Raymond Santana Sr. arrived.

Detective Tom McKenna was more active. The 21-year veteran falsely told Yusef Salaam that fingerprints had been found on the jogger's clothes. "Salaam looks at me and says, 'I was there, but I didn't rape her,'" McKenna recalls. "We are allowed, by law, to use guile and ruse, and we do. People only give things up when you tell 'em you got 'em. But to frame somebody and leave the right son-of-a-bitch out in the street? I'm irate anyone would infer that."

Nor has Sheehan lost any sleep over the convictions. "I used to lie awake at night thinking about cases we had over the years: *I hope to God we have the right guy*," he says. "That's your biggest fear: You never want to put an innocent person in jail.

Mother of God! I didn't worry much on this one. Because they're telling us where they were. *They* are telling *us*—the sequence may be off, but they're essentially telling us the same stuff. They remember a guy they beat and took his food, they remember hitting this guy running around the reservoir. They went through all of these things, each kid. And they also tell you about the jogger. And they place people, so you have a mental picture of where they were around this woman's body. And their parents are with them, not only in the interviews but in the videotape, for the record. That's enough for me. I'm satisfied."

Saul M. Kassin, Steven A. Drizin, Thomas Grisso, Gisli H. Gudjonsson, Richard A. Leo, and Allison D. Redlich, *Police-Induced Confessions: Risk Factors and Recommendations*

34 LAW & HUM. BEHAV. 3, 6–18 (2010)

Current Law Enforcement Objectives and Practices in the U.S.

American police typically receive brief instruction on interrogation in the academy and then more sustained and specialized training when promoted from patrol to detective. Interrogation is an evidence-gathering activity that is supposed to occur after detectives have conducted an initial investigation and determined, to a reasonable degree of certainty, that the suspect to be questioned committed the crime.

Sometimes this determination is reasonably based on witnesses, informants, or tangible evidence. Often, however, it is based on a clinical hunch formed during a pre-interrogation interview in which special "behavior-provoking" questions are asked (e.g., "What do you think should happen to the person who committed this crime?") and changes are observed in aspects of the suspect's behavior that allegedly betray lying (e.g., gaze aversion, frozen posture, and fidgety movements). Yet in laboratories all over the world, research has consistently shown that most commonsense behavioral cues are not diagnostic of truth and deception (DePaulo et al., 2003). Hence, it is not surprising as an empirical matter that laypeople on average are only 54% accurate at distinguishing truth and deception; that training does not produce reliable improvement; and that police investigators, judges, customs inspectors, and other professionals perform only slightly better, if at all—albeit with high levels of confidence (for reviews, see Bond & DePaulo, 2006; Meissner & Kassin, 2002; Vrij, 2008).

The purpose of interrogation is therefore not to discern the truth, determine if the suspect committed the crime, or evaluate his or her denials. Rather, police are trained to interrogate only those suspects whose culpability they "establish" on the basis of their initial investigation (Gordon & Fleisher, 2006; Inbau, Reid, Buckley, & Jayne, 2001). For a person under suspicion, this initial impression is critical because it determines whether police proceed to interrogation with a strong presumption of guilt which, in turn, predisposes an inclination to ask confirmatory questions, use persuasive tactics, and seek confessions (Hill, Memon, & McGeorge, 2008; Kassin, Goldstein, & Savitsky, 2003). In short, the single-minded purpose of interrogation is to elicit incriminating statements, admissions, and perhaps a full confession in an effort to secure the conviction of offenders (Leo, 2008).

Designed to overcome the anticipated resistance of individual suspects who are presumed guilty, police interrogation is said to be stress-inducing by design—structured to promote a sense of isolation and increase the anxiety and despair associated with denial relative to confession. To achieve these goals, police employ a number of tactics. As described in Inbau et al.'s (2001) *Criminal Interrogation and Confessions*, the most influential approach is the so-called Reid technique (named after John E. Reid who, along with Fred Inbau, developed this approach in the 1940s and published the first edition of their manual in 1962). First, investigators are advised to isolate the suspect in a small private room, which increases his or her anxiety and incentive to escape. A nine-step process then ensues in which an interrogator employs both negative and positive incentives. On one hand, the interrogator confronts the suspect with accusations of guilt, assertions that may be bolstered by evidence, real or manufactured, and refuses to accept alibis and denials. On the other hand, the interrogator offers sympathy and moral justification, introducing "themes" that minimize the crime and lead suspects to see confession as an expedient means of escape....

Miranda Warnings, Rights, and Waivers

One of the U.S. legal system's greatest efforts to protect suspects from conditions that might produce involuntary and unreliable confessions is found in the U.S. Supreme Court decision in *Miranda v. Arizona* (1966)....[23]

* * *

In a formal sense, whether one waives his or her rights voluntarily, knowingly, and intelligently does not have a direct bearing on the likelihood of false confessions (Kassin, 2005; White, 2001). The decision to waive one's rights in a police interrogation does not necessarily lead to a confession, much less a false confession. Nevertheless, research cited earlier regarding the lack of attentiveness of persons with disabilities and adolescents to long-range consequences suggests an increased risk that they would also comply with requests for a confession—whether true or false—to obtain the presumed short-term reward (e.g., release to go home). In addition, some studies have found that poor comprehension of Miranda warnings is itself predictive of a propensity to give false confessions (Clare & Gudjonsson, 1995; Goldstein et al., 2003). Sometimes this stems from low intelligence or a desire to comply; at other times it appears to be related to a naive belief that one's actual innocence will eventually prevail—a belief that is not confined to adolescents or persons with disabilities (Kassin & Norwick, 2004).

* * *

Corroboration Rules

The corroboration rule, which requires that confessions be corroborated by independent evidence, was the American take on the English rule known as the *corpus delicti* rule. *Corpus delicti* literally means "body of the crime"—that is, the material substance upon which a crime has been committed. The rule was founded at common law in England in the wake of Perry's Case, a seventeenth-century case in which a mother and two brothers were convicted and executed based upon a confession to a murder that was later discovered to be false when the supposed murder victim turned up alive (Leo et al., 2006). America's version of Perry's Case is the infamous 1819 case of Stephen and Jesse Boom, two brothers who were convicted and sentenced to death in Manchester, Vermont for the murder of their brother-in-law Russell Colvin. Fortunately for the two men, both of whom had confessed to the killing under intense pressure from authorities, their lawyers located Colvin alive before their hangings took place (Warden, 2005).

In American homicide cases, in response to Boom, the rule came to mean that no individual can be convicted of a murder without proof that a death occurred, namely the existence of a "dead body." As the rule evolved in the courts over time, it was applied to all crimes and required that before a confession could be admitted to a jury, prosecutors had to prove: (1) that a death, injury, or loss had occurred and (2) that criminal agency was responsible for that death, injury, or loss (Leo et al., 2006). The rule was designed to serve three purposes: to prevent false confessions,

---

23. 384 U.S. 436 (1966).

to provide incentives to police to continue to investigate after obtaining a confession, and to safeguard against the tendency of juries to view confessions as dispositive of guilt regardless of the circumstances under which they were obtained (Ayling, 1984).

* * *

In place of the *corpus delicti* rule, the Supreme Court, in two decisions released on the same day—*Smith*[24] and *Opper v. United States*[25] (1954)—announced a new rule, dubbed the trustworthiness rule, which requires corroboration of the confession itself rather than the fact that a crime occurred. Under the trustworthiness rule, which was adopted by several states, the government may not introduce a confession unless it provides "substantial independent evidence which would tend to establish the trustworthiness of the confession."

In theory, the trustworthiness standard is a marked improvement on the *corpus delicti* rule in its ability to prevent false confessions from entering the stream of evidence at trial. In practice, however, the rule has not worked to screen out false confessions. Because investigators sometimes suggest and incorporate crime details into a suspect's confession, whether deliberately or inadvertently, many false confessions appear highly credible to the secondhand observer. Without an electronic recording of the entire interrogation process, courts are thus left to decide a swearing contest between the suspect and the detective over the source of the details contained within the confession. Moreover, the quantum of corroboration in most jurisdictions that apply the trustworthiness doctrine is very low, allowing many unreliable confessions to go before the jury (Leo et al., 2006).

Rules Prohibiting Involuntary Confession

Until the late eighteenth century, out-of-court confessions were admissible as evidence even if they were the involuntary product of police coercion. In 1783, however, in *The King v. Warrickshall*,[26] an English Court recognized the inherent lack of reliability of involuntary confessions and established the first exclusionary rule:

> Confessions are received in evidence, or rejected as inadmissible, under a consideration whether they are or are not intitled [sic] to credit. A free and voluntary confession is deserving of the highest credit, because it is presumed to flow from the strongest sense of guilt ... but a confession forced from the mind by the flattery of hope, or by the torture of fear, comes in so questionable a shape ... that no credit ought to be given it; and therefore it should be rejected.

The basis for excluding involuntary confessions in *Warrickshall* was a concern that confessions procured by torture or other forms of coercion must be prohibited because of the risk that such tactics could cause an innocent person to confess. In

---

24. 348 U.S. 147 (1954).
25. 348 U.S. 84 (1954).
26. 168 Eng. Rep. 234 (K.B. 1783).

other words, involuntary confessions were to be prohibited because they were un-reliable....

The Supreme Court adopted a second rationale for excluding involuntary confessions in 1897, in *Bram v. United States*.[27] In Bram, the Court for the first time linked the voluntariness doctrine to the Fifth Amendment's provision that "no person shall be compelled in any criminal case to be a witness against himself." This privilege against self-incrimination was not rooted in a concern about the reliability of confessions. Rather, its origins were grounded in the rule of *nemo tenetur sepsum prodere* ("no one is bound to inform on himself"), a rule dating back to the English ecclesiastical courts which sought to protect individual free will from state intrusion (Leo et al., 2006). The rule of *nemo tenetur*, which was adopted in the colonies and incorporated into the Fifth Amendment, applied only to self-incriminating statements in court, and had never been applied to extrajudicial confessions. By mixing two unrelated voluntariness doctrines, *Bram* rewrote history and provoked considerable confusion by courts and academics alike (Wigmore, 1970). Still, it gave birth to a new basis for excluding involuntary confession evidence—the protection of individual free will.

A third basis for excluding involuntary confessions began to emerge in 1936, in the case of *Brown v. Mississippi*,[28] to deter unfair and oppressive police practices..., holding that confessions procured by physical abuse and torture were involuntary.... [The Supreme Court thus has] relied on different and sometimes conflicting rationales for excluding involuntary confessions throughout the twentieth century (Kamisar, 1963; White, 1998). It was not always clear which of the three justifications the Court would rely on when evaluating the voluntariness of a confession. Nevertheless, the Court did appear to designate certain interrogation methods—including physical force, threats of harm or punishment, lengthy or incommunicado questioning, solitary confinement, denial of food or sleep, and promises of leniency—as presumptively coercive and therefore unconstitutional (White, 2001). The Court also considered the individual suspect's personal characteristics, such as age, intelligence, education, mental stability, and prior contact with law enforcement, in determining whether a confession was voluntary. The template of the due process voluntariness test thus involved a balancing of whether police interrogation pressures, interacting with a suspect's personal dispositions, were sufficient to render a confession involuntary (Schulhofer, 1981).

* * *

The "totality of the circumstances" test, while affording judges flexibility in practice, has offered little protection to suspects. Without bright lines for courts to follow, and without a complete and accurate record of what transpired during the interrogation process, the end result has been largely unfettered and unreviewable discretion by judges. In practice, when judges apply the test, "they exclude only the most egregiously obtained confessions and then only haphazardly." The absence of a litmus

---

27. 168 U.S. 532 (1897).
28. 297 U.S. 278 (1936).

test has also encouraged law enforcement officers to push the envelope with respect to the use of arguably coercive psychological interrogation techniques. Unlike its sweeping condemnation of physical abuse in *Brown v. Mississippi*, the Court's overall attitude toward *psychological* interrogation techniques has been far less condemnatory. In particular, the Court's attitudes toward the use of maximization and minimization (Kassin & McNall, 1991) and the false evidence ploy and other forms of deception — techniques that have frequently been linked to false confessions (Kassin & Gudjonsson, 2004) — has been largely permissive.

* * *

Types of False Confessions

Although it is not possible to calculate a precise incidence rate, it is clear that false confessions occur in different ways and for different reasons. Drawing on the pages of legal history, and borrowing from social-psychological theories of influence, Kassin and Wrightsman (1985) proposed a taxonomy that distinguished among three types of false confession: voluntary, coerced-compliant, and coerced-internalized. This classification scheme has provided a useful framework for the study of false confessions and has since been used, critiqued, extended, and refined by others (Gudjonsson, 2003; Inbau et al., 2001; McCann, 1998; Ofshe & Leo, 1997a, 1997b).

Voluntary False Confessions

Sometimes innocent people have claimed responsibility for crimes they did not commit without prompting or pressure from police. This has occurred in several high-profile cases. After Charles Lindbergh's infant son was kidnapped in 1932, 200 people volunteered confessions. When "Black Dahlia" actress Elizabeth Short was murdered and her body mutilated in 1947, more than 50 men and women confessed. In the 1980s, Henry Lee Lucas in Texas falsely confessed to hundreds of unsolved murders, making him the most prolific serial confessor in history. In 2006, John Mark Karr volunteered a confession, replete with details, to the unsolved murder of young JonBenet Ramsey. There are a host of reasons why people have volunteered false confessions — such as a pathological desire for notoriety, especially in high-profile cases reported in the news media; a conscious or unconscious need for self-punishment to expiate feelings of guilt over prior transgressions; an inability to distinguish fact from fantasy due to a breakdown in reality monitoring, a common feature of major mental illness; and a desire to protect the actual perpetrator — the most prevalent reason for false admissions (Gudjonsson et al., 2004; Sigurdsson & Gudjonsson, 1996, 1997, 2001). Radelet, Bedau, and Putnam (1992) described one case in which an innocent man confessed to a murder to impress his girlfriend. Gudjonsson (2003) described another case in which a man confessed to murder because he was angry at police for a prior arrest and wanted to mislead them in an act of revenge.

Compliant False Confessions

In contrast to voluntary false confessions, compliant false confessions are those in which suspects are induced through interrogation to confess to a crime they did not commit. In these cases, the suspect acquiesces to the demand for a confession to escape a stressful situation, avoid punishment, or gain a promised or implied reward. Demonstrating the form of influence observed in classic studies of social influence (e.g., Asch, 1956; Milgram, 1974), this type of confession is an act of mere public compliance by a suspect who knows that he or she is innocent but bows to social pressure, often coming to believe that the short-term benefits of confession relative to denial outweigh the long-term costs. Based on a review of a number of cases, Gudjonsson (2003) identified some very specific incentives for this type of compliance—such as being allowed to sleep, eat, make a phone call, go home, or, in the case of drug addicts, feed a drug habit. The desire to bring the interview to an end and avoid additional confinement may be particularly pressing for people who are young, desperate, socially dependent, or phobic of being locked up in a police station. The pages of legal history are filled with stories of compliant false confessions. In the 1989 Central Park jogger case described earlier, five teenagers confessed after lengthy interrogations. All immediately retracted their confessions but were convicted at trial and sent to prison—only to be exonerated 13 years later (*People of the State of New York v. Kharey Wise et al.*, 2002).[29]

Internalized False Confessions

In the third type of false confession, innocent but malleable suspects, told that there is incontrovertible evidence of their involvement, come not only to capitulate in their behavior but also to believe that they may have committed the crime in question, sometimes confabulating false memories in the process. Gudjonsson and MacKeith (1982) argued that this kind of false confession occurs when people develop such a profound distrust of their own memory that they become vulnerable to influence from external sources. Noting that the innocent confessor's belief is seldom fully internalized, Ofshe and Leo (1997a) have suggested that the term "persuaded false confession" is a more accurate description of the phenomenon. The case of 14-year-old Michael Crowe, whose sister Stephanie was stabbed to death in her bedroom, illustrates this type of persuasion. After a series of interrogation sessions, during which time police presented Crowe with compelling false physical evidence of his guilt, he concluded that he was a killer, saying: "I'm not sure how I did it. All I know is I did it." Eventually, he was convinced that he had a split personality—that "bad Michael" acted out of a jealous rage while "good Michael" blocked the incident from memory. The charges against Crowe were later dropped when a drifter in the neighborhood that night was found with Stephanie's blood on his clothing (Drizin & Colgan, 2004).

Relevant Core Principles of Psychology

Earlier we reviewed the tactics of a modern American interrogation and the ways in which the U.S. Supreme Court has treated these tactics with respect to the voluntariness and admissibility of the confessions they elicit. As noted, the goal of interrogation is to alter a suspect's decision making by increasing the anxiety associated with denial and reducing the anxiety associated with confession.

---

29. 752 N.Y.S.2d 837 (2002).

Long before the first empirical studies of confessions were conducted, the core processes of relevance to this situation were familiar to generations of behavioral scientists. Dating back to Thorndike's (1911) law of effect, psychologists have known that people are highly responsive to reinforcement and subject to the laws of conditioning, and that behavior is influenced more by perceptions of short-term than long-term consequences. Of distal relevance to a psychological analysis of interrogation are the thousands of operant animal studies of reinforcement schedules, punishment, appetitive, avoidance, and escape learning, as well as behavioral modification applications in clinics, schools, and workplaces. Looking through this behaviorist lens, it seems that interrogators have sometimes shaped suspects to confess to particular narrative accounts of crimes like they were rats in a Skinner box (see Herrnstein, 1970; Skinner, 1938).

More proximally relevant to an analysis of choice behavior in the interrogation room are studies of human decision making in a behavioral economics paradigm. A voluminous body of research has shown that people make choices that they think will maximize their well-being given the constraints they face, making the best of the situation they are in—what Herrnstein has called the "matching law" (Herrnstein, Rachlin, & Laibson, 1997). With respect to a suspect's response to interrogation, studies on the discounting of rewards and costs show that people tend to be impulsive in their orientation, preferring outcomes that are immediate rather than delayed, with delayed outcomes depreciating over time in their subjective value (Rachlin, 2000). In particular, animals and humans clearly prefer delayed punishment to immediate aversive stimulation (Deluty, 1978; Navarick, 1982). These impulsive tendencies are especially evident in juvenile populations and among cigarette smokers, alcoholics, and other substance users.

Rooted in the observation that people are inherently social beings, a second set of core principles is that individuals are highly vulnerable to influence from change agents who seek their compliance. Of direct relevance to an analysis of interrogation are the extensive literatures on attitudes and persuasion (Petty & Cacioppo, 1986), informational and normative influences (e.g., Asch, 1956; Sherif, 1936), the use of sequential request strategies, as in the foot-in-the-door effect (Cialdini, 2001), and the gradual escalation of commands, issued by figures of authority, to effectively obtain self- and other-defeating acts of obedience (Milgram, 1974). Conceptually, Latane's (1981) social impact theory provides a predictive mathematical model that can account for the influence of police interrogators—who bring *power*, *proximity*, and *number* to bear on their exchange with suspects (for a range of social psychological perspectives on interrogation, see Bem, 1966; Davis & O'Donahue, 2004; Zimbardo, 1967).

A third set of core principles consists of the "seven sins of memory" that Schacter (2001) identified from cognitive and neuroscience research—a list that includes memory transience, misattribution effects, suggestibility, and bias. When Kassin and Wrightsman (1985) first identified coerced-internalized or coerced-persuaded false confessions, they were puzzled. At the time, existing models of memory could not account for the phenomenon whereby innocent suspects would come to internalize responsibility for crimes they did not commit and confabulate memories about these nonevents. These cases occur when a suspect is dispositionally or situationally rendered vulnerable to manipulation and the interrogator then misrepresents the evidence, a common ploy. In light of a now extensive research literature on misinformation effects and the creation of illusory beliefs and memories (e.g., Loftus, 1997, 2005), experts can now better grasp the process by which people come to accept guilt for a crime they did not commit as well as the conditions under which this may occur (*see* Kassin, 2008).

Situational Risk Factors

Among the situational risk factors associated with false confessions, three will be singled out: interrogation time, the presentation of false evidence, and minimization. These factors are highlighted because of the consistency in which they appear in cases involving proven false confessions.

Physical Custody and Isolation

To ensure privacy and control, and to increase the stress associated with denial in an incommunicado setting, interrogators are trained to remove suspects from their familiar surroundings and question them in the police station—often in a special interrogation room. Consistent with guidelines articulated by Inbau et al. (2001), most interrogations are brief. Observational studies in the U.S. and Britain have consistently shown that the vast majority of interrogations last approximately from 30 minutes up to 2 hours. In a recent self-report survey, 631 North American police investigators estimated from their experience that the mean length of a typical interrogation is 1.60 hours. Consistent with cautionary advice from Inbau against exceeding 4 hours in a single session, these same respondents estimated on average that their longest interrogations lasted 4.21 hours (Kassin et al., 2007). Suggesting that time is a concern among practitioners, one former Reid technique investigator has defined interrogations that exceed 6 hours as "coercive" (Blair, 2005). In their study of 125 proven false confessions, Drizin and Leo (2004) thus found, in cases in which interrogation time was recorded, that 34% lasted 6–12 hours, that 39% lasted 12–24 hours, and that the mean was 16.3 hours.

* * *

Presentations of False Evidence

Once suspects are isolated, interrogators, armed with a strong presumption of guilt, seek to communicate that resistance is futile. This begins the confrontation process, during which interrogators exploit the psychology of inevitability to drive suspects into a state of despair. Basic research shows that once people see an outcome as inevitable, cognitive and motivational forces conspire to promote their acceptance, compliance with, and even approval of the outcome (Aronson, 1999). In the case of interrogation, this process also involves interrupting the suspect's denials, overcoming objections, and refuting alibis. At times, American police will overcome a suspect's denials by presenting supposedly incontrovertible evidence of his or her guilt (e.g., a fingerprint, blood or hair sample, eyewitness identification, or failed polygraph)—

even if that evidence does not exist. In the U.S., it is permissible for police to outright lie to suspects about the evidence (Frazier v. Cupp, 1969)—a tactic that is recommended in training (Inbau et al., 2001), and occasionally used (Kassin et al., 2007; Leo, 1996b).

Yet basic psychological research warns of the risk of this manipulation. Over the years, across a range of sub-disciplines, basic research has revealed that misinformation renders people vulnerable to manipulation. To cite but a few highly recognized classics in the field, experiments have shown that presentations of false information—via confederates, witnesses, counterfeit test results, bogus norms, false physiological feedback, and the like—can substantially alter subjects' visual judgments (Asch, 1956; Sherif, 1936), beliefs (Anderson, Lepper, & Ross, 1980), perceptions of other people (Tajfel, Billig, Bundy, & Flament, 1971), behaviors toward other people (Rosenthal & Jacobson, 1968), emotional states (Schachter & Singer, 1962), physical attraction (Valins, 1966), self-assessments (Crocker, Voelkl, Testa, & Major, 1991), memories for observed and experienced events (Loftus, 2005), and even certain medical outcomes, as seen in studies of the placebo effect (Brown, 1998; Price, Finniss, & Benedetti, 2008). Scientific evidence for human malleability in the face of misinformation is broad and pervasive.

* * *

Minimization: Promises Implied But Not Spoken

In addition to thrusting the suspect into a state of despair by the processes of confrontation, interrogators are trained to minimize the crime through "theme development," a process of providing moral justification or face-saving excuses, making confession seem like an expedient means of escape. Interrogators are thus trained to suggest to suspects that their actions were spontaneous, accidental, provoked, peer-pressured, drug-induced, or otherwise justifiable by external factors. In the Central Park jogger case, every boy gave a false confession that placed his cohorts at center stage and minimized his own involvement (e.g., 16-year-old Kharey Wise said he felt pressured by peers)—and each said afterward that he thought he would go home after confessing based on statements made by police.

Minimization tactics that imply leniency may well lead innocent people who feel trapped to confess. Two core areas of psychology compel this conclusion. The first concerns the principle of reinforcement. As noted earlier, generations of basic behavioral scientists, dating back to Thorndike (1911), and formalized by Skinner (1938), have found that people are highly responsive to reinforcement and the perceived consequences of their behavior. More recent studies of human decision making have added that people are particularly influenced by outcomes that are immediate rather than delayed, the latter depreciating over time in their subjective value (Rachlin, 2000). The second core principle concerns the cognitive psychology of pragmatic implication. Over the years, researchers have found that when people read text or hear speech, they tend to process information "between the lines" and recall not what was stated per se, but what was pragmatically implied. Hence, people who read that "The burglar goes to the house" often mistakenly recall later that the burglar actually broke into the house; those who hear that "The flimsy shelf weakened under the weight of the books" often mistakenly recall that the shelf actually broke. These findings indicate that pragmatic inferences can change the meaning of a communication, leading listeners to infer something that is "neither explicitly stated nor necessarily implied" (Brewer, 1977).

Douglas Starr, *The Interview: Do Police Interrogation Techniques Produce False Confessions?*
THE NEW YORKER, Dec. 9, 2013

Last winter, I signed up for a basic Reid & Associates training course, in Boston. It lasted three days and cost five hundred and eighty dollars. There were about forty people in the class—mostly police officers, federal agents, and private security workers. The instructor, Lou Senese, joined the firm in 1972, shortly after he graduated from college, and is now a vice-president. A middle-aged Chicagoan who resembles a less edgy Dan Ackroyd with glasses, he has the manner of an affable salesman. He mixed lessons in interrogation with homespun stories about how he used his training to outwit a car dealer, and how his daughters used it to manipulate him. The hallmark of lying is anxiety, he said, and interviewing therefore involves watching for signs of anxiety and occasionally causing it.

The Reid Technique begins with the Behavior Analysis Interview, in which you determine whether the suspect is lying. The interview has its roots in polygraph testing, and involves asking a series of nonthreatening questions to get a sense of the suspect's baseline behavior, and then following up with more loaded questions. Such "behavior-provoking questions" might include "What kind of punishment should they give to the person who committed this crime?" You can also imply that you have evidence, a technique called "baiting." You might say, "We're in the process of analyzing evidence from the crime scene. Is there any reason that your DNA would turn up there?"

Senese asked the class, "What do you think is more important, verbal or nonverbal behavior?" Intuitively, we responded, "Nonverbal." "Yeah," he said. "That's the whole ballgame right there." He told us that a video of an interview without sound would be more likely to reveal lying than one that included the audio. He showed us footage of a dark-haired woman being questioned about having changed her prescription for oxycodone from ten pills to forty. She gave equivocal answers, touched her face, and cast her eyes down and to the left. "I say that's deceptive," Senese pronounced. In another video, a bearded bank-robbery suspect sighed and shrugged while giving meandering answers. A teen-ager accused of setting fire to his family's house responded with details that were oddly specific—such as arriving at school at 7:49 A.M.—while picking at his sock, jiggling his foot, and touching his cheek. When the kid paused to rub his eye, Senese turned and shot us a look.

If you decide that the suspect is lying, you leave the room and wait for five minutes. Then you return with an official-looking folder. "I have in this folder the results of our investigation," you say. You remain standing to establish your dominance. "After reviewing our results, we have no doubt that you committed the crime. Now, let's sit down and see what we can do to work this out."

The next phase—Interrogation—involves prodding the suspect toward confession. Whereas before you listened, now you do all the talking. If the suspect denies the accusation, you bat it away. "There's absolutely no doubt that this happened," you say. "Now let's move forward and see what we can do." If he asks to see the folder, you say no. "There'll be time for that later. Now let's focus on clearing this whole thing up."

"Never allow them to give you denials," Senese told us. "The key is to shut them up." Having headed off denials, you steer the subject toward a confession by offering a face-saving alternative. The process is called "minimization"—downplaying the moral consequences of the crime without mentioning the legal ones. In the case of the woman who tampered with her oxycodone prescription, you can suggest that the dentist did not give her enough pain pills and that she only wanted to save a trip to the pharmacy. "If you were a drug addict, you wouldn't have changed the prescription to forty—you would have changed it to a hundred!" Senese's 2005 book "Anatomy of Interrogation Themes" lists more than two thousand such excuses, in cases ranging from identity theft to murder. No matter how repugnant the crime, he told us, you can come up with a rationalization that makes it easier for the suspect to admit it. The standard Reid Technique manual, first published in 1962 and now in its fifth edition, suggests a way an interviewer can minimize rape:

> Joe, no woman should be on the street alone at night looking as sexy as she did. Even here today, she's got on a low-cut dress that makes visible damn near all of her breasts. That's wrong! It's too much temptation for any normal man. If she hadn't gone around dressed like that you wouldn't be in this room now.

You can further lower barriers to confession by presenting the crime as the lesser of two evils. Was this your idea or did your buddies talk you into it? Did you use that money for drugs or to help feed your kids?

You watch for reactions from the suspect. Averted eyes and folded arms tell you that he is shutting you out; facing you with an open posture says that he's listening. You expand on themes that trigger the right response. It can take minutes or hours. You might even lie: "Why were your fingerprints found on that gun?"

When the suspect finally admits to the crime, you praise him for owning up and press for corroborating details. Then you work together to convert the admission into a full, written confession. If he seems to have trouble remembering the details, you can present multiple-choice questions. Where did you enter the house: the front, the back, through a window? As a finishing touch, you introduce some trivial mistakes into the document, which the suspect will correct and initial. That will show the court that the suspect understood what he was signing.

After three days of Reid training, my classmates and I, newly versed in the subtleties of body language, gestured carefully in the hall and elevators, lest we unintentionally give something away. At the end, Senese gave us our certificates and left us with some closing remarks.

"It's been a real pleasure to teach you," he said. "I can honestly say this is the smartest and best group I've ever had." He sniffed, looked down, picked some lint off his shirt, crossed his arms—and got a laugh. From what he had taught us, we knew he was lying.

Thirty-five years ago, a postdoctoral fellow in psychology named Saul Kassin began researching the psychological factors that affect jury decisions. He noticed that whenever a confession was involved, every juror voted guilty. Alibis and fingerprints didn't matter in these cases. Kassin read the U.S. Supreme Court's 1966 Miranda decision and found that it repeatedly cites the Reid Technique manual as the most authoritative source on American interrogation techniques. When he bought the manual, he says, "my first impression was, my God, this reads like a bad psychology textbook. It was filled with assertions with no empirical proof."

Today, Kassin has appointments at Williams College, in Massachusetts, and at John Jay College of Criminal Justice, in New York, and is widely regarded as a leading expert on false confessions. He believes that the Reid Technique is inherently coercive. The interrogator's refusal to listen to a suspect's denials creates feelings of hopelessness, which are compounded by the fake file and by lies about the evidence. At this point, short-term thinking takes over. Confession opens something of an escape hatch, so it is only natural that some people choose it.

In the mid-nineteen-nineties, Kassin devised an experiment to explore how easy it was to induce false confessions. Two students would sit at a table with a computer. One student, an accomplice of the researchers, would read individual letters from a chart for the other to type, at varying speeds. The experimenter would warn the students not to hit the Alt key—hitting it would cause the computer to crash. The computer was programmed to crash sixty seconds after the experiment began, and the experimenter would angrily ask the participants if they had hit the forbidden key. Ripping a page out of his notebook, he'd scribble an admission and demand that the student sign it. These conditions gave a baseline confession rate, after which various Reid tactics were used to see which ones provoked additional false confessions.

The first time Kassin tried the experiment, with seventy-five participants, the students were so intimidated by the accusatory question that about a quarter of them signed the confession. When the experimenter added false incrimination—instructing the accomplice to say that he had seen the subject hit the Alt key—the rate of false confession nearly doubled. When another of the experiment's accomplices, posing as a fellow-student, asked what had happened, the subjects put the blame on themselves, saying things like "I hit the wrong button" rather than "They accused me of hitting the wrong button." Some even confabulated details, such as "I hit it with the side of my hand." Not only had they internalized their guilt; they had come up with a story to explain it. Although Kassin made sure to inform the students afterward that the experiment was a hoax, they sometimes replied, "You're just trying to make me feel better."

* * *

The Reid interrogation technique is predicated upon an accurate determination, during Behavioral Analysis, of whether the suspect is lying. Here, too, social scientists find reason for concern. Three decades of research have shown that nonverbal signals, so prized by the Reid trainers, bear no relation to deception. In fact, people have little more than coin-flipping odds of guessing if someone is telling the truth, and numerous surveys have shown that police do no better....

Such studies suggest that a troubling chain of events can easily take place in the mind of an interrogator. During the Behavioral Analysis Interview, the detective begins to form an impression, based in part on the suspect's body language. The impression could be wrong, but the detective, sensitized to those responses, notices them more and pays less attention to others—an instance of confirmation bias. Increasingly convinced that he's dealing with a liar, the detective questions more aggressively, and this, in turn, triggers more nervousness. The behaviors create a feedback loop, ratcheting up the suspicion and anxiety to the point where the detective feels duty-bound to get a confession. Psychologists call this cycle the "Othello error," for the tragic escalation of accusation and fear that leads Othello to kill Desdemona.

Gregg McCrary, a retired F.B.I. agent, told me that Reid-style training creates a tendency to see lies where they may not exist, with an unhealthy amount of confidence in that judgment. "They just assume they're interviewing the guilty guy," he said.

* * *

[Example of another way to interrogate (PEACE):]

In 1990, after a flurry of false-confession scandals in Britain, the government appointed a commission of detectives, academics, and legal experts to develop an interview method that would reflect up-to-date psychological research. After two years' work, the commission unveiled their technique, called PEACE, for Preparation and Planning, Engage and Explain, Account, Closure, Evaluate. Training was provided for police departments throughout England and Wales, starting with major-crimes units. By 2001, every police officer in England and Wales had received a basic level of instruction in the method.

The method differed dramatically from previous practices. Police were instructed not to try to obtain confessions but to use the interview as a way to gather evidence and information, almost as a journalist would. They were to focus on content rather than on nonverbal behavior, and were taught not to pay attention to anxiety, since it does not correlate with lying. Instead, police were trained to ask open-ended questions to elicit the whole story, and then go back over the details in a variety of ways to find inconsistencies. For the suspect, lying creates a cognitive load—it takes energy to juggle the details of a fake story. Part of the process involved thorough preparation: police learned to spend hours drawing diagrams of the route they hoped an interview would take. Bluffing about evidence was prohibited. "We were not allowed to lie, coerce, or minimize," Andy Griffiths, a detective superintendent with the Sussex Police Department, told me. Their job was simply to get as much information as possible, which, along with corroborating evidence, would either inculpate the suspect or set him free.

Originally a street cop, Griffiths earned a Ph.D. in criminal-justice studies at the University of Portsmouth. He spent last fall at John Jay College of Criminal Justice.

He showed me a video of British police using the PEACE method to interview a man named David Chenery-Wickens. In January, 2008, Chenery-Wickens, of East Sussex, was accused of murdering his wife, Diane, a makeup artist who worked for the BBC. Two days after her disappearance, he had reported her missing. He told the police that the two had taken the train into London, but she never showed up for the return trip home. He thought she might have run away to Spain.

The officer leading the interview, Detective Constable Gary Pattison, was respectful and polite, asking open-ended questions about Diane's disappearance. He gave the suspect plenty of time to talk. After an hour and a half, when he got all the information that Chenery-Wickens was willing to give, Pattison ended the interview.

A few days later, they reconvened. Chenery-Wickens, a lumpy blond guy in a light-colored sweater and faded blue jeans, sat comfortably in his seat, facing the officers in an open and relaxed posture. ("You can see what a load of bunkum this body-language stuff is," Griffiths said.) As the questions wore on and Pattison kept reexamining certain parts of the story, Chenery-Wickens found it increasingly difficult to keep his facts straight—not because of anxiety, it seemed, but because of the simple cognitive challenge. For example, he had previously denied visiting a nearby town on a certain date and selling his wife's jewelry. Pattison showed him a parking ticket from that date.

"Something is not right, David," Pattison said. "Please help me, David, because I'm struggling with this." Chenery-Wickens spent several minutes trying to prevaricate, and finally said, "I'm baffled. I'm really baffled."

Later in the interview, they discussed David's claim that Diane had sent him text messages while he was on a homeward-bound train from London. Cell-phone records revealed that both phones had been on the train at the same time. Pattison inquired about the issue at length. He spoke slowly, as Chenery-Wickens's explanations for how his wife's phone came to be on the same train became hollower and hollower. Griffiths stopped the video and said, "As you can see, this guy is digging a bigger and bigger hole. And this is what is presented to the jury." At no point did Pattison directly accuse Chenery-Wickens of murder or attempt to get him to confess. But the accumulation of lies and evidence condemned him. He was found guilty of murder and sentenced to eighteen years.

Samuel R. Gross, Kristen Jacoby, Daniel J. Matheson, Nicholas Montgomery, and Sujata Patil, *Exonerations in the United States 1989 through 2003*

95 J. Crim. L. & Criminology 523, 544–46 (2005)

False Confessions: Youth and Mental Disability

In fifty-one of the 340 exonerations between 1989 and 2004—15%—the defendants confessed to crimes they had not committed. In most of these cases it is apparent that the false confessions were coerced by the police. One defendant falsely confessed to larceny; nine falsely confessed to rape; and forty-one—80%—falsely confessed to murder. Twenty percent of murder exonerations involve false confessions, but only 7% of rape exonerations, and that comparison understates the difference. Five of the false confessions in rape exonerations—more than half of the total—were in the Central Park jogger case in New York City in 1989. But when those confessions were taken the investigation was being treated as a homicide because the victim was in a coma from her injuries and was expected to die.

False confessions don't come cheap. They are usually the product of long, intensive interrogations that eventually frighten or deceive or break the will of a suspect to the point where he will admit to a terrible crime that he did not commit. Some of these interrogations stretch over days and involve relays of police interrogators. Not surprisingly, this expensive procedure is generally reserved for the most serious cases where there is no other evidence sufficient to convict—which usually means a murder with no surviving eyewitnesses.

False confessions are heavily concentrated among the most vulnerable groups of innocent defendants. Thirty-three of the exonerated defendants were under eighteen at the time of the crimes for which they were convicted, and fourteen of these innocent juveniles falsely confessed—42%, compared to 13% of older exonerees. Among the youngest of these juvenile exonerees—those aged twelve to fifteen   69% (9/13) confessed to homicides (and one rape) that they did not commit.

False confessions are even more prevalent among exonerees with mental disabilities. Our data indicate that sixteen of the 340 exonerees were mentally retarded; 69% of them—over two thirds—falsely confessed. Another ten exonerees appear to have been suffering from mental illnesses; seven of them falsely confessed. Among all other exonerees (some of who may also have suffered from mental disabilities of which we are unaware) the false confession rate was 11% (33/313). Overall, 55% of all the false confessions we found were from defendants who were under eighteen, or mentally disabled, or both. Among adult exonerees without known mental disabilities, the false confession rate was 8% (23/272). See Table 6.1.

Table 6.1: False Confessions by Age and Mental Disability

Age and Mental Status of the Exonerated Defendants	Proportion Who Falsely Confessed
Juveniles—under 18 at time of crime (33)	42%
12–15 year olds (13)	69%
16–17 year olds (20)	25%
Mentally Ill or Mentally Retarded (26)	69%
Adults Without Known Mental Disabilities (272)	8%

False confessions have more impact on false convictions than their numbers suggest, since quite often they implicate other innocent people in addition to the confessor.

Terry Harrington, a seventeen-year old African American charged with killing a white retired police captain, did not confess to murder in Iowa in 1978—but his sixteen-year-old friend Kevin Hughes did, and that confession, which was later repeatedly retracted, led to false murder convictions for Harrington and his co-defendant Curtis McGhee. Hughes was never prosecuted. Similarly, in 1978 Paula Gray, a seventeen-year-old borderline retarded girl, falsely confessed to participating in a double murder and rape in Chicago, and implicated four innocent men. After she recanted, she was prosecuted for rape, murder and perjury, and sentenced to fifty years in prison. The four men she named were also all convicted, and two were sentenced to death. All five were exonerated after DNA testing cleared the men of the rape; the real killers have since been identified, linked to the rape by DNA, and confessed.

Brandon L. Garrett, *The Substance of False Confessions*
62 Stan. L. Rev. 1051, 1052–1118 (2010)

False confessions present a puzzle: How could innocent people convincingly confess to crimes they knew nothing about? For decades, commentators doubted that a crime suspect would falsely confess. For example, John Henry Wigmore wrote in his 1923 evidence treatise that false confessions were "scarcely conceivable" and "of the rarest occurrence" and that "[n]o trustworthy figures of authenticated instances exist...." That understanding has changed dramatically in recent years, as, at the time of this writing, postconviction DNA testing has exonerated 252 convicts, forty-two of whom falsely confessed to rapes and murders. There is a new awareness among scholars, legislators, courts, prosecutors, police departments, and the public that innocent people falsely confess, often due to psychological pressure placed upon them during police interrogations. Scholars increasingly study the psychological techniques that can cause people to falsely confess and have documented how such techniques were used in instances of known false confessions.

This Article takes a different approach by examining the substance of false confessions, including what was said during interrogations and how confessions were litigated at trial. Doing so sheds light on the phenomenon of confession contamination. Police may, intentionally or not, prompt the suspect on how the crime happened so that the suspect can then parrot back an accurate-sounding narrative....

* * *

In the cases studied here, innocent people not only falsely confessed, but they also offered surprisingly rich, detailed, and accurate information. Exonerees told police much more than just "I did it." In all cases but two (ninety-seven percent—or thirty-six of the thirty-eight—of the exonerees for whom trial or pretrial records could be obtained), police reported that suspects confessed to a series of specific details concerning how the crime occurred. Often those details included reportedly "inside information" that only the rapist or murderer could have known. We now know that each of these people was innocent and was not at the crime scene. Where did those details, recounted at length at trial and recorded in confession statements, come from? We often cannot tell what happened from reading the written records. In many cases, however, police likely disclosed those details during interrogations by telling exonerees how the crime happened. Police may not have done so intentionally or recklessly; the study materials do not provide definitive information about the state of mind of the officers. Police may have been convinced the suspect was guilty and may not have realized that the interrogation had been mishandled.

An illustrative case is that of Jeffrey Deskovic, a seventeen-year-old when he was convicted of rape and murder. Deskovic was a classmate of the fifteen-year-old victim, had attended her wake, and was eager to help solve the crime. Deskovic spoke to police many times and was interrogated for hours over multiple sessions, including a session in which police had a tape recorder, but turned it on and off, only recording thirty-five minutes. During one discussion, he "supposedly drew an accurate diagram," which depicted details concerning "three discrete crime scenes" which were not ever made public. He never actually confessed to raping or murdering the victim, but he offered other details, including that the victim suffered a blow to the temple, that he tore her clothes, struggled with her, held his hand over her mouth, and "may have left it there a little too long." In his last statement, which ended with him in a fetal position and crying uncontrollably, he reportedly told police that he had "hit her in the back of the head with a Gatoraid [sic] bottle that was lying on the path." Police testified that, after hearing this, the next day they conducted a careful search and found a Gatorade bottle cap at the crime scene.

The trial transcripts highlight how central these admissions were to the State's case. DNA tests conducted by the FBI laboratory before the trial excluded Deskovic, providing powerful evidence that he was not the perpetrator. The district attorney asked the jury to ignore that DNA evidence, speculating that perhaps the victim was "sexually active" and "romantically linked to somebody else" who she had sexual relations with shortly before her rape and murder. After all, "[s]he grew up in the eighties." There was no investigation or DNA testing conducted to support this conjecture, either by the prosecution or the defense.

Instead, the district attorney emphasized in closing arguments the reliability of Deskovic's statements, noting that after he told police about the Gatorade bottle, "it was found there," and this was a heavy weapon, "not a small little bottle." Detectives "did not disclose any of their observations or any of the evidence they recovered from Jeffrey nor, for that matter, to anyone else they interviewed." They kept their investigative work nonpublic:

> for the simple reason ... that [if a suspect] revealed certain intimate details that only the true killer would know, having said those, and be arrested could not then say, "Hey, they were fed to me by the police, I heard them as rumors, I used my common sense, and it's simply theories."

The district attorney told the jury to reject the suggestion that Deskovic was fed facts, stating, "Ladies and gentlemen, it doesn't wash in this case, it just doesn't wash."

Deskovic was convicted of rape and murder and served more than fifteen years of a sentence of fifteen years to life. In 2006, new DNA testing again excluded him, but also matched the profile of a murder convict who subsequently confessed and pleaded guilty. Now that we know Deskovic is innocent, how could he have known those "intimate details"? The District Attorney's post-exoneration inquiry noted:

> Much of the prosecution's effort to persuade the jury that Deskovic's statements established his guilt hinged on the argument that Deskovic knew things about the crime that only the killer could know.... Given Deskovic's innocence, two scenarios are possible: either the police (deliberately or inadvertently) communicated this information directly to Deskovic or their questioning at the high school and elsewhere caused this supposedly secret information to be widely known throughout the community.

This confession was contaminated, either by police leaking facts or feeding them. Given the level of specificity reportedly provided by Deskovic, the second and more troubling possibility, that the officers disclosed facts to him, seems far more likely. Yet during the trial, the police and the prosecutor not only denied having told Deskovic those facts, such as the presence of the Gatorade bottle cap and the depiction of the crime scene, but were emphatic they did not leak those facts to the media or to anyone else, such as other high school students interviewed. Whether the police acted inadvertently or intentionally, in hindsight we know that they provided an inaccurate account. Deskovic has commented, "[b]elieving in the criminal justice system and being fearful for myself, I told them what they wanted to hear." Deskovic is currently suing for civil rights violations caused by a "veritable perfect storm of misconduct by virtually every actor at every stage of his investigation and prosecution...." The suit alleges that police disclosed facts to him.

The Deskovic case illustrates how false confessions do not happen simply by happenstance. They are carefully constructed during an interrogation and then reconstructed during any criminal trial that follows. Constitutional criminal procedure does not regulate this critical phase of an interrogation. The Constitution requires the provision of initial Miranda warnings and then requires that the bare admission of guilt have been made voluntarily. That admission of guilt, while important, is only a part of the interrogation process. The "confession-making" phase may be far more involved. Much of the power of a confession derives from the narrative describing how the crime was committed. For a person to confess in a convincing way, he must be able to say more than "I did it." Police are trained to carefully test the suspect's knowledge of how the crime occurred by assessing whether the suspect can freely volunteer specific details that only the true culprit could know.

That confession-making process was corrupted in the cases studied in this Article. This Article examines the substance of the confession statements, how they were litigated at trial, and then on appeal. Just as in Deskovic's case, in almost all of the cases that resulted in trials, detectives testified that these defendants did far more than say "I did it," but that they also stated they had "guilty" or "inside" knowledge. Only two of the thirty-eight exonerees, Travis Hayes and Freddie Peacock, relayed no specific information concerning the crime. Hayes was still convicted, although

DNA testing conducted before trial excluded him and his co-defendant. Peacock was mentally disabled and all he could say to the police about the crime was "I did it, I did it." The other thirty-six exonerees each reportedly volunteered key details about the crime, including facts that matched the crime scene evidence or scientific evidence or accounts by the victim. Detectives further emphasized in twenty-seven cases—or seventy-one percent of the thirty-eight cases with transcripts obtained—that the details confessed were nonpublic or corroborated facts. Detectives sometimes specifically testified that they had assiduously avoided contaminating the confessions by not asking leading questions, but rather allowing the suspects to volunteer crucial facts.

The nonpublic facts contained in confession statements then became the centerpiece of the State's case. Although defense counsel moved to exclude almost all of these confessions from the trial, courts found each to be voluntary and admissible, often citing to the apparent reliability of the confessions. The facts were typically the focus of the State's closing arguments to the jury. Even after DNA testing excluded these people, courts sometimes initially denied relief, citing the seeming reliability of these confessions. The ironic result is that the public learned about these false confessions in part because of the contaminated facts. These false confessions were so persuasive, detailed and believable that they resulted in convictions which were often repeatedly upheld during appeals and habeas review. After years passed, these convicts had no option but to seek the DNA testing finally proving their confessions false.

* * *

A series of reforms could orient our criminal system towards the substance of confessions. First, constitutional criminal procedure could regulate reliability, though such constitutional change may be unlikely. An understanding of the vulnerability of confessions to contamination can also inform courts reviewing trials postconviction, particularly in cases involving persons vulnerable to suggestion, such as juveniles and mentally disabled individuals whose false confessions are studied here. Second, unless interrogations are recorded in their entirety, courts may not detect contamination of facts, especially when no DNA testing can be performed. In response to some of these false confessions, state legislatures, police departments, and courts have increasingly required videotaping of entire interrogations. Third, additional police procedures can safeguard reliability, such as procedures intended to assure against contamination, assess suggestibility, and avoid postadmission coercion.

I. Characteristics of DNA Exonerees' False Confessions

* * *

Unpacking the motive of an innocent person to confess requires a closer examination of what transpired during that interrogation, for which I had incomplete information. Social scientists have developed several categories for causes of false confessions, beginning with Saul Kassin and Lawrence Wrightsman's work. These exonerees' confessions were likely all what Kassin and Wrightsman term "coerced compliant" confessions, referring to those in which the subject complies with law enforcement pressure during the interrogation process. Many involved the subtype which Richard Leo and Richard Ofshe term a "stress compliant" false confession, in which the stress of the interrogation process, but not necessarily illegal coercion, secure a confession. In either type of compliant false confession, the suspect confesses chiefly to obtain a gain, such as "being allowed to go home, bringing a lengthy interrogation to an end, or avoiding physical injury."

Social scientists have long documented how pressure combined with repetition of a crime narrative may cause the suspect to internalize that narrative and repeat it, possibly becoming convinced of his own guilt. Only recently, however, have actual instances of such false confessions been documented. Pressures brought to bear on these exonerees ranged from threats combined with offers of leniency, to threats of physical force. Many described harrowing interrogations lasting many hours or days. Several described verbal or physical abuse. As will be developed below, twenty-two of the interrogations were recorded, but only partially....

Seventeen or forty-three percent of the forty DNA exonerees who falsely confessed were mentally ill, mentally retarded, or borderline mentally retarded. Thirteen or thirty-three percent of those who confessed were juveniles (five in the "Central Park Jogger" case). In twenty-six of the forty cases — or sixty-five percent — the defendant was either mentally disabled, under eighteen at the time of the offense, or both. Mentally disabled individuals and juveniles are both groups long known to be vulnerable to coercion and suggestion. For example, Earl Washington, Jr. and Jerry Townsend — both mentally disabled — each readily confessed to every crime that police asked them about. Several later explained that they confessed in order to avoid threats of the death penalty. For example, Chris Ochoa reported that a detective threatened him, "You're going to get the needle. You're going to get the needle for this. We got you."

Studies suggest that "police-induced false confessions appear to occur primarily in the more serious cases, especially homicides and other high-profile felonies," and consistent with those studies, seventy percent of these false confessions involved a murder. Twenty-five of the forty cases were rape-murder cases, three were murder cases, and twelve were rape cases. Thus, while most DNA exonerees were convicted of rape and not murder, the false confessions are concentrated in the murder cases. Confessions were obtained more frequently in murder and rape-murder cases than in rape cases, presumably because in rape cases a victim identification of the attacker obviates the need to secure a confession....

* * *

The confessions were also often the central evidence at trial. Few of the forty exonerees' cases involved eyewitnesses to the crime. Only twelve involved eyewitnesses, six involved jailhouse informants, and seven involved co-defendant testimony, though twenty-one involved some type of forensic evidence. Twenty-four were black, thirteen were white, and three were Hispanic.

II. Contaminated Confessions

The overwhelming majority of these forty false confession cases were contaminated. Thirty-six of the thirty-eight cases for which transcripts were obtained had confessions that reportedly included specific details about how the crime occurred. The trials of these exonerees then centered on those facts. At trial, law enforcement testified that the suspect had volunteered specific details about how the crime occurred, typically details corroborated by expert evidence or crime scene evidence. In most, the innocent person did not merely guess or repeat one or two facts. Almost all exonerees were reported to have provided detailed statements that included facts likely to be known only by the culprit. As the prosecutor in Robert Miller's case put it, "He supplied detail after detail after detail after detail. And details that only but the killer could have known."

A. Law Enforcement Practices Concerning Contamination of Confessions

Police have long been trained not to contaminate a confession by feeding or leaking crucial facts. The leading manual on police interrogations, originally written by Fred Inbau and John Reid, and now in its Fourth Edition, is emphatic on this point. Feeding facts contaminates a confession because if the suspect is told how the crime happened, then the police cannot ever again properly test the suspect's knowledge. The opportunity to obtain volunteered information is lost. For that reason, when developing the simple admission of guilt into a confession, police are trained to ask open questions, like "What happened next?" Leading questions are not to be asked, at least not as to crucial corroborated details concerning the crime. Inbau and Reid call it "highly important" to "let the confessor supply the details of the occurrence...." They explain that during the interrogation "[w]hat should be sought particularly are facts that would only be known by the guilty person...." Not only does this practice make the confession more convincing by avoiding any suggestion or disclosure of facts, but it allows the investigator to later "evaluate the confession in the light of certain known facts."

Law enforcement has strong practical reasons to test and to safeguard the reliability of a confession. Police are trained to construct a narrative of how the crime occurred, including the motives for committing the crime and a detailed explanation of how it was committed. During a criminal investigation, law enforcement tests the reliability of its work product to try to build as strong a case as possible. If the suspect truly lacks knowledge of how the crime occurred, the bare admission of culpability will not be very convincing to a jury. Indeed, police have long known that suspects may admit to crimes that they did not commit for a range of reasons, including mental illness, desire for attention, desire to protect loved ones, or others. The Inbau and Reid manual cautions that "[t]he truthfulness of a confession should be questioned, however, when the suspect is unable to provide any corroboration beyond the statement, 'I did it.'"

Further, police are trained not to leak facts. Police black out certain key information so that the public does not learn of it during the investigation. Thus, Inbau and Reid advise that, "When developing corroborative information, the investigator must be certain that the details were not somehow revealed to the suspect through the questioning process, news media, or the viewing of crime scene photographs." Police also know how important it is to document their efforts to keep certain facts confidential, because doing so later enhances the power of the confession in a subsequent prosecution or trial. Inbau and Reid recommend documenting in the case file the facts that are to be kept confidential "so that all investigators are aware of what information will be withheld." Even more powerful is corroborative evidence that the interrogators did not yet know, termed "independent corroboration." Thus, a suspect could be asked where the murder weapon was hidden, and if the weapon is found at that location, the confession is strongly corroborated. By carefully avoiding contamination of the confession, the officer can at trial "confidently refute" any defense suggestion that facts had been fed to the suspect.

B. Corroborated and Nonpublic Facts

In most of these cases, police did "confidently refute" at trial that they disclosed none of those detailed facts and instead claimed that the telling facts were volunteered. This is what made the confessions particularly powerful. The defendant reportedly freely offered information that only the perpetrator could have known. As police recognize, if the defendant had merely agreed to a series of leading questions by the police, then the confession would not appear particularly believable.

An example of the power of specific corroborated facts is in the cases of Marcellius Bradford and Calvin Ollins, two fourteen-year-old boys who confessed to the rape and murder of a medical student in Chicago, and who inculpated Calvin's cousin, Larry Ollins, and another boy, Omar Saunders. All four youths were wrongly convicted and served six-and-a-half to thirteen-and-a-half years before DNA testing exonerated them. The case revolved around two facts: the existence at the crime scene of a piece of concrete and a bloody footprint on the body of one victim.

Police stopped Larry Ollins on January 24, 1987, near the crime scene. He denied any knowledge of the crime. Three days later police detained his friend Marcellius Bradford. Bradford eventually told the detectives that he committed the murder along with Calvin and Larry Ollins, Saunders and others. The next morning, Calvin Ollins delivered his written confession and appeared to volunteer the crucial detail: when asked what Larry did next, he said, "That's when he hit her with a piece of concrete."

Police did not take a formal statement from Bradford until two hours after Ollins signed his own statement. A stenographer typed Bradford's admission. Bradford initially described Larry Ollins hitting the victim in the face with a brick. After making repeated references to a brick, the assistant state's attorney posed a leading question to correct Bradford. She asked:

Q. Was this brick a piece of concrete from the ground?

A. Yes. All of the references to a brick in the typed statement were then crossed out, replaced with the word "concrete," and initialed by Bradford.

Where did that detail regarding the concrete come from? A detective conducting the interrogations claimed that Bradford had first mentioned the concrete the night before. But that seems unlikely because the corrections were made in Bradford's written statement, which was elicited only after Calvin Ollins gave a statement.

Regardless where it originated, that detail provided crucial evidence against the two fourteen-year-olds. Officers later testified at trial that they had found at the crime scene a piece of concrete, which they took into evidence. At trial, the Chicago police crime lab analyst described analyzing stains on the piece of concrete and detecting human blood consistent with the blood type of the victim.

A second crucial detail emerged at trial. The medical examiner who conducted the autopsy described the victim's "multiple blunt injuries that included the face." Similarly, Calvin Ollins volunteered that "they started kicking [the victim]." The medical examiner described bloody footprints found on the body. The jury saw a photograph of the bloody footprint.

Bradford pleaded guilty and received a twelve-year sentence in exchange for his testimony against the others at trial. At Larry Ollins's trial, Bradford gave a detailed account of the murder, including the kicking. During this trial testimony, Bradford slipped yet again and several times described Larry Ollins picking up a brick. He was again corrected:

Q. Are we talking about a house brick or some other kind of object?

A. Cement out of the ground, like a rock.

Q. Like a chunk of cement?

A. Chunk of cement.

The prosecutor focused the closing statements on how the confessions were fully consistent with the injuries of the victim: "You will see this photograph and it won't be pleasant. But it shows you how this pointed end of the rock where the blood was ... matches the injury that's on her face." He added, "So, when Marcellius Bradford told you Larry Ollins did that, it fits the evidence. And you know he was telling the truth." Then he described the footprints and noted that they are "more evidence to show you that Marcellius Bradford accurately truly described to you what happened that day."

Ofshe and Leo note: "The only time an innocent person will contribute correct information is when he makes an unlucky guess. The likelihood of an unlucky guess diminishes as the number of possible answers to an investigator's questions grows large." Cases involving unusual, specific, or numerous details raise the most troubling questions. The Bradford confession involving such specific crime scene details suggests a very low likelihood that the teenager could possibly have guessed each of those unusual facts on his own. Indeed, Bradford later claimed police beat him and also that he confessed to avoid a life sentence. DNA testing not only exonerated Bradford, Calvin and Larry Ollins, and Saunders, but after their release, police arrested two others whose DNA did match the crime scene evidence. A

Chicago Tribune investigation also later found that "the alleged confessions mirrored a scenario that an FBI criminal profiler said he provided before the four teenagers were arrested."

* * *

C. Denying Disclosing Facts

In twenty-seven of the thirty-eight cases, the police officers testifying under oath at trial denied that they had disclosed facts to the suspect. Some were asked directly whether they had told the suspect key facts, others themselves noted they had not done so, and others carefully described an interrogation in which the suspect had volunteered each of the relevant facts. The question then arises whether officers were testifying falsely when they claimed that crucial facts were volunteered, where in fact they were disclosed by these police officers.... These officers most likely believed they were interrogating a guilty person. Officers may contaminate a confession unintentionally. During a complex interrogation, they might not later recall that as to important subjects they had in fact asked leading questions. A fascinating column by Detective James Trainum describes how he and his colleagues unintentionally secured a false confession. Trainum explained:

> We believed so much in our suspect's guilt that we ignored all evidence to the contrary. To demonstrate the strength of our case, we showed the suspect our evidence, and unintentionally fed her details that she was able to parrot back to us at a later time. Contrary to our operating procedures at the time, my colleagues and I chose to videotape the interrogation. This is what saved me from making a horrible mistake in the long run. It was a classic false confession case and without the video we would never have known. Similarly, it is possible that officers who did not testify at trial may have disclosed facts without the knowledge of their colleagues, and failed to tell their colleagues what transpired.

* * *

The case of Earl Washington, Jr. provides another example in which the law enforcement denials that facts were disclosed formed the crucial evidence in the State's case. Washington falsely confessed to a rape and murder in Culpepper, Virginia. He came within nine days of execution and was in prison for eighteen years before finally being exonerated by DNA testing. A long string of state and federal courts denied his appeals and postconviction petitions, citing to the reliability of his confession. Although he was borderline mentally retarded, the Fourth Circuit emphasized "Washington had supplied without prompting details of the crime that were corroborated by evidence taken from the scene and by the observations of those investigating the [victim's] apartment."

Lieutenant Harlan Lee Hart and Special Agent Curtis Reese Wilmore told prosecutors and then testified at trial that Washington identified as his a shirt with a torn pocket that was found in the rear bureau of the victim's bedroom many months after the murder. The typed statement read as follows:

Hart: Did you leave any of your clothing in the apartment?

Washington: My shirt.

Hart: The shirt that has been shown you, it is the one you left in apartment?

Washington: Yes sir.

Wilmore: How do you know it is yours?

Washington: That is the shirt I wore.

Hart: What makes it stand out?

Washington: A patch had been removed from the top of the pocket.

Wilmore: Why did you leave the shirt in the apartment?

Washington: It had blood on it and I didn't want to wear it back out.

Wilmore: Where did you put it when you left?

Washington: Laid it on top of dresser drawer in bedroom.

This statement was powerful for several reasons. Washington offers in this statement that he left a shirt, yet the police had not made public that a shirt was found at the crime scene. Further, he knew about an identifying characteristic making that shirt unusual: the torn-off patch. He knew precisely where the shirt had been left, in a dresser drawer in the bedroom. Most remarkable, not only did Earl Washington, Jr. know of the existence of this shirt and appear to volunteer where the shirt had been found, but he said that he left it there because it had blood on it. The shirt that the officers showed Washington no longer had blood on it. The stains had been cut from the shirt for forensic analysis. Thus, this appeared to be no mere lucky guess. Washington appeared to have detailed knowledge concerning this shirt and this crime scene.

The prosecutor emphasized in closing arguments that the police were not "lying" and "didn't suggest to him" how the crime had been committed, but that Washington knew exactly how the crime had been committed. The prosecutor ended the closing statements by discussing the shirt and noting that Washington knew "the patch was missing over the left top pocket." The prosecutor continued, "Now, how does somebody make all that up, unless they were actually there and actually did it? I would submit to you that there can't be any question in your mind about it, the fact that this happened and the fact that Earl Washington Junior did it."

Now that we know Earl Washington, Jr. did not commit the crime, but rather another man later identified through a DNA database who has now pleaded guilty, there are limited explanations for how Washington could have uttered those remarks concerning the shirt, together with other details concerning how the crime had been committed. Either the police offered those facts to him, or the police had actually leaked all of that information to the public and somehow Washington, a mentally retarded farmhand living in the next county, heard it all and carefully incorporated it into his confession. Whether or not the officers intended to misrepresent their interrogation of Washington, they had provided a version of events that is likely false as to crucial details, in a case where Washington was sentenced to death.

This was precisely the issue raised in a civil rights lawsuit brought by Washington after his exoneration. It emerged for the first time during discovery in that civil rights suit that almost ten years after the conviction and near the time that Virginia's Governor was considering a clemency petition based on postconviction DNA testing, Agent Wilmore for the first time expressed doubts concerning the interrogation. He admitted the facts were likely disclosed, telling the Virginia Assistant Attorney General "that he felt like either he or Hart must have mentioned the shirt to Washington ... and that his testimony in the record did not accurately reflect that the shirt had been first mentioned by the police." In 2006, a federal jury found that Wilmore had fabricated the confession and violated Washington's constitutional rights by at minimum recklessly and falsely claiming that Washington volunteered crucial nonpublic facts. That jury awarded Earl Washington, Jr. $2.25 million in compensatory damages.

The Central Park Jogger case also involved a striking detail concerning a shirt. The prosecutor emphasized in closing arguments that Antron McCray knew information that only the jogger's assailant could have known:

> You heard in that video Antron McCray was asked about what she was wearing, and he describes she was wearing a white shirt. This is the shirt that [the victim] was wearing.

> You saw the photograph of what that shirt looked like. There is no way that you knew that that shirt was white unless you saw it before it became soaked with blood and mud.

> I submit to you that Antron McCray describes details and describes them in a way that make you know beyond any doubt, beyond a reasonable doubt, that he was present, that he helped other people rape her and that he helped other people beat her and that he left her there to die.

* * *

D. Recorded False Interrogations

A surprising number of these false confessions were recorded. Twenty-two of the thirty-eight cases—or fifty-eight percent—had recordings, but only part of the interrogation was recorded. Thirteen were audio recorded and nine had video. Five additional confessions or interrogations were at some point transcribed by a stenographer. These create a record of what transpired during selected portions of the interrogations.

Yet where only part of the interrogation was recorded, we do not know what preceded that recording. Thus, four of the five youths in the Central Park Jogger case had their interrogation videotaped, but this recording followed their lengthy initial interrogations. Similarly, three of the Beatrice Six had statements videotaped, but only after multiple interviews and interrogations by police and others. In David Allen Jones's recorded interrogation, when he did not recall the location of a crime, police reminded him that they had earlier shown him photos of the crime scene, asking "You remember yesterday we showed you that picture" and that it was "by the water fountain" and "you remember that gate we showed you right there," finally eliciting a response from Jones that was transcribed as "This right here (Untranslatable)."

Steven Drizin notes that it is "not uncommon" for police to conduct an initial interview in which they "use a gamut of techniques" to secure admissions, but do not tape that interview, perhaps because jurors might be disturbed by coercive or misleading techniques employed; rather police tape a second interview only once the admissions have been secured.

* * *

In the case of David Vasquez..., even in the portion of the interrogation that was recorded, leading questions were asked about key issues. In that case, the crucial nonpublic information contained in the confession was the type of cord used to bind the victim and to hang her. The police determined "that the bindings used to secure [the victim's] hands had been cut from the venetian blinds in the sunroom. The noose employed for her execution had been cut from a length of rope wrapped around a carpet in her basement." It was obvious from the recording of the interrogation that Vasquez had no idea what was used to bind and murder the victim:

Det. 1: Did she tell you to tie her hands behind her back?

Vasquez: Ah, if she did, I did.

Det. 2: Whatcha use?

Vasquez: The ropes?

Det. 2: No, not the ropes. Whatcha use?

Vasquez: Only my belt.

Det. 2: No, not your belt.... Remember being out in the sunroom, the room that sits out to the back of the house? ... and what did you cut down? To use?

Vasquez: That, uh, clothesline?

Det. 2: No, it wasn't a clothesline, it was something like a clothesline. What was it? By the window? Think about the Venetian blinds, David. Remember cutting the Venetian blind cords?

Vasquez: Ah, it's the same as rope?

Det. 2: Yeah.

Det. 1: Okay, now tell us how it went, David—tell us how you did it.

Vasquez: She told me to grab the knife, and, and, stab her, that's all.

Det. 2: (voice raised) David, no, David.

Vasquez: If it did happen, and I did it, and my fingerprints were on it ...

Det. 2: (slamming his hand on the table and yelling) You hung her!

Vasquez: What?

Det. 2: You hung her!

Vasquez: Okay, so I hung her.

* * *

G. Crime Scene Visits

In fourteen of the thirty-eight cases—or thirty-eight percent—police brought the exonerees to the crime scene. The visits allowed police to test the knowledge of how the crime occurred and to gather facts. The visits could also provide a chance to review with the exoneree how the crime occurred. They could also be used to disclose facts....

Earl Washington, Jr. led police to locations all around Culpepper, Virginia, having had no idea where the victim was murdered. Even after being driven right in front of the victim's building several times, he did not identify it. When the police then asked him to point to her building once in the apartment complex he pointed to "the exact opposite end" of the complex, and it was only when the officer pointed to her apartment and asked if that was it, he finally "said that it was." In other exonerees' cases, police did not describe such uncertainty, so it remains quite questionable how absent police prompting, innocent suspects could have described on their own what transpired at these crime scenes.

* * *

L. Litigating Contamination of Confessions at Trial

Although many of these false confessions betrayed indicia of unreliability at the time of trial, the issue was rarely litigated because courts conduct very limited reliability review.... Due to the Court's rejection of the consideration of "probable reliability" of a confession, even grossly unreliable confessions may be admitted if found not to have been the product of affirmative police coercion.

* * *

One third of these defendants—ten—had their attorneys argue at trial that the confession was contaminated, at least in the materials obtained which sometimes omitted pretrial motions. They typically had little evidence to support an allegation that facts had been disclosed. For example, Eddie Joe Lloyd's lawyer did not maintain his client's innocence in his closing arguments and conceded that the confession left him "bewildered." Attorneys typically did not focus on reliability, as no legal theory typically supported relief for an unreliable confession, but rather on criminal procedure claims concerning the voluntariness of the statements and whether the defendant had the capacity to understand Miranda warnings or to be tried.... [W]hile gross unreliability typically lacks any legal remedy, courts often emphasized apparent reliability in denying motions to suppress the seeming reliability of these confessions.

B. Current Law: Overview

The court decision to admit a confession at trial is governed by the voluntariness rule, the corroboration rule, and finally whether the defendant while in custody was advised of his rights to be free from self-incrimination under *Miranda v. Arizona*. The due process clause of the Fourteenth Amendment, and the Fifth Amendment right to be free of self-incrimination, bar the admission of involuntary confessions at trial.

Voluntariness Rule and Due Process

The due process clause of the Fourteenth Amendment bars the admission of involuntary confessions at trial. *Jackson v. Denno* 378 U.S. 368, 385–386 (1964). The trial court must provide the defendant with a pre-trial hearing to determine the voluntariness of the statement or confession, if the defendant requests, before the confession may be admitted at trial. This is referred to as a *Jackson v. Denno* hearing, during which all evidence of the alleged confession is presented to the judge outside of the presence of the jury. In *Jackson v. Denno,* the Supreme Court found it violated due process to allow a jury to make the initial decision of whether a confession or statement was voluntary. At the pre-trial hearing, the prosecution is only required to prove voluntariness by a preponderance of the evidence. *Lego v. Twomey,* 404 U.S. 477, 489 (1972). If the court finds the statement was given voluntarily, the statement can be presented at trial before the jury.

The test for determining whether a statement is involuntary under the Due Process Clause is whether the confession was "extracted by any sort of threats or violence, [or] obtained by any direct or implied promises, however slight, [or] by the exertion of any improper influence." *Hutto v. Ross*, 429 U.S. 28, 30 (1976).

Relevant Factors for Voluntariness

Relevant factors for voluntariness include "the crucial element of police coercion; the length of the interrogation; its location; its continuity" as well as "the defendant's maturity; education; physical condition; and mental health." *Withrow v. Williams* 507 U.S. 680, 693–694 (1993).

In *Brown v. Mississippi*, when Ed Brown denied committing a murder the police hung him from a tree limb repeatedly and then tied him to a tree and whipped him, attempting to coerce Brown into confessing. Ed Brown maintained his innocence and was finally released. Days later the police returned and whipped Ed Brown again; at this point Brown agreed to confess to a statement. The Supreme Court held for the first time that the use of a coerced confession at a state trial violates the due process clause of the Fourteenth Amendment. *Brown v. Mississippi,* 297 U.S. 278 (1936).

In *Chambers v. Florida*, when an elderly Caucasian man was robbed and murdered, police arrested 25–40 African-American men and confined them for five days, without charges, subjecting them to interrogations and isolation. The Supreme Court found that a lengthy and uninterrupted interrogation can show a confession is involuntary. 309 U.S. 227 (1940).

Finally, the due process clause only protects against official or state misconduct in involuntary confessions. In *Colorado v. Connelly,* a mentally ill individual approached a police officer on the street and confessed to a crime; he continued to confess after being taken into custody and read his Miranda rights. Although the suspect felt compelled to confess by "voices" brought on by his mental illness, the Supreme Court found behavior of a private party does not make a confession inadmissible under the due process clause. *Colorado v. Connelly*, 479 U.S. 157 (1987).

Corroboration Rule

Under *Crane v. Kentucky*, even if a judge finds a confession is voluntary, the defendant is entitled under the due process clause and the Sixth Amendment confrontation clause to introduce evidence about the circumstances of the confession, and can contest the reliability of the confession in front of the jury. *Crane v. Kentucky*, 476 U.S. 683 (1986). As the court found, even a voluntary confession can be "insufficiently corroborated or otherwise unworthy of belief."

Miranda and Admissibility

A confession obtained from a defendant in custody can be excluded from trial under the Fifth Amendment if the defendant was not advised of his rights under *Miranda v. Arizona*. In *Miranda v. Arizona*, the Supreme Court held the police must inform a defendant in custody that he has the right to remain silent, anything said will be used against him or her in court, that the person has the right to consult with a lawyer and have a lawyer present during questioning, and that a lawyer will be appointed to represent the defendant if he or she cannot afford a lawyer. If police fail to provide this information, the confession can be excluded at trial as violative of the defendant's Fifth Amendment protection from self-incrimination—unless the defendant "knowingly and intelligently" waives his rights. *Miranda v. Arizona*, 384 U.S. 436 (1966).

C. Legal Materials, Exercises, and Media

1. *Proposed Solutions:*

a. In a portion of their article not excerpted above, Leo and his co-authors argue that all interrogations, absent extraordinary circumstances, should be captured in audio-visual recordings, and that any unrecorded confessions should only be admissible if the state can show that recording was infeasible under the circumstances and that the confession led the state to the discovery of previously unknown corroborating evidence. As to recorded confessions, they further propose that judges only admit such evidence after conducting pretrial reliability hearings to assess three factors: 1) whether the confession contains nonpublic information that can be independently verified, would only be known by the true perpetrator or an accomplice, and cannot likely be guessed by chance; 2) whether the suspect's confession led the police to new evidence about the crime; and 3) whether the suspect's postadmission narrative "fits" (or fails to fit) with the crime facts and existing objective evidence. Leo *et al.*, p. 531–535.

b. Like Leo *et al.*, Kassin and his co-authors strongly advocate for a videotaping requirement. In addition, they urge police to replace the Reid interrogation method with the PEACE method (discussed by Starr, supra), and that time limits be placed on the duration of custodial interrogations, that the use of minimization tactics and false evidence ploys be limited or barred, and that particularly vulnerable populations, such as youth and persons with intellectual disabilities, be afforded special protections. Kassin *et al.*, *id.* at 25–32.

How effective do you think these reforms would be? How aggressively would you implement them? To what extent does Garrett's data on confession contamination raise doubts about the potential effectiveness of pretrial reliability determinations?

2. *Exercise, Testifying Before the Legislature on Videotaped Interrogations*: The state legislature judiciary committee is holding a hearing on whether your state should pass a law mandating that all police interrogations be visually recorded as a prerequisite to the admissibility of a defendant's confession to the police in a criminal case. Prepare your testimony before the Committee in support of, or opposition to, the proposed legislation, limiting it to five minutes.

3. *Exercise, Read and Identify:* Read the transcript below of the real interrogation of Joseph Buffey:

Statement of Joey Buffey (excerpt)

12/08/01

RM. What house did you break into Joe?

J.B. This old lady's house.

R.M. Where was it at, what was the location?

J.B. It was in Hartland.

R.M. Over in Hartland. Was it near any specific place?

J.B. I couldn't tell you exactly where.

R.M. Uh huh, do you know where the Pepsi Cola Plant is?

J.B. Yeah.

R.M. Was it near there?

J.B. I guess so.

R.M. Okay, what happened when you broke into the house?

J.B. This old woman flipped on me, that's all I remember.

R.M. How did she flip on you?

J.B. Went crazy.

R.M. Uh huh, and what did you do?

J.B. I don't remember.

. . .

R.M. Did you do anything to this lady when she flipped out?

J.B. Not that I remember, I don't remember nothing, I don't remember nothing.

R.M. You don't remember nothing but I mean you could have done something but you just don't remember. You feel bad about going in there with that old lady?

J.B. Yeah.

. . .

R.M. And you don't remember anything that happened inside the house?

J.B. Nope.

R.M. Did you have sex with the lady that was in the house?

J.B. I don't remember.

R.M. Possibility?

J.B. I don't remember.

R.M. But I mean, is it a is it a possibility?

J.B. All, all, all I know is what I'm being charged with.

…

R.M. You ever have situations where you've blacked out before or don't remember anything?

J.B. I never have.

…

R.M. Did you hit her, knock her down?

J.B. l don't know.

RM. You don't know, don't remember?

J.B. No.

R.M. Is there anything else that you remember about that incident?

J.B. No.

R.M. Did you sexually assault her?

J.B. l don't remember.

…

D.W. Are you sure you don't want to tell us anymore?

J.B. That's all.

R.M This will probably be your last....

D.W. This is gonna be the last time we're going to talk: to you about this.

R.M. We're gonna give you an opportunity on this particular statement to, to sing. That's it? Okay, the information that you've given me do you swear that it's true and accurate to the best of your knowledge and belief?

J.B. Yes.

R.M. Now you hesitated. I really think you want to tell us what happened in that house; I really think you remember.

D.W. I know you want to tell us you're just scared. What are you scared of?

J.B. You really want to know the truth?

R.M. Yeah. we want the truth.

J.B. I didn't do it.

R.M. Okay.

J.B. I mean, I had (inaudible) breathing down my throat, breathing down my neck, telling me, "I did it, I did", I got people saying that I did. I made up a story, I couldn't say, no, I couldn't tell you what went on in there, I couldn't tell you where I was at, you know. I got everyone telling me that I did it ...

R.M. Uh huh. So you lie a lot then?

J.B. Yeah. I just thought maybe....

D.W. Now you're making us feel real bad cause now you're lying to us and you can see it in your face, you know that's not the truth that you just told both of us that you didn't do it. Let me ask you this, have we done anything to you?

J.B. You guys have been good to me.

D.W. We haven't threatened you or anything like that, we've been on your side because we're trying to do our job. You told us a story, you sounded very remorseful in your whole story and now you're going back saying you didn't do it.

RM. Now the new information that you've given us do you swear it's true and accurate to the best of your knowledge and belief?

J.B. Yes.

R.M. You have anything you want to add to your statement? Okay, that concludes the statement at 3:51.

* * *

Mr. Buffey's final taped statement was taken between 3:25 a.m. and 3:51 a.m. It was his only admission after eight hours of being interrogated by multiple detectives. He was 19 years old at the time.

The victim's recorded account was that a knife-wielding perpetrator woke her while she slept in the upstairs bedroom. She was scared for her life and submitted to him blindfolding her; he then walked her downstairs and around the home in search of cash, commenting on the photos. Part of his face was covered with a white bandana. He finally took her back upstairs and sexually assaulted her in the bedroom.

What interrogation techniques led Joseph Buffey to confess to involvement in the crimes?

4. *Joseph Buffey Postscript:* Brady *Disclosure Pre-Plea:* Joseph Buffey took a guilty plea. At the time of his sentencing the prosecutor had results from the rape kit excluding Buffey, and ultimately including Adam Bowers. Fifteen years after his false confession and guilty plea, Joseph Buffey was able to retract his guilty plea in a decision by the West Virginia Supreme Court of Appeals requiring prosecutors to disclose *Brady* evidence pre-plea. Nationally, it was the first state supreme court decision to order *Brady* evidence disclosed pre-plea rather than pre-trial.

The Clarksburg Prosecuting Attorney then charged Buffey with statutory rape for fathering a child when he was 19 years old with his then 14-year-old girl-friend—in 2001. To avoid registering as a sex offender, Buffey pled guilty—again—to the breaking and entering and the state dropped the statutory rape charge. Buffey maintained his innocence during the Alford plea.

5. *Reflective Essay, Interviewing:* What are similarities between how police interrogate suspects and how attorneys interview clients in criminal cases? What are differences? Explain your answers in a few paragraphs.

6. *The Reid Technique, Science and Eliciting Confessions:* Police are permitted to lie to suspects when interrogating them, however false information provided in interrogations has also been connected to false confessions.

   a.   In this excerpt from "The Wire," a critically acclaimed television series about the drug trade and policing in Baltimore, an officer uses a particular interrogation technique using "science"—a fake lie detector test. https://www.youtube.com/watch?v=rN7pkFNEg5c (3 minutes).

   b.   Dr. Richard Leo has written extensively on the "evidence ploy" used by police to elicit confessions, particularly under the Reid Technique. Read his expert testimony in a post-conviction hearing for Patrick Donley in Wisconsin below:

Q. Okay. Dr. Leo, at this point I'm going to play a second segment. This portion of the interrogation occurs at the 11 minute mark and ends approximately at the 12 minute and 50 second mark. (Plays the video.) Dr. Leo, again, what, if anything, is noteworthy about this portion of the audio?

A. Well, the interrogator is essentially accusing implicitly Mr. Donley of not telling the truth, but what he's focussing on here in this is, is the supposed scientific evidence that would show the injuries contradict Mr. Donley's account, and so we call this the evidence ploy when you confront somebody with evidence of their guilt and it can be true or false as I mentioned earlier, so if this is false, that it would be a false evidence ploy. We know the evidence ploy is very effective technique about getting true and false confessions, but it creates a higher risk of false confessions. And I think this segment also indicates or indicates the beginning of the guilt presumptive nature of the interrogation, so it's the place at which some of the basic interrogation techniques are starting to be applied.

Q. Or. Leo, what is the significance of the evidence ploy being scientific evidence particularly?

A. Well, the idea behind the technique is to convince a suspect that the evidence conclusively, irrefutably demonstrates their guilt and therefore it's pointless for them to continue to deny because no one will believe them and their guilt has been demonstrated to 100 percent certainty. And scientific evidence is particularly potent when it comes to false evidence at establishing that because culturally, particularly people who are don't have PhD's in science, tend to defer to scientific evidence. Well, here is something we scientifically assume to be proven or truthful, so this be would be the most potent kind of evidence ploy one could have and, therefore, the strongest at creating the risk of false or unreliable confessions.

c. *The Reid Technique:* A paper by Reid and Associates, Inc., the company that patented the Reid technique for interrogation training, responds to issues surrounding false confessions by outlining its own position and offering advice on distinguishing between true and false confessions. Read the response—and updated Testimony Data Sheet—below:

John E. Reid and Associates, Inc. Established 1947

www.reid.com

False Confession Cases—The Issues

In the past several years a number of false confession cases have received extensive publicity. In several of these cases the convicted individual has been exonerated by DNA testing and the actual perpetrator, in turn, has been identified. In these cases it is important to examine in detail exactly what happened; what went wrong; what are the lessons to be learned, and what are potential safeguards that can be put into place to prevent future mistakes.

To be sure, in the experience of most professional interrogators the frequency of false confessions is rare. When we do learn of them, however, the interrogation tactics and techniques should be scrupulously examined, as well as the circumstances surrounding the interrogation.

When this has been done, there are four factors that appear with some regularity in false confession cases:

The suspect is a juvenile; and/or

The suspect suffers some mental or psychological impairment; and/or

The interrogation took place over an inordinate amount of time; and/or

The interrogators engaged in illegal tactics and techniques

Confession Corroboration

As we have stated earlier, it is imperative that interrogators do not reveal details of the crime so that they can use the disclosure of such information by the suspect as verification of the confession's authenticity. In each case there should be documented "hold back" information about the details of how the crime was committed; details from the crime scene; details about specific activities perpetrated by the offender; etc. The goal is match the suspect's confession against these details to establish the veracity of the statement. It should be remembered, however, that suspects do not always tell us everything that they did and they do not always remember all of the details themselves.

Factors to Consider

With the above discussion in mind, the following represents some factors to consider in the assessment of the credibility of a suspect's confession. These issues are certainly not all inclusive, and each case must be evaluated on the "totality of circumstances" surrounding the interrogation and confession, but nevertheless, these are elements that should be given careful consideration:

1. The suspect's condition at the time of the interrogation

   a. Physical condition (including drug and/or alcohol intoxication)

   b. Mental capacity

   c. Psychological condition

2. The suspects age

3. The suspect's prior experience with law enforcement

4. The suspect's understanding of the language

5. The length of the interrogation

6. The degree of detail provided by the suspect in his confession

7. The extent of corroboration between the confession and the crime

8. The presence of witnesses to the interrogation and confession

9. The suspect's behavior during the interrogation

10. The effort to address the suspect's physical needs

11. The presence of any improper interrogation techniques

The Testimony Data Sheet provided below will help to document information relevant to these considerations. For more information on these issues go to Helpful Info at our web page www.reid.com and then click on the Critics Corner.

TESTIMONY DATA SHEET

Name: DOB:

Language:

People involved in the interrogation:

1. Was *Miranda* given? Y N time place Witness

2. Behavior Analysis Interview start end

   How do you feel about being interviewed today? Why have you agreed to talk to me about this matter?

   How would you describe your physical health right now? How much sleep did you get in the last 24 hours?

   When was your last full meal?

   Have you had any alcohol or drugs in the last 24 hours?

3. Interrogation start end

   Primary Theme:

   Alternative Question:

   First admission of guilt time

   Suspect left interrogation room time

Did the suspect request an attorney? Y N

Did the suspect say he no longer wanted to answer questions? Y N Did the suspect attempt to leave the room? Y N

4. Document any washroom breaks; beverages; food; cigarette breaks, etc:

5. Confession Witnessed by

Why did you decide to tell the truth about this?

Do you have any complaints about the way you were treated today?

Completed by:

7. *Review Questions:* Based on the readings, "The Wire" excerpt, Dr. Leo's expert testimony, and the Reid Technique discussion, provide a short answer for each of the following questions on confessions.

   a. What is an evidence ploy?

   b. Why is a scientific evidence ploy particularly effective?

   c. What suspects are particularly vulnerable to confessing to a crime they did not commit?

   d. What police behavior can be more likely to elicit a false confession?

   e. Why have a Testimony Data Sheet for interrogations?

8. *Reflective Essay, Dignity and Respect:* Write about a moment where you felt berated, belittled, or misunderstood. Drawing from that experience, what are ways you can create dignity for a client?

9. *The Central Park Five, Discussion:* The false confessions of the "Central Park Five" have been widely documented and provide important insight into false confessions, juveniles, and the role of race in interrogations. For a powerful re-telling, watch Ava DuVernay's television miniseries "When They See Us." For an overview, read and watch the resources below, largely provided by Ken Burns and Sarah Burns documentary coverage of the wrongful convictions on PBS:

   a. *The Central Park Five* is a a two-hour documentary by Ken Burns and Sarah Burns, available here: http://www.pbs.org/kenburns/centralparkfive/.

   b. The following excerpt from *The Central Park Five*, available on PBS, documents how "after hours of intense interrogation, seasoned detectives intimidate the five teenagers into falsely convicting each other": https://wv.pbslearningmedia.org/resource/confessions-central-park-five-video-1231/confessions-ken-burns-the-central-park-five/#.WS8iWoDWQZ0.email (6 min. 16 seconds).

   c. The following are images and news stories provided in connection with *The Central Park Five:* https://wv.pbslearningmedia.org/resource/central-park-five-ken-burns-central-park-five/central-park-five-ken-burns-central-park-five/#.WS8jVOau2KM.email.

d. For a reading particularly on the role of race in the Central Park Five convictions, see Jeremy Duru, *Central Park Five, the Scottsboro Boys and the Myth of the Bestial Black Man*, 25 Cardozo L. Rev. 1315 (2004).

e. Kharey Wise' confession, admitted as evidence at his trial, is excerpted from the trial transcript below:

Figure 6.1

```
 1                      Hartigan/direct/People            2279

 2      make on objections to questions that are asked of

 3      witnesses appearing before you, you're not to

 4      speculate about the reasons for the redactions or

 5      the matters redacted.  The original copy will be

 6      exhibited to you and then a Xerox copy will be

 7      substituted.

 8           So please keep that in mind.  The statement

 9      that you will hear can only be considered by you as

10      it pertains to Kharey Wise.  And you're not to

11      speculate about the matters that are covered with

12      yellow tape or the typing over it.

13           Okay.

14      A    It starts off at "0030 hours.  Interviewed is

15  Kharey Wise," with his date of birth, his address, his phone

16  number.  "Location of interview, 20th Precinct Sex Crimes

17  Squad.

18      "Present is Detective John Hartigan, Manhattan North

19  Homicide Squad, Detective Robert Nugent, Central Park

20  Precinct.  Advised of his rights by Detective Hartigan."

21  And then Kharey began to tell us the story and I began to

22  write.

23      "About 8 p.m. on April 19 I was on Fifth Avenue between

24  110th and 111th Street.  I was with my girlfriend Lisa,

25  Apartment 25, same building as myself.  She was in the
```

Figure 6.1, continued

1	Hartigan/direct/People 2280
2	chicken store when Eddie, 24 D, came across the street and
3	started talking to me. At this time I saw a large crowd,
4	about thirty guys. Both Eddie and I ran to the crowd which
5	was coming out of the plaza and walking towards Central
6	Park. When we got there I saw Yusef, Fedora, apartment 22
7	C, Steve, apartment 8 B, Al, apartment 23 B, and Patrick,
8	who lives at 1295 Fifth Avenue. I also observed Orlando in
9	the crowd.
10	"I asked Yusef what was happening, and he told me to
11	come along. And one guy that yelled out, 'violence'. Steve
12	said,' whoever is not going don't go, but when we start
13	'violence' and the cops come, nobody knows nothing and don't
14	squeal whoever gets caught.'
15	"Steve then told Eddie he couldn't go but Eddie went
16	with me into the park. As we entered the park there was a
17	guy and a girl they were going to hit, but they knew him and
18	left him alone. They continued into the park and they saw a
19	bum walking down. A big guy, dark skin, 5 foot 6, black
20	coat, jumped on the drunk and knocked him down. Everyone,
21	Patrick, Steve, Raymond, apartment 6 D, all jumped on the
22	drunk and beat him. He was lying on the roadway and I told
23	them not to leave him there because he would get hit by a
24	car.
25	"Steve, Raymond, Al all said he was dead, but I told

Figure 6.1, continued

them that he was still breathing, and they dragged him on to the grass. We went further into the park and saw a guy and girl on a bench, but we left them alone. We then saw a clean guy walking on the roadway and everyone asked him if he had any money and he told them no. And they started chasing him, but he ran away.

"We continued further south into the park on the roadway and we saw a guy and a girl on a double bike, and we tried to stop him. Steve and a Spanish guy hit him, but he kept his balance and they rode off.

"A jogger was coming down and he turned around and a biker was also coming along. And the jogger warned him about the crowd, and they went the other way. A car came along and someone threw a rock and the driver stopped and got out. Someone told him to go back into the car, but it looked like he was talking into a walkie-talkie and was calling the cops. Everyone ran into the woods. And there was a police car was coming off 104th Street into the park and they put their spot light on, and everybody ran. I ran west across the park and into the area where there was a fire and waterfall. I was with Al, apartment 13 B, and there was others behind him. I don't know who they were. When we got by the stream where the waterfall is, that's where I left Al and I came north and out of the park to

Figure 6.1, continued

```
1                    Hartigan/direct/People          2282
2   Lenox Avenue.
3       "I went straight home and went to bed.  Today April 20,
4   I went out to the street around 2:30 this afternoon.  I saw
5   Raymond Yusef, apartment 6 E, and Al and Fedore.  I hung
6   around and watched cops on Fifth Avenue.  The above guys
7   were in the basketball court playing basketball, and Yusef
8   came from school.  We started talking of what had happened
9   last night.  Yusef said they jumped a guy at the reservoir,
10  him and some others, and one of them hit this guy with a
11  pipe he took out of Corey's house.
12      "Yusef also stated they all were looking for each other,
13  and they met up with Steve and others.  They saw a lady
14  jogger coming down and they grabbed her, dragged her into
15  the bushes and they punched her and stripped her and cut her
16  up on the legs, took off her shirt and a guy and Steve raped
17  her.  Then Steve and that guy stopped a man in the van beat
18  him up, and that's when the cops got them.
19      "Al also told me that he was there when the girl was
20  getting raped, and he told me it was Steve and that guy.  I
21  knew Yusef to have a knife and the pipe when we went into
22  the park.
23      "One other that I recognize was a male black, 15, named
24  Antron who lives in the Foster Houses."
25      Then he signed the statement is true.  Signed Kharey
```

Figure 6.1, continued

```
 1                          Colloquy                    2283

 2 Wise.  Myself and Detective Nugent also signed it.

 3            MS. LEDERER:  Your Honor, at this time I'd ask

 4       if the exhibits that have just been received 148

 5       and 148 A could be circulated among the jurors.

 6            THE COURT:  Just show them to the jury.  I

 7       think if they can look at both altogether.

 8            (Whereupon, those exhibits are passed among the

 9       jury)

10            THE COURT:  If I might just suggest, if two of

11       the jurors can read it together, that might

12       expedite it somewhat.  But if you want to read it

13       individually, you're certainly entitled to do that

14       also.

15            (Pause)

16            THE COURT:  All right.  Ladies and gentlemen,

17       the two exhibits have apparently been read by the

18       jurors.  We're going to recess for the day.

19       Tomorrow, as you know, Thursday is my calendar day.

20        Normally we resume at 2.15 tomorrow.  We're going

21       to try and resume at 12 o'clock, so we can

22       accommodate the witness' schedule also.

23            And in the meantime, as always, don't discuss

24       this case with anyone, including among yourselves.

25       Don't let anyone else talk to you about the case.
```

f.   On direct appeal, the court denied Kharey Wise relief. Read the court's entire brief opinion below.

People v. Wise

612 N.Y.S.2d 117 (App. Div. 1994)

MEMORANDUM DECISION.

Judgment, Supreme Court, New York County (Thomas B. Galligan, J.), rendered January 9, 1991, convicting defendant, after a jury trial, of assault in the first degree, sexual abuse in the first degree, and riot in the first degree and sentencing him to concurrent terms of 5 to 15 years, 1⅓ to 7 years and 1 to 3 years, respectively, unanimously affirmed.

Defendant does not dispute that the crimes for which he was indicted actually took place. He urges instead that his various statements and admissions should have been suppressed and that, without these statements and admissions, there was inadequate evidence that he was involved. However, the fact findings made by the trial court were amply supported by the evidence, and there is no basis for not giving them due deference on appeal (*People v. Prochilo*, 41 N.Y.2d 759, 761, 395 N.Y.S.2d 635, 363 N.E.2d 1380).

In any event, the record simply does not substantiate defendant's contention that when the police first approached him, they did not know that he was involved in the case. By the time that the detectives went in search of defendant, a full day had elapsed since the mayhem in Central Park, and the police had already interviewed both the victims and many of the suspects. In that regard, the police had taken statements from numerous alleged perpetrators providing them with information concerning most of the details of the crimes committed in the park and the identity of most of the participants. At least two of the suspects had directly implicated defendant. Yet, notwithstanding that there was probable cause to believe that defendant had taken part in the riotous conduct sufficient to furnish a basis for custodial interrogation (*see, People v. Johnson*, 66 N.Y.2d 398, 402–403, 497 N.Y.S.2d 618, 488 N.E.2d 439), the fact is that defendant voluntarily agreed to accompany the detectives to the station house for questioning. Indeed, the Court of Appeals has affirmed this Court's previous determination that Yusef Salaam, who was together with defendant at the time in question, voluntarily agreed to come to the precinct for questioning (*People v. Salaam*, 83 N.Y.2d 51, 607 N.Y.S.2d 899, 629 N.E.2d 371, *affd.* 187 A.D.2d 363, 590 N.Y.S.2d 195), and there is no significant distinction between defendant's situation and that of Salaam.

Defendant maintains that an innocent person like himself, a learning disabled sixteen year old with low intelligence and no prior experience with the criminal justice system, was particularly vulnerable to the coercive pressures of police requests, and thus would have reasonably considered himself to be in custody and not in a position to refuse to be interviewed. There is no indication that defendant is retarded or otherwise incompetent. While some proof was introduced at trial that defendant may be learning disabled, evidence subsequently elicited may not be used to invalidate the findings of a suppression court (*see People v. Giles,* 73 N.Y.2d 666, 543 N.Y.S.2d 37, 541 N.E.2d 37). To the extent that defendant may be so incapacitated, this matter was not educed until after the court had rendered its ruling on defendant's motion to suppress, and, at any rate, there is no authority for the proposition that a learning disability precludes an individual from giving voluntary consent to be questioned. A minor is certainly capable of waiving his or her *Miranda* rights (*Fare v. Michael C.,* 442 U.S. 707, 99 S.Ct. 2560, 61 L.Ed.2d 197; *People v. Stephen J.B.,* 23 N.Y.2d 611, 298 N.Y.S.2d 489, 246 N.E.2d 344; Family Ct Act § 305.2[4] [b]; [7], [8]) and answering questions, and there are no grounds to hold otherwise insofar as defendant is concerned.

Consequently, defendant's various statements and admissions were either spontaneous or provided after the administration of the *Miranda* warnings, and suppression was properly denied. There was, accordingly, sufficient evidence to support the jury's finding of guilt.

Finally, defendant argues that reversal is mandated because the court, during its initial and supplemental charge on accomplice liability, supplied the jury with some examples to illustrate the concept, thereby giving the erroneous impression that defendant could be convicted because of his mere presence at the scene of the crime. Specifically, defendant complains that the court used a theater analogy to explain accomplice liability such that the jury was instructed that an actor is a player regardless of the importance of his role. While defendant does not assert that the court did not properly define the principle of accomplice liability, he, in effect, contends that the otherwise correct definition was rendered erroneous and prejudicial by the addition of certain hypotheticals, only one of which (the theater analogy) resulted in an objection.

However, a trial judge is not precluded from supplying hypothetical examples in its jury instructions as an aid to understanding the applicable law (*People v. Fagan,* 166 A.D.2d 290, 564 N.Y.S.2d 129, *lv. denied* 77 N.Y.2d 838, 567 N.Y.S.2d 206, 568 N.E.2d 655) so long as the hypothetical is fair and will not mislead the jury (*People v. Johnson,* 171 A.D.2d 532, 567 N.Y.S.2d 430, *lv. denied* 77 N.Y.2d 996, 571 N.Y.S.2d 922, 575 N.E.2d 408). Although a fair hypothetical must not be biased or uneven (*People v. Bell,* 38 N.Y.2d 116, 378 N.Y.S.2d 686, 341 N.E.2d 246) or indicate to the jury that the court has an opinion of the defendant's guilt or innocence (*People v. Hommel,* 41 N.Y.2d 427, 393 N.Y.S.2d 371, 361 N.E.2d 1020), the crucial question is whether the charge, in its entirety, conveys an appropriate legal standard and does not engender any possible confusion (*People v. Evans,* 192 A.D.2d 337, 596 N.Y.S.2d 17, *lv. denied* 81 N.Y.2d 1072, 601 N.Y.S.2d 592, 619 N.E.2d 670). Applying that standard, it is clear that the court's instructions, taken as a whole, expressed the proper definition of acting in concert and the hypotheticals used by the court, which were not "strikingly similar" to the facts in the matter herein (*People v. Woods,* 199 A.D.2d 176, 605 N.Y.S.2d 279), were certainly fair and do not require reversal of defendant's conviction.

g. Finally, read Chris Smith's New York Magazine article from October 21, 2002, for interviews with key players in the convictions, available here: http://nymag.com/nymetro/news/crimelaw/features/n_7836/.

10. *Exonerations by State, False Confessions:*

Figure 6.2

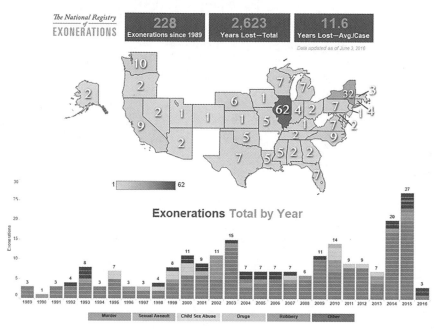

Source: The National Reg. of Exonerations

11. *Explore Further False Confessions Transcripts:* Brandon Garrett and the University of Virginia have compiled a database where you can read and review further transcripts of false confessions cases, including the original confession, the testimony at trial, and even court rulings.

http://www.law.virginia.edu/html/librarysite/garrett_falseconfess.htm

Choose one such case and examine the transcripts. How could this wrongful conviction have happened?

Chapter Seven

Scientific Standards, Statistical Evidence, and the Future of Forensic Science

A. Readings

1. Overview

Vanessa Meterko, *Strengths and Limitations of Forensic Science: What DNA Exonerations Have Taught Us and Where to Go from Here*

119 W. Va. L. Rev. 639, 646 (2016)

[T]he misapplication of forensic science is defined as an instance in which forensic evidence (i.e., analysis and/or testimony) was used to associate, identify, or implicate someone who was later conclusively proven innocent with post-conviction DNA testing, thereby demonstrating that the original forensic evidence was incorrect. To date, 158 DNA exonerees' cases—nearly half (46%) of all 343 DNA exonerees nationwide—meet this definition, making flawed forensics the second most common contributing factor among those we systematically track. In 13 cases, misapplied forensic science was the only evidence that linked an innocent suspect to a crime, but more often (in 145 cases) it appeared in conjunction with other factors, lending an air of credibility to problematic evidence like eyewitness misidentification, false confession, and/or incentivized informant testimony.

Breaking these numbers down further, serology (the study of blood and other bodily fluids) was the discipline that was misapplied most often, with 86 cases featuring flawed serological analysis and/or testimony. Although, according to the NAS, serology—and also DNA testing—are based on solid theory and research, these disciplines can be misapplied through scientific error, misleading testimony, or misconduct. A common example of misapplied serology involves testimony about a phenomenon known as masking. Humans have different blood types, which are inherited from our parents and determined by the presence or absence of different antigens. Type A, Type B, Type AB, and Type O are the four major groups in the ABO blood group system and occur with different frequencies in different ethnic populations. ABO blood group markers can be detected in blood, of course, but approximately 80% of the population also secretes blood group substances in their other bodily fluids (e.g., saliva, semen, vaginal fluid). If a sample of bodily fluid contains a mixture of a relatively large amount of the victim's biological material and a relatively small amount of the perpetrator's biological material (as is often the case in instances of rape), the victim's contribution can overwhelm the perpetrator's, rendering the perpetrator's blood type unidentifiable or masked. Therefore, while ABO blood grouping is a scientifically valid and reliable way to narrow down the pool of possible donors of a biological sample, suggesting that someone is a possible contributor without clarifying that, in instances of potential masking, literally anyone could be the donor is misleading and is a misapplication of forensic science. This is exactly what happened in the most recent (343d) DNA exoneration. Similarly, flawed DNA evidence was involved in nine cases in this sample. In these cases, DNA samples were accidentally switched; an analyst claimed that a sample was too small for testing but it was, in fact, testable with the technology available at the time, and DNA mixtures were misinterpreted (e.g., a mixture was said to have been contributed by two males when in actuality it was contributed by a male and a female).

The remaining disciplines in these cases (e.g., hair microscopy, forensic odontology/bite mark analysis, dog scent evidence, fingerprint analysis) are even more prone to misapplication than the established sciences of DNA and serology because they lack agreed-upon standards for comparison and identification, and their error rates are unknown. While DNA analysis was "originally developed in research laboratories in the context of life sciences research," other forensic disciplines were "developed in crime laboratories to aid in the investigation of evidence from a particular crime scene, and researching their limitations and foundations was never a top priority," and, consequently, they "have never been exposed to stringent scientific scrutiny." Hair microscopy was the second most common type of flawed forensic evidence in this sample of DNA exonerations, with 74 cases involving hair analysis and/or testimony that incorrectly suggested an innocent person was guilty. After several exonerations involving erroneous testimony given by different FBI hair examiners came to light, the FBI and the Department of Justice decided to conduct a review of criminal cases involving microscopic hair analysis in collaboration with the National Association of Criminal Defense Lawyers and the Innocence Project. The preliminary results of their review of trial transcripts with examiner testimony found that at least 90% contained erroneous statements. In a similar development, the Texas Forensic Science Commission recently evaluated the practice of bite mark analysis and recommended a moratorium on the use of bite mark evidence in future criminal prosecutions in Texas until the technique can be scientifically validated. Misleading bite mark evidence was found in ten DNA exoneration cases nationwide. Six cases involved flawed dog scent evidence, three involved flawed fingerprint evidence, and ten involved incorrect testimony about "other" less-common disciplines like shoe print and fiber analysis.

It is also important to acknowledge that many scientists have provided responsible analysis and testimony over the years. There are plenty of examples of proper forensic evidence among these DNA exoneration cases. For instance, early DNA testing in 1989 correctly included Christopher Ochoa—along with 16% of the population—as a potential donor of the biological material recovered from a Texas rape/murder. Later, as DNA testing technology advanced, Christopher was excluded as a possible contributor and his wrongful conviction was finally righted in 2002. Similarly, Andrew Johnson was convicted of a rape in Wyoming in 1989 when a serology expert correctly testified that he was within the 5% of the population who could have contributed the seminal fluid found in the victim's evidence collection kit. Ultimately, DNA testing showed that, in fact, Andrew was not the donor of the seminal fluid and he was exonerated in 2013. The DNA testing in Christopher Ochoa's case and the serology testing in Andrew Johnson's case were not counted as misapplications of forensic science in the Innocence Project's database of contributing factors.

Fortunately, there have been significant advances in forensic science in recent years. Since the comprehensive NAS assessment of the state of forensic science in 2009, groups like the Center for Statistics and Applications in Forensic Evidence ("CSAFE"), the Statistical and Applied Mathematical Sciences Institute ("SAMSI"), the President's Council of Advisors on Science and Technology ("PCAST"), the National Commission on Forensic Science ("NCFS"), and the Organizational Scientific Area Committees ("OSAC"), have made tremendous progress in both improving forensic science and making relevant policy recommendations and changes. However, this does not mean that all the problems related to forensic science have been solved.

Some have noted a decline in DNA exoneration cases involving misapplied forensic science in recent years. While an initial look at this trend may suggest that forensic science is no longer being misapplied, a deeper investigation does not support this conclusion. Notably, the total number of DNA exoneration cases is also decreasing. One reason for this trend may be that the wider use of DNA testing is now helping forestall potential wrongful convictions. We have certainly seen examples of that in recent years. In addition, available data suggest that the apparent decrease in wrongful convictions (and wrongful convictions involving misapplied forensic science) may be an artifact of the exoneration process.

2. Rethinking Traditional Forensic Science

Michael J. Saks, Jonathan J. Koehler, *The Coming Paradigm Shift in Forensic Identification Science*

SCIENCE August 5, 2005
Vol. 309, Issue 5736, pp. 892–895

Little more than a decade ago, forensic individualization scientists compared pairs of marks (handwriting, fingerprints, tool marks, hair, tire marks, bite marks, etc.), intuited whether the marks matched, and testified in court that whoever or whatever made one made the other. Courts almost never excluded the testimony. Cross-examination rarely questioned the foundations of the asserted expertise or the basis of the analyst's certainty.

Today, that once-complacent corner of the law and science interface has begun to unravel—or at least to regroup. The news carries reports of erroneous forensic identifications of hair, bullets, handwriting, footprints, bite marks, and even venerated fingerprints. Scientists have begun to question the core assumptions of numerous forensic sciences. Federal funding has materialized to support research that examines long-asserted but unproven claims. Courts have started taking challenges to asserted forensic science expertise seriously. A dispassionate scientist or judge reviewing the current state of the traditional forensic sciences would likely regard their claims as plausible, under-researched, and oversold.

The traditional forensic individualization sciences rest on a central assumption: that two indistinguishable marks must have been produced by a single object. Traditional forensic scientists seek to link crime scene evidence to a single person or object "to the exclusion of all others in the world." They do so by leaning on the assumption of discernible uniqueness. According to this assumption, markings produced by different people or objects are observably different. Thus, when a pair of markings is not observably different, criminalists conclude that the marks were made by the same person or object.

Although lacking theoretical or empirical foundations, the assumption of discernible uniqueness offers important practical benefits to the traditional forensic sciences. It enables forensic scientists to draw bold, definitive conclusions that can make or break cases. It excuses the forensic sciences from developing measures of object attributes, collecting population data on the frequencies of variations in those attributes, testing attribute independence, or calculating and explaining the probability that different objects share a common set of observable attributes. Without the discernible uniqueness assumption, far more scientific work would be needed, and criminalists would need to offer more tempered opinions in court.

Legal and scientific forces are converging to drive an emerging skepticism about the claims of the traditional forensic individualization sciences. As a result, these sciences are moving toward a new scientific paradigm. [We use the notion of paradigm shift not as a literal application of Thomas Kuhn's concept, but as a metaphor highlighting the transformation involved in moving from a pre-science to an empirically grounded science.] Two such forces are outgrowths of DNA typing: the discovery of erroneous convictions and a model for a scientifically sound identification science. A third force is the momentous change in the legal admissibility standards for expert testimony. A final force grows from studies of error rates across the forensic sciences.

Post-Conviction DNA Exonerations

During the past decade, scores of people who were convicted of serious crimes—including at least 14 who had been sentenced to death—have been exonerated by DNA analyses of crime scene evidence that had not been tested at the time of their trials. It was not surprising to learn that erroneous convictions sometimes occur, and

Figure 7.1

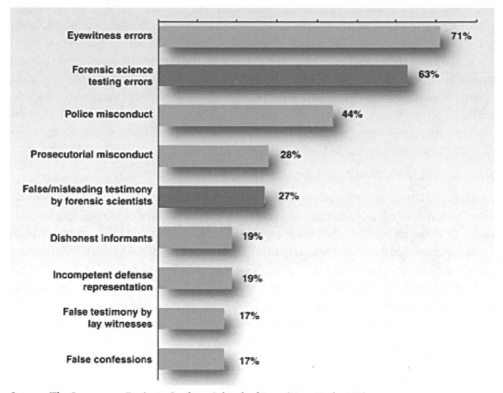

Source: The Innocence Project, Cardozo School of Law (New York, NY)

that new science and technology can help detect and correct those mistakes. Nor was it surprising to learn, from an analysis of 86 such cases (Fig. 1), that erroneous eyewitness identifications are the most common contributing factor to wrongful convictions. What was unexpected is that erroneous forensic science expert testimony is the second most common contributing factor to wrongful convictions, found in 63% of those cases. These data likely understate the relative contribution of forensic science expert testimony to erroneous convictions. Whereas lawyers, police, and lay witnesses participate in virtually every criminal case, forensic science experts participate in a smaller subset of cases—about 10 to 20% of criminal cases during the era when these DNA exonerations were originally tried.[30]

Figure 7.1 also indicates that forensic scientists are the witnesses most likely to present misleading or fraudulent testimony. Deceitful forensic scientists are a minor sidelight to this paper, but a sidelight that underscores cultural differences between normal science and forensic science. In normal science, academically gifted students

---

30. Factors associated with wrongful conviction in 86 DNA exoneration cases, based on case analysis data provided by the Innocence Project, Cardozo School of Law (New York, NY), and computed by us. Percentages exceed 100% because more than one factor was found in many cases. Red bars indicate factors related to forensic science.

receive four or more years of doctoral training where much of the socialization into the culture of science takes place. This culture emphasizes methodological rigor, openness, and cautious interpretation of data. In forensic science, 96% of positions are held by persons with bachelor's degrees (or less), 3% master's degrees, and 1% Ph.D.s. When individuals who are not steeped in the culture of science work in an adversarial, crime-fighting culture, there is a substantial risk that a different set of norms will prevail. As one former forensic scientist noted, this pressure-packed environment can lead to data fudging and fabrication: "All [forensic science] experts are tempted, many times in their careers, to report positive results when their inquiries come up inconclusive, or indeed to report a negative result as positive."

DNA Typing as the New Model for Scientific Forensic Identification

Much of the above criticism does not apply to the science of DNA typing as practiced today. Indeed, DNA typing can serve as a model for the traditional forensic sciences in three important respects. First, DNA typing technology was an application of knowledge derived from core scientific disciplines. This provided a stable structure for future empirical work on the technology. Second, the courts and scientists scrutinized applications of the technology in individual cases. As a result, early, unscientific practices were rooted out. Third, DNA typing offered data-based, probabilistic assessments of the meaning of evidentiary "matches." This practice represented an advance over potentially misleading match/no-match claims associated with other forensic identification sciences.

Immediately after DNA's first courtroom appearance in the 1980s, scientists from disciplines as varied as statistics, psychology, and evolutionary biology debated the strengths and limitations of forensic DNA evidence. Blue-ribbon panels were convened, conferences were held, unscientific practices were identified, data were collected, critical papers were written, and standards were developed and implemented. The scientific debates focused on the adequacy of DNA databases, the computation of DNA match probabilities, the training of DNA analysts, the presentation of DNA matches in the court-room, and the role of error rates. In some cases, disputants worked together to find common ground. These matters were not resolved by the forensic scientists themselves, by fiat, or by neglect. Most exaggerated claims and counterclaims about DNA evidence have been replaced by scientifically defensible propositions. Although some disagreement remains, the scientific process worked.

One of the great strengths of DNA typing is that it uses a statistical approach based on population genetics theory and empirical testing. Experts evaluate matches between suspects and crime scene DNA evidence in terms of the probability of random matches across different reference populations (e.g., different ethnicities). These probabilities are derived from databases that identify the frequency with which various alleles occur at different locations on the DNA strand. The traditional forensic sciences could and should emulate this approach. Each subfield must construct databases of sample characteristics and use these databases to support a probabilistic approach to identification. Fingerprinting could be one of the first areas to make the transition to this approach because large fingerprint databases already exist. The greatest chal-

Figure 7.2

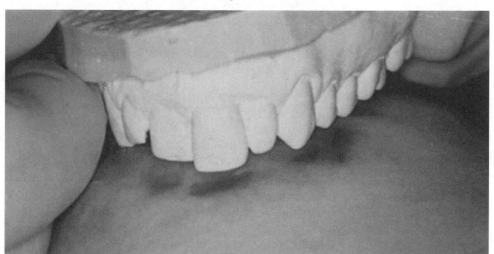

Bite mark evidence exhibit from trial of Ray Krone, suggesting alignment of a cast of Krone's dentition with bite wounds in victim's flesh [State v. Krone, 182 Ariz. 319 (1995)]. A forensic odontologist testified that this showed Krone to be the biter. Krone was convicted of murder and sentenced to death, but a decade later he was exonerated by DNA analysis. [Source: E. Thomas Barham (Los Alamitos, CA) and Alan Simpson (Phoenix, AZ), attorneys for Krone]

lenge in this effort would be to develop measures of the complex images presented by fingerprints, tool marks, bite marks, handwriting, etc. (Figs. 7.2 and 7.3). Forensic scientists will need to work with experts in differential geometry, topology, or other fields to develop workable measures.

A second data collection effort that would strengthen the scientific foundation of the forensic sciences involves estimating error rates. Although the theoretical promise of forensic technology is considerable, the practical value of any particular technology is limited by the extent to which potentially important errors arise. The best way to identify the frequency with which errors occur is to conduct blind, external proficiency tests using realistic samples. A proficiency test requires analysts to make judgments about samples whose properties are known. External proficiency tests are conducted by an agency unaffiliated with the forensic scientist's laboratory. Externality is important to the integrity of proficiency tests because laboratories have strong incentives to be perceived as error-free. An even better test would be a blind proficiency test, in which the analyst believes the test materials are part of ordinary case work. Blindness increases the validity of proficiency test results because it ensures that analysts treat the test sample as they would other case samples. Although proficiency tests are used in many forensic sciences, the tests are generally infrequent, internal, and unrealistic; blind tests are practically nonexistent.

Changes in the Law

Until recently, courts assessed expertise by looking for superficial indicia of validity. In the 19th century, courts were impressed by "qualifications" and success in the mar-

Figure 7.3

Image of two bullets viewed through a comparison microscope. The bullets were fired from two consecutively manufactured Smith & Wesson 38 Special revolver barrels. Whether fired through the same or different barrels, numerous matching and nonmatching striations are engraved onto bullets. To reliably identify the barrel through which a questioned bullet was fired, an examiner must distinguish among class, subclass, and individual characteristics. These two bullets illustrate subclass characteristic agreement of striated markings on a groove impression that could be mistaken for individual characteristics. Without investigating the potential for subclass carryover, the examiner could mistake these as having been fired from the same gun. [Source: Bruce Moran, firearms examiner with the Sacramento County (CA) District Attorney, Laboratory of Forensic Services]

ketplace. If the market valued an asserted expertise or expert, courts generally did, too. In *Frye v. United States* [293 F. 1013 (D.C. Cir. 1923)], a federal appellate court confronted the question of admissibility of an expertise that had no life in any commercial marketplace. The court solved the problem by substituting an intellectual marketplace. The court asked whether the proffered expertise had "gained general acceptance in the particular field in which it belongs." Sixty years later, the *Frye* test had become the dominant expert evidence filter in American courts.

In 1993, the law began to catch up with the scientific method. In *Daubert v. Merrell Dow Pharmaceuticals* [509 U.S. 579 (1993)], the U.S. Supreme Court introduced a new standard for the admissibility of scientific evidence. Under *Daubert*, proffered scientific testimony must be shown to stand on a dependable foundation. The court suggested that trial judges making this determination consider whether the proffered science has been tested, the methodological soundness of that testing, and the results of that testing. The *Daubert* test in effect lowers the threshold for admission of sound cutting-edge science and raises the threshold for long-asserted expertise that lacks a scientific foundation. Seriously applied, the *Daubert* test subjects the forensic sciences to a first-principles scientific scrutiny that poses a profound challenge to fields that lack rigorous supporting data.

United States v. Starzecpyzel [880 F. Supp. 1027 (S.D.N.Y. 1995)] offered an early indication of how *Daubert* could change judicial views. After an extensive hearing on the soundness of asserted handwriting identification expertise, a federal district court concluded that the field had no scientific basis: "[T]he testimony at the *Daubert* hearing firmly established that forensic document examination, despite the existence of a certification program, professional journals and other trappings of science, cannot, after *Daubert*, be regarded as 'scientific ... knowledge'" (p. 1038). However, the court did not exclude this unscientific testimony. It reasoned that handwriting identification did not have to reach the *Daubert* standard because *Daubert* applied only to scientific evidence, and handwriting identification plainly was not scientific evidence. Thus, when a forensic science was found to stand on a weak foundation, the threshold of admission was lowered to accommodate this weakness.

In *Kumho Tire v. Carmichael* [526 U.S. 137 (1999)], the Supreme Court directly confronted the question of whether *Daubert* applies to nonsciences. A consortium of law enforcement organizations prepared an amicus brief urging that *Daubert* scrutiny not be extended to the testimony of police agency expert witnesses. The brief argued that "the great bulk of expert testimony provided by law enforcement officers does not involve scientific theories, methodologies, techniques, or data in any respect.... Instead, law enforcement officers testify about such things as accident reconstruction, fingerprint, footprint and handprint [identification], handwriting analysis, firearms markings and toolmarks and the unique characteristics of guns, bullets, and shell casings, and bloodstain pattern identification." Ironically, then, fields that initially gained entry to the courts by declaring themselves to be "sciences" now sought to remain in court by denying any connection with scientific methods, data, or principles. Despite efforts to preserve the "nonscience" loophole, the Supreme Court doctrinally sealed it shut when *Kumho Tire* held that all expert testimony must pass appropriate tests of validity to be admissible in court.

Error Rates

Although *Daubert's* testing recommendations are familiar to most scientists, there has been remarkably little research on the accuracy of traditional forensic sciences. Proficiency tests in some fields offer a step in the right direction, even though simple tasks and infrequent peer review limit their value. Nonetheless, the available data hint that some forensic sciences are best interpreted in tandem with error rates estimated from sound studies.

Unfortunately, forensic scientists often reject error rate estimates in favor of arguments that theirs is an error-free science. For example, an FBI document section chief asserted that all certified document examiners in the United States would agree

Figure 7.4

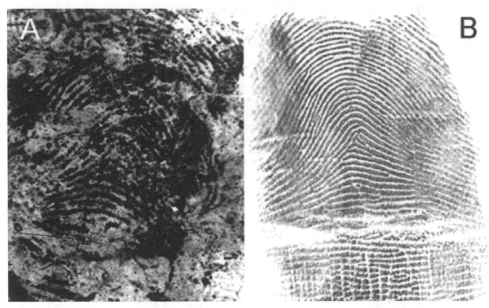

(A) A latent fingerprint believed to belong to a terrorist involved in train bombings in Madrid, Spain, in March 2004. (B) A database print belonging to Brandon Mayfield of Portland, Oregon. On the basis of these prints (though not necessarily these very images), FBI fingerprint examiners erroneously identified Mayfield as the bomber. [Source: Problem Idents, onin.com/fp/problemidents.html#madrid]

with his conclusions in every case. Likewise, fingerprint experts commonly claim that all fingerprint experts would reach the same conclusions about every print. Such hubris was on display in spring 2004 when the FBI declared that a fingerprint recovered from a suspicious plastic bag near the scene of a terrorist bombing in Madrid provided a "100 percent match" to an Oregon attorney (Fig. 7.4). The FBI eventually conceded error when Spanish fingerprint experts linked the print to someone else.

The FBI and other agencies often seek to preserve the illusion of perfection after disclosure of such errors by distinguishing between human errors ("possible") and errors of method ("impossible"). A leading FBI scientist explained the distinction to the court in *United States v. Llera-Plaza* I [58 Fed. R. Evid. Serv. 1 (E.D. Pa. 2002)]:[31] "We have to understand that error rate is a difficult thing to calculate. I mean, people are trying to do this, it shouldn't be done, it can't be done.... An error rate is a wispy thing like smoke, it changes over time.... If you made a mistake in the past, that's certainly valid information, but to say there's an error rate that's definable would be a misrepresentation.... Now, error rate deals with people, you should have a method that is defined and stays within its limits, so it doesn't have error at all. So the method is one thing, people making mistakes is another issue."

Such claims are problematic. First, the suggestion that humans err but forensic techniques do not is unfalsifiable. It is impossible to disentangle "method" errors

---

31. 188 F. Supp. 2d 492, vacated and superseded by 188 F. Supp. 2d 549.

from "practitioner" errors in fields where the method is primarily the judgment of the examiner. Second, even if such disentanglement were possible, it is a red herring. When factfinders hear evidence of a forensic match, a proper assessment of the probative value of that match requires awareness of the chance that a mistake was made. The source of such a mistake is irrelevant for this purpose. If method errors could be distinguished from practitioner errors, a 1% method error affects the probative value of the match in exactly the same way as a 1% practitioner error. Identifying sources of error is relevant for improving forensic science practice, but it plays no role in identifying the probative importance of a match.

Third, the suggestion that error rates do not exist because they change over time and are not specific to the case at hand is a base-rate fallacy. In this fallacy of reasoning, people underuse (or willfully ignore) general background data in judgment tasks because they believe the data are irrelevant to the instant case. However, general background data (or base rates) are relevant for specific predictions. For example, although risk estimates for a disease fluctuate and are developed on patients other than the patient now seeking medical advice, these estimates provide information useful for predicting whether this patient will contract the disease. A 20% base-rate risk of contracting the disease makes it more likely that the patient will get the disease than would a 1% risk. Likewise, an X% base-rate risk of error in a given forensic science provides some indication of the chance that a particular conclusion is in error.

Data from proficiency tests and other examinations suggest that forensic errors are not minor imperfections. Spectrographic voice identification error rates are as high as 63%, depending on the type of voice sample tested. Handwriting error rates average around 40% and sometimes approach 100%. False-positive error rates for bite marks run as high as 64%. Those for microscopic hair comparisons are about 12% (using results of mitochondrial DNA testing as the criterion). Fingerprint examiners generally fare better, although data from a well-known forensic testing program contradict industry boasts of perfect, or even near-perfect, agreement. Since 1995, about one-fourth of examiners failed to correctly identify all latent prints in this test (which includes 9 to 12 latent prints and palm-prints). About 4 to 5% of examiners committed false-positive errors on at least one latent. In one test, 20% of examiners mistook one person's prints for those of his twin. The editor of the leading fingerprint journal called this performance "unacceptable." It is noteworthy that these misidentifications are not confined to a single lab, circumstance, or marking. Moreover, the misidentification rates do not show a clear pattern of improvement (the misidentification rates in 2004 were 4 to 6%). Nor are these errors limited to arguably artificial testing situations; erroneous fingerprint identifications have made their way out of the crime lab and into prosecutions in at least 21 documented cases.

Forensic science proficiency tests and examinations are obviously imperfect indicators of the rate at which errors occur in practice. This fact does not justify ignoring the worrisome data these tests have yielded. Indeed, these data are probably best regarded as lower-bound estimates of error rates. Because the tests are relatively easy (according to test participants), and because participants know that mistakes will be identified and punished, test error rates (particularly the false-positive error rate) probably are lower than those in everyday casework.

The studies mentioned above cry out for attention and follow-up investigations. In light of the law's growing reluctance to accept experts' personal guarantees in lieu of scientific data, these studies should increase candor about performance and create pressure for improvement.

The Future

The traditional forensic sciences need look no further than their newest sister discipline, DNA typing, for guidance on how to put the science into forensic identification science. This effort should begin with adoption of the basic-research model. Just as DNA scientists tested the genetic assumptions that undergirded DNA typing theory (e.g., Hardy-Weinberg equilibrium), traditional forensic scientists should design experiments that test the core assumptions of their fields. As basic research knowledge grows, experts will be able to inform courts about the relative strengths and weaknesses of their theories and methods, and suggest how that knowledge applies to individual cases.

At the same time, data should be collected on the frequency with which markings and attribute variations occur in different populations. In addition to their case-specific benefits, these data may also facilitate the development of artificial intelligence or computer-aided pattern recognition programs for the identification sciences. Forensic scientists might also adopt protocols, such as blind examinations in combination with realistic samples, that minimize the risks that their success rates will be inflated and their conclusions biased by extraneous evidence and assumptions. When matches are identified, forensic scientists in all fields would compute and report random-match probabilities similar to those used in DNA typing. These estimates—in combination with error rate estimates provided by mandatory, well-constructed proficiency tests— would inform fact-finders about the probative value of the evidentiary match.

Simply put, we envision a paradigm shift in the traditional forensic identification sciences in which untested assumptions and semi-informed guesswork are replaced by a sound scientific foundation and justifiable protocols. Although obstacles exist both inside and outside forensic science, the time is ripe for the traditional forensic sciences to replace antiquated assumptions of uniqueness and perfection with a more defensible empirical and probabilistic foundation.

Jennifer L. Mnookin, *The Courts, the NAS, and the Future of Forensic Science*
75 BROOK. L. REV. 1209, 1217–30 (2010)

In what follows, I focus primarily on latent fingerprint identification, but it is important to realize that I could tell an extremely similar tale about a variety of other kinds of forensic science, including firearms identification, handwriting identification, bitemark identification, toolmark identification, and the like. Fingerprint evidence is, in all likelihood, both more probative and less error-prone than some other kinds of forensic identification evidence, and it has a long and extremely substantial courtroom use. It therefore provides an especially good focus, for if the problems I am describing exist within this forensic domain, they are likely to be equally or more acute in other areas of pattern identification.

Fingerprint evidence was first used in the American courtroom nearly a century ago in 1911, and for most of its history it has been seen as the "gold standard" of forensic science. In recent years, however, whatever metal out of which this evidentiary standard was made has rather noticeably begun to tarnish.

The basic approach taken by latent fingerprint experts involves what they call ACE-V. This acronym stands for analysis, comparison, evaluation and verification. First, in the analysis step, the examiner looks closely at the latent print associated with the crime at issue, and decides whether there is enough useful information contained in the image that it is "of value" for further examination. If so, the examiner then looks carefully at the various minutiae that he or she sees in the image, and, depending on local practices and the apparent difficulty of the print, typically marks up the print and documents the minutiae she observes. Second, in the comparison stage, the expert compares the latent print to a particular source print, noting both observed similarities and differences. Third, the analyst evaluates these similarities and differences, and reaches one of three, and only three, conclusions: identification, exclusion, or inconclusive. Note that these are the only permissible options available to a latent fingerprint expert—a match, a non-match, or a conclusion of "I don't know." "Maybe," "possibly," and "probably," are not determinations presently permitted to fingerprint examiners under their professional rules and norms. Finally, in the verification step, if the first examiner has determined that the prints match, a second examiner takes the prints and goes through the same process to re-analyze them. In most laboratories, this step is conducted by an examiner who is informed of the original examiner's conclusion before undertaking his or her own analysis. This verifying examiner typically recognizes both that (a) he or she is verifying a conclusion already reached by someone else; and (b) that the conclusion already reached is that the prints do match.

Latent fingerprint examiners regularly claim that ACE-V is a version of the scientific method and assert that it offers a reliable methodology that establishes that fingerprint evidence is indeed a valid science. Many courts have agreed that ACE-V passes muster under *Daubert*.

In fact, ACE-V's relationship to the scientific method is tenuous at best: as a methodology, it amounts, more or less, to having two different examiners look carefully at a set of fingerprints. To be sure, the "scientific method" is itself a complicated and capacious idea, not altogether easily or adequately defined. But however we might define the critical characteristics of the scientific method, it surely amounts to more than simply careful, semi-structured observation. At root, ACE-V in its current incarnation amounts to no more and no less than a set of procedures to describe the careful comparison of a latent print with a potential source print by an initial examiner and a subsequent verifier. While careful observation and the recording of one's observations may be a necessary part of many scientific practices, careful observation in and of itself cannot be meaningfully said to constitute a method. Moreover, the simple act of labeling this process of careful observation as a methodology does not make it into one. Nor does bestowing upon it the label "scientific" tell us, through the moniker, anything about its likely validity or error rate.

The basic difficulty is that ACE-V is too general in conception and scope to provide much in the way of guidance or constraint for those who practice it. The devil is in the details—what constitutes analysis? How exactly does a competent comparison take place? When are apparent similarities misleading, and when might apparent differences be attributed to something other than the two prints deriving from different sources? ACE-V, as a methodology, does not help answer any of these critical methodological questions, because its categories are too general and insufficiently substantive.

It is as if one were to describe the methodology for fixing a car by the acronym DACT—Diagnose, Acquire, Conduct, and Test. We could describe the DACT car-repair methodology as follows: (1) diagnose the car's problem, (2) acquire the necessary parts for the repair, (3) conduct the repair, and (4) test to verify that the repair fixed the problem. Whether or not such a car-repair methodology actually works, or how well it works, would depend entirely on the content given to these very broad categories in specific instances. If in fact, someone diagnosed the car's problem correctly, located the appropriate parts, and conducted the repair properly, the methodology would work. But if the mechanic misdiagnosed the difficulty, acquired the wrong parts, or made an error when conducting the repair, the repair would fail, even though he or she had, in some sense, followed the methodology. Now, in light of the failed repair effort, a defender of ACE-V (and DACT) might suggest that the mechanic had not in fact followed DACT correctly, because he or she misdiagnosed the problem, made an error in the repair, or made some other mistake in application. The DACT defender might even argue that the mechanic's failure to fix the car established that she failed to follow DACT; that following DACT necessitates doing the steps correctly, not just endeavoring to follow them. But that response would render DACT (or, analogously, ACE-V), in some sense, merely tautological. The method does not describe with any specificity how to complete its requirements correctly. It is therefore illegitimate to argue that the method has not been followed simply because the desired outcome did not occur, precisely because the method itself underspecifies what is required. DACT itself does not explain how to diagnose, or what constitutes a sufficient repair, just as ACE-V does not explain how to analyze or compare (beyond calling for careful looking at a target portion of each print), or what constitutes a sufficient evaluation. To be sure, ACE-V might be a useful description of the basic steps a fingerprint examiner takes in order to conduct his or her examination, but that does not make it a very useful description of a methodology, much less a so-called "scientific method."

Surely, one would think, ACE-V in practice must amount to more than I am suggesting? Latent print examiners do have norms about what kinds of print ridge detail and minutiae they ought to be looking at, and examiners are trained to search both for relevant minutiae and to assess their contextual relationship and position on a fingerprint. And latent print examiners do discuss with one another, informally, their personal notions regarding sufficiency, or the virtues and limitations of different categories of print information.

While individual examiners or even sometimes laboratories may develop working rules of thumb about the quantity of similarity required, latent fingerprint examination as a field lacks any formalized specifications about what is required in order to declare a match. There is no required minimum number of points of resemblance or minimum number of total print features, nor any required quantum of any specific kind of ridge detail. Instead, examiners decide for themselves, based on their training and experience, how much similarity is sufficient to declare a match. Moreover, when examiners look at a print, they may not even be focusing on the same features. Two fingerprint analysts will often focus on different minutiae in their examination of the same print; indeed, sometimes the same examiner, when given the same print at a different time, will focus on different minutiae than he or she did the first time. The judgment is fundamentally a subjective one, not based on any formalized measures of either quantity or sufficiency.

Additionally, latent fingerprint examiners do not generally employ any statistical information or models in the ordinary ACE-V process. The field presently does not have or make use of robust statistically-based data about the frequency of different friction ridge characteristics. Analysts do not make regular or structured use in their comparisons of empirical studies showing how common or how rare different fingerprint details might be. They do not presently make use of any statistically-validated standards to justify how many identifying characteristics must be the same on two prints in order to warrant a finding that they match. Nor do they employ a probabilistic approach to determining the likelihood that a print selected at random would have that quantum of similarity, akin to the use of "random-match probability" in DNA identification. Although significant strides are being made toward developing these kinds of information, technical obstacles still limit the ability to develop a satisfactory statistical measure of the frequency of various ridge characteristics. As of now, there simply is no well-accepted, fully-specified statistical model that is available for latent fingerprint examiners to employ.

The list of difficulties continues. A fundamental tenet of latent fingerprint analysis is the "one discrepancy rule"—if there is even one genuine discrepancy between the latent print and a potential source print, then the two prints cannot have come from the same source. This, however, invites the critical question of how to decide what constitutes a discrepancy, as opposed to a dissimilarity that can legitimately be explained in some other way. The problem is that no two print impressions are ever truly identical—every single impression from a print is distinct from every other impression of a print, different to some extent even from those that came from the same source. A print image can be affected by the pressure with which it was left, the surface on which it was made, the processes by which it was lifted, and many other factors. The question when comparing two prints, then, is not whether they are truly "identical"—for they will never be truly identical—but rather, whether they are sufficiently similar to each other to permit the conclusion that they came from the same source. The examiner needs to determine whether apparent differences are true dissimilarities, or instead, merely artifacts that ought not to be deemed meaningful. Unfortunately, latent fingerprint examiners lack any formalized criteria for determining when a difference between two prints is genuinely a dissimilarity, or when it might appropriately be explained in other ways. At root, this is again a matter of subjective judgment by the trained examiner.

Note, however, that the fact that these judgments are subjective does not necessarily imply that they are incorrect or unreliable. If I were to look at many different photographs of my sister, no two images of her would be identical. And yet, my judgment of whether any given photograph was an image of my sister or actually an image of someone else bearing a certain degree of resemblance to my sister would, I would wager, have a high probability of being correct. I would posit that my ability to identify images containing my sister, and to avoid misidentifying images of other people as my sister would be quite high—notwithstanding my lack of formal criteria for doing so. The absence of formal, validated standards for making such identification of my sister does not mean that I lack all relevant knowledge. My experience of many years of seeing my sister in a great variety of contexts would indeed likely help me with the identification tasks.

However, I also suspect that my ability to identify my sister in photographs would be strong but not perfect. In some images, she might be too far away, or too blurry, or someone else might bear such a strong resemblance to her, that despite my life-long knowledge of her from every angle, I might nonetheless mistake the other person for my sister. Or conversely, I might fail to recognize that some picture truly did show an image of my sister. Of course, to determine how often I was right or wrong, we would also want to make sure we had a good method by which to determine "ground truth," whether or not the photograph truly was of my sister.

The purpose of this analogy is to suggest three points that apply as much to fingerprint identifications as to my hypothetical efforts to identify my sister. First, I want to suggest that experience can be a legitimate basis for knowledge. Second, I want to suggest that knowledge need not necessarily be formalized to count as legitimate or valid. However, and this is the third point, if we wanted to find out just how good my ability to recognize my sister in photographs really was, we would need to depend on something that went beyond my say-so. We would not want simply to take my word for it when I said I was good at the task. We would not want to take the simple fact of my extensive experience looking at my sister as proof of my identification talents. Nor would we want to blindly accept my opinion that particular photos actually were or were not of my sister.

Instead of taking my say-so, my experience, and my conclusions as proof of my accuracy, we should carefully test my actual proficiency at the tasks. We would need to investigate empirically just how well I did identify my sister; in what array of circumstances I succeeded; and when and how often the task proved beyond my capacity. Indeed, ... an equivalent focus on serious, careful proficiency testing of practitioners is precisely what we ought to demand in the realm of forensic science as well. Just as we would want proficiency testing to verify my claimed experience-based ability to identify my sister, so we also ought to require significant proficiency of fingerprint examiners and other pattern identification analysts. And just as we ought not to simply take my assertions about my conclusions' accuracy as proof of actual accuracy, we ought not to take fingerprint examiners' experience-based assertions of accuracy as proof of accuracy either.

* * *

We do know that errors sometimes occur, though it is impossible on the basis of what we presently know to attempt to quantify their frequency. One particular fingerprint error—perhaps the monster of all fingerprint errors, the most high-profile, embarrassing fingerprint mistake in recent history, at least here in the United States— has contributed to shaping and framing the discourse surrounding latent fingerprint identification. This mistake was sufficiently public, serious, and embarrassing that it led to a substantial inquiry into its causes; more generally, it made the fingerprint community—and the legal community—recognize that fingerprint errors were not simply a matter of incompetence or an issue of purely academic concern. I am referring, of course, to the mistaken identification of Brandon Mayfield, an attorney from Portland, Oregon who was held as a material witness in relation to the 2004 Madrid train bombing. The only evidentiary basis for suspecting his involvement was an alleged fingerprint match. Mayfield's print had been one of the possible source prints suggested by a computer database search using an AFIS (Automated Fingerprint Identification System). Mayfield's print appeared fourth down on the computer-generated list of suggestions—and according to the FBI, his print was a definite match.

Mayfield insisted that the identification had to be a mistake. He told authorities he had never set foot in Spain, had remained entirely in the United States during the relevant period, and indeed, lacked a passport. But three separate fingerprint examiners at the FBI, including two of the most respected senior examiners in the office, all concluded that the match was 100% certain. Even an independent, court-appointed expert confirmed the match as well.

The Spanish authorities were less convinced, and after several weeks, located another suspect, an Algerian named Ouhnane Daoud, in a different database, who, they claimed, was the actual source of the print. Eventually, the FBI concurred. The FBI was deeply embarrassed, Mayfield was released from custody, and eventually received compensation of $2 million.

What happened? I will mention just two of the most important causes of the error. First, one portion of one of Brandon Mayfield's prints really does bear a striking resemblance to one portion of one of Ouhnane Daoud's fingers. There is no doubt that portions of the two prints are extremely similar, and the resemblance between Mayfield's finger and the portion of the image most clearly visible on the latent recovered from Madrid was, as it happens, particularly strong. How often are we likely to see such a high degree of resemblance in prints from different sources? No one really knows. The Inspector General's report, an independent investigation conducted in the aftermath of the scandal, insists that this degree of similarity is extraordinarily rare. Perhaps so, but the truth is that we do not actually know how common or rare that degree of apparent similarity may be. It is clear that the growing size of the databases used for fingerprint analysis increase the risks of misidentifications like this one. Latent fingerprint examiners, at present, do make regular use of AFIS systems, computerized databases to generate a set of possible matching prints—possible "cold hits" based on a fingerprint match. But the computer algorithms are far from perfect, and thus the computer search process alone cannot determine whether any of the possible prints actually match. Only the examiner, using ACE-V to compare each AFIS suggestion to the latent print, can make that determination. As the databases grow, so grows the possibility of highly similar near-misses like Brandon Mayfield's—fingerprints so similar that they might fool even crack fingerprint experts.

In addition to the unexpected degree of similarity between the prints from different sources, it appears that cognitive bias also played a role in the debacle. Immigration lawyer Mayfield was a Muslim; he had converted to Islam some time earlier. He had also once represented a known terrorist in a child custody dispute. While it appears that the FBI investigators did not know these facts about Mayfield when they first determined that his print matched the one found on the detonation materials in Madrid, their subsequent awareness of this information made them more reluctant to reopen the issue or contemplate the possibility that they had made an error. More generally, even apart from this contextual information, it seems that once the first FBI examiner declared the prints to match, the verifying examiners expected to find a match. It is no great surprise, then, that they found precisely what they expected to find, likely the result of a mixture of peer pressure and expectation bias.

3. Base Rates, Error Rates, and Proficiency Tests

William C. Thompson and Edward L. Schumann,
Interpretation of Statistical Evidence in Criminal Trials:
The Prosecutor's Fallacy and the Defense Attorney's Fallacy
11 Law & Hum. Behav. 167, 167–85 (1987)

Crime laboratories often play an important role in the identification of criminal suspects. Laboratory tests may show, for example, that blood shed by the perpetrator at the scene of the crime matches the suspect's blood type, that a hair pulled from the head of the perpetrator matches samples of the suspect's hair, or that carpet fibers found on the victim's body match the carpet in the suspect's apartment. Testimony about "matches" found through these comparisons is called associative evidence. It is increasingly common in criminal trials where the defendant's identity is at issue.

Associative evidence is sometimes accompanied by statistical testimony about the incidence rate of the "matching" characteristic. Where tests show the defendant and perpetrator share the same blood type, for example, an expert may provide information on the percentage of people in the general population who possess that blood type. Where microscopic comparisons reveal a match between the defendant's hair and samples of the perpetrator's hair, the expert may provide information on the incidence rate of such "matches" among hairs drawn from different individuals. During the past 15 years, forensic scientists have devoted much effort to studying the incidence rate of various characteristics of hair, soil, glass, paint, and bodily fluids. Statistical data from this literature are increasingly presented in criminal trials. One legal commentator, discussing research on blood typing, concluded that "our criminal justice system is now at the threshold of an explosion in the presentation of mathematical testimony."

The reaction of appellate courts to this type of evidence has been divided. The conflict stems largely from differing assumptions about the way jurors respond to incidence rate statistics. A few appellate courts have rejected such evidence on the grounds that jurors are likely to greatly overestimate its value.[32] The majority of jurisdictions, however, admit such evidence on the grounds that jurors are unlikely to find it misleading and will give it appropriate weight. Legal commentary on the issue appears divided between those who argue that statistical evidence may have an exaggerated impact on the jury (Tribe, 1971), and those who argue that statistical evidence is likely to be underutilized.

Which of these positions is correct? Although no studies have examined people's evaluation of incidence rate statistics directly, research does exist on people's reactions to similar types of statistical information. A number of studies have shown, for example, that when people are asked to judge the likelihood of an event they often ignore or underutilize statistics on the base rate frequency of that event. When judging whether a man is a lawyer or an engineer, for example, people tend to give less weight than they should to statistics on the relative number of lawyers and engineers in the relevant population (Kahneman & Tversky, 1973). This error has been labeled the base rate fallacy.

Because base rate statistics are similar to incidence rate statistics, one is tempted to assume incidence rates will be underutilized as well. There are important differences between the two types of statistics, however, which render this generalization problematic. Base rate statistics indicate the frequency of a target outcome in a relevant population, while incidence rate statistics indicate the frequency of a trait or characteristic that is merely diagnostic of the target outcome. Suppose one is judging the likelihood Joan, who works in a tall building and owns a briefcase, is a lawyer. The percentage of women in Joan's building who are lawyers is a base rate statistic. The

---

32. People v. Robinson, 1970; People v. Macedono, 1977; State v. Carlson, 1978; People v. McMillen, 1984.

percentage of women in the building who own briefcases is an incidence rate statistic. In a criminal trial, the percentage of defendants in some relevant comparison population who are guilty is a base rate statistic,[33] while the percentage of some relevant population who possess a characteristic linking the defendant to the crime is an incidence rate statistic. Because incidence rate statistics are likely to play a different role in people's inferences than base rate statistics, people's tendency to underutilize the latter may not generalize to the former.

Research on the "pseudodiagnosticity phenomenon" has examined people's reactions to a form of statistical data more closely analogous to incidence rate statistics. In one series of studies, Beyth-Marom and Fischhoff asked people to judge the likelihood that a man, drawn from a group consisting of university professors and business executives, is a professor (rather than an executive) based on the fact he is a member of the Bears Club. These researchers were interested in how people respond to information about the percentage of professors and business executives who are "Bears." Data on the percentage of business executives who are Bears are most analogous to incidence rate statistics because they speak to the probability the man would be a Bear if he is not a professor, just as incidence rate statistics speak to the probability a defendant would possess a "matching" characteristic if he is not guilty.

When subjects in these studies were asked what information they would require to evaluate the probability that the man was a professor based on the fact he is a "Bear," most were interested primarily in knowing the percentage of professors who are Bears; only half expressed an interest in knowing the percentage of executives who are "Bears," although the two types of information are equally important. Moreover, those subjects who expressed an interest in the latter percentage often did so based on mistaken or illogical reasoning. Nevertheless, when subjects were informed of the respective percentages, most subjects considered both and adjusted their beliefs in the proper direction. Beyth-Marom and Fischhoff conclude that "people are much better at using [statistical] information … than they are at seeking it out … or articulating reasons for its usage."

Although the findings of Beyth-Marom and Fischhoff are hopeful, anecdotal evidence suggests people sometimes make serious errors when evaluating incidence rate statistics. One of the authors recently discussed the use of incidence rate statistics with a deputy district attorney. This experienced prosecutor insisted that one can

33. Base rate statistics, when used in a trial, are sometimes called "naked statistical evidence" (Kaye, 1982). Where a person is struck by a bus of unknown ownership, evidence that a particular company operates 90% of the buses on that route is "naked statistical evidence" on who owns the bus. Where a man possessing heroin is charged with concealing an illegally imported narcotic, evidence that 98% of heroin in the U.S. is illegally imported is "naked statistical evidence" on whether the heroin possessed by the defendant was illegally imported. Courts have generally treated "naked statistical evidence" differently from incidence rate statistics. Although the majority of jurisdictions admit incidence rate statistics, courts almost universally reject "naked statistical evidence" (see, e.g., Smith v. Rapid Transit, 1945), though there are a few exceptions where its admissibility has been upheld (e.g., Turner V. U.S, 1970; Sindell v. Abbott Labs, 1980). For general discussions of "naked statistical evidence," see Kaye (1982), Cohen (1977), and Tribe (1971).

determine the probability of a defendant's guilt by subtracting the incidence rate of a "matching" characteristic from one. In a case where the defendant and perpetrator match on a blood type found in 10% of the population, for example, he reasoned that there is a 10% chance the defendant would have this blood type if he were innocent and therefore concluded there is a 90% chance he is guilty. This assessment is misguided because it purports to determine the defendant's probability of guilt based solely on the associative evidence, ignoring the strength of other evidence in the case. If a prosecutor falls victim to this error, however, it is possible that jurors do as well.

The fallacy in the prosecutor's logic can best be seen if we apply his analysis to a different problem. Suppose you are asked to judge the probability a man is a lawyer based on the fact he owns a briefcase. Let us assume all lawyers own a briefcase but only one person in ten in the general population owns a briefcase. Following the prosecutor's logic, you would jump to the conclusions that there is a 90% chance the man is a lawyer. But this conclusion is obviously wrong. We know that the number of nonlawyers is many times greater than the number of lawyers. Hence, lawyers are probably outnumbered by briefcase owners who are not lawyers (and a given briefcase owner is more likely to be a nonlawyer than a lawyer). To draw conclusions about the probability the man is a lawyer based on the fact he owns a briefcase, we must consider not just the incidence rate of briefcase ownership, but also the a priori likelihood of being a lawyer. Similarly, to draw conclusions about the probability a criminal suspect is guilty based on evidence of a "match," we must consider not just the percentage of people who would match but also the a priori likelihood that the defendant in question is guilty.

The prosecutor's misguided judgmental strategy (which we shall call the Prosecutor's Fallacy) could lead to serious error, particularly where the other evidence in the case is weak and therefore the prior probability of guilt is low. Suppose, for example, that one initially estimates the suspect's probability of guilt to be only .20, but then receives additional evidence showing that the defendant and perpetrator match on a blood type found in 10% of the population. According to Bayes theorem, this new evidence should increase one's subjective probability of guilt to .71, not .90.

There is also anecdotal evidence for a second error, which we first heard voiced by a criminal defense attorney and therefore call the Defense Attorney's Fallacy. Victims of this fallacy assume associative evidence is irrelevant, regardless of the rarity of the "matching" characteristic. They reason that associative evidence is irrelevant because it shows, at best, that the defendant and perpetrator are both members of the same large group. Suppose, for example, that the defendant and perpetrator share a blood type possessed by only 1% of the population. Victims of the fallacy reason that in a city of 1 million there would be approximately 10,000 people with this blood type. They conclude there is little if any relevance in the fact that the defendant and perpetrator both belong to such a large group. What this reasoning fails to take into account, of course, is that the great majority of people with the relevant blood type are not suspects in the case at hand. The associative evidence drastically narrows the group of people who are or could have been suspects, while failing to exclude the defendant, and is therefore highly probative, as a Bayesian analysis shows. The Defense Attorney's Fallacy is not limited to defense attorneys. Several appellate justices also appear to be victims of this fallacy.[34] If defense attorneys and appellate justices fall victim to this fallacy, it is quite possible that some jurors do as well, thereby giving less weight to associative evidence than it warrants.

Whether people fall victim to the Prosecutor's Fallacy, the Defense Attorney's Fallacy, or neither may depend on the manner in which incidence rate statistics are presented and explained. In criminal trials, forensic experts often present information about incidence rates in terms of the conditional probability the defendant would have a particular characteristic if he were innocent. Where 1% of the population possess a blood type shared by the defendant and perpetrator, for example, experts often present only the conclusory statement that there is one chance in 100 that the defendant would have this blood type if he were innocent. This type of testimony seems especially likely to lead jurors to commit the Prosecutor's Fallacy. On the other hand, a defense tactic used in some actual cases is to point out that, notwithstanding its low incidence rate, the characteristic shared by the defendant and perpetrator is also possessed by thousands of other individuals. Where 1% of the population possess a blood type shared by the defendant and perpetrator, for example, the expert might be forced to admit during cross-examination that in a city of one million people, approximately 10,000 individuals would have the "rare" blood type. Statements of this type may reduce the tendency toward the Prosecutor's Fallacy but induce more errors consistent with the Defense Attorney's Fallacy.

Boaz Sangero and Mordechai Halpert,
Why a Conviction Should Not Be Based on a Single Piece of Evidence: A Proposal for Reform
48 JURIMETRICS J. 43, 44–45 (2007)

Our argument relates to what is termed "the fallacy of the transposed conditional." In the legal community, this has been commonly referred to as "the prosecutor's fallacy." It describes a situation where the fact finder in a trial mistakenly confuses the probability of the evidence given guilt or innocence with the inverse conditional probability crucial for the purposes of reaching a fateful legal verdict — namely, the probability of guilt or innocence given the evidence. In Bayesian language, in order to determine the probability of guilt-innocence given the evidence (as opposed to the probability of the evidence given guilt-innocence), the prior probability of guilt must be taken into account — namely, the probability of guilt without the key evidence against the suspect. For example, when there is a single piece of identification evidence for a conviction, the prior probability could be very low, because, apart from this single piece of evidence, any other person could be the perpetrator. The prior probability in such cases might be as low as the number one divided by the size of the

---

34. See, e.g., People v. Robinson, 1970.

population. When such a low prior probability is ignored, the cognitive illusion reaches extreme proportions and the error by the fact finder could be enormous. We establish our theory also without the use of Bayesian concepts, *inter alia*, by translating probabilities into frequencies in a manner that illustrates this fallacy.

Up until now, only the buds of this theory have been visible—and only in relation to scientific evidence. The legal community has been wary of falling into the trap of this fallacy as it concerns the random match probability in DNA testing. The weight of the evidence regarding the random match probability is not measured independently, but is balanced against the other evidence in the particular case. However, the possibility of a laboratory error, which is much more likely than a random match and is, therefore, much more significant, is examined independently from the other evidence without considering the danger of a conviction based on a single piece of evidence. Counterintuitively, an error rate of only one mistake in every ten thousand tests in a specific laboratory could lead to a wrongful conviction in *most* cases where a conviction is based on a single piece of evidence.

The situation is even worse regarding fingerprint evidence. Not only is there a tendency, as with DNA testing, to ignore the possibility of an error, there is also a tendency to ignore the possibility of a random match between fingerprints (or at least the possibility of a result similar to a random match). As we shall see below, the conventional attitude towards this evidence is erroneous, misleading, and dangerous.

* * *

The Proposed General Theory

A. The Impact of a False Positive in Medical Diagnosis

We start with an example that appears quite surprising. Let us assume that there is a home kit for performing an HIV test and that the manufacturer reports an average false positive rate of 0.1% when this kit is used. Namely, if a thousand healthy people are tested with the kit, only one of them would get a false positive indicating that he is a carrier of the HIV virus. A random person, Mr. Smith, is tested with the kit, and the result is positive. What is the probability that he is actually an HIV carrier?

Most people would answer this kind of question by saying that there is a 99.9% likelihood that the unfortunate Mr. Smith is a carrier of the HIV virus and only a 0.1% possibility that a false positive has occurred. Is this true? There is a big difference between conditional probability and inverse conditional probability. The answer to the question, "what is the probability of a positive test result given that the person tested is healthy?" is 0.1%. But we are asking an entirely different question; "what is the probability that the person tested is actually a carrier of the virus given a positive test result?"

Let us assume that Mr. Smith is in a low-risk group (he practices safe sex, does not use intravenous needles, does not require blood transfusions, etc.) and that in this risk group the frequency of the HIV virus is one case in ten thousand. In the professional jargon, it is said that the base rate (the frequency in a specific population) of the virus in this low-risk population group is 1 in 10,000.

If 10,000 people from Mr. Smith's low-risk group were to be tested with the home kit, the result would be positive in 11 cases: 10 cases of error (false positives) for healthy persons ($9,999 \times 0.1\% \simeq 10$), together with one person who is actually a carrier (because, in this low-risk group, 1 out of 10,000 people is a carrier). Surprisingly, and contrary to our first intuition, it appears that, although the test shows Mr. Smith to be a carrier, the probability that this is actually the case is only 1/11, or about 9%; whereas the probability of a false positive is 10/11, or about 91%. Hence, a test that might be considered quite accurate for members of a high-risk group can be expected to be misleading for members of a low-risk group.

C. The Danger of Conviction Based on a Single Piece of (Scientific) Evidence

1. *General*

Let us assume an expert has determined that fingerprints taken from the scene of a crime are identical to those of a defendant. To simplify this example, let us assume it is impossible for the defendant's fingerprints to have reached the crime scene in a manner unrelated to the commission of the offense (that is, ignoring the possibility that the fingerprint could have been left by the defendant innocently or planted there by someone else). Let us further assume that the error rate for these tests conducted by this expert is one error in every 10,000 tests. Is it right to convict the defendant solely on the basis of this evidence? Is it correct to believe that if we convict 10,000 persons under identical circumstances — with no other inculpatory evidence — we will make an error in only one case?

If we were to compare the fingerprints found at the scene of the crime to the fingerprints of all 300 million U.S. residents, we would get approximately 30,000 false matches. It is obvious that — in the absence of any other inculpatory evidence — we cannot conclude that the defendant is the actual criminal. Thus, with scientific evidence alone, in the overwhelming majority of cases, a false conviction will result.

We should also remember that the defendant should be acquitted if, at the conclusion of a criminal trial, a reasonable doubt remains as to his guilt. When someone is charged solely on the basis of a single piece of scientific evidence, we propose an alternative thesis: that the evidence is not accurate enough, on its own, to establish a conviction. If the scientific evidence does not possess an error rate that is sufficiently low — and absent any other inculpatory evidence — we cannot be sure that we have the right person in custody.

Let us examine what error rate should be required of identification evidence so that a conviction beyond a reasonable doubt may be solely based on such evidence. Let us assume that only the residents of a particular country are taken into consideration (for such an assumption, we must already rely on some other evidence, but we shall assume that it — and only it — does exist). In order to establish a conviction beyond a reasonable doubt on a single piece of scientific evidence, we should demand that the error rate be significantly lower than 1/N (N being the number of residents in the country). Because, even if the error rate is 1/N (for example, in the U.S., a rate of 1/300,000,000), there would be on average one person other than the defendant with a positive test result. In the absence of any other inculpatory evidence, the probability that each one of them is the culprit is 50%, and this is not sufficient for a criminal proceeding.

Of course, we may (and should) take additional evidence into consideration, thus reducing the list of potential suspects—for example, to assume that the perpetrator lives in the same city as the victim or make assumptions about the perpetrator's sex and age. Let us assume that, in this manner, we reduce the list of potential suspects to 100,000 people. A satisfactory error rate of the test still needs to be much lower than 1/100,000. In order to establish such a low error rate, we would have had to examine the work methods of the laboratory in question in at least 100,000 cases, and it is reasonable to assume that no existing laboratory has conducted so many tests (not to mention the fact that it could not have erred more than once).

To the extent that we reduce the list of potential suspects, a less accurate test may suffice. However, in order to reduce the list, we must find and rely on additional evidence, and the scientific evidence is no longer isolated.

Moreover, if there is evidence in the defendant's favor distancing him from the crime, then we should demand a very high level of accuracy from the scientific evidence, even if the list of potential suspects is reduced. If the evidence in the defendant's favor is strong and convincing, (such as a solid alibi) we can almost be sure that we have a laboratory error. In Bayesian language, strong exculpating evidence reduces the prior odds. Therefore, it is very important to examine and take into account evidence in the suspect's favor—like the failure to identify him in a lineup—even if it is not particularly strong, and not allow the glare of scientific evidence to blind us.

The belief that, if we convict 10,000 people under a test with 99.99% accuracy, we will make an error in only one case derives from the fallacy of the transposed conditional. When we fall into the trap of this fallacy, instead of answering the relevant question—what is the probability of innocence given a match—we answer another question—what is the probability of a match given innocence. The latter probability is low (0.01% in our example), but that low probability does not point unambiguously to the guilt of the person matched. Indeed, when the populations are large, even that low probability can implicate many people besides the particular defendant who is matched to the crime solely through the scientific measurement.

* * *

The burden of proof regarding the possibility of error should also be addressed. In our opinion, the onus is on the prosecution—which is requesting to make inculpatory use of scientific evidence—to provide the court with reliable information as to the possibility of error for the relevant test in the specific laboratory where it was performed. First of all, this burden derives from the general burden of proof imposed on the prosecution in a criminal trial. Secondly, knowledge of the error rate is a condition for the admissibility of the scientific evidence, as follows from the *Daubert* ruling. As already indicated, we find it hard to believe that any test can achieve an accuracy of only one error in a million. Laboratory workers and technicians are human and humans make errors from time to time, as we shall see below when we discuss DNA and fingerprint evidence.

2. *The Inherent Limitation of a Single Piece of Evidence*

In the absence of other evidence linking the defendant to the crime—apart from the scientific evidence—the prior odds are low and do not allow for proof of guilt (posterior odds) beyond a reasonable doubt. As long as there is a possibility of testing error—even if only slim—the basic theory shows the unlikelihood that there will be objective scientific evidence that alone could serve as the basis for conviction. Just as the rate of error is particularly high among the low-risk group in the above example of the HIV test, so it is for any single piece of scientific evidence of a person's guilt: the rate of error is particularly high when there is no other inculpatory evidence.

In many cases, the prior odds do not seem as objective as the scientific evidence. That is, the decision maker's belief in the defendant's guilt or innocence, based on the remaining evidence, is not easy to quantify. This is not a problem of math or logic that can be resolved by a non-Bayesian statistical approach. It is a genuine theoretical problem correctly expressing our uncertainty about the defendant's guilt.

The method of inductive probability developed by Jonathan Cohen may provide another way to reach the conclusion that a single piece of evidence is not sufficient. This method is based on the elimination of alternative explanations for a fact, and proof of the final conclusion as the only acceptable possibility that remains. According to this approach, the "beyond a reasonable doubt" standard—as required in a criminal trial—is not met by a specific degree of proof (such as 99%), but rather by disproving any reasonable alternative other than the defendant's guilt. For the purposes of our discussion, we will note that by this method as well, it is still possible to prove the theory proposed in this article. The reason is that if a single piece of evidence is only capable of identifying the suspect as one member of a group of people, each of whom (on his own) could have committed the crime, then according to the inductive method as well, we need additional evidence to disprove the possibility that the other members of the group committed the crime. Furthermore, we need additional evidence to disprove the possibility of a testing error in the initial evidence.

Jonathan J. Koehler, *Error and Exaggeration in the Presentation of DNA Evidence at Trial*

34 Jurimetrics J. 21, 21–39 (1993)

DNA identification evidence has been and will continue to be powerful evidence against criminal defendants. This is as it should be. In general, when blood, semen or hair that reportedly matches that of a defendant is found on or about a victim of violent crime, one's belief that the defendant committed the crime should increase, based on the following chain of reasoning:

Match Report → True Match → Source → Perpetrator

First, a reported match is highly suggestive of a true match, although the two are not the same. Errors in the DNA typing process may occur, leading to a false match report. Second, a true DNA match usually provides strong evidence that the suspect who matches is indeed the source of the trace, although the match may be coincidental. Finally, a suspect who actually is the source of the trace may not be the perpetrator of the crime. The suspect may have left the trace innocently either before or after the crime was committed.

In general, the concerns that arise at each phase of the chain of inferences are cumulative. Thus, the degree of confidence one has that a suspect is the source of a recovered trace following a match report should be somewhat less than one's confidence that the reported match is a true match. Likewise, one's confidence that a suspect is the perpetrator of a crime should be less than one's confidence that the suspect is the source of the trace.

Unfortunately, many experts and attorneys not only fail to see the cumulative nature of the problems that can occur when moving along the inferential chain, but they frequently confuse the probabilistic estimates that are reached at one stage with estimates of the others. In many cases, the resulting misrepresentation and misinterpretation of these estimates lead to exaggerated expressions about the strength and implications of the DNA evidence. These exaggerations may have a significant impact on verdicts, possibly leading to convictions where acquittals might have been obtained.

This Article identifies some of the subtle, but common, exaggerations that have occurred at trial, and classifies each in relation to the three questions that are suggested by the chain of reasoning sketched above: (1) Is a reported match a true match? (2) Is the suspect the source of the trace? (3) Is the suspect the perpetrator of the crime? ...

Is the Reported Match a True Match?

A reported match is a true match if the characteristics that are identified by the analysis as belonging both to the trace and to the suspect's sample are, in fact, characteristics of the trace and the suspect. Forensic scientists are often reluctant to acknowledge that a reported match could be something other than a true match. When asked about the possibility, many respond by discussing their skill, care and experience in typing samples, or by discussing the validity of their protocol. Such discussion provides only a very limited basis for assessing the probability that a reported match is a true match. While it may be true that laboratories that have superior procedures are less likely to commit errors, the primary concern is not with the process that yields conclusions but with the accuracy of the conclusions themselves.

What can go wrong? First, technical errors are possible. According to testimony provided by Dr. Robert Kidd in *People v. Axell*,[35] enzyme failures, abnormal salt concentrations, and mischievous dirt spots can produce misleading DNA banding patterns.

---

35. 235 Cal. App. 3d 836 (1991).

Human errors are also possible. Contaminations, mislabelings, misrecordings, misrepresentations, case mix-ups and interpretive errors may lead to false positive errors.

Some of these errors have been documented in proficiency tests as well as in actual casework. However, many forensic scientists who testify in court are reluctant to acknowledge even the *possibility* of false positive error: "It is technically impossible to make a false/positive identification." "There is no way to get a false positive with this technology." An incorrect match is an "impossible" result. DNA analysis is "failsafe." The accuracy rate is 100%. And so on.

These statements are extremely misleading and may be reversible error. A factfinder needs to know how likely it is that a reported match is not a true match. This probability, in combination with the probability that a suspect who truly matches a trace is not its source, comprises the false positive error rate. Notice that technical errors and human performance errors contribute to the false positive error rate.

Some forensic scientists will object to this definition of false positive error. They prefer a narrower definition that includes only those errors that result from *technical* failures. With this definition in mind, some say, the impossibility statements above are justifiable.

Two points should be made in response. First, technical errors are not only possible, they have occurred in some instances. For this reason alone, the impossibility claims should be forbidden. But even assuming that the probability of technical error is negligible, experts should not be permitted to equate the technical error rate with the false positive error rate. Judges and jurors are (or should be) concerned with identifying the rate at which false positive errors occur for whatever reason, rather than the rate at which false positive errors arise for a particular reason. Those who insist on defining false positive error as error that arises in a particular way are engaged in a sinister semantic game. There is a danger that jurors will understand their testimony to refer to the likelihood of false identification rather than the likelihood of a certain type of false positive error. This is particularly likely in cases such as *Bethune* where the expert repeated his impossibility claim even after being asked about the possibility of a human error.

The best way to measure the rate of false positive error associated with a laboratory or an individual technician is through an ongoing series of blind, external proficiency tests conducted under realistic conditions. In these tests, samples of genetic materials such as blood, semen and hair can be provided to laboratory technicians who are then asked to determine which, if any, match samples taken from possible sources. Erroneous match reports between "recovered" samples and suspected sources constitute false positive error. Failures to detect matches between recovered samples and true sources constitute false negative error. Further investigation of these errors may reveal their causes and lead to procedural modifications and improved performance.

Surprisingly, there have been no blind external proficiency tests conducted to date. In the few tests conducted by outside agencies, the tested laboratories and technicians were aware that they were being tested. This makes inferences from test performance to case work performance difficult. It may be, for example, that the technicians who conduct DNA analyses are more diligent and cautious when they know that they are being observed and tested.

An equally serious problem is that most proficiency tests have not used samples that are representative of casework. Sample stains in tests are usually large and carefully preserved on a clean cotton cloth. Moreover, the laboratories are often told what the samples are composed of and when they were prepared.

Although many DNA laboratories prefer to conduct in-house proficiency tests rather than submit to external testing, some outside tests have been conducted. Tests conducted by the California Association of Crime Laboratory Directors (CACLD) on three DNA laboratories in 1987 and 1988 revealed several false positives.... Taken together, all these results suggest that false positive errors occur in one to four percent of match reports provided in open proficiency tests. Although it is hard to say whether the false positive error rate in actual casework is much different than this, it is clear that reported matches are not always true matches.

Is the Suspect the Source of the Trace?

A. The Reference Population

Even if a reported match is a true match, the suspect will not be the source of the trace if the match is purely coincidental. To the extent that the frequency of the matching traits, F(Traits), is rare, the probability that the suspect actually is the source increases. But before F(Traits) may be estimated, some attention must be given to identifying an acceptable reference population.

The reference population used by forensic science laboratories to derive F(Traits) is usually based on the ethnic group of the suspect (e.g., black, Hispanic, Caucasian). Though convenient, this practice is misguided. It is only appropriate when it is known that the source of the recovered trace is a member of the suspect's ethnic group. When there is *no* information about the ethnic group of the trace source, the general population is a more appropriate reference class. When there is *some* information about the trace source, it would be best to compute F(Traits) based on a case-specific "potential source population."

Practical problems arise in the construction of potential source populations. These include the need to construct them on a case by case basis, and the lack of clear standards for deciding who is and is not a member of the population. When disagreements arise about the composition of the population, F(Traits) can be computed for several different source populations. In many cases, the resultant F(Traits) values will be sufficiently similar that there is no practical effect for using one population rather than another. But in other cases—particularly those in which there is disagreement about whether particular relatives of the suspect should be included in the source population—the differences may be important.

In general, the inclusion of a suspect's close relatives in the potential source population will lead to F(Traits) values that are larger—hence less diagnostic—than F(Traits) values constructed on the general population. This is because a suspect's relatives are more likely to be genetically similar to him or her than a random member of the general population. F(Traits) based on three probes may be one in millions for the general population. But the probability that the suspect and his biological brother will share a set of alleles on each of the three probe sites is approximately $(1/4)^3 = 1/64$.

B. The Source Probability Error

Even in cases where there is no dispute about F(Traits), there may be confusion about its significance for estimating the probability that the suspect is the source of the matching trace. Specifically, there is a tendency to equate F(Traits), with the probability that the suspect is not the source of the trace, P(Not-Source). Equating F(Traits) with P(Not-Source) tends to exaggerate the strength of the DNA evidence, and may be referred to as the "source probability error." Absent an estimate of the size of the potential source population, a source probability statement cannot be made. A Bayesian analysis illustrates the point. Bayes's Theorem states that the odds on the defendant being the source given the reported match are the prior odds on this hypothesis times the likelihood ratio L = P(Reported Match Source)/ P(Reported Match Not-Source). While L is not connected to the size of the source population, the prior odds P (Source)/P(Not-Source) are. Absent other background information, if the source population consists of only ten people, of which the defendant is one, then the prior odds are one to nine. If the source population consists of one million people equally likely to be the source, the prior odds are one to 999,999. In this way, the size of the population informs one's estimate of the prior odds. Since the prior odds affect the posterior odds, estimates of P(Source Reported Match) cannot be made on the basis of forensic identification evidence alone.

Source probability errors are frequently committed in the popular press. They are also committed by the courts and by experts who should know better. After testifying that a DNA match was found between blood from a murder victim and blood recovered from a blanket, an FBI scientist in *Wike v. State* was questioned by a prosecuting attorney as follows:

> Q: And in your profession and in the scientific field when you say match what do you mean?
>
> A: They are identical.
>
> Q: So the blood on the blanket can you say that it came from Sayeh Rivazfar [the victim]?
> A: With great certainty I can say that those two DNA samples match and they are identical. And with population statistics we can derive a probability of it being anyone other than that victim.
>
> Q: What is that probability in this case?
>
> A: In this case that probability is that it is one in 7 million chances that it could be anyone other than the victim.

As we have seen, the expert's claim that population statistics alone enable him to determine the probability that the victim is not the source of the recovered blood trace is false. The Florida Supreme Court in *Wike* interpreted the source probability hyperbole to mean that the blood on the blanket was "positively" identified as belonging to the victim.

Such exaggerations of scientific evidence and testimony are common and troubling in their own right. Many judges are quick to assume that reported DNA matches are dispositive of identity even when such conclusions are *not* expressed by the scientific experts. On occasion, the experts *do* testify that they are 100% certain that a particular trace came from a particular person. From a normative standpoint, such testimony is more egregious than the source probability error because it does not even allow for the *possibility* that someone other than the matchee is the source of the trace. Even if source probability estimates could be made, it is not clear that a forensic scientist should offer personal interpretations, let alone ones that further exaggerate the strength of the DNA evidence.

C. With "Help" From Attorneys

Trial transcripts reveal that courtroom source probability errors are usually committed with the help of statements in the form of questions from attorneys. Consider the following exchange:

> Q: In layman's terms, just so I get this right, are you saying that the probability that the DNA that was found in the question samples came from anyone else besides Amos Lee is one in 7,000,000, it came from another unrelated person other than Amos Lee?
>
> A: Yes, approximately.

Even if F(Traits) were indeed one in seven million, the expert only could say that there is one chance in seven million that a single randomly selected person would match the trace evidence. This is not equivalent to a claim that there is one chance in seven million that the DNA came from someone other than Lee. This would only be true in the special case where Lee was one of two equally likely members of the potential source population. If the potential source population contained more than two people (as it usually does), then the probability that the DNA came from someone other than Lee would be greater.

In some cases, the source probability error is committed in the context of a longer attorney/expert exchange that makes it difficult to catch and correct:

> Q: And are you able to compile all four of those probabilities and determine what is the likelihood of the DNA found in Billy Glover just randomly occurring in some other DNA sample?
>
> A: Yes.
>
> Q: What is the likelihood of that?
>
> A: The way that is done is to multiply each one of those four numbers that I mentioned before together, because each one is separate and independent, and the final number comes out as one in about 18 billion.

Q: So the likelihood that DNA belongs to someone other than Billy Glover is one in 18 billion?

A: That is correct.

The expert was initially asked about F(Traits). But the attorney redescribed this value as a source probability, and the expert confirmed this characterization.

The conversational dynamic that exists between attorneys and experts during direct and cross-examinations may be partially responsible for some source probability errors, including those committed overtly by the experts. In a Missouri case, an expert testified that trace evidence had the "same blood types and the same DNA profile as Mr. Davis." But when the prosecuting attorney restated this testimony as "the staining on the lower part of the jacket that you identified as Jack Davis's blood," the expert made no effort to correct this subtle distortion. Likewise, when the expert stated that a particular blood stain was "consistent with Mr. Davis's," the prosecuting attorney interrupted to ask "Which one consists of Mr. Davis's?" Rather than explain that there is an important difference between blood that is consistent with Mr. Davis's and blood that *is* Mr. Davis's, the expert simply answered the misleading question. Eventually, the persistent mischaracterization of the expert's testimony by the prosecuting attorney broke down the expert's scientific venire:

Q: [W]hose blood was found to be on item 52?

A: Mr. Davis's blood.

The experts are at least partially to blame for committing and confirming source probability errors. They should know enough about the meaning of a match to resist characterizing F(Traits) evidence in P(Source) or P(Not-Source) terms. They certainly should know enough to avoid absolute identity claims. On the other hand, under the stress of direct and cross-examinations, it may not be reasonable to expect an expert to correct all subtle distortions and misunderstandings expressed by attorneys and judges.

Is the Suspect the Perpetrator of the Crime?

An error related to, but more egregious than, the source probability error occurs when F(Traits) is identified as P(Not-Guilty), the probability that the defendant is not guilty. Dubbed the "Prosecutor's Fallacy," its commission by experts and defense attorneys justifies a broader and more descriptive phrase. Because it mistakes F(Traits) for a probability statement about the ultimate issue, the error of presuming that F(Traits) = P(Not-Guilty) is referred to here as the "ultimate issue error."

People v. Collins[36] is the most famous illustration. In *Collins*, the prosecutor obtained a robbery conviction against a couple by equating the probability that a random couple would possess a series of observed characteristics with the probability that the accused couple did not commit the robbery. The California Supreme Court overturned this conviction, identified errors in the prosecution's assumptions and prob-

---

36. 68 Cal 2d 319 (1968).

abilistic logic, and delivered a stern warning about the dangers of "trial by mathematics." This case has been analyzed extensively and the legal community appeared to understand the difference between probability evidence and the probability of the ultimate issue.

But the ultimate issue error has resurfaced with alarming frequency in cases—particularly rape cases—involving DNA evidence. Some have suggested that the discovery of a DNA match between a defendant and semen recovered from a rape victim justifies an assertion that the probability that someone other than the defendant committed the rape equals F(Traits). In a Texas case, the following exchange took place after the statistics in a DNA report were reviewed:

> Q: Is that correct? So that in the event that the accused sitting in this chair would happen to be White, you're telling the members of this jury that there would [be] a one in 5 billion chance that anybody else could have committed the crime; is that correct?

> A: One in 5 billion, correct.

As with source probability errors, judges sometimes commit ultimate issue errors even when the experts do not. Direct evidence that jurors who hear F(Traits) testimony commit ultimate issue errors is harder to come by. But if popular press accounts of DNA testimony indicate or influence how this evidence will be interpreted, ultimate issue errors may be common.

Related Exaggerations

A. The P(Another Match) Error

The mistaken belief that F(Traits) is identical to the probability that there exists another person who matches the defendant's DNA profile, P(Another-Match), is a close cousin of the previous errors. In a Virginia case, an attorney incorrectly restated the expert's F(Traits) testimony:

> Q: I guess I don't understand. You have told the ladies and gentlemen of the jury that the odds are 705 million to 1 against two persons having the pattern that Spencer has; is that correct?

> A: That's correct.

The problem here is especially subtle. On the one hand, it is true that for F(Traits) = one in 705 million, there is one chance in 705 million that a single randomly selected member of the reference population will match the observed trait pattern. But the chance that *some* member of the reference population will match the observed pattern may be much greater.

To determine P(Another Match), an estimate of the size of the potential source population must be made. For populations of size N in which F(Traits) = 1/X,

$$P(\text{Another Match}) = 1 - (1 - 1/X)^N$$

Thus, if F(Traits) = one in 705 million and the potential source population consists of one million unrelated people,

$$P(\text{Another Match}) = 1 - (1 - 1/705{,}000{,}000)^{1{,}000{,}000} = .14\%$$

Although P(Another Match) estimates are commonly provided in cases involving DNA evidence, this computation is never made. Moreover, there appears to be little awareness among experts, attorneys or judges that the size of the potential source population is relevant, let alone necessary, to estimate P(Another Match).

B. The Numerical Conversion Error

Sometimes DNA experts describe the significance of F(Traits) in terms of the number of people who would have to be tested before one should expect another match to occur. This computation is straight-forward, although it is not, as some have said, the denominator of F(Traits). A conclusion that there is one chance in 100 that a randomly selected individual would match as well as the defendant is *not* equivalent to a conclusion that 100 people would need to be tested before another match might be expected. This common mistake may be called the "numerical conversion error."

In a Texas case, the DNA expert was questioned about the F(Traits) = one in 23 million statistic he provided:

> Q: Could you explain briefly to the jury what 1 in 23 million means in reference to this case? What does that mean?
>
> A: It means that we calculated a match for four probes and that the pattern for the suspect in this case occurs in 1 in approximately every 23 million people. If we continued typing people until we reach 23 million, we would not expect to find someone else that matched for those four probes until after we had reached or exceeded 23 million people.

Similar comments were made in other cases involving DNA, blood, and hair analyses.

To estimate the number of people who would need to be tested before we might expect to find a match on a trait common to one in X people, we must compute the smallest N such that $(1 - 1/X)^N < .50$. Thus, for F(Traits) = one in 100, we would expect to find a match after testing 69 people. If 100 people were tested, the probability that at least one would match is about 63%. Because the N that satisfies the equation will always be smaller than the denominator of F(Traits), the numerical conversion error exaggerates the number of people who would need to be tested before a match may be expected. This, in turn, exaggerates the probative strength of the DNA match.

Why Do These Errors Occur?

Having identified errors that can and do occur in connection with DNA evidence, it is important to consider why these errors persist. Admittedly, the conversational context of the attorney-expert exchanges makes it difficult for the expert to catch and correct all probabilistic distortions. But given that all the errors appear to exaggerate the probative strength of DNA and other identification matches, it is reasonable to consider various motivational theories for their appearance. Could it be that the probative strength of DNA evidence is deliberately exaggerated by forensic experts interested in puffing the utility of their science, or prosecutors determined to win their cases? A review of trial transcripts suggests otherwise. DNA experts generally begin the statistical portion of their testimony with statements about estimated population frequencies and comparisons with a "random man." Broader, misguided statements about source and guilt probabilities typically emerge only after the experts redescribe or expand upon their initial testimony in response to attorneys' questions.

Motivational explanations are also weakened by evidence that the errors are routinely committed even by those who would seem to be motivated *not* to commit them. For example, the source probability errors in *Pierce* and *Thomas,* the ultimate issue errors in *Bethune* and *Womack,* and the P(Another Match) error in *Spencer* were all committed by defense attorneys who surely had no incentive to exaggerate the strength of the evidence against their clients.

A better explanation for the plethora of errors is the simplest one: ignorance. Few jurists are trained in probability theory, and most DNA experts who testify at trial know a good deal more about DNA laboratory procedures than the subtleties of probabilistic inference. Indeed, there is a great deal of evidence that people have trouble differentiating probabilistic information from the probabilistic hypotheses that the information informs; such confusion is consistent with the commission of the errors identified here and supports the ignorance hypothesis. Finally, the well-known fact that everyone (save identical twins) has a unique DNA code may contribute to DNA evidence exaggerations; people may confuse that which is biologically inevitable with that which our technology is capable of revealing.

Jonathan J. Koehler, *Fingerprint Error Rates and Proficiency Tests: What They Are and Why They Matter*
59 HASTINGS L.J. 1077, 1077–1100 (2008)

When a fingerprint examiner declares a match between a print from a known source and a latent print recovered from a crime scene, his word may seal a defendant's fate like no other form of evidence save, perhaps, DNA. At trial the fingerprint examiner will offer little in the way of data, statistical tests, or uncertainty. Instead, he will say that latent print could only have been made by the source of the known print, that he is 100% certain, that he has never erred, and that the method he used to make this and other identifications has an error rate of zero. In recent years, the broader scientific community has objected to this form of testimony. Critics charge that fingerprint analysis lacks an empirical foundation and that examiners make exaggerated claims that are likely to mislead jurors.

Regardless of one's views about the scientific underpinnings of fingerprint examination, all agree that jurors need to understand the probative value of fingerprint evidence at trial. Drawing on research by decision theorist David Schum, researchers at U.C. Irvine explain that probative value is a combination of the diagnosticity and reliability of a reported match. The diagnosticity of a reported fingerprint match is the value of shared characteristics for establishing that two prints share a common source. If prints from many different fingers share the observed characteristics, then the match report will be correspondingly less diagnostic of the claim that the two prints share a common source. If the observed characteristics are rare, then the match report will be more diagnostic of the common source claim. The reliability of a reported fingerprint match pertains to whether two reportedly matching prints actually do share a common set of characteristics. That is, is the reported match a true match, or has the examiner made an error? Taken together, the diagnosticity and reliability of a reported match provide rational jurors with the information they need to assess the probative value of a fingerprint examiner's opinion that two prints share a common source.

The sad truth is that there is a dearth of good data that directly pertains to either diagnosticity or reliability. On the diagnosticity side, the fingerprinting profession has made remarkably few attempts to test its uniqueness assumptions or to develop an empirical foundation from which to offer probabilistic claims. We simply do not know the frequency with which various characteristics relied on by fingerprint examiners exist in various populations.

More important, however, is the risk that an examiner has erred, thereby implicating reliability. An examiner is unreliable if he frequently or perhaps even occasionally concludes that: (a) prints made from different sources were made by a common source, or (b) prints made from common sources were made by different sources. In its landmark *Daubert* and *Kumho* decisions, the Supreme Court stated that trial courts "ordinarily should consider the known or potential rate of error" when evaluating the reliability of scientific techniques and other forms of expert testimony. Though the Supreme Court did not require trial courts to seek error rates, fingerprint examination is surely the poster child for the centrality of this *Daubert* factor. Without information about error rates, fact finders have an insufficient basis for assessing the examiner's reliability and assigning weight to his opinion.

Though sufficient data on the diagnosticity and reliability of fingerprint match reports do not exist, there is reason to expect that their diagnosticity will generally be high and that their reliability (as given by rates of error) will be substantially lower. If so, then the issue of error rate is even more important because the probative value of the reported fingerprint match is restricted by the chance that a false positive error has occurred. In other words, if experts make false positive errors, say, one time in 200, then it does not matter whether the chance that two randomly selected prints match is one in a million, billion, or trillion. It does not even matter whether the chance of a coincidental match is zero (as implausible and unscientific as this value is) because in these situations, the false positive error rate limits and controls the probative value of the match report. The relevance of this observation for our purposes here is to note that error rate is so central to an assessment of the reliability and probative value of fingerprint evidence that it is not sufficient to know, simply, that errors might occur or that errors have occurred. Instead, judges who make admissibility decisions and jurors who assess the probative value of fingerprint evidence need to have better information on the risk that an error has occurred in the instant case.

Does scientific data related to the risk of error exist? If not, how shall we go about getting those data? There is much confusion surrounding these questions.... I use a question and answer style to address key issues related to fingerprint error rates and the proficiency tests that are sometimes used to estimate those rates. My focus throughout is on how to assess the various error rates, why they matter, and how we might go about collecting the requisite data. I do not examine individual cases of error, incompetence or fraud; this information can be found elsewhere....

Errors and Error Rates

A. What Constitutes an Error in Fingerprint Examination?

There is no agreed-upon answer to what counts as an error. Obvious errors occur when an examiner either matches a print to a person other than the one who made it or affirmatively excludes the true source of a print. Less obviously, some would argue that an examiner who correctly identifies the source of a print but incorrectly identifies the finger that produced it has made an error. Others would argue that such an error is so inconsequential relative to other types of errors that it does not deserve the "error" label.

Similarly, when an examiner offers an "inconclusive" opinion about whether two prints match, there is a sense in which he has erred. After all, he did not get the answer right, and the consequences of this failure may be serious (e.g., missed opportunity to exonerate a suspect). However, in the more usual sense of the meaning of error, an inconclusive is not an error. It is a pass. An inconclusive means that the examiner offers no judgment about whether two prints do or do not share a common source. Therefore, for purpose of computing the errors and error rates (see below), I set inconclusives aside.

B. What Are the Different Types of Errors?

Table 7.1: States of Nature and Examiner's Judgment

Examiner's Judgment	States of Nature (i. e., Truth)	
	Same Source (S)	Different Source (-S)
Common Source ("S")	True Positives	B False Positives
Different Source ("-S")	C False Negatives	D True Negatives

Table 7.1 above offers a visual aid that helps clarify the different types of errors. Table I crosses the two states of nature pertaining to a pair of fingerprints (S = same source, -S = different source) with the two types of decisions that fingerprint examiners offer for their relation ("S" = says common source, "-S" = says different source). The four aggregate states described in cells A to D are mutually exclusive (non-overlapping) and exhaustive (all situations described). Cells A and B represent states where the examiner reports that two prints share a common source. Cells C and D represent states where the examiner reports that two prints were left by different sources.

Two important types of errors are false positive errors and false negative errors. A false positive error occurs when an examiner concludes that two prints share a common source when, in fact, they do not. This error is captured by judgments in cell B. A false negative error occurs when an examiner concludes that two prints do not share a common source when, in fact, they do. This error is captured by judgments in cell C.

C. What Are the Different Types of Error Rates?

Three error rates are of central importance: the false positive error rate, the false negative error rate and the false discovery rate. None of these error rates lay claim to being "the" error rate because the term error rate has been used in different ways.

The false positive error rate identifies the rate at which an examiner concludes that two prints share a common source when, in fact, they do not. It is computed by dividing the number of false positive errors by the number of examined pairs of prints that are from different sources....

The false negative error rate is the rate at which an examiner concludes that two prints do not share a common source when, in fact, they do. It is computed by dividing the number of false negative errors by the number of examined pairs of prints that are from common sources....

The false discovery rate identifies the rate at which an examiner's claim that two markings share a common source is wrong. It is computed by dividing the number of false positive errors by the number of examined pairs of prints that the examiner judged to share a common source.... The false discovery rate is the inverse of the false positive error rate.... Both are error rates and both provide important information for assessing the accuracy of fingerprint examiners.

It is important to reiterate that there are other ways to report error rates and that there are even different ways to report the false positive error rate. However, in the interests of simplicity and clarity, I limit the discussion of error rates to the central notions mentioned here.

D. Which Error Rate Is More Useful: The False Discovery Rate or the False Positive Error Rate?

There is no easy answer. All error rates are useful, but each has its own unique features and limitations that legal actors must understand.

The false discovery rate is probably what decision makers most want to know and what they assume that an error rate tells them: how often is the examiner wrong when he calls a match? The central problem with false discovery rate is that it varies as a function of the baserate chance that an unknown latent print and known prints handled by the examiner share a common source. Figure I illustrates the point. Suppose that two equally skilled fingerprint examiners each have a 5% false positive error rate, and a 5% false negative error rate. If the first examiner reviews 1,000 pairs of prints, 900 of which share a common source, his false discovery rate will be (on average) 5 out of 860 or 0.6%. In other words, when this examiner concludes that two prints share a common source, he is wrong less than 1% of the time.

Now suppose that the second examiner reviews 1,000 pairs of prints, in which only 100 pairs share a common source. This examiner's false discovery rate will be (on average) 45 out of 140 or 32%! Is the second examiner worse than the first? No. They are identical in terms of their skill level as evidenced by their identical false positive and false negative error rates. However, the second examiner makes more mistakes because he is subjected to a tougher task. The point is that when the false discovery rate is available, special attention should be paid to the mapping between the baserate chance that pairs of prints share a common source in the target case versus in the task (usually a test or series of tests) that generated the false discovery rate. If these chances are similar, then the false discovery rate provides a simple, direct measure of a key error rate in the instant case. If not, then the false discovery rate should be adjusted to account for the difference in chances.

* * *

The false positive error rate does not rely on an assumption about the rate at which prints handled by an examiner share a common source. This is both a strength and a weakness. It is a strength because the mapping issue described above does not threaten the applicability of the statistic to the target case. It is a weakness because the implications of this statistic depend on the baserate chance that latent and known prints in the target case share a common source. In short, there is no getting around the problem of baserate match chance when it comes to applying error rates to individual cases. Either that baserate is built into the statistic as it is for the false discovery rate, or a case-specific baserate must be combined with the "purer" false positive error rate to determine how likely it is that the match call in a particular case is erroneous.

4. Reform Initiatives: The National Academy of Science Report & PCAST

Late in 2005, partly at the request of the leadership of the forensic science community itself, Congress commissioned the well-regarded, independent, and non-partisan National Academy of Sciences to research and write a report on the needs of the forensic science community. In February of 2009, the long-anticipated report was issued.

This report was written by an interdisciplinary panel of distinguished scholars and practitioners, who conducted their own investigation into the state of the research, and also heard numerous days of testimony from a substantial number of leading forensic science professionals, researchers, and others knowledgeable about the state of the forensic scientists.... In essence, the 319-page report substantially confirms the views of the academic critics about the inadequacy of the research basis to support many of the claims routinely made by forensic scientists.

For example, the report finds that there is not an adequate basis for claims of individualization. The report also finds "a notable dearth of peer-reviewed, published studies establishing the scientific bases and validity of many forensic methods." The report claims that research on proficiency, performance, and the role of bias and observer effects is "sorely needed." All in all, "[t]he present situation is seriously wanting, both because of the limitations of the judicial system and because of the many problems faced by the forensic science community."

The report's boldest and perhaps most important recommendation is for the creation of a new independent federal agency to regulate, supervise, and improve the forensic sciences. This agency, dubbed the National Institute of Forensic Science (NIFS), would be responsible for funding research to improve forensic sciences; it would also be responsible for establishing and developing best practices, and, more generally, supporting and overseeing the forensic science infrastructure....

The report makes a number of other significant recommendations. It calls in strong terms for additional research to establish the validity and reliability of forensic sciences, as well as research to examine the extent of biases and observer effects. It calls for mandatory laboratory accreditation and mandatory individual certification of forensic scientists (right now both are entirely optional). Significantly, it calls for the use of incentive funding to motivate states to make their crime laboratories independent from law enforcement and prosecutors.[37]

National Academy of Sciences, *Strengthening Forensic Science in the United States: A Path Forward*

National Research Council (2009)

The Admission of Forensic Science Evidence in Litigation

Forensic science experts and evidence are used routinely in the service of the criminal justice system. DNA testing may be used to determine whether sperm found on a rape victim came from an accused party; a latent fingerprint found on a gun may be used to determine whether a defendant handled the weapon; drug analysis may be used to determine whether pills found in a person's possession were illicit; and an autopsy may be used to determine the cause and manner of death of a murder victim. In order for qualified forensic science experts to testify competently about forensic evidence, they must first find the evidence in a usable state and properly preserve it. A latent fingerprint that is badly smudged when found cannot be usefully saved, analyzed, or explained. An inadequate drug sample may be insufficient to allow for proper analysis. And, DNA tests performed on a contaminated or otherwise compromised sample cannot be used reliably to identify or eliminate an individual as the perpetrator of a crime. These are important matters involving the proper processing of forensic evidence. The law's greatest dilemma in its heavy reliance on forensic evidence, however, concerns the question of whether—and to what extent—there is science in any given forensic science discipline.

---

37. Mnookin, *supra* at pp. 1235–36.

Two very important questions should underlie the law's admission of and reliance upon forensic evidence in criminal trials: (1) the extent to which a particular forensic discipline is founded on a reliable scientific methodology that gives it the capacity to accurately analyze evidence and report findings and (2) the extent to which practitioners in a particular forensic discipline rely on human interpretation that could be tainted by error, the threat of bias, or the absence of sound operational procedures and robust performance standards. These questions are significant. Thus, it matters a great deal whether an expert is qualified to testify about forensic evidence and whether the evidence is sufficiently reliable to merit a fact finder's reliance on the truth that it purports to support. Unfortunately, these important questions do not always produce satisfactory answers in judicial decisions pertaining to the admissibility of forensic science evidence proffered in criminal trials.

In 1993, in *Daubert v. Merrell Dow Pharmaceuticals, Inc.*, the Supreme Court ruled that, under Rule 702 of the Federal Rules of Evidence (which covers both civil trials and criminal prosecutions in the federal courts), a "trial judge must ensure that any and all scientific testimony or evidence admitted is not only relevant, but reliable." The Court indicated that the subject of an expert's testimony should be scientific knowledge, so that "evidentiary reliability will be based upon scientific validity." The Court also emphasized that, in considering the admissibility of evidence, a trial judge should focus "solely" on the expert's "principles and methodology," and "not on the conclusions that they generate." In sum, *Daubert's* requirement that an expert's testimony pertain to "scientific knowledge" established a standard of "evidentiary reliability."

In explaining this evidentiary standard, the *Daubert* Court pointed to several factors that might be considered by a trial judge: (1) whether a theory or technique can be (and has been) tested; (2) whether the theory or technique has been subjected to peer review and publication; (3) the known or potential rate of error of a particular scientific technique; (4) the existence and maintenance of standards controlling the technique's operation; and (5) a scientific technique's degree of acceptance within a relevant scientific community. In the end, however, the Court emphasized that the inquiry under Rule 702 is "a flexible one." The Court expressed confidence in the adversarial system, noting that "[v]igorous cross-examination, presentation of contrary evidence, and careful instruction on the burden of proof are the traditional and appropriate means of attacking shaky but admissible evidence." The Supreme Court has made it clear that trial judges have great discretion in deciding on the admissibility of evidence under Rule 702, and that appeals from *Daubert* rulings are subject to a very narrow abuse-of-discretion standard of review. Most importantly, in *Kumho Tire Co., Ltd. v. Carmichael*, the Court stated that "whether *Daubert's* specific factors are, or are not, reasonable measures of reliability in a particular case is a matter that the law grants the trial judge broad latitude to determine."

Daubert and its progeny have engendered confusion and controversy. In particular, judicial dispositions of *Daubert*-type questions in criminal cases have been criticized by some lawyers and scholars who thought that the Supreme Court's decision would be applied more rigorously. If one focuses solely on reported federal appellate decisions, the picture is not appealing to those who have preferred a more rigorous application of *Daubert*. Federal appellate courts have not with any consistency or clarity imposed standards ensuring the application of scientifically valid reasoning and reliable methodology in criminal cases involving *Daubert* questions. This is not really surprising, however. The Supreme Court itself described the *Daubert* standard as "flexible." This means that, beyond questions of relevance, *Daubert* offers appellate courts no clear substantive standard by which to review decisions by trial courts. As a result, trial judges exercise great discretion in deciding whether to admit or exclude expert testimony, and their judgments are subject only to a highly deferential "abuse of discretion" standard of review. Although it is difficult to get a clear picture of how trial courts handle *Daubert* challenges, because many evidentiary rulings are issued without a published opinion and without an appeal, the vast majority of the reported opinions in criminal cases indicate that trial judges rarely exclude or restrict expert testimony offered by prosecutors; most reported opinions also indicate that appellate courts routinely deny appeals contesting trial court decisions admitting forensic evidence against criminal defendants. But the reported opinions do not offer in any way a complete sample of federal trial court dispositions of *Daubert*-type questions in criminal cases. The situation appears to be very different in civil cases. Plaintiffs and defendants, equally, are more likely to have access to expert witnesses in civil cases, while prosecutors usually have an advantage over most defendants in offering expert testimony in criminal cases. And, ironically, the appellate courts appear to be more willing to second-guess trial court judgments on the admissibility of purported scientific evidence in civil cases than in criminal cases.

Prophetically, the *Daubert* decision observed that "there are important differences between the quest for truth in the courtroom and the quest for truth in the laboratory. Scientific conclusions are subject to perpetual revision. Law, on the other hand, must resolve disputes finally and quickly." But because accused parties in criminal cases are convicted on the basis of testimony from forensic science experts, much depends upon whether the evidence offered is reliable. Furthermore, in addition to protecting innocent persons from being convicted of crimes that they did not commit, we are also seeking to protect society from persons who have committed criminal acts. Law enforcement officials and the members of society they serve need to be assured that forensic techniques are reliable. Therefore, we must limit the risk of having the reliability of certain forensic science methodologies judicially certified before the techniques have been properly studied and their accuracy verified by the forensic science community. "[T]here is no evident reason why ['rigorous, systematic'] research would be infeasible." However, some courts appear to be loath to insist on such research as a condition of admitting forensic science evidence in criminal cases, perhaps because to do so would likely "demand more by way of validation than the disciplines can presently offer."

The adversarial process relating to the admission and exclusion of scientific evidence is not suited to the task of finding "scientific truth." The judicial system is encumbered by, among other things, judges and lawyers who generally lack the scientific expertise necessary to comprehend and evaluate forensic evidence in an informed manner, trial judges (sitting alone) who must decide evidentiary issues without the benefit of judicial colleagues and often with little time for extensive research and reflection, and the highly deferential nature of the appellate review afforded trial courts' *Daubert* rulings. Given these realities, there is a tremendous need for the forensic science community to improve. Judicial review, by itself, will not cure the infirmities of the forensic science community. The development of scientific research, training, technology, and databases associated with DNA analysis have resulted from substantial and steady federal support for both academic research and programs employing techniques for DNA analysis. Similar support must be given to all credible forensic science disciplines if they are to achieve the degrees of reliability needed to serve the goals of justice. With more and better educational programs, accredited laboratories, certified forensic practitioners, sound operational principles and procedures, and serious research to establish the limits and measures of performance in each discipline, forensic science experts will be better able to analyze evidence and coherently report their findings in the courts. The current situation, however, is seriously wanting, both because of the limitations of the judicial system and because of the many problems faced by the forensic science community.

John M. Butler, *U.S. Initiatives to Strengthen Forensic Science and International Standards in Forensic DNA*
18 FORENSIC SCI. INT. GENET. 4–20 (Sept. 2015)

Many disciplines of forensic science, including DNA analysis, are undergoing change in the United States and around the world. New methods are being developed, validated, and put into use to help in criminal investigations. The validity and accuracy of older and even current methods are being challenged. New approaches for interpreting evidence via probabilistic modeling are being introduced. A better appreciation of difficulties that can exist for the field of forensic science is gained when the diverse cultures of scientific laboratories, law enforcement, and the legal community interact.

The publication of the National Academy of Sciences' (NAS) National Research Council (NRC) report in February 2009 calling for improvements in forensic science in the United States has been felt around the world.

Summary of 13 recommendations made in the 2009 National Research Council report entitled "Strengthening Forensic Science in the United States: A Path Forward."

1 Create an independent federal entity called the National Institute of Forensic Science (NIFS)

2 Establish standard terminology to be used in reporting on and testifying about the results of forensic science investigations and establish model laboratory reports with minimum information specified

3 Research (and publish in respected scientific journals) the validity of forensic methods, quantify limits of reliability when forensic evidence conditions vary,

develop measures of uncertainty in the conclusions of forensic analyses, and automate techniques

4   Remove public forensic laboratories from law enforcement or prosecutor's administrative control

5   Research human observer bias and error in forensic examinations and develop standard operating procedures to minimize potential bias and error

6   Work with the National Institute of Standards and Technology (NIST) and partners to develop tools for advancing measurement, validation, reliability, information sharing, and proficiency testing in forensic science and to establish protocols for forensic examinations, methods, and practices

7   Mandate accreditation for all laboratories and facilities (public or private) and mandate individual certification of forensic science professionals

8   Establish routine quality assurance and quality control procedures to ensure the accuracy of forensic analyses and the work of forensic practitioners

9   Establish a national code of ethics for all forensic science disciplines that can be enforced through certification

10 Improve graduate education programs with attractive scholarship and fellowship offerings and establish continuing legal education programs for law students, practitioners, and judges

11 Improve death investigations through establishing a nationwide medical examiner system with all medicolegal autopsies being performed or supervised by a board certified forensic pathologist

12 Work to achieve nationwide fingerprint data interoperability from Automated Fingerprint Identification Systems (AFIS) and work to improve accuracy of computer algorithms used

13 Coordinate local forensic science efforts related to homeland security with the Centers for Disease Control and Prevention and the FBI through planning and conducting preparedness exercises

President's Council of Advisors on Science & Technology, *An Addendum to the PCAST Report on Forensic Science in Criminal Courts*

(2017)

On September 20, 2016, PCAST released its unanimous report to the President entitled "Forensic Science in Criminal Courts: Ensuring Scientific Validity of Feature-Comparison Methods." This new document, approved by PCAST on January 6, 2017, is an addendum to the earlier report developed to address input received from stakeholders in the intervening period.

Background

PCAST's 2016 report addressed the question of when expert testimony based on a forensic feature-comparison method should be deemed admissible in criminal courts. We briefly summarize key aspects of the previous report.

Forensic feature-comparison methods

PCAST chose to focus solely on forensic feature-comparison methods. These methods seek to determine whether a questioned sample is likely to have come from a known source based on shared features in certain types of evidence. Specific methods are defined by such elements as:

(i) the type of evidence examined (e.g., DNA, fingerprints, striations on bullets, bitemarks, footwear impressions, head-hair);

(ii) the complexity of the sample examined (e.g., a DNA sample from a single person vs. a three-person mixture in which a person of interest may have contributed only 1%); and

(iii) whether the conclusion concerns only "class characteristics" or "individual characteristics" (e.g., whether a shoeprint was made by a pair of size 12 Adidas Supernova Classic running shoes vs. whether it was made by a specific pair of such running shoes).

The U.S. legal system recognizes that scientific methods can assist the quest for justice, by revealing information and allowing inferences that lie beyond the experience of ordinary observers. But, precisely because the conclusions are potentially so powerful and persuasive, the law requires scientific testimony be based on methods that are scientifically valid and reliable.

Requirement for empirical testing of subjective methods

In its report, PCAST noted that the only way to establish the scientific validity and degree of reliability of a subjective forensic feature-comparison method—that is, one involving significant human judgment—is to test it empirically by seeing how often examiners actually get the right answer. Such an empirical test of a subjective forensic feature-comparison method is referred to as a "black-box test." The point reflects a central tenet underlying all science: an empirical claim cannot be considered scientifically valid until it has been empirically tested.

If practitioners of a subjective forensic feature-comparison method claim that, through a procedure involving substantial human judgment, they can determine with reasonable accuracy whether a particular type of evidence came from a particular source (e.g., a specific type of pistol or a specific pistol), the claim cannot be considered scientifically valid and reliable until one has tested it by (i) providing an adequate number of examiners with an adequate number of test problems that resemble those found in forensic practice and (ii) determining whether they get the right answer with acceptable frequency for the intended application. While scientists may debate the precise design of a study, there is no room for debate about the absolute requirement for empirical testing.

* * *

Evaluation of empirical testing for various methods

To evaluate the empirical evidence supporting various feature-comparison methods, PCAST invited broad input from the forensic community and conducted its own extensive review. Based on this review, PCAST evaluated seven forensic feature-comparison methods to determine whether there was appropriate empirical evidence that the method met the threshold requirements of "scientific validity" and "reliability" under the Federal Rules of Evidence.

- In two cases (DNA analysis of single-source samples and simple mixtures; latent fingerprint analysis), PCAST found that there was clear empirical evidence.

- In three cases (bitemark analysis; footwear analysis; and microscopic hair comparison), PCAST found no empirical studies whatsoever that supported the scientific validity and reliability of the methods.

- In one case (firearms analysis), PCAST found only one empirical study that had been appropriately designed to evaluate the validity and estimate the reliability of the ability of firearms analysts to associate a piece of ammunition with a specific gun. Because scientific conclusions should be shown to be reproducible, we judged that firearms analysis currently falls short of the scientific criteria for scientific validity.

- In the remaining case (DNA analysis of complex mixtures), PCAST found that empirical studies had evaluated validity within a limited range of sample types.

Responses to the PCAST Report

Following the report's release, PCAST received input from stakeholders, expressing a wide range of opinions. Some of the commentators raised the question of whether empirical evidence is truly needed to establish the validity and degree of reliability of a forensic feature-comparison method.

The Federal Bureau of Investigation (FBI), which clearly recognizes the need for empirical evidence and has been a leader in performing empirical studies in latent-print examination, raised a different issue. Specifically, although PCAST had received detailed input on forensic methods from forensic scientists at the FBI Laboratory, the agency suggested that PCAST may have failed to take account of some relevant empirical studies. A statement issued by the Department of Justice (DOJ) on September 20, 2016, (the same day as the report's release) opined that:

The report does not mention numerous published research studies which seem to meet PCAST's criteria for appropriately designed studies providing support for foundational validity. That omission discredits the PCAST report as a thorough evaluation of scientific validity.

Given its respect for the FBI, PCAST undertook a further review of the scientific literature and invited a variety of stakeholders—including the DOJ—to identify any "published … appropriately designed studies" that had not been considered by PCAST and that established the validity and reliability of any of the forensic feature-comparison methods that the PCAST report found to lack such support. As noted below, DOJ ultimately concluded that it had no additional studies for PCAST to consider.

* * *

In what follows, we focus on three key issues raised.

Issue: Are empirical studies truly necessary?

While forensic-science organizations agreed with the value of empirical tests of subjective forensic feature-comparison methods (that is, black-box tests), many suggested that the validity and reliability of such a method could be established without actually empirically testing the method in an appropriate setting. Notably, however, none of these respondents identified any alternative approach that could establish the validity and reliability of a subjective forensic feature-comparison method.

* * *

(i) The forensic-science literature contains many papers describing variation among features. In some cases, the papers argue that patterns are "unique" (e.g., that no two fingerprints, shoes or DNA patterns are identical if one looks carefully enough). Such studies can provide a valuable starting point for a discipline, because they suggest that it may be worthwhile to attempt to develop reliable methods to identify the source of a sample based on feature comparison. However, such studies—no matter how extensive—can never establish the validity or degree of reliability of any particular method. Only empirical testing can do so.

(ii) Forensic scientists rightly cite examiners' experience and judgment as important elements in their disciplines. PCAST has great respect for the value of examiners' experience and judgment: they are critical factors in ensuring that a scientifically valid and reliable method is practiced correctly. However, experience and judgment alone—no matter how great—can never establish the validity or degree of reliability of any particular method. Only empirical testing of the method can do so.

(iii) Forensic scientists cite the role of professional organizations, certification, accreditation, best-practices manuals, and training within their disciplines. PCAST recognizes that such practices play a critical role in any professional discipline. However, the existence of good professional practices alone—no matter how well crafted—can never establish the validity or degree of reliability of any particular method. Only empirical testing of the method can do so.

In science, empirical testing is the only way to establish the validity and degree of reliability of such an empirical method. Fortunately, empirical testing of empirical methods is feasible. There is no justification for accepting that a method is valid and reliable in the absence of appropriate empirical evidence.

Issue: Importance of other kinds of studies

In its response to PCAST's call for further input, the Organization of Scientific Area Committees' Friction Ridge Subcommittee (OSAC FRS), whose purview includes latent-print analysis, raised a very important issue:

While the OSAC FRS agrees with the need for black box studies to evaluate the overall validity of a particular method, the OSAC FRS is concerned this view could unintentionally stifle future research agendas aimed at dissecting the components of the black box in order to transition it from a subjective method to an objective method. If the PCAST maintains such an emphasis on black box studies as the only means of establishing validity, the forensic science community could be inundated with predominantly black box testing and potentially detract from progress in refining other foundational aspects of the method, such as those previously outlined by the OSAC FRS, in an effort to identify ways to emphasize objective methods over subjective methods (see www.nist.gov/topics/forensic-science/osac-research-development-needs). Given the existing funding limitations, this will be especially problematic and the OSAC RFS is concerned other foundational research will thus be left incomplete.

PCAST applauds the work of the friction-ridge discipline, which has set an excellent example by undertaking both (i) path-breaking black-box studies to establish the validity and degree of reliability of latent-fingerprint analysis, and (ii) insightful "white-box" studies that shed light on how latent-print analysts carry out their examinations, including forthrightly identifying problems and needs for improvement. PCAST also applauds ongoing efforts to transform latent-print analysis from a subjective method to a fully objective method. In the long run, the development of objective methods is likely to increase the power, efficiency and accuracy of methods—and thus better serve the public.

In the case of subjective methods whose validity and degree of reliability have already been established by appropriate empirical studies (such as latent-print analysis), PCAST agrees that continued investment in black-box studies is likely to be less valuable than investments to develop fully objective methods. Indeed, PCAST's report calls for substantial investment in such efforts.

The situation is different, however, for subjective methods whose validity and degree of reliability has not been established by appropriate empirical studies. If a discipline wishes to offer testimony based on a subjective method, it must first establish the method's validity and degree of reliability—which can only be done through empirical studies. However, as the OSAC FRS rightly notes, a discipline could follow an alternative path by abandoning testimony based on the subjective method and instead developing an objective method. Establishing the validity and degree of reliability of an objective method is often more straightforward. PCAST agrees that, in many cases, the latter path will make more sense.

Issue: Completeness of PCAST's evaluation

Finally, we considered the important question ... of whether PCAST had failed to consider "numerous published research studies which seem to meet PCAST's criteria for appropriately designed studies providing support for foundational validity."

* * *

Bitemark analysis

In its report, PCAST stated that it found no empirical studies whatsoever that establish the scientific validity or degree of reliability of bitemark analysis as currently practiced. To the contrary, it found considerable literature pointing to the unreliability of the method. None of the respondents identified any empirical studies that establish the validity or reliability of bitemark analysis. (One respondent noted a paper, which had already been reviewed by PCAST, that studied whether examiners agree when measuring features in dental casts but did not study bitemarks.) One respondent shared a recent paper by a distinguished group of biomedical scientists, forensic scientists, statisticians, pathologists, medical examiners, lawyers, and others, published in November 2016, that is highly critical of bitemark analysis and is consistent with PCAST's analysis.

Footwear analysis

In its report, PCAST considered feature-comparison methods for associating a shoeprint with a specific shoe based on randomly acquired characteristics (as opposed to with a class of shoes based on class characteristics). PCAST found no empirical studies whatsoever that establish the scientific validity or reliability of the method.

IAI member Lesley Hammer ... noted that the first such empirical study is currently being undertaken at the West Virginia University. When completed and published, this study should provide the first actual empirical evidence concerning the validity of footwear examination. The types of samples and comparisons used in the study will define the bounds within which the method can be considered reliable.

Microscopic hair comparison

In its report, PCAST considered only those studies on microscopic hair comparison cited in a recent DOJ document as establishing the scientific validity and reliability of the method. PCAST found that none of these studies provided any meaningful evidence to establish the validity and degree of reliability of hair comparison as a forensic feature-comparison method. Moreover, a 2002 FBI study, by Houck and Budowle, showed that hair analysis had a stunningly high error rate in practice: Of hair samples that FBI examiners had found in the course of actual casework to be microscopically indistinguishable, 11% were found by subsequent DNA analysis to have come from different individuals.

PCAST received detailed responses from the Organization of Scientific Area Committees' Materials Subcommittee (OSAC MS) and from Sandra Koch, Fellow of the American Board of Criminalistics (Hairs and Fibers). These respondents urged PCAST not to underestimate the rich tradition of microscopic hair analysis. They emphasized that anthropologists have published many papers over the past century noting differences in average characteristics of hair among different ancestry groups, as well as variation among individuals. The studies also note intra-individual differences among hair from different sites on the head and across age.

While PCAST agrees that these empirical studies describing hair differences provide an encouraging starting point, we note that the studies do not address the validity and degree of reliability of hair comparison as a forensic feature-comparison method. What is needed are empirical studies to assess how often examiners incorrectly associate similar but distinct-source hairs (i.e., false-positive rate).

Relevant to this issue, OSAC MS states: "Although we readily acknowledge that an error rate for microscopic hair comparison is not currently known, this should not be interpreted to suggest that the discipline is any less scientific." In fact, this is the central issue: the acknowledged lack of any empirical evidence about false-positive rates indeed means that, as a forensic feature-comparison method, hair comparison lacks a scientific foundation.

Based on these responses and its own further review of the literature beyond the studies mentioned in the DOJ document, PCAST concludes that there are no empirical studies that establish the scientific validity and estimate the reliability of hair comparison as a forensic feature-comparison method.

Firearms analysis

In its report, PCAST reviewed a substantial set of empirical studies that have been published over the past 15 years and discussed a representative subset in detail. We focused on the ability to associate ammunition not with a class of guns, but with a specific gun within the class.

The firearms discipline clearly recognizes the importance of empirical studies. However, most of these studies used flawed designs. As described in the PCAST report, "set-based" approaches can inflate examiners' performance by allowing them to take advantage of internal dependencies in the data. The most extreme example is the "closed-set design", in which the correct source of each questioned sample is always present; studies using the closed-set design have underestimated the false-positive and inconclusive rates by more than 100-fold. This striking discrepancy seriously undermines the validity of the results and underscores the need to test methods under appropriate conditions. Other set-based designs also involve internal dependencies that provide hints to examiners, although not to the same extent as closed-set designs.

To date, there has been only one appropriately designed black-box study: a 2014 study commissioned by the Defense Forensic Science Center (DFSC) and conducted by the Ames Laboratory, which reported an upper 95% confidence bound on the false-positive rate of 2.2%.

* * *

Stephen Bunch, a pioneer in empirical studies of firearms analysis, provided a thoughtful and detailed response. He agreed that set-based designs are problematic due to internal dependencies, yet suggested that certain set-based studies could still shed light on the method if properly analyzed. He focused on a 2003 study that he had co-authored, which used a set-based design and tested a small number of examiners (n = 8) from the FBI Laboratory's Firearms and Toolmarks Unit. Although the underlying data are not readily available, Bunch offered an estimate of the number of truly independent comparisons in the study and concluded that the 95% upper confidence bound on the false-positive rate in his study was 4.3% (vs. 2.2% for the Ames Laboratory black-box study).

The Organization of Scientific Area Committee's Firearms and Toolmarks Subcommittee (OSAC FTS) took the more extreme position that all set-based designs are appropriate and that they reflect actual casework, because examiners often start their examinations by sorting sets of ammunition from a crime-scene. OSAC FTS's argument is unconvincing because (i) it fails to recognize that the results from certain set-based designs are wildly inconsistent with those from appropriately designed black-box studies, and (ii) the key conclusions presented in court do not concern the ability to sort collections of ammunition (as tested by set-based designs) but rather the ability to accurately associate ammunition with a specific gun (as tested by appropriately designed black-box studies).

Courts deciding on the admissibility of firearms analysis should consider the following scientific issues:

(i) There is only a single appropriate black-box study, employing a design that cannot provide hints to examiners. The upper confidence bound on the false-positive rate is equivalent to an error rate of 1 in 46.

(ii) A number of older studies involve the seriously flawed closed-set design, which has dramatically underestimated the error rates. These studies do not provide useful information about the actual reliability of firearms analysis.

(iii) There are several studies involving other kinds of set-based designs. These designs also involve internal dependencies that can provide hints to examiners, although not to the same extent that closed-set designs do. The large Miami-Dade study cited in the PCAST report and the small studies cited by Bunch fall into this category; these two studies have upper confidence bounds corresponding to error rates in the range of 1 in 20.

From a scientific standpoint, scientific validity should require at least two properly designed studies to ensure reproducibility. The issue for judges is whether one properly designed study, together with ancillary evidence from imperfect studies, adequately satisfies the legal criteria for scientific validity. Whatever courts decide, it is essential that information about error rates is properly reported.

DNA analysis of complex mixtures

In its report, PCAST reviewed recent efforts to extend DNA analysis to samples containing complex mixtures. The challenge is that the DNA profiles resulting from such samples contain many alleles (depending on the number of contributors) that vary in height (depending on the ratios of the contributions), often overlap fully or partially (due to their "stutter patterns"), and may sometimes be missing (due to PCR dropout). Early efforts to interpret these profiles involved purely subjective and poorly defined methods, which were not subjected to empirical validation. Efforts then shifted to a quantitative method called combined probability of inclusion (CPI); however, this approach also proved seriously problematic.

Recently, efforts have focused on an approach called probabilistic genotyping (PG), which uses mathematical models (involving a likelihood-ratio approach) and simulations to attempt to infer the likelihood that a given individual's DNA is present in the sample. PCAST found that empirical testing of PG had largely been limited to a narrow range of parameters (number and ratios of contributors). We judged that the available literature supported the validity and reliability of PG for samples with three contributors where the person of interest comprises at least 20% of the sample. Beyond this approximate range (i.e. with a larger number of contributors or where the person if interest makes a lower than 20% contribution to the sample), however, there has been little empirical validation.

A recent controversy has highlighted issues with PG. In a prominent murder case in upstate New York, a judge ruled in late August (a few days before the approval of PCAST's report) that testimony based on PG was inadmissible owing to insufficient validity testing. Two PG software packages (STRMix and TrueAllele), from two competing firms, reached differing conclusions about whether a DNA sample in the case contained a tiny contribution (~1%) from the defendant. Disagreements between the firms have grown following the conclusion of the case.

PCAST convened a meeting with the developers of the two programs (John Buckleton and Mark Perlin), as well as John Butler from NIST, to discuss how best to establish the range in which a PG software program can be considered to be valid and reliable. Buckleton agreed that empirical testing of PG software with different kinds of mixtures was necessary and appropriate, whereas Perlin contended that empirical testing was unnecessary because it was mathematically impossible for the likelihood-ratio approach in his software to incorrectly implicate an individual. PCAST was unpersuaded by the latter argument. While likelihood ratios are a mathematically sound concept, their application requires making a set of assumptions about DNA profiles that require empirical testing. Errors in the assumptions can lead to errors in the results. To establish validity with a range of parameters, it is thus important to undertake empirical testing with a variety of samples in the relevant range.

* * *

Notably, one response suggested that the relevant category for consideration should be expanded from "complex mixtures" (defined based on the number of contributors) to "complex samples" (defined to include also samples with low amounts of template, substantial degradation, or significant PCR inhibition, all of which will also complicate interpretation). We agree that this expansion could be useful.

The path forward is straightforward. The validity of specific PG software should be validated by testing a diverse collection of samples within well-defined ranges. The DNA analysis field contains excellent scientists who are capable of defining, executing, and analyzing such empirical studies.

When considering the admissibility of testimony about complex mixtures (or complex samples), judges should ascertain whether the published validation studies adequately address the nature of the sample being analyzed (e.g., DNA quantity and quality, number of contributors, and mixture proportion for the person of interest).

Conclusion

Forensic science is at a crossroads. There is growing recognition that the law requires that a forensic feature-comparison method be established as scientifically valid and reliable before it may be used in court and that this requirement can only be satisfied by actual empirical testing. Several forensic disciplines, such as latent-print analysis, have clearly demonstrated that actual empirical testing is feasible and can help drive improvement. A generation of forensic scientists appears ready and eager to embrace a new, empirical approach—including black-box studies, white-box studies, and technology development efforts to transform subjective methods into objective methods.

PCAST urges the forensic science community to build on its current forward momentum.

* * *

Jennifer E. Laurin, *Remapping the Path Forward: Toward a Systemic View of Forensic Science Reform and Oversight*

91 Tex. L. Rev. 1051, 1076–79 (2013)

[F]orensic evidence is both special and mundane. It is special in its potential to identify and exclude with a degree of reliability that sets it apart from more traditional forms of proof in criminal investigations (eyewitness identification, confessions, informants, and the like). But it is also, like all evidence produced by humans in the crucible of the criminal justice system, susceptible to error, bias, manipulation, rationing, and other dynamics that compromise its reliability both in theory and in practice.

For at least three decades, academic observers (largely legal scholars, joined by a handful of social scientists and a smattering of commentators within the tiny community of academic forensic science) were nearly alone in grappling with this vexing duality. But with the release of the 2009 Report of the National Academy of Sciences (NAS), Strengthening Forensic Science in the United States: A Path Forward (the NAS Report), these critiques have been nudged from the margins into the policy mainstream. In three hundred pages, the NAS Report criticized the absence of validation for virtually every forensic methodology; pointed to widespread deficiencies in funding, training, and standard setting in forensic science; and laid further blame at the feet of courts for "continu[ing] to rely on forensic evidence without fully understanding and addressing the limitations of different forensic science disciplines." Importantly, however, the thrust of the NAS Report was not ultimately pessimistic, but rather, as the title implies, forward-looking: its prestigious authors clearly viewed the future of criminal justice as bound up with the future of forensic science. Toward that end, the NAS Report proffered thirteen recommendations for comprehensive reform of the forensic science field, which, in sum, call for broader training and standardization of laboratory work, an ambitious program for expanding research and education directed at improving forensic science, and most controversially, institutional independence of laboratories from law enforcement institutions and the formation of a new federal agency, the National Institute of Forensic Science (NIFS), charged with funding and agenda setting in the forensic sciences.

The NAS Report has been widely heralded as a watershed, and its analysis and recommendations look to be setting the terms of academic and policy debates concerning forensic science for the foreseeable future. But academic and policy agendas tethered to the NAS Report will be deficient in a critical respect. Like the overwhelming majority of the scholarship and criticism that so heavily influenced it, the light shined by the Report is focused almost exclusively on the primary site of forensic science production—the laboratory—as the relevant site of reform. But this ignores a critical set of dynamics affecting forensic science: namely, the manner in which upstream users of forensic science—police and prosecutors, to be precise—will select priorities, initiate investigations, collect and submit evidence, choose investigative techniques, and charge and plead cases in ways that have critical and systematic, though poorly understood, influences on the accuracy of forensic analysis and the integrity of its application in criminal cases.

These dynamics have featured (albeit often below the surface) in many known and even more unknown cases in which forensic science has failed to live up to, or even frustrated, the truth-facilitating function it is deployed to serve. Consider, for example, the fact that both cases in which the Supreme Court has taken on the question of postconviction access to (putatively exonerative) DNA testing feature challenges not to shoddy science but rather to incomplete science: both William Osborne and Hank Skinner have argued that prosecutors and police in their original investigations opted not to test available and potentially exculpatory evidence and relied in convicting them on less than the best available scientific evidence.[38] Consider, similarly, the fact that in a recent study of the first 250 DNA exonerations in the United States, analysis of investigative documents and trial transcripts revealed that at least 34 defendants were initially tried for their crimes despite the known contemporaneous existence of arguably exculpatory forensic evidence.

The reform agenda of the NAS Report has little to say about the critical questions raised by these cases, which center not on laboratory-based practices, but rather on the exercise of upstream discretion by other law enforcement actors. These actors exercise a range of discretion in selecting, submitting, and utilizing scientific evidence in criminal cases, and they do so within professional, organizational, and legal contexts

---

38. See Brief for the Respondent at 8–9 & n.3, Dist. Attorney's Office for the Third Judicial Dist. v. Osborne, 129 S. Ct. 2308 (2009) (No. 08-6) (discussing the State's decision to not conduct RFLP testing and to rely upon microscopic examination of hairs—an analysis which is no longer accepted as a valid basis for identification standing alone); Appellant's Opening Brief at 31–33, Skinner v. State, No. AP-76,675 (Tex. Crim. App. Feb.2, 2012), 2012 WL 591289, *31–33 (discussing facts); see also Skinner v. Switzer, 131 S. Ct. 1289, 1298 (2011) (holding that a convicted state prisoner seeking DNA testing of evidence may assert that claim in a civil rights action); Osborne, 129 S. Ct. at 2323 (declining to recognize a freestanding constitutional right of access to DNA testing).

that create particular incentives and, at times, pathologies in regard to these tasks. Critically, not only do these dynamics at times play a dispositive role in determining the impact of science in an investigation—as illustrated by the Osborne and Skinner examples above—but they also, perhaps more commonly, play a contributory role by reacting and adjusting, perhaps unexpectedly and perhaps perversely, to the work of laboratory actors. Accounting for these dynamics thus requires a broader view— a systemic view—than is afforded by a laboratory-centric lens.

* * *

Upstream Discretion: Evidence Collection.

It is perhaps too obvious to state that the quality and reliability of forensic science is entirely dependent upon the quality and reliability of the processes by which the analyzed evidence is collected.

By "collection," I refer to a range of activities that occur in relation to spatial or physical locations—primarily, a geographic location where a crime occurred, the body of a victim (as when a sexual assault kit is collected), or the body of a suspect (as when reference samples are collected for comparison to evidence found on a victim or at a crime scene). In addition to evidence gathering, other activities such as transportation (typically first to a police storage facility to await possible transmittal to a laboratory) and documentation also must occur in this stage. The stakes are high. If evidence is not identified and gathered, or if it is collected, transported, and stored in a deficient manner, items that could have established an element of a crime, implicated a perpetrator, or exculpated a suspect, could be destroyed or lost—or worse, could generate inaccurate results. Somewhat less obviously and far less glamorously, if the steps of evidence collection are not documented to show what, how, and when physical evidence was collected, exploitation of that evidence could be compromised (by, for example, precluding admissibility under chain-of-custody rules), and the ability for downstream actors to evaluate the integrity of the evidence and the investigation that uncovered it will be compromised.

Evidence collection practices and priorities unquestionably suppress forensic analysis in at least some cases in which it might be thought to aid in detection or arrest, though as discussed below the prevalence and magnitude of this effect is difficult to estimate. The consequences of deficient evidence collection are borne by identifiable, putatively innocent suspects as well. O.J. Simpson's highly publicized criminal trial popularized such concerns, when his attorneys successfully neutralized evidence of a DNA match between Simpson's blood and that found at the scene of his wife's (and her companion's) murder by arguing that police and laboratory sloppiness and corruption, rather than Simpson's presence at the crime scene, explained the inculpatory evidence. In New York's notorious Central Park Jogger case, failure to properly handle evidence likely led to the identification of hairs that were transferred at the police station and not the crime scene. One of the Supreme Court's recent forays into actual innocence claims concerned plausible allegations of flawed blood spatter analysis as a result of poor evidence handling and transport. The recent exoneration of Texan Michael Morton, convicted in 1987 of murdering his wife, featured a near miss in this regard: a bandana, initially overlooked by investigators because it was located beyond the confines of what they adjudged the crime scene, was recovered by an enterprising relative of the victim and became critical in identifying the actual murderer and exonerating Morton nearly twenty-five years after his conviction. There is fair reason to think that Morton's (tragically delayed) near miss is not an isolated occurrence.

This is in part because the degree of selectivity that is occurring at this early stage is more dramatic than might commonly be appreciated. The best (albeit limited) empirical data that exists indicates that, across the board, significantly less physical evidence is collected in most cases than is available; that the rates of collection vary widely across categories of crime; and that this gap between collection potential and actuality has not meaningfully diminished even as forensic science has become a more central feature of criminal cases....

B. Current Law: Overview

Frye, Daubert, and Kumho Tire

Frye v. United States, 293 F. 1013 (D.C. Cir. 1923), articulated a highly-influential standard for assessing the admissibility of scientific evidence. According to *Frye*, the test for admissibility was whether the evidence or technique is "sufficiently established to have gained general acceptance in the particular field in which it belongs." This standard was widely adopted in state and federal courts and relied on for decades.

Following enactment of Federal Rule of Evidence 702, however, which the Court concluded had superseded *Frye*, the Supreme Court articulated a new test in *Daubert v. Merrell Dow Pharmaceuticals, Inc.*, 509 U.S. 579 (1993). *Daubert* requires federal judges to perform a "gatekeeping" function, in which the judge must "ensure that any and all scientific testimony or evidence admitted is not only relevant, but reliable." In making this assessment, the judge is instructed to consider four criteria:

(1) Whether the expert's theory or technique can be (and has been) tested;

(2) Whether the theory or technique has been subjected to peer review and publication;

(3) Whether the theory or technique has an acceptable known or potential rate of error and the existence and maintenance of standards controlling the technique's operation; and

(4) Whether the theory or technique has attained "general acceptance."

The *Daubert* case is the subject of an enormous literature, much of it critical.

Kumho Tire Co. v. Carmichael, 526 U.S. 137 (1999), further clarified that the standard announced in *Daubert* applies to both scientific expertise and experience-based, technical fields.

Admissibility of New Forensic Evidence in Post-Conviction Proceedings

In *McDaniel v. Brown*, 558 U.S. 120 (2010), the Court considered a habeas action brought by a prisoner who complained that his trial lawyer had been ineffective by failing to challenge the testimony of a DNA expert and arguments made by the prosecutor reflecting classic "prosecutor's fallacy" reasoning. The expert testified that the chance that a member of the general population might match the DNA sample in the case was, in her opinion, only 1 in 3,000,000. Based on that testimony, the prosecutor argued that "the jury could be "99.999967 percent sure" in this case that Brown was guilty. "And when the prosecutor asked Romero, in a classic example of erroneously equating source probability with random match probability, whether 'it [would] be fair to say ... that the chances that the DNA found in the panties—the semen in the panties—and the blood sample, the likelihood that it is not Troy Brown would be .000033,' Romero ultimately agreed that it was 'not inaccurate' to state it that way." Not only is this a textbook example of the fallacy, both the DNA expert and the prosecutor failed to consider that Brown's brothers were also suspects in the case, and the chances of a DNA match between one of the brothers and the DNA sample was far greater than that testified to by the expert. Rather than 1 in 3 million, depending on assumptions, the actual chance of a random match was potentially as high as 1 in 66. Although the Court found that those errors occurred, it refused to grant habeas relief to Brown, holding that the district court erred in admitting a report by defendant's new DNA expert for purposes of establishing defendant's Jackson v. Virginia claim because the new evidence was not relevant to the Jackson claim, and holding that Brown procedurally forfeited his claim that errors by the state's expert witness in describing the statistical meaning of DNA evidence constituted unnecessarily suggestive identification testimony in violation of due process. The Court did not foreclose the possibility that a properly preserved claim of error in similar circumstances might be sufficient to warrant due process relief.

Confrontation Clause Limits on Expert Forensic Testimony and Reports

A relatively recent line of cases has dealt with application of the Confrontation Clause to the admission of forensic lab tests. *See Melendez-Diaz v. Massachusetts*, 557 U.S. 305 (2009) (holding that "certificates of analysis" showing the results of the forensic analysis performed on seized substances and identifying the substances as cocaine were testimonial statements, and the analysts were "witnesses" for purposes of the Sixth Amendment. Absent a showing that the analysts were unavailable to testify at trial and that petitioner had a prior opportunity to cross-examine them, petitioner was entitled to "'be confronted with'" the analysts at trial); *Bullcoming v. New Mexico*, 564 U.S. 647 (2011) (defendant had right to confront analyst who certified blood-alcohol analysis report); *Williams v. Illinois*, 567 U.S. 50 (2012) (where DNA expert's reference to the DNA profile provided by Cellmark, a forensic laboratory, as having been produced from semen found on the victim's vaginal swabs was not admitted for the truth of the matter asserted, the Confrontation Clause does not bar the admission of such statements).

As the Court explained in *Williams*:

> When an expert testifies for the prosecution in a criminal case, the defendant has the opportunity to cross-examine the expert about any statements that are offered for their truth. Out-of-court statements that are related by

the expert solely for the purpose of explaining the assumptions on which that opinion rests are not offered for their truth and thus fall outside the scope of the Confrontation Clause. Applying this rule to the present case, we conclude that the expert's testimony did not violate the Sixth Amendment.

As a second, independent basis for our decision, we also conclude that even if the report produced by Cellmark had been admitted into evidence, there would have been no Confrontation Clause violation. The Cellmark report is very different from the sort of extrajudicial statements, such as affidavits, depositions, prior testimony, and confessions, that the Confrontation Clause was originally understood to reach. The report was produced before any suspect was identified. The report was sought not for the purpose of obtaining evidence to be used against petitioner, who was not even under suspicion at the time, but for the purpose of finding a rapist who was on the loose. And the profile that Cellmark provided was not inherently inculpatory. On the contrary, a DNA profile is evidence that tends to exculpate all but one of the more than 7 billion people in the world today. The use of DNA evidence to exonerate persons who have been wrongfully accused or convicted is well known. If DNA profiles could not be introduced without calling the technicians who participated in the preparation of the profile, economic pressures would encourage prosecutors to forgo DNA testing and rely instead on older forms of evidence, such as eyewitness identification, that are less reliable. See *Perry v. New Hampshire*, 565 U.S. ___, 132 S.Ct. 716 (2012). The Confrontation Clause does not mandate such an undesirable development. This conclusion will not prejudice any defendant who really wishes to probe the reliability of the DNA testing done in a particular case because those who participated in the testing may always be subpoenaed by the defense and questioned at trial.

Williams, 567 U.S. at 58.

C. Legal Materials, Exercises, and Media

1. *Reflective Essay, Forensic Odontology:* Bite mark identification lacks scientific reliability, and yet bite marks continue to be admitted in the criminal courtroom. For background on bite mark evidence, read Radley Balko, *How the Flawed 'Science' of Bite Mark Analysis Has Sent Innocent People to Prison*, WASHINGTON POST (Feb. 13, 2015), https://www.washingtonpost.com/news/the-watch/wp/2015/02/13/how-the-flawed-science-of-bite-mark-analysis-has-sent-innocent-people-to-jail/?utm_term=.44c82b435780, and find other articles at *The Marshall Project* webpage on bite marks at https://www.themarshallproject.org/records/1001-bite-mark-evidence. What role do you think cognitive bias plays in the bite mark findings of forensic odontologists and in the acceptance of bite mark evidence in the courtroom? What steps can be taken by courtroom players to prevent wrongful convictions due to bite mark evidence?

Figure 7.5

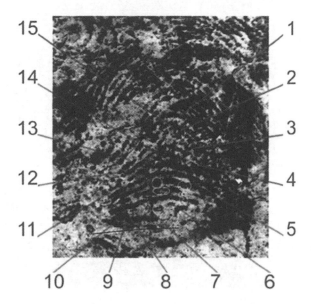

2. *Discussion, Brandon Mayfield and Faulty Fingerprint Evidence:* Brandon Mayfield was wrongly charged of being the bomber in the 2004 Madrid train bombings when FBI agents "matched" his fingerprint to one found at the scene. *Frontline* discusses the case in Season 10, Episode 30, "The Real CSI" http://www.pbs.org/wgbh/frontline/film/real-csi/ (3:10–13:30). In these images, Figure 7.5 is the print from the crime scene, Figure 7.6 is Brandon Mayfield, and Figure 7.7 is the confirmed bomber. Based on your readings, how do you think courtrooms should handle fingerprint evidence?

Figure 7.6

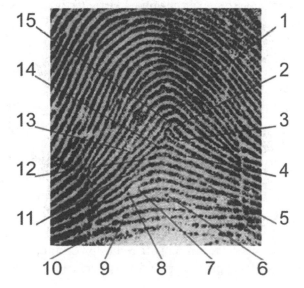

Figure 7.7

3. *Reflective Essay, Comparing Forensic Disciplines:* Compare and contrast fingerprint analysis with microscopic hair analysis. Discuss the challenges to these two forms of analysis, as well as how you think they are viewed by the general public or by a jury.

4. *Exercise, Oral Advocacy:* Read West Virginia Code § 15-2B-14. The FBI has admitted to testifying falsely about hair analysis in your client's case, and has now offered to test any DNA evidence to remedy the testimony by the FBI analyst. Imagine that the state prosecutor opposes DNA testing, and you have filed a motion with the state trial court for DNA testing in this case by the FBI at Quantico. At the hearing, what arguments will you make for testing, in light of the statutory requirements of § 15-2B-14?

5. *Comparing the Admissibility of Forensic Evidence in Civil and Criminal Cases:*

    Why do judges frequently fail to keep faulty forensics out in criminal cases despite the fact that they rigorously enforce *Daubert's* gatekeeping requirements when presiding over civil cases? *Daubert* requires trial judges in both civil and criminal proceedings to determine "whether the reasoning or methodology underlying the testimony is scientifically valid...." As the relevant research reveals, however, judges are far more willing to fulfill their gatekeeping roles in civil cases than criminal ones. Challenges to forensic evidence pretrial, including *Daubert* hearings, are rare in the criminal context. As the NAS Report makes clear, "the vast majority of the *reported* opinions in criminal cases indicate that trial judges rarely exclude or restrict expert testimony offered by prosecutors...." The evidentiary standards that apply to expert forensic evidence should be identical in civil and criminal proceedings according to the Federal Rules of Evidence and relevant precedent, yet courts rigorously engage in gatekeeping of such evidence in civil proceedings while giving broad leeway to prosecutors in criminal proceedings.

Jennifer D. Oliva & Valena E. Beety, *Discovering Forensic Fraud*, 112 Nw. U. L. Rev. 121 (2017).

Listen to Professor Jennifer Oliva discuss this piece, *Discovering Forensic Fraud*, on the *Excited Utterance* podcast hosted by Professor Edward Cheng, Episode 29. Professor Oliva discusses the "*Daubert* Gap" in how forensic evidence is challenged in civil versus criminal cases pre-trial (0:00–9:45), and the gap in discovery disclosure in civil versus criminal cases (11:45–16:00). https://www.excited utterancepodcast.com/listen/2017/9/11/32-jennifer-oliva.

6. *Recommended Listening, "Perfect Accuracy" and Error Rates in Forensics:* Professor Jonathan Koehler, author of the *Error and Exaggeration in the Presentation of DNA Evidence at Trial* excerpt, discusses error rates on the *Excited Utterance* podcast with Edward Cheng, Episode 14, "Testing for Accuracy in the Forensic Sciences." To better understand error rates, listen to 1:00–5:25; for a discussion about human error, listen to 7:30–9:00; and to query whether judges should address error rates through increased discovery or *Daubert* hearings, listen to 10:30–13:15. https://www.excitedutterancepodcast.com/listen/2016/11/21/14-jay-koehler.

7. *Recommended Reading, DNA evidence and the Death Penalty:* For a discussion of the role of DNA evidence in Robin Lovitt's conviction, read William C. Thompson & Rachel Dioso-Villa *Turning a Blind Eye to Misleading Scientific Testimony: Failure of Procedural Safeguards in a Capital Case*, 18 Alb. L.J. Sci. & Tech. 151 (2008).

8. *Late Night Forensic Evidence:* Watch John Oliver's *Last Week Tonight*, October 1, 2017 episode, "Forensic Science," for a comedic take on the very real harms of faulty forensic evidence: https://www.youtube.com/watch?v=ScmJvmzDcG0 (0:00–18:50).

9. *Flawed Forensics Local Media Coverage:* National news outlets now cover wrongful convictions due to faulty forensic science, however for a collection of in-depth Wisconsin coverage see the *Flawed Forensics* series by the Wisconsin Center for Investigative Journalism, covering faulty microscopic hair analysis, false confessions, and fiber comparisons at www.wisconsinwatch.org/series/flawed-forensics/.

10. *Recommended Listening, Machine Testimony as Evidence:* Andrea Roth, in her article *Machine Testimony*, 126 Yale L.J. 1972 (2017), discusses the problems with admitting scientific evidence from a machine without any checks. She points out that with machine expert testimony, defendants need to know the analytical assumptions underlying the machine processes that provide results admitted in court as impartial and scientific. Listen to her interview on Ed Cheng's podcast, *Excited Utterance*, where she discusses how *Daubert* can be applied to expert machine testimony, using corroboration requirements similar to that of confessions by requiring two machine results before admitting evidence, and ways to better

inform the jury about machine testimony: https://www.excitedutterancepodcast.com/listen/2017/1/23/17-andrea-roth (5:25–13:15) (16:30–18:57, access to databases).

11. *Short Answers, Forensic Autopsies:* Death investigations are a crucial analysis of scientific evidence—the body of the deceased—that are often underfunded and can be influenced by police reports, eyewitness testimony, and police or prosecutor presence at the autopsy.

    a.   Look at this map of death investigations nationally:

        http://www.pbs.org/wgbh/pages/frontline/post-mortem/map-death-in-america/

        What kind of death investigation system does your state have?

    b.   Now read this short article, *Autopsies 101:*

        http://www.pbs.org/wgbh/pages/frontline/post-mortem/things-to-know/autopsy-101.html

        Name a well-known case you know of, where the autopsy was particularly relevant to the death investigation. Why was it important? Who conducted the autopsy?

    c.   Now read *How Qualified is your Coroner?:*

        http://www.pbs.org/wgbh/pages/frontline/post-mortem/things-to-know/how-qualified-is-your-coroner.html

        What are some qualifications to be coroner in different states?

12. *The 2009 National Academy of Sciences Report, Forensic Science: A Path Forward:* On February 18, 2009, the National Academy of Sciences released its groundbreaking report on forensic evidence, *A Path Forward*. The Committee, which was composed of scientific and legal experts, spent two years holding public hearings at the request of Congress. The report that resulted electrified the field of forensics.

A Path Forward found that forensic sciences were failing in the courtroom. In court, analysts were routinely over-representing the accuracy of their findings. Analysts testified to perfect "matches" of crime scene evidence to defendants, when such a match—"individualization"—was impossible. Chastising decades of courtroom representations of exact matches, the report found that no forensic discipline was capable of individualization, save DNA analysis.

Outside of the courtroom, analysts needed increased oversight, forensic disciplines needed heightened research, and crime labs needed financial support. The majority of crime labs are located within police departments. When police departments underfund the scientific work of their labs, problems of fraud, incompetence, cheating, backlogged tests, and drug theft become rampant. Indeed, one study shows at least fifty national laboratories reported destruction of evidence, analyst fraud, failed proficiency tests, misleading testimony, or drug tampering between 2005–2011. *A Path Forward* demanded a reckoning of these issues.

A Path Forward also spotlighted the lack of rigorous scientific evaluation of hair microscopy, bite mark comparison, firearms, tool marks, and shoe print analysis. This historical lack of scientific evaluation is rooted in the creation of forensic sciences, which occurred at crime scenes rather than in laboratories. Such forensic disciplines relied on subjective assessments without objective standards and protocols. For example, the general analysis for fingerprints relies on a subjective interpretation of markings and on finding "that sufficient quantity and quality of friction ridge detail is in agreement between the latent print and the known print." What constitutes "sufficient" varies from analyst to analyst. The subsequent use and representation of these subjective forensic findings in criminal cases compounded the concerns of the Forensics NAS Report Committee. *A Path Forward* questioned how forensic techniques could lack scientific validity yet be used freely in a courtroom.

Chapter Eight

DNA and Junk Science

"The nonscience forensic sciences, as the paradoxical phrase suggests, are those fields within forensic science that have little or no basis in actual science. They neither borrow from established science nor systematically test their hypotheses. Their primary claims for validity rest on anecdotal experience and proclamations of success over time.... Whereas in most scientific fields experience and observation are designated as the first steps of the scientific method, for many forensic fields they constitute the final stages of confirmation. Indeed, in a way, many practitioners of the forensic arts have turned the scientific method on its head. So long as their hypotheses and suppositions have not been tested, they are assumed true...."

—Michael J. Saks & Davis L. Faigman, *Failed Forensics:*
How Forensic Science Lost Its Way and How It Might Yet Find It,
4 Ann. Rev. L. & Soc. Sci. 149, 150 (2008)

A. Readings

1. Forensic DNA: A Double-Edged Helix

Simon A. Cole, *Forensic Science and Wrongful Convictions:*
From Exposer to Contributor to Corrector
46 New Eng. L. Rev. 711, 712–19 (2012)

I. Early Studies of Wrongful Conviction

Historically, forensic science and miscarriages of justice were rarely reflected upon in concert. Certainly, forensic science has been cited as a contributor to miscarriages of justice since as long ago as the Dreyfus case. But until recently, forensic science—compared to other issues like eyewitness identification, perjury, official misconduct, and interrogation practices—has tended to take a back seat in discussions of miscarriages of justice. Although the earliest U.S. study of miscarriages of justice mentioned "[t]he unreliability of so-called 'expert' evidence" as a contributor to wrongful convictions, most of the early studies that attempted to systematically identify causes of wrongful conviction discussed: eyewitness identification; false confessions; police and prosecutorial misconduct; bad lawyering; race; failures of the discovery process; and public pressure for a conviction, making scant mention of forensic science. Two Royal Commissions issued reports addressing problems with forensic science in Australia during the 1980s attracting little international attention. As Schiffer and Champod observed, "forensic science (to convict and to exonerate) is underrepresented and often wrongly understood in research concerning wrongful convictions."

This made some intuitive sense because the characteristics popularly associated with "science" seem antithetical to the characteristics of wrongful convictions. Wrongful convictions were thought to be caused by unclear, misguided, or fallacious reasoning, but science is supposed to embody clear, rational reasoning. Wrongful convictions were also thought to be caused by unjustified biases against people of certain races or classes, against persons with prior criminal records, or even simply against the police's preferred suspect. By contrast, science is supposed to be objective and free of bias. Wrongful convictions were thought to be caused by deceitful and otherwise unreliable information given by witnesses, informants, co-conspirators, and the like. But science, goes the truism, "never lies." Wrongful convictions were thought to be caused by evidence that was less reliable than it appeared — like eyewitness identification evidence — but science is by nature associated, in the popular imagination, with high reliability, indeed often with certainty.

II. Forensic Science as Exposer of Miscarriages of Justice

The development of forensic DNA profiling during the 1980s caused people to begin associating forensic science with miscarriages of justice. Beginning with Gary Dotson, and then David Vasquez in 1989, post-conviction DNA testing exposed a number of miscarriages of justice in the United States. Realizing the potential of post-conviction DNA testing to expose miscarriages of justice, in 1992, American attorneys Peter Neufeld and Barry Scheck founded the Innocence Project at Cardozo Law School as a legal clinic dedicated to such testing. Over the next two decades, the Innocence Project and other independent efforts exposed more than 250 wrongful convictions in the United States through post-conviction DNA testing. This set of wrongful convictions has taken on a degree of significance beyond the parties involved in the underlying cases themselves. These cases have acquired significance in drawing attention to the issue of miscarriages of justice, to flaws in the American justice system, and to capital punishment. In part, their significance derives from their ability to be packaged and conceptualized as a "data set" through media such as reports, books, and the Innocence Project's own website. Additionally, their significance derives from their ability to achieve supposed "scientific certainty" or "epistemological closure." Alleged miscarriages of justice exposed through post-conviction DNA testing were less vulnerable to disputes over whether they should be characterized as miscarriages of justice at all. While some post-conviction DNA exonerations may be challenged, even the most determined "innocence skeptics" concede that the vast majority of post-conviction exonerations were miscarriages of justice.

III. Forensic Science as Contributor to Miscarriages of Justice

Thus, forensic science was initially perceived as a powerful tool for exposing wrongful convictions. However, the earliest analyses of post-conviction DNA exonerations as a data set revealed a paradox. Forensic science was not merely the engine for exposing miscarriages of justice; it also appeared to be a contributor to miscarriages of justice. An analysis of the first twenty-eight cases of post-conviction DNA exonerations noted:

> A majority of the cases involved non-DNA-tested forensic evidence that was introduced at trial. Although not pinpointing the defendants, that evidence substantially narrowed the field of possibilities to include them. Typically, those cases involved comparisons of nonvictim specimens of blood, semen, or hair at the crime scene to that of the defendants. Testimony of prosecution experts also was used to explain the reliability and scientific strength of non-DNA evidence to the jury.

Thus, post-conviction DNA exoneration introduced forensic science into the discourse on miscarriages of justice in two ways: (1) as a tool for exposing miscarriages of justice in a way that allowed for bypassing debates over whether the alleged miscarriages of justice were, in fact, miscarriages of justice; and (2) as a potentially important cause of miscarriages of justice. Paradoxically, forensic science was little discussed as a cause of miscarriages of justice until its role was exposed — by forensic science.

During this same period, a miscarriage of justice "crisis" arose in the United Kingdom. Among the most prominent alleged miscarriages of justice were three 1974 Irish Republic Army ("IRA") bombing cases. These cases resulted in the convictions of the so-called "Guildford Four," "Birmingham Six," and "Maguire Seven." All of the cases involved explosive residue evidence. These cases prompted two official inquiries, which highlighted the role of forensic science in miscarriages of justice. The Royal Commission on Criminal Justice's 1993 "Runciman Report" discussed a number of issues concerning forensic science including: failure to adhere to objectivity and impartiality; problems with interpretation of evidence; failure to communicate findings clearly; inequalities between defense and prosecution resources; defense access to samples; pro-prosecution bias; expert shopping; and the low accuracy of the residue detection techniques themselves. In 1994, the "May Inquiry" discussed the role of forensic science in the Guildford Four and Maguire Seven cases. The May Inquiry primarily blamed individual forensic scientists for the failings of forensic science in cases involving miscarriages of justice.

In Canada, the 1998 "Kaufman Report" discussed the role that microscopic hair comparison played in the wrongful conviction of Guy Paul Morin for murder. Morin had been exonerated by post-conviction DNA testing. Among other things, the "Kaufman Report" noted that both the overstatement of the probative value of forensics analysts' findings and the failure to disclose contamination problems contributed to Morin's wrongful conviction. In 2000, Barry Scheck, Peter Neufeld, and Jim Dwyer published Actual Innocence, which analyzed the first sixty-two post-conviction DNA exonerations. The book devoted two chapters to forensic science as a contributor to miscarriages of justice, splitting the issue into scientific misconduct ("White Coat Fraud") and the unreliability of forensic science ("Junk Science"). The former discussed notorious forensic vigilantes, such as Fred Zain. The latter discussed the unreliability of microscopic hair analysis and bite mark comparison. It also addressed the need for regulation of forensic laboratories, proficiency testing, clear reporting of error rates in order for fact-finders to assign weight to forensic evidence, transparency, and independence from law enforcement. In addition, the book revealed that the Innocence Project's founders became familiar with forensic DNA profiling by working on the Coakley case, which involved serology evidence that was misleadingly interpreted. The authors cited "serology inclusion" as the second leading contributor, after "mistaken identification," to the wrongful convictions exposed by post-conviction DNA testing—contributing to thirty-two of the sixty-two wrongful convictions. "Defective or Fraudulent Science" was listed as the fifth leading cause with twenty-one cases, "microscopic hair comparison" was sixth with eighteen cases, "other forensic inclusions" was the eleventh leading cause with five cases, and "DNA inclusions" was the twelfth leading cause with one case.

Michael Saks and Jonathan Koehler cited the role of forensic science as a contributor to miscarriages of justice to support their claim that forensic science was not as reliable as it was often claimed to be and reform of forensic science was urgently needed.[39] Saks and Koehler suspected that Scheck et al.'s splitting of forensic science into multiple categories might obscure the significant role that forensic science plays as a contributor to miscarriages of justice. As a result, they published a slight reanalysis of the Innocence Project data—which at that time represented the first eighty-six post-conviction DNA exonerations—by aggregating all forensic contributors into just two categories. Errors in forensic science testing were found to be present in sixty-three percent of cases, second only to eyewitnesses misidentifications. The giving of false or misleading testimony by forensic scientists was found to be present in twenty-seven percent of cases, the fifth most common contributor. The article's placement in the prestigious journal Science helped ignite renewed efforts to reform forensic science in the United States. Some forensic scientists, upset by the article's portrayal of their field, questioned "the data sampling techniques, methods, [and] criteria" that went into Saks and Koehler's representation of the forensic sciences as a leading contributor to miscarriages of justice. Saks and Koehler responded that "[r]esearch on DNA exonerations is obviously in its infancy, and we support calls for a more complete and scientific review of these cases."

Of course, post-conviction DNA testing is only one method of exposing miscarriages of justice. In a comprehensive study of U.S. exonerations from 1989, the beginning of the post-conviction DNA exoneration era, to 2003, Gross and colleagues found a total of 340 exonerations, slightly less than half of which were exposed by post-conviction DNA testing.[40] Gross and his colleagues devised their own system for categorizing the causes of these wrongful convictions; forensic science was lumped into their "perjury" category. The study found that twenty-four of the wrongful convictions involved perjury by a forensic scientist. This analytic approach narrowed the apparent contribution of forensic science to miscarriages of justice.

---

39. The article is reproduced infra, Ch. 9.
40. See supra, Ch. 3.

In 2008, Garrett published an extensive analysis of the first 200 post-conviction DNA exonerations. He reported that "[f]orensic evidence was the second leading type of evidence supporting these erroneous convictions," appearing in fifty-seven percent of the cases.[41] A more extensive analysis of the role of forensic science in wrongful convictions reported that "[t]wo hundred thirty-two innocent persons have now been exonerated by post-conviction DNA testing[]" and offered an extensive analysis of these cases.[42]

Jessica Gabel Cino, *Tackling Technical Debt: Managing Advances in DNA Technology That Outpace the Evolution of Law*
54 Am. Crim. L. Rev. 373, 377–82 (2017)

A. History of DNA Testing

DNA, an acronym for deoxyribonucleic acid, is the building block of all organisms. Swiss scientist Friedrich Miescher originally identified nucleic material in white blood cells in 1869. In 1953, American biologist James Watson and English physicist Francis Crick discovered the three dimensional, double helix configuration of DNA that is well-known today.

The future of DNA changed forever on the morning of September 10, 1984, when Dr. Alec Jeffreys discovered genetic fingerprinting in the Genetics Department at the University of Leicester in the United Kingdom. Almost immediately, Dr. Jeffreys realized the implications of his discovery and its application not only to paternity testing, its chief application, but also to criminal investigations.

Jeffreys put his novel discovery to the test for the first time in 1986 after two young girls were raped and murdered in Leicestershire, England. The police had a suspect in custody who had already confessed to one murder but refused to confess to the second. The police asked Jeffreys to use his new technique, DNA profiling, to connect the suspect to both murders. The results were "completely unexpected": they did not match the man in custody. Because the police now had DNA samples from semen found on both victims and the support of the police, a manhunt was initiated to find the man who matched the DNA fingerprint identified by Jeffreys' work. The search eventually led to Colin Pitchfork, who was arrested and convicted of the crimes in 1988.

The first person in the United States to be convicted using DNA evidence was in 1988 as well, when Tommie Lee Andrews was convicted of two violent sexual assaults/murders in Florida. Two separate juries convicted Andrews of the two murders when DNA evidence was only an "emerging science." At the time it was used to identify Andrews, DNA evidence had only been used once: in the conviction of Colin Pitchfork in Leicester.

---

41. See supra, Ch. 3 at *Judging Innocence*.

42. Brandon L. Garrett & Peter J. Neufeld, Invalid Forensic Science Testimony and Wrongful Convictions, 95 Va. L. Rev. 1, 5 (2009).

Since the conviction of Andrews and Pitchfork, DNA evidence has become a crucial part of the criminal justice system in the United States and the United Kingdom. Globally, DNA was instrumental in recent war-crimes and genocide investigations in Kosovo and Bosnia.

The United States passed the DNA Identification Act of 1994. The Act detailed the requirements of maintaining an NDIS for convicted offenders, arrestees, and forensic casework. NDIS is just one part of the larger Combined DNA Index System ("CODIS"), which is the generic term for the FBI's program that supports criminal justice databases. Furthermore, all fifty states now have laws requiring the collection of DNA samples from certain categories of offenders.

Since the 1990s, Congress has devoted a large amount of funds to forensic DNA research and development. This is directly related to the amplified use of DNA in criminal investigations. As DNA continued to become the so-called "gold standard" in law enforcement, this new reverence—bordering on obsession—meant that a tremendous amount of the federal funding was designated for DNA research and development.

Two decades later, DNA testing is the focal point of many labs, forcing other traditional forensic areas to reduce or even shut down their units. Police departments now include routine DNA swabs of evidence and persons in everyday investigations, from stolen cars to burgled homes, because "the justice system's hunger for DNA evidence just keeps growing."

B. How DNA Testing Works

1. DNA Description

Like a serial number or bar code is used to identify a particular product, people can be identified based on their specific genetic makeup. Within a person's cells, strings of nucleotides—made up of Adenine, Cytosine, Guanine, and Thymine—match up with the corresponding proteins in the form of a double helix. Though these patterns are highly predictable—A matches with T and C matches with G—the discrete differences can distinguish each person's genetic makeup.

Variations in DNA patterns may be seen at the single nucleotide level or through an unexpected, repetitive pattern of nucleotides. The addition, deletion, or unexpected change of one nucleotide is recognized as a single nucleotide polymorphism ("SNP"). The repeat of a series of nucleotides within a sequence, also known as a short tandem repeat ("STR"), may also be indicative of a person's traits. Gender may be easily determined based on the presence or absence of a Y-chromosome in a person's DNA. But as DNA analysts delve further into these genetic details, they are uncovering more ways that parts of sequences and individual allele variances can be predictive of a person's appearance.

2. DNA Collection

"Protection of the crime scene is essential to the protection of evidence." Generally, the use of DNA evidence in crime solving involves a lab's comparison of a known match, taken from a suspect or from the DNA database, with an unidentified sample taken from a crime scene. Investigators may find samples of DNA from a number of sources, but because biological evidence is not always visible and can be mixed with other sources, there is always a chance that the evidence gathered may lead to imprecise results. Very little DNA is required in order to perform an analysis, but that does not mean that the quality of that small sample is adequate for testing. Sufficient amounts and types of DNA must be collected on the scene for this technology to work properly.

3. Short Tandem Repeats

Short tandem repeats—repeat nucleotides within a sequence—is one attribute of DNA that could be indicative of a person's traits. To find these STRs, a small sample of DNA—typically less than fifty base pairs—is obtained from a physical sample, copied through polymerase chain reaction, and analyzed for patterns of nucleotides. The current standard method for developing a DNA profile first utilizes polymerase chain reaction analysis ("PCR") prior to examining STRs.

The STRs used for forensic DNA profiling are warehoused in an area of the chromosome—often termed junk, or noncoding DNA. New research suggests that STRs may be indicative of genetic history, as relatives and people from similar regions often share the same repeated pattern of nucleotides. The benefit of using STRs in analyzing DNA is that the product may be a highly accurate match, but obtaining this match depends on the sample having decent quality DNA from which to create the STRs. By examining several STR loci one can establish the unique genetic profile of an individual, linking biological evidence from a crime to the perpetrator or to other crimes by the same person.

Generally, DNA found in crime scene samples is tested in a lab and compared with known samples to exclude suspects. Traditional autosomal STR profiling (which excludes the X and Y sex chromosomes) involves taking certain loci in DNA and comparing these STR patterns with a known match to discover whether there are variances. Thirteen loci in DNA are predesignated test sites for comparing the gathered sample to the CODIS profiles. Side-by-side comparison of the samples shows whether the DNA produces a match. This technique is highly accurate, but also leaves the donor's privacy intact since no other information is gathered from the unknown DNA sample. That sample will either become known, based on information already legally acquired and stored, or the sample will remain unidentified.

Erin Murphy, *The Art in the Science of DNA: A Layperson's Guide to the Subjectivity Inherent in Forensic DNA Typing*
58 EMORY L.J. 489, 492–96 (2008)

Serious concerns pervade the use of forensic evidence in criminal cases. Despite efforts by a dedicated coterie of scholars who have long endeavored to expose fraudulent forensic methods, it perhaps took the DNA-exoneration cases to finally bring the breadth and depth of the problems to light. Much of the critical attention has centered upon what I have elsewhere termed "first-generation forensic techniques"—methods such as ballistics, handwriting analysis, and tool or bite mark analyses.

Although the judicial and executive branches have been slow to respond, some incremental changes have finally started to occur. Scrutiny has revealed that the methodological foundations that purport to legitimate many longstanding methods either do not exist or are woefully inadequate. While renewed efforts to scientifically validate some techniques—such as fingerprint typing—may prove effective, other methods have already fallen into disrepute. For instance, after a national expert panel discredited the forensic technique of bullet lead analysis, the Federal Bureau of Investigation (FBI) issued a statement that it would no longer conduct such testing. Similarly, courts have also recently called into question other long-accepted forensic techniques.

Often omitted from critiques of forensic methods, however, is a robust discussion of nuclear DNA typing. If anything, DNA typing is typically held out as the pinnacle of "good" forensic evidence, in that it exemplifies the kind of scientific rigor that first-generation techniques lack. After all, DNA analysis emerged from scientific processes, and it is a testable, reproducible, and falsifiable technique. DNA analysts even testify to their findings with expressions of statistical probabilities rather than arbitrary and unsupportable statements of certain identity.

Without question, this praise is well-deserved. DNA typing represents a marked advance beyond the shamanistic "sciences" of the first generation. Yet the seeming corollary—that DNA typing is therefore an exercise in purely objective, indisputable science—does not hold true. This is not to suggest that DNA has no basis in objective science, or even that it is as subjective as other forensic techniques; comparing most first-generation methods to DNA typing is like comparing astrology to neuroscience. Nevertheless, not unlike neuroscience, the fact that DNA typing is scientifically grounded does not mean that there are not plenty of things that we still do not understand about it, and plenty of instances in which the best conclusions we can draw are nonetheless tentative ones.

Many people know this, but a surprising number of laypersons, and even lawyers, do not. To be clear, I am not saying that DNA typing done poorly entails an exercise of subjective judgment. Rather, DNA typing—done perfectly and precisely according to protocol—still often entails making discretionary calls and choices. But just because DNA typing is not wholly objective does not mean that it is wholly indeterminate—it simply means that it may be more like meteorology than mathematics.

* * *

I. Fundamentals of DNA Typing

To understand the nature of the subjective decision making required by forensic DNA typing, it is first necessary to have some general notion of how it works. At the outset, it is worth spending a moment to resolve what, for many readers, may be a nagging preliminary contradiction. That is, some may wonder why criticisms of forensic DNA typing used to inculpate suspects should not likewise call into question the legitimacy of DNA typing used to exculpate people. After all, DNA typing has grabbed headlines for its use to exonerate wrongfully convicted persons, and thus the suggestion that it might have shortcomings understandably causes alarm. However, the use of DNA typing to inculpate a person—by which I mean to say that a suspect is the likely source of a sample—fundamentally differs from its use to exculpate. The simplest analogy is to blood typing. Imagine a murder scene at which police find a blood sample certain to belong to the killer. Crime scene technicians test the blood sample and show that it is type O+. Later, the police find and draw blood from two suspects. One suspect is type AB; the other is type O+. We can, with unreserved confidence, say that the first suspect is not the killer, but regarding the second suspect, we can only say that she is included within the class of people that includes the killer. The probability that she is the actual killer turns on how many other people have that blood type, along with any other evidence that we might be able to adduce.

DNA typing works in a similar fashion. When a genetic profile is generated, it is far easier to determine with confidence those individuals from whom the sample could not have come than to identify with certainty the individual to whom the sample absolutely belongs. The difficulty is in determining the parameters of inclusion—how to define the characteristics and size of the class of persons to whom it may belong. To provide another analogy, one can imagine that a witness glimpses a six-digit license plate and detects some symbols, but not others, which can be written as follows: "??2 3?6" or "??2 3? 8." That makes a suspect out of all those with plates of "XX2 3X6" and "XX2 3X8" (using "X" to represent the variable), but it does not call into question the certainty with which we can exclude all those with plates of "XX8 4X9."

Next, it is important to note that the general labels "DNA typing" or "forensic DNA" comprise a variety of techniques and methodologies. Most generally, forensic DNA typing currently consists largely of two different forms—nuclear DNA and mitochondrial DNA (mtDNA). As the name suggests, nuclear DNA typing looks at the strands of DNA found in the nucleus of cells—specifically those pieces of DNA found on a person's chromosomes. However, mtDNA typing examines DNA found in the mitochondria—organelles in the cell outside of the nucleus. The greatest advantage of mtDNA is that it is present in copious quantities and, therefore, may be more resilient to cell degradation. However, because mtDNA typing is both more time-intensive and produces less specific results (in terms of individuating persons), it is typically used only when nuclear DNA typing is not possible. For this reason, and for reasons of clarity, this Essay focuses only on nuclear DNA typing; however, it is worth noting that mtDNA also entails a large number of subjective determinations.

Lastly, even within the practice of nuclear DNA typing, many different individuation techniques have emerged. When DNA typing first appeared in 1986, a method known as restriction fragment length polymorphism (RFLP) was used to measure the length of certain parts of the DNA strand known as variable number tandem repeats (VNTRs). Ultimately, the technique that has prevailed and reflects contemporary practice is known as short tandem repeat multiplexing (STR), and thus it is that technique which this Essay discusses. The attractiveness of this particular method stems largely from its efficacy; it offers a high degree of discriminatory power at a rapid speed and relatively low cost.

A. Basics of STR Typing

How does STR typing work? I have explained that nuclear DNA typing looks at pieces of the genome found on chromosomes within the nucleus of the cell. The whole human genome is incredibly long—if unraveled it would stretch to more than six feet. Although examining the entire genome would be an excellent means of individuating persons, it would take a very long time and expend a great deal of resources. It would also be largely unnecessary: over 99% of the genomes of two human beings are identical. In fact, human DNA is roughly 98% identical to that of a chimpanzee.

It is on some of these regions of difference among people, then, that DNA typing focuses. Specifically, STR typing looks to particular regions of the genome where certain known sequences of the four DNA base pairs (GATC) repeat themselves, and then measures how many times those repeats occur. These repetitive sections are particularly useful because, presently, they have no known function. That is why they are sometimes called "junk" DNA—because unlike sections (called genes) of the DNA strand that "code" for something and have a purpose (such as determining hair color), these genes are "non-coding."

In light of the standard set by the FBI when it put together the national database of genetic profiles, known as CODIS (Combined DNA Index System), most crime laboratories look at thirteen different places (or "loci," the plural of "locus") where these repeats occur. To make matters somewhat more complicated, at each place there are two possibilities for the number of repeats. The reason for this is that individuals have two sets of chromosomes—one from their father and one from their mother—and the number of repeats they have in a particular section might be different on each chromosome. In the end, a genetic profile is expressed as a list of twenty-six numbers—two numbers for each of the thirteen places. Those numbers represent the repeats present at the thirteen specific sites on both chromosomes.

For example, looking at a particular locus on the gene strand, an analyst might observe six repeats on one chromosome, and fifteen on another. The person would therefore be a 6, 15 at that locus. The repeats at a particular locus are called the alleles. Thus, in the example, the person would have a 6 allele and a 15 allele. All twenty-six alleles together—the two alleles from each of the thirteen loci—constitute the forensic DNA profile.

By crude analogy, you can imagine a DNA profile as a composition of the size measurements of a person. If we measure precisely, we might find a person—let's call her Jean—has a 34-inch bust, a 28-inch waist, 38-inch hips, and a 34-inch inseam. We could then think of Jean's profile as 34x28x38x34. By comparison, Jean's friend Dana might have a profile of 28x28x32x26. If we had a big pile of clothing, and we knew both Jean's and Dana's profiles, then we could probably separate the clothes accordingly.

Similarly, DNA typing allows us to take the measurements of the individual in two respects at thirteen different places and then compare them to the measurements of another individual. Like the example given above, the range of "sizes" at each spot is not limitless — there is a finite degree of possibilities. Of course, the variation in body sizes is both less diverse and less precise than the variation in genetic material, but the general idea is the same.

* * *

When a crime scene sample arrives at a laboratory, an analyst must check to see if the item contains any usable biological material — most typically blood, semen, or saliva. Once detected, the DNA must be "extracted" from the item, a delicate process that creates a high risk of sample contamination or further degradation. The analyst then measures the amount of DNA present to select an optimal quantity for testing, and to ensure that the sample is human DNA.

Once the sample is ready, the first step is to amplify the genetic material so that testing it is easier. Again, to use a crude illustration, imagine you saw something that looked like a termite in your house. You want to know if it was a termite or just an ant, whether there are more termites, and if so, where they are. But it is very hard to figure that out from observing just one termite. If you saw one hundred termites, then you could not only more readily conclude that, in fact, you have a termite problem, but it would also be easier to determine the specific type of termite and where they have nested. DNA amplification, through a process known as polymerase chain reaction (PCR), takes the DNA strand, cuts it, and then creates identical copies of only the part of the DNA strand important for testing. Thus, it not only eliminates the irrelevant parts of the genetic strand, but it also amplifies, through replication, the relevant bit so it is easier to measure its characteristics.

The actual testing and measuring of the DNA sample is conducted using kits made by commercial companies and a process called electrophoresis. Detailed explanation of this process is not necessary for the purposes of this Essay, and even a brief description can be surprisingly complex. What matters for our purposes is that the results of this process are interpreted by computer software that separates out the relevant pieces of information. In this phase, DNA testing appears to the analyst not as a list of numbers, but rather as a kind of graph with peaks and valleys. Different computer software then assigns values to those peaks and valleys, based on a template of information. For a single-source sample — that is, a sample known to contain the DNA of only one person like that collected in clinical conditions from prisoners or parolees — the graphical representation is typically a fairly clean and easily interpreted chart, such as Figure 8.1.

When the DNA of more than one person is involved, this entire process can become a bit more complicated. To return to the clothing analogy above, imagine that both

Figure 8.1

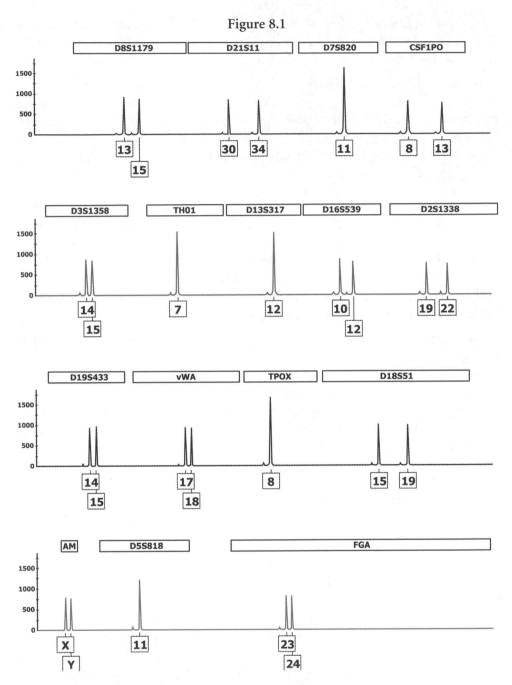

Jean and Dana take their clothes to the same dry cleaner. Unfortunately, the cleaner is having a bad day and instead of putting the clothes in the "to clean" bag, he accidentally throws them into the garbage. Fortunately, he realizes his mistake in time and grabs the bag before it leaves the shop. Also fortunately, the cleaner knows the relative sizes of Dana and Jean, and that both of them brought in five different items: a skirt, a blouse, slacks, a jacket, and a sweater.

In trying to straighten things out, the cleaner might first sort through the pile—separating out the trash from the clothes, and then separating out skirts from pants and so on. The cleaner hopes, at this point, to have one of each—and to only have to figure out which belongs to Dana and which to Jean. Assume that the cleaner finishes separating and identifying the relevant clothes, but the cleaner still does not know to whom each article of clothing belongs. The next step he might undertake is to assess the relative sizes of each of the items in each category—distinguishing the larger from the smaller skirt, blouse, slacks, jacket, and sweater.

But our cleaner still is not finished. He has not yet reached his goal of ultimate attribution. He has separated the clothes from the garbage, and even the types of clothes from one another. He has figured out which is the larger and which is the smaller of each kind of item. But recall that he knows both Jean and Dana's relative sizes. Now he must take what he knows and make inferences about to whom each piece of clothing belongs. For instance, he should be able to surmise that the longer pants belong to Jean and the shorter ones to Dana. Or the tighter fitting blouse is likely to fit only Dana, and thus the looser one is probably Jean's. And in most cases, he will be right.

This somewhat silly example of the bumbling cleaner mirrors the process of DNA typing. In the first stage, a machine and computer software work together to amplify and then observe the relevant characteristics of the pieces of genetic material passing through the machine. This is akin to the cleaner looking into the trash bag and distinguishing between both clothes and trash, and between types of clothes, like skirts and pants. In the second stage, the software assigns values to those characteristics based on an internal sizing standard that tells it how to quantify what it detected. This is akin to the cleaner looking at the clothing and determining that the inseam on one pair of pants is about 28" and on another it is about 34".

The last part—where the cleaner determines that the shorter pants go with Dana and the longer pants with Jean—is done not by a machine, but by the forensic analyst. And although as a general rule such determinations can be made with confidence, they are nonetheless fraught with the potential for erroneous inferences. The cleaner, for instance, might be wrong in assuming that just because Jean is taller she prefers longer pants. Perhaps the shorter pants belong to Jean, and Dana, in turn, buys her pants long so that she can roll them up.

Still more complicated, imagine that the cleaner accidentally overlooked a third pair of pants that were in the trash bag. Suppose further that this overlooked pair in fact belonged to Jean, and so not only was the cleaner wrong in assuming that the longer pants were Jean's, but also that there were only two people's clothing mixed up in the pile. Or maybe he looked carefully, but somehow only one pair of pants was found in the bag—he now knows that he has lost one set of pants, but he is not sure whose they were or how they got lost.

These examples of the mixed-up cleaner help to illustrate how this act of sorting and labeling may in fact be more difficult than it seems at first blush. In much the same way, forensic DNA typing churns out an unsorted mass of information, which must be deciphered by an analyst, and which is not always amenable to only one interpretation. This leads us to the necessary subjectivity of forensic DNA typing.

II. Subjective Determinations in DNA Typing

The job of the DNA analyst, like the mixed-up cleaner, often involves taking the information processed by the computer and attributing it meaning. As in the case of the cleaner, this process relies largely on reasoning abilities, processes of elimination, subjective judgment calls, and inferences; it is not a mathematically certain, objective enterprise. If it was, we would not need DNA analysts at all because there would be no need for interpretation of DNA results. This is not to say that interpretation involves unbounded discretion—a DNA analyst works within a range of assumptions and knowledge that forms the basis of the inferences and conclusions drawn. But DNA interpretation is a discretionary act—more like stepping outside and predicting the afternoon weather than like reciting multiplication tables.

* * *

In providing the examples below, I want to make clear that I have focused on ordinary, run-of-the-mill issues that arise in forensic DNA typing. I have specifically avoided discussion, for instance, of contamination—either at the crime scene or in the laboratory—even though it constitutes a significant problem. I have also avoided discussion of transfer—the phenomenon by which DNA may appear to be present in a place where it was not directly deposited. For example, my DNA may show up on a towel simply because I shook hands with a person who later grabbed that towel himself. And lastly, I am not discussing any ongoing methodological disputes or vanguard technologies, such as "low copy number" (LCN) DNA typing.

Rather, my focus ... is on forensic samples collected in typical crime scene conditions, and the subjective determinations that often go into interpreting them. Figure 1 illustrated the typical clarity of a single-source forensic DNA result. But for a forensic sample collected from more chaotic conditions and with an unknown number of contributors, the results can be a bit more difficult to interpret. Consider, for instance, the image reproduced as Figure 8.2.

At each locus—identified by the boxed-off information at the top of different sections and typically abbreviated to the first few letters or numbers (for instance, locus "vWA" on the top row)—there are multiple identifiable peaks representing the alleles. For instance, locus vWA shows at least four identifiable peaks with clearly observable alleles—16, 17, 18, and 19. The amount of the genetic material (the quantity, not the length) is reflected by the numbers off to the right. At locus vWA, there is a large amount of material for the 16, 18, and 19 alleles, and much less for the 17 allele. The differences in quantity can be significant for typing purposes; a large amount of material may reflect that one person has two of the same allele at that locus or that multiple persons share the same allele. On the contrary, very little material may indicate any number of things—for instance, it could mean nothing; it could mean that the peak is "spurious" (not a real indication of genetic material); or it could

Figure 8.2

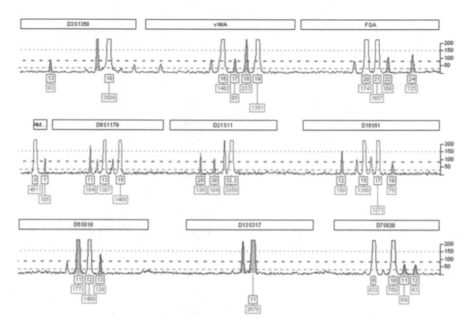

mean simply that fewer persons in the mixture possess that allele than others. That is why, for instance, there is an unlabeled peak to the left of the 16 allele.

This is the essential difficulty in interpreting forensic DNA samples—determining what to count and what not to count, while also recognizing that the logical inference is not necessarily the only or correct inference. When analysts are given the known suspect's profile—as opposed to being asked what profiles are possible, given the results they have generated—the risk of erroneous attribution becomes heightened. An analyst may unwittingly fall prey to confirmation bias—seeing in the results what she expects to see, rather than what may or may not be there. The paragraphs below give additional examples of the ways in which even the most conscientious forensic analyst may make the kind of subjective calls that risk an erroneous interpretation of DNA test results.

A. Deciding Which Peaks Should Count: Peak-Height Thresholds

As explained in the previous section, the first thing an analyst must do is determine what information matters. The peaks and valleys of a forensic DNA sample are not always indisputably clear, but instead require interpretation that labels some as legitimate and others as spurious. The height of the peak (literally, how tall it looks) reflects the amount of genetic material measured at that allele. The amount of measured material can be a function of many different things.... Regardless, analysts typically aim for a peak height within an optimal range to ensure that what is observed is genuine genetic material. For instance, the FBI Protocol allows only peaks over 200 relative fluorescence units (RFU) to "be considered conclusive for match purposes," though it recommends interpretation of any peak over 50 RFU, including for exculpatory purposes. The makers of commercial equipment for DNA testing recommend a minimum of 150 RFU. Other laboratories allow thresholds as low as 50 RFU for inculpation.

The importance of peak heights in interpreting DNA results is several-fold. If the threshold is set too low, then many small peaks that do not represent true alleles, but appear for other reasons, will be treated as representing genetic material. Without minimum thresholds, an analyst might think that a peak belongs to the suspect, when in fact it is not from the suspect. Conversely, a very large quantity of genetic material raises risks of a spillover effect, wherein additional peaks that are relics of the excess of material, rather than a reflection of a true allele, are created. A very large peak might also (correctly or erroneously) suggest that one person has two copies of the same allele at that locus (recall that each locus has genetic material from the father and mother), or that multiple persons share that allele. Almost always, a forensic profile does not contain only perfectly formed peaks that reflect true genetic alleles; rather, before making any conclusions, an analyst must first determine which peaks should factor into consideration at all.

B. Choosing How to Interpret Peaks of Different Sizes: Peak-Height Imbalance

When interpreting which peaks are significant, the analyst is typically guided by some rules of thumb. For instance, a genetic profile should have relatively balanced material across the loci. A pristine, single-source sample collected in clinical conditions will often reflect relatively consistent peak heights, with the primary exception being loci where the individual has two copies of the same allele at that locus (known as homozygosity). In those places, the peak height should be roughly twice the size of the other peaks because twice as much genetic material was observed for that allele.

But perfect balance can be difficult to achieve with crime scene samples. Such samples, as previously noted, often arrive at the crime laboratory in imperfect condition, both in terms of quantity and quality. For a variety of reasons ... peak heights can vary dramatically. As a result, an analyst often must interpret that variation and decide what, if any, significance it carries.

For instance, suppose the analyst knows that the defendant is homozygotic at a locus. The analyst might then interpret a very large peak as evidence of that homozygosity, and dismiss any additional peaks at that locus as spurious. Even if the peak is not extremely high, the analyst might still claim that it represents a "true" allele that matches the defendant, while at the same time dismissing another peak for various reasons. Such determinations would not necessarily be wrong, but they also would not necessarily be right. The key is that these decisions involve the exercise of (hopefully reasoned) discretion, and no analyst can state without reservation which peaks will always, and which will never, count as "true."

C. Ignoring Some Peaks Altogether: Artifacts and Stochastic Effects

What are some of the reasons, then, that an analyst might ignore or dismiss a peak— even a peak that is taller (and thus suggests a significant quantity of material) than other peaks in the same profile? There are numerous responses, but I will only discuss a few. Notably, at times an analyst may not have any explanation for the presence of a peak, but often the presence of a particular peak may be explained by one of several recognizable phenomena. These phenomena are typically lumped under the label "artifacts"—because they create spurious peaks rather than true alleles, or "stochastic effects"—meaning that they occur as a result of a random variable. Such effects have very expressive names like stutter, pull-up or bleed through, spikes, and blobs.

Some artifacts are "reproducible," meaning that repeat testing should generate identical artifacts, while others are not. The occurrence of artifacts, however, requires human interpretation of DNA testing results in order to separate true peaks from spurious peaks. Again, to be clear, a good laboratory will have standards and protocols for undertaking this effort, but even such standards are apt to be mere guidelines— not precise, unalterable rules. Ultimately, the decision to dismiss a peak as an artifact, or label it a true allele, is a discretionary decision left to the analyst.

D. Assigning Meaning to Missing Peaks: Allelic Dropout

At times, the difficulty in interpreting DNA evidence is not the presence of extraneous peaks, but the absence of an expected peak or allele. One way to interpret such an absence would be to identify it as an exclusion; that is, if the suspect has a particular profile that matches the crime scene sample in all but one place, it might simply be assumed that the suspect is then excluded as the source. Commonly, however, analysts will explain the absence of an anticipated or expected allele as a function of "allelic dropout."

Dropout often occurs when the DNA is not properly amplified so that it can be detected. This commonly results from degraded or low quantity DNA samples, where some material fails to amplify. A similar result can also occur as a result of genetic mutations that cause an allele not to amplify properly, creating what is commonly referred to as a null allele.

The fact that an allele may simply fail to appear—for any number of reasons— obviously causes problems in interpreting DNA typing results. A missing allele could mean any number of things; for example, it could represent grounds for excluding a suspect as a possible source because the suspect, unlike the sample, has a typeable allele at that locus. Or it could simply generate ambiguity in the possible interpretations of the results because it is not known with certainty why the allele did not appear. What matters is that the analyst reading the crime scene profile has the opportunity to ascribe significance to the missing material. It is like evidence that the perpetrator lives at 55 Jones Street; if a suspect in fact lives at 55 Jones Court, but matches the evidence in every other way, we might not be too worried. But if that address is the only evidence, we might not feel comfortable concluding it was just a trivial mistake.

E. Labeling Peaks as Belonging to Particular Profiles: Mixture Deconvolution

In the area of mixture deconvolution, forensic DNA analysts have another major opportunity for interpretive discretion. This is simply a fancy way of saying that crime scene samples often contain the DNA of multiple persons, and analysts frequently attempt to reach conclusions about the number and characteristics of the various contributors. Recall Figure 2, which contained the DNA typing results of a fictive crime scene stain. The interpreted data does not arrive labeled with the number of contributors or their particular profiles; rather, the technology simply analyzes all the DNA present and identifies the results indiscriminately. It is up to the analyst to try to separate out and ascribe relevant profiles, much like our bumbling cleaner had to do with the mixed up clothing.

Because deciphering mixtures constitutes such an important part of forensic DNA typing, many efforts are underway to improve the available technology. One recent, significant advance is the capacity to separate male DNA from female DNA, and then focus on amplifying only the male fragment. This technique, known as Y-STR typing, is particularly helpful in rape cases, in which samples are commonly a mixture of DNA (frequently, a male perpetrator and a female victim). However, because this form of typing only examines half of the quantity of material as a full DNA profile (i.e., just the male fraction), it is less discriminating and therefore less determinate than a full profile.

As with most aspects of DNA interpretation, the discretion exercised by analysts is not limitless. There are principles and guidelines that instruct analysts on how to separate out a mixture, assign the number of contributors, and perhaps even tentatively identify major or minor contributor profiles. The FBI Protocol, for instance, permits an analyst to label a major and minor contributor in a mixed specimen sample "if there is a distinct contrast in peak intensities between the alleles, and the alleles contributing the largest peak height values satisfy the conditions of a single source specimen."

The problem with mixtures is that they exacerbate all of the above issues regarding the interpretation of stutter, pull-ups, spikes, blobs, or dropout. Not only may it be more difficult to distinguish true from false peaks, but even in the cleanest of profiles, contributors can readily mask one another's contributions. Studies have shown that roughly 3% of three-person mixtures are easily misidentified as two-person mixtures, and that over 70% of four-person mixtures would be wrongly labeled two- or three-person mixtures. And even where the number of contributors is known, there may be an extraordinarily large number of ways of interpreting the evident genetic material to create possible individual profiles.

2. Studies in Junk Science: Shaken Baby Syndrome and Arson

"In light of current information, it is unlikely that the prosecution's experts would testify today as adamantly as they did in 1997."

—*Cavazos v. Smith*, 565 US 1, 14 (2011) (J. Ginsberg, dissenting)

Deborah Tuerkheimer, *Science-Dependent Prosecution and the Problem of Epistemic Contingency: A Study of Shaken Baby Syndrome*

62 Ala. L. Rev. 513, 513–69 (2011)

Imagine that you are the parent of a young child who is just learning to crawl. When you look away for a moment, you hear a "thud" and turn to see your baby bump her head on the ground. She seems fine at first, but hours later, when she vomits, you become concerned and take her to the hospital. After performing a battery of tests, doctors inform you that they have detected cerebral edema (brain swelling), subdural hematoma (bleeding between the hard outer layer and the spongy membranes that surround the brain), and retinal hemorrhaging (bleeding of the inside surface of the back of the eye). You are told that these three symptoms—the diagnostic "triad"—are the telltale signs of Shaken Baby Syndrome (SBS), and that, because you were with the baby during the window of time when forceful shaking necessarily occurred, doctors know that you are the abuser. Within hours, the state has removed your baby—along with her sibling—from your custody, and you are being interrogated by police detectives.

Around the country, parents and caregivers confront a similar medical insistence that shaking caused their babies' injuries and a criminal justice apparatus primed to respond accordingly....

Each year in this country, up to 1,500 babies are given an SBS diagnosis. While a portion of cases present medical corroboration of some type of abuse (e.g., long bone fractures and grip marks), the classic formulation of SBS is based exclusively on the diagnostic "triad"—again, cerebral edema, subdural hematomas, and retinal hemorrhages. Approximately 200 defendants a year are convicted of crimes related to SBS, and hundreds of people are currently serving lengthy prison sentences for shaking babies.

With rare exception, SBS prosecutions rest entirely on the testimony of medical experts. All elements of the charge are proven by the claims of science: testimony regarding the force necessary to cause the infant's injuries establishes the mechanism of death, as well as the perpetrator's criminal state of mind; testimony that the baby's symptoms would invariably present themselves immediately upon the infliction of injury demonstrates the killer's identity. In essence, SBS is a medical diagnosis of murder.

First, research has shown that retinal hemorrhages and subdural hematomas can result from forces other than shaking. In effect, the myth of pathonomony—which told that the diagnostic triad was necessarily and exclusively induced by shaking—has been debunked. Second, the existence of lucid intervals has been established, proving that an earlier trauma (i.e., one occurring before the infant came under the suspect's care) can cause an infant's later symptoms. Doctors now concede the possibility of a lag between injury and neurological manifestation.

Third, there has been increasing awareness of a variety of medical disorders that can "mimic" the symptoms of SBS. As a result, doctors must consider not only accidental trauma as a cause of the constellation of symptoms previously associated with SBS, but also the possibility of congenital malformations, metabolic disorders, hematological diseases, infectious diseases, autoimmune conditions, birth effects, rebleeds, and hypoxia. In sum, depending on the clinical picture presented, the "differential diagnosis" for symptoms previously associated exclusively with SBS now contemplates a wide range of nontraumatic possibilities. Thus, with hardly any notice, scientific advances effectively undermined the validity of triad-based criminal convictions. In 2008, an appeals court in Wisconsin was the first to recognize this.

In a ruling without precedent, the court concluded that "a shift in mainstream medical opinion" had eroded the basis of the SBS diagnosis. Audrey Edmunds, a day care provider serving an eighteen-year sentence at the time, was freed.

The implications seemed enormous. Edmunds's case was prototypical of SBS prosecutions. Now that she had been exonerated by the science that just a decade before had convicted her, what of the hundreds of convictions based on functionally indistinguishable factual predicates?

* * *

As its default mode, the criminal justice system continues to process SBS cases as it has for decades, seemingly without regard to fundamental revision of the science once believed to support a diagnosis of shaking. Police and prosecutors still move forward based on the exclusive presence of retinal hemorrhages and subdural hematomas; judges still allow experts to testify to speculative claims; juries still convict in triad-only cases; courts still deny appeals and motions for post-conviction relief.

* * *

The SBS prosecution paradigm is utterly dependent on the claims of science. As I have explained:

> With rare exception, the case turns on the testimony of medical experts. Unlike any other category of prosecution, all elements of the crime—mens rea and actus reus (which includes both the act itself and causation of the resulting harm)—are proven by the science. Degree of force testimony not only establishes causation, but also the requisite state of mind. Unequivocal testimony regarding timing—i.e., that symptoms necessarily would appear instantaneously upon the infliction of injury—proves the perpetrator's identity. In its classic formulation, SBS comes as close as one could imagine to a medical diagnosis of murder: prosecutors use it to prove the mechanism of death, the intent to harm, and the identity of the killer.[43]

Deborah W. Denno, *Concocting Criminal Intent*
105 Geo. L.J. 323, 349, 341–43 (2017)

Three key interrelated factors distinguish [studied SBS] cases from other kinds of criminal cases: (1) the prosecution depends almost entirely on the medical diagnosis of SBS for its theory and argument, without which there would most likely be no case or, at most, a case involving a substantially lesser charge; (2) the prosecution focuses on proving, however dubiously, that the defendant intended his or her actions, as opposed to a lower level of *mens rea* such as recklessness, despite no direct evidence of intentionality; and (3) the prosecution emphasizes a causal connection between the defendant's *mens rea* and *actus reus*, which suggests that the defendant was aware that the actions he or she engaged in would cause the victim's harm. As a result, for

---

43. Deborah Tuerkheimer, *The Next Innocence Project: Shaken Baby Syndrome and the Criminal Courts*, 87 Wash. U. L. Rev. 1, n.58 (2009).

many cases involving SBS, courts convict defendants for the most serious offenses, and those defendants receive the harshest punishments.

* * *

The link between SBS and criminality developed gradually. The first SBS case, that of John Schneider, took place in 1984, but it would be one of only fifteen such appellate cases decided before 1990. In sharp contrast, there would be hundreds more cases in the early 1990s and beyond. Indeed, by the late 1990s, in the legal community, SBS had garnered a substantial level of "acceptance and enormously widespread popularity, with no real investigation or even question as to its scientific validity." A constellation of factors contributed to this status, ranging from the establishment of mandatory reporting laws for health care and other professionals to the increased use of clinical medicine in legal cases to a growing presumption that any child's unexplained injury was likely to have been inflicted by a culpable adult.

Also by this time, the ties between SBS and the requisite elements of a crime had become firmly entrenched: shaking was the act that caused harm to the infant; the force with which the baby was shaken indicated the perpetrator's mental state, especially intent; and finally, the caretaker who was last with the conscious baby was the defendant. The very term "shaken baby syndrome" fuels the causal perception of these associations, with its suggestion that there is a singular origin of the act—"shaking"—and its implication of intent because shaking a baby is only rarely accidental. In other words, the caretaker presumably fulfills both the *actus reus* requirement and the *mens rea* requirement. It is highly unusual for a medical syndrome to be identified using terms that so readily connote wrongdoing; the vast majority of syndromes are named either by the person who discovered them or by their medical characteristics. By 2012, even Guthkelch, the creator of SBS, published an article severely deriding how the syndrome had been misapplied over the years, particularly as a vehicle for connoting a caretaker's intent to harm.

The initial SBS research proposed that shaking was merely a possible method by which the triad symptoms could occur and that it was often considered an acceptable response to a crying infant. However, influential medical organizations took the causal suggestion one step further. In 1992, the National Center on Child Abuse and Neglect supported a groundbreaking nationwide strategy to promote awareness of SBS. As a result, prosecutors throughout the country were instructed about the SBS triad symptoms in order to pursue cases. A year later, the American Academy of Pediatrics, the leading U.S. organization of pediatricians, made statements suggesting that evidence of the triad symptoms supported a medical presumption of abuse, thereby prompting both doctors and prosecutors to equate those symptoms with shaking.

Likewise, in 1998, a number of leading pediatricians who specialized in child abuse endorsed a published letter to the editor of the journal Pediatrics insisting that SBS "is now a well-characterized clinical and pathological entity." The group questioned "those who would challenge the specificity of [the SBS] diagnostic features" in court by way of suggesting other causes for an infant's injury. Therefore, by reinforcing the presumption of abuse, the medical community created a scenario in which presumption of abuse could be treated as intentionality in the legal context. Recent findings and investigation into the original research, however, have seriously questioned both the scientific and legal underpinnings of SBS.

Doubts About the Science

There is a debate in much of the modern literature on SBS concerning whether the science behind the diagnosis is problematic. For example, despite many reported cases of shaken infants, there has not been a single documented instance in which someone has witnessed shaking alone cause brain injury in an infant, nor has such damage been replicated in a controlled laboratory setting. Furthermore, no study has shown that human beings are capable of creating the necessary rotational acceleration through manual shaking to cause brain injuries in infants without impact. These and other findings conflict with Guthkelch's original hypothesis that manual shaking alone can manifest in triad symptoms.

* * *

The controversy surrounding SBS in no way invalidates the horrifying fact that some caregivers do inflict injury or death upon children. Child abuse and SBS are devastating issues for families and society, and there is no question that nonaccidental brain trauma in babies is medically diagnosable within the confines of medical practice in a hospital. Yet there is a growing recognition of the legal problems raised by SBS. The doctors who make and corroborate such diagnoses are not trained in the forensics of child abuse. Their sole concern is to immediately treat their patients and to protect them from future harm. Therefore, these doctors are not capable of determining whether the patient was in fact criminally abused, let alone whether the alleged abuser intended to cause such harm. As one neurosurgeon and expert noted, "[w]ith regard to treatment of cranio-cerebral trauma, the differentiation between accidental and inflicted injury is of limited practical importance: injuries are injuries. For social purposes, however, the distinction is critical."

Swedish Agency for Health Tech. Assessment & Assessment of Social Services, *Traumatic Shaking: The Role of the Triad in Medical Investigations of Suspected Traumatic Shaking—A Systematic Review*

(2016)

The systematic review showed the following graded results:

- There is limited scientific evidence that the triad and therefore its components can be associated with traumatic shaking (low quality evidence).
- There is insufficient scientific evidence on which to assess the diagnostic accuracy of the triad in identifying traumatic shaking (very low quality evidence).

* * *

Although relatively many studies met the criteria for inclusion, the literature search identified only two studies of moderate quality. This is disconcerting, because traumatic shaking is very serious and has dramatic consequences for both the child and its family. The research field is complex, but this does not excuse, for example, circular reasoning and inadequate presentation of data collection....

Other possible causes (differential diagnoses) of the triad and its components

In cases presenting with the triad, it is important to determine whether these can be attributed to causes other than traumatic shaking.

Subdural hematoma, retinal hemorrhages and encephalopathy have been described after delivery and in association with such conditions as various convulsive states, certain hemorrhagic diseases, infectious diseases, metabolic disorders, immunological diseases, skeletal diseases and vascular malformations (see Table 8.1 for details).

Table 8.1: Other possible causes of the components of the triad

Other possible causes (differential diagnosis) of the triad and its components.	Disease/condition	Reported findings from the triad	Reference number (number of cases, or cases/study population size) Reported finding from the triad
Diseases or conditions causing hemorrhagic symptoms	von Willebrand's disease	SDH, RH	[78] (1)
	Delta storage pool disease	SDH, BE, RH	[79] (1)
	Hyperfibrinogenemia	RH (including vitreous hemorrhage)	[80] (1)
	Hemophilia A	SDH/RH	[81] (2) RH [82] (1) SDH
	Factor X deficiency	SDH	[83] (2)
	Idiopathic thrombocytopenic purpura	ICH	[84] (1)
	Kasabach-Merrit syndrome thrombocytopenia	RH	[85] (1)
	Hepatitis	RH, BE, SDH	[86] (1)
	Albers-Schönberg disease	SDH	[87] (1)
	Vitamin K deficiency	SDH (ICH)/BE/RH	[88] (3) SDH [89] (17) SDH [90] (1) SDH [91] (16) SDH, [92] (1) SDH, BE, RH [93] (1) SDH, BE
	Menkes disease (Copper deficiency)	SDH	[94] (1)
	Unspecified	RH, SDH	[95] (1) [96] (3)
Infections	Infection	RH	[97] (4)
	Infection with or without hypoxia	SDH (intradural bleeding)	[21] (10/30)
Vascular malformations	Aneurysm, Arterio-venous malformation	SDH (SAH)/BE/RH	[98] (1) SDH [99] (1) SDH, BE [100] (1) SDH, BE [101] (1) SDH, RH
Prenatal and birth-related injuries	Prematurity	RH	[102] (11)
	Delivery injury	SDH (ICH)/RH	[18] (2) SDH [103] (3) ICH [96] (3) SDH [56] (53) RH [104] (10) RH
	Normal delivery (or prenatal)	SDH/RH	[77] (17/97) SDH [39] (94/252) RH [76] (32/63) SDH
	Prenatal trauma	RH	[105] (2)
	Congenital SDH	SDH	[106] (1)
	Congenital heart disease	SDH	[22] (66/152)

The table continues on the next page

Source: Appendix to the Swedish Agency for Health Tech.

Table 8.1, Continued

	Disease/condition	Reported findings from the triad	Reference number (number of cases, or cases/study population size) Reported finding from the triad
Large head size	Enlarged SA space/ External hydrocephalus/ Benign enlargement of the subarachnoid spaces	SDH	[31] (6/108) [32] (4/177) [107] (7) [33] (3) [96] (6)
	External hydrocephalus	RH, SDH	[108] (1) [109] (6)
Metabolic diseases	Glutamic aciduria	SDH/RH	[110] (1) SDH [111] (1) SDH [112] (1) SDH, RH
Immunological diseases	Hemo-phagocytic lymphohistiocytosis	SDH, SAH (ICH), BE, RH	[113] (1)
	Transplacental acquisition of anti-Ro antibodies	SDH	[114] (2)
Skeletal diseases	Osteogenesis imperfecta	SDH, RH	[115] (3)
	Brittle bone disease	SDH/RH	[116] (20/20) SDH (11/20) RH
Other	Hypoxia and resuscitation	RH	[117] (1/33) [118] (1)
	Hypoxia	SDH/intradural bleeding	[21] (20/30)
	Choking and resuscitation	SDH (SAH), RH	[119] (1)
	Resuscitation in patients with retinopathy of prematurity	RH	[118] (2) [117] (1/33)
	Hypernatremia and dehydration	ICH, BE	[120] (1)
	Leukemia	RH	[95] (3)
	Vaccine-induced vitamin C deficiency	SDH, BE	[121] (2)

BE = Brain edema; **ICH** = Intracranial hemorrhage; **RH** = Retinal hemorrhage; **SAH** = Subarachnoid hemorrhage; **SDH** = Subdural hematoma

Source: Appendix to the Swedish Agency for Health Tech.

Deborah Tuerkheimer, *Arson and SBS* excerpt from *Science-Dependent Prosecution and the Problem of Epistemic Contingency: A Study of Shaken Baby Syndrome*

62 ALA. L. REV. 513, 553 (2011)

The crime of arson has striking parallels to SBS. In fire investigations, as in forensic medicine, "mistakes can lead to the belief that there is a crime when none was committed." Here, too, expert testimony establishes the actus reus—the damaging of real property by means of fire or explosive. The requisite mens rea—typically knowl-edge—is proven by the fire investigator's conclusion that the fire was purposely set. In contrast to a diagnosis of SBS, which effectively demonstrates the perpetrator's identity by framing a small temporal window in which the injuries could have been inflicted, techniques of fire investigation do not generally allow for a determination of who perpetrated the alleged arson. But, notwithstanding this distinction, arson shares with SBS an enormous dependence on a body of technical knowledge—which may or may not be scientific—thought to prove guilt beyond a reasonable doubt.

I raise the arson example to make a fairly modest point: SBS is not the only crime that is almost fully embedded in the domain of science. However, it should also be noted that, apart from this similarity, the two areas of criminal justice share a dependence on scientific claims that have been undermined. As is becoming more widely known, the science of fire investigations has evolved dramatically raising many of the same issues that have arisen in the SBS context, in particular, the problem of innocence.

* * *

Triad-based SBS convictions raise the distinct possibility that, notwithstanding a criminal judgment to the contrary, no crime whatsoever occurred. Just as new scientific consensus regarding the diagnosis undermines the proposition that the three symptoms establish the identity of a perpetrator, it also belies the notion that the triad is necessarily caused by shaking. Put differently, in some cases, the "wrong" suspect may have been pursued by law enforcement; but in many, there is no killer because there was no homicide. Here, the old science has (falsely) constructed a crime.

Kristine Bunch, Exoneree

As the interrogation wore on [Sheriff Oldham] asked her repeatedly who set the fire. Kristine didn't know.

"Kristy, you realize what I'm telling you don't you?" Oldham asked her a few minutes later. "Accelerant was on the thing. There is no way that you— if his room was on fire, the living room would have been on fire too. I mean, it was not an accidental fire. It was set."

Kristine struggled to think who could be responsible.

"Did you set it?"

"No."

"Then who did?"

"I can't tell you."

"You can."

"What am I going to do, make wild stabs at people that just don't like me?"

—excerpt from *Exoneree Diaries: The Fight for Innocence, Independence, and Identity*, by Alison Flowers

Caitlin M. Plummer and Imran J. Syed,
"Shifted Science" Revisited: Percolation Delays and the Persistence of Wrongful Convictions Based on Outdated Science
64 Clev. St. L. Rev. 483, 483–518 (2016)

It is easy enough to grasp that changes in scientific understanding and theory take some time to be accepted within the scientific community, and even longer to be perceived by the largely unscientific legal community. But there is much more gravity to that simple truth than our legal system has so far accounted for....

[S]hifts in science take years to percolate down into the average courtroom—and the delay causes unjust convictions to continue for years after the science is recognized as flawed. Describing shifts pulled from the fields of fire science, comparative bullet lead analysis, and the medical diagnosis that was for years referred to as "Shaken Baby Syndrome," this Article outlines some of the problems arising from delays in percolation of new scientific ideas into the local legal communities where criminal convictions occur....

* * *

On the evening of September 8, 1995, [Andrew] Babick visited a drug house to purchase crack cocaine. After returning a second time to make another purchase, he was told that the dealer was not there, so Babick waited on the porch for the dealer to return. During that time, he smoked a cigarette and fell asleep on the couch on the porch. Waking up shortly afterward, Babick could not find his cigarette. Seeing that the dealer had still not returned, Babick ambled home.

A fire consumed the drug house shortly after Babick's departure. Two adults escaped from the burning home, but two children died. Babick was arrested and charged with felony murder for intentionally setting the fire, allegedly because he was angry with the dealer.

No one saw Babick set the fire. He had no traces of gasoline on him, and there was no explanation given of how he had acquired or transported gasoline. There was no explanation for how he got into the house, and why no one in the house heard him, despite the allegation that he spread gasoline only a few feet away from the inhabitants. Babick insisted he did not set the fire. Nevertheless, the State concluded that he broke into the house, poured gasoline throughout, and ignited it. And the State had no trouble convincing the jury about that version of events, because "science" was on its side.

At trial the State's case consisted of two vital lines of scientific argument. The first was based on the physical markers present at the fire scene, testified to by two fire investigators, Wayne Etue and Joan Tuttle. They stated that present in the house were "liquid pour patterns" on the floor, suspicious "even burning" on the stairs, an abundance of "low burning" and "deep burning" into the carpet, and evidence of especially intense, extremely high temperature burning. The experts testified that all of these things were unmistakable markers of arson. Specifically, they said that the evidence showed that someone had walked into the house, poured gasoline in various places, including the living room, stairs and upstairs landing, and then ignited the accelerant. Indeed, reading what was then often called the "fingerprint of arson," the two experts claimed even to be able to read and follow the particular pour trail left by Babick as he spread the gasoline through the house.

The second line of scientific argument was based on the alerts given at the scene by an accelerant-detection canine. The dog's handler, Jeff Austin, testified that the dog alerted in various places throughout the house, and that her alerts were direct evidence that an accelerant was used in those locations. Austin went so far as to say that his dog was "100% correct every time" and her nose was 1,000 times more sensitive than laboratory equipment used to detect gasoline. The latter statement was necessary because lab testing failed to detect the presence of gasoline on any of the debris samples taken from inside the house. The prosecutor asked the jury to overlook that fact, stating, "a dog's nose on a trained dog is a mystical thing ... a thousand times more sensitive than the lab equipment."

In light of that dynamic duo of scientific implication and insinuation, Babick's defense team faced a severe uphill battle. Given that juries often attribute a "mystic infallibility" to scientific evidence presented in court, a defendant's options are inevitably limited when confronted with a situation where (not just one but) two lines of scientific argument, and multiple scientific experts, heavy handedly negate any possibility of innocence or mitigation. Babick maintained his innocence, but because the experts seemed to decisively conclude that the fire was arson, his attorney did not even bother with a "not-arson" defense, and tried instead to just point the finger at possible alternative arsonists.

The strategy failed. Babick was convicted and sentenced in December 1996 to life in prison without the possibility of parole—the most severe punishment permitted in Michigan, given that the state outlawed the death penalty nearly two centuries ago. His direct appeal was denied by the state court of appeals in 1999, and higher courts denied his applications and petitions for relief. As far as the law was concerned, Babick's story was over.

But science was already working on a sequel.

A Revolution in the Backdrop

Unbeknownst to Babick or his defense counsel was the fact that the very sort of evidence the State was using to convict him was being invalidated even as his trial proceeded. Since the late 1980s, a select group of fire investigators had begun to question the conventional wisdom that went into the diagnosis of arson in cases like Babick's....

Roots of Revolution

The story of the revolution in fire science is best told by John J. Lentini, who was among its chief catalysts and is certainly its most recognized documenter. In his book *Scientific Protocols in Fire Investigation* Lentini notes that as a profession, "[f]ire investigation developed on a parallel track" from advances in fire science, and "until the mid-1980s, very little of the newly discovered knowledge about the behavior of fire was passed on to fire investigators...."[44]

The Forging of NFPA 921: A New Way of Doing Things

Noting "the perception of a profession plagued by misconceptions," the Standards Council of the NFPA formed a Technical Committee on Fire Investigations in 1985. "After 7 years, the first edition of NFPA 921, Guide for Fire and Explosion Investigations, was released." Intended to "assist in improving the fire investigation process and the quality of information on fires resulting from the fire investigation process," NFPA 921 "is currently updated every 3 or 4 years" and "is the single most important treatise ever published in the field of fire investigation."

The exact changes to the fire investigation profession wrought by NFPA 921 were truly substantial....

[F]ire scientists began to note that many of the physical artifacts previously thought to only occur in arson fires could actually occur in innocent fires that have reached flashover. NFPA 921 noted that physical markers—such as alligatoring of wood, crazed glass, depth and location of char, lines of demarcation in the burn patterns, sagged furniture springs, spalled concrete, low burning and holes in the floor, and time and temperature of the fire—were vastly misunderstood prior to the understanding of flashover. Previously, the presence of one or more of these markers would have led to a quick conclusion that the fire was arson, but flashover deepened the narrative. Given that the same physical markers could be present in both accidental and arson fires, investigators needed more than just those physical markers to make a call of arson....

As Lentini notes, the advancements in scientific knowledge codified in the initial and successive editions of NFPA 921, were not immediately or universally accepted and implemented: "To say that the early editions of NFPA 921 were not universally embraced by the fire investigation community would be a serious understatement."

* * *

As [the affidavit of David M. Smith in *People v. Babick*] notes,

> Only since the early 2000's has the scientific method embodied in NFPA 921 come to be generally accepted by the relevant scientific community. Specifically, the execution of Cameron Todd Willingham in 2004 was the first major event that exposed the old myths of the fire investigation profession to the general public. Only after that point did non-scientists really begin to appreciate the importance of the decisive shift in methodology and paradigm that the fire investigation profession was undergoing.

---

44. John J. Lentini, Scientific Protocols in Fire Investigation 13 (2d ed. 2013).

A Parallel Revolution in Fire Science: Canine-Accelerant Alerts

"Dog said it. I believe it. That settles it."

[A]s the 1995 edition of NFPA 921 went to print, the official position of the relevant scientific community on canine accelerant alerts was what it had been for a decade or more: trained dogs have a mystical ability to detect accelerants at fire scenes, even where lab testing fails to show anything....

Indeed, in 1995, the then-latest edition of the leading fire investigation treatise Kirk's Fire Investigation advised that canine alerts, even without lab confirmation, can be "accepted as proof of the presence of accelerants." Babick's attorney at his November 1996 trial thus had no real way to contest the prosecution's claim that gasoline was present on the debris samples taken from the house. Even though lab testing failed to confirm the canine accelerant alerts, the State could, and certainly did, argue that there was gasoline present in the debris at the fire scene....

* * *

Ten years after the NFPA's and Kirk's Fire Investigation's [ultimate] recognition of the problems surrounding canine evidence, *United States v. Hebshie*[45] resulted in a significant habeas opinion repudiating canine evidence. In that case, canine handler Douglas Lynch presented alerts given by his dog, Billy, though they were not properly confirmed or contextualized for the jury. As federal judge Nancy Gertner described in granting Hebshie's petition for writ of habeas corpus,

> It is not an understatement to say that Lynch, the dog handler, was permitted to testify to an almost mystical account of Billy's powers and her unique olfactory capabilities. He presented unsubstantiated claims about the dog's accuracy. He was allowed to go on at great length about his emotional relationship with the dog and his entirely subjective ability to interpret her face, what she thought, intended, and the "strength" of the alert she gave in this case. Finally, Lynch was permitted to testify that the dog did not alert to anything else on the premises, as if the dog had been allowed to range widely on the fire scene (she was not), and as if the dog's failure to alert had evidential value (it does not).[46]

Moreover, the court found that proper investigation by trial counsel would have revealed the problems with the dog testimony and, more likely than not, trial counsel could have succeeded in having the canine evidence suppressed. And had such evidence been suppressed, a different outcome would have been likely at trial. Implicitly, then, *Hebshie* is significant because it marks an era where not only have unconfirmed canine alerts been repudiated, but also, that repudiation has sunk in enough that a reasonable defense attorney is expected to be aware of it in order to meet the Strickland standard of providing constitutionally sufficient assistance of counsel to a defendant.

---

45. 754 F. Supp. 2d 89, 91–95 (D. Mass. 2010).
46. *Id.*

In the world of fire science, the prevailing fact of life is that holdouts die out: Wrongful convictions based on previously repudiated science become less likely as the years go by. Such has been the case in the realm of canine accelerant alerts, though the percolation has taken an alarmingly long time in some places. It is for that reason that the 2012 declaration by CADA, perhaps the last of the official organizational holdouts, is so significant. Although CADA had previously butted heads with the IAAI to argue that unconfirmed canine alerts could be used as affirmative evidence of accelerants being present, CADA reversed course entirely in 2012. In no uncertain terms, it proclaimed:

> The Canine Accelerant Detection Association (CADA) does not support, nor do we recommend, Accelerant Detection Canine Handlers testifying in criminal or civil court to the presence of an ignitable liquid without having received confirmation through laboratory analysis.... [N]o Prosecutor, Attorney or ADC Handler should ever testify or encourage testimony that an ignitable liquid is present without confirmation through laboratory analysis.

CADA's declaration was, one would hope, the closing of the book on unconfirmed canine alerts.

John J. Lentini, *Confronting Inaccuracy in Fire Cause Determinations*

FORENSIC SCIENCE REFORM: PROTECTING THE INNOCENT 66, 81–82, 86, 90
(Wendy Koen et al. eds., 2017)

Fire investigation is different from many sciences, and even from many forensic sciences, by virtue of the fact that its practitioners largely lack any formal scientific education. Yet every day, we ask them to make sophisticated decisions about chemistry, heat transfer, fluid dynamics, and electricity. Fire investigators are generally drawn from the ranks of the police and fire services. Training historically has been done "on the job" with an experienced mentor passing on his belief system to new recruits. Thus, fire investigation suffers from two major challenges to its reliability: unqualified practitioners and invalid methodology.

* * *

The Questionable Validity of Fire Origin Determination

The situation today is dramatically improved from 30 years ago, but the fire investigation profession is still struggling to understand the complexities of fire behavior. Recent developments have made abundantly clear that as with many disciplines, "the more one learns, the less one knows." This point was brought home in 2005 and 2007 when agents of the US Bureau of Alcohol, Tobacco, Firearms and Explosives (ATF), which investigates many of the high-profile fires in the US today, conducted studies that reflected rather poorly on the reliability of fire investigators' determinations of where a fire started. It is axiomatic that unless one finds the correct origin (defined as the place where fuel, oxygen, and an ignition source come together), one is likely to come up with an incorrect cause determination. In the 2005 study, two test fires were set in single-room structures and allowed to burn for 2 min after flashover.

Flashover is a transition point in a structure fire's development where a "fire in a room" becomes a "room on fire." This happens when a hot gas layer develops at the ceiling. The fire serves as a "pump" to increase the volume and temperature of that hot gas layer until it begins to radiate its heat in all directions, including downward. When the temperature approaches 1200°F, every exposed combustible surface in the room ignites more or less simultaneously.

Fifty-three investigators were shown the two rooms and asked to write down the quadrant in which they believe the fire originated. Relying on their interpretation of the fire patterns and their belief that the lowest and deepest char indicated the origin, 50 of the 53 selected the wrong quadrant. In the second room, the results were the same. Only 3 of 53 correctly identified the quadrant of origin.

* * *

Of course, the problem with identifying the wrong point of origin or area of origin is that the ignition source and the first fuel ignited will not be there. Using the discredited methodology called "negative corpus," investigators will state that there were no potential sources of accidental ignition at the "origin," and therefore the fire "must have been" intentional. Investigators might then opine that the first fuel ignited "must have been" a flammable liquid, and the ignition source "must have been" an open flame that whoever poured flammable liquid took with them. There may even be a ventilation induced "irregular pattern" on the floor at the base of the fire pattern determined to have been located just above the "origin." When one considers how fires can be ventilated, keep in mind that usually the hot gases and flames exit the top of the opening, while cool fresh air is drawn in at the bottom. This will result in floor level burning, which, prior to the 1990s, was believed to indicate flammable liquids burning on the floor because as we all know, "heat rises...."

* * *

Canine Alerts to Arson

Another wrongful conviction overturned was that of Weldon Wayne Carr in Georgia. He was convicted in 1994, despite the fact that 12 samples collected by the fire investigator tested negative at two different laboratories. Prosecutor Nancy Grace, in her last trial before hiring on at CNN, used the positive alerts of a canine named Blaze to persuade the jury that ignitable liquids were involved in the fire. The Georgia Supreme Court found that using unconfirmed canine alerts was akin to the earliest lie detector tests.

> The first recorded lie detector test was in ancient India where a suspect was required to enter a darkened room and touch the tail of a donkey. If the donkey brayed when his tail was touched the suspect was declared guilty, otherwise he was released. Modern science has substituted a metal electronic box for the donkey but the results remain just as haphazard and inconclusive.[47]

---

47. Carr v. State, 482 S.E.2d 314, 317–18 (Ga. 1997).

The use of unconfirmed canine alerts is an insult to the collective intelligence of courts and juries, but overzealous prosecutors will present this pseudoscience anyways. Analogies to drug dogs and explosive dogs are inapt. If a drug dog or an explosive dog alerts to a suitcase, and no drugs or explosives are found, nobody is even arrested. But in the case of accelerant-detecting canines, the handlers (who are not scientists) believe their dogs are more sensitive than the laboratory and insist that the alerts, which are presumptive tests at best, mean that the fire was intentionally set. The sensitivity argument is bogus. A competent laboratory analyst can detect quantities of ignitable liquid as small as 1/500th of a drop (0.1 µL).

Rachel Dioso-Villa, *Scientific and Legal Developments in Fire and Arson Investigation Expertise in* Texas v. Willingham

14 MINN. J.L. SCI. & TECH. 817, 817–48 (2013)

Fire and Arson Expert Testimony

Texas v. Willingham — *Case Study*

In 1992, Cameron Todd Willingham was convicted for setting fire to his home and killing his three children. Twelve years later, the State of Texas executed him by lethal injection. The state's key evidence came from two fire investigators who testified that the fire was intentionally set. The indicators of arson included a sample taken from the front porch floorboard that tested positive for petroleum-based chemicals; burn patterns on the floor in the home where a liquid accelerant was believed to have been poured and ignited; broken glass patterns; and melted aluminum believed to be caused by abnormally high temperatures associated with fires fueled by accelerants. The fire experts' investigative techniques and their reliance on the interpretation of arson indicators and burn patterns were not based on scientific testing, but on heuristics consistent with practices employed in the 1980s and, in some cases, still relied upon today.

* * *

In [fire investigator] Vasquez's explanation to the jury of his assertion of arson, there is little science involved:

> Heat rises. In the winter time when you are going to the bathroom and if you don't have any carpet on the rug and you are barefooted, and you step on that cold floor, that floor is colder than the ceiling. It always is. Like right now, this floor is colder than this ceiling here.
>
> So when I found that the floor is hotter than the ceiling, that's backwards, upside down. It shouldn't be like that. The only reason that the floor is hotter is because there was an accelerant. That's the difference. Man made it hotter or woman or whatever. Human being[s] made it hotter.

Vasquez explained fire investigation and fire dynamics as logical and common sense, such that jurors themselves could evaluate with their senses and experiences to arrive at the same conclusions....

* * *

[Fire investigators] Fogg and Vasquez chemically analyzed over a dozen samples taken from "suspicious" areas of the house that showed severe burning and where the fire investigators hypothesized were the origins of the fires using gas chromatography with mass spectrometry (GC-MS). All samples, with the exception of the front porch taken from the barbecue area, tested negative for any traces of an accelerant.

Vasquez explained the chemical results:

A[:] And so there won't be any — anything left; it will burn up. The only thing left is a burn pattern. Because the fire, itself, leaves the evidence of what was there. Although the evidence — the liquid is burned, the evidence, by the fire left there, is that there was a liquid there.

Q[:] Similar to a fingerprint?

A[:] Yes, sir.

. . .

A[:] . . . [T]he fire leaves the burn patterns. You can't — you can't alter the burn patterns. You cannot pollute the fire scene. You can try, but you can't.

Here, he argued that the lack of GC-MS evidence of an accelerant should not be interpreted as evidence of its absence. . . .

Extra-Legal Factors

Vasquez reviewed Fogg's investigation report prior to commencing his examination and based his conclusion in part on external factors independent from his inspection of the physical evidence:

Q[:] Based on your experience, your training, your investigation, examination of the scene, do you have an opinion as to whether this particular fire was arson or [incendiary] in nature?

. . .

A[:] It's a set fire. It's an incen[dia]ry fire, and consequently is a crime of arson.

Q[:] What led you to believe this fire was incen[dia]ry?

A[:] Besides what I've already said [about an investigation of the fire debris], I've talked to the occupant of the house, and I let him talk and he told me a story of pure fabrication.

[The Defense raised an objection on the basis that the conclusions are hearsay. The Court overrules the Defense's objection.]

. . .

Q[:] Deputy Vasquez, on your investigation and examination of this, did you interview witnesses, including the occupants of this house?

A[:] Yes, sir.

Q[:] Why?

A[:] If I am going to have a complete investigation, I have to have all the information I can possibly get.

...

Q[:] ... You investigated the scene, examined the fire scene. Based on your experience and training and interviews that you conducted of, say, witnesses and the occupants of the house, do you have an opinion as to whether it's incen[dia]ry or arson?

A[:] Yes, sir.

Q[:] And how did you arrive at that decision?

A[:] From what I have already reiterated and explained on the diagram and on the photographs and the interview with the defendant.

...

[Defense raises objections on the basis of hearsay. Court overrules objection.]

A[:] I listened to him. I never questioned him. I never asked him any questions. He just talked and he talked, and all he did was lie.

Despite the defense's objections, the court permitted Vasquez to name Willingham as the person who set the fire:

Q[:] Based upon all your investigation and interviews and experience as a fire or arson investigator, do you have an opinion as to the person or persons who started this particular fire?

...

A[:] Yes, sir.

Q[:] What is that opinion?

A[:] The occupant, Mr. Willingham.

Vasquez was admitted as an expert witness to testify as to the cause and origin of the fire, yet the court gave him latitude to opine that the defendant intended to commit arson, that the fire was incendiary, and that the defendant was guilty....

* * *

Incorporating investigative facts into scientific analysis, contextual bias, overreaching claims, and testifying to the ultimate issue of a case are serious problems that the legal system and forensic science community must contend with regarding the use of fire investigation expertise. Despite empirical evidence that discredits existing investigation methodologies and techniques, members of the fire community remain resistant to acknowledge or correct such errors, or adopt national standards and protocols.

Sandra Guerra Thompson and Nicole Bremner Cásarez, *Building the Infrastructure for "Justice Through Science": The Texas Model*
119 W. Va. L. Rev. 711, 711–748 (2016)

This Article surveys the important reforms adopted by the Texas legislature to advance the quality of forensic science that form what we call the "infrastructure" of forensic science in the state. In all, the legislature put into place six key components that now form the Texas forensic science infrastructure: (1) the Texas Forensic Science Commission; (2) the Texas Criminal Justice Integrity Unit (a stakeholder committee that hosts discussion meetings and training programs); (3) the Michael Morton Act, which instituted expansive prosecutorial disclosure from pre-plea to post-conviction; (4) the "junk science" writ, a habeas petition that allows challenges to the forensic science used to obtain a conviction if new evidence undermines the validity of the evidence; (5) the Office of Capital and Forensic Writs, a statewide public defender for habeas petitions; and (6) state laws requiring the preservation and testing of biological evidence.

* * *

The story about how Texas came to lead the nation in criminal justice reforms has many leading figures. However, to understand why Texas — of all states — has adopted more reforms to prevent wrongful convictions than any other, one has to mention the avalanche of negative headlines from 2002 to 2009 surrounding two separate problems: (1) the Houston Police Department Crime Laboratory and (2) the controversial execution of Cameron Todd Willingham, including Texas Governor Rick Perry's decision not to grant his request for a stay of execution. While the two situations were unrelated, they both laid bare the shoddy forensic science that supported many criminal convictions, and they both generated bad press at roughly the same time.

The problems in the Houston Police Department ("HPD") Crime Laboratory came first, beginning in 2002, when news reports exposed its deplorable conditions. Two years later, in 2004, a man named George Rodriguez walked out of prison after serving 17 years behind bars for a rape he did not commit. Rodriguez became the first of several high-profile exonerations in which HPD Crime Laboratory analysts were found to have given invalid scientific testimony. The widespread and serious nature of the problems in the laboratory led one auditor to conclude that the Houston laboratory was "the paradigmatic example of a failed forensic agency." From the initial reports in 2002 until at least 2008, the Houston laboratory continued to generate scathing news stories.

At about the same time that the HPD Crime Laboratory scandal unfolded in the early 2000s, Cameron Todd Willingham's death penalty case was reaching the end. Willingham, a white man from Corsicana, Texas, had been convicted of capital murder by arson of his three young daughters who died in a house fire on a cold December morning, two days before Christmas, in 1991. His conviction rested on the testimony of two arson investigators as well as that of a jailhouse informant.

After all of Willingham's appeals had been exhausted, his court-appointed attorney asked Gerald Hurst, a leading fire investigator and fire scientist, to search for new evidence to include in a clemency petition. In reviewing the evidence from Willingham's trial, Hurst determined that the arson investigators' testimony was based on invalid fire science and that the fire was most likely accidental. Willingham filed a petition seeking clemency based on this new scientific evidence, which was unanimously denied by the Texas Board of Pardons and Parole. Willingham's lawyer then sought a stay of execution from Governor Perry, providing the same scientific proof that Willingham's conviction had been secured through invalid forensic testimony. On Willingham's scheduled execution date, February 17, 2004, the governor denied the stay of execution "based on the facts of the case." Willingham was executed. He had begged his parents to never stop trying to vindicate him.

News stories after Willingham's death caused many to believe that Texas had executed an innocent man, and Governor Perry's decision to deny his petition for a stay of execution gained notoriety. Whether Willingham was innocent or not, it is clear that the ostensible "scientific" evidence in his case was patently incorrect and not based on valid scientific principles. (Years after his execution, the jailhouse informant would recant, and other evidence came to light that the prosecutor in Willingham's case had withheld exculpatory evidence, further intensifying doubts about his guilt.)

* * *

Having erected an elaborate infrastructure to support the practice of forensic science, the state has been in a unique position to respond to large-scale problems that develop whenever a problem with a forensic discipline is discovered. In addition to its role implementing regulations prospectively to improve the quality of forensic investigations, the TFSC has also examined entire forensic disciplines to determine whether they measure up to today's scientific standards. When particular areas of forensic science are found to be scientifically invalid, the Commission has partnered with other agencies and groups, including the state fire marshal and the Innocence Project of Texas ("IPOT"), to conduct retroactive reviews of Texas convictions that were based, at least in part, on faulty evidence or testimony. To organize these large-scale reviews of old convictions, the TFSC has mobilized criminal justice stakeholders representing all facets of the forensic science infrastructure to work cooperatively. In the most recent instance, the Texas Criminal Justice Integrity Unit called a meeting of prosecutors (mostly from CIUs), public defenders, innocence project representatives, academics, and others to meet with the General Counsel of TFSC so that the entire group could learn about a forensic science problem and to devise strategies for conducting the large-scale systemic review.

As a result, the TFSC has been described as one of the most important forensic science reform groups in the nation—a remarkable accomplishment given that the Commission's mission was almost derailed by politics in relation to the Willingham case described above.

After the controversy over the Willingham case, the TFSC decided to ensure that other cases involving questionable arson testimony were reviewed. The TFSC reached out to the state fire marshal's office, and asked it to reexamine arson convictions where unscientific methods may have been used. Not only did the state fire marshal agree, but he also accepted an offer from the IPOT to assist in the case review. After initially contacting 1,085 Texas defendants who had been convicted of arson, IPOT lawyers identified 33 arson convictions that warranted further investigation. By 2014, nine of those cases had been reviewed by an advisory panel of legal and forensic experts assembled by the state fire marshal and IPOT, and five of those nine convictions were found to rely on scientifically unsound arson techniques. In June, 2016, a district court ruled that the defendant in one of those cases had presented overwhelming evidence of actual innocence, and in November 2016, the Court of Criminal Appeals affirmed this finding and granted relief.

B. Current Law: Overview

Fire science and Shaken Baby Syndrome ("SBS") are issues of changing science and determining intent. Changes in science in these areas can undermine the required component of intent and whether there was even a crime.

Court Decisions and Shaken Baby Syndrome

Audrey Edmunds became the first SBS exoneree when the Wisconsin Court of Appeals reversed her conviction in 2008. *State v. Edmunds,* 746 N.W.2d 590 (Wis. App. 2008). This nationally relevant decision recognized the change in science around SBS as newly discovered evidence for post-conviction relief:

> [T]here has been a shift in mainstream medical opinion since the time of Edmunds's trial as to the cause of the types of injuries Natalie suffered.... However, it is the emergence of a legitimate and significant dispute within the medical community as to the cause of those injuries that constitutes newly discovered evidence.

Id. at para. 23, 598–99.

In *Cavazos v. Smith*, the United States Supreme Court decided an SBS case on a procedural matter. The dissent, however, stated that "[r]ecent scientific opinion undermines [the trial] testimony," such that "[i]n light of current information, it is unlikely that the prosecution's experts would testify today as adamantly as they did in 1997." *Cavazos v. Smith*, 132 S.Ct. 2, 14 (2011) (Ginsburg, J., dissenting).

Finally, Judge Richard Posner confronted false confessions and circular reasoning in SBS cases, observing that a caretaker confronted with supposed medical proof of shaking as the cause of death would have no basis for denying it.

> They told him the only possible cause of Joshua's injuries was that he'd been shaken right before he collapsed; not being an expert in shaken-baby syndrome, Aleman could not deny the officers' false representation of medical opinion. And since he was the only person to have shaken Joshua immediately before Joshua's collapse, it was a logical necessity that he had been responsible for the child's death.

Aleman v. Village of Hanover Park, 662 F.3d 897, 907 (7th Cir. 2011).

Court Decisions and Arson

Fire science has encountered a scientific about-face, where fire investigation findings avowed as true for decades were ultimately no better than myth. The U.S. Court of

Appeals for the Third Circuit found in *Han Tak Lee v. Glunt* that when an analysis of the evidence cannot conclusively determine the cause of the fire, there exists "a prima facie case for granting [petitioner] habeas corpus relief on his due process claim." *Han Tak Lee v. Glunt*, 667 F.3d 397, 407 (3d Cir. 2012). The U.S. District Court in reversing Mr. Han Tak Lee's conviction concluded, "[t]oday, with the benefit of extraordinary progress in human science regarding fire science over the past two decades it is now uncontested that this fire science evidence—which was a critical component in the quantum of proof that led to Han Tak Lee's conviction—is invalid, *and that much of what was presented to the jury as science is now conceded to be little more than superstition.*" *Han Tak Lee v. Tennis*, No. 4:08-CV-1972, 2014 WL 3894306 (M.D. Pa. June 13, 2014). In similar litigation, courts recognized new developments in fire science as newly discovered evidence, sufficient to undermine the original conviction and entitle the defendant to a new trial.

As noted above, the most important reform to fire science has been the National Fire Protection Agency Guide for Fire and Explosion Investigations NFPA 921, an effort to introduce the scientific method to fire experts. NFPA 921 "establish[ed] guidelines and recommendations for the safe and systematic investigation or analysis of fire and explosion incidents ... intended for use by *both* public-sector employees who are responsible for fire investigation and private sector professionals who conduct investigations for insurance companies or litigation purposes." NFPA 921 § 1.2.1. The new guidelines when created in 1993 undermined hundreds of incorrect conclusions of arson, implicating fire investigators in causing wrongful convictions.

Increasingly, state and federal courts recognize NFPA 921 as the standard of care for fire investigations. *See, for example, Bryte v. Am. Household Co.*, 429 F.3d 469 (4th Cir. 2005); *Fireman's Fund Ins. Co. v. Canon U.S.A., Inc.*, 394 F.3d 1054 (8th Cir. 2005). Notably, these have largely been civil, rather than criminal, cases. For more on this development and comparing fire science in civil and criminal cases, see Valena Beety & Jennifer Oliva, *Evidence on Fire*, 97 N.C. L. Rev. (2019). Equally important, NFPA 921 has been accepted within the fire science community by the International Association of Arson Investigators.

Another important case of note, *United States v. Hebshie*, 754 F.Supp.2d 89, 92 (D. Mass. 2010), condemned the trial court's admission of unconfirmed accelerant-detection canine alerts. Canine alerts for detecting accelerant have now been criticized by every major fire science organization, including the Canine Accelerant Detection Association (CADA), the largest organization of professional accelerant-detection canine handlers.

Changed Science Statutes

A few states have passed changed science statutes to provide an avenue for post-conviction habeas litigation of changed sciences such as Shaken Baby Syndrome, fire science, and other forensic fields. Colloquially known as "junk science writs," Texas enacted its changed-science statute, Article 11.073 of the Code of Criminal Procedure, in 2013 and amended it in 2015; California enacted California Penal Code Chapter 623 § 1493 in 2014.

Under the Texas statute, the key question is "whether the field of scientific knowledge, a testifying expert's scientific knowledge, or a scientific method on which the relevant scientific evidence is based has changed." The California statute states that "'false evidence' shall include opinions of experts that have either been repudiated by the expert who originally provided the opinion at a hearing or trial or that have been undermined by later scientific research or technological advances."

C. Legal Materials, Exercises, and Media

DNA

1. *Recommended Viewing, DNA:* Two Minute Science Lesson: How Forensic DNA Testing Works with Huy Dao. https://youtu.be/qZeYu76bOsQ.

2. *Forensic Crime Lab Reform*: Professor Sandra Guerra Thompson, author of *The Texas Model* excerpt, discusses the Houston Crime Lab scandal and reform on the Excited Utterance podcast with Ed Cheng, Episode 8, *Cops in Lab Coats,* interviewing Sandra Guerra Thompson. For an overview on crime lab scandals, listen to 3:00–9:00, or a discussion on the importance of independent crime labs from 18–20:45. https://www.excitedutterancepodcast.com/listen/2016/10/10/08-sandra-guerra-thompson.

   For further reading on forensic crime lab reform, Mark Hansen's thorough 2013 ABA Journal piece, "Crime Labs Under the Microscope," is available here: http://www.abajournal.com/magazine/article/crime_labs_under_the_microscope_after_a_string_of_shoddy_suspect_and_fraudu/.

3. *Lab Misconduct and Prosecutorial Lack of Disclosure, Massachusetts:* "Twice in recent years, chemists used by the state of Massachusetts to test drugs in criminal cases committed massive misconduct in their testing, affecting tens of thousands of cases. And twice, prosecutors in Massachusetts failed to act promptly to notify most defendants of the problem. Instead, the prosecutors have taken years to seek justice for the defendants affected by the bad drug testing in both episodes, causing some people to wrongly spend years in prison. In the first case, after five years, the Massachusetts supreme court eventually forced state prosecutors to compile a list of affected defendants and ultimately dismiss 98.5 percent of the cases involved, with more than 21,000 drug convictions erased. In the second case, discovered in 2013 but still unfolding, a judge concluded recently that two prosecutors committed 'intentional, repeated, prolonged and deceptive withholding of evidence from the defendants' and that 'their misconduct evinces a depth of deceptiveness that constitutes a fraud upon the court.'" Tom Jackman, *Prosecutors Slammed for 'Lack of Moral Compass,' Withholding Evidence in Widening Mass. Drug Lab Scandal,* Washington Post, October 4, 2017: https://www.washingtonpost.com/amphtml/news/true-crime/wp/2017/10/04/prosecutors-slammed-for-lack-of-moral-compass-withholding-evidence-in-widening-mass-drug-lab-scandal/; *see also 21,587 Reasons to Fix Forensic Sci-*

ence, NY Times, April 27, 2017: https://mobile.nytimes.com/2017/04/27/opinion/21587-reasons-to-fix-forensic-science.html?referer=.

Shaken Baby Syndrome

1. *Shaken Baby Syndrome In-Depth Media*: As part of the New York Times Retro Report, the newspaper reviewed the SBS conviction of the "Boston Nanny" Louise Woodward in 1997, and compared the case to current SBS charges through interviewing New York School of Law Innocence Project Director Adele Bernhard and Norman Guthkelch, the pediatric neurosurgeon who first identified Shaken Baby Syndrome as a theory and who later in life questioned the liberal use of the diagnosis. Clyde Haberman, *Shaken Baby Syndrome: A Diagnosis That Divides the Medical World*, NY TIMES (Sept. 13, 2015), https://www.nytimes.com/2015/09/14/us/shaken-baby-syndrome-a-diagnosis-that-divides-the-medical-world.html.

2. *Recommended Viewing*: The Syndrome: The film *The Syndrome* discusses the ongoing controversy over Shaken Baby Syndrome and Abusive Head Trauma, interviewing doctors as well as individuals who have been wrongfully convicted. http://www.resetfilms.com.

3. *Recommended Viewing, False Confessions and SBS*: Melissa Calusinski in Illinois discusses her false confession to shaking a toddler, after 79 denials, on CBS Chicago: https://www.youtube.com/watch?v=OTHzxCn3_Qw (0:00–2:14).

4. *Recommended Listening, SBS exoneree*: Paul Bieber, co-author of the *Folklore and Forensics* excerpt, is also the director of the Arson Project and interviews exonerees nationally. Listen to his interview of one Shaken Baby Syndrome exoneree in West Virginia, Jeremiah Mongold at www.ourcommonbonds.net (3:00).

5. *Exercise, Short Answer:* What does Deborah Tuerkheimer mean by a "medical diagnosis of murder"?

6. *Exercise, Read and Identify:* Read the transcript below of the real interrogation of Christopher Brandon:

JJ: I hold before you the autopsy report right here that I've shown you before.

CB: Yes, sir.

JJ: Okay. And what did I tell you this baby, according to the medical examiner, has died from?

CB: Shaken Baby Syndrome.

JJ: Okay. And you do understand that a Shaken Baby Syndrome is vigorously shaking a baby.

CB: Yes, sir.

JJ: To the point that it causes death.

CB: Yes, sir. But, I never shook him.

JJ: And the only way that this baby can be shaken to that degree is someone has to do that.

CB: Yes, sir.

JJ: And you are agreeing with me today that the care for that child, that particular day, during this period of time, was who?

CB: On me.

JJ: No one else was in the room?

CB: No, sir.

JJ: Is that the only injury that you know of that this baby sustained while it was in your care is when the baby somehow or another fell or jumped off the bed ...

CB: Yes, sir.

JJ: ... and possibly bumped its head on that toy?

CB: Yes, sir. And just ... like I said, as far as the shaking part, I never shook him that hard. I had him right up on my body doing him like this right here....

JJ: But, you did shake him to some degree.

CB: Yes, sir. I didn't shake him like ... that or whatever. You know. He's right here on my body on my chest ... I shook him like this.

JJ: Have you ever shook a baby to the point that it died?

CB: No, sir. I ... I ... no, sir.

JJ: How do you know how hard it takes to shake one?

CB: I really don't. It had to be really hard to ... for a baby to die ... to shake a baby like that.

JJ: But, that's your opinion?

CB: Just ... yeah, that's what I'm thinking.

...

JJ: But, you again agree with me ... that the only time ... and be truthful ...

CB: Yes, sir.

JJ: ... the only time that this could have happened ...

CB: Yes, sir.

JJ: To the child ... there was only

CB: When I was trying to revive him ...

JJ: ... there was only one person in that room taking care of that baby. And that was who?

CB: It's me.

JJ: Okay, so you will take full responsibility ...

CB: Yes, sir.

JJ: ... for whatever happened while you had this baby?

CB: Yes, sir.

What interrogation techniques led Christopher Brandon to confess to shaking his stepchild?

At trial, the shaking was characterized by the forensic pathologist as, "a child is shaken, without impacting the child's head on a hard surface. And the force is equivalent to … a motor vehicle crash."

Brandon's confession to shaking was used in the prosecutor's closing argument to challenge Brandon's description of what happened: "Fell of the bed, fell off the bed … That doesn't make sense, Ladies and Gentlemen, because lies don't add up … I'm not going to insult you, you know that's a lie."

The Mississippi Supreme Court granted Christopher Brandon a post-conviction hearing on his habeas petition in 2014; to date the Lee County Circuit Court has not yet held the hearing. You can learn more about Brandon's case in news articles by journalist Radley Balko: "New case again demonstrates duplicity of embattled Mississippi medical examiner," WASHINGTON POST, May 15, 2014, available at https://www.washingtonpost.com/news/the-watch/wp/2014/05/15/new-case-again-demonstrates-duplicity-of-embattled-mississippi-medical-examiner/?utm_term=.55e8cc56a922 and "Mississippi prosecutors say ex-medical examiner can travel through time," WASHINGTON POST, July 28, 2014, available at https://www.washingtonpost.com/news/the-watch/wp/2014/07/28/mississippi-prosecutors-say-ex-medical-examiner-can-travel-through-time/?utm_term=.4232412b8083.

Fire Science

1. *Exercise, Read and Review*: David Grann won the George Polk Award in Journalism for his piece covering Cameron Todd Willingham's trial, execution, and redemption. "Trial By Fire," published by the *New Yorker* in 2009, is available here: http://www.newyorker.com/magazine/2009/09/07/trial-by-fire.

    Based on your reading of "Trial by Fire," identify as either TRUE or FALSE each of the following statements:

    a) Because police and prosecutors could not determine a motive for Willingham to murder his three daughters, they presented him as a sociopath, and the children were interfering with his drinking beer and throwing darts.

    b) At the time of Cameron Todd Willingham's trial, it cost on average 2.3 million dollars to execute a prisoner in Texas.

    c) Cameron Todd Willingham accepted a plea offer.

    d) Justice Scalia in an opinion upholding the death penalty in a Kansas case opined that not one person had been executed who was innocent.

    e) The listed cause of death on a death certificate for an execution is "homicide."

2. *Recommended Viewing*: Indiana exoneree Kristine Bunch opens up about her wrongful conviction of killing her son by arson with Crime Watch Daily (8 minutes): https://www.youtube.com/watch?v=RXB60YzprSM&t=61s.

For a more extensive interview with Kristine Bunch, listen to the podcast *Wrongful Conviction* with Jason Flom, Season 2, Episode 13, "Justice Had Just Begun: Stories from the 2017 Innocence Network Conference, Part Two": https://art19. com/shows/wrongful-conviction-with-jason-flom?month=5&perPage=100& year=2017 (1:15–23:30 to learn about her case; 9:45–12:35 when she discusses being separated from her child while in prison).

3. *Recommended Viewing, Arson and False Confessions:* The Netflix series *The Confession Tapes* documents how innocent people can falsely confess, particularly when confronted with "scientific" evidence. Watch Season 1, episode 4, "Trial by Fire," where Karen Boes, convicted of murder by arson in Michigan, confessed after being confronted with a failed polygraph test result and guided by police through a "dream" confession.

4. Daubert *Exercise:* You are representing the defendant in a criminal arson case. Read the fire investigation report below, and in 1–2 pages draft your arguments for a *Daubert* hearing on whether the fire science evidence and testimony should be admitted at trial.

Figure 8.3

TEXAS COMMISSION ON FIRE PROTECTION
State Fire Marshal's Office

Report [XX]
Synopsis [ ]   Supplement [ ]
Investigation [XX]   Continuation [ ]
Photo Index [ ]

Case #: _923-037-12_   City / County: _Corsicana/Navarro_   P.R. _1_
Investigator: _Manuel R. Vasquez_   Date of Report: _1-24-92_

ORIGIN-CAUSE

The origin and cause examination was conducted on December 30, 1991, and January 2, 1992. Other persons present during the examination were: Doug Fogg, Corsicana Assistant Fire Chief; James Palos, Corsicana Fire Marshal; Jimmie Hensley and Rex Givens, Corsicana Police Detectives; Edward Cheever and Donald Turk, State Fire Marshal Deputy Investigators.

The perimeter examination disclosed that the burned structure was located in a residential neighborhood of Corsicana, Texas. The structure was surrounded by a chain link fence on the east, south and west side. The structure had a tree on the north front yard, two trees on the east side, and regular back yard on the south. The structure has the front facing north. The examination of the perimeter did not disclose anything of significance.

The exterior examination of the burned structure disclosed the following burn patterns on the walls.

The north wall to the northeast bedroom was charred and scorched by the fire from the bottom to the top. The door on the west side of the north wall of the northeast bedroom was totally consumed by the fire. The east side of the north wall to the northeast bedroom had the paint blistered below the windows. The east wall of the northwest living room was also charred and scorched by the fire from the bottom to the top. The north wall of the northwest living room was not charred or scorched, except near the east side of the wall next to the porch. The examination also disclosed that the fire had not vented up through the roof.

The examination of the east wall of the northeast bedroom disclosed that flames and smoke vented out the east windows. The flames and smoke vented out the south window of the northeast bedroom. The flames that vented out the south window of the northeast bedroom reached under the roof outside the window and burned off the corner of the roof. Also, the flames traveled south along and below the eaves of the rest of the east wall.

The examination of the south wall of the structure disclosed that smoke vented out from under the eaves. Also, heavy smoke vented out the top of the south door to the kitchen. The examination of the west

Received By: _oR_   Date: _1-21-92_

INV04

Figure 8.3, continued

TEXAS COMMISSION ON FIRE PROTECTION
State Fire Marshal's Office

	Report	☐
Synopsis ☐	Supplement	☐
Investigation ☒	Continuation	☒
	Photo Index	☐

Case #:   923-037-12   City / County: Corsicana/Navarro   P.R.   1

Investigator: Manuel R. Vasquez   Date of Report: 1-24-92

---

outside wall disclosed that smoke vented out from under the eaves. The west windows were smoke stained.

The entrance to conduct the interior examination was through the south door of the southeast kitchen. A large refrigerator had blocked the south door from inside the kitchen before and during the fire. The kitchen door on the north and the entrance into the hallway had burn patterns on top of the north side that faced the hallway. There was only smoke damage to the kitchen.

The southwest bedroom that was being used as a utility room was entered from the kitchen. In this room smoke debris had settled down on top of everything.

The master bedroom located at the center of the west side disclosed that a tremendous amount of heat entered the room at the southeast door from the hallway. The west window to the bedroom had brown and streaky smoke stains. A plastic item on the south side of the bed had melted half-way down from on top. The top of the southeast door from the hallway had flame and heat damage. The mattress on the bed in the center of the room had slight stains of heat and smoke.

The northwest living room was also covered with smoke soot. The southeast entrance to the living room from the hallway disclosed burn patterns from the outside or from the hallway.

The bathroom in the center of the east side disclosed that flames and smoke entered the bathroom through the west door from the hallway. The west door was burned on top and the smoke line reached halfway down the walls. All the glass in the bath room was smoke stained.

The view of the hallway toward the south disclosed that the east and west walls on the north end had burn patterns from the base of the floor to the ceiling. The fire did not burn through the ceiling. The burn pattern on the east and west wall of the hallway disclosed a gradual climb in a 45 degree angle toward the south end and clearly showed a "V" pattern. This "V" pattern is an indicator that the fire originated on the floor near the north end. An examination of the

Received By: LR   Date: 1-21-92

INV04

Figure 8.3, continued

TEXAS COMMISSION ON FIRE PROTECTION
State Fire Marshal's Office

		Report	[X]
Synopsis	[ ]	Supplement	[ ]
Investigation	[X]	Continuation	[ ]
		Photo Index	[ ]

Case #: 923-037-12 City / County: Corsicana/Navarro P.R. 1
Investigator: _Manuel R. Vasquez_ Date of Report: _1-24-92_

ORIGIN-CAUSE

The origin and cause examination was conducted on December 30, 1991,
and January 2, 1992. Other persons present during the examination
were: Doug Fogg, Corsicana Assistant Fire Chief; James Palos, Corsicana
Fire Marshal; Jimmie Hensley and Rex Givens, Corsicana Police Detectives;
Edward Cheever and Donald Turk, State Fire Marshal Deputy Investigators.

The perimeter examination disclosed that the burned structure was located
in a residential neighborhood of Corsicana, Texas. The structure was
surrounded by a chain link fence on the east, south and west side.
The structure had a tree on the north front yard, two trees on the
east side, and regular back yard on the south. The structure has the
front facing north. The examination of the perimeter did not disclose
anything of significance.

The exterior examination of the burned structure disclosed the following
burn patterns on the walls.

The north wall to the northeast bedroom was charred and scorched by
the fire from the bottom to the top. The door on the west side of
the north wall of the northeast bedroom was totally consumed by the
fire. The east side of the north wall to the northeast bedroom had
the paint blistered below the windows. The east wall of the northwest
living room was also charred and scorched by the fire from the bottom
to the top. The north wall of the northwest living room was not charred
or scorched, except near the east side of the wall next to the porch.
The examination also disclosed that the fire had not vented up through
the roof.

The examination of the east wall of the northeast bedroom disclosed
that flames and smoke vented out the east windows. The flames and
smoke vented out the south window of the northeast bedroom. The flames
that vented out the south window of the northeast bedroom reached under
the roof outside the window and burned off the corner of the roof.
Also, the flames traveled south along and below the eaves of the rest
of the east wall.

The examination of the south wall of the structure disclosed that smoke
vented out from under the eaves. Also, heavy smoke vented out the
top of the south door to the kitchen. The examination of the west

Received By: _OR_   Date: _1-21-92_

INV04

Figure 8.3, continued

TEXAS COMMISSION ON FIRE PROTECTION
State Fire Marshal's Office

		Report	☐
Synopsis	☐	Supplement	☐
Investigation	XX	Continuation	XX
		Photo Index	☐

Case #: ___923-037-12___   City / County: ___Corsicana/Navarro___   P.R. 1

Investigator: ___Manuel R. Vasquez___   Date of Report: _1-24-92_

The examination of the open space heater in the southeast corner and the area disclosed that the space heater was a victim of the fire.

Two spots were painted on the floor of the northeast bedroom where the burned bodies of the one-year old twin girls were found. One body was under the baby crib just about 12-18 inches to the left of the west door to the bedroom. The other body was 2 feet east of the body under the crib.

The burn trailers, pour patterns, and puddle configurations were followed from the west door into the northeast bedroom. The patterns went straight east to the center of the bedroom and they also branched to the right (south) in front and under the bed on the south side of the west wall. An examination of the north end under the bed disclosed that the bed was burned from underneath. The metal bed frame sustained discolorations from the intense heat to half of the bed rail. The floor under the bed had burn trailers, pour patterns, and puddle configurations. The center of the northeast bedroom was examined. The entire floor disclosed burn trailers, pour patterns, and configurations. In the center of the bedroom several puddle configurations disclosed that the fire had burned through 3 layers of floor material and then charred the wooden floor. In the center of the floor a liquid accelerant flowed under the tile squares and burned. The burn trailers, pour patterns, puddle configurations, burning under the tiles, and the charred wooden floor is evidence that the floor of the Northeast bedroom was poured with a combustible liquid accelerant and was ignited.

Upon completion of the interior examination, a closer examination of the front north wall and the porch was conducted. The windows to the northeast bedroom disclosed that the fire behavior was not consistent. Neither were the burn patterns consistent on the north wall, the front door, and the outside east wall to the northwest living room. This inconsistency is apparent, because the normal behavior of fire is up and out. That is not true of the north window to the northeast bedroom and the north door to the central hallway. The closer examination disclosed a low char burn pattern at the base of the north wall, the north door, and the east wall to the northwest living room. This wall was burned from the outside. Also, the north wall to the northeast bedroom disclosed a "V" burn pattern. The pieces of broken window glass on the ledge of the north windows to the northeast bedroom

Received By: _X R_   Date: _1-21-92_

INV04

Figure 8.3, continued

TEXAS COMMISSION ON FIRE PROTECTION
State Fire Marshal's Office

	Report	☐
Synopsis ☐	Supplement	☐
Investigation [XX]	Continuation	[X]
	Photo Index	☐

Case #: 923-037-12   City / County: Corsicana/Navarro   P.R. 1

Investigator: Manuel R. Vasquez   Date of Report: 1-24-92

disclosed a crazed (spiderwebbing) condition. This condition is an indication that the fire burned fast and hot. The examination of the porch concrete floor disclosed an area of brown discoloration at the base of the north wall and in front of the door to the central hallway. This discoloration, or brown condition, is also an indication that a liquid accelerant burned on the concrete. The bottom of the screen door was examined and it disclosed that the base was burned from underneath. This is also an indication that a liquid accelerant flowed underneath the door and burned. The examination of the concrete floor disclosed a burned can of charcoal lighter fluid near the east end of the porch next to the north wall. A sample of wood debris from the base of the front door was analyzed and the results were positive for a combustible liquid accelerant-Kerosene.

Based on the fire scene examination and statements from eyewitnesses, it was determined that the fire had multiple origins. The origins of the fire were the northeast bedroom, the north end area of the center hallway, and on the concrete porch outside the entrance at the bottom of the door to the hallway. The fire scene examination eliminated the electrical and natural gas accidental causes. The fire scene examination determined that the cause of the fire was incendiary. The fire scene examination established the direction of fire travel.

Further, based on the more than 20 indicators of incendiarism and the behavior of fire, the account given by the occupant on how he escaped the fire is not consistent with the facts. The account is determined to be pure fabrication. A fire does not lie.

SUMMARY OF INVESTIGATION

On December 27, 1991, this investigator was assigned to investigate a fire with three (3) fire deaths at ████ █ ████ ██████, Navarro County, Texas.

On December 27, 1991, this investigator traveled to the Corsicana Fire Department and met with Assistant Fire Chief Doug Fogg, Fire Marshal James Palos, and two Police Department Detectives-Jimmie Hensley and Rex Givens. This investigator was briefed on the fire incident that resulted in the fire death of 3 children.

Received By: XR   Date: 1-21-92

INV04

Figure 8.3, continued

TEXAS COMMISSION ON FIRE PROTECTION
State Fire Marshal's Office

Report	☐
Synopsis ☐	Supplement ☐
Investigation ☒	Continuation ☒
	Photo Index ☐

Case #: 923-037-12   City / County: Corsicana/Navarro   P.R. 1

Investigator: Manuel R. Vasquez   Date of Report: 1-24-92

On December 27, 1991, this investigator, accompanied by Assistant Fire Chief Doug Fogg, made a visual survey of the burned structure.

On December 30, 1991, this investigator traveled to the Corsicana Fire Department and met Assistant Fire Chief Doug Fogg, Fire Marshal James Palos, Police Detectives Jimmie Hensley and Rex Givens. The meeting was to coordinate the fire scene examination.

On December 30, 1991, this investigator traveled with Fire Marshal James Palos to a residence on ███████ ██ , Texas and met the occupants of the burned structure. The occupant, Cameron Todd Willingham, signed a consent to search document.

On December 30, 1991, went to the fire scene of the burned structure accompanied by the Fire and Police officials. This investigator started the fire scene examination.

On December 31, 1991, this investigator traveled to the Corsicana Fire Department and met Assistant Fire Chief Doug Fogg and Detective Jimmie Hensley. We had an appointment with the occupants of the burned structure, Cameron Todd Willingham and his wife Stacy Willingham. Both occupants were interviewed and they gave a voluntary written statement.

On January 2, 1992, this investigator traveled to the Corsicana Fire Department and met the Fire and Police officials. Also, this investigator was accompanied by two deputies from the Region 3 office, State Fire Marshals-Edward Cheever and Don Turk. We had a conference on the fire incident at the fire department.

On January 2, 1992, this investigator, accompanied by the Fire and Police officials and the two State Fire Marshal Deputies, went to the fire scene. This investigator completed the fire scene examination.

On January 4, 1992, this investigator traveled to the Corsicana Fire Department and obtained a voluntary written statement from a witness.

On January 4, 1992, this investigator, accompanied by Assistant Fire Chief Doug Fogg and Detective Jimmie Hensley, went to the fire scene and canvassed the neighborhood for witnessses. Three voluntary, written statements were taken from witnesses.

Received By: XR   Date: 1-21-92

INV04

Figure 8.3, continued

Page 7

TEXAS COMMISSION ON FIRE PROTECTION
State Fire Marshal's Office

Report ☐
Synopsis ☐ Supplement ☐
Investigation [XX] Continuation ☒
Photo Index ☐

Case #: 923-037-12   City / County: Corsicana/Navarro   P.R. 1

Investigator: Manuel R. Vasquez   Date of Report: 1-24-92

On January 4, 1992, this investigator and the Fire and Police officials held a conference on the fire incident and prepared to present the case to the District Attorney.

On January 6, 1992, this investigator went to the Dallas County Forensic Institute and met Dr.'s C. D. Odom and J. L. Zamora, M.E.'s. Others present were Assistant Fire Chief Doug Fogg, Detective Jimmie Hensley, and Justice of the Peace Judge Connie Mayfield. The two doctors from the Medical Examiner's Office ruled the deaths of the three (3) children as homicide. The weapon used to kill them was fire.

On January 7, 1992, this investigator traveled to the studios of KXAS-TV, Chanel 5, and picked up a video tape of an interview with the parents of the dead children.

On January 7, 1992, this investigator and the Fire and Police officials visited the office of the District Attorney and had a conference with First Assistant Criminal District Attorney, John Jackson.

On January 7, 1992, the parents of the dead children were invited to the Police Department. Assistant Fire Chief Doug Fogg, Detective Jimmie Hensley, and this investigator conducted an extensive interview with the mother. Cameron Todd Willingham was interrogated, but he did not confess.

On Janury 8, 1992, this investigator traveled to the Corsicana Police Department, because the father was scheduled to take a polygraph exam. He called the Police Department and refused to take it.

On January 8, 1992 Cameron Todd Willingham was arrested and placed in custody on suspicion of homicide.

This case remains open/active.

Received By: _____   Date: 1-21-92

INV04

Chapter Nine

Informants and Snitches

A. Readings

Alexandra Natapoff, *Beyond Unreliable: How Snitches Contribute to Wrongful Convictions*

37 GOLDEN GATE U. L. REV. 107, 107–12 (2006)

Thanks to new DNA technologies and the heroic efforts of innocence advocates, there is increasing public recognition that our criminal justice system often convicts the wrong people. Criminal informants, or "snitches," play a prominent role in this wrongful conviction phenomenon. According to Northwestern University Law School's Center on Wrongful Convictions, 45.9 percent of documented wrongful capital convictions have been traced to false informant testimony, making "snitches the leading cause of wrongful convictions in U.S. capital cases." Horror stories abound of lying jailhouse snitches and paid informants who frame innocent people in pursuit of cash or lenience for their own crimes. In recognition of the dangers of informants who lie, capital reform proposals often contain provisions designed to restrain the use of informant testimony.

But informants do not generate wrongful convictions merely because they lie. After all, lying hardly distinguishes informants from other sorts of witnesses. Rather, it is how and why they lie, and how the government depends on lying informants, that makes snitching a troubling distortion of the truth-seeking process. Informants lie primarily in exchange for lenience for their own crimes, although sometimes they lie for money. In order to obtain the benefit of these lies, informants must persuade the government that their lies are true. Police and prosecutors, in turn, often do not and cannot check these lies because the snitch's information may be all the government has. Additionally, police and prosecutors are heavily invested in using informants to conduct investigations and to make their cases. As a result, they often lack the objectivity and the information that would permit them to discern when informants are lying. This gives rise to a disturbing marriage of convenience: both snitches and the government benefit from inculpatory information while neither has a strong incentive to challenge it. The usual protections against false evidence, particularly prosecutorial ethics and discovery, may thus be unavailing to protect the system from informant falsehoods precisely because prosecutors themselves have limited means and incentives to ferret out the truth.

* * *

Wrongful Conviction Data

In 2000, the groundbreaking book Actual Innocence estimated that twenty-one percent of wrongful capital convictions are influenced by snitch testimony. Four years later, a study by the Center on Wrongful Convictions doubled that number. Another recent report estimates that twenty percent of all California wrongful convictions, capital or otherwise, result from false snitch testimony. The Illinois Commission on Capital Punishment, in reviewing that state's wrongfully convicted capital defendants, identified "a number of cases where it appeared that the prosecution relied unduly on the uncorroborated testimony of a witness with something to gain. In some cases, this was an accomplice, while in other cases it was an in-custody informant." Professor Samuel Gross's study on exonerations likewise reports that nearly fifty percent of wrongful murder convictions involved perjury by someone such as a "jailhouse snitch or another witness who stood to gain from the false testimony."

Behind these general statistics lie numerous stories of informant crime, deceit, secret deals and government duplicity. In Texas, in the so-called "sheetrock scandal," a group of police officers and informants set up dozens of individuals with fake drugs, which were actually gypsum, the main, non-narcotic component of sheetrock. The suspects were typically Mexican workers, and many pleaded guilty or were deported before the scandal was uncovered. In Los Angeles, DEA informant Essam Magid not only avoided jail for his many crimes but earned hundreds of thousands of dollars by serving as an informant. During this time, he framed dozens of innocent people before one person he targeted finally refused to plead guilty and revealed the arrangement. The now-infamous Leslie White, the prototypical jailhouse snitch, sent dozens of suspects to prison by fabricating confessions and evidence, reducing his own sentences by years.

Although such horror stories provoke outcry, little has been done to cabin the law enforcement discretion that makes such informant operations possible, or to impose greater transparency and oversight onto the process in order to curtail such abuses.

Inextricably Intertwined: Law Enforcement Dependence on Snitches

Informants have become law enforcement's investigative tool of choice, particularly in the ever-expanding world of drug enforcement. Informants are part of a thriving market for information. In this market, snitches trade information with police and prosecutors in exchange for lenience, the dismissal of charges, reduced sentences, or even the avoidance of arrest. It is a highly informal, robust market that is rarely scrutinized by courts or the public. And it is growing. While data is hard to come by, federal statistics indicate that sixty percent of drug defendants cooperate in some fashion. Informants permeate all aspects of law enforcement, from investigations to plea-bargaining to trial.

The growth in the sheer number of informants reflects the increasing dependence of police and prosecutors on informants. Professor Ellen Yaroshefsky describes prosecutors' own complaints: "These [drug] cases are not very well investigated.... [O]ur cases are developed through cooperators and their recitation of the facts. Often, in

DEA, you have agents who do little or no follow up so when a cooperator comes and begins to give you information outside of the particular incident, you have no clue if what he says is true." Another prosecutor revealed that "the biggest surprise is the amount of time you spend with criminals. You spend most of your time with cooperators. It's bizarre." Another prosecutor describes the phenomenon of "falling in love with your rat":

> You are not supposed to, of course.... But you spend time with this guy, you get to know him and his family. You like him.... [T]he reality is that the cooperator's information often becomes your mind set.... It's a phenomenon and the danger is that because you feel all warm and fuzzy about your cooperator, you come to believe that you do not have to spend much time or energy investigating the case and you don't. Once you become chummy with your cooperator, there is a real danger that you lose your objectivity....

Because investigations and cases rely so heavily on informants, protecting and rewarding informants has become an important part of law enforcement. Police and prosecutors are well known for protecting their snitches: all too often, when defendants or courts seek the identity of informants, cases are dismissed or warrant applications are dropped. More fundamentally, police and prosecutors become invested in their informants' stories, and therefore may lack the objectivity to know when their sources are lying.

Informants are thus punished for silence and rewarded for producing inculpatory information, even when that information is inaccurate. The system protects them from the consequences of their inaccuracies by guarding their identities and making their information the centerpiece of the government's cases. The front line officials who handle informants—police and prosecutors—are ill equipped to screen that information, and once they incorporate it into their cases, they acquire a stake in its validity. This phenomenon explains in part why snitch testimony generates so many wrongful convictions: it permeates the criminal system and there are few safeguards against it.

Robert P. Mosteller, *The Special Threat of Informants to the Innocent Who Are Not Innocents: Producing "First Drafts," Recording Incentives, and Taking a Fresh Look at the Evidence*
6 OHIO ST. J. CRIM. L. 519, 554–57 (2009)

Types of Informants

Informants are usefully divided into two categories. In one group are jailhouse informants; the second includes all other informants, who are most commonly coparticipants in the crime or other members of the suspect's criminal group.

A. Jailhouse Informants

The typical story from a jailhouse informant is that, while in custody, the defendant made an incriminating statement to the informant. Judge Stephen Trott of the Ninth

Circuit, writing from his experience as a prosecutor said, "Sometimes these snitches tell the truth, but more often they invent testimony and stray details out of the air...."

Although sharing similarities with other informants, jailhouse informants generally present the dangers at a consistently higher degree. They are by definition incarcerated (hence the term "jailhouse"), and as a result, all such informers have a strong interest in securing their freedom, which is in the government's control. Probably more important to their suspect classification is the high degree of difficulty in most cases of corroborating or refuting the truth of what such informers claim they were told. The role is an easy one to play in that virtually anyone could invent a plausible story.

* * *

B. Informants Drawn from Crime Co-Participants or Members of the Suspect's Criminal Group

One important difference between jailhouse informants and other types of informants is that the latter is limited to a smaller, more selective group of crime associates and that limitation provides at least some indirect support for the informant's basic story. Their ranks are restricted to a small number of individuals who can plausibly claim that they had contact with the crime suspect while he was engaged in crime. Moreover, these other informants do not typically self-identify and seek out the authorities but instead attempt to avoid exposure because it may lead to their own prosecution.

This class of informants also differs in that their stories are not as frequently entire fabrications. Instead, when lies are told, they more commonly fit into a pattern of the informant describing a crime largely accurately but changing the roles or identities of the individuals who committed crime. One of the most common alterations is for an involved informant to describe a crime accurately but to diminish his or her own role and enhance that of others. Such stories nicely mesh with the prosecution's typical goal of gathering evidence against a "big fish" by securing the testimony of "little fish," whose criminal liability they reduce or extinguish. One major fault line for prosecutors, which reveals that the process has been subverted, is when they turn out to have made a deal with a "big fish" to secure the conviction of those lower down in the operation.

Unfortunately, if the informant was involved in the crime or has talked with those who were, then he or she has the information to present or to reformulate to fit the needs of the situation. The prosecutor is generally not in a position to know how the informant may have altered the facts and thus can be misused by the informant. Prosecutors can also be misled by the police. Because investigators rather than prosecutors generally have the initial contact with the individuals who become informants, critical alterations in the informants' stories may occur without the prosecutor's knowledge, which effectively hides from the prosecutor's scrutiny key data for evaluating informants' veracity.

[I]f it were possible, a procedural protection might be used to partially compensate for the lack of corroboration: those having contact with the informant, like the investigator in a "double blind" experiment, would not know what response is desired. Yet the world of informants is not "blind" in the experimental sense at all. Instead, those who have first contact with the informant—the police or other investigative personnel—sometimes have personal relationships with the informant. Quite often they have preconceptions and/or some knowledge of how the crime occurred. Also, they will generally have a sense who the "bad actors" in the community are and the "usual suspects" for the type of crime at issue. Accordingly, those having contact with the informant typically have both the ability and some inclination to help the informant shape the story line in a particular direction. They may act inadvertently in supplying information, but they may also push the informant to tell what they believe is the accurate version of events. In either situation, one source of data in the informant's story may be investigating officers who sought to "turn" into a cooperating witness a person who likely began by denying any knowledge or involvement and only gradually moved to recite the version that the investigator believed all along to be the truth.

Russell D. Covey, *Abolishing Jailhouse Snitch Testimony*
49 Wake Forest L. Rev. 1375, 1375–1429 (2014)

Jailhouse Snitch Testimony is Fundamentally and Pervasively Unreliable

Exoneration studies have identified a set of recurrent causes of wrongful convictions, including false confessions, mistaken eyewitness testimony, and faulty forensic evidence. However, no evidence is more intrinsically untrustworthy than the allegations of a jailhouse snitch. According to some wrongful conviction scholars, jailhouse snitch testimony is the single greatest cause of wrongful convictions. This should not be surprising. It is hard to imagine more facially untrustworthy evidence. One federal court characterized the practice of using jailhouse snitches as "one of the most abused aspects of the criminal justice system," another as a "fertile field[] from which truth-bending or even perjury could grow," and a third called jailhouse snitch testimony "inherently unreliable." In an address intended as advice for prosecutors, federal judge Stephen Trott warned prosecutors not to trust criminal informants:

> Criminals are likely to say and do almost anything to get what they want, especially when what they want is to get out of trouble with the law. This willingness to do anything includes not only truthfully spilling the beans on friends and relatives, but also lying, committing perjury, manufacturing evidence, soliciting others to corroborate their lies with more lies, and double-crossing anyone with whom they come into contact, including—and especially—the prosecutor. A drug addict can sell out his mother to get a deal, and burglars, robbers, murderers[,] and thieves are not far behind. Criminals are remarkably manipulative and skillfully devious. Many are outright conscienceless sociopaths to whom "truth" is a wholly meaningless concept. To some, "conning" people is a way of life. Others are just basically unstable people. A "reliable informer" one day may turn into a consummate prevaricator the next.

Judge Trott warned that, among informants, jailhouse snitches are indisputably the worst of the bunch:

> The most dangerous informer of all is the jailhouse snitch who claims another prisoner has confessed to him. The snitch now stands ready to testify in return for some consideration in his own case. Sometimes these snitches tell the truth, but more often they invent testimony and stray details out of the air.

The practice of using jailhouse snitches in serious criminal cases is both pervasive and, as a direct result, a major cause of error in the criminal justice system. Although it had long been apparent that jailhouse snitch testimony was sometimes extremely unreliable, the strong link between jailhouse snitches and wrongful convictions has only become clear recently thanks to the still-breaking wave of DNA exonerations. Analysis of the causes of wrongful convictions in these cases reveals that jailhouse snitches have been involved in a surprisingly large percentage of known wrongful convictions—twenty-one percent—according to Innocence Project founders Barry Scheck, Peter Neufeld, and Jim Dwyer. The Scheck, Neufeld, and Dwyer study looked at exonerations resulting from DNA testing, a sample that included a disproportionately large percentage of sexual assault cases.

Jailhouse informants play an even more pernicious role in capital cases. One criminal defense attorney testified before a Los Angeles County grand jury that she had conducted a study of all cases in which a California defendant received the death penalty and concluded that jailhouse informant testimony was used in approximately one-third of those cases. According to the Northwestern University Law School's Center on Wrongful Convictions, 45.9 percent of documented wrongful convictions in capital cases involved testimony by jailhouse informants or by "killers with incentives to cast suspicion away from themselves," making "snitches the leading cause of wrongful convictions in U.S. capital cases." The Commission on Capital Punishment convened by former Illinois Governor George Ryan concluded that testimony from jailhouse informants appeared to be a major cause of wrongful convictions in the cases it looked at involving persons sentenced to death in Illinois.

A. Jailhouse Informants Face Overwhelming Temptations to Commit Perjury

Jailhouse snitches testify not out of the goodness of their hearts but to obtain one or more of a variety of incentives typically offered to them. These incentives range from almost trivial benefits, like cigarettes, to improved jail conditions and cash payments, up to the gold standard of "cooperation benefits"—release or reduction of jail sentences. Indeed, testifying against fellow inmates may often constitute a prisoner's only hope of escaping a substantial prison term. The unscrupulous inmate thus faces powerful temptations to serve as a jailhouse snitch. As the Fifth Circuit has observed, "It is difficult to imagine a greater motivation to lie than the inducement of a reduced sentence." Another court noted that it was "obvious" that cooperation premised on promises of leniency or immunity "provide[s] a strong inducement to falsify" testimony. Even in cases where leniency or immunity is not at stake, the prospect of receiving some tangible reward for false testimony can be irresistible. As one attorney commented, "When you dangle extra rewards, furloughs, money, their own clothes, stereos, in front of people in overcrowded jails, then you have an unacceptable temptation to commit perjury."

Not only are the temptations to manufacture false snitch testimony powerful, the difficulty of doing so is minimal. As a Canadian commission created to investigate the causes of one wrongful conviction observed, "In-custody confessions are often easy to allege and difficult, if not impossible, to disprove." To generate a credible confession, a snitch need only learn some basic details about a fellow inmate's case. A lying jailhouse snitch might gather information about a high profile case simply by reading newspaper stories or watching television broadcasts about the case. Snitches can also obtain details about fellow prisoners' cases by speaking with complicit friends and relatives who can monitor preliminary hearings and other case proceedings and feed details to the aspiring snitch. In some cases, informants share knowledge about case facts with each other, permitting multiple informants to corroborate each other's testimony. Investigators have documented cases in which prison inmates purchased information from others outside of prison in an attempt to trade it for reduced sentences. And now there is the Internet. As one commentator has observed, "The combination of the increasing availability of information over the internet and inmate internet access makes fabricating confessions even easier than ever before."

The ease with which jailhouse informants can fabricate credible confessions was demonstrated by one particularly industrious snitch, Leslie Vernon White, a "convicted kidnapper, robber[,] and car thief." In 1990, the CBS news program *60 Minutes* aired a segment featuring White, a self-proclaimed jailhouse snitch. Two years earlier, White demonstrated for jailers how simple it was to concoct a confession and convince prosecutors it was genuine. He repeated the performance while on camera for the CBS news program. White's methods were shocking in their audacity. To get information, he simply picked up the telephone and asked for it. To get government officials to talk, White posed as a law enforcement official or a government worker, and in that guise, contacted various government agencies, including the sheriff's information bureau, the county coroner, and the district attorney handling the case, from whom he obtained details about the facts and evidence of the case. Then he arranged to be transported to or from the courthouse with the defendant who supposedly made the confession so that he could plausibly establish an opportunity for the defendant's alleged confession to have been made to him.

Having gathered the basic case information and established a context in which the supposed confession occurred, it was easy for White to approach a homicide detective or a prosecutor with a deal. "The key thing is they want to win," White explained.

> So if I come forward with the information as detailed as that they're gonna use it. Because the jury not knowing the system or how it works, is going to believe when I get up there with all these details and facts, that this guy sat in the jail cell, or he sat on the bus, or he sat in the holding tank somewhere, or told me through a door or something, they're gonna believe me.

Over the course of several years, White appeared as a government witness in numerous cases and offered to appear in even more. In return, he received various rewards, including a letter recommending parole from a high-ranking official in a district attorney's office. These benefits did not always work out well for the citizens of California. On White's last furlough, he used the opportunity to beat his wife, snatch a purse, and assault his landlady with a knife.

As a result of the furor caused by White's confession and his startling demonstration of the ease with which he could manufacture false jailhouse confessions, Los Angeles County convened a grand jury investigation. The Los Angeles County Grand Jury commenced a year-long examination of the jailhouse informant problem in the county. What it found was even more shocking than White's demonstration. Based on extensive documentary and witness testimony, the Grand Jury learned of the existence of a complex and pervasive "informant system" at work in Los Angeles County, one that was driven by "the unwritten understanding between prosecutors and informants as to the benefits to be derived from their testimony." In its report, the Grand Jury described a system set up to manufacture false jailhouse informant testimony. At the county jail, known informants were segregated and housed in a special unit — known as the "K-9 unit." Police officers and prosecutors in need of additional evidence could request that an inmate be housed in the K-9 unit, and those requests were routinely granted. The delivery of fresh meat to the K-9 unit typically set off a feeding frenzy among the seasoned snitches housed there, and it was not unusual for several K-9 inmates to contact officials with reports of alleged confessions only hours after the unsuspecting prisoner's arrival. Attempts to obtain information from the unwitting inmate might begin in minutes.

The Grand Jury found evidence that not only did clever informants like Leslie Vernon White find ways to gather facts needed to fool police and prosecutors into believing that they had heard a defendant confess to a crime, but in some cases police and prosecutors actively colluded with jailhouse informants to manufacture false evidence. These officials, some informants testified, provided them with copies of arrest reports, trial transcripts, and case files; took the informants to crime scenes; and sometimes simply fed them the facts of the crime in order to help the informants develop convincing testimony.

Snitches, moreover, risk little by fabricating false testimony. Perjury prosecutions of lying jailhouse informants are almost nonexistent. As a case in point, following the Los Angeles County Grand Jury's investigation of the jailhouse informant problem, and despite discovery of large-scale and pervasive deception by jailhouse informants, the only two individuals prosecuted for providing perjured testimony in any court or case were the grand jury witnesses who had helped to expose the problems in the jailhouse snitch system. In contrast, snitches who helped convict other innocent defendants were never prosecuted. The message is clear — lying snitches have little to lose and everything to gain by falsely reporting to police and testifying to juries that fellow inmates have confessed to crimes.

Witnesses suspected of lying to benefit criminal defendants, on the other hand, do not fare nearly so well. When a witness is thought to have lied on behalf of a criminal defendant, the witness is far more likely to be prosecuted for perjury. In one prominent Illinois case involving the killing of a Chicago police officer, six witnesses initially gave statements to police implicating Jonathan Tolliver as a suspect. Those same witnesses later recanted their statements. According to the witnesses, the original statements had been coerced from them by police. The witnesses, however, paid dearly for the recantations. Five of the witnesses were charged with perjury and ultimately pled guilty to avoid even more serious sanctions. Prosecutors then trumpeted the convictions as proof that the allegations that the witnesses' testimony had been coerced by police were false.

Inmates thus find it easy to fabricate incriminating evidence against fellow defendants and costly to retract incriminating statements once made. Where the rewards for providing incriminating evidence are great, and where the costs of providing false testimony on behalf of the State are negligible, the "frequency of fabrication by witnesses who have made 'deals' with the government," as one commentator has observed, "while impossible to ascertain with accuracy, is potentially staggering."

* * *

The ease with which false jailhouse snitch testimony can be manufactured also plays into the hands of corrupt police officers and prosecutors who are seeking shortcuts to conviction or are engaged in corrupt conduct. Research on wrongful convictions, for example, demonstrates that police are likely to set up innocent people, when they do, by using evidence that is easy to manufacture and hard to disprove. Jailhouse snitch testimony fits that description. As the first-hand accounts provided by seasoned snitches prove, it is almost laughably simple to conjure up a plausible, albeit false, claim that a criminal defendant made a jailhouse confession. Once such allegations have been made by an informant, the informant has much to gain by sticking to his story, and even more to lose by retracting it.

B. Compensated Witnesses Are Inherently Biased

A jailhouse informant is the quintessential self-interested witness. Anglo-American law has long recognized the potentially distorting effects of self-interest on the accuracy and reliability of legal proceedings. Indeed, "[s]elf-interested witnesses were barred from testifying under early common law," and informers in particular were viewed as incompetent witnesses if they stood to directly gain some material benefit from their testimony. Although the common law bar on self-interested witnesses has generally been abandoned, awareness of the effect of self-interest on decision making continues to grow. Cognitive researchers have documented the powerful biasing effect of self-interest on objectivity. Human judgment is almost inevitably influenced, consciously or unconsciously, by perceived self-interest. Where persons must decide which of two positions to adopt or accept as true, those who stand to benefit from taking one position rather than another tend to favor the position that furthers their own self-interest. Recognition of the biasing effect of self-interest provides a basis for a wide variety of legal rules. Self-interest bars some witnesses from testifying in probate proceedings, for instance, and "self-serving bias" has been recognized in some contexts as grounds for regulating the types of compensation that a witness might be provided for testifying.

For example, normally "payments to witnesses in return for testimony are considered unethical and illegal." Lawyers who provide such incentives to witnesses are subject to professional sanctions. There are, however, exceptions to the rule. Expert witnesses, who are retained by parties and paid significant sums to testify on the party's behalf in court, are an obvious example. Ethical rules attempt to constrain the degree to which compensated expert witnesses have a stake in the outcome of the cases in which they testify. Almost every jurisdiction forbids expert witnesses from being paid on a contingent fee basis in recognition that such a fee arrangement would unduly bias the expert's testimony and be likely to induce the witness to tailor her testimony to favor the party on whose behalf she is testifying. Ethics experts have continued to express concern about even non-contingent fee arrangements with expert witnesses. The mere act of soliciting an initial opinion in a case provides expert witnesses with incentives to provide a favorable assessment because doing so greatly enhances the likelihood that they will be retained and paid for future testimony.

In criminal law, aside from experts and the parties themselves, the most common type of compensated or incentivized witness is the informant. Informants come in many shapes and sizes. There are informants on the street who are paid to feed information to police. There are accomplices, codefendants, and coconspirators who seek cooperation deals with prosecutors in order to reduce or avoid their criminal exposure. The use of informants pervades the criminal justice system. According to one account, approximately one in eight federal prisoners had his or her sentence reduced as a result of providing information to federal prosecutors. All such witnesses are prone to self-serving bias, as are the police and prosecutors who benefit from their testimony. One might argue, therefore, that all informant testimony, and perhaps all incentivized testimony more generally, is compromised as a result of self-serving bias.

Jailhouse snitches, however, pose more of a problem than paid expert witnesses or even other types of snitches. The impact of a biased expert witness can be muted in many cases by the proffer of competing expert testimony. In a classic "battle of experts," each side can call out an opposing expert whose opinion strays too far from the facts or mainstream science, or at least make clear to the jury that the opposing expert's interpretation is subject to debate. In addition, most credible expert witnesses face reputational constraints that limit the expert's willingness to proffer knowingly false or misleading testimony. The same cannot be said for jailhouse snitches whose reputations are already marginal. Nor is it realistic to think that criminal defendants can combat jailhouse snitch testimony, or even the testimony of cooperating accomplice witnesses, street snitches, and the like, by calling comparable witnesses of their own. A criminal defendant lacks the ability to commandeer helpful testimony from such witnesses because, unlike the prosecutor, he lacks any power to reward such witnesses with leniency or immunity from prosecution. And whereas prosecutors routinely reward street informants for information and testimony, a criminal defendant who paid a street informant to testify on his behalf would likely be charged with tampering or bribing witnesses. Nonetheless, it is not implausible to assume that in many cases some types of cooperating accomplices and street snitches do have a credible basis for their testimony. Testimony provided by a codefendant who admits to being present at the crime scene, for example, can be tested against the known facts and evidence in the case, including the defendant's own account where the defendant chooses to testify.

In contrast, a criminal defendant is typically helpless to counter testimony provided by a lying jailhouse informant. Unlike with experts, defendants cannot usually put on their own "jailhouse snitch," so criminal defendants lack any opportunity to fight back on an even playing field. In criminal trials there is no "battle of snitches" that might balance competing versions of events. The criminal defendant can try, as many have, to call other inmates to testify that the defendant did not make any jailhouse confession. But such testimony is, on its face, usually irrelevant, and courts will often bar it as such. Even when allowed, however, it is not likely to be effective. After all, such witnesses cannot prove the negative—that an alleged confession did not actually occur—if the jailhouse informant testifies, as an untruthful jailhouse informant invariably will, that the confession was made out of earshot of other prisoners. Finally, whereas ethical rules bar contingent fee agreements with experts out of fear that such arrangements will bias witness testimony, jailhouse informants—and indeed all informants—testify almost exclusively under arrangements that create de facto contingent payment arrangements. Because "payment" in terms of leniency almost always is granted by the prosecutor after the informant testifies, the informant readily understands that the informant's chances of getting rewarded are contingent on his delivery of credible incriminating evidence against the defendant.

Jailhouse Snitch Testimony Is Highly Persuasive Evidence

Jailhouse snitch testimony is problematic for another reason. There is, by and large, only one thing to which a jailhouse snitch can testify: that a fellow inmate confessed, and confession evidence is widely acknowledged to possess unique potency. The Supreme Court has observed that confessions are "probably the most probative and damaging evidence that can be admitted." One prominent evidence scholar asserted that "introduction of a confession makes the other aspects of a trial in court superfluous." Research confirms that evidence that the defendant has confessed greatly increases the odds of conviction. In a study conducted by Kassin and Neumann, researchers presented mock jurors with a variety of evidence of guilt and found that jurors were far more likely to convict suspects when the evidence included a confession than when other types of traditional evidence, such as eyewitness identifications or physical evidence, were presented. They thus concluded that "confession evidence has a greater impact on jurors—and is seen as having a greater impact by jurors—than other potent types of evidence."[48]

Secondary confessions—that is, confessions made to witnesses (other than police officers)—are likely not as persuasive to jurors as direct confessions. Jurors do, as a general matter, discount secondary confession evidence to some extent, and jurors may often be unwilling to convict based on secondary confession evidence alone. However, secondary confession evidence remains extremely potent. "Since few species of evidence are as powerful as an acknowledgement of guilt from the mouth of the accused, jailhouse informant testimony can be highly persuasive." Secondary confession evidence is likely to be particularly critical in "close cases." That is, jailhouse snitch testimony is likely to be most influential where the State has some other evidence of guilt, but that other evidence is weak. And these cases are precisely the ones in which jailhouse snitches are most likely to be used. After all, the State must pay a price to induce the jailhouse snitch to testify, and it can be expected to avoid doing so unless prosecutors believe that the testimony is needed. Accordingly, jailhouse snitch testimony will typically only be introduced when the prosecutor is concerned about the sufficiency of her case, and the testimony will tend to have the greatest impact in precisely those cases.

The prevailing assumption by courts, and the justification for admitting jailhouse snitch testimony absent any significant reliability review or assessment, is that jurors are capable of discounting unreliable snitch testimony as the facts and circumstances warrant. This assumption is almost certainly incorrect. Research on fundamental attribution error demonstrates that jurors cannot properly discount snitch testimony, even when they know that snitches have incentives to lie.

In a recent study, a team of researchers set out to test the claim that jurors are able to effectively discount secondary confession evidence provided by a cooperating witness with incentives to fabricate evidence.[49] Their findings undercut the assertion that jurors are able to properly take into account the degree to which witness incentives undermine reliability. In the study, the researchers recruited 345 college students and persons from the community to act as mock jurors. All of the mock jurors were given an abbreviated trial transcript drawn from a real criminal case. The transcript set forth the testimony of two State's witnesses, one who provided fiber evidence and another who presented knife evidence, and included opening and closing statements. The control group received this transcript only. Other groups received the same transcript, plus the testimony of an additional witness who claimed to have heard the defendant confess to the crime. In some cases, mock jurors were told that the witness had inadvertently learned of the crime and came forward as an act of civic duty. In other cases, they were told that the witness was testifying pursuant to a cooperation

---

48. Saul M. Kassin and Katherine Neumann, On the Power of Confession Evidence: An Experimental Test of the Fundamental Difference Hypothesis, 21 Law and Hum. Behav. 469 – 481 (1997).

49. Jeffrey S. Neuschatz et al., The Effects of Accomplice Witnesses and Jailhouse Informants on Jury Decisionmaking, 32 Law and Hum. Behav. 137, 142 (2008).

deal in which the witness would directly benefit from his testimony. The researchers then asked all of the mock jurors to assess the guilt of the defendant. Consistent with prior research, researchers found that mock jurors who were given the confession evidence convicted the defendant at significantly higher rates than those who were not presented the confession evidence.

More disturbing, however, the researchers found that the mock jurors who were presented with the confession evidence convicted at the *same* rate regardless of the source of the evidence. Conviction rates, their data indicated, "were unaffected by the explicit provision of information indicating that the witness received an incentive to testify." Although the mock jurors' questionnaire responses demonstrated that they understood that the "civic duty" witness was more interested in serving justice than the "incentivized" witness, the mock jurors failed to discount the reliability of the incentivized witness.

The most plausible explanation for these results, as the researchers suggest, is that the mock jurors were committing "fundamental attribution error." As they explain, "According to the fundamental attribution hypothesis, perceivers will ignore the contextual and situational factors in favor of a dispositional attribution. In application to a jury situation, jurors should perceive a witness' behavior as influenced by personal factors rather than situational demands."

The vast majority of participants in the experiment seemed to make just this mistake, dismissing the possibility that important contextual factors like incentives for incriminating another suspect might influence the witness's motives to provide truthful testimony. The mock jurors instead simply accepted the witness's testimony at face value.

Prior studies similarly have concluded that "attributors attach insufficient weight to situational causes and accept behavior at 'face value.'" To be sure, some of these studies have found evidence that subjects were able to engage in some critical assessment of certain types of confession evidence. For instance, where subjects were told that a confession was coerced through threats or violence, they tended to more heavily discount the credibility of the confession. After conducting one such study in which investigators provided subjects with trial transcripts from a mock case presenting a variety of evidence to the subjects, the investigators found that the subjects consistently gave some types of evidence more weight than others. Although subjects continued to be more likely to convict in confession cases than nonconfession cases, subjects generally viewed confessions made in exchange for positive rewards as more credible than confessions made in response to threats. When the coercive influence was operationally defined as a threat of harm or punishment, subjects clearly discounted the confession evidence—they viewed the confession as involuntary and manifested a relatively low rate of conviction. However, when coercion took the form of an offer or a promise of leniency, subjects were unable or unwilling to dismiss the prior confession.

Although this research demonstrates that jurors have the capacity to overcome fundamental attribution bias and discount certain types of confession evidence, it does nothing to increase confidence in jurors' capacity to properly assess jailhouse snitch testimony induced through positive incentives. Rather, these findings cast further doubt on jurors' ability to adequately discount the reliability of jailhouse snitch testimony that has been induced through positive incentives.

Juror insensitivity to the increased unreliability of incentivized witness testimony is magnified by two additional factors. First, as discussed above, typical jurors almost certainly do not understand how easy it is for jailhouse snitches to manufacture detailed false confessions. If jailhouse snitches testify about details that seem like they could only have been learned if the perpetrator had actually confessed to the snitch, but were actually gathered through the variety of approaches that snitches like Leslie White have admitted to using, then jailhouse snitch testimony will often be viewed as more credible than it should be.

Second, many jurors might perceive jailhouse snitch testimony as worthy of enhanced credence because of implicit or explicit prosecutorial bolstering of the witness's credibility. The mere fact that a prosecutor calls a jailhouse informant to serve as a State's witness suggests that the prosecutor has already determined the witness to be credible and truthful. Although the amount of presumptive credit the jury extends to State's witnesses will vary depending on both the local community's and the individual juror's views regarding prosecutorial honesty and integrity, in many jurisdictions the State begins with the benefit of the doubt.

Moreover, even though it constitutes improper practice, it is not uncommon for prosecutors to affirmatively vouch for, or bolster, the credibility of the jailhouse snitches they put on the witness stand. Take the controversial case of Troy Davis, who was executed in 2011. Davis was tried for the 1989 murder of Savannah police officer Mark McPhail. At Davis's trial in 1991, the State called a jailhouse snitch named Kevin McQueen to testify about an alleged confession made by Davis while the two men were on the prison basketball court. The snitch's testimony was suspect. Not only had McQueen served as an informant for the State in other cases, but his testimony was also seemingly implausible on its face. Numerous witnesses testified at Davis's trial that the persons who were involved with the police officer shooting had been playing pool at a local pool hall, that a man named Sylvester "Red" Coles had gotten into an argument with a homeless man outside the pool hall, and that Troy Davis and a friend—who had both also been playing pool at the hall at the time—had followed Coles and his victim up the street to a Burger King parking lot where the police officer—who was responding to the fight between Coles and the homeless man—was shot.

When the State called jailhouse snitch McQueen to testify at trial, however, McQueen claimed that Troy Davis had "confessed" to him a very different set of facts. According to McQueen, Davis told him that he had gone to a party in Cloverdale, a Savannah suburb, and that after the party, he had gone to his girlfriend's house, that they had decided to get breakfast at Burger King, and that he ran into someone who owed Davis money that was loaned to buy "dope." According to McQueen, Davis told him that "they got into some beef there, and then a whole bunch of commotion started, and a dude came in what turned out to be Officer McPhail, and there were some shots fired." On cross-examination, McQueen admitted that he had seen a story about the shooting on the news but denied "hoping to gain any advantage by testifying on behalf of the State, claiming that he had already been sentenced for his crimes."

The supposed confession recounted by McQueen failed to match up in almost any way with the other evidence in the case. McQueen's version of the confession put Davis in the wrong place, at the wrong time, for the wrong reasons, in light of the evidence presented at trial and the State's own theory of the case. In fact, McQueen's account of this supposed confession was deemed, by the federal district court judge who years later conducted a three-day habeas hearing on Troy Davis's contention of actual innocence, to be patently false because it "totally contradict[ed] the events of the night as described by numerous other State witnesses." Indeed, the judge found that McQueen's trial testimony "was so clearly fabricated" that the Court could not understand "why the State persist[ed] in trying to support its veracity."

But the State's position at trial and beyond was that McQueen's testimony was solid and credible. In his closing argument to the jury, Savannah District Attorney Spencer Lawton beseeched the jury to credit McQueen's testimony. As he told the jury:

> You heard from Kevin McQueen. Kevin McQueen was, in Mr. Barker's terms, the jailbird. Well, if you're going to talk to Troy Anthony Davis about what he did, you've got to be where Troy Anthony Davis is, and Kevin McQueen told you that he was told by Troy Anthony Davis that ... Davis had shot Officer McPhail. *There's not a reason on earth to doubt his word.* There was nothing, no reason why he had to be here, except that we subpoenaed him when we learned what he had to say.

Notwithstanding that the jailhouse snitch's testimony was later dismissed as "clearly fabricated," jurors were assured by the District Attorney that "there's not a reason on earth to doubt his word." It is difficult, in retrospect, to ascertain the weight that the jury ultimately gave to McQueen's testimony, but the attempt by prosecutors to bolster McQueen's testimony and convince the jury that the jailhouse snitch was a reliable witness certainly could have contributed to the jury's decision to convict.

Jessica A. Roth, *Informant Witnesses and the Risk of Wrongful Convictions*

53 AM. CRIM. L. REV. 737, 743–44 (2016)

Although courts and commentators have long recognized the inherent unreliability of informant testimony, little research has been dedicated to understanding how informant testimony contributes to wrongful convictions, and practically none to how it might be improved. While the federal government recently has played a more active role with respect to, for example, forensic science, it has done nothing to jumpstart research or reform on the use of informants. The United States Government has failed even to assemble an official commission to investigate and make recommendations regarding the use of informants. This is a missed opportunity, since an official report, or even the expectation of one, can be a major catalyst for change.

To the extent that there has been any recent policy movement regarding informant testimony, it has been modest and largely has been confined to jailhouse informants, who also have been the focus of recent popular and academic attention. A few states now require pretrial reliability hearings for jailhouse informants, at least in capital cases. Largely the same states also impose enhanced disclosure requirements on prosecutors with respect to jailhouse informants, and a few states have enacted legislation providing that a defendant may not be convicted solely on the basis of a single jailhouse informant's testimony, in effect extending to jailhouse informants the corroboration requirement that a number of jurisdictions have long applied to the testimony of accomplices. However, these jurisdictions that are actively exploring reform with regard to jailhouse informants are in the minority. Indeed, there are no discernible signs of change regarding the use of other kinds of informants, including accomplices.

* * *

Informant testimony is also the only one of the four suspect categories of evidence associated with wrongful convictions (i.e., confessions, eyewitness identification, forensic science, and informants) that is not universally subject to any judicial check. Confessions are subject to voluntariness review and compliance with *Miranda v. Arizona*; identifications are subject to suggestiveness and reliability review pursuant to Manson v. Brathwaite and, increasingly, more stringent state standards; and expert forensic testimony is subject to judicial gatekeeping pursuant to *Daubert v. Merrell Dow Pharmaceuticals, Inc.*, or *Frye v. United States*. As prior innocence scholarship has demonstrated, none of these review procedures is perfect, but at least they provide some pretrial screening before evidence is presented to a jury, thereby lending some accountability and feedback to police and prosecutors. By contrast, the use of informant testimony is virtually unregulated by the courts, except in the minority of jurisdictions that recently have introduced modest reforms — and even those reforms are limited only to jailhouse informants.

* * *

Recommendations for Reform

* * *

A. Pretrial Reforms

1. Better Disclosure

The first recommended reform is to expand prosecutors' disclosure requirements so that defendants obtain earlier and more fulsome disclosure whenever prosecutors intend to use informants at trial. Already, defendants generally receive such pretrial notice when a prosecutor intends to use any of the other three categories of suspect evidence associated with wrongful convictions — confessions, eyewitness identifications, and expert testimony. Concerns about informants' safety and the integrity of ongoing investigations must be taken into account. However, given the numerous studies showing the relationship between informant testimony and wrongful convictions, and the other reasons for concerns about informants' reliability, ... it no longer seems tenable for prosecutors to maintain, as a blanket matter, that disclosure of informant use always poses such grave dangers to witness security and ongoing investigations that greater and earlier disclosure cannot be made safely to defense counsel.

The disclosure ought to include the type of informants involved, [and] the form of compensation provided to the informant and the context in which the informant obtained his or her information. It also should include information such as the informant's criminal history, prior record of cooperation with authorities, the terms of any cooperation agreement, and statements made by the informant during the debriefing process.

Such disclosures (which ultimately are required in any event by Brady, Giglio, the Jenks Act, and similar state rules) would advance the cause of reliability along a number of vectors. First, the process of preparing the disclosures will focus the prosecutor on issues related to the informant's reliability and to the completeness of disclosures to the defense, at a time when the prosecutor still has the opportunity to investigate and correct any deficiencies before the cost of doing so seems prohibitive. Second, those disclosures would help defense counsel decide whether to accept any plea offer that is made, taking into account the significance and credibility of the informant's anticipated testimony. Third, defense counsel would be in a better position to evaluate whether there is any particularized basis for doubting an informant's reliability and whether any required disclosures appear to be missing, at a time when there is still an opportunity to raise these issues with the prosecutor (and the court, if necessary). Finally, if a defendant opted to proceed to trial, his or her defense attorney would be better able to prepare an effective cross-examination of the informant witness.

Whether such enhanced disclosure in fact yields "reliability gains" should be the subject of ongoing study. For example, as jurisdictions experiment with different disclosure regimes, it should be possible to study the relationship between discovery practices and the likelihood that unreliable informant witnesses are detected by counsel (defense attorneys, prosecutors, or both in combination) before trial such that an informant, once deemed reliable but subsequently called into doubt, is not called as a witness at trial. Similarly, it would be valuable (although likely harder) to study the relationship between informant disclosure practices and the incidence of innocent defendants' pleading guilty. It also would be useful to study in an experimental setting the impact of a robust and tailored cross-examination of an informant, as contrasted to a relatively weaker and generic one, on jurors' ability to detect false informant testimony. To the extent that research supports a connection between enhanced disclosure and any of these hypothesized reliability gains, the cause for insisting on such reforms more broadly would be strengthened. Such an outcome might even persuade law enforcement agencies to adopt reforms voluntarily, as many have adopted evidence-based practices for eyewitness identification and confessions.

2. Pretrial Reliability Hearings

The second recommended reform—which builds on the first—is to create the space for pretrial judicial review of informants before a judge. We already have the mechanisms for pretrial hearings on the other three suspect categories of evidence associated with wrongful convictions, as well as on searches and wiretaps. A few state jurisdictions already require pretrial judicial hearings for jailhouse informant testimony. Such hearings should be available for all informant witnesses upon a threshold showing of grounds to believe the informant is unreliable.

Reliability hearings would provide a number of benefits. First, they would provide an external check on prosecutorial decisions regarding informant witnesses. Although not all cases involving informants would proceed to that stage, the possibility of such hearings would operate as a powerful incentive to prosecutors and agents to think more carefully about their choice of informants, since it is not always possible to tell ex ante which case will result in a reliability hearing. Thus, hearings would pry open the "black box" of informant use, to a far greater extent than does current practice, providing greater accountability for prosecutorial use of informants.

Second, reliability hearings would provide courts with the opportunity to develop a common law regarding the factors and practices associated with greater informant reliability. Initially, courts likely would employ factors familiar from other evidence contexts — such as the extent to which government agents engaged in suggestive behavior, the prior basis for an informant's claim of knowledge, the existence of any corroborating evidence of an informant's testimony, and any other circumstance suggesting trustworthiness or lack thereof. On the last point, courts might consider as bearing on trustworthiness whether the particular law enforcement agencies involved had policies regarding informant use and, if so, whether those policies were followed in the particular case. Courts also could consider the content of such policies and whether they were reasonably calculated to ensure informant reliability.

* * *

B. Evidence Rule Reforms

[C]hanges to evidence rules, or courts' application thereof … could supplement general pretrial reliability hearings for informants.

1. Inquire into the Reliability of Coconspirator Statements

First, courts should be more careful about admitting informant testimony about oral communications, especially coconspirator statements that are not electronically recorded. One possible fix would be to provide the defendant against whom the statements are offered the opportunity to show that the declarant, or the circumstances in which the statement was made, indicate a lack of trustworthiness. The rules of evidence explicitly provide such an opportunity for many other types of evidence deemed potentially unreliable. Even absent a formal amendment to the rules, courts could, in their discretion, make such an inquiry.

* * *

[T]he coconspirator exception stands out for the breadth of the hearsay that it admits with no requirement that there be any particularized showing of reliability.

Adding a reliability inquiry to the coconspirator exception would eliminate this discrepancy.

2. Admit "Other Act" Evidence More Sparingly

Another evidence tweak that would enhance the reliability of convictions obtained using cooperator testimony would be to reconsider the current approach to the admission of evidence of a defendant's character and other acts. [T]he rules and doctrine applied in many courts result in the admission, through cooperator testimony, of considerable other act evidence, on the theory that it is intrinsic to the crime on trial (especially in conspiracy cases) or explains the formation of the relationship between the defendant and the cooperator. In many cases, it is appropriate to admit such evidence on one or both bases. But there is tension between the current approach, which has become quite liberal in admitting such evidence, and our jurisprudential commitment to limiting evidence about character, which runs deep for good reason.

In recognition of this potentially unfairly prejudicial effect, courts should rigorously examine the probative value of such evidence in the context of the case. If a court would be reluctant to admit evidence about the same acts through other types of proof, then cooperator testimony about those same subjects should also be approached with caution. If offered primarily to explain the background of the conspiracy and the development of a trusting relationship, each act discussed actually should be probative of those issues, and the balance of probative value versus unfair prejudice should take into account the extent to which those issues are contested. Courts also should think more carefully about the instructions they give juries about such testimony, including the rationales for any limitations on the use of such evidence, to ensure they make sense and actually are responsive to the concerns such testimony raises....

3. Rethink Corroboration Requirements

Third, courts should rethink the corroboration rules, if any, that constrain when cases based primarily on informant testimony may be submitted to the jury. [S]uch rules formally protect against conviction based solely on the testimony of an informant as to a defendant's involvement in a crime. However, in practice, they often provide cover for cases to be submitted to a jury when the corroboration is weak or is itself suspect. They also do not account for the possibility that law enforcement witnesses have disclosed the corroborating facts to the informant.

Rather than a formal requirement of corroboration, a more substantive inquiry into the reliability of the evidence of a defendant's guilt—as would be required by a pretrial reliability hearing on an informant—might be more protective of innocence. In reality, it would be a rare case where an informant's account of a defendant's guilt would be deemed reliable absent any independent corroboration. The ultimate inquiry, however, should be the reliability of the informant's evidence, with emphasis on the procedures used to debrief and incentivize the informant and on the quality of the record of that process. Moreover, when evaluating the extent of corroboration, courts should take into account the nature of the corroborating evidence and whether it, too, requires greater scrutiny.

C. Trial Practice Reforms

In addition to the foregoing tweaks to the evidence rules and their application, courts also should consider the following additional reforms to existing trial practices in an effort to improve the reliability of proceedings involving informants.

1. Limit Implicit Prosecutorial Vouching

First, courts should consider limiting the implicit prosecutorial vouching that occurs when prosecutors introduce cooperation agreements and reference their truth-telling incentives in their jury addresses. At a minimum, when an informant witness lies after entering into a cooperation agreement, or after progressing substantially in the cooperation process, the prosecutor should not be permitted to make arguments premised on these provisions. In those circumstances, these incentives plainly have not been sufficient to assure full candor. I suspect that prosecutors would be more reluctant to call some informant witnesses at trial if they knew that they would be prohibited from making such arguments. In the meantime, it would be very useful to study whether such provisions in fact result in more reliable testimony and the effect that prosecutorial vouching has on jurors' appraisal of informant witnesses' credibility.

2. Improve the Substance and Timing of Jury Instructions About Informants

Second, courts should give juries instructions about informant witnesses at various stages during the trial that are tailored to address some of the most salient risks associated with them.... Currently, many judges instruct juries to scrutinize the testimony of informant witnesses carefully because of their incentives to curry favor with the government. Such instructions are substantively insufficient and likely are given too late — at the end of the trial along with the other instructions of law.

Although more study is needed, at a minimum, judges should instruct juries about some of the other specific reasons why informant testimony may be unreliable, and such instructions should be given closer in time to the informant's testimony. Judges also should give well-timed instructions to counter some of the psychological effects that otherwise may cause juries to overvalue informant testimony. For example, while courts routinely tell juries that what the lawyers say in their jury addresses are not evidence, a specific instruction about framing and repetition effects, given after the prosecutor gives an opening statement, or after an informant is permitted to offer an interpretation of other evidence, would be an entirely different kind of experience. It therefore would be worthwhile to study the impact of variations of instructions on the unreliability of informant testimony, the effect of giving those instructions at different times, and whether instructions that call jurors' attention to the effects of framing, primacy, and repetition are effective in countering them.

D. Reforms in Prosecutor Offices

The foregoing reforms, which center around the pretrial and trial processes, hold considerable promise for reliability gains. However, the most important reforms likely would be those that occur within prosecutors' offices. As other commentators have called for, offices should adopt formal policies—in the place of mere custom and practice—addressing directly the criteria for selecting and developing informant witnesses and should train their prosecutors around those policies. These criteria should include not only the value of the information that a witness offers, but also criteria tied to markers of reliability, informed by the most recent social science and the wrongful conviction literature. Policies also should provide guidance on the conduct of the debriefing and trial preparation process, requiring that prosecutors not disclose information to the witness (with examples of how disclosure can occur inadvertently) and that they conduct more investigation as needed to evaluate the witness' reliability. Policies also should address the kinds of benefits that may be provided to an informant witness and the permissible terms of cooperation agreements and should require that all benefits and cooperation agreements be reduced to writing.

Policies also should require that prosecutors and agents keep careful records of all their communications with informant witnesses from the beginning until the end of the cooperation process, as well as of the investigative efforts to corroborate the witnesses' accounts and the results thereof. Such policies should address the form those records should take (i.e., whether sessions should be recorded electronically), who should maintain the records, the extent to which they should be disclosed to defense counsel, and when such disclosure should occur. Each office should maintain a central file containing the office's cooperation policies, memoranda explaining the prosecutor's decision to offer a cooperation agreement to a particular witness, all cooperation agreements, and a record reflecting the results of each witness' cooperation.

Further, prosecutors should be required to report errors or "near misses" that are discovered regarding cooperating witnesses—i.e., when it is discovered that the cooperator provided false testimony or lied at a late stage in the cooperation process—to the highest levels in the office, so that they can be examined in consultation with the line prosecutors to understand what went wrong, and so the lessons learned can be incorporated into the office's ongoing training. These reports, and a written analysis of them, also should be included in the central file. Policies also should address when a cooperation agreement must be rescinded in light of new information suggesting that a witness once deemed reliable lied or withheld information. Finally, policies should provide mechanisms for holding prosecutors accountable when they repeatedly, or intentionally, fail to comply with office policies regarding informants.

The foregoing policies would help prosecutors on a number of vectors. First, they would facilitate compliance with existing Brady obligations, which has consistently proven challenging, and any more demanding disclosure regime that might be adopted.... Second, they would help prosecutorial offices evaluate their use of cooperating witnesses, including for the value they are getting (in terms of crimes solved and culpable offenders brought to justice) and the extent to which they are succeeding in propounding only reliable cooperator testimony. Third, such requirements would enable cross-jurisdictional research comparing the experiences of different offices to determine whether certain policies and practices are associated with better outcomes than others. Fourth, they would provide prosecutors the material they will need at pretrial reliability hearings and potentially at trial to respond to attacks on a cooperator's reliability. Fifth, they would help send an important signal to line prosecutors regarding the importance of cooperator reliability to the office's culture—and would help weed out those prosecutors whose conduct is inconsistent with that culture.

Until more is known about what constitutes "best practices" for informants, the precise content of some aspects of these policies, like rules about the permissible benefits and structure of cooperation agreements, should be left to the individual prosecutors' offices. At least initially, the priority should be that offices have policies in effect and that the policies be followed. Locally developed rules often are better suited to local conditions, and—as much of the new governance literature suggests—organizations may be more likely to comply with rules that they played a role in developing than those imposed upon them. Moreover, simply requiring that offices adopt policies may have the salutary effect of prompting high-ranking individuals within prosecutorial offices to educate themselves about the relevant literature on wrongful convictions to better inform their policies.

American Bar Association, Section of Criminal Justice, *Report to the House of Delegates*
(2005)

RECOMMENDATION

RESOLVED, That the American Bar Association urges federal, state, local and territorial governments to reduce the risk of convicting the innocent, while increasing the likelihood of convicting the guilty, by ensuring that no prosecution should occur based solely upon uncorroborated jailhouse informant testimony.

REPORT

Witnesses who receive benefits from the government for their testimony include jailhouse informants, immunized witnesses, and accomplices. This Resolution is directed at the former. A jailhouse informant is "someone who is purporting to testify about admissions made to him or her by the accused while incarcerated in a penal institution contemporaneously."

Prosecution Screening

The first check (and perhaps the most important) on unreliable testimony by informants is the prosecutor. The Canadian ("Kaufman") Commission in the Guy Paul Morin case provided the following list of factors that prosecutors should review:

(1) The extent to which the statement is confirmed;

(2) The specificity of the alleged statement. For example, a claim that the accused said "I killed A.B." is easy to make but extremely difficult for any accused to disprove;

(3) The extent to which the statement contains details or leads to the discovery of evidence known only to the perpetrator;

(4) The extent to which the statement contains details or leads which could reasonably be accessed by the in-custody informer, other than through inculpatory statements by the accused.... Crown counsel should be mindful that, historically, some informers have shown great ingenuity in securing information thought to be unaccessible to them. Furthermore, some informers have converted details communicated by the accused in the context of an exculpatory statement into details which purport to prove the making of an inculpatory statement;

(5) The informer's general character, which may be evidenced by his or her criminal record or other disreputable or dishonest conduct known to the authorities;

(6) Any request the informer has made for benefits or special treatment (whether or not agreed to) and any promises which may have been made (or discussed with the informer) by a person in authority in connection with the provision of the statement or an agreement to testify;

(7) Whether the informer has, in the past, given reliable information to the authorities;

(8) Whether the informer has previously claimed to have received statements while in custody. This may be relevant not only to the informer's reliability or unreliability but, more generally, to the issue of whether the public interest would be served by utilizing a recidivist informer who previously traded information for benefits;

(9) Whether the informer has previously testified in any court proceeding, whether as a witness for the prosecution or the defence or on his or her behalf, and any findings in relation to the accuracy and reliability of that evidence, if known;

(10) Whether the informer made some written or other record of the words allegedly spoken by the accused and, if so, whether the record was made contemporaneous to the alleged statement of the accused;

(11) The circumstances under which the informer's report of the alleged statement was taken (e.g. report made immediately after the statement was made, report made to more than one officer, etc);

(12) The manner in which the report of the statement was taken by the police (e.g. though use of non-leading questions, thorough report of words spoken by the accused, thorough investigation of circumstances which might suggest opportunity or lack of opportunity to fabricate a statement).... ;

(13) Any other known evidence that may attest to or diminish the credibility of the informer, including the presence or absence of any relationship between the accused and the informer;

(14) Any relevant information contained in any available registry of informers. Judge Trott has also provided step-by-step guidance for prosecutors. Nevertheless,

the little empirical data on the subject and the exoneration cases indicate that there is often difficulty in screening out unreliable informant testimony.

Corroboration Requirement

The inherent skepticism of the testimony of accomplices has led many jurisdictions to require corroboration. A significant number mandate this requirement by statute. However, a greater number of states do not require corroboration and are satisfied with only a cautionary jury instruction. Corroboration should be required in jailhouse informant cases; no person should lose liberty or life based solely on the testimony of such a witness. As Judge Trott has observed, "The most dangerous informer of all is the jailhouse snitch who claims another prisoner has confessed to him."

"Corroborative evidence is usually considered to be that which, when viewed independent of the accomplice, would tend to connect the defendant with the commission of the crime charged. The existence of corroboration is usually a threshold question for the judge; if found, she may then submit the accomplice testimony to the jury."

B. Current Law: Overview

Jailhouse Informants and the Supreme Court

The Supreme Court has not yet decided any case directly addressing the problem of unreliable jailhouse informant testimony, but the following cases are relevant:

- *Kansas v. Ventris*, 556 U.S. 586 (2009) (statements obtained by jailhouse informant in violation of the Sixth Amendment right to counsel under Massiah/Henry doctrine are admissible for impeachment purposes).

- *Van de Kamp v. Goldstein*, 555 U.S. 335 (2009) (holding that district attorney and chief deputy district attorney were entitled to absolute prosecutorial immunity where plaintiff alleged that the district attorney's office failed to institute a system of information-sharing among deputy district attorneys regarding jailhouse informants, and that failure to adequately train or supervise sharing of information concerning informants, resulting in Giglio violation at his trial).

- *Kuhlmann v. Wilson*, 477 U.S. 436 (1986) (Sixth Amendment does not forbid admission of accused's statements to a jailhouse informant who is placed in close proximity but makes no effort to stimulate conversations involved in crime charged).

- *United States v. Henry*, 447 U.S. 264 (1980) (defendant's incriminating statements made to paid informant who had engaged the defendant in conversations and "had developed a relationship of trust and confidence with [the defendant] such that [the defendant] revealed incriminating information" while confined in same cellblock as defendant were "deliberately elicited" from defendant in violation of his Sixth Amendment right to counsel).

• *Massiah v. United States*, 377 U.S. 201 (1964) (holding that once a defendant's Sixth Amendment right to counsel has attached, he is denied that right when federal agents "deliberately elicit" incriminating statements from him in the absence of his lawyer, either through direct questioning or through "'indirect and surreptitious interrogations'").

State Law Measures to Regulate the Use of Jailhouse Informants

As Professor Roth notes:

> A few states now require pretrial reliability hearings for jailhouse informants, at least in capital cases. Largely the same states also impose enhanced disclosure requirements on prosecutors with respect to jailhouse informants, and a few states have enacted legislation providing that a defendant may not be convicted solely on the basis of a single jailhouse informant's testimony, in effect extending to jailhouse informants the corroboration requirement that a number of jurisdictions have long applied to the testimony of accomplices.

Jessica A. Roth, Informant Witnesses and the Risk of Wrongful Convictions, 53 Am. Crim. L. Rev. 737, 743–44 (2016).

State Evidence Codes

For example, California adopted a corroboration requirement in 2011. CAL. PEN. CODE § 1111.5 (West 2016):

> § 1111.5. Conviction on testimony of in-custody informant; corroboration; "in-custody informant" defined
>
> (a) A jury or judge may not convict a defendant, find a special circumstance true, or use a fact in aggravation based on the uncorroborated testimony of an in-custody informant. The testimony of an in-custody informant shall be corroborated by other evidence that connects the defendant with the commission of the offense, the special circumstance, or the evidence offered in aggravation to which the in-custody informant testifies. Corroboration is not sufficient if it merely shows the commission of the offense or the special circumstance or the circumstance in aggravation. Corroboration of an in-custody informant shall not be provided by the testimony of another in-custody informant unless the party calling the in-custody informant as a witness establishes by a preponderance of the evidence that the in-custody informant has not communicated with another in-custody informant on the subject of the testimony.
>
> (b) As used in this section, "in-custody informant" means a person, other than a codefendant, percipient witness, accomplice, or coconspirator, whose testimony is based on statements allegedly made by the defendant while both the defendant and the informant were held within a city or county jail, state penal institution, or correctional institution....

State Evidence Codes: Accomplice Testimony

Legislatures in many states have enacted evidentiary provisions requiring corroboration for the testimony of accomplices. See, e.g., Tex. Code Crim. Proc. Ann., Art. 38.14 (Vernon Supp. 2000) ("A conviction cannot be had upon the testimony of an accomplice unless corroborated by other evidence tending to connect the defendant with the offense committed....").

The "Informant's Privilege"

When informants are involved with reference to trial proceedings, we are confronted with the principle established by Roviaro v. United States. In Roviaro, the Supreme Court ruled that the identity of the confidential informant which led to the arrest of the defendant and the charges need not be disclosed, nor must that person be produced at trial, unless his or her potential testimony would be relevant and helpful to the defense of the accused, or is essential to a fair determination of the cause. This has been referred to as the common law "informer's privilege," a qualified privilege, which a court can only override if the test established in Roviaro can be met. The determination whether to disclose the identity of the confidential informant requires the court to balance "the public interest in protecting the flow of information to law enforcement officials against the individual's right to prepare his defense." Indeed, it may well implicate the constitutional right of a defendant to call witnesses in his own behalf such as where the defendant asserts an entrapment defense in a drug case and the informant was a participant in the transaction with the defendant and the undercover police officer involved.

Senior Judge Arthur L. Burnett, Sr., *The Potential for Injustice in the Use of Informants in the Criminal Justice System*, 37 Sw. L. Rev. 1079, 1082–83 (2008).

C. Legal Materials, Exercises, and Media

1. *Recommended Listening, Exoneree Franky Carrillo:* Listen to Franky Carrillo, an exoneree from southern California, describe how snitch testimony led to his wrongful conviction on Season 2, Episode 10, "Mistaken Identity: The Wrongful Murder Conviction of Franky Carrillo," *Wrongful Conviction with Jason Flom* (7:00–13:00). Franky also discusses the line-up procedure, another factor in his wrongful conviction (18–19:30): https://art19.com/shows/wrongful-conviction-with-jason-flom?month=4&perPage=50&year=2017.

2. *Recommended Viewing, Snitching.org:* For a complete resource on informants, see the website www.snitching.org, created by Professor Alexandra Natapoff, author of the *Beyond Unreliable* excerpt above as well as the book *Snitching: Criminal Informants and the Erosion of American Justice*. In this short video, Professor Natapoff discusses problems with informants: https://www.youtube.com/watch?v=Aacl73Z6ThI (2:54).

3. *Recommended Listening, Informant Witnesses and Risking Wrongful Convictions:* Jessica Roth discusses parts of her article not included in the excerpt above in her interview on *Excited Utterance* with Edward Cheng, Episode 19, "Informant Witnesses and the Risk of Wrongful Convictions." Roth discusses repetition and framing effects (9:15–11:15) and proposes pre-trial hearings on informants (11:15–15:00): https://www.excitedutterancepodcast.com/listen/2017/2/6/19-jessica-roth.

4. *Discussion, College Students as Confidential Informants:* Have you ever thought other students could be CIs? *60 Minutes* investigated this practice after Andrew Sadek, a 20-year-old college student, was killed possibly due to his work as a CI for the police: https://www.youtube.com/watch?v=VBiXcfrP_4s (0:00–4:35). Who do you think police should recruit to be CIs?

5. *Discussion, OC Snitch Tank:* Orange County, California, law enforcement officials and the District Attorney's Office were investigated for a coordinated jailhouse informant system used in multiple cases.

   a. *Inside the Snitch Tank:* The Orange County Register reported on this "secret jail-informant network," uncovered in the well-known case of mass murderer Scott Dekraai, but used in cases across Orange County for decades: https://www.youtube.com/watch?v=xi9XLnxRCHU (14:48).

   b. *Lack of Accountability:* Orange County prosecutors who put on false testimony have not faced accountability, nor has a neighboring Riverside County prosecutor who presented false testimony, as noted in R. Scott Moxley, *Why Is California's AG Turning a Blind Eye to Orange County Deputies' Perjury?*, OC Weekly (Sept. 27, 2017): http://www.ocweekly.com/news/california-attorney-general-lets-oc-sheriffs-department-get-away-with-perjury-8457185.

   c. *No "Organized Formal Program," No Indictments:* An Orange County Grand Jury found no evidence of an "organized formal program," instead finding uncoordinated use of informants and behavior by "rogue" officers. KCAL9 report on June 13, 2017: https://www.youtube.com/watch?v=xVLLgVH0qUA.

6. *Reflective Essay, Who Is Responsible for Telling the Jury about False Government Testimony:* "When a key prosecution witness lies on the stand during a murder trial, and the judge and the lawyers know it, who has the responsibility to tell the jury?" Andrew Cohen of *The Marshall Project* covers the case of *Long v. Pfister*, where the U.S. Court of Appeals for the Seventh Circuit ruled in favor of prosecutors who failed to disclose—and misrepresented—false testimony, in "Getting Away with Perjury," October 30, 2017: https://www.themarshallproject.org/2017/10/30/getting-away-with-perjury. How far do you think prosecutors must go to acknowledge a lie by one of their witnesses?

7. *Oral Advocacy Exercise:* Prepare to argue on behalf of the State of Kansas or Donnie Ray Ventris after reading either the State's brief or Ventris' Reply brief below. Both sides will be argued by students in class.

Brief for Respondent, Kansas Appellate Defender Office, *State of Kansas v. Ventris*

On Writ of Certiorari to the Supreme Court of the State of Kansas
2008 WL 5369542 (U.S.), 1–4 (2008)

Statement Of Facts

The prosecutor filed a complaint with an accompanying affidavit and application for arrest warrant charging Rhonda Theel and Donnie Ray Ventris with felony murder and other charges. After the state arrested Mr. Ventris, the State recruited an informant, Johnnie Doser, and placed him in Mr. Ventris' cell. Doser said that he "was asked if [he] could get any information out of [Mr. Ventris]." Doser indicated that the first day in the cell with Mr. Ventris, he did not obtain any incriminating statements. On the second day in the cell together, Doser told Mr. Ventris that he "could tell by the look in [Mr. Ventris'] eyes that he had something more serious weighing in on his mind." Doser testified that Mr. Ventris asked whether Doser could be trusted. Doser testified that he assured Mr. Ventris of his trustworthiness. Doser claimed that Mr. Ventris then made incriminating statements regarding the alleged offenses.

The state entered into a plea bargain with Theel to procure her testimony against Mr. Ventris on capital charges. At jury trial, Theel implicated Mr. Ventris in the murder. Mr. Ventris testified in his own behalf, denying culpability in the incident. The state subsequently sought to introduce Doser's testimony regarding Mr. Ventris' alleged statements. Mr. Ventris objected, asserting that any statements obtained by Doser violated Mr. Ventris' right to counsel. The prosecutor indicated that "I will grant that [Doser] was placed in there and there's probably a violation. However, that doesn't give the Defendant unlicensed—a license to just get on the stand and lie."

The state trial court overruled the objection and allowed Doser's testimony. "In exchange for Doser's testimony, the State released him from probation." The jury acquitted Mr. Ventris of felony murder and theft, but convicted him of aggravated robbery and aggravated burglary.

Mr. Ventris filed a timely motion for new trial renewing the Sixth Amendment claim. Specifically, Mr. Ventris alleged that:

> Johnnie Doser, then an inmate at the Montgomery County Jail, was solicited by the Montgomery County Attorney to be a cell mate of the defendant's following the defendant's arrest, and following the defendant's assertion of his right to counsel. Upon Doser's agreement to cooperate with police, he became an agent of the state.

In its written response to the motion for new trial, the prosecutor indicated that "[t]he State agrees with the defendant's statement of the facts," and further conceded that "[i]n the case at bar, the defendant's sixth amendment right to counsel may have been violated." The state trial court found that the statements obtained by Doser were voluntary and overruled the motion for new trial.

After the state trial court imposed a 281-month prison sentence, ... [t]he Kansas Supreme Court granted review and, in its decision, reiterated that "[t]he State concedes that it violated Ventris' Sixth Amendment right to counsel when it surreptitiously planted Doser in Ventris' jail cell as a human listening device." The Kansas Supreme Court went on to hold that the statements obtained in direct violation of the Sixth Amendment right to counsel could not be used for any purpose in the trial of the charges to which that right to counsel had attached and that the erroneous admission was not harmless beyond a reasonable doubt.

[The State then sought review in the United States Supreme Court, which granted the State's petition, in which the following briefs, excerpted and *inter alia*, were filed:]

Brief of the National Association of Criminal Defense Lawyers as *Amicus Curiae* in Support of Respondent *State of Kansas v. Ventris*

2008 WL 5409458 (U.S.)

Because testifying for the prosecution promises remuneration, reduced sentences, and other benefits, snitches face strong—and sometimes irresistible—incentives to lie.... Snitches who are already serving time often have their sentences reduced in exchange for their testimony. For example, a snitch who testified against Charles Fain— who was charged with rape and murder in 1983—had been facing 230 years in prison before he testified. After testifying, some of the charges against him were dropped and others were reduced; he was released just three years later.[50] As a result of these snitches' testimony, Fain was sentenced to death and spent nearly eighteen years on death row before being exonerated by DNA evidence. Ventris's case illustrates this very point: the informant Doser was in jail because he had violated his probation and was facing the possibility of prison time, but prosecutors recruited him and agreed to release him from probation in exchange for his testimony against respondent....

In addition to the benefits that snitches in general receive in exchange for their testimony, some snitches have an additional incentive to lie: they are the actual perpetrators of the crime at issue, and concocting a false confession shifts the prosecution's focus away from them. With personal knowledge of the crime, perpetrator-snitches are particularly well-placed to fabricate a convincing "confession" that describes how the crime was committed and thereby frame another individual for the crime....

The incentives for false testimony potential snitches face are further exacerbated when snitches are affirmatively recruited by the police. In such a scenario, the pressure placed on a would-be informant can be overwhelming: the snitch fears retaliation if she fails to return with the confession she was recruited to obtain.

---

50. Hans Sherrer, Charles Fain Proved Innocent of Murder, and Released After Almost 18 Years On Idaho's Death Row, Forejustice, available at http:// forejustice.org/wc/charles_fain.htm; The Innocence Project, Know the Cases, Charles Irvin Fain, http://www.innocenceproject.org/Content/149.php.

Obviously, fabricated confessions cannot further the truth-seeking process. Instead, they result in unreliable convictions of innocent defendants. Consider, for example, Dennis Fritz and Ron Williamson, who were charged with murder years after the crime occurred.[51] The case against the two men depended almost entirely on snitch testimony: none of the myriad fingerprints at the crime scene belonged to either man, and although the hairs at the scene supposedly "matched" Fritz and Williamson's, the prosecutors knew this evidence alone was insufficient to obtain a conviction. Based primarily on snitch testimony, both men were convicted of murder, with Fritz sentenced to life in prison and Williamson sentenced to death. Finally, after spending twelve years in prison, both men were exonerated by DNA evidence, which proved not only that they were not the perpetrators, but that one of the prosecution's other informants, Glen Gore, had actually committed the murder....

Ironically, prosecutors have the strongest incentives to rely on snitches in cases in which they are least able to ensure veracity. "[I]n most situations a cooperator's value increases in inverse proportion to the [other] information in possession of the prosecutor."[52] Snitch testimony is most valuable when the prosecutor otherwise has a weak case — for example, when there is little to no physical evidence and no eyewitness testimony — both because the prosecutor needs evidence and because the lack of other sources of information makes it more difficult for a defendant to rebut informant testimony. And sometimes prosecutors must choose between relying on unreliable snitch testimony and dropping charges altogether. For example, in the case of Dennis Fritz, the snitch came forward with his testimony only one day before prosecutors would have been forced to drop charges for lack of evidence....

Especially in cases involving serious crimes, and therefore high stakes, prosecutors will be tempted to supplement thin evidence with snitch testimony. Thus, it is not surprising that reliance on incentivized testimony is the "leading cause of wrongful convictions" in capital cases. For example, in the case of Gary Gauger, who was convicted and sentenced to death for the murder of his parents in 1994, prosecutors needed testimony to corroborate a disputed confession to the police that occurred after hours of interrogation. So they relied on Raymond Wagner, a convicted felon and snitch, to testify that Gauger had also confessed to him. The true killers later admitted to the murders and were convicted. Gauger received a gubernatorial pardon based on actual innocence in 2002, six years after his conviction had been reversed on other grounds.[53]

---

51. The Innocence Project, Know the Cases, Dennis Fritz, http://www.innocenceproject.org/Content/152.php.

52. Steven M. Cohen, What is True? Perspectives of a Former Prosecutor, 23 Cardozo L. Rev. 817, 822 (2002).

53. Northwestern Center on Wrongful Convictions Website, Gary Gauger, available at http://www.law.northwestern.edu/wrongfulconvictions/exonerations/ilGaugerSummary.html; see also C. Blaine Elliott, Life's Uncertainties: How to Deal with Cooperating Witnesses and Jailhouse Snitches, 16 Cap. Def. J. 1 (2003) (describing the case of Earl Bramblett, who was sentenced to death and executed, based in part on testimony by a snitch who later recanted); Grand Jury Report, supra, at 37

In these cases involving thin evidence, "[the] very lack of evidence tends to make it much more difficult to evaluate the veracity of the would-be cooperator." Corroboration becomes even more difficult when an informant's testimony includes few details about the alleged crime, but instead only vague statements — such as "the defendant told me he pulled the trigger" — that are "easy to make but extremely difficult ... to disprove." Again, this case offers an illustration: the snitch testified simply "that the Hicks robbery 'went sour' and that Ventris shot Hicks before robbing him of money, keys, and a vehicle."

Additionally, the ever-present danger of false snitch testimony materializing at the last moment impedes the truth-seeking function for an independent reason: it interferes with defense counsel's ability to prepare and present their strongest case. Because snitch testimony is so damaging and difficult to rebut, defense counsel may decide for strategic reasons not to have the defendant testify if a snitch materializes and is available for impeachment. Therefore, the possibility of snitch testimony may dissuade a defendant from taking the stand even when he otherwise might have done so. And defense counsel may learn of such a snitch only just before trial, as snitches often come forward only at the last second.

In other areas of the law, this Court has held that the Constitution requires exclusion of types of evidence that are especially prone to unreliability absent additional safeguards. Thus, for example, this Court has excluded identifications obtained under unduly suggestive circumstances unless the identifications "possess[] sufficient aspects of reliability."

By contrast, Kansas provides none of these safeguards. In this case, for example, although law enforcement officials "recruited Doser to share a cell with Ventris and to 'keep [his] ear open and listen' for incriminating statements," the State failed to take any steps to ensure the reliability of Doser's testimony by tape-recording conversations between the two cellmates or otherwise seeking to corroborate Doser's testimony....

The practicability of requiring corroboration, or other safeguards, for the admission of snitch testimony is ... illustrated by a related development: the adoption of such measures in cases involving accomplice testimony.[54] If anything, this development only strengthens the case for requiring such safeguards in snitch cases, since the problems with reliability here are even greater.

Sixteen states have statutes mandating corroboration for accomplice informants. Thirteen of those require corroboration for all accomplice testimony, regardless whether the informant was in custody. California's law is illustrative: "A conviction cannot be had upon the testimony of an accomplice unless it be corroborated by such

---

(referring to a survey showing that snitches were used in approximately one-third of an extensive sample of cases in which defendants were sentenced to death).

54. Cf. Lee v. Illinois, 476 U.S. 530, 546 (1986) (describing "the time-honored teaching that a co-defendant's confession inculpating the accused is inherently unreliable, and that convictions supported by such evidence violate the constitutional right of confrontation").

other evidence as shall tend to connect the defendant with the commission of the offense; and the corroboration is not sufficient if it merely shows the commission of the offense or the circumstances thereof."[55]

In addition to the states that require some form of corroboration for accomplice testimony, an even greater number of states also require "cautionary jury instruction[s]" in cases involving accomplice testimony.

This Court should not allow lower courts to admit unreliable jailhouse snitch testimony for impeachment purposes. But if the Court chooses to do so at all, it should at the very least require that these statements meet the same type of corroboration requirements that apply to confessions offered by accomplices that connect the defendant with the charged offense.

Reply Brief for Petitioner, *State of Kansas v. Ventris*
2009 WL 97751, 7–21 (U.S. 2009)

I. The Fundamental Purpose Of The Sixth Amendment Right To Counsel Is To Ensure A Fair Trial Through An Adversary Process, Which Occurred In This Case.

A. Both parties and all amicus curiae in this case agree that the fundamental purpose of the Sixth Amendment right of a defendant "to have the Assistance of Counsel for his defence," is to ensure a fair trial through an adversary process. Respondent received precisely such assistance and a fair trial.

First, counsel fully assisted Respondent in his defense in the adversary trial setting. Doser's testimony was offered only after Respondent testified that he did not shoot the murder victim. Respondent's counsel confronted and fully cross-examined Doser, exploring whether law enforcement officials, other inmates, or anyone else told Doser anything about Respondent's alleged crimes before Doser and Respondent were placed together, what instructions law enforcement agents gave to Doser, and whether Doser received any benefit in exchange for his assistance to law enforcement.

Second, the trial judge, as is commonly done, gave the jury a cautionary instruction, directing them that "[y]ou should consider with caution the testimony of an informant who, in exchange for benefits from the State, acts as an agent for the State in obtaining evidence against a defendant, if that testimony is not supported by other evidence."

---

55. Cal. Penal Code § 1111 (West 2008). Three more states impose similar safeguards for accomplice testimony in felony cases. Ala. Code § 12-21-222 (2008); Ark. Code Ann. § 16-89-111(e) (West 2008); Ga. Code Ann. § 24-4-8 (West 2008) (corroboration also required when accomplice is sole witness in cases of treason or perjury). And Tennessee requires accomplice corroboration under common law. See, e.g., State v. Shaw, 37 S.W.3d 900, 903 (Tenn. 2001) ("[A] conviction may not be based solely upon the uncorroborated testimony of an accomplice.").

* * *

II. The Costs Of Excluding, For All Purposes, Relevant And Probative Voluntary Statements Unlawfully Obtained Far Outweigh Any Marginal Benefit In Deterring Government Misconduct

A. Significant Incentives Already Exist For Police And Prosecutors To Follow The Law.

Respondent and its amicus appear to endorse the propositions that no prosecutor is to be trusted and that all police seek to violate constitutional standards whenever doing so might result in obtaining evidence that may be useful in some way at some time. The truth, however, is much more complicated than that, and there already exist several significant deterrents to police and prosecutorial misconduct.

First, as the Court has said in other contexts, such as describing the anticipated behavior of the States and state judges, there is a presumption that the States and their officials will act in good faith to follow and uphold the Constitution. See, e.g., Alden v. Maine, 527 U.S. 706, 755 (1999) ("We are unwilling to assume the States will refuse to honor the Constitution or obey the binding laws of the United States. The good faith of the States thus provides an important assurance that" federal standards will be followed.) The Court has never assumed, nor should it, that state prosecutors systematically and intentionally violate, or encourage police to violate, a defendant's constitutional rights. Rather, the Court long has assumed that prosecutors follow the Constitution and the rules of professional ethics, and that ethical standards and professional discipline in particular will act as a significant deterrent to prosecutorial misconduct. Similarly, the Court recently recognized that police professional standards and discipline create important incentives for police to follow the law, much more so than when the Court first adopted the exclusionary rule decades ago. Combined with much stronger professional training and supervision than once may have been the case, police professional norms and discipline provide significant protection against police misconduct. Indeed, there is no evidence in this case of either prosecutorial or police bad faith or improper motives. Here, at worst, the informant failed to follow his instructions carefully.

As explained previously, there are strong incentives to follow the law in this context. Because placing an informant in a cell to act as a "listening post" does not violate the Sixth Amendment right to counsel at all, Kuhlmann v. Wilson, 477 U.S. 436 (1986), any statements obtained from a defendant in that scenario will be admissible for all purposes. Having a defendant's inculpatory statements available for use in the government's case in chief is far more helpful than (1) purposefully violating the Massiah rule (2) in the hope of obtaining something that might be useful (3) if and only if the defendant both (a) actually testifies at trial and (b) does so inconsistently with statements previously made to an informant.

B. Total Exclusion Of Informant Testimony Would Prevent The Jury From Hearing Often Relevant, Probative, And Reliable Evidence While Permitting Criminal Defendants To Commit Perjury.

Respondent's amicus, and to a great extent Respondent himself, suggest in essence that informants are inherently unreliable and that their uncorroborated testimony should be per se inadmissible, or else subject to special evidentiary and procedural rules. Such claims are radical, running contrary to two centuries of American (and even longer British) reliance upon cross-examination in an adversary process before a jury to determine the credibility of testimonial evidence in pursuit of the truth in criminal cases.[56] Not surprisingly, the Constitution provides no basis for such special rules, and the Court long ago rejected any such proposition. Indeed, Sixth Amendment right to counsel cases such as Massiah and Kuhlmann stand in direct contradiction of the argument. In none of those cases did the Court even suggest, much less hold, that informant testimony is inherently unreliable. To the contrary, the Court long has recognized that such evidence is admissible, subject to the normal rules of evidence, cross-examination, and trial procedure.

In fact, informant testimony regarding voluntary statements a defendant has made to a person the defendant believed (erroneously) to be a friend, ally, or confidante, may be extremely reliable. Furthermore, informants often have no prior knowledge of the crimes with which a defendant is charged, or the circumstances of those crimes, prior to talking with the defendant, making it impossible for them to fabricate the substance of a defendant's statements to match non-existent prior knowledge of the crime and its circumstances. In this case, Doser testified, on cross-examination, that the police did not tell him that Respondent was charged with murder, nor had he heard such information from other inmates, from visitors, or from any other source prior to his conversations with Respondent. Further, there are reasons to think that statements made to informants may be even more reliable than statements elicited by direct police interrogation, where the possibility of coercion or intimidation may exist.... Jailhouse informants themselves have incentives not to be aggressive or too active in questioning cellmates. Jails can be dangerous places, and being discovered as a government informant could have significant, negative consequences, a fact of which Doser was well aware in this case. See J.A. at 155 ("I didn't want to push for any information. I didn't want to subject myself to being injured.") Thus, informants, too, have significant incentives to follow Kuhlmann rather than violate Massiah. To the extent Respondent and his amicus argue that informants are inherently unreliable, they actually bolster the Court's longstanding concern about perjury by criminal defendants. By necessity, jailhouse informants themselves are criminal defendants. If such informants are inherently unreliable, logic suggests that criminal defendants as a group may be inherently unreliable. Certainly, it is not lost on juries (nor has it ever been lost on the Court) that criminal defendants may have incentives to be less

---

56. See, e.g., 5 J. Wigmore, Evidence § 1367 p.32 (J. Chadbourn rev. 1974) (cross-examination is "beyond any doubt the greatest legal engine ever invented for the discovery of truth.").

than forthcoming or candid when they testify in their own defense. That is a basis for the Court's repeated warnings about condoning or encouraging perjury, and a fundamental reason for jury trials—to permit a cross-section of citizens to evaluate the credibility of all witnesses, including criminal defendants.

Moreover, it is common for trial judges to instruct the jury, as the trial judge did in this case, to evaluate an informant's testimony with caution, particularly when the informant has received a benefit from the government in exchange for testifying. There is no constitutional basis for imposing additional restrictions or more severe and unique limitations on informant testimony.

III. The Alternative Proposals That Respondent And His Amicus Offer Are Fundamentally Flawed.

As an alternative to a rule of total exclusion, Respondent proposes that statements obtained in violation of the Massiah rule be admissible only "when necessary to prevent intentional false testimony." His amicus offers a different alternative, namely that such a statement be admissible "only if it satisfies a basic reliability requirement: corroboration." These "alternative" proposals are fundamentally flawed, run contrary to two centuries of American jurisprudence and, if adopted, would prove to be a "cure" with far worse consequences for the criminal justice system than any current perceived problems with informant testimony.

Respondent's alternative proposal effectively acknowledges that perjury by criminal defendants is a serious concern, and that impeachment of at least some criminal defendants who testify is critical to protecting the integrity of the criminal justice system. But even cursory consideration of the proposed alternative demonstrates that the only workable and constitutionally justified approach is to permit impeachment whenever a defendant testifies and the informant's testimony will contradict the defendant, just as the Court has held repeatedly in the Fourth Amendment, Miranda, and Jackson cases. Fundamentally, the alternative proposals invite this Court to create special, unique rules on the basis of policy judgments, not constitutional requirements. There are two centuries of American jurisprudence in place to deal with informant testimony, as demonstrated by this case. Here, Respondent's counsel had information regarding any benefits Doser received from the government for his testimony, was able to cross-examine Doser aggressively on a variety of topics, and the trial judge gave the jury a cautionary instruction regarding informant testimony. These rules and measures protected Respondent's rights in this case, just as they long have been deemed adequate to protect criminal defendants' rights in general. Indeed, such measures proved quite effective here. Given the opportunity to assess Doser, the jury apparently did not believe him, at least not beyond a reasonable doubt, because it acquitted Respondent of murder, the primary charge Doser's testimony addressed.

Further, there is no constitutional "corroboration" requirement applicable to criminal defendants' testimony, though Respondent and his amicus must acknowledge that, by definition, informants placed in cells with defendants generally are themselves criminal defendants. Surely Respondent and his amicus are not intending to suggest that all criminal defendants are inherently unreliable and untrustworthy. If that is their suggestion, then any rule applied to informants logically should be extended also to criminal defendants generally. Because the right of a defendant to testify does not include the right to commit perjury, the logic of the amicus alternative proposal is that the courts should require "corroboration" before a criminal defendant is permitted to testify.

Respondent and his amicus are inviting this Court to create unique new rules for informant testimony without any basis in constitutional text, history, or precedent. Equally important, it is not at all obvious that the alternatives are workable or would improve rather than undermine the criminal justice system. For example, under Respondent's proposal, would a trial court have to hold a mini-trial—putting the main trial on hold—to hear evidence to determine whether the defendant committed perjury during his trial testimony (in order to decide, under Respondent's alternative, whether the prosecution could then use the testimony of an informant to contradict the defendant's "perjury")? Would such a proceeding itself have to be conducted with a jury which, after all, is charged with determining the credibility of witnesses in our constitutional system? Moreover, by what standard of proof would the trial court have to determine that a defendant's testimony was perjurious? And would a finding that perjury had been committed be given collateral estoppel effect in a subsequent criminal prosecution for perjury? These questions are merely illustrative, and hardly exhaustive, of the many problems and complexities that Respondent's alternative proposal would create.

Similarly, adopting a "corroboration" alternative also would create complex and difficult questions. Respondent's amicus necessarily cannot really answer questions such as what would constitute sufficient "corroboration" to justify the admission of informant testimony, or when and how a trial court would determine whether such corroboration existed. Indeed, Respondent's amicus acknowledges that existing corroboration policies have been created by state legislatures and prosecutor offices as a matter of policy, not by courts as a matter of constitutional law.

In recent years, particularly in the *Apprendi v. New Jersey*, 530 U.S. 466 (2000), line of cases, the Court has emphasized the primary and fundamental role that juries play in determining the critical facts in criminal cases. Respondent and his amicus seek to create rules of law that limit the jury's ability both to hear witnesses and to evaluate fully the credibility of those witnesses. Furthermore, there is no suggestion in this case that the jury was somehow fooled or duped by the prosecution; indeed, it appears that the jury was skeptical of Doser's testimony because it in fact acquitted Respondent of the murder charge, the focus of Doser's testimony.

Ultimately, there is no reason to think that the traditional safeguards—among them disclosure of any benefits an informant receives from the government, an opportunity by defendant's counsel for vigorous cross-examination of an informant, cautionary jury instructions by the trial judge, and faith in a jury's ability to judge credibility—are insufficient to protect against untruthful informant testimony. The Court need not and should not accept the invitation of Respondent and his amicus to substitute unproven policy judgments for settled jurisprudence.

Kansas v. Donnie Ray Ventris

556 U.S. 586 (2009)

Justice SCALIA delivered the opinion of the Court.

We address in this case the question whether a defendant's incriminating statement to a jailhouse informant, concededly elicited in violation of Sixth Amendment strictures, is admissible at trial to impeach the defendant's conflicting statement.

I

In the early hours of January 7, 2004, after two days of no sleep and some drug use, Rhonda Theel and respondent Donnie Ray Ventris reached an ill-conceived agreement to confront Ernest Hicks in his home. The couple testified that the aim of the visit was simply to investigate rumors that Hicks abused children, but the couple may have been inspired by the potential for financial gain: Theel had recently learned that Hicks carried large amounts of cash.

The encounter did not end well. One or both of the pair shot and killed Hicks with shots from a .38-caliber revolver, and the companions drove off in Hicks's truck with approximately $300 of his money and his cell phone. On receiving a tip from two friends of the couple who had helped transport them to Hicks's home, officers arrested Ventris and Theel and charged them with various crimes, chief among them murder and aggravated robbery. The State dropped the murder charge against Theel in exchange for her guilty plea to the robbery charge and her testimony identifying Ventris as the shooter.

Prior to trial, officers planted an informant in Ventris's holding cell, instructing him to "keep [his] ear open and listen" for incriminating statements. According to the informant, in response to his statement that Ventris appeared to have "something more serious weighing in on his mind," Ventris divulged that "[h]e'd shot this man in his head and in his chest" and taken "his keys, his wallet, about $350.00, and ... a vehicle."

At trial, Ventris took the stand and blamed the robbery and shooting entirely on Theel. The government sought to call the informant, to testify to Ventris's prior contradictory statement; Ventris objected. The State conceded that there was "probably a violation" of Ventris's Sixth Amendment right to counsel but nonetheless argued that the statement was admissible for impeachment purposes because the violation "doesn't give the Defendant ... a license to just get on the stand and lie." The trial court agreed and allowed the informant's testimony, but instructed the jury to "consider with caution" all testimony given in exchange for benefits from the State. The jury ultimately acquitted Ventris of felony murder and misdemeanor theft but returned a guilty verdict on the aggravated burglary and aggravated robbery counts.

The Kansas Supreme Court reversed the conviction, holding that "[o]nce a criminal prosecution has commenced, the defendant's statements made to an undercover informant surreptitiously acting as an agent for the State are not admissible at trial for any reason, including the impeachment of the defendant's testimony." 285 Kan. 595, 606, 176 P.3d 920, 928 (2008).

II

The Sixth Amendment, applied to the States through the Fourteenth Amendment, guarantees that "[i]n all criminal prosecutions, the accused shall ... have the Assistance of Counsel for his defence." The core of this right has historically been, and remains today, "the opportunity for a defendant to consult with an attorney and to have him investigate the case and prepare a defense for trial." We have held, however, that the right extends to having counsel present at various pretrial "critical" interactions between the defendant and the State, *United States v. Wade*, 388 U.S. 218 (1967), including the deliberate elicitation by law enforcement officers (and their agents) of statements pertaining to the charge, *Massiah v. United States*, 377 U.S. 201, 206 (1964). The State has conceded throughout these proceedings that Ventris's confession was taken in violation of *Massiah*'s dictates and was therefore not admissible in the prosecution's case in chief.... The only question we answer today is whether the State must bear the additional consequence of inability to counter Ventris's contradictory testimony by placing the informant on the stand.

A

Respondent argues that the Sixth Amendment's right to counsel is a "right an accused is to enjoy a[t] trial." The core of the right to counsel is indeed a trial right, ensuring that the prosecution's case is subjected to "the crucible of meaningful adversarial testing." *United States v. Cronic*, 466 U.S. 648, 656 (1984). But our opinions under the Sixth Amendment, as under the Fifth, have held that the right covers pretrial interrogations to ensure that police manipulation does not render counsel entirely impotent — depriving the defendant of "'effective representation by counsel at the only stage when legal aid and advice would help him.'"

Now that we are confronted with the question, we conclude that the *Massiah* right is a right to be free of uncounseled interrogation, and is infringed at the time of the interrogation. That, we think, is when the "Assistance of Counsel" is denied.

It is illogical to say that the right is not violated until trial counsel's task of opposing conviction has been undermined by the statement's admission into evidence. A defendant is not denied counsel merely because the prosecution has been permitted to introduce evidence of guilt — even evidence so overwhelming that the attorney's job of gaining an acquittal is rendered impossible. In such circumstances the accused continues to enjoy the assistance of counsel; the assistance is simply not worth much. The assistance of counsel has been denied, however, at the prior critical stage which produced the inculpatory evidence. Our cases acknowledge that reality in holding that the stringency of the warnings necessary for a waiver of the assistance of counsel varies according to "the usefulness of counsel to the accused at the particular [pretrial] proceeding." It is *that* deprivation which demands a remedy.

The United States [in an amicus brief] insists that "post-charge deliberate elicitation of statements without the defendant's counsel or a valid waiver of counsel is not intrinsically unlawful." That is true when the questioning is unrelated to charged crimes—the Sixth Amendment right is "offense specific." We have never said, however, that officers may badger counseled defendants about charged crimes so long as they do not use information they gain. The constitutional violation occurs when the uncounseled interrogation is conducted.

B

On the other side of the scale, preventing impeachment use of statements taken in violation of *Massiah* would add little appreciable deterrence. Officers have significant incentive to ensure that they and their informants comply with the Constitution's demands, since statements lawfully obtained can be used for all purposes rather than simply for impeachment. And the *ex ante* probability that evidence gained in violation of *Massiah* would be of use for impeachment is exceedingly small. An investigator would have to anticipate both that the defendant would choose to testify at trial (an unusual occurrence to begin with) *and* that he would testify inconsistently despite the admissibility of his prior statement for impeachment. Not likely to happen—or at least not likely enough to risk squandering the opportunity of using a properly obtained statement for the prosecution's case in chief.

In any event, even if "the officer may be said to have little to lose and perhaps something to gain by way of possibly uncovering impeachment material," we have multiple times rejected the argument that this "speculative possibility" can trump the costs of allowing perjurious statements to go unchallenged.

We hold that the informant's testimony, concededly elicited in violation of the Sixth Amendment, was admissible to challenge Ventris's inconsistent testimony at trial. The judgment of the Kansas Supreme Court is reversed, and the case is remanded for further proceedings not inconsistent with this opinion.

Justice STEVENS, with whom Justice GINSBURG joins, dissenting.

In this case, the State has conceded that it violated the Sixth Amendment as interpreted in *Massiah v. United States*, when it used a jailhouse informant to elicit a statement from the defendant. No *Miranda* warnings were given to the defendant, nor was he otherwise alerted to the fact that he was speaking to a state agent. Even though the jury apparently did not credit the informant's testimony, the Kansas Supreme Court correctly concluded that the prosecution should not be allowed to exploit its pretrial constitutional violation during the trial itself. The Kansas Court's judgment should be affirmed.

This Court's contrary holding relies on the view that a defendant's pretrial right to counsel is merely "prophylactic" in nature. The majority argues that any violation of this prophylactic right occurs solely at the time the State subjects a counseled defendant to an uncounseled interrogation, not when the fruits of the encounter are used against the defendant at trial. This reasoning is deeply flawed.

We have never endorsed the notion that the pretrial right to counsel stands at the periphery of the Sixth Amendment. To the contrary, we have explained that the pretrial period is "perhaps the most critical period of the proceedings" during which a defendant "requires the guiding hand of counsel." Placing the prophylactic label on a core Sixth Amendment right mischaracterizes the sweep of the constitutional guarantee.

When counsel is excluded from a critical pretrial interaction between the defendant and the State, she may be unable to effectively counter the potentially devastating, and potentially false,[57] evidence subsequently introduced at trial. Inexplicably, today's Court refuses to recognize that this is a constitutional harm. Yet in *Massiah,* the Court forcefully explained that a defendant is "denied the basic protections of the [Sixth Amendment] guarantee when there [is] used against him at his trial evidence of his own incriminating words" that were "deliberately elicited from him after he had been indicted and in the absence of counsel." Sadly, the majority has retreated from this robust understanding of the right to counsel.

---

57. The likelihood that evidence gathered by self-interested jailhouse informants may be false cannot be ignored. See generally Brief for National Association of Criminal Defense Lawyers as Amicus Curiae. Indeed, by deciding to acquit respondent of felony murder, the jury seems to have dismissed the informant's trial testimony as unreliable.

Chapter Ten

Police and Prosecutorial Misconduct

A. Readings

Russell Covey, *Police Misconduct as a Cause of Wrongful Convictions*

90 WASH. U. L. REV. 1133, 1137–61 (2013)

The Rampart and Tulia Exonerations

On December 16, 1997, the L.A.P.D. arrested police officer David Mack on charges of stealing $722,000 from a Los Angeles area Bank of America. Three months later, the department fired two other officers, Brian Hewitt and Daniel Lujan, for severely beating a handcuffed prisoner in an interrogation room. The common thread was that all three officers were either former or current members of the Rampart CRASH, or Community Resources Against Street Hoodlums, unit. Rampart is an area covering 7.9 square miles to the northwest of downtown Los Angeles. It is the most densely populated portion of Los Angeles, with 36,000 people per square mile, and is widely known as a locus of gang activity. At the same time, the Rampart CRASH unit had a reputation for operating in a largely autonomous fashion with little to no oversight. The arrest of Officer Mack and termination of Officers Hewitt and Lujan motivated L.A.P.D. Chief of Police Bernard C. Banks to form a special task force to investigate the Rampart CRASH unit.

Then, on March 2, 1998, six-and-a-half pounds of cocaine disappeared from an evidence room in Los Angeles. Within a week, the special task force investigators honed in on Los Angeles police officer Raphael Perez, a member of Rampart CRASH, as the primary suspect. A year later, trial on the charge ended with a hung jury. Shortly thereafter, Perez cut a deal with prosecutors, agreeing to cooperate with a government investigation of police wrongdoing in the Rampart CRASH unit. Perez worked with investigators over the next year, divulging over 4,000 pages of interrogation transcripts. Perez's testimony revealed police corruption on an unimagined scale, implicating police officers in wrongful killings, indiscriminate beatings and violence, theft, and drug dealing. Perez's testimony also implicated dozens of police officers in systematic acts of dishonest law enforcement, exposing hundreds of instances in which evidence or contraband was planted on suspects, false statements were coerced or fabricated, and police officers offered perjured testimony in court.

Perez's confessions prompted the L.A.P.D. to re-name its investigative task force the "Rampart Task Force." The Task Force was charged with corroborating Perez's allegations of corruption within Rampart CRASH. What followed was, in the words of one independent commission, one of the "worst police scandals in American history." Ultimately, the District Attorney was able to corroborate hundreds of Perez's allegations and the L.A.P.D. entered into a consent decree with the U.S. Department of Justice, submitting to federal oversight of departmental operations. As a result of the scandal, more than three hundred prisoners filed writs of habeas corpus seeking to overturn allegedly tainted convictions, and approximately 156 felony convictions were dismissed or overturned as a result of "Rampart related" writs, 110 of which were either initiated or unopposed by the District Attorney.

The extent of wrongdoing by the L.A.P.D., however, remains a mystery to this day largely due to the overall ineffectiveness of the L.A.P.D.'s internal investigation of the police force. Although Officer Perez claimed that "ninety percent of the officers that work CRASH, and not just Rampart CRASH, falsify a lot of information" and "put cases on people," no investigation or follow-up was ever undertaken to explore, or even clarify, those allegations. In speaking with an investigative panel, some officers, who spoke anonymously out of fear of retribution, expressed concerns that the department did not genuinely seek to uncover the extent of the corruption. In fact, the L.A.P.D. failed to produce a promised "after-action" report which, according to the department, was going to include "the exact nature and disposition of each allegation." Consequently, whatever the department may have uncovered about widespread corruption throughout the force remains outside the public domain.

In the spring of 2003, while the Rampart story was winding down, news of another major police scandal broke, this time not out of a major metropolitan police force but instead in the tiny west Texas town of Tulia, located in Swisher County. The Tulia operation began as a roundup of suspected drug dealers in the summer of 1999, but transformed into what some described as a wholesale assault on the black residents of Tulia. The operation was spearheaded by a freelance agent named Tom Coleman. Working undercover, Coleman claimed to have bought powder cocaine from more than 20% of the adult black residents of Tulia. In all, nearly fifty persons were convicted of selling drugs to Coleman, in most cases based solely on Coleman's uncorroborated testimony.

The first several Tulia defendants fought the drug charges at trial and were convicted and sentenced to draconian prison terms. After seeing the writing on the wall, however, most of the remaining defendants agreed to plead guilty. In all, forty-seven persons were charged and thirty-five were convicted. Of the twelve who were not convicted, several were placed on deferred adjudication.

As these cases were tried, however, it became increasingly evident that Coleman's testimony was not credible. Defense attorneys discovered that Coleman had been arrested on theft charges in a neighboring county and lied about it on his employment application to the task force. They also learned that Coleman had a history of employment problems, mental health problems, and significant unpaid debts. Worse still, it became increasingly evident that Coleman's bosses in Tulia, as well as the prosecutor in the Tulia cases, knew of Coleman's problems and lied about them under oath in the course of the Tulia trials.

After the Texas Court of Criminal Appeals remanded four of the Tulia convictions for evidentiary hearings on claims that the prosecutor had failed to turn over material exculpatory evidence as required by Brady v. Maryland, hearings were conducted before a different trial judge. In the course of the hearings, it became clear that Coleman had perjured himself on numerous occasions during the Tulia trials, and that other law enforcement officials may have done so as well. Ultimately, the state agreed to a global settlement with defense attorneys in which it stipulated that Coleman was not a credible witness, vacated every conviction obtained as a result of the sting operation without seeking new trials against any of the defendants, and provided $250,000 to be divided among the defendants. In exchange, the defendants agreed not to sue the county. The state judge who presided at the hearing found "that Mr. Coleman had engaged in 'blatant perjury' and was 'the most devious, nonresponsive law enforcement witness this court has witnessed in twenty-five years on the bench in Texas.'" Coleman was eventually tried and convicted of one count of perjury and sentenced to ten years probation.

Although the settlement was contingent on approval by the Court of Criminal Appeals, when that approval was not immediately forthcoming, the Texas legislature passed a bill "specifically authorizing" the judge "to grant bond to the defendants." Texas Governor Rick Perry then asked the Texas Board of Pardons and Paroles to review the cases. Pardons were granted to all thirty-five Tulia defendants convicted as a result of the sting operation. Two more individuals later were exonerated by courts.

Rampart and Tulia together account for nearly two hundred cases of wrongful conviction and represent two large sets of exonerations stemming from police corruption scandals. But these are not the only major scandals that have recently beset law enforcement organizations in the United States, or even in Texas. In Hearne, Texas, numerous cases in 2001 were dismissed following revelations that a drug task force was systematically targeting black residents in an effort, allegedly, to drive them from the community. As in Tulia, the evidence against the defendants in these cases consisted solely of the uncorroborated assertions of a single, unreliable, police informant. Although most cases were dismissed prior to conviction, some innocent defendants pleaded guilty before the police wrongdoing was exposed. A year later, in the so-called "Dallas Sheetrock scandal," at least thirty-nine criminal cases were dropped or dismissed after it was discovered that white powder allegedly recovered from criminal suspects and identified through field-tests as cocaine was actually ground up sheetrock packaged to look like cocaine. All of the victims in the scandal were blue-collar Mexican immigrants who spoke little or no English.

Another Tulia-like scandal erupted more recently in St. Charles Parish, Louisiana, where seventy narcotics cases made by a single undercover officer were dismissed following revelations that the undercover officer had lied under oath in a criminal investigation. Before the scandal broke, at least twenty persons in cases made by the undercover officer had already pled guilty. An even larger Rampart-style corruption case has unfolded in Camden, New Jersey. Other incidents have also grabbed recent headlines. Gross and Shaffer have identified twelve separate incidents involving group exonerations based on police misconduct involving exonerations of at least 1,100 people.

In short, Rampart and Tulia produced numerous exonerations and received a significant amount of national attention, but they are not unique. Revelations of large-scale police misconduct both preceded and post-dated them, suggesting that police misconduct leading to the wrongful conviction of innocent persons is a disturbingly common feature of the criminal justice system.

* * *

Of the two, the Rampart material provides the greatest insight into how police misconduct "on the ground" can trigger a disastrous chain of events for innocent persons directly resulting in criminal convictions. Because the writs filed on behalf of wrongly convicted Rampart defendants often included narrative accounts of the circumstances of arrest, the Rampart cases provide an illuminating glossary of the many ways that police misconduct can lead to wrongful convictions. Study of these cases in the aggregate provides a fairly detailed empirical picture of wrongful convictions resulting from dishonest policing. The data pertaining to the Tulia cases shows less variation in the factual circumstances surrounding the charges, primarily because of the relatively uniform way in which the Tulia convictions were generated: each Tulia defendant was convicted based almost exclusively on the uncorroborated testimony of a single corrupt undercover agent. However, the Tulia data permits useful observations about the adjudicative procedures in such cases, and deepens the data pool in this regard.

* * *

Police misconduct in these scandals took many forms. Police officers filed false police reports detailing observations of criminal conduct the defendants never engaged in, or describing circumstances that if true would have established criminal conduct. In most of the cases, police either physically planted drugs or weapons on the defendants and then lied about how they found the contraband, or simply misstated that they had found drugs or weapons when they had not. Police officers then testified to these same false facts at preliminary hearings and at trial in those rare cases that did not end in guilty pleas. For example, Emmanuel Chavez was arrested and ultimately convicted of possession of a firearm by a minor. In the arrest report, Officer Perez stated that "he and his partners observed" Emmanuel Chavez pass "a sawed-off shotgun" to another minor named Sergio Salcido. According to later evidence gathered by investigators, however, police never saw either minor handle a gun. Instead, Chavez and Salcido were stopped because police knew them to be members of a "tagging crew." As Perez frisked Salcido, a gun dropped down Salcido's pant leg and struck the pavement. The officers then made up a story that allowed them to charge Chavez as well as Salcido for possession of the gun.

Similar police misconduct led to the wrongful conviction of Diego Barrios. Barrios and several others were socializing in the parking lot of a Jack-In-the-Box fast food restaurant when a "police car drove up to the group and shined its high-beam lights on the group." The officers ordered everyone in the group to kneel down. They then searched and questioned each person. Four persons, including a juvenile by the name of Raymond C., were placed into a police car and taken to the police station. Unknown to the police, Raymond C. had a handgun in his possession at the time which he deposited, during the ride, behind the back seat of the squad car. Police discovered the gun after searching the car at the station and demanded to know who had dropped the gun. Raymond C. admitted the gun was his, but according to Barrios, "the officers said they did not 'want' a juvenile," and instead " 'put the gun' on Barrios." Barrios pled guilty to a charge of unlawful gun possession.

On a different occasion, police approached another group of youths in a parking lot. After police recovered a handgun from underneath a parked car, they arrested one of the youths and brought him to the station where they asked him, among other things, who owned the gun. When he failed to provide an answer, the interrogating officer "told him that he was going to jail for the gun and rubbed it against Lobos' fingers." Lobos pled guilty at his arraignment to a charge of unlawful possession of a firearm by a felon.

In these cases, contraband discovered by police in the possession of one person, or an unknown person, was attributed to others in order to permit an arrest to be made or to facilitate additional arrests. In other cases, police planted guns or drugs obtained elsewhere on suspects, or simply claimed that they found guns or drugs on suspects who in fact were not in possession of them. This is precisely what officers did in the Ovando case, where, after shooting Ovando, the officers planted a weapon on him picked up elsewhere to falsely implicate him in criminal conduct and cover up their own misdeeds.

Other examples include the case of Ivan Oliver, who was charged with unlawful possession of a gun after police raided a party at which he was present. In Oliver's case, police searched the residence where the party was held and located several guns. One officer then, investigators concluded, "arbitrarily decided who would be arrested for possessing them," while other "CRASH officers created scenarios accounting for the recovery of each gun and ... wrote the arrest report accordingly." In several cases, defendants did not even know what offenses they were alleged to have committed until long after being arrested. One defendant, who was charged with narcotics possession, stated that he "did not find out why he was being arrested until he got to the jail and asked a jailer to tell him what his 'pink slip' indicated."

Although present in every Rampart case, police perjury was not the sole cause of the false convictions. In some cases, police coerced an individual to make false statements inculpating the defendant. George Alfaro, for instance, was arrested for violating a gang injunction based on such evidence. According to police officers, Alfaro and two other suspects were arrested after police recovered a baggie of rock cocaine at the scene. The officers claimed that one of the suspects admitted that he possessed the drugs for sale. Rampart investigators, however, concluded that the drugs were planted at the scene, and the officers coerced the admission. As a result of the incident, Alfaro's probation was revoked and Alfaro was sentenced to two years in state prison.

In other cases, police simply falsely reported incriminating statements made by others. This happened in the case of Gregorio Lopez. Lopez and another man named Omar Alonso were arrested after police claimed they saw Alonso in possession of a magnetic key holder containing cocaine and Lopez attempt to discard a similar item. According to the arrest report, police searched Lopez and recovered a gun from his waistband. In fact, investigators found, the drugs said to belong to Lopez were planted, and the gun was found in his car rather than on his person. The prosecution's case was also bolstered by inculpatory statements allegedly made by Alonso. No such statements, it turns out, were ever made, nor did the officers administer Miranda warnings as they claimed to have done.

Several of the Rampart exonerees falsely confessed, or were reported to have done so. Clinton Harris, for example, was convicted of possession of a firearm by a felon after police reported that they had observed Harris wearing a gun in the waistband of his pants, and that he had admitted that the gun was his, saying "[d]amn, I knew I shouldn't have bought the gun. . . ." In fact, Harris never made any such statement. At the time of arrest Harris was seated on the couch of a friend's apartment. Police officers entered the apartment without consent and found a gun on a table. According to Officer Perez, they decided to attribute the gun to Harris "because he was an ex-con."

Delbert Carrillo was arrested after police officers allegedly "'noticed a large bulge in his front shirt pocket.'" The arresting officers explained in the police report:

> Knowing defendant to be on active parole and having a criminal history, we asked him what he had in his pocket (to ensure that it was not a weapon or narcotics). The defendant's expression went from that of being calm to nervous, and he hesitantly reached into his pocket and removed a clear plastic baggy containing approximately nine white paper bindles, the type routinely used to package rock cocaine, and stated, "its [sic] rocks." [W]e recovered the bag and found it to contain nine paper bindles, each one, containing approximately ten off-white wafers resembling rock cocaine.

After Carrillo was arrested, police obtained a signed statement reading, with original misspellings, as follows:

> I DelBert Carrillo contacted officer Cohan and BRehm to discouse a matter at the time I had cocane in my posseion. and Because I new them I thought It would not Be a proBlem. Officers then overed it in my Shirt pocket. DEC. I make this statement freely.

Carrillo was charged with possession for sale of cocaine base and ultimately pleaded guilty to an amended complaint that charged him with possession for sale of a controlled substance. He was sentenced to the statutory minimum term of two years. Carrillo later alleged that the drugs were planted and police officers coerced him into signing the statement by threatening to file additional charges against him if he refused. His conviction was vacated after the state discovered evidence corroborating Carrillo's account of the incident.

In short, then, the primary "cause" of false convictions in the Rampart and Tulia scandals was police perjury, some form of which was present in 100% of the cases. Innocent defendants who won exonerations primarily had been convicted in the first instance on the basis of the false reports and false testimony of corrupt police officers. That same police misconduct, however, was also responsible for the generation of other types of false evidence, including false witness statements and false confessions that supported the police officers' false reports and perjurious testimony in court.

After police perjury, the most common "causes" of false convictions were the false confessions generated through police misconduct. False confessions were present in about 13% of the Rampart cases. Interestingly, that figure is consistent with findings by Gross and Garrett on the approximate frequency of false confessions in wrongful conviction cases. While a substantial amount of commentary has focused on the problem of false confessions, and commentators have probed how innocent defendants might be induced to confess to crimes they did not commit, very little discussion exists regarding the problem of entirely fabricated confessions. Yet, as the Rampart cases show, some false confessions "occur" simply because police lie about what suspects actually said.

* * *

The data suggests that efforts to reform the criminal justice system in order to prevent wrongful convictions should include greater focus on the prevention of police misconduct. During the last decade, a major effort has been made to improve the reliability of lineup identification procedures. The revised data set suggests that those concerned with decreasing the incidence of wrongful convictions should devote similar attention to enhancing the integrity and reliability of police officer statements and testimony.

Peter A. Joy, *The Relationship between Prosecutorial Misconduct and Wrongful Convictions: Shaping Remedies for a Broken System*
2006 Wis. L. Rev. 399, 399–427 (2006)

With impunity, prosecutors across the country have violated their oaths and the law, committing the worst kinds of deception in the most serious of cases.

They have prosecuted black men, hiding evidence the real killers were white. They have prosecuted a wife, hiding evidence her husband committed suicide. They have prosecuted parents, hiding evidence their daughter was killed by wild dogs.

They do it to win.

They do it because they won't get punished.

They have done it to defendants who came within hours of being executed, only to be exonerated.

Introduction

Citing malfeasance on the part of some prosecutors across the country, two journalists researched thousands of court files and documented hundreds of homicide cases that were reversed because of prosecutors' misconduct that denied the accused fair trials. Since that exposé, the growing number of exonerated persons who were wrongfully convicted due, at least in part, to prosecutorial misconduct provides us with a lens through which we can view the shortcomings of both the current norms guiding prosecutors and the remedies for addressing prosecutorial misconduct. Although some of the other factors leading to wrongful convictions, such as mistaken identification, are more prevalent, prosecutorial misconduct is the most troubling, not only because it occurs so frequently, but for both normative and practical reasons as well.

If one agrees that the innocent should not be convicted, then we need to explore ameliorative actions to reduce prosecutorial misconduct as a cause of wrongful convictions. The starting point is to understand the institutional conditions that facilitate prosecutorial misconduct. Once we understand the conditions contributing to prosecutorial misconduct, achievable steps to remedy those conditions can take place.

My thesis is that prosecutorial misconduct is not chiefly the result of isolated instances of unprincipled choices or the failure of character on the part of some prosecutors. Rather, prosecutorial misconduct is largely the result of three institutional conditions: vague ethics rules that provide ambiguous guidance to prosecutors; vast discretionary authority with little or no transparency; and inadequate remedies for prosecutorial misconduct, which create perverse incentives for prosecutors to engage in, rather than refrain from, prosecutorial misconduct. These three conditions converge to create uncertain norms and a general lack of accountability for how prosecutors view and carry out their ethical and institutional obligations.

I. Understanding Prosecutorial Misconduct and Its Relationship to Wrongful Convictions

In *Berger v. United States*,[58] Justice Sutherland defined prosecutorial misconduct as "overstepp[ing] the bounds of that propriety and fairness which should characterize the conduct of such an officer in the prosecution of a criminal offense." In the decision, Justice Sutherland identified a laundry list of misconduct by the prosecutor at Berger's trial including:

> misstating the facts in his cross-examination of witnesses; of putting into the mouths of such witnesses things which they had not said; of suggesting by his questions that statements had been made to him personally out of court, in respect of which no proof was offered; of pretending to understand that a witness had said something which he had not said and persistently cross-examining the witness upon that basis; of assuming prejudicial facts

---

58. Berger v. United States, 295 U.S. 78 (1935).

not in evidence; of bullying and arguing with witnesses; and in general, of conducting himself in a thoroughly indecorous and improper manner.

* * *

In addition to the types of prosecutorial misconduct the Supreme Court identified in *Berger*, the Court has identified other examples, including: prosecutors knowingly using perjured testimony, suppressing evidence favorable to the accused that might have led to a not guilty verdict, and misstating the law in argument to the jury. Lower courts have identified additional examples of prosecutorial misconduct, including: prosecutors threatening witnesses with loss of immunity if they testify for the defense, ignoring the obligation to disclose to the defense special treatment or promises of immunity given to a government witness in exchange for testimony against the accused, failing to remedy or disclose the government's presentation of false evidence, making inflammatory remarks to the jury based on racial bias against the accused, presenting perjured testimony to the grand jury, and a host of other situations where the prosecutor ignores the obligation to accord procedural justice to the accused.

In the years since the Court's decision in *Berger*, prosecutorial misconduct has proven to be one of the most common factors that causes or contributes to wrongful convictions. An initial study of the first sixty-two persons exonerated by DNA evidence found some degree of prosecutorial misconduct in twenty-six cases, and a subsequent study of seventy persons exonerated by DNA evidence found some degree of prosecutorial misconduct in thirty-four cases. Studies of DNA exonerations have identified wrongful convictions based on prosecutorial misconduct that included: suppressing exculpatory evidence, knowingly using false testimony, fabricating evidence, coercing witnesses, making false statements to the jury, and engaging in improper closing arguments. Similarly, grand jury and journalistic studies into wrongful convictions have found that prosecutorial misconduct is a leading cause of wrongful convictions.

From a normative perspective, we strive to design a criminal justice system that protects the innocent and convicts the guilty. The very concept of justice requires that the innocent should not be prosecuted, and, if mistakenly prosecuted, they should go free. The presumption of innocence, the right to remain silent, the right to a public trial by an impartial jury, and the requirement that the prosecutor must prove each case beyond a reasonable doubt all reinforce the public's perception that the criminal justice system operates under the precautionary principle announced by Blackstone more than two hundred years ago: "better that ten guilty persons escape than that one innocent suffer." We teach school children this principle of criminal justice, and law students have it "drilled into [their] head[s] over and over."

The unique role of the prosecutor is a key component in the social compact that requires our justice system to protect the innocent. As the Supreme Court explained, the prosecutor "is in a peculiar and very definite sense the servant of the law, the twofold aim of which is that guilt shall not escape or innocence suffer." Rather than simply acting as a partisan advocate seeking convictions, the ethics rules admonish a prosecutor to be a "minister of justice" and to seek justice. In this role as a minister of justice, the prosecutor has the responsibility "not simply ... of an advocate," but to adopt a somewhat neutral stance "to see that the defendant is accorded procedural justice and that guilt is decided upon the basis of the sufficient evidence."

Yet, from a normative perspective, there are some societal pressures working against a prosecutor's duty to justice. At the state level, nearly all chief prosecutors are elected, thus directly accountable to the public. Despite the ideal that the criminal justice system should protect the innocent and convict only the guilty, public support for the rights of the accused is not clear. Some studies show that the public believes "the courts undo the work of the police to get criminals off the street[s]," and although a majority of African-Americans are concerned with the rights of the accused "only 29 percent of Whites held the view that disregarding a defendant's rights was a problem." On the other hand, the number of Americans who oppose the death penalty because of the potential for wrongful convictions has more than doubled in recent years.

Even if public support for protecting the accused is ambivalent or weak, the Supreme Court has acknowledged that "the moral force of the criminal law" relies on safeguards that keep the innocent from being convicted. From a practical perspective, this requires the prosecutor to monitor how the enormous resources of the government are used in each prosecution. In this role, the prosecutor has a duty to ensure that police investigators and government witnesses act properly and testify truthfully. Thus, the prosecutor bears oversight responsibility for procedures for searches, obtaining confessions, the making of eyewitness identifications, introducing lab reports, and using jailhouse informants and other cooperating witnesses. The courts even give standing to the prosecutor in some instances to raise a claim that the defense counsel is failing to provide competent representation. For example, a prosecutor may raise a claim if a defense lawyer seeks to represent the accused, but has a conflict of interest based on the representation of a codefendant or government witness.

Practically speaking, the prosecutor is the first line of defense against many of the common factors that lead to wrongful convictions. The prosecutor's supervisory authority to evaluate the quality and quantity of evidence holds the potential for assuring the accused both procedural and, when the accused is actually innocent, substantive justice. When prosecutors do not critically examine the evidence against the accused to ensure its trustworthiness, or fail to comply with discovery and other obligations to the accused, rather than act as ministers of justice, they administer injustice.

It may be impossible to know with any certainty the reasons for prosecutorial misconduct in every case where a prosecutor ignores legal and ethical obligations in order to gain a conviction. But whatever the motivation, the misconduct is wrong. If the prosecutorial misconduct occurs to frame an innocent person, it is corrupt. It is still inexcusable if it is instead designed to facilitate the conviction of a person the prosecutor believes is guilty. It is wrong because each act of prosecutorial misconduct is a rejection both of the prosecutor's oath of office to uphold the law and oath as a lawyer to adhere to ethical responsibilities. It is wrong because prosecutorial misconduct undermines the due process afforded to the accused. It often results in relevant evidence being kept from the fact finder and contributes to wrongful convictions. It is also wrong because placing a thumb on the scales of justice not only invades the province of the fact finder but, if the prosecutor is mistaken, it may result in an innocent person going to prison and the actual wrongdoer remaining free to commit future crimes.

II. Understanding the Prosecutor's Role and Developing More Effective Ethics Rules for Prosecutors

Prosecutors wield enormous power in the criminal justice system. They decide whom to prosecute and what crimes to charge. They chart pretrial and trial strategies. And they decide, or at least greatly influence, what the sentence will be through charging decisions, plea-bargaining, or sentencing guideline choices. Because the prosecutor represents the government whose goal is "not that it shall win a case, but that justice shall be done," there is a need for special ethics rules to govern the conduct of prosecutors. Yet, the history of ethics rules directed toward prosecutors demonstrates that the ethics rules generally have been limited to nonspecific pronouncements that the prosecutor has "special" responsibilities, different from other lawyers, and that the prosecutor should "seek justice."

* * *

[T]he ABA Prosecution Function Standards provide examples of the types of norms that should be considered in clearly defining the prosecutor's ethical duties. The Standards address the various functions of the prosecutor, and cover all phases of the prosecutor's work, including investigation, the charging decision, plea discussions, trial, and sentencing. The ABA states that the Standards are "to be used as a guide to professional conduct and performance," but to date the ABA has not promoted adoption of the Standards at the state level as it had the Model Code and the Model Rules. Nevertheless, the Standards are a rich source of thoughtful requirements that, if incorporated into the ethics rules, would greatly improve upon the minimal guidance currently provided to prosecutors. The Supreme Court has relied upon the Defense Function Standards as norms of practice or guides to determining what is reasonable, and the Prosecution Function Standards similarly set forth reasonable expectations. A brief discussion of some of the Standards will illustrate this point.

The Standards state that a prosecutor shall not "knowingly fail to disclose to the grand jury evidence which tends to negate guilt or mitigate the offense." A norm such as this would provide the grand jury with sufficient evidence to evaluate whether there is sufficient probable cause to issue an indictment. Other provisions in the Standards require the prosecutor not only to have probable cause before instituting a criminal charge but also to have "sufficient admissible evidence to support a conviction" in order to permit the pendency of criminal charges, and prohibit a supervisor from compelling a subordinate "to prosecute a case in which he or she has a reasonable doubt about the guilt of the accused." These provisions are aimed at ensuring that once charges are brought the prosecutor will not pursue them when there are doubts as to the sufficiency of the evidence.

In terms of disclosure obligations to the accused, the Standards require "timely disclosure ... at the earliest feasible opportunity, of the existence of all evidence or information which tends to negate the guilt of the accused or mitigate the offense charged or which would tend to reduce the punishment of the accused." And, "[a] prosecutor should not intentionally avoid pursuit of evidence because he or she believes it will damage the prosecution's case or aid the accused." These obligations would prohibit two practices that some prosecutors employ: withholding exculpatory evidence until the eve of trial, or indeed during trial, when the defense has too little time to develop the evidence; and failing to follow investigatory leads that may exonerate the accused.

With regard to advocacy obligations during trial, the Standards prohibit the prosecutor from using cross-examination to discredit or undermine a truthful witness, asking a question that implies the existence of a fact in which the prosecutor does not have a good faith belief, and making arguments to the jury that would divert them from deciding the case on the evidence. Each of these provisions reinforces the prosecutor's duty to ensure procedural justice for the accused and to be concerned with truth more than winning during the trial process.

As these examples from the Standards indicate, there is room for much more guidance and clearer ethical obligations for prosecutors. Some states have incorporated some aspects of the Standards into their versions of Model Rule 3.8, but no state has done the "ground up review" recommended in the Report on Model Rule 3.8. Until each state does such a review, prosecutors will continue to operate under existing ethics rules that provide minimal guidance. As the following Part discusses, in addition to the minimal ethics rules, the prosecutor often has few internal guideposts or other explicit legal requirements defining how to discharge duties and exercise prosecutorial discretion.

III. Increasing Transparency and Setting Clearer Limits on Prosecutorial Discretion

The prosecutor has a great deal of discretion, and in many areas a prosecutor exercises this discretion with little or no oversight or transparency. For example, a prosecutor has discretion over the evidence to present to a grand jury or in a preliminary hearing, and a prosecutor is not required to present any exculpatory evidence in either proceeding. Similarly, a prosecutor has discretion under Brady and through most state discovery rules to make the determination of what constitutes exculpatory evidence, and when to disclose it. In these and other instances, the prosecutor makes these decisions in secret, based on personal judgment that often is not subject to any established guidelines or public oversight.

* * *

Prosecutors' offices that do not have a written manual or set of guidelines addressing the exercise of discretion would benefit from creating such a document and making it accessible to the public. Such steps would help to establish norms in the offices that could be subject to review and, when necessary, enforcement. As a recent study into police integrity by the Department of Justice's National Institute of Justice found, having a "culture of integrity, as defined by clearly understood and implemented policies and rules, may be more important in shaping the ethics … than hiring the 'right' people." This finding is consistent with studies of lawyer ethics that the ethical culture of the law office is critical to the ethical behavior of lawyers.

In addition, prosecutors' offices should consider two recommendations that the National Institute of Justice study found important to enhancing police integrity that would appear equally applicable to prosecutors' offices. First, it is important "to consistently address relatively minor offenses with the appropriate discipline" so that one "may infer that major offenses, too, are likely to be disciplined." Second, "disclose the disciplinary process and resulting discipline to public scrutiny."

Implementing internal policies that value ethical conduct, and implementing and enforcing internal discipline when those norms are violated, would go a long way toward addressing the issue of prosecutorial misconduct. In the absence of such policies, prosecutors simply do not know the limits of their authority, nor do they have guidance on how to exercise discretion. Without internal controls, especially when external controls, such as the ethics rules for prosecutors, are incomplete and underenforced, it is easy for the prosecutor to value winning over ensuring fairness for the accused.

Internal controls, though, are unlikely to be enough. Innocence commissions, state supreme courts, and legislatures should consider changes in some areas, such as the prosecutor's discovery obligation and use of informants and other cooperating witnesses who receive something of value from the prosecutor. For example, an open file discovery obligation would help to eliminate one of the major forms of prosecutorial misconduct—the suppression of material evidence, which is a leading cause of wrongful convictions. Under an open file discovery regime, the prosecutor could still seek a protective order to withhold some information from the defense counsel, but such a system would require a court to review the request.

With regard to the use of informants, requiring the prosecutor to file a pretrial notice, much like a notice of alibi that the accused is required to file, could help stem abuses.…

IV. Creating More Accountability and Effective Remedies for Prosecutorial Misconduct

Studies of wrongful convictions have demonstrated that when prosecutorial misconduct caused or contributed to a wrongful conviction, the prosecutors involved were rarely disciplined, either internally or through external bodies. Additionally, prosecutors normally have immunity from civil lawsuits, which limits their personal liability for bad acts. And appellate courts impose strict standards of review and rarely reverse a conviction based on prosecutorial conduct, usually finding the misconduct to constitute harmless error. These factors have led courts and commentators to observe that current restraints on prosecutorial misconduct "are either meaningless or nonexistent."

The general lack of accountability for prosecutorial misconduct has also been demonstrated by various studies and is the subject of much debate among commentators. As one commentator remarked, there is "the human tendency to push margins when there are no sufficiently demanding external controls." In addition, psychological literature demonstrates that when one is not held accountable for decisions several biases come into play that negatively affect the quality of those decisions. Thus, the overall lack of accountability is a condition contributing to prosecutorial misconduct.

The lack of oversight and accountability for prosecutorial misconduct needs to be addressed by anyone interested in remedying prosecutorial misconduct as a factor contributing to wrongful convictions. A more proactive approach is needed. Prosecutors' offices should be required to implement a system of graduated discipline each time there is a finding by a trial judge or appellate court of prosecutorial misconduct. Bar disciplinary authorities should implement a system to review reported instances of prosecutorial misconduct and, when they deem it appropriate, conduct investigations or recommend discipline. Without reasonable attempts to exercise internal and external controls on the conduct of prosecutors, prosecutorial misconduct will continue to contribute to future wrongful convictions.

Kara MacKillop and Neil Vidmar, *Decision-Making in the Dark: How Pre-Trial Errors Change the Narrative in Criminal Jury Trials*
90 Chi.-Kent L. Rev. 957, 970–72 (2015)

How do Brady and other evidentiary issues impact juror decision-making? Unfortunately, probably more than judges and prosecutors want to acknowledge. The obvious problem is that in some wrongful conviction cases the jury was served an incomplete or misleading set of facts and expected to essentially play "choose your own adventure"—filling in the holes in the narrative with their own knowledge, experiences, and biases.

A recent exoneration litigated by the Duke Wrongful Convictions Clinic (Duke Clinic) presents an interesting story of a case predicated on just these types of issues. LaMonte Armstrong was convicted of first-degree murder and sentenced to life in prison in August 1995. The crime charged was the July 1988 murder of Ms. Ernestine Compton, a faculty member at North Carolina A&T University and a neighbor of Mr. Armstrong's family. Mr. Armstrong emerged as a suspect as a result of a CrimeStoppers call made by a distant acquaintance of Armstrong, Mr. Charles Blackwell. The police soon interviewed Armstrong by phone, then three months later in person, during which he mentioned that he had received a few phone calls from Mr. Blackwell asking Mr. Armstrong for information about the case. Mr. Armstrong denied any knowledge of the murder, both to the police in the interviews and to Mr. Blackwell during these odd phone calls. Post-conviction investigation would later reveal that the investigating officers, in fact, orchestrated the phone calls, as well as a recorded drop-in visit from Mr. Blackwell.

For the next six years, no further interaction occurred between the police and Mr. Armstrong regarding the Compton murder. However, in 1994, the police took an inexplicably renewed interest in the case, and the lead detective and the then-assistant district attorney decided to file charges against Mr. Blackwell as "a participant" in Ms. Compton's murder based on information he fabricated or otherwise gleaned through his repeated contacts with the investigating officers. With no apparent physical evidence at hand, Mr. Blackwell was plucked from prison in Person County, returned to Greensboro, and charged with the murder of Ms. Compton in March of 1994. In April, Mr. Armstrong was arrested and charged as well, presumably because of Mr. Blackwell's statements. Mr. Blackwell eventually pled guilty to accessory to murder and agreed to a five-year sentence. Mr. Armstrong consistently denied involvement in the crime, refused two plea offers from the State (for sentences of twenty and fifteen years), and was subsequently tried, convicted, and sentenced to life in 1996.

With the absence of any physical evidence connecting either defendant to this crime, the State's case rested on creating a narrative through witness testimony. The prosecution's theory was that Mr. Armstrong, who had known the victim for many years, was in the habit of borrowing money from her and when she refused to give him money on this occasion, Mr. Armstrong became enraged and murdered her. The key witnesses included Mr. Blackwell and three other incentivized witnesses, including two jail inmates, all of whom received some favorable treatment in exchange for their testimony. Of course, the jury heard Mr. Blackwell testify that he had pled guilty to playing a role in the murder and was present at the scene with Mr. Armstrong right up until the murder occurred. One witness testified to seeing Mr. Armstrong and Mr. Blackwell leaving the scene. The other two witnesses testified that Mr. Armstrong confessed to each of them, on separate occasions while jailed together, that he had committed the murder. Although there essentially was no other evidence, it was reasonable, given the available data and a fairly simple storyline, that the jury could easily develop a rational narrative leading to a guilty verdict.

Unfortunately for those jurors, they were denied access to significant evidence ranging from the basic facts of the case to the troublesome realities surrounding each of the key witnesses. Brady violations included nondisclosure of witness statements that established a different time frame for the murder — one that inconveniently coincided with a solid alibi for Mr. Armstrong. Additionally, the state withheld evidence that directly contradicted the prosecution's theory of the case. The victim actually did lend money to the young men in her neighborhood on occasion, and she kept records of those loans on her refrigerator. However, Mr. Armstrong's name was not on any of these lists, and there was no evidence he had ever borrowed money from her.

Also, the state failed to disclose the entirety of the detectives' relationship with Mr. Blackwell, including evidence that his story changed significantly over a number of interviews and included innumerable inaccuracies; that he was paid cash on multiple occasions to obtain incriminating statements from Mr. Armstrong; that recordings of Mr. Armstrong's repeated and consistent denials existed; and that Mr. Blackwell, as well as the other three informants, were provided other incentives for their testimony. Furthermore, each of the three jailhouse informants, including the one who claimed to witness Mr. Armstrong and Mr. Blackwell at the scene, were first in contact with the police regarding this case more than five years after the crime, and only after the police had set their sights on Mr. Armstrong. Additionally, the police denied the existence of alternative suspects at trial, though the Duke Clinic's review of their files indicated otherwise.

Perhaps it is fair to say that any of these issues, individually, could be considered "harmless" in terms of deciding Mr. Armstrong's guilt and each was, in fact, denied on direct appeal on that basis. However, it is disingenuous to assume that none of the twelve jurors would have viewed this case differently, and would have developed a different narrative, given any or all of this additional evidence. Taken from the jurors' perspectives, there is little question that Mr. Blackwell's plea deal and admission of involvement in the crime provided him otherwise unwarranted credibility. Still, had the jurors heard the totality of the background of the case it seems possible, if not likely, that they would have at least developed a different and more accurate narrative, if not a different verdict.

Ironically, Armstrong's case was not resolved on the basis of any of the evidentiary issues discussed above. The Duke Clinic managed to encourage cooperation from the current police department and district attorney, and, in 2012, they reran prints found at the scene. In a stroke of unbelievable luck, the actual perpetrator's prints had been entered into the system just a few weeks before, and thus, after languishing as an "unknown" palm print over the murdered Ms. Compton's body for years, the mystery was solved. The State agreed to release Mr. Armstrong.

Unfortunately, as in other exonerations, the evidentiary issues did not make the front page, or the pages of precedent. Although the Armstrong case is a remarkable example of justice gone awry, the reality is that an argument can be made that the jury still did its job. Given an "admitted" co-conspirator as a key witness, multiple "confession" witnesses, a plausible if unproven motive, and little else to go on, the jurors had little choice but to develop a narrative that encompassed all those details. That, combined with a natural bias toward the prosecutor's position resulted in a supportable, if entirely incorrect, verdict.

Jon B. Gould, Julia Carrano, Richard A. Leo, and Katie Hail-Jares, *Predicting Erroneous Convictions*
99 Iowa L. Rev. 471, 494–502 (2014)

[*Editor's note:* In this study, the authors examined the factors that statistically explain why an innocent defendant, once indicted, ends up erroneously convicted rather than released. The analysis identified several predictors that distinguish erroneous convictions and near misses, the most significant of which were the age and criminal history of the defendant, punitiveness of the state, *Brady* violations, forensic error, weak defense, weak prosecution case, family defense witness, non-intentional misidentification, and lying by a non-eyewitness.]

[These predictors] help explain why an innocent defendant's case, after indictment, is either dismissed or leads to an erroneous conviction. These factors include several of the traditional legal sources of erroneous convictions as well as sociological (but not procedural) variables, suggesting that the difference in case outcome for an innocent defendant is the result of a relatively complex and diverse process.

* * *

The Prosecution's Case: Weak Facts, Brady Violations, and False Non-Eyewitness Testimony

Of all the statistically significant factors that harm an innocent defendant, a weak prosecution case is hardest to explain. Intuitively, we might expect the opposite — that cases with weaker evidence against the defendant would be more likely to end in dismissal or acquittal. But in fact, a qualitative assessment of the cases revealed a number of reasons for our finding. Many of our erroneous conviction cases lacked good evidence from the start. In a typical scenario, the only inculpatory evidence was a microscopic hair comparison and an identification of the defendant by the rape victim, who admitted she only saw the perpetrator briefly in the dark. This type of evidence is relatively difficult for the defense to combat — the hair and face could be his — and the lack of alternative evidence to evaluate makes it difficult for the prosecution to uncover a mistake. By contrast, in the near misses, the inculpatory evidence may seem stronger on its face — a victim who identifies the perpetrator by name or a supposed DNA match. But it might actually be easier for either the prosecution or the defense to debunk this type of "conclusive" evidence with, for example, proof that the victim is lying or that the DNA sample was mislabeled. In addition, more pieces of evidence in a case means that there is more for defense counsel to attack or for the prosecution to use to find an alternative suspect.

Weak facts may also encourage prosecutors to engage in certain behaviors designed to bolster the case, which our statistics show help predict an erroneous conviction. In several of our erroneous convictions, a prosecutor, convinced of the defendant's guilt despite a lack of conclusive proof, failed to recognize and turn over exculpatory evidence or enlisted a snitch or other non-eyewitness to provide dubious corroborating testimony. These types of actions compound, rather than rectify, previous errors or misconduct in the case.

Specifically, the prosecution's failure to turn over exculpatory evidence severely harms the system's ability to self-correct from initial errors because it hamstrings the defense and reduces the effectiveness of the jury's decision-making process. For example, a prosecutor, convinced of the defendant's guilt, may withhold what she considers to be a "red herring" from the defense — such as a report of another suspect seen in the neighborhood. Of course, if she is correct and the defendant is really guilty, then the harm may be minimal. But if her judgment is incorrect, she has deprived the other participants in the system (i.e., defense attorney, judge, and jury) from forming an alternative opinion. By contrast, when prosecution, police, and defense attorneys have the opportunity to fully evaluate both sides' evidence, the innocent defendant stands a better chance of achieving justice.

In addition, our finding that intentionally false statements by a non-eyewitness predict an erroneous conviction suggests that police and prosecutors may rely on questionable testimony to obtain a conviction in cases with weak facts. Lying non-eyewitnesses include jailhouse informants and snitches. Thus, our results partially support prior literature that argues snitch testimony plays a substantial role in producing erroneous convictions for the obvious reason—there are strong incentives and few disincentives for the snitch to lie. However, because snitch testimony alone was not significant in our quantitative analysis, our research indicates that the danger of lying non-eyewitness testimony is not limited to instances where money or reduced sentencing is offered to jailhouse informants, but can include scenarios in which family, friends, co-workers, or neighbors want to hurt the defendant or cast suspicion away from the real perpetrator. Regardless of whether the false evidence is from a jailhouse informant or another type of non-eyewitness, our qualitative analysis revealed that such testimony is particularly dangerous because it is often specifically elicited by the prosecution when case facts are weak, which means the state may not be inclined to rigorously vet it in the same way as it would for other types of evidence.

Valena Beety, *Changing the Culture of Disclosure and Forensics*
73 Wash. & Lee L. Rev. Online 580, 581–82 (2017)

Joseph Buffey was 19 years old when, on the advice of his attorney, he pled guilty to a rape and robbery he did not commit. Only afterward did he learn that the DNA evidence exonerating him of the crime, and inculpating the true perpetrator, was available to prosecutors at the time Joe pled guilty. Thirteen years later, Joe was finally released from prison when the West Virginia Supreme Court of Appeals ruled the prosecution should have disclosed the exculpatory DNA evidence pre-trial.

This small case from West Virginia is the first decision nationally to require pre-trial disclosure of Brady material. The criminal justice system failed Joseph Buffey. But does blame fall on the prosecutors who failed to disclose the exculpatory DNA evidence and violated their duties under Brady? Or does it fall on the defense attorney who pressured Joe to take a plea deal and never followed up on requesting the forensic results?

* * *

The Supreme Court may ultimately determine that when counsel fails to request a Daubert hearing or query forensic evidence pre-trial, this dereliction is equally as damaging as failing to cross-examine experts at trial. The determination that counsel is effective, or not, is tied to "reasonableness under prevailing processional norms," and those norms are changing.

* * *

A. Prosecutorial Disclosure Pre-Trial

Prosecutorial culture, on the other hand, appears slower to change.... When prosecutors are the only individuals with full access to the forensic findings and the underlying methods and files, the same bias and tunnel vision that plagues prosecutors in their refusal to re-examine cases post-conviction can likewise play a detrimental role in the initial prosecution.

Our court system is now dependent on plea bargains to function. As Judge Rakoff of the Southern District of New York remarked, the plea bargaining system is unjust, excessive, and "so totally untransparent it is going to lead to some serious mistakes." These mistakes have already been made: the National Registry of Exonerations has found that 40% of people exonerated in 2015 were convicted based on taking a guilty plea; these cases range from drug crimes to homicides. One easy and effective solution to more informed plea agreements is open case-file discovery. A closed-file system exacerbates timing concerns and disclosure issues by allowing prosecutors to only produce critical evidence on the eve of, or at, trial.

In response to wrongful convictions caused by prosecutorial misconduct, the Texas legislature passed the Michael Morton Act in 2013 requiring open file discovery. The Act requires prosecutors to disclose any information favorable to the defense, including exculpatory, impeaching, and mitigating evidence. This disclosure is required "as soon as practicable" after the prosecution receives a request, and extends even after conviction. This Act serves as an example of open-file discovery, and its implementation has highlighted resistance by some prosecutors to comply. Indeed, the State Bar of Texas recently issued an ethics opinion chastising prosecutors who attempt to circumvent the Act by requiring defendants give up discovery rights in exchange for a plea offer.

Perhaps these prosecutors are concerned because in cases of a plea agreement, the prosecutor may not have yet examined the case as fully as she would in preparation for trial, and may not have even discovered Brady evidence, particularly forensic evidence. Federal Rule of Criminal Procedure Rule 16 provides prosecutors with some discovery leeway for forensics. Rule 16 only requires discovery of scientific reports and examinations if such evidence "is material to preparing the defense" or "the government intends to use the item in its case-in-chief at trial." At the time of a plea, a prosecutor may only have given a cursory glance at crime lab results.

The expectation of prosecutors is changing. Joseph Buffey's case is particularly instructive as the first coherent opinion requiring *Brady* disclosure of exculpatory— not impeachment—evidence during plea negotiations before trial. While the U.S. Supreme Court has ruled impeachment evidence does not need to be disclosed in plea negotiations, the Court has not ruled on exculpatory evidence. The West Virginia Supreme Court of Appeals ruled that the constitutional due process rights in Brady extend to the plea negotiation stage of criminal proceedings. The Court found "that the DNA results were favorable, suppressed, and material"; thus nondisclosure violated Buffey's due process rights and was prejudicial. In Justice Loughry's concurrence, he stated that *Brady* disclosure requirements "extend to evidence in the State's control that is favorable to the defendant regardless of whether a plea agreement or trial ensues." Furthermore, the Court found that the evidence does not need to be exonerative, and the standard for materiality "does not require a demonstration by a preponderance that disclosure of the suppressed evidence would have resulted ultimately in the defendant's acquittal."

B. Prosecutorial Ethical Obligations Post-Conviction

When discussing prosecutorial disclosure, prosecutors face a different ethical standard than defense attorneys. Prosecutors do not represent an individual client; rather, they represent the state and the government. The duty of a prosecutor is to ensure justice, even if that means "losing" an individual case. Under the ABA Rules of Professional Conduct 3.8:

> [A] prosecutor has the responsibility of a minister of justice and not simply that of an advocate. This responsibility carries with it specific obligations to see that the defendant is accorded procedural justice, that guilt is decided upon the basis of sufficient evidence, and that special precautions are taken to prevent and rectify the conviction of innocent persons.

This responsibility requires disclosure of evidence that helps a defendant and undermines the state's case.

In 2008, the ABA amended Rule 3.8 to affirmatively require a prosecutor to disclose evidence of a defendant's innocence found after the conviction. A minister of justice seeks the truth whether before or after a conviction. And yet while the fear of wrongful convictions has galvanized defense attorneys to advocate more robustly for clients and has led courts to chastise a lack of defense, prosecutors often remain planted all the more firmly in their original positions. Instead of "seek[ing] to remedy the conviction," prosecutors challenge the testing of DNA evidence, argue against its relevancy, and often re-bring charges if a conviction is reversed in court. Indeed, less than half the states have adopted—or even considered—Rule 3.8 (g) and (h) for state law. Prosecutors proclaim the amendments are insulting and resent the insinuation of poor behavior.

Insinuations? In Joseph Buffey's case, prosecutors re-filed the exact same charges as soon as the West Virginia Supreme Court of Appeals vacated them—even after they had prosecuted and convicted the true perpetrator, identified by DNA, of the same single-assailant crime. Instead of following Rule 3.8's admonition that "guilt is decided upon the basis of sufficient evidence" and that prosecutors are obliged to "rectify the conviction of innocent persons," prosecutors in Clarksburg, West Virginia, convicted the true perpetrator, Adam Bowers, of this single-assailant crime and then re-charged Buffey with the same assault. Additionally, prosecutors charged Joe with statutory rape from 2002 because as a 19-year-old he fathered a child with his then 14-year-old girlfriend. To avoid being registered as a sex offender for life, Joe took an Alford plea to the original crime he did not commit, and the state dropped the statutory rape charge. Thirteen years after his original conviction, Joseph Buffey pled guilty—again—to a crime he did not commit on October 11, 2016. In his own words, he told the court he did not commit the crime, but thought it was in his best interest to plead guilty. As is often the case in these re-prosecutions, the prosecutors asked only for a sentence of time served.

Professor Keith Findley has documented the accompanying "time served" plea offer to re-brought charges, usually for particularly heinous and memorable crimes.

Do even the prosecutors believe the person they re-charged committed the crime if they are allowing a perpetrator to be free on the streets? Yet prosecutors can be reluctant to consent even to DNA testing to determine if the convicted person is truly guilty. Although courts are increasingly receptive to allowing DNA testing to determine the true perpetrator, prosecutors continue to oppose it.

* * *

In summary, prosecutors hold a duty to disclose evidence of innocence under Rule 3.8 and also to serve as ministers of justice rather than simply as advocates. Their duty to uphold justice extends after a conviction, particularly when evidence exposes a wrongful conviction. The disclosure of forensic evidence is key to an accurate conviction and to upholding the requirements of the position as prosecuting attorney.

* * *

A final suggestion ... put forward by Professor Jason Kreag, is for courts to routinely ask prosecutors if they have disclosed *Brady* evidence pre-trial. In this "*Brady* colloquy," the judge questions the prosecutor about her compliance with disclosure on the record. Some prosecutors refute the idea of a *Brady* colloquy, insisting that this questioning is demeaning, and they are insulted by the inference of not complying with their duties. The reality of opposition to DNA testing, re-filing debunked charges, and retributive actions against defendants who have been proven innocent lessen the alleged insult of these questions, in my opinion. Even Judge Kozinski of the Ninth Circuit has opined, "There is an epidemic of Brady violations abroad in the land ... only judges can put a stop to it." A *Brady* colloquy is yet another tool for judges to ensure accurate disclosure, the first step to admitting accurate forensics in the courtroom.

Jacqueline McMurtrie, *The Unindicted Co-Ejaculator and Necrophilia: Addressing Prosecutors' Logic-Defying Responses to Exculpatory DNA Results*
105 J. Crim. L. & Criminology 853, 854–76 (2015)

Prosecutors' willingness to acknowledge the exculpatory value of post-conviction DNA results has varied widely among jurisdictions. Some prosecutors have embraced DNA's power to free innocent prisoners, going so far as to create "conviction integrity units" within their offices to investigate claims of actual innocence. The nation's first Conviction Integrity Unit, established in Dallas County, has proactively worked to exonerate thirty-four people, including someone who did not seek out the DNA testing that proved his innocence.

However, other prosecutors have developed new and bizarre theories, particularly in cases involving confession evidence, to explain away exculpatory DNA results. Many of the most outlandish and insidious theories were advanced against innocent suspects who falsely confessed and whose cases were championed by Rob Warden, the warrior for justice honored by this symposium. Warden, the co-founder and longtime Executive Director of the Center on Wrongful Convictions at Northwestern University School of Law, dedicated his career to freeing innocent prisoners and remedying causes of wrongful conviction. His focus on exposing and eradicating false confessions is appropriate since the majority of Illinois's known wrongful conviction cases involved false confessions. Warden's work has had a profound impact on innumerable people including Juan Rivera, the Dixmoor Five, and Jerry Hobbs. Each falsely confessed and were prosecuted despite exculpatory DNA tests which led to only one logical conclusion: They were innocent.

In Rivera's case, the prosecutor's theory for why sperm found inside the eleven-year-old victim did not belong to Rivera was that she had sex with someone on the day she was murdered before Rivera came along and raped (but didn't ejaculate) and murdered her. The unnamed-lover theory is used so often by prosecutors that it has its own moniker: "the unindicted co-ejaculator." In the case of the Dixmoor Five, teenagers convicted of the rape and murder of a fourteen-year-old girl were exonerated after DNA from semen found on the victim's body was linked to a man with a lengthy record of sexual assault and armed robbery. When the exculpatory post-conviction evidence was presented to the Cook County State's Attorney's Office, the State opined the convicted rapist engaged in necrophilia after wandering through a field and finding the deceased fourteen-year-old victim's body. And in the last example, Hobbs was detained and charged with murdering his eight-year-old daughter and her friend, but DNA testing later excluded Hobbs as the source of semen, spermatozoa, and other biological material found on evidence gathered from his daughter's skirt and hands. A single male was determined to be the source of all of the DNA profiles. The prosecutor explained away the exculpatory DNA results by claiming the victim came into contact with the sperm while playing around the crime scene, a park where couples went to have sex. Two years later the DNA profile was matched to a convicted sex offender who was serving a sentence for attacking three women and also was awaiting trial on a murder charge. Moreover, the sex offender was friends with the second victim's older brother. The same prosecutor then switched theories to posit — and this is hard to follow — that Hobbs' daughter got the biological material on her hands while visiting the house and then transferred it to her clothes and genital area after the sex offender masturbated at the second victim's home.

These and other examples demonstrate the extreme lengths to which some prosecutors will go to protect flawed convictions. The logic-defying theories advanced by prosecutors run counter to the government's fundamental interest in criminal prosecutions, "not that it shall win a case, but that justice shall be done."

An overarching principle of our criminal justice system is that a prosecutor owes a duty of fairness to a defendant. The majority of prosecutors are conscientious public servants who adhere to their ethical and constitutional obligations to ensure "that guilt shall not escape or innocence suffer." The consequences of violating this principle are damaging and far-reaching. Litigating cases against innocent suspects drains resources, devastates innocent defendants and their families, and harms public safety by allowing the actual perpetrator to remain free, often to commit additional crimes, which leads to an erosion of trust in the criminal justice system. The question becomes why our criminal justice system lacks sufficient safeguards to prevent a case built upon a logic-defying theory of guilt from moving forward to trial. Although prosecutors enjoy largely unfettered discretion, they must account for their actions at different stages of the criminal proceedings before bringing cases to trial.

* * *

Nearly ten months after his exoneration, Rivera filed a federal lawsuit against law enforcement officials, alleging police coerced him into falsely confessing. As the civil proceeding moved forward, additional claims of misconduct surfaced. Rivera's civil attorneys discovered that after his conviction, law enforcement found a knife near the crime scene that more closely matched the knife wounds inflicted on the victim, and did not tell the defense or the prosecution of its existence. The knife was subsequently destroyed. Moreover, additional DNA testing of Rivera's gym shoes supported a claim the victim's blood was planted on his shoes. Finally, the DNA profile obtained from semen found in the victim's body was matched to a profile retrieved from crime scene evidence in a subsequent 2000 murder. This match, Rivera's lawyers suggested, established that the State's focus on Rivera had allowed the actual perpetrator to remain free and commit an additional murder.

* * *

Prosecutors who make egregious charging decisions should, as Medwed and other scholars urge, face disciplinary proceedings and sanctions.

Ultimately, the damaging consequences of prosecuting innocent defendants occur regardless of whether prosecutors pursue an improbable case theory, "not because they are bad, but because they are human," through overzealousness, or because of misconduct. Judicial pre-trial interventions, which do not rely on prosecutorial discretion or self-regulation, have been advanced as means to prevent a case built upon a logic-defying theory of guilt from moving forward to trial. These solutions include the doctrines of judicial estoppel and judicial admission and the proposed reform of criminal summary judgment.

When prosecutors develop a new theory of guilt in response to exculpatory post-conviction DNA evidence, it often contradicts the position they asserted at the defendant's trial to obtain the conviction. For example, in Rivera's case, the prosecutor argued at the 2009 trial that the eleven-year-old victim was sexually active, a theory that was not advanced at previous trials. However, Rivera's case is not the only example of a prosecutor advancing new theories in the face of exculpatory DNA results. For example, when post-conviction DNA testing excluded Earl Washington as the source of semen found on a rape and murder victim, Virginia prosecutors argued that an unidentified accomplice — the unindicted co-ejaculator — joined Washington in the crime. And in Florida, the State also took a position inconsistent with what it had presented at trial in Wilton Dedge's case. Although prosecutors argued at Dedge's trial that pubic hairs found on the victim's bed matched Dedge, when postconviction DNA testing (which the prosecution opposed) excluded him as the source of the hair, they argued the results were insignificant.

Scholars have suggested, and case law supports, using the doctrine of judicial estoppel to prevent prosecutors from responding to exculpatory DNA test results by advancing a new theory of guilt that contradicts the factual theory relied upon at the defendant's original trial. Judicial estoppel is an equitable doctrine precluding a party who asserts one position in a court proceeding from later seeking an advantage by taking a clearly inconsistent position in another court proceeding. A court may properly apply judicial estoppel when the following elements are shown: (1) a party asserts a position that is clearly inconsistent with an earlier position; (2) judicial acceptance of the inconsistent position would indicate that either the first or second court was misled; and (3) the party seeking to assert an inconsistent position would derive an unfair advantage or impose an unfair detriment on the opposing party. Although these factors are not exhaustive, they help guide a court's decision. Judicial estoppel protects the integrity of the judicial process by precluding litigants from "playing fast and loose with the courts" by "deliberately changing positions according to the exigencies of the moment." However, judicial estoppel is largely a creature of civil law and when it has been applied in criminal cases, it has often been used to prevent a defendant from taking a position on appeal which is different from what was asserted at trial. Despite its current lack of use against prosecutors, judicial estoppel could protect defendants from implausible arguments in response to exculpatory DNA results.

Dan Simon, *Criminal Law at the Crossroads: Turn to Accuracy*
87 S. Cal. L. Rev. 421, 437–39 (2014)

There is good reason to believe that in excessive doses, the adversarial system compromises the goal of accuracy more than it promotes it. The zeal that accompanies excessive adversarialism is the likely explanation for the occasional misconduct by state officials, which readily wreaks havoc on the factfinding task. Indeed, the annals of false conviction cases are replete with suggested testimony, coercion of witnesses, fabrication of evidence, and concealment of exculpating evidence. Forty-four percent of the convictions listed in the Registry of Exonerations involved official misconduct, as did some half of the DNA exonerations.

But the ill effects of excessive adversarialism are present even when all actors execute their roles honestly and diligently. Adversarialism can compromise the process by influencing the selection of witnesses on grounds other than the accuracy of their testimony. Lawyers might elect not to call to the stand an honest and reliable witness who might seem unappealing to the factfinder or who might not hold up well to the vigor of cross-examination due to a personality trait, low intelligence, and the like. By the same token, a lawyer would be tempted to call a witness who can be trusted to stand up to the task, even in the face of doubts over the integrity of the witness or the reliability of his account.

The accuracy of the process can be readily thwarted by witness preparation. Lawyers routinely prepare witnesses before the trial, and while the practice verges on subornation of perjury, failing to do so can amount to a breach of the professional responsibility the lawyer owes her client in an adversarial system. As observed by Judge

Frankel, witness preparation is a "major item of battle planning, not a step toward the revelation of objective truth." Lawyers are permitted to explain the applicable law to the witness, to discuss the witness's probable testimony, to inform the witness of other testimony to be presented, and to ask the witness to reconsider his or her recollection in light of all this information. Lawyers are also permitted to prepare the witness for hostile cross-examination, to rehearse the testimony, and to suggest alternative word choices. In short, lawyers have considerable latitude to mold the witness's testimony to fit a particular conclusion, thus weakening its correspondence to the actual criminal event.

Adversarialism can also obstruct accuracy through the excessive application of trial procedures. For one, lawyers frequently drench their courtroom presentation with all sorts of affective matter and emotional appeals that paint defendants and witnesses in either a contemptible or venerable light. Oftentimes, these depictions have little or nothing to do with the facts of the case. Studies have found that exposing jurors to emotionally arousing or gruesome evidence can increase the propensity of the jurors to vote to convict, even in "whodunit" cases, in which the evidence has no probative value whatsoever.

Cross-examination is generally touted as the "greatest legal engine ever invented for the discovery of truth," but in the hands of the zealous lawyer it easily becomes a weapon to sway the factfinder toward his client's preferred version of the facts. Skilled lawyers can use cross-examination to undermine the testimony of even honest and accurate witnesses, a feat that is considered by some commentators to be another professional duty that lawyers owe their clients. One contemporary trial advocacy manual evokes images of hunting the adversary's witnesses during cross-examination: "Close all the gaps he might try to slither through" and "pin him down—don't spring the trap too soon." Studies show that subjecting witnesses to cross-examination can also result in substantive changes in their testimony, especially when confronted with questions phrased in "lawyerese," that is, leading questions, questions phrased in the negative or double negative form, and multipart questions.

B. Current Law: Overview

Police and Prosecutor Misconduct

With respect to the disclosure of exculpatory evidence, and the use of false, and misleading evidence, the three most important lines of precedent stem from *Brady v. Maryland*, 373 U.S. 83 (1963), *Giglio v. United States*, 405 U.S. 150 (1972), and *Napue v. Illinois*, 360 U.S. 264 (1959). *Brady* and its progeny[59] establish a prosecutorial duty to disclose material exculpatory evidence in the State's possession to criminal

---

59. See, e.g., United States v. Bagley, 473 U.S. 667, 677 (1985) (limiting Brady disclosure requirement to material evidence); United States v. Agurs, 427 U.S. 97, 104 (1976) (explaining that suppressing material evidence violates a defendant's due process rights).

defendants prior to trial. The *Brady* doctrine is undoubtedly one of the most significant tools available to prevent official misconduct that contributes to wrongful convictions. *Giglio* extends the *Brady* rule to the disclosure of information that could be used to impeach the credibility of a witness, and is thus especially important with regard to the state's handling of prosecution witnesses, particularly informants. In *Napue v. Illinois,* the Court held that "[t]he prosecution cannot present evidence it knows is false and must immediately correct any falsity of which it is aware even if the false evidence was not intentionally submitted." *Id.* at 269.

The Due Process Clause also regulates other types of prosecutorial misconduct, including improper prosecutorial argument or conduct at trial, see e.g., *Connelly v. De Christoforo,* 416 U.S. 637 (1974) ("The relevant question is whether the prosecutors' comments 'so infected the trial with unfairness as to make the resulting conviction a denial of due process.'"); *Darden v. Wainwright,* 477 U.S. 168 (1986) (same).

As the Supreme Court has long held, prosecutors have a duty to conduct themselves with a high level of integrity. In the oft-quoted words of the Court in *Berger v. United States,* 295 U.S. 78, 84 (1935), the prosecutor "is the representative not of an ordinary party to a controversy, but of a sovereignty whose obligation to govern impartially is as compelling as its obligation to govern at all; and whose interest, therefore, in a criminal prosecution is not that it shall win a case, but that justice shall be done." Accordingly, the Court condemned such prosecutorial conduct as

> misstating the facts in his cross-examination of witnesses; of putting into the mouths of such witnesses things which they had not said; of suggesting by his questions that statements had been made to him personally out of court, in respect of which no proof was offered; of pretending to understand that a witness had said something which he had not said and persistently cross-examining the witness upon that basis; of assuming prejudicial facts not in evidence; of bullying and arguing with witnesses; and, in general, of conducting himself in a thoroughly indecorous and improper manner.

Id. (holding that misconduct necessitated new trial).

C. Legal Materials, Exercises, and Media

1. *John Thompson, Exoneree Epitaph:* Louisiana exoneree John Thompson died on October 4, 2017, at the age of 55. At least five prosecutors were complicit in sending him to death row and hiding exculpatory evidence, yet in *Connick, District Attorney v. Thompson,* 563 U.S. 51 (2011), the U.S. Supreme Court ruled in a 5–4 decision that there was no pattern of misconduct—and no §1983 civil rights violation— by the New Orleans District Attorney's Office. After his release, Thompson founded Resurrection After Exoneration to assist exonerees with re-entry. You can read more about J.T.'s life here: Sam Roberts, *John Thompson, Cleared After 14 Years on Death Row, Dies at 55,* NY Times (Oct. 4, 2017) https://www.nytimes.com/2017/10/04/ obituaries/john-thompson-cleared-after-14-years-on-death-row-dies-at-55.html?

hpw&rref=obituaries&action=click&pgtype=Homepage&module=well-region&
region=bottom-well&WT.nav=bottom-well; Jesse Wegman, *An Innocent Man Who
Imagined the World as It Should Be*, NY TIMES (Oct. 5, 2017) https://www.nytimes.
com/2017/10/05/opinion/john-thompson-exonerated.html.

2. *Oral Advocacy Exercise, Prosecutorial Discretion and ABA Rule 3.8(g) & (h):* In
2008, the American Bar Association amended Model Rule 3.8: Special Responsibilities of a Prosecutor to place an affirmative duty on prosecutors to investigate
"new, credible and material evidence" of innocence and to remedy a wrongful
conviction. Seventeen states have adopted Rule 3.8(g) and (h), and the Rules
Committees of other states are considering adoption. Read the excerpted Rule
below, and prepare a five-minute oral presentation to your state Rules Committee
on whether to adopt Rule 3.8(g) and (h) or whether to oppose adoption.

> (g) When a prosecutor knows of new, credible and material evidence cre-
> ating a reasonable likelihood that a convicted defendant did not commit
> an offense of which the defendant was convicted, the prosecutor shall:
>
> (1) promptly disclose that evidence to an appropriate court or authority,
> and
>
> (2) if the conviction was obtained in the prosecutor's jurisdiction,
>
> (i) promptly disclose that evidence to the defendant unless a court au-
> thorizes delay, and
>
> (ii) undertake further investigation, or make reasonable efforts to cause
> an investigation, to determine whether the defendant was convicted of an
> offense that the defendant did not commit.
>
> (h) When a prosecutor knows of clear and convincing evidence establishing
> that a defendant in the prosecutor's jurisdiction was convicted of an offense
> that the defendant did not commit, the prosecutor shall seek to remedy
> the conviction.

3. *Prosecutorial Misconduct, Then and Now:*

   a. *Accountability 1999:* In January 1999, reporters Ken Armstrong and Maurice
   Possley wrote a series of articles titled *Trial and Error*, exploring how prosecutors sacrifice justice to win. *Part 1: The Verdict: Dishonor*, CHICAGO TRIBUNE
   (January 11, 1999) http://www.chicagotribune.com/news/watchdog/chi-020
   103trial1-story.html; see also *Part 5: Break Rules, Be Promoted*, (Jan. 14, 1999)
   http://www.chicagotribune.com/chi-020103trial-gallery-storygallery.html.

   The authors noted:

   > The appellate courts denounced the prosecutors' actions with words
   > like "unforgivable," "intolerable," "beyond reprehension," and "illegal,
   > improper and dishonest." At least a dozen of the prosecutors were in-
   > vestigated by state agencies charged with policing lawyers for miscon-
   > duct.... One was fired, but appealed and was reinstated with back

pay. Another received an in-house suspension of 30 days. A third prosecutor's law license was suspended for 59 days, but because of other misconduct in the case. Not one received any kind of public sanction from a state lawyer disciplinary agency.

b. *Accountability 2009*: Reporter Maurice Possley and Professor Cookie Ridolfi of the Northern California Innocence Project (NCIP) co-authored *Preventable Error: A Report on Prosecutorial Misconduct in California 1997–2009*, Veritas Initiative (October 1, 2010). In the report, they compare court determinations of prosecutorial misconduct that was determined to be harmless error and the court upheld the conviction versus harmful error where the conviction was reversed. They conclude that "the egregiousness of a prosecutor's misconduct does not determine the harmfulness of the error; the issue for harmless error review is whether despite the misconduct, the defendant received a fair trial."

Figure 10.1: Misconduct Committed by Multiple Offenders

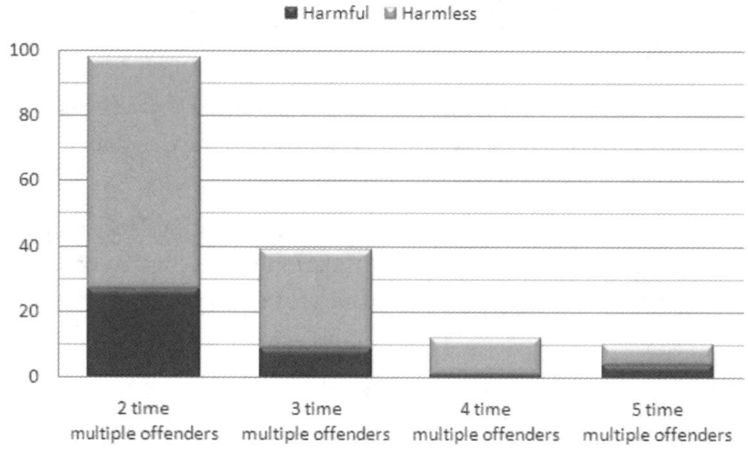

Misconduct Committed by Multiple Offenders: NCIP researchers found that multiple offenders committed misconduct in both harmful (convictions or sentences set aside, mistrials declared, or evidence barred) and harmless (convictions upheld) cases. This chart details the breakdown of cases by how many cases were handled by multiple offenders who committed misconduct two, three, four, and five times. For example, the first bar details the number of cases handled by two-time multiple offenders broken down into harmful and harmless.

Source: Maurice Possley and Cookie Ridolfi, *Preventable Error: A Report on Prosecutorial Misconduct in California 1997–2009*.

Figure 10.2: Comparing How Courts Characterize Misconduct

Harmful Error Conduct	Harmless Error Conduct
Perlaza, 439 F.3d 1149 (2006)	*Flores-Perez, 311 Fed.Appx 69 (2009)*
Shifting the Burden of Proof	Shifting the Burden of Proof
"That presumption [of innocence], when you go back in the room behind you, is going to vanish when you start deliberating. And that's when the presumption of guilt is going to take over…" (at 1169)	"when you retire to the jury room to deliberate, the presumption [of innocence] is gone. You are no longer obligated to presume innocence, but you are obligated to draw rational conclusions from the evidence." (at 71)
Combs, 379 F.3d 564 (2004)	*Brown, 2006 WL 1062095 (2006)*
Improper Examination	Improper Examination
"compel Combs to impugn the veracity of agent Bailey's testimony, pitting Comb's credibility against agent Bailey's." (at 573)	"forcing [defendant] to characterize all the witnesses, including police officers as liars." (at 22)
Sandoval, 231 F.3d 1140 (2000)	*Welch, 20 Cal.4th 701 (1999)*
Appeal to Religious Authority	Appeal to Religious Authority
"prosecutor argued to the jury that the death penalty was sanctioned by God." He paraphrased Romans 13 saying, "But if you do what is evil, be afraid for it does not bear the sword for nothing for it is a minister of God an avenger who brings wrath upon one who practices evil." (at 1150)	"prosecutor read various passages of the Bible apparently sanctioning capital punishment, including Exodus, chapter 21, verse 12, which states, 'He that smiteth a man, so that he die, shall be surely put to death'."(at 761)
R. Guzman, 96 Cal.Rptr.2d 87 (2000)	*G. Guzman, 2005 WL 435452 (2005)*
Improper Comment on Right to Silence	Improper Comment on Right to Silence
The prosecutor "repeatedly emphasized Hall's (the other party in the incident) decision to testify… [and] rather clumsily alerted the jury to the fact that, unlike Hall, Guzman was not willing to explain his side of the story in court." (at 90)	The prosecutor argued that "the prosecution on this case has provided to you two out of the three murderers who come in here and tell you themselves from their own mouths what really happened" which "brought Guzman's failure to testify into sharper focus than might otherwise have been the case." (at 19)
Rodrigues, 159 F.3d 439 (1998)	*Jordan, 2005 WL 1766387 (2005)*
Impugning Defense	Impugning Defense
The prosecutor argued, "Mr. Neal [defense counsel] has tried to deceive you from the start in this case about what this case is really about…. [Mr. Neal] has tried to introduce a number of nonissues, false issues." (at 449)	The prosecutor argued, "What has gone on in this case is a mockery of the system. You've seen from start to finish the defense pull all sorts of games and all sorts of tricks." (at 13)

Comparing How Courts Characterize Misconduct: Courts have found the same types of misconduct in both cases where convictions or sentences were set aside, mistrials declared, or evidence barred and cases where convictions were upheld. The misconduct does not determine whether a trial is called fair by a court.

Source: Maurice Possley and Cookie Ridolfi, *Preventable Error: A Report on Prosecutorial Misconduct in California 1997–2009.*

    c. *Accountability Today:* The U.S. Court of Appeals for the Ninth Circuit heard oral arguments in *Johnny Baca v. Derral Adams* on January 8, 2015. When the deputy attorney general argued the convictions be upheld, the panel of judges surprisingly asked if then-Attorney General for California Kamala Harris intended to defend a conviction "obtained by lying prosecutors." Read more about this unusual exchange in this article by Maura Dolan, *U.S. Judges See 'Epidemic' of Prosecutorial Misconduct in State,* Los Angeles Times (January 31, 2015) and view the oral arguments, beginning at 15:50, here: http://www.latimes.com/local/politics/la-me-lying-prosecutors-20150201-story.html.

4. *Discussion, Exoneree Michael Morton and the Michael Morton Act:* In Texas, Michael Morton was wrongfully convicted of his wife's murder after his prosecutor—who later became a judge—hid exculpatory evidence. The Texas legislature responded by passing the Michael Morton Act, which requires full open-file discovery of favorable evidence "as soon as practicable" after the prosecution receives a request. Tex. Code Crim. Proc. Ann. Art. 39.14 (2013).

    a. *Recommended Viewing:* Watch Michael Morton discuss his experience as an innocent man in prison in *An Unreal Dream: Evidence Witheld,* CNN (1:17; 00:47) http://www.cnn.com/2013/12/04/justice/prisoner-exonerations-facts-innocence-project/index.html.

    b. *Recommended Listening:* Listen to exoneree Michael Morton describe his wrongful conviction due to prosecutorial misconduct, and the creation of the Michael Morton Statute, on Season 1, Episode 10, The Wrongful Conviction of Michael Morton, of *Wrongful Conviction with Jason Flom* (11:45–16:05, prosecutorial fabrication of evidence) (39:30–46:00, prosecutorial misconduct and the Michael Morton Act): https://art19.com/shows/wrongful-conviction-with-jason-flom?month=12&perPage=100&year=2016.

    c. *Prosecutor Ken Anderson:* Williamson County District Attorney Ken Anderson, who withheld exculpatory evidence leading to Michael Morton's wrongful conviction, received a 10-day jail sentence for his misconduct. Michael Morton served 25 years for a crime he did not commit. Read editorial *Justice for Ken Anderson,* Dallas Morning News (Nov. 11, 2013), here: https://www.dallasnews.com/opinion/editorials/2013/11/11/editorial-justice-for-ken-anderson.

5. *Police Misconduct, an Example of Accountability:* As you've read, rarely are police and prosecutors held accountable for their misconduct in criminal cases. However, in the unusual case of exoneree Barry Gibbs, the N.Y.P.D. detective who framed Gibbs was later convicted of arranging and covering up multiple murders on behalf of an organized crime family. Hear Gibbs discuss his wrongful conviction and the behavior of Detective Louis Eppolito on *The Moth* podcast, "Exonerated," https://themoth.org/storytellers/barry-gibbs (11:13), or watch the same *Moth* monologue at "The Moth Presents Barry Gibbs: Exonerated," https://www.youtube.com/watch?v=W2si1-qi1CY (11:13).

6. *Reflective Essay, The Ethics of Conflicting Prosecutor Theories:* What if you were in prison for rape and new DNA evidence proved someone else committed the crime—but prosecutors opposed your release and instead charged, tried, and convicted the true culprit of the same single perpetrator crime? This happened to Joseph Buffey in West Virginia, and nationally prosecutors have used conflicting theories to convict co-defendants in separate trials. Is it ethical for a prosecutor to argue Jim shot the victim at Jim's trial, and then argue that Bob is the true perpetrator at Bob's trial? Explain your thoughts, and read more in Ken Armstrong's article, *Two Murder Convictions For One Fatal Shot,* THE NEW YORKER (Nov. 13, 2017): https://www.newyorker.com/magazine/2017/11/13/two-murder-convictions-for-one-fatal-shot.

7. *Collected Articles on "Epidemic of Brady Violations":* For a collection of articles and news stories discussing *Brady* evidence, prosecutorial misconduct, and prosecutorial accountability, read Jessica Brand, *The Epidemic of Brady Violations: Explained,* IN JUSTICE TODAY (Nov. 6, 2017): https://injusticetoday.com/the-epidemic-of-brady-violations-4a8733d6ccf. For a scholarly account that explores the risk factors identified in Gould, *et al.*'s study, *Predicting Erroneous Convictions,* see Catherine Hancock, Reflections on the *Brady* Violations in Milke v. Ryan: *Taking Account of Risk Factors for Wrongful Conviction,* 38 N.Y.U. REV. L. & SOC. CHANGE 437, 438–39 (2014).

8. *Comedy and Accountability:* Watch Samantha Bee's *Full Frontal with Samantha Bee,* March 14, 2018 episode, "Elected Prosecutors: Doin' Whatever They Want," for a comedian's response to prosecutorial abuse of power: https://www.youtube.com/watch?v=XC2jpKfgKko (0:00–3:58).

Chapter Eleven

Incompetent Lawyering

A. Readings

Barry Scheck, Peter Neufeld, and Jim Dwyer, *Sleeping Lawyers,* excerpt from *Actual Innocence: When Justice Goes Wrong and How to Make It Right*

NEW YORK: SIGNET 2000, 237–241

Convicted murderer Dennis Williams had been given all the rights a person had coming. He had a trial. He had twelve jurors. He had a lawyer. He could march himself right into the death chamber, the Illinois Supreme Court ruled on April 16, 1982. In particular, the court said that his defense lawyer had met all the constitutional requirements for competency. These standards are written in highly technical legal jargon, but laypeople can understand them by thinking of a "breath test." If a mirror fogs up when placed beneath the lawyer's nostrils, he or she is not ineffective, as a matter of law.

Of the seven judges on the Supreme Court, one complained that Dennis Williams had not gotten a decent day's work from his attorney. Justice Seymour Simon said that it didn't make sense for one lawyer to defend three men on the same charge, as had happened in the Williams case. Plus, the standard for competent lawyering in a capital case had to be better than simply the breath test. "If the court can safely reduce every attorney to the level of a novice," he wrote, "we may as well all take the novice; he's cheaper."

The defense lawyer, Archie Weston, had sat quietly as the prosecution systematically excluded blacks from the jury, finally creating a panel of eleven whites and one black woman. The defendants were four black men from the Ford Heights section of Chicago, charged with kidnapping a white couple from a suburban gas station, murdering the man, gang-raping the woman, then murdering her. For starters, the lawyer might have taken more care with the jury selection. Then came the trial, and the Kojak issue.

An important prosecution witness said he turned off Kojak, played a guitar piece for forty-five minutes, then saw the four men running into an abandoned building where the bodies were later found. He put the time at 3:00 A.M. Anyone who checked the time Kojak ended would have known something was wrong. That night, the episode had finished airing at 12:50 A.M.—so even forty-five minutes later, after the witness finished his guitar recital, the victims were still alive. They were last heard from at 2:30 A.M. If the four men were seen in Ford Heights at 1:30 or 2:00 in the morning, they hardly were available to kidnap the couple in Homewood at 2:30 A.M. But the defense attorney didn't make mention of the timing problem.

And then there was the Caucasian hair collected from the backseat of Williams's car. The state's lab expert said three of the hairs matched the victims' hair. Weston didn't talk to any other forensic experts. Years later, it would be shown that the hair was nothing like the victims'.

In all, it was an uninspiring performance by Attorney Weston, but lawyers have gotten away with much worse. Weston was well liked among his peers, considered to be a man who took on the problems of too many clients who couldn't pay — making it necessary for him to carry a caseload that was un-manageable. He did a lot of volunteer work as the head of the black bar association. The majority of judges on the Illinois Supreme Court decided that Dennis Williams could die. "A defendant is entitled to competent, not perfect, representation," wrote Justice Robert Underwood. Of course, different tactics might look better in hindsight, but no case would ever end if every move made by a losing lawyer were subject to scrutiny by appellate courts.

And so the matter of Dennis Williams might have rested until he was executed — except for a critical development. A few weeks after the court voted six to one to affirm his conviction, the justices were presented with disciplinary cases of lawyers who had broken the rules. Justice Simon, who had been the sole vote against upholding the Williams conviction, was an old-line Chicago politician who had risen to the bench from the ranks of ward captain, alderman, and president of the Cook County Board. Among his gifts was the ability to remember a name. When he heard that a lawyer named Archie Benjamin Weston was in hot water for mishandling his clients' business affairs, the justice paid attention.

In 1978, the same year Dennis Williams was tried, Weston had been accused of mishandling the estate of an elderly woman. Within days of Williams's conviction for first-degree murder, a civil judge removed defense attorney Weston as administrator of the estate and held him in contempt. A $23,000 judgment was entered against the attorney. After he failed to pay, his home was seized and sold at a sheriff's auction. In Illinois, the conduct of lawyers falls under the jurisdiction of the State Disciplinary Commission, which opened an investigation and subpoenaed Weston's financial records. When he ignored the subpoena, the commission initiated disbarment proceedings.

Justice Simon privately called an investigative journalist named Rob Warden, who had been covering the Williams case, and met him for drinks at the City Tavern. The judge wanted to make sure he had his facts lined up — that the Archie Weston now in trouble with the bar association was the same fellow who had represented Dennis Williams. The very same man, Warden told the judge.

When Weston appeared before the Illinois Supreme Court, pleading to save his law license, Justice Simon asked Weston why he had failed to defend himself before the Attorney Registration and Disciplinary Commission, which had leveled the disbarment charges against him.

Well, said Weston, at the time of the disciplinary proceedings, he was hard up and under so much stress that he had not been thinking straight.

When the court retired to consider the fate of Counselor Weston, Simon convinced his colleagues to investigate the dates to see whether the trial of Dennis Williams coincided with Weston's fall from grace. Justice Simon knew the score. And faced with evidence that a man sentenced to death had been represented by a lawyer in the midst of a personal collapse, the Illinois Supreme Court began a slow, spectacular reverse somersault. The judges sent for the prosecution and new defense lawyers from the Williams case.

First, they asked the state's attorney and the Williams appellate lawyers if it mattered that Weston had been falling apart when he was fighting for Williams's life.

Of course, said Williams's new lawyers.

Absolutely not, said the state's attorney. Unless someone could show big errors in how Weston handled the trial, it didn't matter that he was going bankrupt, no more than if he were actually psychotic and hallucinating for eighteen days.

Finally, the Court ruled. Sure, Archie Weston may not have been Clarence Darrow, but the justices would not describe his performance "as actual incompetence or as of such a low caliber as to reduce the trial to a farce or sham." Still, the court reversed the conviction of Williams and ordered a new trial, concluding that under "the unique circumstances and sequence of events in this capital case, which will rarely, if ever, be duplicated, that the interests of justice require that Dennis Williams be granted a new trial." Nearly in the same judicial breath, the justices also disbarred Archie Weston.

Old-fashioned Chicago politics, it turned out, had saved the life of Dennis Williams, an innocent man. The case would linger for years. Williams and his three co-defendants would be proven innocent, primarily through the extraordinary efforts of journalists Warden, Margaret Roberts, a Northwestern University journalism professor named David Protess, and Protess's students. Along the way, the licenses of three other defense lawyers for the Ford Heights Four were either suspended or revoked.

Meghan J. Ryan and John Adams,
Cultivating Judgment on the Tools of Wrongful Conviction
68 SMU L. Rev. 1073, 1096–99 (2015)

With so many potential sources of wrongful conviction, vigilant defense attorneys are vital to avoid wrongful convictions. For example, knowledge and training are necessary to exclude, object to, and preserve error relating to the admission and use of forensic evidence. A defense attorney should be able to challenge forensic science and eyewitness identifications with expert testimony about the reliability of these types of evidence. A defense attorney should also be engaged throughout a suspect's journey through the criminal justice system to ensure lineups are conducted with appropriate safeguards, protect against coercive interrogation techniques, and defend against overzealous prosecution. Unfortunately, defense attorneys are not always this vigilant.

One example of inadequate defense counsel leading to a wrongful conviction can be found in the case of Jimmy Ray Bromgard. The government's rape case against Bromgard was penetrable; it consisted of: (1) victim testimony that she was "not too sure" that Bromgard was the perpetrator and (2) unsupported (and ultimately false) testimony that hair found at the crime scene was "indistinguishable" from Bromgard's hair. Although this second piece of evidence might seem damning, effective lawyering could have exposed the inaccuracy of this testimony. Instead, Bromgard's lawyer did not present an opening statement or prepare a closing one. Further, he did no independent investigation and failed to hire an expert to contradict the State's flawed forensic evidence. The attorney did not even file a motion to suppress the victim's shaky identification. And the attorney then failed to appeal Bromgard's conviction. Bromgard spent over fourteen years in prison before ultimately being exonerated by postconviction DNA testing.

Most criminal defendants are represented by publicly funded counsel, and the limits on resources available for these attorneys likely contribute to instances of ineffective assistance of counsel in criminal cases. In the worst cases, defense counsel falls asleep at trial, fails to appear for hearings, or is disbarred shortly after working on a case. But the current state of affairs makes good criminal defense difficult for even the best publicly funded lawyers. In some states, public defenders are working over 1,700 cases each year, including over 200 felony cases. With only a few hours to dedicate to each case, it is understandable that these lawyers often adopt a transactional approach and for plea bargaining to be the norm. Publicly funded defense attorneys also tend to be poorly compensated. Although some states offer an hourly rate of approximately $90 per hour, there may be caps in particular cases, such as the Virginia cap of $112 total for a juvenile felony case. Such poor compensation disincentivizes attorneys from spending more time on each case. It also tends to make recruitment and retention of experienced attorneys difficult.

One manifestation of the inadequate resources indigent defendants and their counsel receive is the abundance of "meet 'em and plead 'em" lawyers. One report found that more than 80% of indigent clients never met their attorneys out of court and were given pre-negotiated plea agreements when they finally met their attorneys at trial. And a study of all felony cases in one county over a five-year period found that over 40% of cases were resolved by a guilty plea on the day of arraignment at the same time clients first met their attorneys. Sadly, though, many defendants are not even appointed counsel in time for their first appearances. Some jurisdictions admit to thousands of such unconstitutional failures each year.

The compensation for publicly funded defense attorneys is also often significantly less than the compensation for the district attorneys prosecuting the cases. Because the prosecution often has greater resources, it is not uncommon for there to be more, and better qualified, prosecutors working on a particular case. Recognizing these problems and the need for greater funding for indigent defense, former Attorney General Janet Reno explained that this defense work is an "essential element of the criminal justice process" and that it is necessary to the legitimacy of convictions.

Jacqueline McMurtrie, *Strange Bedfellows: Can Insurers Play a Role in Advancing Gideon's Promise?*
45 HOFSTRA L. REV. 391, 395–97 (2016)

There are few empirical studies on how often poor defense representation leads to wrongful conviction. A study of the first sixty-two DNA exonerations concluded that about twenty-seven percent were caused by "bad lawyering." The National Registry of Exonerations attributes "inadequate legal defense" as a contributing factor in about twenty-three percent of identified wrongful convictions. However, the rate of error stemming from inadequate defense representation is difficult to quantify because other known causes of wrongful conviction, such as mistaken eyewitness identification, faulty scientific evidence, and police misconduct, can be challenged and refuted by competent counsel. As Professor Adele Bernhard explains, "[I]t [is] defense counsel's responsibility to protect [the innocent] from the mistakes of others: from witnesses' misidentifications, police officers' rush to judgment, and prosecution's reluctance to reveal potentially exculpatory material."

Challenging a conviction based on counsel's incompetence is an uphill battle. Individuals asserting they were deprived of their Sixth Amendment right to effective assistance of counsel must show more than "bad lawyering" or "inadequate defense." Under the two-part test established by the Supreme Court in *Strickland v. Washington*,[60] convicted persons must demonstrate their defense counsel's performance was deficient and that the deficient performance prejudiced the defense. Judicial scrutiny of counsel's performance is highly deferential; the convicted person must overcome the "strong presumption" that counsel rendered adequate assistance and exercised reasonable professional judgement when making strategic decisions. To show prejudice, the convicted person must establish that there is a "reasonable probability that, but for counsel's unprofessional errors, the result of the proceeding would have been different." If a court can dispose of an ineffectiveness claim under the prejudice prong, it may dismiss the claim without deciding whether counsel's performance was deficient. In many cases of egregious attorney performance, the conviction is affirmed because the court finds defense counsel's deficiencies did not affect the result of the trial.

Strickland claims seldom prevail. A recent study of over 2500 such claims found that only four percent were granted. Even innocent people who are eventually released because of DNA testing rarely obtain relief on ineffective assistance of counsel claims brought prior to their exoneration. A study of the first 250 DNA exonerations revealed that ineffective assistance of counsel claims were raised in thirty-two percent of the cases, but in the overwhelming majority of the cases (about ninety-seven percent), the court rejected the claim.

Individuals who obtain a conviction reversal on the ground that their Sixth Amendment rights were violated may, like Clarence Gideon, face retrial. They can, even if factually innocent, be convicted again. Fifteen of twenty-one exonerees who obtained

---

60. 466 U.S. 668, 690–92 (1984).

reversals on ineffective assistance of counsel claims were retried after their convictions were reversed and all were reconvicted. Each was later exonerated through post-conviction DNA testing after enduring two, and sometimes three, trials. If a person is acquitted after retrial or the prosecutor elects to dismiss charges, constitutional tort actions for monetary damages related to the ineffectiveness claim are generally barred under immunity doctrines and prudential concerns. If a person seeks monetary damages through a criminal malpractice action, they face additional hurdles. In many states, the individual must first litigate and win an ineffective assistance of counsel claim in order to be successful in bringing a criminal malpractice suit. In several states, an individual must additionally prove actual innocence in order to recover monetary damages against a former criminal defense attorney.

Eve Brensike Primus, *Defense Counsel and Public Defense*

In ACADEMY FOR JUSTICE, A REPORT ON SCHOLARSHIP AND CRIMINAL JUSTICE REFORM, 121–45 (Erik Luna, ed., 2017)

As criminal codes proliferated in the 1970s and '80s as part of the war on drugs, and legislatures earmarked more funding for law enforcement, criminal court dockets exploded but without corresponding increases in public-defense funding. Numerous investigative reports now document a public-defense crisis characterized by funding problems, a lack of independence, and a failure of training and oversight. These structural problems create a culture of indifference in criminal courts, leading to the wrongful conviction of innocent people and undermining the legitimacy of the criminal justice system.

A. Funding Problems

The vast majority of American criminal defendants are indigent, and funding for public defense is grossly insufficient for providing adequate legal representation to such a large client base. A few numbers should make the point. According to the American Bar Association (ABA), no defender should handle more than 400 misdemeanor cases in a year. In Chicago and Atlanta, however, public defenders have had to handle more than 2,000 misdemeanor cases annually. In New Orleans, funding shortages have forced public defenders to handle almost 19,000 misdemeanor cases per year. Similarly, the ABA recommends that no defender handle more than 150 felony cases each year, but public defenders in Florida's Miami-Dade County have had to handle more than 700. Countless reports document excessive defender caseloads arising from the lack of funding. The sheer volume of cases means that many defendants sit in jail for months before speaking to their court-appointed lawyers.

In addition to lacking the funds to pay an adequate number of attorneys, public-defender offices lack the funds necessary to provide the attorneys they do have with training, mentorship, or supervision. Lacking training and support, and asked to handle far more cases than is feasible, defenders commonly feel overwhelmed. They often burn out and quit after only a year or two on the job, leaving much indigent-defense representation to a rotating crop of new, inexperienced attorneys.

A lack of funding also means insufficient resources for adequate investigative assistance. In 2013, six states reported that they had fewer than 10 total investigators on staff for all of the state's public-defender offices. Many cases are resolved with no investigation whatsoever.

This lack of funding is striking when compared to the funding for the prosecution and law enforcement. Prosecutors often have higher salaries than defenders, lighter caseloads, and more access to investigative and expert assistance. Prosecutors have the police department and state crime labs to help with their investigations, whereas defense attorneys often have neither investigative nor expert assistance readily available.

The source of public-defense funding is also troubling. A 2010 report found that only 23 states completely fund their indigent-defense systems at the state level. In 19 states, counties shoulder the burden for more than half of the funding. Pennsylvania requires its counties to provide all of the funding for indigent defense. A lack of state funding means that financial resources cannot be spread across the state. Urban counties with large indigent populations are overwhelmed and have resorted to conscripting unwilling and inexperienced attorneys who have no criminal-defense background and no financial incentive to be zealous advocates to represent indigent criminal defendants. Other urban counties resort to flat-fee contract systems to save money, resulting in defense lawyers who carry large caseloads for little compensation. These contract lawyers often have to supplement their incomes with other work, resulting in less time for their indigent-defense clients.

Many less-populous rural counties rely on assigned-counsel systems under which attorneys are paid as little as $40 per hour with hard caps on how much an attorney can earn per case. With caps as low as $500 per felony case, these attorneys have no financial incentive to go to trial, do legal research, or investigate. They are better off pleading out a case, getting the fee, and getting a new client.

Even in counties that can afford public-defender offices, the reliance on county funds often means that the income stream for the office is not stable. In New Orleans, for example, the public-defense budget relies on traffic-ticket revenue. If the police do not issue enough tickets, there is no money for indigent defense.

B. Lack of Independence

Many indigent-defense attorneys cannot provide effective representation, because they are not sufficiently independent of the judiciary. A statewide survey of Nebraska judges revealed that some judges punish court-appointed attorneys who take cases to trial rather than pleading them out by not reappointing those attorneys in future cases. In Texas, there are reports of judges appointing those with whom they have personal relationships. And in Detroit, Michigan, some claim that judges give cases to attorneys who make contributions to their re-election campaigns.

Independence problems also exist when elected legislative or executive officials have too much control over public-defender offices. A recent report documented nine states in which the governor had the power to fire the chief public defender, and claims persist that governors have used their removal power to fire especially zealous defenders. In Onondaga County, New York, the Legal Aid Society lost a contract to handle city court cases after the director was questioned by a legislative committee about why she was filing motions and making discovery requests instead of pleading cases. And in some jurisdictions, the public defender is chosen by an advisory board that consists entirely of law enforcement personnel and prosecutors who have a vested interest in ensuring that prosecutions are successful.

Such independence problems are built in to the federal defender system, because the Criminal Justice Act vests control over the structure of appointment and funding for indigent defense in the local courts. This means local judges decide which attorneys can be panel attorneys and whether to approve their payment vouchers or expense requests. Similarly, circuit courts hire the heads of the federal defender organizations and determine how many attorneys can work in the offices. Moreover, the judiciary is charged with asking Congress for funding for both the courts and the defense function at the same time. A 2015 report documented judicial concern that the Executive and Budget Committees sought to reduce the defender budget in order to protect and grow the judiciary's own budget.

C. Failure to Train and Oversee

Too often, defenders are thrown into the job without training, and their performance is never evaluated. Many offices do not have training directors or funds for training programs. Attorneys learn in court, and defenders often get no constructive feedback from, or substantive review by, supervisors. In assigned-counsel and contract systems, there is often no supervisor at all—just a bureaucrat who coordinates appointments. And the local bar associations do a terrible job of finding and removing ineffective attorneys.

Courts have done little to address these problems. Citing separation-of-powers principles, judges have been loath to inject themselves into state funding issues. Moreover, given the prevailing constitutional standard for judging the adequacy of trial representation, the very fact that defenders are persistently underfunded and overwhelmed prevents courts from ruling that any particular failure of representation is a constitutional violation for which a court could order a remedy. Under Strickland v. Washington, there is no constitutional violation of the right to effective counsel unless the defendant shows that (a) his attorney performed unreasonably given prevailing norms of practice (with a heavy measure of deference to the trial attorney's strategic decisions and a presumption that decisions were strategic) and (b) the attorney's deficient performance prejudiced the case outcome. When prevailing norms of practice require attorneys to carry excessive caseloads and meet clients for the first time on the trial date, it is hard to show deficient performance. And when there is little to no pretrial investigation, it is hard to demonstrate prejudice.

Given the difficulty of getting courts to rule that the representation in any given trial was inadequate under Strickland, some public defenders and advocacy groups have filed pretrial lawsuits arguing that funding and independence problems in particular jurisdictions violate the Sixth Amendment, because they constructively deny indigent defendants counsel altogether. These lawsuits present courts not just with individual cases of abysmal representation, but with data demonstrating the gross inadequacy of public-defense delivery systems as a whole. Nonetheless, many courts have been reticent to get involved. Some courts have dismissed the cases on procedural grounds; other cases have settled. And even in the few places where courts have found systemic constitutional violations, the process has been extremely time- and resource-intensive, and the long-term impact of favorable decisions remains unclear.

D. A Broken System with Serious Consequences

The lack of funding, excessive caseloads, minimal training, lack of independence, and failure of oversight make it impossible for defense attorneys to do their jobs. The result is a breakdown in the adversarial system that results in wrongful convictions and undermines the legitimacy and fairness of the system. In too many jurisdictions, criminal-defense attorneys show up on the day of court having never met their clients and having conducted no investigation or legal research into their cases. After a hurried five-minute conversation, the client is pushed into a plea and forced down the assembly line to prison. Many indigent criminal defendants do not even get that five-minute conversation with an attorney; their constitutional rights to counsel are simply ignored, and they are forced to navigate the justice system without any help whatsoever. No one listens to the defendant's side of the story, questions the adequacy of the prosecution's proof, or even explains to the defendant what is happening. All that the defendant's family and friends see is another poor person of color being processed through the system. Sometimes defendants' pleas are taken en masse as group after group of men in orange jumpsuits are corralled into the courtroom and carted off to prison.

This failure to provide defendants with adequate representation contributes to the wrongful imprisonment of innocent people. Scientific advances like DNA testing have made the public more aware that wrongful convictions happen. Defense lawyers are supposed to fight to prevent the conviction of innocent people, but crushing caseloads and a lack of time and funding to investigate cases inhibits their ability to perform that vital role. The chief district defender for Orleans Parish in Louisiana recently acknowledged that his office is not able to guarantee "the timely retrieval of ... important evidence before it [is] routinely erased" and, as a result, innocent people can be imprisoned.

The fact that our system does not care about or listen to the people it imprisons is problematic not just for the innocent. It also undermines the legitimacy of the system in the eyes of the public. As a matter of procedural justice, when people do not feel that they have been treated fairly, it is hard for them to respect the system's results. That lack of respect, in turn, encourages lawlessness and undermines the goals of the criminal justice system. Indigent criminal defendants routinely complain that their trial attorneys assume that they are guilty, don't listen to them, and don't communicate with them. That is a problem in any system that wants to be perceived as legitimate, but it is particularly problematic in an adversarial system that relies on zealous defenders to justify its results.

The failure to provide defendants with adequate trial representation also creates inefficiencies in the system and generates larger costs later in the process. Society pays to imprison people who would have been released had they had competent counsel to argue for them. And money is wasted at the appellate and post-conviction stages relitigating cases that would not be in the system if they had been properly litigated at trial.

Mark Godsey, *Blind Injustice: A Former Prosecutor Exposes the Psychology and Politics of Wrongful Convictions*
University of California Press, 84 (2017)

It is not uncommon for a murder prosecution to cost the state millions of dollars. While other types of cases often cost the prosecution less, the state has nearly unlimited resources at its disposal to prosecute its cases, with a host of investigators and state crime labs to help it. But when it comes to funding the cost of a proper defense, the reality tends to be quite different. The public often sees only the celebrity trials, where defendants like Michael Jackson or O. J. Simpson are able to hire an expensive defense team that allows them to wage a somewhat fair head-to-head match with the prosecution. But that kind of defense rarely occurs in the real world. Most criminal defendants are given a public defender, or court-appointed attorney working on contract with the local public defender's office, who is grossly underpaid and so overloaded that he or she has little time to devote to any given case.

The Netflix docu-series *Making a Murderer* did an excellent job depicting this problem. One of the two defendants in the case of the murder of Teresa Halbach, Steven Avery, was able to afford two top-notch defense attorneys who were on top of the case from start to finish, and who assembled an impressive team of experts and investigators, because Avery had recently settled a civil case for $400,000 for his wrongful conviction of the rape of Penny Bernstein. He was able to dump that money into his defense in the Teresa Halbach case. But the other defendant in the Halbach case, Brendan Dassey, had no money and was left with a court-appointed attorney, Len Kachinsky, who sold him down the river by assuming his client was guilty and admitting as much to the media before doing any investigation or even bothering to meet his new client. Kachinsky then allowed his sixteen-year-old cognitively impaired client to be interrogated by the police without him being present in the interrogation room. The difference in the quality of representation for the two defendants was striking. While the rare criminal defendant who has significant wealth is able to mount the type of quality defense that many in the public believe is routine, many of the rest are left with the Len Kachinskys.

The structural imbalance between the prosecution and the defense bar has been widely reported. In any given year, one can find media reports from all across the country in which public defenders, who represent 80 percent of those charged with crimes in this country, complain that they simply are unable to do their jobs due to underfunding and overloaded dockets. In fact, in several jurisdictions the ACLU has filed suit against public defender offices because they are unable to operate effectively, depriving their clients of their constitutional right to adequate counsel. These lawsuits, or threats of such lawsuits, are common. But nothing ever changes. In Missouri, the state's head public defender became so exasperated by the governor's refusal to adequately fund his department that he used an obscure law to appoint the governor, a licensed attorney, to represent an indigent defendant. Of course, the governor refused the assignment. But this maneuver reflects the frustration that public defenders feel around the country.

Many public defenders are forced to carry dockets two or three times the number of cases that the American Bar Association recognizes as the maximum. In New Orleans, for example, public defenders are so overloaded that they are able to devote an average of just seven minutes of work on each misdemeanor case. Seven minutes! In 2016, the public defender's office in New Orleans had the courage to refuse to take new felony cases for serious crimes, as the lawyers were so overloaded that they simply didn't have time to provide an appropriate defense in each case. In 2017, five public defenders from New Orleans appeared on a segment of 60 Minutes and declared their belief that they have represented innocent clients who have gone to prison because they lacked the time and resources to defend them properly.

Tigran W. Eldred, *Prescriptions for Ethical Blindness: Improving Advocacy for Indigent Defendants in Criminal Cases*
65 Rutgers L. Rev. 333, 344–51 (2013)

Despite the importance of investigation, too often lawyers across the county— whether public defenders, contract lawyers, or appointed counsel—fail to properly investigate in a substantial number of cases. The results can be and often are disastrous.

On this point, statistics are telling. For example, in one of the largest studies conducted of defense lawyers in a single locale, researchers evaluated the percentage of cases in which appointed lawyers in New York City engaged in various representational activities—including investigating their cases—in both homicide and non-homicide felonies. Shockingly, lawyers engaged in any form of investigation in approximately 27% of homicide cases, 12% of non-homicide felonies, and only 8% of misdemeanor cases. Delving into the details of these statistics is even more disturbing. In cases in which the defendant was accused of homicide, lawyers failed to interview their clients in 75% of the cases—meaning that the matter was resolved by the lawyer without any attempt to gather essential factual information from the most important source for the defense: the client. This number increased to over 80% in nonhomicide cases.

Unfortunately, the results of the New York City study are not unique. In another study conducted of defense attorneys in Phoenix, Arizona, 47% of lawyers "entered plea agreements without interviewing any prosecution witnesses," and in 30% of the cases where a plea was entered, no defense witnesses were interviewed. In addition, defense attorneys visited the crime scene in only 55% of the felony cases that went to trial, and only 31% of defense lawyers interviewed all the prosecution's trial witnesses. Remarkably, 15% of lawyers interviewed none of the prosecution's trial witnesses. Others studies have come to similar conclusions.

Investigatory failure is also evident by how infrequently defense attorneys utilize the services of trained investigators. Underfunded defenders often must request appointment of trained investigators from the court, having no funds to hire them on their own. Yet rarely are such requests made, much less granted. For example, in one study in Pennsylvania, few public defenders reported speaking to an investigator in the representation of a client. Appointed counsel, who must also seek court appointment for investigators, similarly fail to seek these services. For example, in one study conducted in Alabama, virtually no attorneys requested the assistance of a court appointed investigator, despite the statutory and constitutional ability to do so. When asked for an explanation, lawyers indicated there was an unwritten rule created by the judges in the courthouse: do not seek the assistance of an investigator or an expert witness. Similar experiences have been recounted in other jurisdictions, including in New York, California, and Michigan.

The net result of these persistent investigative failures can be devastating. Potentially innocent clients invariably will be lost in the shuffle of excessive caseloads. And clients who may be factually guilty lose the potential benefits that a dedicated lawyer with adequate resources can provide. As one scholar has noted:

> The lack of careful investigation that characterizes most felony prosecutions virtually guarantees that a significant number of innocent defendants are pressured to plead to crimes they did not commit. And within the much larger universe of guilty defendants, those who are punished most severely are often those who made the worst deals, not those who committed the worst crimes.

Explaining Inadequate Advocacy

A variety of reasons have been offered to explain why defense lawyers so often fail in their duties. The most obvious is a matter of simple arithmetic. As many have noted, systemic underfunding of defender services frequently means that too many lawyers handle too many cases with too few resources. The result is that many lawyers labor under excessive caseloads where they are unable to provide adequate representation. For example, it is not uncommon in some jurisdictions for lawyers to be responsible for caseloads that exceed national guidelines by more than 500%. Some lawyers respond by effectively abdicating their responsibilities to their clients. Others engage in a form of legal "triage" in which some clients are selected to receive adequate representation, while the rest are relegated to the "assembly line" of quick, standardized guilty pleas in which the lawyer expends only minimal efforts. In either case, time-consuming and labor-intensive tasks, such as investigations, too often are dispensed with out of expediency.

The problem of too much work is augmented by what some have described as "perverse incentives" that can discourage defenders from providing competent representation. The agency costs that adhere in every attorney-client relationship are exacerbated by the economic realities of indigent defense practice. Take, for example, the situation involving Robert Surrency, who was awarded a low-bid contract to represent indigent defendants. The contract itself ensured that Surrency's caseload would be excessive, given the number of people requiring representation in the county. In addition, Surrency had no economic incentive to do anything but provide minimal efforts for most of his clients. After all, greater effort on any given case did not increase the amount that he was paid in most instances. To the contrary, because each segment of effort he expended reduced the overall profitability of the contract, his economic incentive was to resolve most cases with the least amount of effort possible. For Surrency and lawyers like him, any activity that diverts attention away from quick disposition of cases—such as pretrial investigations, which can take hours, days, or longer to accomplish—is discouraged by the nature of the contract itself.

One might expect a different result for appointed lawyers who are paid per case to represent clients. However, because the hourly rate of pay is often so low, and the total amount of pay available per case often is capped well below the amount needed to compensate for competent representation, appointed lawyers also have economic incentives to expend minimal efforts per case. Pushing quick plea bargains is the name of the game. This is particularly true when the lawyer's appointed clients pay worse than the lawyer's paying clients, meaning that the lawyer has an incentive to minimize time spent on appointed cases so that more time can be focused on better compensated cases. Many judges augment these incentives by making appointments not based on the competency of counsel, but rather on how quickly the lawyer can dispose of cases.

Public defenders also have incentives to minimize the amount of work they expend on each case. Of course, public defenders are not paid on a per case basis, meaning that they do not have the same economic incentives to turn over cases as quickly as appointed counsel. But because so many defenders carry excessive caseloads, the only way that all of the cases can be resolved is to cap the amount of time devoted to each client. Otherwise, they would be required to work around the clock—and even then would likely be unable to meet their professional obligations. Additionally, because the public defender's office itself does not receive additional payments when a lawyer engages in robust advocacy, the incentive is for lawyers to neglect activities that do not produce financial benefits to the organization, such as expending resources to investigate cases or to take cases to trial. In some cases, the economic incentives are more direct: because the defender's office is not paid on a per case basis, lawyers who expend too much time on each case may risk alienating supervisors who want cases resolved expeditiously. Job security can be very motivating.

The incentives that encourage minimal effort by lawyers are counterbalanced by few disincentives for subpar performance. Unfortunately, there are few costs for lawyers who fail to meet their professional duties. Because indigent clients do not control the appointment process, they are powerless to fire their attorneys without court approval. Nor are there any likely penalties for poor performance. As a matter of professional ethics, few defenders are sanctioned for failing to provide the type of representation expected by the rules of professional responsibility. Nor is there much risk of civil liability. The only other possible sanction is reputational harm that could result from a finding of ineffective assistance of counsel. Unfortunately, the well-known obstacles to proving a claim of ineffectiveness — including the deep deference that is afforded to the choices of defense counsel and the almost insurmountable prejudice requirement — make it highly unlikely that most lawyers will ever be found ineffective.

Given these realities, a lawyer whose primary focus is on his or her personal self-interest in deciding how to represent clients can be expected to engage in virtually no investigation on cases. For these lawyers, the best way to maximize self-interest is for the lawyer to minimize the amount of work to the extent possible. Because there is little incentive to provide competent representation, and every incentive to do otherwise, the rational calculation is to perform the minimum amount necessary to convince clients to plead guilty as quickly as possible. Investigations that divert attention from expediency are naturally avoided.

Stephen B. Bright, *Counsel for the Poor: The Death Sentence Not for the Worst Crime but for the Worst Lawyer*
103 Yale L.J. 1835, 1841–62 (1994)

Inadequate legal representation does not occur in just a few capital cases. It is pervasive in those jurisdictions which account for most of the death sentences. The American Bar Association concluded after an exhaustive study of the issues that "the inadequacy and inadequate compensation of counsel at trial" was one of the "principal failings of the capital punishment systems in the states today."

* * *

Death sentences have been imposed in cases in which defense lawyers had not even read the state's death penalty statute or did not know that a capital trial is bifurcated into separate determinations of guilt and punishment. State trial judges and prosecutors — who have taken oaths to uphold the law, including the Sixth Amendment — have allowed capital trials to proceed and death sentences to be imposed even when defense counsel fought among themselves or presented conflicting defenses for the same client, referred to their clients by a racial slur, cross-examined a witness whose direct testimony counsel missed because he was parking his car, slept through part of the trial, or was intoxicated during trial. Appellate courts often review and decide capital cases on the basis of appellate briefs that would be rejected in a first-year legal writing course in law school.

* * *

Many death penalty states have two state-funded offices that specialize in handling serious criminal cases. Both employ attorneys who generally spend years — some even their entire careers — handling criminal cases. Both pay decent annual salaries and provide health care and retirement benefits. Both send their employees to conferences and continuing legal education programs each year to keep them up to date on the latest developments in the law. Both have at their disposal a stable of investigative agencies, a wide range of experts, and mental health professionals anxious to help develop and interpret facts favorable to their side. Unfortunately, however, in many states both of these offices are on the same side: the prosecution.

One is the District Attorney's office in each judicial district, whose lawyers devote their time exclusively to handling criminal matters in the local court systems. These lawyers acquire considerable expertise in the trial of criminal cases, including capital cases. There are, for example, prosecutors in the District Attorney's office in Columbus, Georgia, who have been trying death penalty cases since the state's current death penalty statute was adopted in 1973.

The other office is the state Attorney General's office, which usually has a unit made up of lawyers who specialize in handling the appeals of criminal cases and habeas corpus matters. Here, too, lawyers build expertise in handling capital cases. For example, the head of the unit that handles capital litigation for the Georgia Attorney General has been involved in that work since 1976, the same year the Supreme Court upheld Georgia's death penalty statute. She brings to every case a wealth of expertise developed in seventeen years of litigating capital cases in all the state and federal courts involved in Georgia cases. She and her staff are called upon by district attorneys around the state for consultation on pending cases and, on occasion, will assist in trial work. It is the normal practice in Georgia that briefs by *both* the district attorney and the attorney general are filed with the Georgia Supreme Court on the direct appeal of a capital case.

The specialists in the offices of both the district attorneys and the attorneys general have at their call local, state, and, when needed, federal investigative and law enforcement agencies. They have a group of full-time experts at the crime laboratory and in the medical examiner's offices to respond to crime scenes and provide expert testimony when needed. If mental health issues are raised, the prosecution has a group of mental health professionals at the state mental facilities. No one seriously contends that these professional witnesses are objective. They routinely testify for the prosecution as part of their work, and prosecutors enjoy longstanding working relationships with them.

In Alabama, Georgia, Mississippi, Louisiana, Texas, and many other states with a unique fondness for capital punishment, there is no similar degree of specialization or resources on the other side of capital cases. A poor person facing the death penalty may be assigned an attorney who has little or no experience in the defense of capital or even serious criminal cases, one reluctant or unwilling to defend him, one with little or no empathy or understanding of the accused or his particular plight, one with little or no knowledge of criminal or capital punishment law, or one with no understanding of the need to document and present mitigating circumstances. Although it is widely acknowledged that at least two lawyers, supported by investigative and expert assistance, are required to defend a capital case, some of the jurisdictions with the largest number of death sentences still assign only one lawyer to defend a capital case.

In contrast to the prosecution's virtually unlimited access to experts and investigative assistance, the lawyer defending the indigent accused in a capital case may not have any investigative or expert assistance to prepare for trial and present a defense. A study of twenty capital cases in Philadelphia in 1991 and 1992 found that the court "paid for investigators in eight of the twenty cases, spending an average of $605 in each of the eight" and that the court "paid for psychologists in two of them, costing $400 in one case, $500 in the other." It is impossible even to begin a thorough investigation or obtain a comprehensive mental health evaluation for such paltry amounts.

Although the Supreme Court has held that indigent defendants may be entitled to expert assistance in certain circumstances, defense attorneys often do not even request such assistance because they are indifferent or know that no funds will be available. Courts often refuse to authorize funds for investigation and experts by requiring an extensive showing of need that frequently cannot be made without the very expert assistance that is sought. Many lawyers find it impossible to maneuver around this "Catch 22," but even when a court recognizes the right to an expert, it often authorizes so little money that no competent expert will get involved.

* * *

B. The Lack of Indigent Defense Programs

In many jurisdictions where capital punishment is frequently imposed, there are no comprehensive public defender systems whose resources can parallel the prosecutorial functions of the district attorneys' offices. There are no appellate defender offices that parallel the function of the capital litigation sections of the attorneys general's offices. In fact, there is no coherent system at all, but a hodgepodge of approaches that vary from county to county.

In many jurisdictions, judges simply appoint members of the bar in private practice to defend indigents accused of crimes. The lawyers appointed may not want the cases, may receive little or no compensation for the time and expense of handling them, may lack any interest in criminal law, and may not have the skill to defend those accused of a crime. As a result, the poor are often represented by inexperienced lawyers who view their responsibilities as unwanted burdens, have no inclination to help their clients, and have no incentive to develop criminal trial skills.

* * *

C. Compensation of Attorneys: The Wages of Death

The United States Court of Appeals for the Fifth Circuit, finding that Federico Martinez-Macias "was denied his constitutional right to adequate counsel in a capital case in which [his] actual innocence was a close question," observed that, "The state [Texas] paid defense counsel $11.84 per hour. Unfortunately, the justice system got only what it paid for." What is unusual about the case is not the amount paid to counsel, but the court's acknowledgement of its impact on the quality of services rendered.

As we have seen, in many jurisdictions poor people facing the death penalty are not assigned specialists who work for indigent defense programs, but individual attorneys, often sole practitioners. In some jurisdictions, the hourly rates in capital cases may be below the minimum wage or less than the lawyer's overhead expenses.

Many jurisdictions limit the maximum fee for a case. At such rates it is usually impossible to obtain a good lawyer willing to spend the necessary time.

Alabama limits compensation for out-of-court preparation to $20 per hour, up to a limit of $1000. In one rare Alabama case where two lawyers devoted 246.86 and 187.90 hours respectively to out-of-court preparation, they were still paid $1000 each, or $4.05 and $5.32 per hour.

In some rural areas in Texas, lawyers receive no more than $800 to handle a capital case. Generally, the hourly rate is $50 or less. Attorneys appointed to defend capital cases in Philadelphia are paid an average of $6399 per case. In the few cases where a second attorney has been appointed, it is often at a flat rate of $500. A study in Virginia found that, after taking into account an attorney's overhead expenses, the effective hourly rate paid to counsel representing an indigent accused in a capital case was $13. In Kentucky, the limit for a capital case is $2500.

Sometimes even these modest fees are denied to appointed counsel. A capital case in Georgia was resolved with a guilty plea only after the defense attorneys, a sole practitioner and this author, agreed not to seek attorneys fees as part of the bargain in which the state withdrew its request for the death penalty.

In cases involving financial as opposed to moral bankruptcy, Atlanta law firms charge around $125 per hour for their associates, $200 per hour for partners, and $50 to $80 per hour for paralegals. In civil rights and other civil litigation, courts routinely order attorneys fees much higher than those paid to appointed lawyers in capital cases. Paralegals and law clerks in civil rights cases may be compensated at rates equal to or better than what experienced attorneys are paid in capital cases. A new attorney at the Southern Center for Human Rights, straight out of law school, was awarded $65 per hour by a federal court in 1990 for work on a prison conditions case. More experienced lawyers on that case were paid at rates of $90, $100, and $150 per hour. Attorneys appointed to death penalty cases in state courts can never expect compensation at such rates.

*   *   *

Not surprisingly, a recent study in Texas found that "more experienced private criminal attorneys are refusing to accept court appointments in capital cases because of the time involved, the substantial infringement on their private practices, the lack of compensation for counsel fees and expert expenses and the enormous pressure that they feel in handling these cases." "In many counties, the most qualified attorneys often ask not to be considered for court appointments in capital cases due to the fact that the rate of compensation would not allow them to cover the expense of running a law practice." The same unwillingness to take cases because of the low fees has been observed in other states. Consequently, although capital cases require special skills, the level of compensation is often not enough even to attract those who regularly practice in the indigent defense system.

D. The Role of Judges: Appointment and Oversight of Mediocrity and Incompetence

Even if, despite the lack of indigent defense programs and adequate compensation, capable lawyers were willing to move to jurisdictions with many capital cases, forego more lucrative business, and take appointments to capital cases, there is still no assurance that those lawyers would be appointed to the cases. It is no secret that elected state court judges do not appoint the best and brightest of the legal profession to defend capital cases. In part, this is because many judges do not want to impose on those members of the profession they believe to have more important, financially lucrative things to do. But even when choosing from among those who seek criminal appointments, judges often appoint less capable lawyers to defend the most important cases.

Judges have appointed to capital cases lawyers who have never tried a case before. A study of homicide cases in Philadelphia found that the quality of lawyers appointed to capital cases in Philadelphia is so bad that "even officials in charge of the system say they wouldn't want to be represented in Traffic Court by some of the people appointed to defend poor people accused of murder." The study found that many of the attorneys were appointed by judges based on political connections, not legal ability. "Philadelphia's poor defendants often find themselves being represented by ward leaders, ward committeemen, failed politicians, the sons of judges and party leaders, and contributors to the judge's election campaigns."

An Alabama judge refused to relieve counsel even when they filed a motion to be relieved of the appointment because they had inadequate experience in defending criminal cases and considered themselves incompetent to defend a capital case. Georgia trial judges have repeatedly refused to appoint or compensate the experienced attorneys who, doing pro bono representation in post-conviction stages of review, had successfully won new trials for clients who had been sentenced to death. In several of those cases, the Georgia Supreme Court ordered continued representation at the new trials by the lawyers who were familiar with the case and the client. Despite those precedents, a Georgia judge refused to appoint an expert capital litigator from the NAACP Legal Defense and Educational Fund to continue representation of an indigent defendant, even though the Legal Defense Fund lawyer had won a new trial for the client by showing in federal habeas corpus proceedings that he had received ineffective assistance from the lawyer appointed by the judge at the initial capital trial. And the lower court judges who have been reversed for failing to allow continuity in representation are still appointing lawyers when new cases come through the system. Those new defendants have no one to assist them in securing competent representation.

A newly admitted member of the Georgia bar was surprised to be appointed to handle the appeal of a capital case on her fifth day of practice in Columbus, Georgia. Two days earlier she had met the judge who appointed her when she accompanied her boss to a divorce proceeding. Only after she asked for help was a second attorney brought onto the case. Another lawyer in that same circuit was appointed to a capital case, but after submitting his first billing statement to the judge for approval was told by the judge that he was spending too much time on the case. He was summarily replaced by another lawyer and the defendant was ultimately sentenced to death. For a number of years, judges in that circuit appointed a lawyer to capital cases who did not challenge the underrepresentation of black citizens in the jury pools for fear of incurring hostility from the community and alienating potential jurors. As a result, a number of African-Americans were tried by all-white juries in capital cases even though one-third of the population of the circuit is African-American.

The many other examples of exceptionally poor legal representation documented by the American Bar Association (ABA), the *National Law Journal,* and others indicate that judges either are intentionally appointing lawyers who are not equal to the task or are completely inept at securing competent counsel in capital cases. The reality is that popularly elected judges, confronted by a local community that is outraged over the murder of a prominent citizen or angered by the facts of a crime, have little incentive to protect the constitutional rights of the one accused in such a killing. Many state judges are former prosecutors who won their seats on the bench by exploiting high-publicity death penalty cases. Some of those judges have not yet given up the prosecutorial attitude.

United States Congressman William J. Hughes, a former New Jersey prosecutor and leader on crime issues in the Congress, observed: "With some of the horror stories we've heard—lawyers who didn't call witnesses, who waived final argument— it is incredible that the courts allowed these cases to move forward." What is even more incredible is that in most of these instances the judges appointed the lawyers to the case.

E. The Minimal Standard of Legal Representation Tolerated in Capital Cases

This sad state of affairs is tolerated in our nation's courts in part because the United States Supreme Court has said that the Constitution requires no more. Instead of actually requiring *effective* representation to fulfill the Sixth Amendment's guarantee of counsel, the Court has brought the standard down to the level of ineffective practice. Stating that "the purpose of the effective assistance guarantee of the Sixth Amendment is not to improve the quality of legal representation," the Court in *Strickland v. Washington* adopted a standard that is "highly deferential" to the performance of counsel. To prevail on a claim of ineffective assistance of counsel, a defendant must overcome "a strong presumption that counsel's conduct falls within the wide range of reasonable professional assistance," show that the attorney's representation "fell below an objective standard of reasonableness," and establish "prejudice," which is defined as a reasonable probability that counsel's errors affected the outcome.

As Judge Alvin Rubin of the Fifth Circuit concluded:

> The Constitution, as interpreted by the courts, does not require that the accused, even in a capital case, be represented by able or effective counsel.... Consequently, accused persons who are represented by "not-legally-ineffective" lawyers may be condemned to die when the same accused, if represented by *effective* counsel, would receive at least the clemency of a life sentence.

Much less than mediocre assistance passes muster under the *Strickland* standard. Errors in judgment and other mistakes may readily be characterized as "strategy" or "tactics" and thus are beyond review. Indeed, courts employ a lesser standard for judging the competence of lawyers in a capital case than the standard for malpractice for doctors, accountants, and architects.

The defense lawyer in one Texas case failed to introduce any evidence about his client at the penalty phase of the trial. The attorney's entire closing argument regarding sentencing was: "You are an extremely intelligent jury. You've got that man's life in your hands. You can take it or not. That's all I have to say." A United States district court granted habeas corpus relief because of the lawyer's failure to present and argue evidence in mitigation, but the Fifth Circuit, characterizing counsel's nonargument as a "dramatic ploy," found that the attorney's performance satisfied *Strickland*. The lawyer was later suspended for other reasons. The defendant was executed.

* * *

The same ineptitude is frequently tolerated on appeal. The brief on direct appeal to the Alabama Supreme Court in the case of Larry Gene Heath, executed by Alabama on March 20, 1992, consisted of only one page of argument and cited only one case, which it distinguished. Counsel, who had filed a six-page brief on the same issue in the Alabama Court of Criminal Appeals, did not appear for oral argument in the case. Although the United States Court of Appeals later found counsel's performance deficient for failing to raise issues regarding denial of a change of venue, denial of sixty-seven challenges for cause of jurors who knew about the defendant's conviction in a neighboring state arising out of the same facts, and use of the defendant's assertion of his Fifth Amendment rights against him, it found no prejudice.

While such incompetence as has been described here passes muster as "effective assistance of counsel" under the Supreme Court's view of the Sixth Amendment, counsel's performance often fails to satisfy the increasingly strict procedural doctrines developed by the Supreme Court since 1977. Failure of counsel to recognize and preserve an issue, due to ignorance, neglect, or failure to discover and rely upon proper grounds or facts, even in the heat of trial, will bar federal review of that issue. A lawyer whose total knowledge of criminal law is *Miranda* and *Dred Scott* may be "not legally-ineffective" counsel under *Strickland*, but such a lawyer will of course not recognize or preserve many constitutional issues. The result has been what Justice Thurgood Marshall described as an "increasingly pernicious visegrip" for the indigent accused: courts refuse to address constitutional violations because they were not preserved by counsel, but counsel's failure to recognize and raise those issues is not considered deficient legal assistance.

Together, the lax standard of *Strickland* and the strict procedural default doctrines reward the provision of deficient representation. By assigning the indigent accused inadequate counsel, the state increases the likelihood of obtaining a conviction and death sentence at trial and reduces the scope of review. So long as counsel's performance passes muster under *Strickland*, those cases in which the accused received the poorest legal representation will receive the least scrutiny on appeal and in post-conviction review because of failure of the lawyer to preserve issues.

Bruce A. Green, *Access to Criminal Justice: Where Are the Prosecutors?*

3 Tex. A&M L. Rev. 515, 522–31 (2016)

Individual criminal injustices abound, both historically and in recent years. The paradigmatic criminal injustices are wrongful convictions—convictions of innocent individuals. In Texas alone, these have included, most prominently, the prosecution of Cameron Todd Willingham, who was wrongly convicted and executed; Michael Morton's case, which led to legislative reform; and the convictions of the individuals who were ultimately exonerated by Dallas District Attorney Craig Watkins before he was voted out of office. But Texas holds no monopoly on injustice. In any one of these wrongful convictions cases, and others around the country, one might profitably ask, "Where were the prosecutors?"

Consider the case of a recent Alabama exoneree, Anthony Ray Hinton, who spent approximately thirty years in prison, mostly on death row, until the U.S. Supreme Court intervened. Hinton's prosecution dates to 1985 when three restaurant managers were separately robbed and shot in Birmingham over the course of several months. Two died, and there were no eyewitnesses. The survivor of the third shooting picked Hinton's photo out of a photo array, but other witnesses placed Hinton at his job in a warehouse at the time of that robbery. The critical evidence against Hinton came from the state's firearms analysts who claimed to be able to discern through microscopic analysis whether a particular bullet was fired from a particular gun. They testified that the six bullets recovered from the three shootings were fired from the same gun—a revolver found in a search of Hinton's home and belonging to his mother.

Before trial, Hinton's defense lawyer asked the court for funds to hire a defense expert to rebut the state's forensic testimony, but the judge granted only $1,000—not enough to hire an expert with qualifications comparable to those of the state's witnesses. Mistakenly believing that the judge could not award more if asked, the defense lawyer made do, hiring a low-cost, one-eyed expert who the prosecutor effectively discredited at trial based on his lackluster qualifications, his difficulty handling a microscope, and his impaired vision. Hinton was found guilty and sentenced to death.

Hinton maintained his innocence. Once the appeals court upheld his conviction, however, he had no right to a court-appointed lawyer and of course he could not afford to hire one. That could easily have ended Hinton's pursuit of justice, but he was fortunate to have his case championed by the Equal Justice Initiative, directed by the legendary Bryan Stevenson. Few convicted defendants are as fortunate.

In the years following Hinton's conviction, the scientific community discredited the very premise of firearms analysis as used at Hinton's trial. The National Academy of Sciences (NAS) issued a report observing that this type of analysis is subjective, has no accepted protocols, and has a fairly limited scientific basis. In light of more current understandings, and based on their own experts' analysis, Hinton's new lawyers raised serious doubts about whether Hinton's mother's gun had fired the bullets from the three shootings as well as whether the bullets were even fired by the same gun. They asked the state's lawyers to reexamine the case. But the state's lawyers were not interested.

Doubts about the reliability of the forensic evidence standing alone provided no basis for an effective legal challenge to Hinton's conviction. The Supreme Court has never found it unconstitutional for a state to secure a criminal conviction based on dubious forensic evidence; indeed, the Court has not found a constitutional basis to set aside a criminal conviction simply because the convicted person is innocent. But the Court *has* recognized a Sixth Amendment right to competent trial counsel. In fact, many or most post-appeal challenges allege a denial of this right, especially in death penalty cases, where the claim is virtually required. And so Hinton's lawyers challenged the adequacy of his trial lawyer's representation rather than simply attempting to relitigate his guilt or innocence in light of new forensic understandings. But the suggestion of actual innocence was important in advocating the claim, which the Attorney General's Office opposed.

The nature of the legal claims that the defense can and cannot bring is essential to understanding why prosecutors largely escape blame for wrongful convictions. The bar has traditionally focused on defense lawyers as opposed to prosecutors in part because there is no right to a competent prosecution comparable to the right to a competent defense. Most of what prosecutors do is a matter of virtually unreviewable discretion. With the limited exception of alleged discovery violations, post-conviction legal challenges rarely bring prosecutors' role out of the shadows. This is not to say that competent prosecuting is unimportant, but just to say that it is impossible in most cases to have enough information to form a judgment about whether the prosecutor is proceeding competently and it is even harder to find an occasion on which a judge will pass judgment on a prosecutor's competence.

After a decade during which the state courts rejected Hinton's claim, the U.S. Supreme Court reviewed the case and found unanimously that Hinton's lawyer was remiss in not requesting additional funding for a better-qualified defense expert. The Court sent the case back to the state court to decide whether Hinton was prejudiced as a result, and a state judge, finding that he was, overturned his conviction. Both the Supreme Court decision and the ensuing state court decision were questionable from a doctrinal perspective but entirely understandable given that there was no reliable evidence proving Hinton's guilt. The state prosecutor initially scrambled around for witnesses to testify at a retrial, until a new set of state experts reexamined the forensic evidence—the gun and bullets—and reported, as the defense had maintained for years, that a match could not be made.

Upon his release in April 2015, Hinton said, "I got news for them, everybody who played a part in sending me to death row, you will answer to God." Who played a part? The Supreme Court's narrative suggests laying blame at the feet of the prosecution's forensic witnesses who testified unreliably, whether knowingly or just incompetently; the trial judge who afforded inadequate funding to hire a defense expert to expose the flaws in the state's evidence; and most especially Hinton's trial lawyer who did not know or think to ask for more funding. In general, commentators have criticized defense lawyers for failing to develop the necessary expertise to challenge forensic evidence. Conversely, some have argued that prosecutors are generally *not* to blame for wrongful convictions, at least in cases where they did not engage in affirmative misconduct, and that prosecutorial misconduct has been a material or predominant factor in a minority of exoneration cases.

Should the prosecutors get a pass? Hinton's case provides a useful one in which to consider prosecutors' role and responsibilities. Nothing suggests that the prosecutors violated the law or otherwise engaged in prosecutorial misconduct, as conventionally understood. But, at least as a matter of good prosecuting, trial prosecutors have a duty to prevent unjust convictions. And they have a general duty of competence, which presupposes that they will take reasonable steps to avoid convicting innocent people. That Hinton was wrongly convicted suggests at least on the face of it that the prosecutor did not act reasonably.

For one thing, the prosecutor had a gatekeeping responsibility, as Bennett Gershman and others have discussed. A prosecutor is not just a trial lawyer in the adversary process. The prosecutor decides whether or not a defendant will be charged with a crime. The grand jury does not have sole responsibility: It cannot initiate a prosecution without the prosecutor's assent. Knowing the fallibility of the criminal justice system, good prosecutors should not prosecute a case unless they are reasonably convinced that the accused is guilty. In hindsight, one might explore whether a prosecutor in good conscience could have been convinced of Hinton's guilt, or whether the prosecutor should have viewed the evidence more skeptically. For example, did the prosecutor fairly evaluate the credibility of Hinton's alibi witnesses? Did the prosecutor sufficiently scrutinize the reliability of the one eyewitness's photo identification and of the forensic testimony? Prosecutors review evidence critically when it is exculpatory or otherwise inconsistent with the prosecution's theory. Did the prosecutors examine the inculpatory evidence in the same manner?

Further, to protect against wrongful convictions, good prosecutors should not introduce unreliable evidence, even if, for disciplinary purposes, they *may* do so. It is unfair for prosecutors to leave it to lay juries to determine the credibility of dubious evidence. A prosecutor has a gate-keeping function to assure the credibility of evidence: If prosecutors themselves do not reasonably believe testimony, they should not present it to the jury. And particularly in the case of forensic evidence that a jury lacks the scientific and technical capability to evaluate, prosecutors should ensure the reliability of the testimony. Was that done by Hinton's prosecutors?

When the defense lawyer presented the best expert he could find for the money, the prosecutors attacked his qualifications, giving the misimpression that no well-qualified expert would support the defense. Good prosecutors have a duty to ensure that the criminal trial is procedurally fair—that the defense has the ability to put the prosecution's proof to the test in an adversary proceeding. Was it fair for the trial prosecutors to exploit the defense's lack of funding by attacking its expert's credentials in this manner?

Consider the state lawyers who defended the conviction over the course of decades, as scientific understandings evolved regarding the unreliability of firearms analysis as used in Hinton's trial. Given all we now know about wrongful convictions, shouldn't the Alabama state lawyers develop a conviction integrity process, like those in some states and localities, to review plausible claims of wrongful convictions in light of new evidence and new scientific understandings? At some earlier point, given that Hinton's conviction rested fundamentally on the forensic evidence—the supposed match between Hinton's mother's gun and the bullets from the three shootings— didn't the prosecutors have a responsibility to reconsider state experts' trial testimony and ascertain whether it would be confirmed using contemporary forensic techniques? As Hinton put it when he was released: "All they had to do was to test the gun, but when you think you're high and mighty and you're above the law, you don't have to answer to nobody."

And what of the state lawyers who opted vigorously to justify Hinton's conviction despite the unfairness of his trial—the absence of an adversary testing of the state's forensic testimony—because the defense lawyer did not know to ask for funding for an expert witness with credentials equaling those of the state's experts? The state's lawyers insisted implausibly that Hinton's lawyer performed just fine—an argument ultimately rejected by every Supreme Court Justice from the most moderate to the most pro-law-enforcement. And to the bitter end, through the course of the Supreme Court argument and thereafter, the state Attorney General maintained that a better-qualified defense expert would not have made a difference. Do prosecutors have a duty to refrain from making legal arguments that they do not reasonably believe, and could the state lawyers here actually have believed what they were saying?

When the U.S. Supreme Court sent the case back down and an Alabama state court judge set aside Hinton's conviction, for how long should the state prosecutor have waited before owning up to the fact that there was no genuine case against Hinton?

And finally, after the courts found that Hinton had been denied a fair trial because his defense was underfunded, and after contemporary forensic experts found that there was no evidentiary foundation for a retrial, and after Hinton was released, should any of the state's lawyers have engaged in public reflection or issued a public apology? According to the *New York Times*: "The prosecutors who filed the motion to dismiss the case did not respond to messages seeking comment, and, through a spokesman, the Alabama attorney general declined to be interviewed."

In contrast, the public recently heard from a lawyer who had prosecuted a Louisiana man, Glenn Ford, who was exonerated and freed after thirty years on death row. The former prosecutor expressed remorse, supported a call for state compensation of Ford, apologized to Ford and his family, to the victim's family, and to the judge and jury, and acknowledged his responsibility as a prosecutor for the miscarriage of justice. The former prosecutor had not acted unlawfully—he had not, for example, withheld exculpatory evidence. But he acknowledged that obeying the law is not the full measure of a prosecutor's ethical responsibility. He reflected:

Had I been more inquisitive, perhaps the evidence [of Ford's innocence] would have come to light years ago. But I wasn't, and my inaction contributed to the miscarriage of justice in this matter.... My mindset was wrong and blinded me to my purpose of seeking justice, rather than obtaining a conviction of a person who I believed to be guilty. I did not hide evidence, I simply did not seriously consider that sufficient information may have been out there that could have led to a different conclusion.

The former prosecutor acknowledged that he had given no thought to the defense lawyers' inexperience and lack of adequate funding, to the unfairness of trying a Black man before an all white jury, and to the use of forensic testimony that was predicated on "junk science." He described his attitude as a prosecutor in the following terms: "In 1984, I was 33 years old. I was arrogant, judgmental, narcissistic and very full of myself. I was not as interested in justice as I was in winning."

Prosecutors are not legally obligated to account for themselves like this when it is discovered that they secured or defended wrongful convictions. But do they have a moral obligation to do so — an obligation not only to the exonerated person but to the public, so that current prosecutors can learn from their mistakes and procedures can be adopted to reduce the risk of wrongful convictions? The state's lawyers had a central role in putting Anthony Ray Hinton on death row for half a lifetime for crimes for which there is no reason to think he was responsible. Where are the prosecutors and why are they silent?

The Supreme Court's decision in Hinton's case might lead one to conclude that defense counsel was principally to blame for Hinton's wrongful conviction, but that seems unfair. Even assuming the defense lawyer had alerted the court to its legal authority to provide additional funds for a defense expert, it is not certain the court would have exercised its authority. Had the court done so, it is not certain that a better-credentialed defense expert would have been retained, that the prosecutor would have been significantly less effective in discrediting the better-credentialed expert, or that, even if the prosecution were less effective, the jury would have found a reasonable doubt. At every turn, the prosecutor had significantly more power to avert an injustice and to do so without reliance on any other actor — the judge, the jury, or opposing counsel.

The ABA, the National Association of District Attorneys, and other institutional representatives of the bar develop disciplinary, prudential, and aspirational standards of conduct for prosecutors. But these institutions rarely examine the facts of particular cases to determine whether prosecutors adhered to the standards and, if so, whether the standards are adequate to avert injustices. In cases of demonstrable injustice such as Hinton's, the bar should measure the prosecutors' conduct against its standards for several purposes: to elaborate on the meaning of the standards in actual practice; to critique prosecutors' work; and to determine the adequacy of existing standards. As to the last, it is important to learn whether existing norms are up to the task of averting and correcting injustices.

B. Current Law: Overview

Ineffective Assistance of Counsel

The leading case on ineffective assistance of counsel, *Strickland v. Washington*, 466 U.S. 668 (1984), establishes a two-pronged test to determine whether an attorney provided constitutionally-adequate representation. To establish a claim, the claimant must show that his or her attorney's legal representation was objectively deficient, and that the deficient performance prejudiced the defendant — that is, that there is a reasonable probability that, but for the errors, the outcome would have been different. As Justice Alito has explained, "*Strickland*'s definition of prejudice is based on the reliability of the underlying proceeding. 'The benchmark for judging any claim of ineffectiveness must be whether counsel's conduct so undermined the proper functioning of the adversarial process that the trial cannot be relied on as having produced a just result.'"[61]

The Court has held in several cases that deficient advice during plea-bargaining can constitute a violation of the Sixth Amendment right to counsel. See *Lafler v. Cooper*, 566 U.S. 156 (2012) (petitioner was prejudiced by counsel's deficient performance in advising petitioner to reject the plea offer and go to trial); *Missouri v. Frye*, 566 U.S. 133 (2012) (counsel was deficient in failing to communicate to defendant prosecutor's written plea offer before it expired).

Under the doctrine of procedural default, the Supreme Court has long held that criminal defendants are presumptively barred from raising procedurally defaulted claims in federal habeas proceedings. Two exceptions to that rule, however, have been recognized. First, a procedurally defaulted issue may be heard where there was "cause and prejudice" for the default. Second, habeas courts will overlook the procedural default if the petitioner presents evidence that he or she is actually innocent of the crime of conviction.

In the past, the courts have been stingy in finding either of these exceptions. Although ineffective assistance of counsel is cause for procedural default, *Murray v. Carrier*, 477 U.S. 478 (1986), attorney errors not rising to the level of constitutional ineffectiveness under Strickland are not. For instance, in *Coleman v. Thompson*, 501 U.S. 722 (1991), where Coleman's appeal was summarily dismissed after his lawyers filed his notice of appeal in state court one day late, the Supreme Court held that such attorney errors did not excuse procedural default so as to permit habeas review. The rule in Coleman was modified somewhat in *Martinez v. Ryan*, 566 U.S. 1 (2012) (holding that where, under state law, ineffective-assistance-of-trial-counsel claims must be raised in an initial-review collateral proceeding, a procedural default will not bar a federal habeas court from hearing those claims if, in the initial-review collateral proceeding, there was no counsel or counsel in that proceeding was ineffective).

---

61. Weaver v. Massachusetts, 137 S. Ct. 1899, 1915 (2017) (quoting Strickland at 687).

C. Legal Materials, Exercises, and Media

1. *Reflective Essay, Ineffective Defense Counsel and Ethical Duties of Prosecutors*: In Bruce Green's "Access to Criminal Justice: Where are the Prosecutors?" you learned of prosecutor A.M. "Marty" Stroud's soul-searching acknowledgment of his role in the wrongful conviction of Glenn Ford in Louisiana. While Stroud did not violate the law, he also personally felt as though he did not do enough to fulfill his ethical responsibility. You can read his candid op-ed to the Shreveport Times in its entirety at "Lead Prosecutor apologizes for role in sending man to death row," and watch Mr. Stroud's interview with the Shreveport Times (6:28): http://www.shreveporttimes.com/story/opinion/readers/2015/03/20/lead-prosecutor-offers-apology-in-the-case-of-exonerated-death-row-inmate-glenn-ford/25049063/.

    Do prosecutors have any affirmative duties when defense counsel is apparently ineffective? Should they?

2. *From Defendant to Defender:* Shortly after being exonerated, Jarrett Adams went back to school to earn his law degree and then clerked on the U.S. Court of Appeals for the Seventh Circuit — the same court that granted his post-conviction habeas petition for relief. Adams' trial counsel failed to investigate the case and called no witnesses on his behalf. Adams has now represented defendants in challenging their own wrongful convictions, working with the same attorneys at the Wisconsin Innocence Project who represented him in post-conviction. Read about his journey and watch a short documentary (4:37), Elizabeth Chuck & Dan Slepian, *From Defendant to Defender: One Wrongfully Convicted Man Frees Another*, NBC News (Aug. 2, 2018) https://www.nbcnews.com/news/us-news/defendant-defender-one-wrongfully-convicted-man-frees-another-n788886.

3. *Discussion, Ethical Duties of Confidentiality and Disclosure for Defense Attorneys:* What if your client confesses to you that he committed a crime — a crime for which someone else is charged? Under attorney-client confidentiality, are you required to keep that knowledge secret, even when another person is charged and convicted with the crime?

    Alton Logan had served 26 years in prison when Andrew Wilson — the true culprit — died. Wilson's attorneys then provided Logan with a signed affidavit from Wilson, confessing to the crime. With the affidavit, Logan was able to prove his innocence and finally be released from prison. Read more about his case and life in Alton Logan's book with Berl Falbaum, *Justice Failed: How "Legal Ethics" Kept Me in Prison for 26 Years*, (Counterpoint Press 2017). You can read an excerpt from his book at *I Served 26 Years for Murder Even Though the Killer Confessed*, The Marshall Project (October 19, 2017): https://www.themarshallproject.org/2017/10/19/i-served-26-years-for-murder-even-though-the-killer-confessed?utm_medium=email&utm_campaign=newsletter&utm_source=opening-statement&utm_term=newsletter-20171020-872.

4. *Reflective Essay: Trust, Interpretation, and Effective Representation:* Sometimes lawyers talk about the "trust coin"—that a client has to be able to trust the lawyer to tell her story, and to ultimately trust the process. Lawyers thus act as interpreters for the client to the court, while also interpreting the law and the legal system to the client. Discuss a moment where you've culturally been a translator and developed trust. Are there any insights or lessons from that experience that can be brought to effective legal representation?

Chapter Twelve

Cognitive Bias and Tunnel Vision

DAVID'S DEFENSE: He was questioned without benefit of counsel, despite his request to his interrogators to call his mother and obtain legal assistance. At eleven p.m., Keaton was taken to the jail in Tallahassee, where questioning resumed and continued until the next morning.

DAVID'S PROSECUTOR: Now, Keaton could have said in his statement anything he wanted to. There was nobody making those defendants say anything, and this jury knows anyway that of course that would be impossible, impractical. You just can't *make* somebody say something; nobody can!

> —excerpt from *The Exonerated*, a play by Jessica Blank and Erik Jensen; recounting the arguments at exoneree David Keaton's trial

A. Readings

Keith A. Findley and Michael S. Scott,
The Multiple Dimensions of Tunnel Vision in Criminal Cases
2006 WIS. L. REV. 291, 291–397 (2006)

[The] burgeoning inquiry [into wrongful convictions] has identified many of the recurrent causes of error, including fallible eyewitness identification evidence and flawed eyewitness identification procedures, false confessions, jailhouse snitch testimony, police and prosecutorial misconduct, forensic science error or fraud, and inadequate defense counsel. A theme running through almost every case, that touches each of these individual causes, is the problem of tunnel vision.

Tunnel vision is a natural human tendency that has particularly pernicious effects in the criminal justice system. By tunnel vision, we mean that "compendium of common heuristics and logical fallacies," to which we are all susceptible, that lead actors in the criminal justice system to "focus on a suspect, select and filter the evidence that will 'build a case' for conviction, while ignoring or suppressing evidence that points away from guilt." This process leads investigators, prosecutors, judges, and defense lawyers alike to focus on a particular conclusion and then filter all evidence in a case through the lens provided by that conclusion. Through that filter, all information supporting the adopted conclusion is elevated in significance, viewed as consistent with the other evidence, and deemed relevant and probative. Evidence inconsistent with the chosen theory is easily overlooked or dismissed as irrelevant, incredible, or unreliable. Properly understood, tunnel vision is more often the product of the human condition as well as institutional and cultural pressures, than of maliciousness or indifference.

Tunnel vision both affects, and is affected by, other flawed procedures in the criminal justice system. For example, mistaken eyewitness identifications—the most frequent single cause of wrongful convictions—can convince investigators early in a case that a particular individual is the perpetrator. Convinced of guilt, investigators might then set out to obtain a confession from that suspect, producing apparently inculpatory reactions or statements from the suspect, or leading investigators to interpret the suspect's innocent responses as inculpatory. The process of interrogating an innocent suspect might even produce a false confession. Police and prosecutors, convinced of guilt, might recruit or encourage testimony from unreliable jailhouse snitches, who fabricate stories that the defendant confessed to them, in hopes that they will benefit in their own cases from cooperation with authorities. Forensic scientists, aware of the desired result of their analyses, might be influenced—even unwittingly—to interpret ambiguous data or fabricate results to support the police theory. All of this additional evidence then enters a feedback loop that bolsters the witnesses' confidence in the reliability and accuracy of their incriminating testimony and reinforces the original assessment of guilt held by police, and ultimately by prosecutors, courts, and even defense counsel.

Tunnel vision, in a general sense at least, is a well-recognized phenomenon in the criminal justice system. Most official inquiries into specific wrongful convictions have noted the role that tunnel vision played in those individual cases of injustice. For example, former Illinois Governor George Ryan's Commission on Capital Punishment concluded that tunnel vision played a significant role in most of the thirteen Illinois cases studied in which an innocent person was sentenced to death before being exonerated and released from death row. The official investigation of the wrongful convictions in Chicago's "Ford Heights Four" case also concluded that tunnel vision was largely to blame. Official Canadian governmental inquiries, held after high-profile exonerations, have repeatedly identified tunnel vision as a significant problem in those cases. And the Innocence Commission for Virginia issued a report finding that tunnel vision played a significant role in many of Virginia's thirteen proven wrongful convictions.

Most discussions of tunnel vision have focused on its effects in the initial stages of criminal cases—during the police investigation. That is indeed where tunnel vision begins, and in many respects where it can be most damaging, because all later stages of the process feed off the information generated in the police investigation. But tunnel vision in the criminal justice system is more pervasive than that. Considerable literature also examines various pressures on prosecutors that can cause them to act in ways that subvert justice, whether intentionally or, as is more often the case, unintentionally. That literature also depicts a form of tunnel vision. But the problem is more pervasive than even that literature suggests. In this Article, we explore the ways in which tunnel vision infects all phases of criminal proceedings, beginning with the investigation of cases and then proceeding through the prosecution, trial or plea-bargaining, appeal, and postconviction stages. We seek to expose some of the myriad expressions of this tunnel vision, and to come to some understanding of its multiple causes. We examine the roots of the problem in cognitive biases, institutional pressures, and deliberate policies reflected in rules and training throughout the system. In the end, we attempt to draw from this inquiry some understanding of the measures that might be taken to mitigate the harmful effects of tunnel vision.

Case Studies in Tunnel Vision

A. Marvin Anderson

After a trial that lasted less than five hours, Marvin Anderson was convicted of robbery, forcible sodomy, abduction, and two counts of rape of a twenty-four-year-old woman in Hanover, Virginia, in 1982. In 2002, DNA testing proved that he did not commit the crime. Police investigators had focused on Anderson because the rapist, who was African American, had mentioned to the victim that he had a white girlfriend, and Anderson was the only black man police knew of who was living with a white woman.

Anderson did not fit the victim's description of her attacker in several respects; Anderson was taller than the man the victim described and, unlike the attacker, Anderson had a dark complexion, no mustache, and no scratches on his face. Nonetheless, investigators obtained a photo of Anderson from his employer (he had no prior record and hence no mug photo) and presented it to the victim in an array of six to ten photos. Anderson's photo was the only one in color, and the only one with his social security number printed on it. The victim selected Anderson's photograph. Thirty minutes later, police put together a live-person lineup that again included Anderson. Anderson was apparently the only person in the lineup whose photo had also been included in the photo array. Police told the victim to "go in and look at the people in the line up to see if she could pick out the suspect," and she again picked Anderson. Many of the procedures used in Anderson's identification process are now widely recognized as suggestive or flawed in ways that can lead an eyewitness to mistakenly identify an innocent person.

There were other reasons to doubt the identification as well. DNA testing was not yet available at the time, but a forensic scientist testified that she had performed blood typing on swabs from both Anderson and the victim and was unable to identify Anderson as the source of semen samples collected in the rape kit. In addition, Anderson presented four alibi witnesses, including his mother, his girlfriend, and two neighbors, who all testified that they saw him outside his mother's house washing his car at the time of the attack. None of this evidence, however, was enough to overcome the eyewitness identification.

Tunnel vision infected Anderson's case from the beginning, leading police, prosecutors, defense counsel, and eventually the jury and reviewing courts, to minimize and discredit the alibi evidence, the mismatch between the victim's description of the perpetrator and Anderson's appearance, and the absence of physical evidence. Even more significantly, the premature focus on Anderson meant that no one pursued evidence that was available before trial that pointed toward the true perpetrator. As the Virginia Innocence Commission concluded, "[o]nce the victim identified Anderson ... the police did not pursue additional leads."

The DNA testing that exonerated Anderson in 2002 identified the true perpetrator—a man named Otis "Pop" Lincoln. The match to Lincoln should not have come as a surprise. Lincoln's name had been circulating in the community as a likely suspect for some time prior to Anderson's conviction, but no one investigated him. Two friends of the Anderson family said before trial that just before the rape they saw Lincoln riding a bicycle toward the shopping center where the attack occurred—a fact of particular significance because the attacker rode a bicycle. Moreover, these witnesses heard Lincoln make sexually suggestive comments to two young white girls, and then boast as he rode past that he would force himself onto a woman if she refused his advances. The owner of the bicycle that was used by the assailant also said that Lincoln had stolen it from him approximately thirty minutes before the rape. After Anderson was arrested, others in the community reported to Anderson's mother that Lincoln drove by her house one day because he wanted to see "the young boy who was taking his rap." Moreover, unlike Anderson, Lincoln had a criminal record for sexual assault and was awaiting trial for another sexual attack at the time. Nonetheless, even Anderson's defense lawyer declined to investigate or call any witnesses who could have linked Lincoln to the crime at trial.

Eventually, six years later, at proceedings on Anderson's application for habeas corpus, Lincoln confessed fully to the crime in court under oath and provided details of the attack. Nevertheless, the same judge who presided over the original trial refused to credit Lincoln's confession, finding that it was untruthful. The Governor subsequently refused to intervene and denied clemency. Anderson remained in prison, and then on parole, for several more years until DNA testing confirmed that Lincoln, not Anderson, was the attacker.

Other aspects of the case also reveal just how stubborn erroneous beliefs in guilt can be. Despite the weakness of the case against Anderson, and the abundance of evidence that should have alerted authorities to investigate Lincoln, the original prosecutor in the case claimed that, from his perspective and until the exoneration, the Anderson case was "the clearest case he had ever had." Although Anderson's trial lawyer made numerous egregious errors, the trial court was unwilling to grant a new trial on a claim of ineffective assistance of counsel. The court concluded that it made no difference that: (1) counsel had a conflict of interest because he had previously represented Lincoln on a previous attempted rape charge; (2) although the lawyer knew there was evidence against Lincoln, and admitted that he suspected Lincoln, he failed to disclose his prior representation of Lincoln, his suspicions about Lincoln, and his conflict of interest to Anderson; (3) despite Anderson's mother's repeated pleas, the lawyer failed to call Lincoln or the other witnesses who had watched Lincoln harass the young women, make threats, and ride off on a bicycle toward the crime scene just before the attack in this case; and (4) the lawyer failed to ask that the bicycle ridden by the attacker on the day of the rape be fingerprinted or introduced into evidence, even though the bicycle was in police custody. The trial court found that all of this was insufficient to meet the two-pronged test for ineffective assistance of counsel.

B. Steven Avery

Like Marvin Anderson, Steven Avery was convicted of a brutal rape primarily on the strength of the victim's eyewitness identification. Like Anderson, Avery was convicted despite strong alibi evidence, and even though the true perpetrator was well known to police and prosecutors and should have been a prime suspect. Also like Anderson, Avery was wrongly convicted because tunnel vision prevented system actors from considering alternative theories about the crime until DNA evidence finally proved in 2003 that Avery was innocent, and that another man, Gregory Allen, was guilty. By then, Avery had served more than eighteen years in prison.

The rape and attempted murder in Avery's case was committed in broad daylight on a beach in Manitowoc County, Wisconsin, in 1985. While being treated in the hospital after the attack, the victim gave police a description of her attacker and helped create a composite sketch. Based on that description and sketch, local sheriff's deputies thought the attacker might be Avery. Law enforcement knew Avery because Manitowoc was a small community, he had relatives who worked in the sheriff's department, he had previously been convicted of two counts of burglary and one count of cruelty to an animal, and he was being prosecuted at the time for allegedly forcing the wife of a deputy off the road at gunpoint as part of an ongoing feud.

The sheriff presented Avery's photo to the victim as part of a nine-photo simultaneous array, telling her that "the suspect might be in there." The victim later said that the sheriff's statement led her to "believe[] that the suspect's photograph was included in the group of nine photos." However, a photograph of Allen, the true perpetrator, was not included in the array and the victim instead selected Avery's photo. Three days later, after the victim had been informed that police had arrested the man she identified, police conducted a live-person lineup to confirm her identification. Avery was the only person in the lineup whose photo had also been in the previous photo array. Avery was also the shortest, youngest, and fairest person in the lineup. Unlike Avery, a few of the people in the lineup wore professional attire such as neck ties, and some wore glasses. Records from the lineup indicate that one lineup member looked at Avery during most of the lineup. Again, the victim picked Avery.

The State bolstered its eyewitness evidence with circumstantial evidence. Deputies swore that the night of the arrest they told Avery only that he was being arrested for attempted murder, yet they claimed Avery told his wife that he was being accused of attempting to murder a "girl." Despite the ambiguous nature of that evidence, the deputies, the prosecutor, and, ultimately, the courts thought it was highly incriminating that Avery seemed to know the gender of the victim. In addition, to rebut Avery's alibi—his claim that he had spent the day pouring concrete with his extended family and friends—the State offered evidence that the State Crime Laboratory could find no traces of concrete dust on his clothing. The State also offered evidence that a hair found on Avery's tee shirt was microscopically similar to the victim's head hair.

Avery's defense was unusually strong. He presented sixteen alibi witnesses who confirmed that he had been pouring concrete during the day and then had taken his wife and five young children—including six-day-old twins—to Green Bay, more than an hour's drive away, for supper and to shop for paint. Instead of taking pause from this evidence, the State sought a way to minimize its significance. The prosecutor impeached the testimony of Avery's family and friends as biased. When Avery presented the testimony of unbiased witnesses—the clerk and the manager at the Shopko store where Avery purchased his paint in Green Bay—sheriff's deputies sought a way around their testimony. The clerk and the manager, who had not known Avery previously, remembered him checking out because it was unusual to see a family with five young children, including twins who were less than a week old. And they produced the cash register tape showing that Avery and his family had checked out at 5:13 p.m.—a little over an hour after the victim claimed the attack had begun. Sheriff's deputies countered that they had done a timed drive from the location of the assault to the Green Bay Shopko and had been able to make it to the checkout line in fifty-seven minutes. But, as the Attorney General concluded after investigating Avery's wrongful conviction in 2003:

> [T]he officers admitted that they went ten miles per hour over the speed limit to reach those numbers and the officers did not account for potential delays resulting from the presence of five children, including six-day old twins, all of whom were seen with Avery and his wife at the Shopko. Moreover, the reenactment did not allow any time for picking up Avery's family and would therefore assume that Avery's wife and five children were at the beach somewhere or in the car while he committed the assault. Simply put, tunnel vision prevented the deputies, the prosecutor, the judge, and the jury from appreciating the implausibility of that scenario.

Even more startling, however, the sheriff's department and prosecutor refused to consider or investigate the true perpetrator, even though he was in their sights all along. Allen, who was identified as the true perpetrator by a cold hit in the DNA database in 2003, was a known sexual offender in Manitowoc County prior to this offense, and his offenses were escalating. Two years earlier, the same prosecutor who prosecuted Avery had convicted Allen of a very similar attempted sexual assault—Allen masturbated while walking behind a woman and then lunged at her—on the same beach as the site of the attack in 1985. At the time of the 1985 offense, Allen was a chief suspect in the murder of a fifteen-year-old girl in North Carolina, and was suspected of a series of attempted sexual assaults, attempted burglaries, window peepings, and acts of exposing himself in Manitowoc County. Allen was considered such a threat to commit a sexual assault that Manitowoc police maintained daily surveillance on him, checking on his whereabouts as many as fourteen times each day, during the two weeks prior to the 1985 assault for which Avery was wrongly convicted. The day of the attack, police were called away to other duties and were only able to check on Allen once. In fact, before Avery was convicted, at least two employees in the district attorney's office expressed concern that they believed Allen, not Avery, was responsible for the assault for which Avery stood charged.

Nonetheless, the sheriff's department and prosecutor steadfastly refused to consider that Avery might not be guilty, or to investigate Allen. When the police department suggested to the sheriff's department that Allen might be the perpetrator, the sheriff simply responded that Allen had been ruled out as a suspect. When the victim inquired about the police department's concerns regarding Allen, the sheriff's department told her, "Do not talk to the Manitowoc Police Department. It will only confuse you. We have jurisdiction." and all "other suspects ha[ve] been looked at and were ruled out...."

The resilience of the view that Avery was guilty also infected the postconviction and appellate stages of the case. On direct appeal, the court of appeals rejected challenges to the out-of-court identifications, concluding that, despite the now-apparent deficiencies in the identification procedures that were employed, "the photo array constitute[d] one of the fairest ones this court ha[d] seen." Subsequently, in 1995, Avery obtained postconviction DNA testing in an attempt to prove his innocence. Unfortunately, the technology was not advanced enough at that time to produce dispositive results. The DNA taken from the victim's fingernail scrapings (she said she had scratched at her attacker) showed the presence of DNA from the victim and an unknown third person, but could not conclusively exclude (or include) Avery. Avery argued that the third-party DNA had to be the real attacker's, but the courts denied relief, concluding that the foreign DNA could have gotten under the victim's fingernails innocently. Despite the now-apparent weaknesses in the State's case, including Avery's sixteen alibi witnesses, the court of appeals asserted that it did not "view this case as 'extremely close,'" and accordingly concluded that the new DNA evidence was not enough to warrant a new trial.

In September 2003, the Wisconsin State Crime Laboratory was able to use previously unavailable technologies to extract a DNA profile from the victim's pubic hair combings. That DNA profile conclusively excluded Avery. Moreover, when laboratory analysts ran that profile through the State DNA Databank, they obtained a cold hit on Allen, whose profile was in the databank because he had subsequently committed another sexual assault, for which he was by then serving sixty years in prison. By stipulation of the parties and order of the court, Avery was exonerated and released the following day.

Sherry Nakhaeizadeh, Itiel E. Dror, and Ruth M. Morgan, *The Emergence of Cognitive Bias in Forensic Science and Criminal Investigations*
4 Brit. J. Am. Legal Stud. 527, 534–42 (2015)

Human Cognition and Cognitive Bias

In order to understand how judgments and interpretations in forensic science and criminal investigations can be affected by cognitive mechanisms, it is important to recognize the strengths and weakness of human cognition in decision-making. The information processing approach is known as human cognition, and defines the acquisition, organization and the use of knowledge. The study of human cognition addresses human perception, judgment and decision-making, which are all influenced by a variety of cognitive processes. However, in order for the brain to organize information and new perceptions the human mind will use schemata to comprehend the data derived. The power of schemata plays a vital role in judgment and decision-making, which could be defined as "scripts" that help the brain analyze the perception and judgment of an individual based on their prior beliefs. The human mind does encode passively the information coming in, which is known as "bottom up" and is considered to be purely raw data derived from the environment. The processing and interpretation of incoming data (bottom-up information) is mediated by a variety of "top down" cognitive mechanisms such as knowledge, experience, motivations expectations and emotional states. Top-down processing makes the processing of information much more efficient however, in some cases top-down components interfere with and distort the processing of the bottom-up component. For example, research within psychology and social science has demonstrated that the emotional state of individuals can have a significant impact upon the way information is processed and interpreted as perceptions and understandings are highly related to emotional conditions. Mock juror studies that have addressed the issue of emotional state and decision-making have demonstrated that emotional state can influence verdict outcomes. Results have shown that presenting emotionally disturbing evidence influences the verdict of mock jurors. Within forensic science, it is now acknowledged that forensic evidence can also potentially be influenced by a variety of top-down processing, with much forensic analysis arguably occurring in highly emotional contexts where evidence is associated with specific crimes against a victim(s).

Therefore, relying exclusively on top down cognitive mechanisms and operative information processing is liable to cause weakness in the interpretation of evidence. This type of information may affect the analytical methods and influence the decision-making procedure when generating the final conclusion and thereby cause a biasing effect. These types of errors could be referred to as cognitive biases, potentially defined as the psychological and cognitive factors that unconsciously manipulate and interfere with the data processing, causing judgment and decision-making to be unreliable. This issue is also part of a concept commonly known as heuristics.

Heuristics are strategies that use mental shortcuts in decision-making, including ignoring part of the information to make decisions quicker, more prudent and accurate. For enhanced and frugal cognition, heuristics trade off some loss in accuracy, which could lead to faulty reasoning. There are differing methods where cognitive heuristics can operate, such as through anchoring and adjustments, whereby the tendency is to rely on the first piece of information presented when making a decision. For example studies regarding sentencing guidelines have demonstrated that judges use different judgmental anchors when making sentencing decisions. It has been demonstrated that judges were influenced by sentencing demands which resulted in people who had committed very similar crimes receiving different sentences. Tversky and Khaneman (1974) demonstrated in their study that people tend to rely on various cognitive heuristics, and whilst this is considered generally to be beneficial, it could also create systematic errors in judgment and decision-making. This has been specifically demonstrated when it comes to prior expectations which could provide a sufficient and unconscious tendency to perceive and interpret evidence that would confirm pre-existing beliefs, otherwise known as confirmation bias.

Confirmation bias is the tendency to selectively gather and process information to confirm a hypothesis or preconception by looking for evidence that would validate existing beliefs and expectations, in terms of rejecting, excusing or ignoring evidence that could contradict the current assumption. Studies within reasoning have demonstrated that people attempt to find evidence, which confirms to a rule rather than finding evidence that would disconfirm it. The fundamental mechanisms upon which confirmation bias operates are selective information search and biased interpretation of available information. Selective information search within legal perspectives occurs when an individual examines information or evidence to incriminate a suspect based on a personal hypothesis, and ignores the search for evidence that could exonerate or lead to an alternative hypothesis. Biased interpretations occur when experts only interpret evidence that supports, and will be in favor of their own hypotheses. This inhibits the expert from observing the evidence from multiple angles, often resulting in a subjective conclusion. For example, the majority of criminal investigations are driven by a theory, which leads investigators in their search for evidence guided by their initial hypothesis regarding when, why, how and by whom a crime was committed. These working hypotheses could arguably be affected by preconceptions and expectations of the investigators due to the way the brain processes and stores information, especially when dealing with ambiguous and complex evidence. Thus, a variety of influences that have nothing to do with the case drive and guide the investigation, and can affect its outcome. As described earlier, a preference for confirmation over falsification could arguably result in investigators searching for and finding confirmatory evidence against a suspect in contrast to find disconfirming and exonerating information.

An article by Kassin et al. (2013) "*The Forensic Confirmation Bias: Problems, Perspectives and Proposed Solutions*" outlined both some of the earliest and the most contemporary work on confirmation biases. The authors traced the concept of confirmation bias back to the philosopher Francis Bacon who acknowledged the impact of it in his work of 1620, by recognizing various obstacles that influence the human mind. The body of literature within psychology has over the years recognized different sources and fuels of cognitive bias, and confirmation bias in particular, such as time pressure, expectations, pre-existing beliefs, and motivation. Empirical research has demonstrated that the beliefs held by people are resistant to change. Once people form a hypothesis they fail to adjust the tenacity of their beliefs in the light of evidence that will challenge the accuracy of those beliefs. This is also known as belief perseverance, which is the tendency to continue to confirm a theory even though the evidence underlying the theory is confounded. One of the earliest studies in belief perseverance was to study the effect of what is known as the *debriefing paradigm*. In a study conducted by Anderson et al. (1980) subjects were presented with allegedly authentic reports of fire-fighters. After reading the reports subjects were asked to write an explanation of the relationship between fire-fighting abilities and risk preference observed in the case histories given. This was done to investigate whether fictitious information about the relationship between the personality trait such as risk taking and fire fighter ability could produce a perseverant social theory. The case histories reports given to the subjects were manipulated whereby participants were led to perceive that there was either a positive or negative correlation between risk preference and fire-fighting abilities. The results demonstrated that even after participants were debriefed concerning the fiction of the case reports, they persisted in the theories that they had formed from those case histories. Participants led to believe that risk taking makes better fire-fighters and those initially led to believe that risk taking makes poorer fire-fighters persevered in their initial beliefs, even after being debriefed about the fictional nature of the initial information. The study demonstrated that the participants adhered to their conclusions even though the evidence fundamental to the conclusions were confounded. Similarly, mock juror studies have found that jurors tend to be unable to disregard evidence that has been ruled inadmissible. Equally, in a criminal investigation, the act of considering someone "accountable" (which is a condition necessary for turning a person into a suspect) is in itself likely to increase the belief of the investigator in the culpability of the suspect(s).

The fact that people can be unaware of pre-existing beliefs has potential consequences in forensic settings. This is also known as the observer effect, which in general terms could be described as when the result of an observation in a particularly set of circumstances is affected by the observer. In forensic science the term observer effect is used when the motives or preconceptions of the observer are thought to influence the perception and interpretation of evidence, resulting in examiner bias. Context effect is highly related to observer effect and is used in the forensic sciences to describe situations in which forensic analysis are affected by the context of the crime or by the contextual information available to the analyst prior to their assessment.

Studies have demonstrated that it is difficult for people to evaluate the strength of evidence independent of pre-existing beliefs and that there is a tendency to devalue disconfirming evidence. This is because evidence is weighed to support prior beliefs to a greater degree than evidence that contradicts those beliefs. The psychology and social science literature suggests that people not only demonstrate confirmation bias when seeking new information but also in the memory of stored information; meaning that people search their memories in biased ways. The product of various cognitive biases that could obstruct accuracy in what is perceived, how it is perceived, and how it is interpreted is also known in criminal cases as tunnel vision. Tunnel vision has been shown to have an effect in the initial stages of criminal investigations and this is a significant issue because all subsequent stages of the investigation will potentially be impacted by the information generated at this initial stage.

Cognitive Bias and the Legal System

Research regarding cognitive biases and decision-making has also been applied within the legal system. Studies conducted by Phillips et al. (1999) in eyewitness misidentification demonstrated the power of information by indicating that when the suspect is known, it is more likely for the investigator to unconsciously steer the witness towards the suspect. Similarly, research in facial recognition and decision-making has demonstrated that when information is given concerning a suspect with regard to their guilt, people have the tendency to perceive more similarities between a facial composite and the suspect.

Studies carried out by Kassin and Fong (1999) demonstrated variations in interrogation methods when an assumption of guilt had previously been established. The findings demonstrated that when investigators had a presumption of guilt there was sometimes an unconscious tendency to be more aggressive and intimidating in interrogation towards the suspect. Mock jury studies have demonstrated that confessions of a crime have more impact on verdicts than other forms of evidence. This is considered to be because most people believe that people do not confess to a crime they did not commit.

For prosecutors it has also been identified that there are some cognitive pitfalls when involved in an investigation. For example, it has been observed that the prosecution can shape the investigative direction for example, by determining who to investigate, and once an arrest is made, they determine whether to bring charges or not, what charges to bring and what sentence to seek. This processing approach for prosecutors may lead to potential ways that cognitive bias may impact upon decision-making. Indeed, the phenomenon of confirmation bias could in complex cases lead to the natural tendency to review the case report for confirming evidence and not exculpatory evidence that might contradict the given hypothesis. It has also been shown that people can fail to look for evidence that disconfirms a given hypothesis and this can lead to tunnel vision in investigations where investigators could potentially fail to investigate alternative theories of the crime. People are motivated to consolidate their beliefs in a manner that strengthens their initial perspective. Numerous studies have demonstrated that expectations and motivations can affect how events, people and evidence are perceived. For example in studies where subjects were told in advance that a person had particular personality characteristics, they had the tendency to see those qualities in that person regardless of whether those characteristics were present or not. In criminal investigations this could have severe effects, especially if an individual is being judged by investigators where the initial belief presented to each actor in the system is that the defendant is guilty.

Research and policy makers have started to realize the significant role the science of psychology plays in the study and prevention of wrongful convictions. It is estimated that over 300 individuals have been exonerated by post-conviction DNA testing. Miscarriages of justice have been identified where there have been a range of causes of error, including fallible eyewitness identification, false confessions, police and prosecutorial misconduct and forensic science error.

Forensic science plays a complex role in the study of wrongful convictions where it has been argued to be both part of the problem but also the solution. For example, DNA evidence has helped to exonerate scores of wrongfully convicted suspects, however in some cases, errors in the DNA evidence were identified. One example of this discussed by Thompson et al. (2009) is the case of Josiah Sutton's (1998) wrongful conviction for rape, where DNA and eyewitness identification was involved in the original case. The analyst testing for DNA in the case was aware that the victim had identified Sutton as one of the rapists. It has been argued that this information may have induced a confirmation bias and led the analyst to focus on evidence supporting Sutton's guilt and ignoring facts inconsistent with that theory. It has been asserted that if forensic scientists are aware of the desired outcome, it is possible that they might unwittingly be influenced to interpret ambiguous data to support a given theory formulated by investigators such as the police and prosecutors. The criminal justice system presumes the independence of different types of evidence but these findings suggest that the reality of criminal investigations may not afford such independence of evidence where in some cases the judgments of forensic scientists could significantly be influenced by psychological factors.

Cognitive Bias and Forensic Science

The judgments of forensic scientists being influenced by cognitive factors are very different from the effects in investigators' bias, problems in eyewitness identification, and other elements in criminal cases, as discussed above. The problems in these areas are well known, and jurors (as well as judges) have started to take them into account. However, scientific evidence by experts has a different status. Forensic evidence has predominantly been viewed as immune to bias effects, and regarded as objective and impartial. Myers and Booker (1991) and Dror et al. (2005) highlighted the mental cognitive process behind the opinion of an expert known as elicitation. This consists of four cognitive tasks: defining the question, remembering the accurate information, making a decision and reaching a conclusion. In a forensic context this would be known as "what is classified as evidence, what is recognized as collected evidence, and what is examined and how it is interpreted." The expert must first understand what has been asked of them in order to answer a question. This demands a specific focus on the accurate information, and the limitation of personal speculation. However, when an expert tries to consider the accuracy of information, different cognitive factors (as mentioned previously) will play a vital role, and might cause selective attention towards information causing an observer effect. This essentially means that what is remembered and perceived by the expert depends upon the perceiver themselves.

Alafair S. Burke, *Improving Prosecutorial Decision Making: Some Lessons of Cognitive Science*

47 WM. & MARY L. REV. 1587, 1588–613 (2006)

Earl Washington Jr., a black mentally retarded farmhand, spent seventeen years in prison—nearly ten of them on death row—for the rape and murder of a white woman before DNA tests linked another man to the crimes. The evidence originally implicating him was questionable. The victim provided little identifying information, indicating before her death only that a black man had attacked her. Washington was convicted based largely on his own confession, even though he simultaneously provided factually inconsistent confessions to four other crimes and did not know the location of the crime scene, whether other people were present, or even the victim's race without the assistance of leading questioning from police. When defense counsel sought postconviction relief based on the discovery of another man's DNA on a blanket linked to the crime, prosecutors resisted. Even after Washington was pardoned because of exonerating evidence, prosecutors insisted that he remained a viable suspect.

Earl Washington's case raises questions about the discretionary decisions his prosecutors made from the moment they received the case. Why did they look past apparent problems with the confession? Why did they resist the evidentiary testing that ultimately exonerated an innocent man? Why would they still not concede innocence after his exoneration? Traditionally, commentators have clothed the study of prosecutorial decision making in the rhetoric of fault, attributing normatively inappropriate outcomes to bad prosecutorial intentions and widespread prosecutorial misconduct. From this perspective, Earl Washington's conviction, and his prosecutors' refusal to concede his innocence even after a gubernatorial pardon, result from prosecutorial overzealousness, a culture that emphasizes winning, the absence of "moral courage," and the failure of prosecutors to act as neutral advocates of justice.

This focus upon incentives, priorities, and values as potential taints upon the exercise of prosecutorial discretion reveals an implicit but important assumption about prosecutors: they are rational, utility-maximizing decision makers. Prosecutors choose to overcharge defendants, withhold exculpatory evidence, and turn a blind eye to claims of innocence; therefore, the traditional inference goes, they must value obtaining and maintaining convictions over "doing justice." To ensure that prosecutors do not rationally opt for misconduct to maximize their conviction rates, the fault-based literature recommends reform through changes to the prosecutorial cost-benefit analysis. Common strategies include more stringent ethical rules, increased disciplinary proceedings and sanctions against prosecutors, and professional and financial rewards based on factors other than just obtaining convictions.

Consider, however, a different explanation for the failure of prosecutors always to make just decisions. Perhaps prosecutors sometimes fail to make decisions that rationally further justice, not because they fail to value justice, but because they are, in fact, irrational. They are irrational because they are human, and all human decision makers share a common set of information-processing tendencies that depart from perfect rationality. A compelling body of cognitive research demonstrates that people systematically hold a set of cognitive biases, rendering them neither perfectly rational information processors, nor wholly random or irrational decision makers. Drawing on the cognitive literature, the growing literature of behavioral law and economics explores the limitations of cost-benefit rationality, challenging the assumption of traditional economists that people are perfect wealth maximizers. From both the cognitive and behavioral economics literature emerges a theory of bounded rationality that seeks to explain how cognitive biases and limitations in our cognitive abilities distort perfect information processing in nonrandom, predictable ways.

Others have suggested how cognitive bias and bounded rationality can affect juries, judges, the regulation of risk, federal rulemaking, corporate disclosures, contract law, consumer choice, employment discrimination, and group deliberations.... Viewing cases like Earl Washington's through a lens of human cognition, rather than fault, colors not only the description of the problem, but also the recommended solutions. When the underlying problem is human irrationality, rather than the malicious intentions of a single prosecutor or the indifference of a prosecutorial culture, the result is a far more complicated story about the criminal justice system. If prosecutors fail to achieve justice not because they are bad, but because they are human, what hope is there for change?

Cognitive Bias: Four Examples of Imperfect Decision Making

Decades of empirical research demonstrate that people's beliefs are both imperfect and resistant to change. Once people form theories, they fail to adjust the strength of their beliefs when confronted with evidence that challenges the accuracy of those theories. Indeed, theory maintenance will often hold even when people learn that the evidence that originally justified the theory is inaccurate. At the same time that people fail to consider information that disconfirms a theory, they tend both to seek out and to overvalue information that confirms it.

[A]spects of cognitive bias that can contribute to imperfect theory formation and maintenance [include] confirmation bias, selective information processing, belief perseverance, and the avoidance of cognitive dissonance. Confirmation bias is the tendency to seek to confirm, rather than disconfirm, any hypothesis under study. Selective information processing causes people to overvalue information that is consistent with their preexisting theories and to undervalue information that challenges those theories. Belief perseverance refers to the human tendency to continue to adhere to a theory, even after the evidence underlying the theory is disproved. Finally, the desire to avoid cognitive dissonance can cause people to adjust their beliefs to maintain existing self-perceptions....

A. Confirmation Bias

When testing a hypothesis's validity, people tend to favor information that confirms their theory over disconfirming information. Good evidence suggests that this information-seeking bias results because people tend to recognize the relevance of confirming evidence more than disconfirming evidence. This is true even when an effort to disconfirm is an essential step towards confirmation of the hypothesis under test.

For example, in a classic study of confirmation bias in hypothesis testing, Peter Wason presented subjects with four cards and told them that each card contained a letter on one side and a number on the other. The revealed sides of the four cards displayed one vowel, one consonant, one even number, and one odd number. Subjects were then asked which of the four cards needed to be turned over to test the following rule: If a card has a vowel on one side, then it has an even number on the other side.

Proper scientific method requires that researchers seek to disprove their working hypotheses. Accordingly, the rational test of Wason's "if vowel, then even number" card test is to turn over the vowel and odd number cards. The vowel card provides a relevant test because discovery of an odd number on its backside would disprove the tested rule. The odd number card provides an equally relevant test because the discovery of a vowel on the backside of the odd number card would disconfirm the proposed "if vowel, then even number" rule in the same way as any odd number on the other side of the vowel card.

However, to test the rule that all vowel cards had even numbers on the other side, subjects overwhelmingly selected from their four choices either just the vowel card, or the vowel and the even number cards. They failed to select the odd number card that was necessary to test the rule properly. Moreover, subjects who chose the even number card erred still further because that card's backside offered no probative value to the rule at hand. The subjects' choice of cards demonstrated that the subjects failed to recognize the importance of disconfirming evidence and instead sought information that would tend to confirm the working rule.

In another classic study, Mark Snyder and William Swann replicated confirmation bias in the context of social inference. Subjects were asked to select questions from a list for the purpose of interviewing a target person. Half of the subjects were instructed to choose questions that would test whether the target person was an extrovert, and half were told to test whether the target person was an introvert. The results demonstrated a strong confirmation bias. Subjects selected questions that could only prove, and never disprove, their working hypothesis. For example, subjects testing for extroversion chose questions like "What would you do if you wanted to liven things up at a party?," while subjects testing for introversion chose questions like "In what situations do you wish you could be more outgoing?"

The social science literature suggests that people demonstrate confirmation bias not only in seeking new information, but also in the recollection of stored information. In one study, subjects were given the same list of traits about a woman named Jane. Some of the listed traits were characteristic of extroversion, some of introversion, and others neutral. Two days later, subjects were asked to determine Jane's suitability for a job either as a real estate agent or as a librarian. Even though all subjects were exposed to the same information about Jane, those subjects testing Jane's suitability for real estate work tended to recall more extroverted than introverted facts about her, whereas the reverse was true for subjects testing her suitability as a librarian. The researchers concluded that subjects were searching their memories in a biased manner, preferring information that tended to confirm the hypothesis presented.

B. Selective Information Processing

A good deal of empirical research demonstrates that people are incapable of evaluating the strength of evidence independent of their prior beliefs. People not only demonstrate search and recall preferences for information that tends to confirm their preexisting theories, they also tend to devalue disconfirming evidence, even when presented with it. As a result of selective information processing, people weigh evidence that supports their prior beliefs more heavily than evidence that contradicts their beliefs.

Charles Lord, Lee Ross, and Mark Lepper conducted what is perhaps the most well-known study demonstrating this bias against disconfirmation. Based on prior questioning, the researchers knew that half of their subjects were proponents of the death penalty who believed that the death penalty deterred murder, while the other half were opponents who did not believe that the death penalty deterred. Subjects were asked to evaluate two studies, one that supported a deterrent efficacy of the death penalty, and one that suggested the death penalty's inefficacy as a deterrent. The researchers found that proponents of the death penalty judged the prodeterrence study as more convincing than the nondeterrence study, whereas opponents of the death penalty reached the opposite conclusion. Even though the studies described the same experimental procedures but with differing results, subjects articulated detailed justifications to support their conclusion that the study supporting their preexisting view was superior. Moreover, as a result of the biased evaluation of the two studies, subjects became more polarized in their beliefs. In other words, even though all subjects read two contradictory studies on the death penalty, proponents of the death penalty reported that they were more in favor of capital punishment after reading the studies, while opponents reported that they were less in favor.

Other researchers have replicated the phenomenon of selective information processing in a variety of contexts. Social scientists have suggested that the mechanism for selective information processing is attributable at least in part to motivational factors. As an initial matter, people choose to expose themselves to information that is consonant with their beliefs rather than dissonant. Moreover, when exposed to dissonant information, they are motivated to defend their beliefs, giving more attention and heightened scrutiny to information that challenges those beliefs. They will search internally for material that refutes the disconfirming evidence, and, once that material is retrieved from memory, a bias will exist to judge the disconfirming evidence as weak. In contrast, when presented with information that supports prior beliefs, people allocate fewer resources to scrutinizing the information and are more inclined to accept the information at face value.

At a general level, selective information processing may be normatively rational. When new information is compatible with what we already know, it is probably accurate. Careful scrutiny and a search for contradictory material would expend cognitive resources unnecessarily. On the other hand, information that is incompatible with existing information may be fallacious, and cognitive work to reveal the fallacy is well spent. Of course, disconfirmation bias leads to effective decision making only when the prior beliefs that bias the assimilation of new information are themselves supported by accurate information. In criminal cases, prosecutors enjoy no such guarantee, potentially basing their theories of guilt on retracted confessions, flawed eyewitness testimony, and false testimony from jailhouse informants.

C. Belief Perseverance

Although selective information processing can prevent rational, incremental adjustments in response to new information, the phenomenon of belief perseverance describes the tendency to adhere to theories even when new information wholly discredits the theory's evidentiary basis. With belief perseverance, human cognition departs from perfectly rational decision making not through biased assimilation of ambiguous new information, but by failing to adjust beliefs in response to proof that prior information was demonstrably false.

In a well-known experiment by Lee Ross, Mark Lepper, and Michael Hubbard, subjects were asked to discern between fake and actual suicide notes. By manipulating false feedback given to subjects as they performed the dummy task, the experimenters led subjects to believe that they had average performance, above average performance (success condition), or below average performance (failure condition). Following their completion of the task, subjects were fully debriefed and learned that the feedback had been false, predetermined, and random. Subjects were even shown the experimenters' instruction sheet, which preassigned subjects to each of the three performance conditions and stipulated the corresponding feedback to be delivered.

After subjects were debriefed, they were asked to assess their actual performance on the task, to estimate the average performance, and to predict their probable performance if they were to repeat the task. The researchers found considerable belief perseverance among subjects, despite the debriefing. Subjects assigned the "success condition" rated both their actual and future task performance more favorably than other subjects, while subjects assigned the "failure condition" showed the opposite pattern, continuing to rate their performance unfavorably.

Moreover, the study found that belief perseverance was not limited to self-evaluation, but extended to perceptions of others. Observer subjects who watched both the feedback sessions and the subsequent debriefings from behind a one-way glass also continued to demonstrate belief perseverance after the debriefings. In other words, observers tended to maintain their beliefs about the observed subject's ability to distinguish between fake and actual suicide notes, even after learning that the feedback was false.

Similarly, in another study, Anderson, Lepper, and Ross presented subjects with purportedly authentic histories of firefighters and asked the subjects to write an explanation of the relationship between risk preference and firefighting abilities observed in the case histories. By manipulating the case histories, the experimenters led subjects to perceive either a positive or negative correlation between the two traits. The researchers reported that, even after subjects were debriefed concerning the fictitious nature of the case histories, they continued to cling to the theories they formed from those histories. In other words, the subjects adhered to their conclusions, even after the evidence underlying the conclusions was wholly discredited. As the researchers concluded, "[i]nitial beliefs may persevere in the face of a subsequent invalidation of the evidence on which they are based, even when this initial evidence is itself … weak."

D. The Avoidance of Cognitive Dissonance

Another phenomenon that can affect prosecutorial cognition is the desire to find consistency between one's behavior and beliefs. The social science evidence suggests that inconsistency between one's external behavior and internal beliefs creates an uncomfortable cognitive dissonance. To mitigate the dissonance, people will adjust their beliefs in a direction consistent with their behavior.

For example, in a classic study, Leon Festinger and James Carlsmith paid subjects either one or twenty dollars to misinform another person, a confederate who was supposedly waiting to serve as a subject, that a long, boring task was actually interesting. Even though subjects were all required to complete the same mundane task, the subjects who were paid only a dollar to deceive the confederate reported that they found the task more interesting than either the subjects who received the more substantial payment or the control subjects, who had performed the task but had not been asked to deceive the confederate.

The researchers concluded that cognitive dissonance was created by the conflict between the subjects' beliefs that the task was boring and the subjects' behavior in telling someone that the task was interesting. To reconcile this dissonance, subjects who were paid only a dollar to mislead adjusted their own beliefs about the task. In contrast, those who were paid twenty dollars had an additional consonant cognition — "I was paid twenty dollars to lie" — and therefore had no need to adjust their beliefs to be consistent with their conduct. Since Fester and Carlsmith's original study, other researchers have reported robust effects of cognitive dissonance in other settings.

The Ethical Prosecutor and Cognitive Bias

No reason exists to believe that lawyers are immune from the documented bounds of rationality, and yet the literature on prosecutorial decision making continues to describe prosecutors as rational, wealth-maximizing actors who would make better, more just decisions if they only had better, more just values. Through the lens of the cognitive phenomena summarized [above], a more complicated story is evident. That prosecutors should be motivated by justice, not conviction rates, should go without saying. The harder question to answer is whether good motives, both individually and institutionally, are enough. The implications of the cognitive literature suggest not.

The broad powers of the prosecutor are familiar. If brought into an investigation prior to a suspect's arrest, prosecutors can shape the investigation's direction and scope by, for example, determining whom to investigate and through what tactics. Once an arrest is made, the prosecutor's full powers come into play as she determines whether to bring charges, what charges to bring, whether to drop charges once brought, whether to negotiate a plea and under what terms, whether to grant immunity, and what sentence to seek upon conviction....

A. Investigation and Charging Decisions

The potential for cognitive bias to creep into prosecutorial decision making starts from the earliest case-screening stages, when prosecutors must determine whether sufficient evidence exists to proceed with a prosecution. In hypothesis testing terms, they are testing the hypothesis that the defendant is guilty. The phenomenon of confirmation bias suggests a natural tendency to review the reports not for exculpatory evidence that might disconfirm the tested hypothesis, but instead for inculpatory, confirming evidence. In Earl Washington's case, for example, the prosecutor might have been looking for the fact of the confession, not for the surrounding circumstances that might undermine its reliability.

If the investigation is still ongoing, confirmation bias might cause law enforcement officers to conduct searches and to ask questions that will yield either further inculpatory evidence or nothing at all. Just as Snyder and Swann's subjects primarily asked suspected extroverts questions like "What would you do if you wanted to liven things up at a party?," police eyeing an initial suspect might ask, "What were you and the victim fighting about the night before the murder?" Confirmation bias will reduce the likelihood that the investigation will be directed in a manner that would yield evidence of innocence.

Recent attention to the risks of wrongful convictions has brought to light the influence of "tunnel vision," whereby the belief that a particular suspect has committed the crime might obfuscate an objective evaluation of alternative suspects or theories. In Illinois, a special commission on capital punishment identified tunnel vision as a contributing factor in many of the capital convictions of thirteen men who were subsequently exonerated and released from death row. Similarly, in Canada, a report issued under the authority of federal, provincial, and territorial justice ministers concluded that tunnel vision was one of the eight most common factors leading to convictions of the innocent. In cognitive terms, the tunnel vision phenomenon is simply one application of the widespread cognitive phenomenon of confirmation bias. Law enforcement fails to investigate alternative theories of the crime because people generally fail to look for evidence that disconfirms working hypotheses.

B. Sticky Presumptions of Guilt

If the prosecutor decides to pursue charges, the potential of cognitive bias to taint decision making only worsens. Prosecutorial reluctance to revisit a theory of guilt is difficult to explain when prosecutors are viewed as rational actors. Attempts to do so often rely on accounts of either individual or institutional indifference to the truth. However, widespread prosecutorial skepticism of innocence claims is wholly understandable, and in fact predictable, in light of disconfirmation bias, belief perseverance, and cognitive consistency. Although some have argued to the contrary, many commentators believe that the ethical prosecutor brings charges only when she is sufficiently certain in her own mind of the accused's guilt. Accordingly, if charges are brought, the prosecutor has presumably made a personal determination about the defendant's guilt. If additional evidence arises, selective information processing comes into play. The prosecutor will accept at face value any evidence that supports the theory of guilt and will interpret ambiguous evidence in a manner that strengthens her faith in the case. Should any potentially exonerative evidence arise, she will scrutinize it carefully, searching for an explanation that undermines the reliability of the evidence or otherwise reconciles it with the existing theory of guilt. As a result of selective information processing, she will continue to adhere to her initial charging decision, regardless of the new information.

Indeed, even if the inculpatory evidence that initially supported the charges is wholly undermined, belief perseverance suggests that the theory of guilt will nevertheless linger. Others have noted the large number of cases, such as Earl Washington's, in which prosecutors continue to insist that a released defendant remains a suspect. Although prosecutorial resistance to claims of factual innocence is often attributed to a prosecutorial culture tainted by politics and an indifference to justice, sticky beliefs about guilt may simply be the result of belief perseverance.

Consider, for example, the government's much criticized spy charges against Ahmad Al Halabi, an Air Force translator at the U.S. naval base at Guantanamo Bay. The initial evidence appeared damning. Al Halabi had stored nearly two hundred detainee notes in his personal laptop, had taken prohibited photographs of the base's guard towers, and had plans to travel to Syria. A computer analyst concluded from an inspection of Al Halabi's laptop that he had already e-mailed some of the stored documents over the Internet.

Within weeks, a different computer investigator concluded that the initial analysis of the laptop was flawed and that Al Halabi had not sent any material over the Internet. Nevertheless, for nearly four months prosecutors continued to seek additional analysis from the "best places." Even when prosecutors concluded that absolutely no evidence existed to show that Al Halabi e-mailed any materials, the government dismissed only those charges that alleged the transmittal of classified information; sixteen charges, including espionage, remained.

Still, the government's case had problems. The supposedly secret documents on Al Halabi's laptop were innocuous communications, such as letters from detainees to parents. Moreover, he had an explanation for their presence on his laptop: translators, including himself, had been asked to alleviate a shortage of computers on the base by using their personal computers. Al Halabi did admit to photographing the base, but only to remember his military service there, not to conduct espionage. He also offered a justification for his anticipated travel to Syria—his upcoming wedding. Nevertheless, prosecutors persisted, arguing that the wedding was a ruse to conceal Al Halabi's true intentions of delivering secret information to an enemy.

Ultimately, the government conceded that only one of the nearly two hundred documents on Al Halabi's computer was classified as secret. Nearly all charges were dropped, and Al Halabi agreed to plead guilty to relatively minor charges relating to the mishandling of a document, the prohibited photographs of the camp, and his false statements concerning the photographs. What was once a death penalty case ended with a discharge and demotion, but no additional jail time.

Some have suggested that Al Halabi was the victim of an anti-Muslim witch hunt at Guantanamo. Although Al Halabi's Muslim faith undoubtedly contributed to the government's willingness to believe that he was a spy, belief perseverance may have played a larger role in the government's unwillingness to yield that belief. After the evidence of e-mailing was demonstrated to be inaccurate, the theory of guilt continued to taint the prosecutor's evaluation of the remaining evidence. Indeed, even after the government's case unraveled, Al Halabi's prosecutor insisted, "He was engaged in suspicious behavior. He took prohibited photographs."

C. The Disclosure of Exculpatory Evidence

The fallibility of human cognition raises especially disturbing questions about a prosecutor's ability to determine whether evidence is exculpatory. Under *Brady v. Maryland*[62] and its progeny, prosecutors must disclose materially exculpatory evidence to the defense. The problem lies in the Court's definition of "materiality." Borrowing from the Court's standard in *Strickland v. Washington*[63] for granting a new trial based on ineffective assistance of counsel, the Court held in *United States v. Bagley*[64] that evidence is material and therefore required to be disclosed to the defense "only if there is a reasonable probability that, had the evidence been disclosed to the defense, the result of the proceeding would have been different." The Court defined a "reasonable probability" as "a probability sufficient to undermine confidence in the outcome." The Court subsequently made clear that the materiality standard is not whether the trial's outcome would more likely than not have been different with the evidence at issue, but whether "the favorable evidence could reasonably be taken to put the whole case in such a different light as to undermine confidence in the verdict."

Because *Brady's* materiality standard turns on a comparison of the supposedly exculpatory evidence and the rest of the trial record, applying the standard prior to trial requires that prosecutors engage in a bizarre kind of anticipatory hindsight review. They must anticipate what the other evidence against the defendant will be by the end of the trial, and then speculate in hypothetical hindsight whether the evidence at issue would place "the whole case" in a different light. Others have previously criticized *Brady* for relying on prosecutors to determine the materiality of evidence in their own files. Prosecutors, some say, are in a poor position to evaluate the materiality of evidence because they are unaware of the planned defense strategy and are, in any event, conflicted by their desire to win. Moreover, if a prosecutor wrongly decides to withhold materially exculpatory evidence, the misapplication of the standard may never be detected, and there will never be judicial review of the prosecutor's decision.

[C]ognitive psychology [may] provid[e] a potential basis for explaining the mechanism underlying the prosecutor's bias. From this perspective, the prosecutor's application of *Brady* is biased not merely because she is a zealous advocate engaged in a "competitive enterprise," but because the theory she has developed from that enterprise might trigger cognitive biases, such as confirmation bias and selective information processing.

Brady requires a prosecutor who is determining whether to disclose a piece of evidence to the defense to speculate first about how the remaining evidence will come together against the defendant at trial, and then about whether a reasonable probability exists that the piece of evidence at issue would affect the result of the trial. During

---

62. 373 U.S. 83 (1963).
63. 466 U.S. 668 (1984).
64. 473 U.S. 667 (1985).

the first step, a risk exists that prosecutors will engage in biased recall, retrieving from memory only those facts that tend to confirm the hypothesis of guilt. Moreover, because of selective information processing, the prosecutor will accept at face value the evidence she views as inculpatory, without subjecting it to the scrutiny that a defense attorney would encourage jurors to apply.

Cognitive bias would also appear to taint the second speculative step of the *Brady* analysis, requiring the prosecutor to determine the value of the potentially exculpatory evidence in the context of the entire record. Because of selective information processing, the prosecutor will look for weaknesses in evidence contradicting her existing belief in the defendant's guilt. In short, compared to a neutral decision maker, the prosecutor will overestimate the strength of the government's case against the defendant and underestimate the potential exculpatory value of the evidence whose disclosure is at issue. As a consequence, the prosecutor will fail to see materiality where it might in fact exist.

D. Stickier Presumptions of Guilt Post-conviction

A further barrier to prosecutorial neutrality arises upon the defendant's conviction. Just as the majority of commentators believe that prosecutors should bring charges only when they are personally convinced of an accused's culpability, prosecutors also have an obligation to seek post-conviction redress if they believe that an innocent person has been convicted. Even if prosecutors do not seek the defendant's release sua sponte, one would at least expect a conscientious prosecutor not to oppose relief for an innocent person who requests it. The problem, of course, is convincing the prosecutor that the defendant is, in fact, innocent.

Whether the conviction was obtained through a jury verdict or the defendant's own guilty plea, the prosecutor will view the conviction as further evidence confirming the accuracy of her initial theory of guilt. The prosecutor's strengthened belief in her theory will continue to taint her analysis of any new evidence submitted by the defense postconviction.

Moreover, cognitive dissonance will further hinder the prosecutor's ability to conduct a neutral evaluation of potentially exculpatory evidence. The conviction of an innocent person is inconsistent with the ethical prosecutor's belief that charges should be brought only against suspects who are actually guilty. To avoid cognitive dissonance, an ethical prosecutor might cling to the theory of guilt to reconcile her conduct with her beliefs, especially after the defendant has been convicted. From this perspective, prosecutorial bias against postconviction exculpatory evidence is not an indication of corrupt ethics at all; rather, it may indicate a deep but biasing adherence to the edict that prosecutors should only do justice. A prosecutor may give short shrift to claims of innocence, in other words, not because she is callous about wrongful convictions, but because she cannot bring herself to believe that she has played a part in one.

Jennifer L. Mnookin, *The Courts, the NAS, and the Future of Forensic Science*

75 Brook. L. Rev. 1209, 1230–32 (2010)

Bias and Sequential Unmasking

Forensic experts frequently have access to information about a case that goes beyond whatever information is actually necessary for their forensic testing. They may be told by detectives or investigators about other powerful evidence linking the suspect to the crime. They may be told details about the suspect that bear no relation to the pattern identification evidence itself—that he is a known gang member, or that she has prior convictions, or that he has confessed, or that this match is critical because it is the only strong evidence in the case. No information of this kind bears in any way on the actual forensic science inquiry, and risks creating an unconscious biasing effect on the examiner. Indeed, in most scientific fields, there is a careful and often formalized effort to shield researchers from this kind of contextual information. It's too dangerous. We human beings have a cognitive tendency to see what we expect to see. Think of the way that medical researchers make use, whenever possible, of carefully controlled studies to ensure that not even the treating physicians know who is receiving the medication under investigation and who may be getting the placebo. These protections exist to protect physicians from unconscious bias that might influence their interpretation of the effects of either the medicine or the placebo. Currently, in the forensic sciences, there are generally no such procedures to protect examiners from extraneous information that may have an unconscious influence on their findings.

To be sure, some information, though potentially biasing, may nonetheless be necessary for conducting the forensic test. A fingerprint examiner, for example, will likely need to know what surface a print came from, notwithstanding that the information may provide context clues about the crime itself. The point is not that examiners should lack all access to non-forensic information relating to the case. Rather, to the maximum extent practicable, they should only be given the case-related information that is actually relevant and helpful to their forensic inquiry. Dan Krane and others have coined the name "sequential unmasking" as a label for this approach, in order to emphasize that forensic analysts ought to learn only that information that they actually need, and only when they actually need it. All information, in other words, should be unmasked—that is to say revealed—to the examiner in sequence, and only when it is necessary. The examiner should have access to all the information necessary to do his or her analysis effectively—no more, and no less.

The concern about the danger and power of biasing information is not simply theoretical. In a clever experiment, cognitive psychologist Itiel Dror used the Mayfield case to show the possibility of contextual bias effects on fingerprint examiners' interpretations. A small handful of fingerprint examiners were each given a pair of prints, a latent print and a potential source print, and told that they were the prints from the Mayfield case. Each examiner was asked to evaluate whether or not the prints matched, using only the information contained in the print.

In fact, however, unbeknownst to the examiners, the prints were not the Mayfield prints. Each examiner was actually given a set of prints that he or she personally had previously testified in court were a 100% certain, positive, error-free individualization. But now, when provided with this biasing contextual information suggesting that the prints were those involved in the Mayfield scandal, 60% of the examiners (three of the five examiners tested) reached the opposite conclusion, determining that the two prints in front of them did not in fact match. A fourth examiner judged the prints to be inconclusive. Only one of the five examiners reached a conclusion consistent with his or her original judgment that the prints matched. To be sure, the Mayfield incident was a significant scandal, so the potential biasing effect of this context information was obviously quite extreme. Nonetheless, given some fingerprint experts' insistence that their methodology is not vulnerable to unconscious bias or general human fallibilities, Dror's findings generated a great deal of interest and a certain amount of both surprise and anxiety within the fingerprint community. The experiment was, in a sense, a possibility proof, showing that bias could indeed, at least in some circumstances, be significant enough to affect examiners' conclusions. Follow up experiments by Dror and his collaborators on a larger number of examiners and with less starkly biasing information still revealed the potentially biasing effect of contextual information on analysts' judgments.

Molly J. Walker Wilson,
Defense Attorney Bias and the Rush to the Plea
65 U. KAN. L. REV. 271, 273–76 (2016)

Traditional analyses of the role of the public defender in the criminal justice system have not explored how limited resources can exacerbate decisional biases, and have therefore underestimated the public-defense crisis. Empirical research has provided a wealth of information regarding how cognitive and social biases can influence choice in a variety of contexts. This research has received widespread attention from the most influential thinkers and policy makers, and the legitimacy of using behavioral data to shape policy and practice is well established. Yet, although psychological findings have been applied to consumer contexts, voting behavior, economic trends, politics, judicial analysis, and many other areas, the behavioral science lens is rarely applied to public defenders. And yet, research on cognitive and behavioral biases has special importance for the public defender context.

Priming, anchoring, belief perseverance, and the confirmation and over-confidence biases lead public defenders to form an impression of a case based upon incomplete evidence, which results in the failure to adequately discount questionable inculpating evidence and the undervaluing of exculpating evidence. Research on motivated reasoning suggests that public defenders will be overly confident and self-serving in their evaluations to cases, and will be "blind" to legitimate ethical issues in how they represent their clients. A number of features of the criminal justice system increase the defense attorney's susceptibility to these biases. First, when cognitive resources are stretched, as is the case when a public defender is representing a large number of defendants, biased judgments are more likely. Psychologists refer to this type of situation as high "cognitive load." Scores of studies have shown that cognitive shortcuts—also called "heuristics"—are far more likely when individuals are under cognitive load. Hence, a public defender is more vulnerable to these biases than she would be were she not under severe time and resource constraints. Another feature of the criminal justice system that can contribute to bias is the process by which law enforcement extracts information from suspects. Common police interrogation practices are known to encourage false confessions. In addition to influencing police, prosecutors, and jurors, confessions also impact defense attorney evaluations of the strength of a case.

The same factors that lead attorneys to make errors—limited resources and time and early exposure to the prosecutor's evidence—also make the plea more attractive to the defense attorney. The vulnerable defendant who is most at risk for falsely confessing is also the defendant who is most likely to agree to accept a plea, even when he is innocent. The more harried and rushed the defense attorney, the less likely she is to perceive weaknesses in the prosecution's case. When a defense attorney has very little time to spend with her client, research tells us that the client is likely to lack confidence in the quality of representation, and may be more likely to view a deal as being his best choice. Under these circumstances, an innocent defendant may conclude that his best bet is to take the deal and avoid the risk of a longer sentence.

Even in the case of guilty defendants, accepting plea bargains without carefully weighing the strength of the case is problematic. Criminal defendants likely underestimate the opportunity costs associated with plea deals—namely, giving up the right to force the prosecutor to prove her case. Considering what the defendant is surrendering, the deals offered by prosecutors do not sufficiently discount the penalty. Because prosecutors routinely overcharge, many charges would not hold up at trial—when the burden of proof is on the state. Accordingly, the "discount" offered with a plea is often close to what the defendant would receive at trial anyway, in which case the defendant would fare best by going to trial. A trial would afford him Fifth, Sixth, and Fourteenth Amendment protections, as well as judicial oversight and a variety of other procedural benefits.

Judges, who suffer the effects of overloaded dockets, generally encourage plea bargains, and courts rarely provide defendants with after-the-fact remedies for shabby lawyering—particularly where plea bargains are concerned. Meanwhile, plea bargains are subject to the least amount of supervision because they occur behind closed doors and away from even minimal judicial supervision. So, although defense attorneys admit that they use psychological pressure to encourage their clients to accept deals, there is virtually no remedy available to defendants who regret their choice later.

In sum, defense lawyers are prone to biased decision-making and are incentivized to make concessions to get their clients' cases settled efficiently. Their choices are accorded deference by courts and members of the public, both for practical reasons and because of an assumption that lawyers make better decisions. Simultaneously, the criminal defendant's opinion regarding pretrial and trial decisions is minimalized, trivialized, or even mocked. There is widespread dismissal and even condemnation of efforts of defendants to take control of their cases.

B. Legal Materials, Exercises, and Media

1. *David Keaton, Exoneree Epitaph:* Is the excerpt at the beginning of this chapter from David Keaton's trial an example of tunnel vision? David Keaton was the first man exonerated from death row in the modern era of the death penalty (1973–present); he died on July 3, 2015, at the age of 63. Keaton was convicted and sentenced to death in Florida in 1971 for the murder of an off-duty police officer. His conviction was based on a coerced confession and erroneous eyewitness testimony. In 1973, the actual perpetrator was discovered because of new evidence, and Keaton was exonerated. In 2003, Keaton became a founding member of Witness To Innocence, an organization of death row exonerees who share their stories to educate the public about the death penalty. Kathy Spillman, director of programs and outreach at Witness To Innocence, said of Keaton, "His life was very difficult. He was sentenced to Death Row as a teenager. And like all exonerees, he struggled with issues related to being on Death Row and integrating back into a society that does not provide support for these men and women. [Yet], he was stoic and very gentle. He was a poet and a singer and whenever he got the chance, he participated in activities against the death penalty so that nobody else had to go through what he did." *See* Gerald Ensley, *Quincy Five's Keaton, Exonerated from Death Row, Dies,* TALLAHASSEE DEMOCRAT (July 7, 2015) available at http://www.tallahassee.com/story/news/2015/07/07/quincy-fives-keaton-exonerated-death-row-dies/29835733/.

2. *Recommended Reading, Prosecutors and True Perpetrators*: Hella Winston of *The Daily Beast* documents that in 263 reversed murder convictions, new suspects were charged in only 16 of the cases. Often, the prosecutor continues to allege the original defendant was the perpetrator or otherwise involved. One instance of tunnel vision is noted by Ms. Winston, "[w]hile the first defendant, Rayshard Darnell Futrell, was exonerated after a video surfaced that showed him near the scene of the crime but dressed in a way that eliminated him as the possible gunman, the district attorney agreed to dismiss the murder and gun charges against him only on the condition that he plead guilty to perjury for falsely testifying at trial that he was not present at the scene of the shooting." Read more at: http://www.thedailybeast.com/263-vacated-murder-convictionsjust-16-new-suspects-charged.

3. *Discussion, Prosecutorial Tunnel Vision and DNA Evidence:* What if the standard for reversing a conviction were not whether the new evidence (or ineffective assistance of counsel) would have led to a different result at trial, but whether the prosecution, knowing this evidence, would have brought charges in the first place? Or do prosecutors simply fit new facts to new theories about the same defendant? In Chapter Ten, we considered this problem from the perspective of prosecutorial misconduct, but maybe it's better thought of as a problem of cognitive bias. Consider the Chicago murder of victim Nina Glover, and the conviction of juveniles based on a false accusation and coerced confessions. When confronted with DNA testing of semen from the victim that excluded all four defendants and implicated a repeat violent sexual offender, prosecutors created a new theory of how the

crime was committed. To learn more, read Erica Goode, *When DNA Evidence Suggests 'Innocent,' Some Prosecutors Cling to 'Maybe,'* NEW YORK TIMES (Nov. 15, 2011) available at https://mobile.nytimes.com/2011/11/16/us/dna-evidence-of-innocence-rejected-by-some-prosecutors.html; and watch the "60 Minutes" episode on the case: https://www.youtube.com/watch?v=YSo_9Xo_78E&t=25s (7–10:45).

4. *Recommended Listening, Exoneree Floyd Bledsoe*: Listen to exoneree Floyd Bledsoe of Kansas discuss his shocking wrongful conviction due to prosecutorial and police tunnel vision on Season 2, Episode 12, "We Are A Family: Stories From The 2017 Innocence Network Conference Part One," of *Wrongful Conviction with Jason Flom*: https://art19.com/shows/wrongful-conviction-with-jason-flom?month=4&perPage=100&year=2017 (12:00–23:30).

5. *Tunnel Vision and Cognitive Bias Exercise:*

   a. *Recommended viewing, Human Factors in Forensics*: Dr. Itiel Dror, co-author of the excerpt above, *The Emergence of Cognitive Bias in Forensic Science and Criminal Investigations*, is known for his research on contextual bias. Watch his presentation on cognitive and human factors to the National Commission on Forensic Science: https://youtu.be/hNaljIMK_hY (21:30).

   b. *Review Questions*: Based on the above video presentation of Dr. Itiel Dror to the National Commission on Forensic Science, identify as either TRUE or FALSE each of the following statements regarding the issues surrounding eyewitness identification:

      1. When given fingerprints and told that the fingerprints were not a match, fingerprint experts were more likely to determine the fingerprints did not match—even when they did.

      2. If an analyst is given contextual information, this often changes the analyst's determination.

      3. With statistics and technology, human bias will no longer be an issue in forensics.

      4. Communication, how people understand results, is part of human factors concerns.

      5. The "contextual management tool kit" gives ideas on limiting the impact of human factors and limiting cognitive contamination.

6. *Reflective Essay, Shared Tunnel Vision of Prosecutors, Police, and Lab Analysts:* Given the intimate—indeed integral—association between forensics and law enforcement, police crime labs have been influenced by bias and an impetus to create results for the prosecution, rather than the impartial search and study of science. Explain potential actions by labs to limit the influence of human factors, discuss whether forensic analysts can be both ethical and biased, and identifying at least two types of bias or situations of bias.

7. *Discussion, Tunnel Vision and Miscommunication:* How do tunnel vision and communication errors lead to the misrepresentation of science in the courtroom?

Misrepresentation of forensic sciences in court is partly attributable to communication errors between law and science. The National Commission on Forensic Science issued a recommendation on inconsistent terminology, namely that forensic disciplines should seek to standardize terms within individual disciplines as well as across disciplines. The lack of standard language further widens the gap between forensic analysts and attorneys. If prosecutors and analysts do not currently share a common language concerning the meaning of "accuracy" and results, then forensic reports are ripe for misconstrual in the courtroom. How does tunnel vision make this problem even worse?

One example of compounded misrepresentation and tunnel vision comes from the trial transcript of *Commonwealth of PA v. Drew Whitley* (1989):

> Prosecutor: "you can't say it belongs to the defendant?"
>
> Forensic Analyst: "that is correct."
>
> Prosecutor's closing argument: "But it's only when the scientists come in and say, hey, we have a standard, we know this hair to be of Drew Whitley and they compare it all microscopically. Exact. No doubt about it. (Pointing) Him."

8. *Discussion, Presumed Innocent or Presumed Guilty?* Throughout its history, the criminal justice system in Mexico began with the presumption that the defendant is guilty until proven innocent, police reports are fact, and prosecutors don't need to build cases—indeed, judges don't even need to appear in court for these bureaucratic written proceedings. In 2016, Mexico implemented a new criminal justice system that shifted from a written-based system to an adversarial oral-based system. "Presumed Guilty," a documentary filmed largely by two Mexican attorneys, follows a wrongful conviction through the old Mexican criminal justice system. Listen to the filmmakers discuss the wrongful conviction and the system in "Imprisoned in Mexico and 'Presumed Guilty'" on *Talk of the Nation*, July 27, 2010: https://www.npr.org/templates/story/story.php?storyId=128800611 (11:33). What are the differences between a system that begins with a presumption of innocence versus a presumption of guilt? The film is available with English subtitles here: https://www.youtube.com/watch?v=jw901iRgSh4.

9. *Resource on Wrongful Convictions from a Former Prosecutor:* Professor Mark Godsey, a former federal prosecutor and current director of the Ohio Innocence Project, addresses his own tunnel vision in his book *Blind Injustice: A Former Prosecutor Exposes the Psychology and Politics of Wrongful Convictions* (University of California Press, 2017). You can also watch him discuss tunnel vision and other causes of wrongful conviction at the 2016 West Virginia Law Review Symposium, "Flawed Forensics & Innocence," https://www.youtube.com/watch?v=wivAanNp8k0 (24:21–36:07).

Chapter Thirteen

Guilty Pleas, Pretrial Procedure, and Innocence

Today, over 95 percent of defendants in the criminal justice system plead guilty and, in most cases, such confessions are prompted by offers of leniency or other benefits from the prosecution. It is unclear how many of these defendants are innocent, but it is clear that plea-bargaining has an innocence problem. At least one study has concluded that as many as 27 percent of defendants who plead guilty would not have been convicted at trial, though this estimate seems exceptionally high. Another more empirically driven study examined DNA evidence in capital rape-murder cases and determined that between 3.3 and 5 percent of those convicted, either through trial or a guilty plea, were factually innocent. Other studies have placed the number of defendants who plead guilty as a result of inducements by the government but who are factually innocent between 1.6 percent and 8 percent. Taking even the lowest of these estimates, the reality is striking and means that in 2009 there were over 1,250 innocent defendants forced to falsely admit guilt in the federal system alone. Extrapolated out to the entire American criminal justice system since 1970, there are conservatively tens of thousands of innocent persons who have been induced to plead guilty by overpowering plea bargains. If this is the case, plea-bargaining certainly has a significant and unacceptable innocence problem.

—Lucian E. Dervan, *Bargained Justice: Plea-Bargaining's Innocence Problem and the Brady Safety-Valve*, 2012 UTAH L. REV. 51, 84–86 (2012)

A. Readings

1. Plea Bargaining and Guilty Pleas

John H. Blume and Rebecca K. Helm, *The Unexonerated: Factually Innocent Defendants Who Plead Guilty*

100 Cornell L. Rev. 157, 158–61 (2014)

> "It's a total injustice.... These three men are being made to plead guilty to something they didn't do...."

> —John Mark Byers, father of one of the alleged
> West Memphis Three victims

On August 19, 2011, Damien Echols, Jason Baldwin, and Jessie Misskelley, also known as the "West Memphis Three," were released from prison nearly eighteen years after they were first arrested in connection with the murders of three eight-year-old boys in West Memphis, Arkansas. Their freedom came at a significant cost however; to obtain their release they pled guilty to crimes they almost certainly did not commit. The deal offered by prosecutors was too "good" to turn down. We might like to think that such things do not happen, or if they do, only very rarely, but innocent defendants do plead guilty more often than most people think and certainly more often than anyone cares to admit....

Let us begin with a more detailed discussion of the West Memphis Three case to set the stage. The defendants were arrested in 1993 after the bodies of three young boys — Christopher Byers, Stevie Branch, and Michael Moore — were found naked and hogtied with their own shoelaces. The victims' clothing was found in a nearby creek. Byers had deep lacerations and injuries to his scrotum and penis. An autopsy revealed that Byers died from multiple injuries, and the other two boys from multiple injuries with drowning. Misskelley confessed to the murders following a twelve-hour police interrogation and implicated Echols and Baldwin in his confession. Misskelley later recanted but was convicted in February 1994 on the strength of his confession and sentenced to life imprisonment plus two twenty-year sentences. The prosecution's case against Misskelley was based almost entirely on his confession. In fact, without the statements, the prosecution's case could not have survived a directed verdict motion.

Echols and Baldwin were convicted of three counts of capital murder. The convictions were largely based on prosecution evidence that the defendants had been motivated as members of a satanic cult and witnesses who said they had heard the teenagers speak of the murders. Echols was sentenced to death and Baldwin received a sentence of life imprisonment.

In 2007, new evidence came to light. DNA testing revealed that biological material found at the crime scene did not belong to the victims or the three convicted defendants. However, a hair found in one of the knots on one of the hogtied bodies was determined to be "not inconsistent" with a DNA sample obtained from the stepfather of one of the victims. Evidence of juror misconduct involving the foreperson of the jury was discovered, and a witness who allegedly told police she had seen the defendants in the area where the crime occurred recanted her testimony.

On November 4, 2010, the Arkansas Supreme Court ordered a state trial judge to determine whether the new DNA evidence rendered the convictions invalid. However, before the hearing took place, the prosecution offered the West Memphis Three a "get out of jail" (but not free) opportunity. Although they would have to plead guilty to lesser charges, the three men would not have to admit their guilt; they would be permitted to plead guilty while still maintaining their innocence using what is commonly called an Alford plea. The agreed-upon sentence would be time served, thus each defendant would be released immediately from prison after entering the pleas. But it was a "package" deal, and was null and void unless all three defendants said yes. After some hesitation, all three defendants accepted the bargain, entered the pleas, and were released.

Was justice served? The plea bargain did secure the defendants' freedom after eighteen years of confinement. It also ensured that Echols would not be executed. Almost any criminal defense lawyer, including the authors of this Essay, would have advised them to take it (and would have cajoled them to take it if they hesitated). However, their freedom came at a high price; the three men pled guilty to a murder they adamantly maintained they did not commit, which the overwhelming weight of the evidence suggested they did not commit, and which almost no one in the community where the crime occurred believed they committed. Furthermore, because a plea is a conviction, the three men are now all "convicted murderers." This will continue to have significant effects on their ability to find employment, and furthermore, they are deprived of most of their civil rights and of any civil remedy they possibly had against either the police or prosecutors, leaving them without any compensation for the eighteen years of wrongful imprisonment.

The prosecution's plea offer was (and was designed to be) highly coercive. The chances that any one of the three would have been found guilty at a new trial were slim; the prosecutors admitted as much. But the prospect of immediate release from prison made "rolling the dice" at a new trial (assuming the judge ordered one) a risky proposition, and one not many persons imprisoned for nearly two decades would be likely to take, or one any competent attorney would advise them to take. Adding to the coercion was the condition that if any of the three rejected the offer, the other two could not take advantage of the deal. This put great pressure on Misskelley and Baldwin to accept the plea for their friend's sake; Echols was still on death row and faced the possibility of execution. In fact, press accounts revealed that Baldwin did not want to plead guilty and would have preferred to take his chances before a new jury. "This was not justice," he said immediately following the plea. "However, they're trying to kill Damien. Sometimes you've just got to bite down to save somebody." Echols later thanked Baldwin at a press conference for his decision to accept the plea despite his misgivings.

The "deal" in this case almost certainly resulted in three innocent men pleading guilty to something they did not do. They were offered a deal they could not realistically refuse. They now stand "convicted" of the murders of three young boys. Should such a result be tolerated? Should prosecutors be allowed to coerce factually innocent defendants to plead guilty to crimes they did not commit? It is a question worth asking because although the West Memphis Three case was unusual in terms of the publicity it attracted, this type of case is not unusual. Innocent defendants plead guilty quite frequently—one of many dark secrets of the criminal justice system.

* * *

Why Do Innocent Defendants Plead Guilty?

In an ideal world, factually innocent defendants would not be charged with crimes they did not commit. In that same world, innocent defendants who were wrongly charged would never plead guilty, but would go to trial and be acquitted by a jury of their peers. But that is not the world we live in. We now know, for example, due to the availability of DNA testing, that at least twenty-nine individuals who pled guilty to crimes they did not commit served a combined total of more than one hundred fifty years in prison before their exonerations, and the National Registry of Exonerations now lists defendants who pled guilty and were subsequently exonerated. Why do they do it?

There are three principal reasons why innocent defendants plead guilty. First, innocent persons charged with relatively minor offenses often plead guilty in order to get out of jail, to avoid the hassle of having criminal charges hanging over their heads, or to avoid being punished for exercising their right to trial. Second, defendants who were wrongfully convicted, but have their conviction vacated on direct appeal or in post-conviction review proceedings, plead guilty to receive a sentence of time served and obtain their immediate (or at least imminent) freedom. Third, some innocent defendants plead guilty due to the fear of a harsh alternative punishment, e.g., the death penalty.

A. Defendants Charged With Minor or Relatively Minor Offenses

The largest category is the first: innocent persons charged with relatively minor offenses. Spend time talking to any "frontline" public defender or persons in our poorest communities, and they will tell you that many innocent defendants charged with relatively minor crimes plead guilty in order to get out of jail or avoid spending additional time in jail. In many of these cases, the defendants do not have a constitutional right to an attorney or a jury trial, and, especially if they are incarcerated pretrial, will plead guilty just to get out of jail. The incentives are quite strong; most of these defendants are poor and thus unable to afford bond, retain counsel, or care for their families. Even in cases where defendants are represented, their court-appointed lawyers will be overworked and underpaid and thus motivated to resolve the case through a quick guilty plea. In many instances, the defendant will already have some kind of criminal record, and in the communities in which they live the stigma of a criminal conviction, especially for a minor offense, is low. Even if they are released on bail, the trial will not be for months, possibly longer, and it is often inconvenient or expensive to go to court for things like "roll-call." And, defendants frequently know, and will be advised, that if they reject a favorable plea and are found guilty, the judge will punish them for exercising their right to trial. Thus, many defendants will do whatever it takes to get out of jail or avoid a trial — including pleading guilty to a crime they did not commit.

Erma Faye Stewart, for example, was thirty and a single mother of two when she was arrested as part of a drug sweep based on the word of a confidential informant. With no one to take care of her two small children, Stewart decided to plead guilty to delivery of a controlled substance. She was sentenced to ten years probation and $1800 in fines, and was required to report to her parole officer monthly. She was released an hour later. The confidential informant was later exposed as a fraud, and the charges were dropped against the other defendants charged in the sweep, who had not pled guilty. The reality is that, for many defendants like Erma Stewart, a guilty plea often represents the only readily available key to the cellblock door.

These defendants can be significantly harmed by their convictions. Their criminal records can "deprive them of employment, as well as educational and social opportunities," and a minor conviction can also "affect eligibility for professional licenses, child custody, food stamps, student loans, [and] health care."

B. Defendants Who Prevail During the Appellate Process

Second, innocent defendants who are wrongfully convicted and then win a new trial may plead guilty in order to secure their immediate or imminent release. This was true of the West Memphis Three and, under the right circumstances, can be an appealing option to an innocent defendant. Why? Think about it from the wrongfully convicted person's perspective. The defendant has been to trial and, despite knowing he was innocent, the jury found him guilty. It is not hard to imagine that such a defendant, having seen the criminal justice system in operation, "up close and personal" so to speak, would be reluctant to "roll the dice" at a retrial. Even in cases where new evidence has come to light (e.g., the DNA evidence in the case of the West Memphis Three), the prosecution will often attempt to bargain with the defendants in order to secure a guilty plea and maintain the conviction. Most prosecutors and law enforcement officers are hostile to post-conviction claims of innocence. This has been described as a "conviction psychology" that leads prosecutors and police to resist claims of innocence in order to maintain the integrity of the criminal justice system (by not admitting that the system made a mistake), improve their own chances of promotion (by maintaining conviction rates), and avoid wasting time (as they still believe defendants are guilty regardless of how persuasive the evidence of innocence is). Even in cases where a prosecutor believes that the defendant is (or at least may be) innocent, a guilty plea is an attractive option because it generally precludes the defendant from filing a civil suit seeking money damages. Therefore, prosecutors will often offer highly coercive deals involving immediate or near immediate release from jail to secure a conviction.

* * *

C. Avoiding Harsh Alternative Punishments

Finally, factually innocent defendants may plead guilty because they are afraid that they will be punished (often quite severely) for exercising their Sixth Amendment right to a jury trial. In capital murder cases, for example, the prosecution will threaten the defendant with capital punishment if he does not plead guilty. After being notified that the prosecution was seeking the death penalty against them, Phillip Bivens and Bobby Ray Dixon pled guilty to a 1979 Mississippi rape and murder in exchange for a sentence of life imprisonment. In 2010, DNA testing conclusively established their innocence. This was also a factor in the West Memphis Three case; the fact that Damien Echols was on death row contributed to the decisions of the three men to plead guilty. But even where death is not a sentencing option, prosecutors often have other potential harsh sentences, including lengthy terms of imprisonment and life without parole, as well as enhancements for second- or third-time offenders that can be used to induce reluctant defendants, even innocent ones, to plead guilty in exchange for a reduction in the amount of time that will have to be served.

Reducing the Number of the Unexonerated?

There is clearly a problem; in a fair criminal justice system innocent defendants would not plead guilty to crimes they did not commit. But they do. We are not exactly sure how often it occurs, but the numbers are not so small that the phenomena can be dismissed as artifact. On the other hand, it is possible that innocent defendants pleading guilty is simply the cost of doing plea business. In the South there is an old saying: "People like sausage and justice, but no one likes to see how either one is really made." Maybe that is true in the plea bargaining context. If the system must induce virtually all defendants, somehow and someway, to plead guilty, then not only the guilty but also the innocent will in some instances agree to plead guilty. And no feasible solutions come readily to mind. This seems especially true for the persons charged with relatively minor offenses who plead guilty for time served to get out of jail. But we are not quite ready to throw up our hands and give up. So, let us discuss some possibilities.

First, the criminal justice system could eliminate plea bargaining. While this is viewed by many people, including members of the current Supreme Court, as unthinkable, some European criminal justice systems do not allow the practice. In a world without the ability to plea bargain, we would expect to see two adjustments benefitting innocent (and also guilty) defendants. First, charges would be dismissed in more cases. Without the ability to use many of the currently sanctioned highly coercive practices, prosecutors would dismiss weak cases rather than working to get the "best" deal possible. And since, on average, weak cases are more closely associated with innocence, innocent defendants would benefit from a no-bargaining regime. Second, charging decisions would likely become more rational. In today's plea-driven market, prosecutors have incentives to overcharge in order to start the "bidding" so to speak. Without the ability to bargain, however, prosecutors would be forced to charge more appropriately, at least in regard to the expected disposition of cases. Another benefit that would protect the innocent would be that the prosecutors would not be able to freely "purchase" the testimony of jailhouse informants by offering them a dismissal or reduction in charges or sentence in exchange, thus eliminating a leading cause of wrongful convictions.

* * *

Another needed reform in the area of judicial supervision of plea bargaining is to allow trial and appellate courts to consider the "voluntariness" of the plea. Current legal doctrine focuses myopically on whether the plea was knowing and intelligent. This, in turn, focuses on questions like: Was the defendant aware of the rights he was waiving by entering the plea (the right to jury trial, the right to testify, the right to confront witnesses)? Was the defendant aware of the nature of the charges he was pleading guilty to? Was the defendant aware of the maximum punishment? And, was there a factual basis for the plea? But very little attention is given to whether the plea was truly voluntary. For example, the pleas entered by the West Memphis Three easily satisfied the knowing-and-intelligent inquiry. But that was not what was wrong with the pleas they were offered. The problem was that virtually no rational defendant, even an innocent one, would turn the deal down. Thus courts should recognize, and more importantly enforce, a stricter voluntary guilty plea requirement. The requirement would be somewhat akin to a voluntariness challenge to an incriminating statement. Current confession law doctrine uses a totality of the circumstances test and asks courts to inquire whether, considering the totality of the circumstances, the individual's will was overborne by coercive interrogation practices. The same could be done for guilty pleas; the test would be whether, considering the totality of the circumstances, the individual's will was overborne by a coercive plea bargain....

Lucian E. Dervan and Vanessa A. Edkins,
The Innocent Defendant's Dilemma: An Innovative Empirical Study of Plea Bargaining's Innocence Problem
103 J. Crim. L. & Criminology 1, 2–48 (2013)

In 1989, Ada JoAnn Taylor sat quietly in a nondescript chair contemplating her choices. On a cold February evening four years earlier, a sixty-eight-year-old woman was brutally victimized in Beatrice, Nebraska. Police were now convinced that Taylor and five others were responsible for the woman's death. The options for Taylor were stark. If she pleaded guilty and cooperated with prosecutors, she would be rewarded with a sentence of ten to forty years in prison. If, however, she proceeded to trial and was convicted, she would likely spend the rest of her life behind bars.

Over a thousand miles away in Florida, and more than twenty years later, a college student sat nervously in a classroom chair contemplating her options. Just moments before, a graduate student had accused her of cheating on a logic test being administered as part of a psychological study. The young student was offered two choices. If she admitted her offense and saved the university the time and expense of proceeding with a trial before the Academic Review Board, she would simply lose her right to compensation for participating in the study. If, however, she proceeded to the review board and lost, she would lose her compensation, her faculty advisor would be informed, and she would be forced to enroll in an ethics course.

In Beatrice, Nebraska, the choice for Taylor was difficult, but the incentives to admit guilt were enticing. A sentence of ten to forty years in prison meant she would return home one day and salvage at least a portion of her life. The alternative, a lifetime behind bars, was grim by comparison. After contemplating the options, Taylor pleaded guilty to aiding and abetting second-degree murder. Twenty years later, the college student made a similar calculation. While the loss of compensation for participating in the study was a significant punishment, it was certainly better than being forced to enroll in a time-consuming ethics course. Just as Taylor had decided to control her destiny and accept the certainty of the lighter alternative, the college student admitted that she had knowingly cheated on the test.

That Taylor and the college student both pleaded guilty is not the only similarity between the cases. Both were also innocent of the offenses of which they had been accused. After serving nineteen years in prison, Taylor was exonerated after DNA testing proved that neither she nor any of the other five defendants in her case were involved in the murder. As for the college student, her innocence is assured by the fact that, unbeknownst to her, she was actually part of an innovative new study into plea bargaining and innocence. The study, conducted by the authors, involving dozens of college students and taking place over several months, not only recreated the innocent defendant's dilemma experienced by Taylor, but also revealed that plea bargaining's innocence problem is not isolated to an obscure and rare set of cases. Strikingly, the study demonstrated that more than half of the innocent participants were willing to falsely admit guilt in return for a perceived benefit. This finding brings new insights to the long-standing debate regarding the possible extent of plea bargaining's innocence problem and ignites a fundamental constitutional question regarding an institution the Supreme Court reluctantly approved of in 1970 in return for an assurance that it would not be used to induce innocent defendants to falsely admit guilt.

* * *

As noted by other scholars in the field, three problems exist with exoneration data when applied to plea-bargaining research. First, exoneration data predominantly focuses on serious felony cases such as murder or rape where there is available DNA evidence and where the defendants' sentences are lengthy enough for the exoneration process to work its way through the system. This means that exoneration data does not examine the role of innocence and plea bargaining in the vast majority of criminal cases, those not involving murder or rape, including misdemeanor cases. Second, because many individuals who plead guilty do so in return for a reduced sentence, it is highly likely that innocent defendants who plead guilty have little incentive or insufficient time to pursue exoneration. Finally, even if some innocent defendants who pleaded guilty had the desire and time to move for exoneration, many would be prohibited from challenging their convictions by the mere fact that they had pleaded guilty. As such, innocent defendants who plead guilty are not accurately captured by the exoneration data sets and, therefore, it is highly likely that the true extent of plea bargaining's innocence problem is significantly underestimated by these studies. Consequently, one must look elsewhere to determine the true likelihood that an innocent defendant might falsely condemn himself in return for an offer of leniency in the form of a plea bargain.

* * *

The Constitutionality of the Innocent Defendant's Dilemma

While the Supreme Court acknowledged the need for plea bargaining in [*United States v.*] *Brady* and approved bargained justice as a form of adjudication in the American criminal justice system, the Court also offered a cautionary note regarding the role of innocence. At the same time the Court made clear its belief that innocent defendants were not vulnerable to the powers of bargained justice, the Court reserved the ability to reexamine the entire institution should it become evident it was mistaken. The Court stated:

> For a defendant who sees slight possibility of acquittal, the advantages of pleading guilty and limiting the probable penalty are obvious—his exposure is reduced, the correctional processes can begin immediately, and the practical burdens of a trial are eliminated. For the State there are also advantages— the more promptly imposed punishment after an admission of guilt may more effectively attain the objectives of punishment; and with the avoidance of trial, scarce judicial and prosecutorial resources are conserved for those cases in which there is a substantial issue of the defendant's guilt or in which there is substantial doubt that the State can sustain its burden of proof.

Continuing to focus more directly on the possibility of an innocence issue, the Court stated:

> This is not to say that guilty plea convictions hold no hazards for the innocent or that the methods of taking guilty pleas presently employed in this country are necessarily valid in all respects. This mode of conviction is no more fool-proof than full trials to the court or to the jury. Accordingly, we take great precautions against unsound results, and we should continue to do so, whether conviction is by plea or by trial. We would have serious doubts about this case if the encouragement of guilty pleas by offers of leniency substantially increased the likelihood that defendants, advised by competent counsel, would falsely condemn themselves.

This caveat about the power of plea bargaining has been termed the Brady safety valve, because it allows the Supreme Court to reevaluate the constitutionality of bargained justice if the persuasiveness of plea offers becomes coercive and surpasses a point at which it begins to ensnarl an unacceptable number of innocent defendants.

Interestingly, *Brady* is not the only Supreme Court plea-bargaining case to include mention of the innocence issue and the safety valve. In *Alford*,[65] for instance, the Court made clear that this form of bargained justice was reserved only for cases where the evidence against the defendant was overwhelming and sufficient to overcome easily the defendant's continued claims of innocence. Where any uncertainty remained, the Supreme Court expected the case to proceed to trial to ensure that "guilty pleas are a product of free and intelligent choice," rather than overwhelming force from

---

65. North Carolina v. Alford, 400 U.S. 25 (1970).

the prosecution. The same language requiring that plea bargaining be utilized in a manner that permits defendants to exercise their free will was contained in the 1978 case of *Bordenkircher v. Hayes*.[66] In *Bordenkircher*, the Court stated that the accused must be "free to accept or reject the prosecution's offer." Just as the Court had stated in *Brady* and *Alford*, it concluded its discussion in *Bordenkircher* by assuring itself that as long as such free choice existed and the pressure to plead guilty was not overwhelming, it would be unlikely that an innocent defendant might be "driven to false self-condemnation."

As is now evident from the study described herein, the Supreme Court was wrong to place such confidence in the ability of individuals to assert their right to trial in the face of grave choices. In our research, more than half of the study participants were willing to forgo an opportunity to argue their innocence in court and instead falsely condemned themselves in return for a perceived benefit. That the plea-bargaining system may operate in a manner vastly different from that presumed by the Supreme Court in 1970 and has the potential to capture far more innocent defendants than predicted means that the Brady safety valve has failed. Perhaps, therefore, it is time for the Court to reevaluate the constitutionality of the institution with an eye towards the true power and resilience of the plea-bargaining machine.

Russell Covey, *Police Misconduct as a Cause of Wrongful Convictions*
90 WASH. U. L. REV. 1133, 1166–74 (2013)

[T]he mass exoneration cases [resulting from the criminal justice scandals in Tulia, Texas and in the Rampart Division in south-central Los Angeles] vividly illustrate how and why actually innocent defendants plead guilty. In general, there appear to have been three main factors driving innocent Rampart and Tulia defendants to plead guilty: an outsized trial penalty, a lack of viable strategies to contest the charges, and presumptively or actually unsympathetic forums....

A. New Data on the Trial Penalty

Without a doubt, the overwhelming reason that innocent Rampart and Tulia exonerees pleaded guilty to crimes they did not commit was that they feared that they would do much worse at trial if they did not plead guilty. Typical are the sentiments expressed by one innocent Rampart exoneree who on advice of his attorney pleaded guilty in exchange for a three-year term of probation, believing that "he would face a stiffer penalty if he chose to fight the charges in a trial and lost." That exoneree likely was not wrong. The existence of a trial penalty has been long acknowledged, albeit bemoaned by many. It is an institutionalized feature of contemporary criminal justice. Nonetheless, the coercive impact of the trial penalty is unmistakable, and is plainly evident in the Rampart and Tulia cases.

---

66. 434 U.S. 357 (1978).

Tulia provides an extreme example of the coercive impact of the trial penalty. Of the thirty-seven innocent Tulia exonerees, seven went to trial and were convicted, twenty-seven pleaded guilty, one did both, and two others had their probation revoked. The first defendant to go to trial, Joe Moore, was convicted and sentenced to ninety years in prison for allegedly dealing 4.5 grams of cocaine. Moore had been offered an opportunity to plead guilty in exchange for a twenty-five-year sentence (the minimum available given the charges and Moore's prior record), but he declined. Six more defendants stood trial, and were convicted and sentenced to prison terms ranging from 20 to 361 years. In light of this precedent, and with cases substantively indistinguishable in terms of the nature of the charges and the strength of the evidence, the remaining defendants all chose to plead guilty. Although the sentences imposed on those who pleaded guilty in Tulia were often quite harsh, the harshness of their sentences paled in comparison to those who were convicted at trial. On average, Tulia defendants who pleaded guilty were sentenced to approximately four years in prison. The Tulia defendants who contested their guilt at trial received an average sentence of 615.4 months, or 51.3 years. Trial sentences at Tulia, in other words, were nearly thirteen times harsher than sentences imposed following guilty pleas.

The trial penalty evident in Tulia might be attributed, at least in part, to an apparently intentional prosecutorial strategy to frighten defendants into foregoing trial. Such an express strategy was made easier in small-town Tulia, where word of harsh sentences quickly spread among Tulia's small defense bar and the defendants themselves.

These dynamics were noticeably absent in Rampart. Unlike Tulia, there is no indication that prosecutors were aware of the defects in the cases they brought against innocent defendants. Indeed, after the scandal broke, the Los Angeles District Attorney's Office took affirmative steps to investigate the scope of wrongdoing and to vacate convictions resulting from police misconduct. In terms of size and population, the L.A. justice system also obviously dwarfs Tulia's. There is far less reason to believe that prosecutors sought to send any messages to specific classes of defendants by seeking harsh trial sentences. Any implicit threat inherent in the harsher trial sentences would seem to be endemic to the justice system in general.

Nonetheless, the observable trial penalty in the Rampart cases, though not on the same order as the average trial penalty in Tulia, was still quite large. On average, actually innocent Rampart defendants who were convicted at trial were sentenced to 101.25 months, or nearly 8.5 years. Actually innocent Rampart defendants who pleaded guilty were sentenced to an average term of 18.5 months, or just over 1.5 years. Defendants who contested their cases at trial, in other words, received sentences on average more than five times harsher than those who agreed to plead guilty. The trial penalty for the larger sample of all Rampart exonerees, including those who did not appear to be actually innocent, was even bigger. For this group, the average plea sentence was 20.3 months. The average trial sentence was 136.3 months. Trial sentences were therefore on average 6.7 times longer than plea sentences, with no apparent qualitative differences among the types of crimes charged or the criminal history of the defendants.

The longest sentence imposed on any Rampart exoneree was a term of fifty-four years to life, later reduced on appeal to twenty-nine years to life, for Lorenzo Nava. Like most of the other Rampart exonerees, Nava was convicted of drug and gun offenses and contested the charges at trial. After conviction, Nava received an initial fifty-four-year sentence under California's three-strikes law. Nava's case, however, can be compared to Joseph Jones, another Rampart defendant, to show that the long trial sentence imposed on Nava was not simply a function of the three-strikes law or other factors unique to his case. Like Nava, Jones was charged with multiple drug counts and was potentially subject to prosecution under the three-strikes law. According to Detective Chris Barling, who interviewed Jones in the Rampart investigation, "Jones believed that he was facing a life term," and notwithstanding his contention that he was innocent, decided to plead guilty on the advice of counsel. Pursuant to the plea, Jones was sentenced to a prison term of eight years. The disparity in sentence outcome between Nava and Jones is roughly consistent with the average trial penalty evident in the Rampart cases, amounting to at least a seven-fold penalty increase based on Nava's initial trial sentence, and a four-fold penalty increase based on Nava's reduced sentence on appeal.

This data provides further evidence that the real trial penalty could be far larger than estimated in some studies. With trial sentences ranging anywhere from four to thirteen times longer than plea sentences, the costs of contesting a typical felony charge are prohibitive. Few defendants can afford to run the risk. The experience of those wrongly convicted in the Rampart and Tulia scandals demonstrates that the coercive power of the trial penalty causes innocent defendants as well as guilty ones to plead guilty.

* * *

B. Innocence as a Minor Factor in Plea Bargaining

Although the empirical evidence from the mass exoneration cases leaves no doubt that innocent defendants plead guilty, the question remains: does innocence have a measurable impact on whether a defendant will hold out for trial? Anecdotally speaking, we know that some innocent defendants turn down favorable plea bargains because of innocence. One Rampart exoneree to do so was Alex Umana. Umana was returning from a barbecue with his daughter and her mother when police stopped him and placed him among a group of four to six people who had been detained by police in the lobby of an apartment building. Although Umana was not in possession of any drugs at the time, he was nevertheless charged with possession of cocaine. Prosecutors offered a plea bargain for a probationary sentence, but Umana rejected the offer "because he was innocent and wanted to fight the charges." Umana was convicted at trial and sentenced to five years in state prison. Several Tulia defendants also refused to plead guilty to drug charges because they were innocent. Take the case of Freddie Brookins, Jr., who was accused of selling an eight-ball of powder cocaine to Coleman. Before trial, the prosecutor offered Brookins a plea of five years. The maximum sentence for the offense was twenty years. Brookins discussed the offer with his father, and the following colloquy reportedly occurred: "Did you do it," his father asked him. "No, I didn't," Brookins replied. "Well then," his father responded, "don't take the deal." Against the advice of counsel, Brookins declined the plea offer. He went to trial, was convicted, and was sentenced to the maximum term of twenty years.

Although we know that some defendants decline plea offers because of innocence, it is also possible that other innocent defendants plead guilty at equal or higher rates to avoid draconian trial penalties. The question therefore remains: does innocence materially alter guilty plea rates? The Rampart data sheds some additional light. For purposes of this analysis, I identified three groups of Rampart cases resulting in exonerations. The first group, discussed above, consisted of those who were actually innocent of the crimes of conviction. There were thirty-eight such defendants in the data set. Of the remaining forty-nine, twenty-seven were identified as clearly "not actually innocent." This group consisted of defendants who in fact were in possession of contraband or who admitted that they were engaged in criminal conduct at the time of arrest, but whose convictions were reversed based on procedural violations. The remaining group of twenty-two consisted of defendants whose guilt or innocence remains unclear given the record evidence. I identify this group as the "may be innocent" group.

Although the numbers are small, they are large enough to permit some tentative comparisons. With respect to plea rates, the data shows that innocence does appear to make some difference. Twenty-five actually innocent Rampart exonerees pleaded guilty, while seven were convicted at trial. Actually innocent exonerees thus pleaded guilty at a rate of 77%. In comparison, twenty-two of those who were not actually innocent pled guilty while three were convicted at trial. In other words, 88% of those who were not innocent pleaded guilty. Finally, of the remaining group of "may be innocents," seventeen pled guilty while two were convicted at trial, providing an 89% guilty plea rate.

It thus appears from the data that actual innocence does induce some defendants to refuse a guilty plea and hold out for trial, but that the incentive has only a marginal effect, leading the innocent to contest their cases at trial at an approximately 10% greater rate than those who are actually guilty. Nonetheless, the data underscore that the vast majority of the actually innocent resolve false charges against them by pleading guilty. Very few held out for trial, and, as the numbers above documenting the size of the trial penalty demonstrate, those who did and lost paid a heavy price for that decision.

Lisa Kern Griffin, *State Incentives, Plea Bargaining Regulation, and the Failed Market for Indigent Defense*
80 Law & Contemp. Probs. 83, 88–95 (2017)

The regulation of plea agreements "through the common-law process is fundamentally no different from the way courts treat other contracts" between civil parties. The Court has adopted wholesale the idea that plea bargaining proceeds from a "mutuality of advantage." The government saves resources, and defendants receive reduced sentences. The courts' "market-based rationality is at times almost comically explicit."

In *United States v. Mezzanatto*, for example, the Supreme Court flatly stated that "[a] defendant can 'maximize' what he has to 'sell' only if he is permitted to offer what the prosecutor is most interested in buying." Or, as Easterbrook writes, "judges must be careful not to override real people's actual views about their actual interests in favor of what judges think those views and interests ought to be."

In accordance with this conception, the plea system is "built around prosecutorial discretion, defense autonomy to trade away procedural entitlements, and a largely passive judiciary." The passivity of courts in the face of market justifications leads to disregard for fairness, indifference to accuracy, only superficial assessments of potential coercion, and assumptions about the competency of counsel representing defendants in the plea bargaining process.

First, courts assess fairness to the defendant in the sense of due process as more or less coextensive with a conception of fairness in private markets. The parties to plea bargains retain similar "autonomy from state regulation to compete against or negotiate with others and enter into contracts, with few legal standards about fair bargaining practices, conditions, and contract terms." Plea negotiations tend to be informal and take place in private. The plea bargain itself is announced in open court and becomes a matter of record only after agreement is reached. In that process, the standards for prosecutorial conduct are no higher than those for other private actors competing in a free market. The Court has deemed the prosecutor's interest in persuading the defendant to forgo trial rights "constitutionally legitimate." Nor does the good or bad faith of the prosecutor's negotiation tactics make any difference, as long as there is no evidence of invidious discrimination such as racial bias. Thus, for negotiated pleas, as for private contracts, "the law permits terms and outcomes widely condemned as unfair."

Second, courts do not account for the factual accuracy of the outcomes that plea bargaining produces. Actually innocent defendants often reach the rational decision to plead guilty. Indeed, innocent defendants may be more likely to plead under imperfect information and may be more risk averse than guilty defendants. Recent studies of DNA exonerations reveal substantial numbers of wrongful convictions obtained by guilty pleas. Plea bargaining masks factual questions about whether a defendant committed the crime and "is perhaps the most prominent example of the criminal justice system operating collateral to a quest for truth." The ultimate goal is a completed agreement, often at the expense of reliable conclusions about the nature or severity of the crime. Courts thus permit defendants to plead guilty even when they persist in professing their legal innocence. In addition, misdemeanor defendants with strong defense claims frequently enter guilty pleas because they are being held without bail or cannot afford bail. The rational choice is a plea to time served despite convincing evidence of innocence because that resolution is clearly preferable to remaining incarcerated for a longer period pending trial.

Although fairness and accuracy do not play a significant role in the regulation of plea bargaining, courts do reference two constitutional limitations when defendants enter pleas: a Fifth Amendment concern with potential coercion and the Sixth Amendment right to counsel. The Constitution itself makes no mention of plea bargaining, but limited constitutional oversight of the process dates to the 1971 decision in *San-tobello v. New York*.[67] There, the Court recognized that plea bargaining was "essential" to an efficient system of criminal justice but also subject to some "safeguards to insure the defendant what is reasonably due in the circumstances." Specifically, the Court held that prosecutors are bound by the promises they make in plea hearings.

The only bargaining tactics constrained by due process, however, are illegal fraud and outright coercion. Prosecutors may constitutionally threaten any punishment that the law allows. So long as the range of potential charges and sentences has legal justification, manipulating offense and punishment to induce a plea is considered an offer rather than a threat. Accordingly, although defendants no doubt face tough choices, the Court still regards them as free ones. If a plea appears "knowing and voluntary," and the parties articulate some "factual basis" for the agreement, almost anything goes in the negotiation process.

Defense lawyers play a key role in justifying limited judicial scrutiny under this free-market approach. Commitment to the idea of plea bargaining as an efficient negotiation has important implications when it comes to a second market at work: publicly funded counsel. A defendant must be formally "knowing" with respect to the terms of the bargain, the nature of the charges, the rights being waived, and the potential sentence to be imposed. But a represented defendant makes an "intelligent" plea notwithstanding actual ignorance "of the evidence admissible at trial or the likelihood that trial will result in conviction." Courts assume that having counsel present provides the requisite notice. That further supposes that the defense lawyer in question is a sophisticated player with a good sense for market prices and customary practices.

* * *

Recall that the free-market logic of plea bargaining depends on a system in which rational choices are made with sufficient information. The "meet 'em and plead 'em" model of representation common in jurisdictions across the United States does not fulfill that condition. Many public defenders are juggling more than one hundred active cases at any given time. They cannot interview clients, investigate the facts of the case, or file appropriate motions, let alone effectively negotiate plea bargains. In addition, face-to-face meetings with clients often require travel to distant detention facilities. Hurried conversations in the courtroom itself, or perhaps a hallway or holding cell, are the best that most public defenders can do.

As a result, defendants who have waited weeks or months for representation may then have a five-minute meeting with a defense lawyer before entering a guilty plea and facing substantial penalties. In one Mississippi county, almost half of the indigent defense cases are resolved by guilty plea on the same day that the public defender first meets the client. Seventy percent of the clients represented by a California public defender office plead guilty at their first court appearance, in some cases after less than a minute of explanation about the deal being offered. In market terms, clients achieve no sense of the sales value of their trial rights from these brief encounters.

---

67. 404 U.S. 257 (1971).

They have insufficient information to make the rational choice on which market justifications for plea bargaining depend.

Stephanos Bibas, *Harmonizing Substantive-Criminal-Law Values and Criminal Procedure: The Case of Alford and Nolo Contendere Pleas*
88 Cornell L. Rev. 1361, 1370–87 (2003)

A. The Law of Nolo Contendere and Alford Pleas

At common law, a defendant could ask the court to impose a merciful sentence without confessing guilt and without estopping himself from later pleading not guilty on the same facts. This procedure became the formal plea of nolo contendere, under which the defendant admits guilt for purposes of the present case but creates no estoppel. Today, the Federal Rules of Criminal Procedure allow defendants to plead nolo contendere with the permission of the court. Most states likewise allow nolo contendere pleas, which are sometimes called no contest pleas, although many of these states require the court's consent.

The *Alford* plea gives defendants another way to plead guilty without admitting guilt. In *North Carolina v. Alford*,[68] Henry Alford was charged with the capital crime of first-degree murder and "faced ... strong evidence of guilt." Rather than go to trial, he pleaded guilty to second-degree murder, a noncapital crime, while protesting his innocence. The U.S. Supreme Court held that defendants may knowingly and voluntarily plead guilty even while protesting their innocence if the judge finds "strong evidence of [the defendant's] actual guilt." In *Alford*, two witnesses testified that the defendant had left his house with a gun saying he would kill the victim and had returned saying he had killed the victim. The Court noted that Alford's plea was similar to a plea of nolo contendere. It held that if a defendant can plead nolo contendere while refusing to admit guilt, he should also be able to plead guilty while protesting his innocence. The Court also suggested that Alford's decision to plead was a reasonable choice to cap his maximum sentence, and therefore the courts should honor it. Although these pleas are not forbidden by the Constitution, neither are they required. Because defendants have no right to plead guilty, judges may refuse to accept *Alford* pleas and states may forbid them by statute or rule. Most states, however, have followed suit and permitted *Alford* pleas (sometimes called best-interests pleas).

* * *

B. The Scholarly Literature

Commentators who have considered *Alford* and nolo contendere pleas have endorsed them for varying reasons. The most common argument in favor of them is that they resolve cases efficiently and cheaply. Easterbrook and others support these pleas because they further the interests of defendants, including innocent defendants, who want to avoid worse outcomes at trial. In other words, these pleas promote au-

---

68. 400 U.S. 25 (1970).

tonomy by giving defendants a choice that may benefit their interests. Others contend that these pleas protect defendants' dignity, privacy, and autonomy by obviating humiliating public admissions of guilt. Still others argue that nolo pleas protect "the respectable citizen" who is "technically guilty" but does not deserve such civil disabilities as losing the rights to vote and hold office. Finally, some commentators claim that *Alford* pleas foster openness between lawyer and client. Without *Alford* pleas, they claim, innocent defendants would lie to their lawyers about their guilt in order to reap the benefits of pleading guilty.

Even Alschuler, who would prefer to abolish plea bargaining altogether, reluctantly endorses *Alford* pleas. He argues that the *Alford* plea can be a necessary psychological "crutch" when defendants, against their best interests, refuse to admit guilt because of psychological obstacles, egos, and shame. Even innocent defendants, he argues, should be able to choose *Alford* pleas if they decide that pleading is in their best interests. Alschuler further claims that if lawyers and judges insist on admissions of guilt, defendants will lie to their lawyers and the court, and defense counsel will pressure clients to confess or lie. He argues that Alford pleas, though distasteful and offensive, are more honest and fair and less hypocritical. They keep defendants from having to lie, prevent defense lawyers from coercing confessions, and avoid forcing defendants into disadvantageous trials.

* * *

C. Convicting Innocent Defendants Is Wrong

It should go without saying that it is wrong to convict innocent defendants. Thus, the law should hinder these convictions instead of facilitating them through *Alford* and nolo contendere pleas. Nonetheless, Easterbrook, Alschuler, and others favor *Alford* and nolo pleas in part because they enable innocent defendants to plead guilty without lying. Some of these commentators, notably Easterbrook, assume that increasing the range and ease of choices is always good. But increasing the ease of convicting innocent defendants is a vice, not a virtue. If the law made it harder for innocent defendants to plead guilty, it would minimize both actual and perceived injustices.

Easterbrook contends that innocent defendants will plead guilty only when the expected sentence at trial, discounted by the probability of acquittal, is greater than the plea terms offered. Defendants who are advised by competent counsel and have private knowledge of the facts will be in a good position to assess their own chances at trial. Because trials are imperfect and sometimes convict innocent defendants, innocent defendants benefit by having the option of pleading guilty whenever they might be convicted at trial. As Alschuler puts it, "both courts and defense attorneys should recognize a 'right' of the innocent to plead guilty. So long as a defendant has something to gain by entering a plea agreement, it is unfair to deny him the choice."

Easterbrook's argument mistakenly treats innocent defendants as fully informed, autonomous, rational actors. Many defendants, however, receive poor advice from overburdened appointed counsel of varying quality whose caseloads and incentives lead them to press clients to plead guilty. In addition, criminal discovery is not nearly as extensive as civil discovery, which hampers defendants' accurate assessments of their prospects at trial. Thus, innocent defendants who want to enter Alford or nolo pleas are likely overestimating their risk of conviction at trial. Innocent defendants may also plead guilty because of pressure or misinformation; thus their pleas may not be fully intelligent and voluntary. Defendants poor enough to qualify for over-burdened appointed counsel and those of low intelligence are most likely to make these mistakes. The result may well be troubling disparities based on wealth, mental capacity, and education. The law should instead encourage these innocent defendants to go to trial.

There is also a deeper moral objection to Easterbrook's purely utilitarian argument. One should recoil at the thought of convicting innocent defendants. It is all the more troubling to trumpet this fact as an advantage. Not all of ethics is reducible to a con-sequentialist calculus. There is something profoundly troubling about knowingly fa-cilitating injustice, more so than inadvertently allowing it to happen. No promise of good consequences can erase the repugnance of promoting an evil in the hope of averting a worse evil. To use Dostoyevsky's example, no hope of good consequences can justify society's murdering a single innocent child. Kant would agree that society cannot knowingly facilitate the punishment of those who do not deserve it, even if they agree to it.

The criminal justice system probably does not charge and prosecute many innocent defendants. Some innocent defendants do exist, however, and may be tempted to use *Alford* and nolo pleas instead of going to trial. Though it is impossible to know how many defendants are innocent, many of the lawyers whom I interviewed thought that innocent defendants occasionally used these pleas. Anecdotal evidence also indicates that innocent defendants use these pleas. For example, in the notorious Wenatchee case, twelve defendants entered *Alford* or nolo contendere pleas to child molestation-related charges. Two of them later adduced evidence that a complaining child had never been abused but had falsely incriminated them because of coercive police inter-rogation. After the child recanted, these two defendants were eventually allowed to withdraw their pleas. Extensive media coverage later suggested that the police investigator had led children to fabricate these and thousands of other allegations of sexual abuse.

D. Public Perceptions of the Justice System

The justice system must consider not only what the parties want, but also public perceptions of accuracy and fairness. As Schulhofer points out, justice and punishment are classic public goods. Allowing innocent defendants to plead guilty creates "serious negative externalities" because society has a strong interest in ensuring that criminal convictions are both just and perceived as just. Though one lawyer whom I interviewed cynically suggested that criminal justice is not and should not be about the truth, the public cares a great deal about truth.

Alschuler, however, turns this concern for public perceptions on its head. He praises *Alford* pleas as an honest way to avoid hypocrisy instead of tempting innocent defendants to confess falsely. But Alschuler's own evidence shows that many lawyers and judges are deeply uncomfortable with this prospect. The public may be even more uncomfortable, as Alschuler recognizes when he characterizes refusals to accept Alford pleas as a "public relations measure." *Alford* and nolo contendere pleas send mixed messages, breeding public doubt, uncertainty, and lack of respect for the criminal justice system. Far from encouraging honesty, they let guilty defendants cloak their pleas in innocence. In contrast, jury verdicts and unequivocal guilty pleas suppress residual doubts and promote public confidence.

The justice system should forestall cynicism by forbidding practices that openly promote injustice or public doubts about guilt. As the Supreme Court noted in Winship, the law goes to great lengths to minimize the risk of erroneous convictions. The perception of accuracy is needed "to command the respect and confidence of the community.... It is critical that the moral force of the criminal law not be diluted by a standard of proof that leaves people in doubt whether innocent men are being condemned."

2. Suggested Reforms

Samuel R. Gross, *Pretrial Incentives, Post-Conviction Review, and Sorting Criminal Prosecutions by Guilt or Innocence*

56 N.Y.L. Sch. L. Rev. 1009, 1022–24 (2012)

Our process of post-conviction review is a major reason why rape and murder convictions at trial dominate the set of cases that end in exoneration. It is extremely difficult to get American courts or executive officers to seriously consider new evidence that a convicted defendant is innocent, let alone to actually exonerate him. All actors in the process, from governors to innocence projects to the media to the courts themselves, concentrate their time and attention on those cases with the most extreme outcomes: death sentences, life imprisonment, and other extreme sentences. Innocent defendants who plea bargain, even in rape and murder prosecutions, are far less likely to be exonerated. Their sentences are on average much lighter than those imposed at trial: that's what they bargain for. And they have a harder procedural row to hoe. One of the rights they waive by pleading guilty is the right to a direct appeal; and many statutes and procedural rules that deal with alternative modes of review—from state habeas corpus to post-conviction DNA testing—limit or foreclose access by defendants who pled guilty. And innocent defendants who plead guilty are handicapped by a common assumption on all sides, held by potential allies and state officers alike, that those who plead guilty are guilty.

[T]he pretrial choice that American criminal defendants now face is stark: plead guilty and accept the conviction and punishment the prosecutor offers, or go to trial and risk far worse. Almost all defendants have overwhelming incentives to plead guilty, but those incentives are similar for defendants who are guilty and for those who are not. For both, the main effect of plea bargaining is to make conviction cheaper and more certain but less onerous; a significant side effect is that the limited prospects of post-conviction review become even more minimal.

The Trade

Consider a new pretrial option that we could offer to defendants alongside the common choice of plea bargain or jury trial. We'll call it an Investigative Trial. Under this procedure, a criminal defendant would waive major procedural rights at trial, but not plead guilty, in return for procedural advantages on post-conviction review. If properly structured, this alternative might be more attractive to innocent defendants, who are most likely to benefit from full disclosure and open consideration of evidence both before and after conviction, and less attractive to guilty defendants, who have more to gain from procedural rigor before trial and at trial and little to gain from open presentation of evidence from all sources. If so, this new choice might separate innocent defendants from guilty defendants more effectively than our current pretrial procedure. That would reduce the number of innocent defendants who plead guilty; help focus official attention on cases of possible innocence, both before conviction and after; and provide better and cheaper evidence in those cases of possible innocence.

What might this new tradeoff look like? There are, of course, two sides to any trade: (1) What would the defendant gain? Here's a rough cut. A defendant who chooses an investigative trial and is then convicted would have two new rights: (i) the right to reopen the question of his guilt if he presents substantial new evidence that casts doubt on his conviction and (ii) the right to a retrial if, at that review proceeding, a de novo assessment of all the evidence leads to the conclusion that there is a substantial doubt that he is guilty.

(2) What would the defendant give up in return? Again, these are preliminary thoughts. Two obvious rights to waive are (i) the Fifth Amendment privilege against self-incrimination and (ii) the right to exclude evidence that was obtained in violation of the Fourth Amendment prohibition of warrantless and unreasonable searches. Both of these rights limit the accuracy of fact finding in favor of other interests. Next in line is (iii) the right to a jury trial. There is no strong reason to believe that judges are in general better (or worse) as fact finders than juries, or specifically that judges are more likely (or less likely) than juries to detect false accusations. But jury trials are famously time consuming, expensive, and inflexible. That's a major reason why we have come to depend on plea bargaining. We can more easily afford a procedure that is likely to increase the frequency of trials if the trial process it uses is correspondingly less costly than our current practice, and on that score bench trials have a big advantage.

If it works, this option would look quite different to guilty and to innocent defendants. Innocent defendants have comparatively little to lose by giving up the privilege against self-incrimination: if they tell the truth and are believed, they will be released. Many innocent defendants are anxious to tell the authorities whatever they know. Needless to say, innocent defendants are sometimes harmed by talking to the police. About 15% of the false felony convictions we know about are based on false confessions, and many other false confessions do not ultimately produce convictions. I do not propose that defendants who choose this procedure subject themselves to the type of police-dominated interrogations that may produce involuntary and sometimes untrue confessions. Rather, I mean that a defendant who chooses an investigative trial will be required to answer pretrial questions from state officials in the presence of his attorney, possibly under oath, and will be required to testify at trial. This may be a benign process for the innocent, but almost all guilty defendants would have a lot to lose by submitting to formal pretrial questioning, especially under oath, and in most cases even more to lose by testifying at trial.

Similarly, as far as we know, innocent defendants are rarely convicted on the basis of illegally seized evidence (although it's easy to imagine how that could happen). But many guilty defendants can only hope that essential evidence against them will be suppressed under the Fourth Amendment.

On the other side of the equation, innocent defendants have a lot to gain from open-minded reconsideration of their case in light of new evidence, if they are convicted. Since they are in fact innocent, any new evidence is likely to point in that direction. That is the lasting hope of so many of the wrongly convicted, that someday the truth will out. This procedure would make that prospect more likely. It would reduce the risk of trial for innocent defendants and make plea bargains comparatively less attractive. But open consideration of new evidence after conviction is not likely to help the guilty, especially since the guilty defendant must waive the privilege against self-incrimination.

Jed S. Rakoff,[*] *Why Innocent People Plead Guilty*
The New York Review of Books, November 20, 2014 Issue

[T]he prosecutor-dictated plea bargain system, by creating such inordinate pressures to enter into plea bargains, appears to have led a significant number of defendants to plead guilty to crimes they never actually committed. For example, of the approximately three hundred people that the Innocence Project and its affiliated lawyers have proven were wrongfully convicted of crimes of rape or murder that they did not in fact commit, at least thirty, or about 10 percent, pleaded guilty to those crimes. Presumably they did so because, even though they were innocent, they faced the likelihood of being convicted of capital offenses and sought to avoid the death penalty, even at the price of life imprisonment. But other publicized cases, arising with disturbing frequency, suggest that this self-protective psychology operates in noncapital cases as well, and recent studies suggest that this is a widespread problem. For example, the National Registry of Exonerations (a joint project of Michigan Law School and Northwestern Law School) records that of 1,428 legally acknowledged exonerations that have occurred since 1989 involving the full range of felony charges, 151 (or, again, about 10 percent) involved false guilty pleas.

It is not difficult to perceive why this should be so. After all, the typical person accused of a crime combines a troubled past with limited resources: he thus recognizes

---

[*] Senior United States District Judge, United States District Court, Southern District of New York.

that, even if he is innocent, his chances of mounting an effective defense at trial may be modest at best. If his lawyer can obtain a plea bargain that will reduce his likely time in prison, he may find it "rational" to take the plea.

Every criminal defense lawyer (and I was both a federal prosecutor and a criminal defense lawyer before going on the bench) has had the experience of a client who first tells his lawyer he is innocent and then, when confronted with a preview of the government's proof, says he is guilty. Usually, he is in fact guilty and was previously lying to his lawyer (despite the protections of the attorney-client privilege, which many defendants, suspicious even of their court-appointed lawyers, do not appreciate). But sometimes the situation is reversed, and the client now lies to his lawyer by saying he is guilty when in fact he is not, because he has decided to "take the fall."

In theory, this charade should be exposed at the time the defendant enters his plea, since the judge is supposed to question the defendant about the facts underlying his confession of guilt. But in practice, most judges, happy for their own reasons to avoid a time-consuming trial, will barely question the defendant beyond the bare bones of his assertion of guilt, relying instead on the prosecutor's statement (untested by any cross-examination) of what the underlying facts are. Indeed, in situations in which the prosecutor and defense counsel themselves recognize that the guilty plea is somewhat artificial, they will have jointly arrived at a written statement of guilt for the defendant to read that cleverly covers all the bases without providing much detail. The Supreme Court, for its part, has gone so far (with the *Alford* plea of 1970) as to allow a defendant to enter a guilty plea while factually maintaining his innocence.

While, moreover, a defendant's decision to plead guilty to a crime he did not commit may represent a "rational," if cynical, cost-benefit analysis of his situation, in fact there is some evidence that the pressure of the situation may cause an innocent defendant to make a less-than-rational appraisal of his chances for acquittal and thus decide to plead guilty when he not only is actually innocent but also could be proven so. Research indicates that young, unintelligent, or risk-averse defendants will often provide false confessions just because they cannot "take the heat" of an interrogation. Although research into false guilty pleas is far less developed, it may be hypothesized that similar pressures, less immediate but more prolonged, may be in effect when a defendant is told, often by his own lawyer, that there is a strong case against him, that his likelihood of acquittal is low, and that he faces a mandatory minimum of five or ten years in prison if convicted and a guidelines range of considerably more— but that, if he acts swiftly, he can get a plea bargain to a lesser offense that will reduce his prison time by many years.

How prevalent is the phenomenon of innocent people pleading guilty? The few criminologists who have thus far investigated the phenomenon estimate that the overall rate for convicted felons as a whole is between 2 percent and 8 percent. The size of that range suggests the imperfection of the data; but let us suppose that it is even lower, say, no more than 1 percent. When you recall that, of the 2.2 million Americans in prison, over 2 million are there because of plea bargains, we are then talking about an estimated 20,000 persons, or more, who are in prison for crimes to which they pleaded guilty but did not in fact commit.

What can we do about it? If there were the political will to do so, we could eliminate mandatory minimums, eliminate sentencing guidelines, and dramatically reduce the severity of our sentencing regimes in general. But even during the second Obama administration, the very modest steps taken by Attorney General Eric Holder to moderate sentences have been met by stiff opposition, some from within his own department. For example, the attorney general's public support for a bipartisan bill that would reduce mandatory minimums for certain narcotics offenses prompted the National Association of Assistant US Attorneys to send an "open letter" of opposition, while a similar letter denouncing the bill was signed by two former attorney generals, three former chiefs of the Drug Enforcement Administration, and eighteen former US attorneys.

Reflecting, perhaps, the religious origins of our country, Americans are notoriously prone to making moral judgments. Often this serves salutary purposes; but a by-product of this moralizing tendency is a punitiveness that I think is not likely to change in the near future. Indeed, on those occasions when Americans read that someone accused of a very serious crime has been permitted to plea bargain to a considerably reduced offense, their typical reaction is one of suspicion or outrage, and sometimes not without reason. Rarely, however, do they contemplate the possibility that the defendant may be totally innocent of any charge but is being coerced into pleading to a lesser offense because the consequences of going to trial and losing are too severe to take the risk.

I am driven, in the end, to advocate what a few jurisdictions, notably Connecticut and Florida, have begun experimenting with: involving judges in the plea-bargaining process. At present, this is forbidden in the federal courts, and with good reason: for a judge to involve herself runs the risk of compromising her objectivity if no bargain is reached. For similar reasons, many federal judges (including this one) refuse to involve themselves in settlement negotiations in civil cases, even though, unlike the criminal plea bargain situation, there is no legal impediment to doing so. But the problem is solved in civil cases by referring the settlement negotiations to magistrates or special masters who do not report the results to the judges who handle the subsequent proceedings. If the federal rule were changed, the same could be done in the criminal plea bargain situation.

As I envision it, shortly after an indictment is returned (or perhaps even earlier if an arrest has occurred and the defendant is jailed), a magistrate would meet separately with the prosecutor and the defense counsel, in proceedings that would be recorded but placed under seal, and all present would be provided with the particulars regarding the evidence and issues in the case. In certain circumstances, the magistrate might interview witnesses or examine other evidence, again under seal so as not to compromise any party's strategy. He might even interview the defendant, under an arrangement where it would not constitute a waiver of the defendant's Fifth Amendment privilege against self-incrimination.

The prosecutor would, in the meantime, be precluded from making any plea bargain offer (or threat) while the magistrate was studying the case. Once the magistrate was ready, he would then meet separately with both sides and, if appropriate, make a recommendation, such as to dismiss the case (if he thought the proof was weak), to proceed to trial (if he thought there was no reasonable plea bargain available), or to enter into a plea bargain along lines the magistrate might suggest. No party would be required to follow the magistrate's suggestions. Their force, if any, would come from the fact that they were being suggested by a neutral third party, who, moreover, was a judicial officer that the prosecutors and the defense lawyers would have to appear before in many other cases.

Would a plan structured along these lines wholly eliminate false guilty pleas? Probably not, but it likely would reduce their number. Would it present new, unforeseeable problems of its own? Undoubtedly, which is why I would recommend that it first be tried as a pilot program. Even given the current federal rules prohibiting judges from involving themselves in the plea-bargaining process, I think something like this could be undertaken, since most such rules can be waived and the relevant parties could here agree to waive them for the limited purposes of a pilot program.

I am under no illusions that this suggested involvement of judges in the plea-bargaining process is a panacea. But would not any program that helps to reduce the shame of sending innocent people to prison be worth trying?

3. The "Direct Connection" Rule

David S. Schwartz and Chelsey B. Metcalf, *Disfavored Treatment of Third-Party Guilt Evidence*

2016 Wis. L. Rev. 337, 338–39 (2016)

Forty-five states and ten federal circuits impose some type of disfavored treatment on a criminal defendant's evidence that a person other than himself committed the crime. When the defendant disputes that he is the perpetrator of a crime whose occurrence is undisputed, evidence having any tendency to increase the likelihood that a third party committed the crime is relevant in the clearest sense. But the so-called direct connection doctrine and its variants impose additional burdens that a defendant must meet before this relevant evidence will be admitted. This disfavored treatment stems from discredited and abandoned concepts of evidence law....

* * *

Jury research has long established that jurors tend to base decisions on the presentation of a persuasive story, the strength of which is judged in part on the completeness of key story elements. Jurors expect the parties to tell a story that has "narrative integrity." Technically, criminal defendants can, and often do, present "reasonable doubt cases" that merely attempt to reduce confidence in the prosecution's narrative of guilt rather than offering a competing narrative. But trial lawyers and scholars alike have recognized that reasonable doubt cases are comparatively ineffective in criminal trials, which are essentially "story battles." As one experienced criminal defense attorney puts it, "if you have to use the term 'reasonable doubt' you've lost your case." Where the central issue is the identity of the perpetrator, even a reasonable doubt case implies a story that someone else did it. But it is a story with a huge hole, and one likely to be ineffective. The jury might speculate that, if this defendant did not do it, there should be at least some evidence suggesting that someone else did. Although such evidence may have been excluded by a pretrial ruling that the jury doesn't know about, the jury could draw a rational, but mistaken, inference that the absence of such evidence increases the probability of the defendant's guilt.

There is thus often a compelling need for a criminal defendant disputing his identity as the perpetrator to offer at least some evidence relevant to show that someone else committed the crime. This evidence can take many forms. Three common types of third-party guilt evidence are opportunity, motive, and propensity. The defendant could offer evidence that the third party had opportunity to commit the crime by demonstrating that the third party had access to a weapon and was near the victim at the time of the crime. Likely, the defendant will want to pair this with the third party's motive to commit the crime, such as revenge, jealousy, money, and the like. Frequently, defendants will try to show the third party's propensity to commit the crime by offering other acts of the third party, such as past violent conduct or criminal charges.

Third-party guilt evidence varies in strength as well as kind. Undisputed evidence that the third party was at the scene of the crime and that the third party had motive is relatively strong. Weaker evidence may be limited to motive or opportunity alone. In one case, a third party merely knew the victim and had the same first name as the victim's identified attacker. Much third-party guilt evidence falls in the middle, like a defendant's offer of proof that (1) the third party's fingerprints were found on the victim's car; (2) the third party lied to the police about not knowing the victim; (3) the third party had a related prior offense; and (4) the third party was known to carry a shotgun in his vehicle.

The direct connection doctrines exclude virtually all weak, and much strong, third-party guilt evidence. This disfavored approach to what may be a very important type of evidence to criminal defendants presents two core problems. First, sometimes seemingly weak evidence does not have a low probative value because the defendant has a great need for it. Second, once a direct connection doctrine is in place, there is a heightened risk of excluding very strong third-party guilt evidence where the third party is in fact guilty.

Steven Avery

The first problem is illustrated by *State v. Avery*,[69] the murder case made (in)famous by the recently aired Netflix documentary *Making a Murderer*. Steven Avery, a forty-four-year-old man from Manitowoc, Wisconsin, had already spent eighteen years in prison for a wrongful conviction from a 1985 rape. Conclusively proven innocent

---

69. 804 N.W.2d 216 (Wis. Ct. App. 2011).

through DNA testing in 2003, Avery was in the midst of a civil suit against several Manitowoc police and prosecutors when, in November 2006, he was charged with a murder that seemed to have occurred in the general area of his property. The State's theory of the case was that Avery lured the victim, twenty-five-year-old part-time photographer Teresa Halbach, to his family's salvage yard with a photography assignment, murdered her with the help of his nephew, Brendan Dassey, and then burned her body and buried her remains in his backyard. While the State had contended in highly publicized pre-trial press conferences that this was a sex crime, involving a brutal rape prior to the murder, the State dropped that charge at the start of the trial and offered no evidence of rape.

At trial, the State presented a circumstantial case against Avery consisting largely of five or six items of physical evidence found in or near Avery's trailer: the victim's SUV itself; traces of Avery's blood inside the SUV; traces of Avery's DNA on the hood latch to the SUV; the key to the SUV, found in Avery's bedroom; burned bone fragments of the victim; and a bullet found in Avery's garage which purportedly had rendered the fatal gunshot to the victim.

But the evidence was dubious. The defense presented strong evidence that the bones had been moved from the actual burn site and argued that it was implausible that Avery would have moved the bones toward his own residence if he were the killer. The SUV key had not been found in several prior searches of Avery's bedroom, and the defense presented evidence strongly suggesting that the key was planted by a detective who had been accused of misconduct in the civil suit; this same officer would have had access to numerous DNA samples of Avery through the search and seizure of toiletries from Avery's bathroom. The defense presented evidence consistent with the possibility that this same detective planted Avery's blood in the vehicle: the detective had access to a vial of blood from the 1985 rape case, and there was evidence that the vial had been tampered with in the clerk's office where it was non-securely stored. The defense presented evidence that Avery's DNA was negligently transferred to the hood latch by an investigating officer who opened the hood after unsuccessfully attempting to start the SUV using the key with Avery's planted DNA on it. The bullet had Avery's DNA on it but not the victim's; and there was strong evidence questioning whether Avery's DNA was really on the bullet, since the lab test was tainted.

At the same time, there was a disturbing absence of the sort of evidence that one would expect to find had Avery been guilty. Aside from the bone fragments and the SUV, which may have been moved, there were no traces of the victim's blood or DNA anywhere on the Avery property, such as Avery's bedroom or garage.

Despite a strong case of reasonable doubt stemming from faulty and possibly fraudulent investigative procedures and evidence, the jury convicted Avery. Missing from the defense case was an innocence narrative suggesting alternative suspects. At trial, the jury was left asking, "If not Steven Avery, then who?" Prior to the start of the trial, Avery's defense team had moved to offer evidence suggesting that other named persons—various customers and family members who visited or lived on or near the salvage yard—could have murdered Teresa Halbach. The defense proposed to name one or more such persons, introduce evidence of their opportunity and suspicious behavior, and argue that these persons would have known that Avery would be easy to frame for the crime. Given Steven Avery's ongoing dispute with the Manitowoc sheriff's department, the real culprit could well know that law enforcement would like nothing better than to be able to show Avery guilty of a new crime.

But the trial court granted the prosecution's motion to exclude all evidence of third-party guilt. Expressing worry about "[t]he danger of degenerating the proceedings into a trial of collateral issues," the court excluded the defendant's third-party guilt evidence, relying on Wisconsin authority requiring that a defendant must offer evidence of the third-party suspect's motive to commit the crime, in addition to his opportunity, and a "direct connection" to the crime. The court ruled that the evidence of motive was absent here. The ruling was particularly ironic given that the prosecution offered no evidence that Avery had a motive to commit the crime. Avery was therefore thrown into a murder trial, a story battle for his life, without an affirmative narrative of his own. The jury was left to wonder why Avery was not explaining what really happened to Teresa Halbach. Jerome Buting anticipated this very problem:

> We're really worried that the jury might think "God you know, can we really acquit this man when we don't know," when we can't tell them who we think did it? That's gonna be on a human level, the hardest thing I think, and the judge has really tied our hands on that.

The Avery trial thus illustrates the potential limitations of even a strong case of police misconduct and tainted evidence toward producing reasonable doubt in the minds of jurors when no third-party guilt evidence is presented.

B. Current Law: Overview

Guilty Pleas

Plea bargaining has been the subject of constitutional regulation at least since *Brady v. United States*, 397 U.S. 742 (1970), definitively established that the practice does not violate the constitution. Moreover, the parameters of that law have been fixed for decades. Brady, along with other decisions such as *Boykin v. Alabama*, 395 U.S. 238 (1969) established a constitutional framework within which plea bargaining can be conducted. At the center of that framework is the requirement that, to pass constitutional muster, guilty pleas must be voluntary and intelligent. *Id.* at 242. The Court in *Brady* identified two reasons for the requirement. First, because a guilty plea was an "admission in open court that he committed the acts charged in the indictment," the defendant's plea would violate the self-incrimination clause of the Fifth Amendment if the plea was not voluntary. Accordingly, criminal defendants may not be physically or mentally coerced into pleading guilty and prosecutors may not materially misrepresent the terms of bargains. At the same time, a guilty plea provides the "defendant's consent that judgment of conviction may be entered without a trial" and thus is "a waiver of his right to trial before a jury or a judge." As the Court long has held, "[w]aivers of constitutional rights not only must be voluntary but must be knowing, intelligent acts done with sufficient awareness of the relevant circumstances and likely consequences." Defendants are thus constitutionally entitled, before pleading guilty, to be informed of certain critical information necessary to make informed plea-bargaining choices, including the nature of the charges, the rights waived by pleading guilty, and the potential sentence that can lawfully be imposed. Although plea bargains are less than fully-enforceable executory agreements, *Mabry v. Johnson*, 467 U.S. 504 (1984), promises upon which a defendant relies in pleading guilty are enforceable and provide a minimum floor of constitutional protection in the plea-bargaining process. *Santobello v. New York*, 404 U.S. 257 (1971).

The Court added another important component to its regulatory plea-bargaining framework by making clear that the right to the effective assistance of counsel extends to the plea process. In *McMann v. Richardson*, 397 U.S. 759, 771 (1970), and then more fully in *Hill v. Lockhart*, 474 U.S. 52, 58 (1985), the Court held that defendants have a Sixth Amendment right to competent legal advice regarding guilty pleas. Hill specifically clarified that the two-pronged test set forth in *Strickland v. Washington* governs in the context of guilty pleas as well. The Court recently supplemented this body of "constitutional plea-bargaining law" in two cases — *Lafler v. Cooper*, 132 S. Ct. 1376 (2012) and *Missouri v. Frye*, 132 S. Ct. 1399 (2012) — which established that defense counsel's failure to provide constitutionally adequate advice during plea bargaining can serve as the basis of an ineffective assistance of counsel claim, even if the defendant later receives an otherwise fair trial or enters a voluntary guilty plea.

Specifically with regard to innocence issues, the Court held in *Alford v. North Carolina*, 400 U.S. 25 (1970), that "the Constitution does not bar imposition of a prison sentence upon an accused who is unwilling expressly to admit his guilty but who, faced with grim alternatives, is willing to waive his trial and accept the sentence" in a procedure that has come to be known as an "Alford plea."

In *Bousley v. United States*, 523 U.S. 614 (1998), the Court held that a defendant who had pled guilty and, as a result, had procedurally defaulted his challenge to his conviction, would nonetheless be entitled to habeas relief if he could make a sufficient showing of "actual innocence" to satisfy the "fundamental miscarriage of justice" exception to the procedural default bar. Actual innocence, the Court emphasized, meant not only innocence of the offense of conviction but also innocence as to any more serious charges that the Government might have forgone in the course of plea bargaining. On remand, the Government would be entitled to rebut any showing that petitioner might make with "any admissible evidence of petitioner's guilt even if that evidence was not presented during petitioner's plea colloquy."

C. Legal Materials, Exercises, and Media

Misdemeanors and Guilty Pleas

1. *Exercise, the Guilty Plea Problem:* Innocent people plead to crimes they did not commit. Why? The Guilty Plea Problem webpage discusses this question from the perspective of exonerees and judges: http://guiltypleaproblem.org.

   a. Watch U.S. District Court Judge Jed Rakoff, author of *Why Innocent People Plead Guilty*, further discuss his answer: http://guiltypleaproblem.org/#judge-jed (4:45).

   b. Watch an exoneree discuss how he or she pled guilty to a charge despite being completely innocent: http://guiltypleaproblem.org.

   c. In a few sentences, answer the following questions:

      i. Why did your exoneree plead guilty?

      ii. How did any of the factors discussed in the readings or by Judge Rakoff impact your exoneree's decision to plead guilty?

      iii. What were the consequences of the guilty plea?

2. *Misdemeanors:* As Professor Jenny Roberts observes, the pressures to surrender procedural rights in plea bargaining are arguably even greater in misdemeanor cases:

   > As the Supreme Court has noted, "the volume of misdemeanor cases, far greater in number than felony prosecutions, may create an obsession for speedy dispositions, regardless of the fairness of the result." With such a high volume of misdemeanors and other minor cases, judges, defense counsel, and prosecutors all have enormous incentive to pursue early guilty pleas—as early as the initial arraignment in some jurisdictions. There is serious institutional pressure from all quarters to quickly "dispose of" misdemeanor cases, often before defense counsel can undertake any investigation or adequately review any discovery material. A study for New York State's then-high court Chief Judge revealed that by the year 2000 in New York City, private attorneys representing indigent defendants through an assigned-counsel plan "were disposing of 69 percent of all misdemeanor cases at arraignment." The same study described how the Legal Aid Society, New York City's largest provider of indigent defense services, had "permanent arraignment lawyers who ... only take misdemeanor arraignments and ... 'know the going rate of a case' on misdemeanors and violations and therefore try to take only those cases that can be disposed of at arraignment."

   Why Misdemeanors Matter: Defining Effective Advocacy in the Lower Criminal Courts, 45 U.C. Davis L. Rev. 277, 306–07 (2011).

3. *Misdemeanors and Pre-Trial Detention*: The Misdemeanor Justice Project at John Jay College collects and analyzes data on pre-trial detention for misdemeanors in cities across the United States. Find out more here: http://misdemeanorjustice.org.

Figure 13.1: Arrest — Pre-Trial Detention — Bail (Prison Policy Initiative)

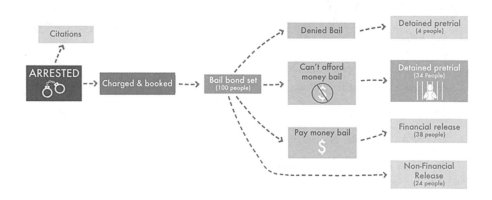

Source: The Prison Policy Initiative

4. *Women and Pre-Trial Detention:* "Fully sixty percent of women in jails have not been convicted of a crime," according to Ryan Cooper's article, *How American Women are Left to Rot in Jail*, THE WEEK (Oct. 23, 2017). Detained women are disproportionately incarcerated pre-trial because they have lower incomes than detained men and are less able to afford cash bail, even though they are also generally the primary caretakers of children on the outside. One study showed that women who could not make bail had an annual median income of $11,071, making the typical cash bail amount of $10,000 unfeasible. Read more at: http://the week.com/articles/732281/how-american-women-are-left-rot-jail.

5. *Exercise, Mock Bail Argument:* Before class, break into teams of two and interview your teammate. Your teammate has been charged with assault and firmly states that she is innocent, but if she isn't granted bail, she may plead guilty so she can take care of her kids and hopefully keep her job.

    While interviewing your teammate, find out information about an important event in his or her life. Learn why this event is considered so important and what it can tell us about the person — about his or her personality, how he/she was before the event as compared to after, why knowledge of it would be helpful to a better knowing/understanding of the person. After you complete the interview, then prepare a not more than five minute bail argument to be presented in court. While you must also consider the seriousness of the crime, likelihood of flight, ties to the community etc. in determining bail, consider also how well you can translate the event that your classmate described to you into a story about them, about their slice of life, and convince the court to grant bail. You will present your bail argument in class.

6. *"The Trial Penalty" and a History of Guilty Pleas:* In *Innocence Is Irrelevant*, Emily Yoffe tracks an innocent Nashville woman who wants nothing more than a guilty plea with no time in prison. Yoffe analyzes the "trial penalty" and the history of guilty pleas in our criminal system: https://www.theatlantic.com/magazine/archive/2017/09/innocence-is-irrelevant/534171/.

7. *Holistic Discussion and Media on Plea Bargains: The Plea*, a PBS Frontline Documentary, examines plea bargains in detail. *The Plea* webpage answers frequently asked questions about guilty pleas, interviews well-known scholars, defense attorneys, and prosecutors, and provides four stories of people who were innocent but pled guilty, including Kerry Max Cooke and his *Alford* plea. http://www.pbs.org/wgbh/pages/frontline/shows/plea/.

8. *Exercise, Plea Negotiation:* Read the following excerpt from Jenny Roberts & Ronald F. Wright, *Training for Bargaining*, 57 WILLIAM & MARY L. REV. 1446 (2016):

> Many defenders view themselves as simply begging or as needing to threaten to take everything to trial to get anything good out of a negotiation.... The whole purpose of a negotiation is to get a more desirable outcome than you would get without the negotiation. To determine whether a deal is worth taking, a negotiator must figure out what would happen if the parties do not reach agreement.
>
> The Best Alternative To a Negotiated Agreement (BATNA) is a concept that gives a negotiator a reference point for knowing when to walk away from the negotiating table ... Fisher and Ury, who coined the term, recommend a three-step process for determining a BATNA: brainstorming a list of actions to be taken if there is no agreement, converting the most promising ideas into tangible alternatives, and selecting the best alternative....
>
> Training about BATNAs would emphasize the importance of early investigation and planning to the negotiation process. Using the BATNA method would lead to a different calculation of the best alternative to agreement, and thus a stronger position from which to negotiate, as well as a better sense of when to walk away from the negotiation....
>
> Anchoring describes a phenomenon in which the initial value given to a particular item strongly influences the ultimate valuation of that item. The first offer in a negotiation serves as an anchor and can thus advantage the negotiator willing to make the initial move. As one negotiation scholar put it, "[p]roficient negotiators generally attempt to develop the most extreme positions they can rationally defend."
>
> Responses to our surveys show that public defenders do not often try a first offer or a low offer ... when asked to characterize their own first offers in typical cases, defenders typically answered that their offers were closer to unfavorable than favorable for their own clients....

Figure 13.2

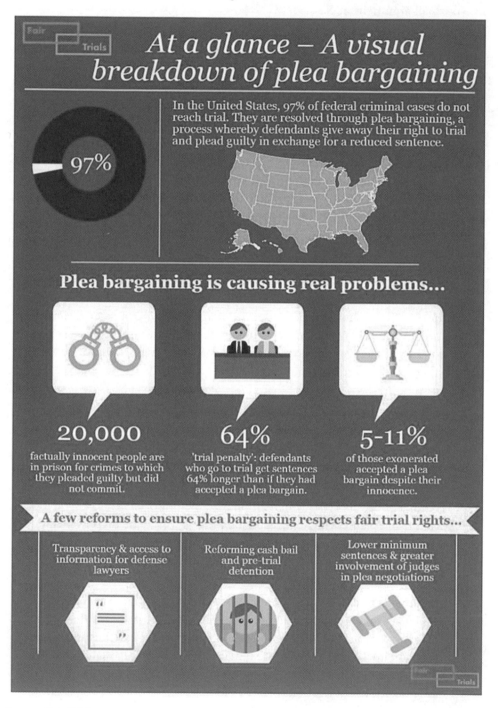

Source: Fair Trials

Another aspect of communication during the actual negotiation is strategic information exchange—formulating a specific plan in advance of the bargaining session for what information to seek out, what information to share, and what information to withhold. Plea bargaining discussions offer an excellent opportunity to learn something about the state's evidence, case theory, and views on sentencing in the particular case.

Indeed, G. Nicholas Herman's treatise, Plea Bargaining, recommends that practitioners prepare a "Plea Bargaining Preparation Outline" that includes lists of "Information 'To Find Out,' Information 'To Reveal,' and Information 'To Protect.'"

Now, break into teams where one person is the prosecutor and the other is the defense attorney. Each student will receive detailed information from the professor relevant to the case, and known only to the defense attorney or the prosecutor. Using your knowledge, negotiate with your teammate for a plea bargain.

9. *Late Night Commentary on Guilty Pleas:* John Oliver discusses guilty pleas, wrongful convictions, and overwhelming public defender caseloads on *Last Week Tonight* (Sept. 13, 2015: Public Defenders): https://www.youtube.com/watch?v=USkEz LuzmZ4 (15:00).

Alford Pleas

10. *"The Freedom Plea":* When a conviction is reversed and an innocent person is released from prison, more and more frequently the prosecutor is re-bringing the charges—and offering an *Alford* plea to time served. The American Bar Association Resolution against *Alford* pleas noted concerns about these post-conviction pleas. In *The Freedom Plea: How Prosecutors Deny Exonerations by Dangling the Prison Keys*, Megan Rose at ProPublica examines the cases of four men who took *Alford* pleas to obtain freedom: https://www.propublica.org/article/freedom-plea-prosecutors-deny-exonerations-dangling-prison-keys.

Listen to or read the cases of James Owens and James Thompson—two men wrongfully convicted of the same murder who were exculpated by DNA evidence—both of whom were offered *Alford* pleas. Same case, same exculpatory evidence, but very different life outcomes based on their plea choices: Megan Rose, *What Does an Innocent Man Have to Do to Get Free? Plead Guilty.* PROPUB-LICA (Sept. 7, 2017) https://www.propublica.org/article/what-does-an-innocent-man-have-to-do-alford-plea-guilty.

11. *American Bar Association Resolution on Alford Pleas:* On February 6, 2017, the American Bar Association (ABA) House of Delegates adopted a Resolution for an "internal conviction-integrity policy" on Alford pleas:

RESOLUTION

RESOLVED, That the American Bar Association urges each federal, state, and territorial prosecutor's office to adopt and implement the following internal conviction-integrity policy: When the prosecutor's office supports a defendant's motion to vacate a conviction based on the office's doubts about the defendant's guilt of the crime for which the defendant was convicted, or about the lawfulness of the defendant's conviction, *the office should not condition its support for the motion on an Alford plea, a guilty plea, or a no contest plea by the defendant to the original or any other charge.* Nevertheless, the office may independently pursue any charge it believes is supported by admissible evidence sufficient to prove guilt beyond reasonable doubt, and may seek to resolve that matter with an *Alford* plea, no contest plea, or guilty plea to that charge.

Read the reasoning behind the Resolution in the brief accompanying ABA Report at https://webcache.googleusercontent.com/search?q=cache:MwJfMoPU7qkJ: https://www.americanbar.org/content/dam/aba/directories/policy/2017_hod_mid year_112B.authcheckdam.docx+&cd=1&hl=en&ct=clnk&gl=us.

12. *Reflective Essay on Alford Pleas:* In 1–2 pages, reflect on these questions:

Would you advise an innocent client who had been wrongfully convicted to plead guilty in order to walk free? Why or why not?

Why do you think a prosecutor, who truly believed your client was guilty, would offer your client time served for a serious crime? If the prosecutor didn't believe your client committed the crime, why would the prosecutor re-bring the charges?

13. *Bringing Constitutional Claims after a Guilty Plea, Texas:* Texas blog *Grits for Breakfast* recaps the Texas Supreme Court of Appeals decision *Ex Parte Tuley*, which allowed criminal defendants to challenge the constitutionality of their convictions regardless of whether they pled guilty or went to trial. Judge Tom Price, writing for the court, stated, "I think it is colossal hypocrisy to exclaim, 'we are shocked, positively shocked,' that a person who has pleaded guilty pursuant to a negotiated plea bargain would never do so unless he were truly guilty and believed himself guilty."

Read a longer excerpt of *Ex Parte Tuley* at *Why An Innocent Person Would Plea Bargain*, Grits for Breakfast (Oct. 3, 2017), available at http://gritsforbreakfast. blogspot.com/2017/10/why-innocent-person-would-plea-bargain.html?utm_ source=feedblitz&utm_medium=FeedBlitzEmail&utm_content=79553&utm_ campaign=0&m=1.

Chapter Fourteen

Appellate and Post-Conviction Review of Innocence: The Cases

A. Readings

Jackson v. Virginia

443 U.S. 307 (1979)

Mr. Justice STEWART delivered the opinion of the Court.

The Constitution prohibits the criminal conviction of any person except upon proof of guilt beyond a reasonable doubt.[70] The question in this case is what standard is to be applied in a federal habeas corpus proceeding when the claim is made that a person has been convicted in a state court upon insufficient evidence.

I

The petitioner was convicted after a bench trial in the Circuit Court of Chesterfield County, Va., of the first-degree murder of a woman named Mary Houston Cole. Under Virginia law, murder is defined as "the unlawful killing of another with malice afore-thought." Premeditation, or specific intent to kill, distinguishes murder in the first from murder in the second degree; proof of this element is essential to conviction of the former offense, and the burden of proving it clearly rests with the prosecution.

That the petitioner had shot and killed Mrs. Cole was not in dispute at the trial. The State's evidence established that she had been a member of the staff at the local county jail, that she had befriended him while he was imprisoned there on a disorderly conduct charge, and that when he was released she had arranged for him to live in the home of her son and daughter-in-law. Testimony by her relatives indicated that on the day of the killing the petitioner had been drinking and had spent a great deal of time shooting at targets with his revolver. Late in the afternoon, according to their testimony, he had unsuccessfully attempted to talk the victim into driving him to North Carolina. She did drive the petitioner to a local diner. There the two were observed by several police officers, who testified that both the petitioner and the victim had been drinking. The two were observed by a deputy sheriff as they were preparing to leave the diner in her car. The petitioner was then in possession of his revolver,

---

70. In re Winship, 397 U.S. 358 (1970).

and the sheriff also observed a kitchen knife in the automobile. The sheriff testified that he had offered to keep the revolver until the petitioner sobered up, but that the latter had indicated that this would be unnecessary since he and the victim were about to engage in sexual activity.

Her body was found in a secluded church parking lot a day and a half later, naked from the waist down, her slacks beneath her body. Uncontradicted medical and expert evidence established that she had been shot twice at close range with the petitioner's gun. She appeared not to have been sexually molested. Six cartridge cases identified as having been fired from the petitioner's gun were found near the body.

After shooting Mrs. Cole, the petitioner drove her car to North Carolina, where, after a short trip to Florida, he was arrested several days later. In a post-arrest statement, introduced in evidence by the prosecution, the petitioner admitted that he had shot the victim. He contended, however, that the shooting had been accidental. When asked to describe his condition at the time of the shooting, he indicated that he had not been drunk, but had been "pretty high." His story was that the victim had attacked him with a knife when he resisted her sexual advances. He said that he had defended himself by firing a number of warning shots into the ground, and had then reloaded his revolver. The victim, he said, then attempted to take the gun from him, and the gun "went off" in the ensuing struggle. He said that he fled without seeking help for the victim because he was afraid. At the trial, his position was that he had acted in self-defense. Alternatively, he claimed that in any event the State's own evidence showed that he had been too intoxicated to form the specific intent necessary under Virginia law to sustain a conviction of murder in the first degree.[71]

The trial judge, declaring himself convinced beyond a reasonable doubt that the petitioner had committed first-degree murder, found him guilty of that offense. The petitioner's motion to set aside the judgment as contrary to the evidence was denied, and he was sentenced to serve a term of 30 years in the Virginia state penitentiary. A petition for writ of error to the Virginia Supreme Court on the ground that the evidence was insufficient to support the conviction was denied.

The petitioner then commenced this habeas corpus proceeding in the United States District Court for the Eastern District of Virginia, raising the same basic claim. Applying the "no evidence" criterion of *Thompson v. Louisville*,[72] the District Court found the record devoid of evidence of premeditation and granted the writ. The Court of Appeals for the Fourth Circuit reversed the judgment. The court noted that a dissent from the denial of certiorari in a case in this Court had exposed the question whether the constitutional rule of *In re Winship*, might compel a new criterion by which the validity of a state criminal conviction must be tested in a federal habeas corpus proceeding. But the appellate court held that in the absence of further guidance from

---

71. Under Virginia law, voluntary intoxication although not an affirmative defense to second degree murder is material to the element of premeditation and may be found to have negated it. Hatcher v. Commonwealth, 218 Va. 811.

72. 362 U.S. 199 (1960).

this Court it would apply the same "no evidence" criterion of *Thompson v. Louisville* that the District Court had adopted. The court was of the view that some evidence that the petitioner had intended to kill the victim could be found in the facts that the petitioner had reloaded his gun after firing warning shots, that he had had time to do so, and that the victim was then shot not once but twice. The court also concluded that the state trial judge could have found that the petitioner was not so intoxicated as to be incapable of premeditation.

We granted certiorari to consider the petitioner's claim that under *In re Winship*, supra, a federal habeas corpus court must consider not whether there was any evidence to support a state-court conviction, but whether there was sufficient evidence to justify a rational trier of the facts to find guilt beyond a reasonable doubt.

II

Our inquiry in this case is narrow. The petitioner has not seriously questioned any aspect of Virginia law governing the allocation of the burden of production or persuasion in a murder trial. As the record demonstrates, the judge sitting as factfinder in the petitioner's trial was aware that the State bore the burden of establishing the element of premeditation, and stated that he was applying the reasonable-doubt standard in his appraisal of the State's evidence. The petitioner, moreover, does not contest the conclusion of the Court of Appeals that under the "no evidence" rule of *Thompson v. Louisville*, his conviction of first-degree murder is sustainable. And he has not attacked the sufficiency of the evidence to support a conviction of second-degree murder. His sole constitutional claim, based squarely upon *Winship*, is that the District Court and the Court of Appeals were in error in not recognizing that the question to be decided in this case is whether any rational factfinder could have concluded beyond a reasonable doubt that the killing for which the petitioner was convicted was premeditated. The question thus raised goes to the basic nature of the constitutional right recognized in the *Winship* opinion.

III

A

This is the first of our cases to expressly consider the question whether the due process standard recognized in *Winship* constitutionally protects an accused against conviction except upon evidence that is sufficient fairly to support a conclusion that every element of the crime has been established beyond a reasonable doubt. . . .

It is axiomatic that a conviction upon a charge not made or upon a charge not tried constitutes a denial of due process. These standards no more than reflect a broader premise that has never been doubted in our constitutional system: that a person cannot incur the loss of liberty for an offense without notice and a meaningful opportunity to defend. A meaningful opportunity to defend, if not the right to a trial itself, presumes as well that a total want of evidence to support a charge will conclude the case in favor of the accused. Accordingly, we held in the *Thompson* case that a conviction based upon a record wholly devoid of any relevant evidence of a crucial element of the offense charged is constitutionally infirm. The "no evidence" doctrine of *Thompson v. Louisville* thus secures to an accused the most elemental of due process rights: freedom from a wholly arbitrary deprivation of liberty.

The Court in *Thompson* explicitly stated that the due process right at issue did not concern a question of evidentiary "sufficiency." The right established in *In re Winship*, however, clearly stands on a different footing. *Winship* involved an adjudication of juvenile delinquency made by a judge under a state statute providing that the prosecution must prove the conduct charged as delinquent — which in *Winship* would have been a criminal offense if engaged in by an adult — by a preponderance of the evidence. Applying that standard, the judge was satisfied that the juvenile was "guilty," but he noted that the result might well have been different under a standard of proof beyond a reasonable doubt. In short, the record in *Winship* was not totally devoid of evidence of guilt.

The constitutional problem addressed in *Winship* was thus distinct from the stark problem of arbitrariness presented in *Thompson v. Louisville*. In *Winship*, the Court held for the first time that the Due Process Clause of the Fourteenth Amendment protects a defendant in a criminal case against conviction "except upon proof beyond a reasonable doubt of every fact necessary to constitute the crime with which he is charged." In so holding, the Court emphasized that proof beyond a reasonable doubt has traditionally been regarded as the decisive difference between criminal culpability and civil liability. The standard of proof beyond a reasonable doubt, said the Court, "plays a vital role in the American scheme of criminal procedure," because it operates to give "concrete substance" to the presumption of innocence to ensure against unjust convictions, and to reduce the risk of factual error in a criminal proceeding. At the same time by impressing upon the factfinder the need to reach a subjective state of near certitude of the guilt of the accused, the standard symbolizes the significance that our society attaches to the criminal sanction and thus to liberty itself.

The constitutional standard recognized in the *Winship* case was expressly phrased as one that protects an accused against a conviction except on "proof beyond a reasonable doubt...." In subsequent cases discussing the reasonable-doubt standard, we have never departed from this definition of the rule or from the *Winship* understanding of the central purposes it serves. In short, *Winship* presupposes as an essential of the due process guaranteed by the Fourteenth Amendment that no person shall be made to suffer the onus of a criminal conviction except upon sufficient proof — defined as evidence necessary to convince a trier of fact beyond a reasonable doubt of the existence of every element of the offense.

B

Although several of our cases have intimated that the factfinder's application of the reasonable-doubt standard to the evidence may present a federal question when a state conviction is challenged, the Federal Courts of Appeals have generally assumed that so long as the reasonable-doubt instruction has been given at trial, the no-evidence doctrine of *Thompson v. Louisville* remains the appropriate guide for a federal habeas corpus court to apply in assessing a state prisoner's challenge to his conviction as founded upon insufficient evidence. We cannot agree.

The *Winship* doctrine requires more than simply a trial ritual. A doctrine establishing so fundamental a substantive constitutional standard must also require that the factfinder will rationally apply that standard to the facts in evidence. A "reasonable doubt," at a minimum, is one based upon "reason."[73] Yet a properly instructed jury may occasionally convict even when it can be said that no rational trier of fact could find guilt beyond a reasonable doubt, and the same may be said of a trial judge sitting as a jury. In a federal trial, such an occurrence has traditionally been deemed to require reversal of the conviction. Under *Winship*, which established proof beyond a reasonable doubt as an essential of Fourteenth Amendment due process, it follows that when such a conviction occurs in a state trial, it cannot constitutionally stand.[74]

A federal court has a duty to assess the historic facts when it is called upon to apply a constitutional standard to a conviction obtained in a state court. For example, on direct review of a state-court conviction, where the claim is made that an involuntary confession was used against the defendant, this Court reviews the facts to determine whether the confession was wrongly admitted in evidence. The same duty obtains in federal habeas corpus proceedings.

After *Winship* the critical inquiry on review of the sufficiency of the evidence to support a criminal conviction must be not simply to determine whether the jury was properly instructed, but to determine whether the record evidence could reasonably support a finding of guilt beyond a reasonable doubt. But this inquiry does not require a court to "ask itself whether it believes that the evidence at the trial established guilt beyond a reasonable doubt." Instead, the relevant question is whether, after viewing the evidence in the light most favorable to the prosecution, any rational trier of fact could have found the essential elements of the crime beyond a reasonable doubt. This familiar standard gives full play to the responsibility of the trier of fact fairly to resolve conflicts in the testimony, to weigh the evidence, and to draw reasonable inferences from basic facts to ultimate facts. Once a defendant has been found guilty

---

73. FN9. A "reasonable doubt" has often been described as one "based on reason which arises from the evidence or lack of evidence." Johnson v. Louisiana, 406 U.S. 356, 360 (citing cases). For a discussion of variations in the definition used in jury instructions, see Holland v. United States, 348 U.S. 121, 140 (rejecting contention that circumstantial evidence must exclude every hypothesis but that of guilt).

74. FN10. This, of course, does not mean that convictions are frequently reversed upon this ground. The practice in the federal courts of entertaining properly preserved challenges to evidentiary sufficiency, see Fed. Rule Crim. Proc. 29, serves only to highlight the traditional understanding in our system that the application of the beyond-a-reasonable-doubt standard to the evidence is not irretrievably committed to jury discretion. To be sure, the factfinder in a criminal case has traditionally been permitted to enter an unassailable but unreasonable verdict of "not guilty." This is the logical corollary of the rule that there can be no appeal from a judgment of acquittal, even if the evidence of guilt is overwhelming. The power of the factfinder to err upon the side of mercy, however, has never been thought to include a power to enter an unreasonable verdict of guilty. Any such premise is wholly belied by the settled practice of testing evidentiary sufficiency through a motion for judgment of acquittal and a post-verdict appeal from the denial of such a motion.

of the crime charged, the factfinder's role as weigher of the evidence is preserved through a legal conclusion that upon judicial review all of the evidence is to be considered in the light most favorable to the prosecution. The criterion thus impinges upon "jury" discretion only to the extent necessary to guarantee the fundamental protection of due process of law.[75]

That the *Thompson* "no evidence" rule is simply inadequate to protect against misapplications of the constitutional standard of reasonable doubt is readily apparent. "[A] mere modicum of evidence may satisfy a 'no evidence' standard...." Any evidence that is relevant — that has any tendency to make the existence of an element of a crime slightly more probable than it would be without the evidence, cf. Fed. Rule Evid. 401 — could be deemed a "mere modicum." But it could not seriously be argued that such a "modicum" of evidence could by itself rationally support a conviction beyond a reasonable doubt. The *Thompson* doctrine simply fails to supply a workable or even a predictable standard for determining whether the due process command of *Winship* has been honored.[76]

IV

Turning finally to the specific facts of this case, we reject the petitioner's claim that under the constitutional standard dictated by *Winship* his conviction of first-degree murder cannot stand. A review of the record in the light most favorable to the prosecution convinces us that a rational factfinder could readily have found the petitioner guilty beyond a reasonable doubt of first-degree murder under Virginia law.

There was no question at the trial that the petitioner had fatally shot Mary Cole. The crucial factual dispute went to the sufficiency of the evidence to support a finding that he had specifically intended to kill her. This question, as the Court of Appeals recognized, must be gauged in the light of applicable Virginia law defining the element of premeditation. Under that law it is well settled that premeditation need not exist for any particular length of time, and that an intent to kill may be formed at the moment of the commission of the unlawful act. From the circumstantial evidence in the record, it is clear that the trial judge could reasonably have found beyond a reasonable doubt that the petitioner did possess the necessary intent at or before the time of the killing.

---

75. FN13. The question whether the evidence is constitutionally sufficient is of course wholly unrelated to the question of how rationally the verdict was actually reached. Just as the standard announced today does not permit a court to make its own subjective determination of guilt or innocence, it does not require scrutiny of the reasoning process actually used by the factfinder — if known.

76. FN14. Application of the Thompson standard to assess the validity of a criminal conviction after Winship could lead to absurdly unjust results. Our cases have indicated that failure to instruct a jury on the necessity of proof of guilt beyond a reasonable doubt can never be harmless error. Thus, a defendant whose guilt was actually proved by overwhelming evidence would be denied due process if the jury was instructed that he could be found guilty on a mere preponderance of the evidence. Yet a defendant against whom there was but one slender bit of evidence would not be denied due process so long as the jury has been properly instructed on the prosecution's burden of proof beyond a reasonable doubt. Such results would be wholly faithless to the constitutional rationale of *Winship*.

The prosecution's uncontradicted evidence established that the petitioner shot the victim not once but twice. The petitioner himself admitted that the fatal shooting had occurred only after he had first fired several shots into the ground and then reloaded his gun. The evidence was clear that the two shots that killed the victim were fired at close, and thus predictably fatal, range by a person who was experienced in the use of the murder weapon. Immediately after the shooting, the petitioner drove without mishap from Virginia to North Carolina, a fact quite at odds with his story of extreme intoxication. Shortly before the fatal episode, he had publicly expressed an intention to have sexual relations with the victim. Her body was found partially unclothed. From these uncontradicted circumstances, a rational factfinder readily could have inferred beyond a reasonable doubt that the petitioner, notwithstanding evidence that he had been drinking on the day of the killing, did have the capacity to form and had in fact formed an intent to kill the victim.

The petitioner's calculated behavior both before and after the killing demonstrated that he was fully capable of committing premeditated murder. His claim of self-defense would have required the trial judge to draw a series of improbable inferences from the basic facts, prime among them the inference that he was wholly uninterested in sexual activity with the victim but that she was so interested as to have willingly removed part of her clothing and then attacked him with a knife when he resisted her advances, even though he was armed with a loaded revolver that he had just demonstrated he knew how to use. It is evident from the record that the trial judge found this story, including the petitioner's belated contention that he had been so intoxicated as to be incapable of premeditation, incredible.

Only under a theory that the prosecution was under an affirmative duty to rule out every hypothesis except that of guilt beyond a reasonable doubt could this petitioner's challenge be sustained. That theory the Court has rejected in the past. We decline to adopt it today. Under the standard established in this opinion as necessary to preserve the due process protection recognized in *Winship*, a federal habeas corpus court faced with a record of historical facts that supports conflicting inferences must presume — even if it does not affirmatively appear in the record — that the trier of fact resolved any such conflicts in favor of the prosecution, and must defer to that resolution. Applying these criteria, we hold that a rational trier of fact could reasonably have found that the petitioner committed murder in the first degree under Virginia law.

For these reasons, the judgment of the Court of Appeals is affirmed.

Herrera v. Collins
506 U.S. 390 (1992)

Chief Justice REHNQUIST delivered the opinion of the Court.

Petitioner Leonel Torres Herrera was convicted of capital murder and sentenced to death in January 1982. He unsuccessfully challenged the conviction on direct appeal and state collateral proceedings in the Texas state courts, and in a federal habeas petition. In February 1992 — 10 years after his conviction — he urged in a second federal habeas petition that he was "actually innocent" of the murder for which he was sentenced to death, and that the Eighth Amendment's prohibition against cruel and unusual punishment and the Fourteenth Amendment's guarantee of due process of law therefore forbid his execution. He supported this claim with affidavits tending to show that his now-dead brother, rather than he, had been the perpetrator of the crime. Petitioner urges us to hold that this showing of innocence entitles him to relief in this federal habeas proceeding. We hold that it does not.

Shortly before 11 p.m. on an evening in late September 1981, the body of Texas Department of Public Safety Officer David Rucker was found by a passer-by on a stretch of highway about six miles east of Los Fresnos, Texas, a few miles north of Brownsville in the Rio Grande Valley. Rucker's body was lying beside his patrol car. He had been shot in the head.

At about the same time, Los Fresnos Police Officer Enrique Carrisalez observed a speeding vehicle traveling west towards Los Fresnos, away from the place where Rucker's body had been found, along the same road. Carrisalez, who was accompanied in his patrol car by Enrique Hernandez, turned on his flashing red lights and pursued the speeding vehicle. After the car had stopped briefly at a red light, it signaled that it would pull over and did so. The patrol car pulled up behind it. Carrisalez took a flashlight and walked toward the car of the speeder. The driver opened his door and exchanged a few words with Carrisalez before firing at least one shot at Carrisalez' chest. The officer died nine days later.

Petitioner Herrera was arrested a few days after the shootings and charged with the capital murder of both Carrisalez and Rucker. He was tried and found guilty of the capital murder of Carrisalez in January 1982, and sentenced to death. In July 1982, petitioner pleaded guilty to the murder of Rucker.

At petitioner's trial for the murder of Carrisalez, Hernandez, who had witnessed Carrisalez' slaying from the officer's patrol car, identified petitioner as the person who had wielded the gun. A declaration by Officer Carrisalez to the same effect, made while he was in the hospital, was also admitted. Through a license plate check, it was shown that the speeding car involved in Carrisalez' murder was registered to petitioner's "live-in" girlfriend. Petitioner was known to drive this car, and he had a set of keys to the car in his pants pocket when he was arrested. Hernandez identified the car as the vehicle from which the murderer had emerged to fire the fatal shot. He also testified that there had been only one person in the car that night.

The evidence showed that Herrera's Social Security card had been found alongside Rucker's patrol car on the night he was killed. Splatters of blood on the car identified as the vehicle involved in the shootings, and on petitioner's blue jeans and wallet were identified as type A blood—the same type which Rucker had. (Herrera has type O blood.) Similar evidence with respect to strands of hair found in the car indicated that the hair was Rucker's and not Herrera's. A handwritten letter was also found on the person of petitioner when he was arrested, which strongly implied that he had killed Rucker.

Petitioner appealed his conviction and sentence, arguing, among other things, that Hernandez' and Carrisalez' identifications were unreliable and improperly admitted. The Texas Court of Criminal Appeals affirmed, and we denied certiorari. Petitioner's application for state habeas relief was denied. Petitioner then filed a federal habeas petition, again challenging the identifications offered against him at trial. This petition was denied, and we again denied certiorari.

Petitioner next returned to state court and filed a second habeas petition, raising, among other things, a claim of "actual innocence" based on newly discovered evidence. In support of this claim petitioner presented the affidavits of Hector Villarreal, an attorney who had represented petitioner's brother, Raul Herrera, Sr., and of Juan Franco Palacious, one of Raul, Senior's former cellmates. Both individuals claimed that Raul, Senior, who died in 1984, had told them that he — and not petitioner — had killed Officers Rucker and Carrisalez. The State District Court denied this application, finding that "no evidence at trial remotely suggest[ed] that anyone other than [petitioner] committed the offense."

In February 1992, petitioner lodged the instant habeas petition — his second — in federal court, alleging, among other things, that he is innocent of the murders of Rucker and Carrisalez, and that his execution would thus violate the Eighth and Fourteenth Amendments. In addition to proffering the above affidavits, petitioner presented the affidavits of Raul Herrera, Jr., Raul Senior's son, and Jose Ybarra, Jr., a schoolmate of the Herrera brothers. Raul, Junior, averred that he had witnessed his father shoot Officers Rucker and Carrisalez and petitioner was not present. Raul, Junior, was nine years old at the time of the killings. Ybarra alleged that Raul, Senior, told him one summer night in 1983 that he had shot the two police officers. Petitioner alleged that law enforcement officials were aware of this evidence, and had withheld it in violation of *Brady v. Maryland*.

Petitioner asserts that the Eighth and Fourteenth Amendments to the United States Constitution prohibit the execution of a person who is innocent of the crime for which he was convicted. This proposition has an elemental appeal, as would the similar proposition that the Constitution prohibits the imprisonment of one who is innocent of the crime for which he was convicted. After all, the central purpose of any system of criminal justice is to convict the guilty and free the innocent. But the evidence upon which petitioner's claim of innocence rests was not produced at his trial, but rather eight years later. In any system of criminal justice, "innocence" or "guilt" must be determined in some sort of a judicial proceeding. Petitioner's showing of innocence, and indeed his constitutional claim for relief based upon that showing, must be evaluated in the light of the previous proceedings in this case, which have stretched over a span of 10 years.

A person when first charged with a crime is entitled to a presumption of innocence, and may insist that his guilt be established beyond a reasonable doubt.[77] Other constitutional provisions also have the effect of ensuring against the risk of convicting an innocent person. *See, e.g., Coy v. Iowa*, 487 U.S. 1012 (1988) (right to confront

---

77. In re Winship, 397 U.S. 358 (1970).

adverse witnesses); *Taylor v. Illinois*, 484 U.S. 400 (1988) (right to compulsory process); *Strickland v. Washington*, 466 U.S. 668 (1984) (right to effective assistance of counsel); *Winship, supra* (prosecution must prove guilt beyond a reasonable doubt); *Duncan v. Louisiana*, 391 U.S. 145 (1968) (right to jury trial); *Brady v. Maryland, supra* (prosecution must disclose exculpatory evidence); *Gideon v. Wainwright*, 372 U.S. 335 (1963) (right to assistance of counsel); *In re Murchison*, 349 U.S. 133, (1955) (right to "fair trial in a fair tribunal"). In capital cases, we have required additional protections because of the nature of the penalty at stake. *See, e.g., Beck v. Alabama*, 447 U.S. 625 (1980) (jury must be given option of convicting the defendant of a lesser offense). All of these constitutional safeguards, of course, make it more difficult for the State to rebut and finally overturn the presumption of innocence which attaches to every criminal defendant. But we have also observed that "[d]ue process does not require that every conceivable step be taken, at whatever cost, to eliminate the possibility of convicting an innocent person." To conclude otherwise would all but paralyze our system for enforcement of the criminal law.

Once a defendant has been afforded a fair trial and convicted of the offense for which he was charged, the presumption of innocence disappears. Here, it is not disputed that the State met its burden of proving at trial that petitioner was guilty of the capital murder of Officer Carrisalez beyond a reasonable doubt. Thus, in the eyes of the law, petitioner does not come before the Court as one who is "innocent," but, on the contrary, as one who has been convicted by due process of law of two brutal murders.

Based on affidavits here filed, petitioner claims that evidence never presented to the trial court proves him innocent notwithstanding the verdict reached at his trial. Such a claim is not cognizable in the state courts of Texas. For to obtain a new trial based on newly discovered evidence, a defendant must file a motion within 30 days after imposition or suspension of sentence. Tex. Rule App. Proc. 31(a)(1) (1992). The Texas courts have construed this 30-day time limit as jurisdictional.

Claims of actual innocence based on newly discovered evidence have never been held to state a ground for federal habeas relief absent an independent constitutional violation occurring in the underlying state criminal proceeding. Chief Justice Warren made this clear in *Townsend v. Sain, supra*, 372 U.S., at 317:

> Where newly discovered evidence is alleged in a habeas application, evidence which could not reasonably have been presented to the state trier of facts, the federal court must grant an evidentiary hearing. Of course, such evidence must bear upon the constitutionality of the applicant's detention; the existence merely of newly discovered evidence relevant to the guilt of a state prisoner is not a ground for relief on federal habeas corpus.

This rule is grounded in the principle that federal habeas courts sit to ensure that individuals are not imprisoned in violation of the Constitution—not to correct errors of fact. *See, e.g., Moore v. Dempsey*, 261 U.S. 86 (1923) (Holmes, J.) ("[W]hat we have to deal with [on habeas review] is not the petitioners' innocence or guilt but solely the question whether their constitutional rights have been preserved").

Our decision in *Jackson v. Virginia*, 443 U.S. 307 (1979), comes as close to authorizing evidentiary review of a state-court conviction on federal habeas as any of our cases. There, we held that a federal habeas court may review a claim that the evidence adduced at a state trial was not sufficient to convict a criminal defendant beyond a reasonable doubt. But in so holding, we emphasized:

> [T]his inquiry does not require a court to 'ask itself whether it believes that the evidence at the trial established guilt beyond a reasonable doubt.' Instead, the relevant question is whether, after viewing the evidence in the light most favorable to the prosecution, any rational trier of fact could have found the essential elements of the crime beyond a reasonable doubt. This familiar standard gives full play to the responsibility of the trier of fact fairly to resolve conflicts in the testimony, to weigh the evidence, and to draw reasonable inferences from basic facts to ultimate facts.

We specifically noted that "the standard announced ... does not permit a court to make its own subjective determination of guilt or innocence."

The type of federal habeas review sought by petitioner here is different in critical respects than that authorized by *Jackson*. First, the *Jackson* inquiry is aimed at determining whether there has been an independent constitutional violation—i.e., a conviction based on evidence that fails to meet the *Winship* standard. Thus, federal habeas courts act in their historic capacity—to assure that the habeas petitioner is not being held in violation of his or her federal constitutional rights. Second, the sufficiency of the evidence review authorized by *Jackson* is limited to "record evidence." *Jackson* does not extend to non-record evidence, including newly discovered evidence. Finally, the *Jackson* inquiry does not focus on whether the trier of fact made the correct guilt or innocence determination, but rather whether it made a rational decision to convict or acquit.

Petitioner is understandably imprecise in describing the sort of federal relief to which a suitable showing of actual innocence would entitle him. In his brief he states that the federal habeas court should have "an important initial opportunity to hear the evidence and resolve the merits of Petitioner's claim." Acceptance of this view would presumably require the habeas court to hear testimony from the witnesses who testified at trial as well as those who made the statements in the affidavits which petitioner has presented, and to determine anew whether or not petitioner is guilty of the murder of Officer Carrisalez. Indeed, the dissent's approach differs little from that hypothesized here.

The dissent would place the burden on petitioner to show that he is "probably" innocent. Although petitioner would not be entitled to discovery "as a matter of right," the District Court would retain its "discretion to order discovery ... when it would help the court make a reliable determination with respect to the prisoner's claim." And although the District Court would not be required to hear testimony from the witnesses who testified at trial or the affiants upon whom petitioner relies, the dissent would allow the District Court to do so "if the petition warrants a hearing." At the end of the day, the dissent would have the District Court "make a case-by-case determination about the reliability of the newly discovered evidence under the circumstances," and then "weigh the evidence in favor of the prisoner against the evidence of his guilt."

The dissent fails to articulate the relief that would be available if petitioner were to meets its "probable innocence" standard. Would it be commutation of petitioner's death sentence, new trial, or unconditional release from imprisonment? The typical relief granted in federal habeas corpus is a conditional order of release unless the State elects to retry the successful habeas petitioner, or in a capital case a similar conditional order vacating the death sentence. Were petitioner to satisfy the dissent's "probable innocence" standard, therefore, the District Court would presumably be required to grant a conditional order of relief, which would in effect require the State to retry petitioner 10 years after his first trial, not because of any constitutional violation which had occurred at the first trial, but simply because of a belief that in light of petitioner's new-found evidence a jury might find him not guilty at a second trial.

Yet there is no guarantee that the guilt or innocence determination would be any more exact. To the contrary, the passage of time only diminishes the reliability of criminal adjudications. Under the dissent's approach, the District Court would be placed in the even more difficult position of having to weigh the probative value of "hot" and "cold" evidence on petitioner's guilt or innocence.

This is not to say that our habeas jurisprudence casts a blind eye toward innocence. In a series of cases culminating with *Sawyer v. Whitley*, 505 U.S. 333 (1992), decided last Term, we have held that a petitioner otherwise subject to defenses of abusive or successive use of the writ may have his federal constitutional claim considered on the merits if he makes a proper showing of actual innocence. This rule, or fundamental miscarriage of justice exception, is grounded in the "equitable discretion" of habeas courts to see that federal constitutional errors do not result in the incarceration of innocent persons. But this body of our habeas jurisprudence makes clear that a claim of "actual innocence" is not itself a constitutional claim, but instead a gateway through which a habeas petitioner must pass to have his otherwise barred constitutional claim considered on the merits.

Petitioner in this case is simply not entitled to habeas relief based on the reasoning of this line of cases. For he does not seek excusal of a procedural error so that he may bring an independent constitutional claim challenging his conviction or sentence, but rather argues that he is entitled to habeas relief because newly discovered evidence shows that his conviction is factually incorrect. The fundamental miscarriage of justice exception is available "only where the prisoner supplements his constitutional claim with a colorable showing of factual innocence." We have never held that it extends to freestanding claims of actual innocence. Therefore, the exception is inapplicable here.

* * *

Alternatively, petitioner invokes the Fourteenth Amendment's guarantee of due process of law in support of his claim that his showing of actual innocence entitles him to a new trial, or at least to a vacation of his death sentence. "[B]ecause the States have considerable expertise in matters of criminal procedure and the criminal process is grounded in centuries of common-law tradition," we have "exercis[ed] substantial deference to legislative judgments in this area." Thus, we have found criminal process lacking only where it "'offends some principle of justice so rooted in the traditions and conscience of our people as to be ranked as fundamental.'" "Historical practice is probative of whether a procedural rule can be characterized as fundamental."

The Constitution itself, of course, makes no mention of new trials. New trials in criminal cases were not granted in England until the end of the 17th century. And even then, they were available only in misdemeanor cases, though the writ of error *coram nobis* was available for some errors of fact in felony cases.

* * *

The practice in the States today, while of limited relevance to our historical inquiry, is divergent. Texas is one of 17 States that requires a new trial motion based on newly discovered evidence to be made within 60 days of judgment. One State adheres to the common-law rule and requires that such a motion be filed during the term in which judgment was rendered. Eighteen jurisdictions have time limits ranging between one and three years, with 10 States and the District of Columbia following the 2-year federal time limit. Only 15 States allow a new trial motion based on newly discovered evidence to be filed more than three years after conviction. Of these States, four have waivable time limits of less than 120 days, two have waivable time limits of more than 120 days, and nine States have no time limits.

In light of the historical availability of new trials, our own amendments to Rule 33, and the contemporary practice in the States, we cannot say that Texas' refusal to entertain petitioner's newly discovered evidence eight years after his conviction transgresses a principle of fundamental fairness "rooted in the traditions and conscience of our people." This is not to say, however, that petitioner is left without a forum to raise his actual innocence claim. For under Texas law, petitioner may file a request for executive clemency. Clemency is deeply rooted in our Anglo-American tradition of law, and is the historic remedy for preventing miscarriages of justice where judicial process has been exhausted.

* * *

Of course, although the Constitution vests in the President a pardon power, it does not require the States to enact a clemency mechanism. Yet since the British Colonies were founded, clemency has been available in America. The original States were reluctant to vest the clemency power in the executive. And although this power has gravitated toward the executive over time, several States have split the clemency power between the Governor and an advisory board selected by the legislature. Today, all 36 States that authorize capital punishment have constitutional or statutory provisions for clemency.

Executive clemency has provided the "fail safe" in our criminal justice system. It is an unalterable fact that our judicial system, like the human beings who administer it, is fallible. But history is replete with examples of wrongfully convicted persons who have been pardoned in the wake of after-discovered evidence establishing their innocence. In his classic work, Professor Edwin Borchard compiled 65 cases in which it was later determined that individuals had been wrongfully convicted of crimes. Clemency provided the relief mechanism in 47 of these cases; the remaining cases ended in judgments of acquittals after new trials.[78] Recent authority confirms that over the past century clemency has been exercised frequently in capital cases in which demonstrations of "actual innocence" have been made. See M. Radelet, H. Bedau, & C. Putnam, *In Spite of Innocence* 282–356 (1992).

* * *

As the foregoing discussion illustrates, in state criminal proceedings the trial is the paramount event for determining the guilt or innocence of the defendant. Federal habeas review of state convictions has traditionally been limited to claims of constitutional violations occurring in the course of the underlying state criminal proceedings. Our federal habeas cases have treated claims of "actual innocence," not as an independent constitutional claim, but as a basis upon which a habeas petitioner may have an independent constitutional claim considered on the merits, even though his habeas petition would otherwise be regarded as successive or abusive. History shows that the traditional remedy for claims of innocence based on new evidence, discovered too late in the day to file a new trial motion, has been executive clemency.

We may assume, for the sake of argument in deciding this case, that in a capital case a truly persuasive demonstration of "actual innocence" made after trial would render the execution of a defendant unconstitutional, and warrant federal habeas relief if there were no state avenue open to process such a claim. But because of the very disruptive effect that entertaining claims of actual innocence would have on the need for finality in capital cases, and the enormous burden that having to retry cases based on often stale evidence would place on the States, the threshold showing for such an assumed right would necessarily be extraordinarily high. The showing made by petitioner in this case falls far short of any such threshold.

Petitioner's newly discovered evidence consists of affidavits. In the new trial context, motions based solely upon affidavits are disfavored because the affiants' statements are obtained without the benefit of cross-examination and an opportunity to make credibility determinations. Petitioner's affidavits are particularly suspect in this regard because, with the exception of Raul Herrera, Jr.'s affidavit, they consist of hearsay. Likewise, in reviewing petitioner's new evidence, we are mindful that defendants often abuse new trial motions "as a method of delaying enforcement of just sentences." Although we are not presented with a new trial motion per se, we believe the likelihood of abuse is as great — or greater — here.

The affidavits filed in this habeas proceeding were given over eight years after petitioner's trial. No satisfactory explanation has been given as to why the affiants waited until the 11th hour — and, indeed, until after the alleged perpetrator of the murders himself was dead — to make their statements. Cf. *Taylor v. Illinois*, 484 U.S., at 414 ("[I]t is … reasonable to presume that there is something suspect about a defense

---

78. E. Borchard, Convicting the Innocent (1932).

witness who is not identified until after the 11th hour has passed"). Equally troubling, no explanation has been offered as to why petitioner, by hypothesis an innocent man, pleaded guilty to the murder of Rucker.

Moreover, the affidavits themselves contain inconsistencies, and therefore fail to provide a convincing account of what took place on the night Officers Rucker and Carrisalez were killed. For instance, the affidavit of Raul, Junior, who was nine years old at the time, indicates that there were three people in the speeding car from which the murderer emerged, whereas Hector Villarreal attested that Raul, Senior, told him that there were two people in the car that night. Of course, Hernandez testified at petitioner's trial that the murderer was the only occupant of the car. The affidavits also conflict as to the direction in which the vehicle was heading when the murders took place and petitioner's whereabouts on the night of the killings.

Finally, the affidavits must be considered in light of the proof of petitioner's guilt at trial—proof which included two eyewitness identifications, numerous pieces of circumstantial evidence, and a handwritten letter in which petitioner apologized for killing the officers and offered to turn himself in under certain conditions. That proof, even when considered alongside petitioner's belated affidavits, points strongly to petitioner's guilt.

This is not to say that petitioner's affidavits are without probative value. Had this sort of testimony been offered at trial, it could have been weighed by the jury, along with the evidence offered by the State and petitioner, in deliberating upon its verdict. Since the statements in the affidavits contradict the evidence received at trial, the jury would have had to decide important issues of credibility. But coming 10 years after petitioner's trial, this showing of innocence falls far short of that which would have to be made in order to trigger the sort of constitutional claim which we have assumed, arguendo, to exist.

Justice O'CONNOR, with whom Justice KENNEDY joins, concurring.

I cannot disagree with the fundamental legal principle that executing the innocent is inconsistent with the Constitution. Regardless of the verbal formula employed— "contrary to contemporary standards of decency," "shocking to the conscience," or offensive to a " "'principle of justice so rooted in the traditions and conscience of our people as to be ranked as fundamental,'" "—the execution of a legally and factually innocent person would be a constitutionally intolerable event. Dispositive to this case, however, is an equally fundamental fact: Petitioner is not innocent, in any sense of the word.

As the Court explains, petitioner is not innocent in the eyes of the law because, in our system of justice, "the trial is the paramount event for determining the guilt or innocence of the defendant." In petitioner's case, that paramount event occurred 10 years ago. He was tried before a jury of his peers, with the full panoply of protections that our Constitution affords criminal defendants. At the conclusion of that trial, the jury found petitioner guilty beyond a reasonable doubt. Petitioner therefore does not appear before us as an innocent man on the verge of execution. He is instead a legally guilty one who, refusing to accept the jury's verdict, demands a hearing in which to have his culpability determined once again.

Consequently, the issue before us is not whether a State can execute the innocent. It is, as the Court notes, whether a fairly convicted and therefore legally guilty person is constitutionally entitled to yet another judicial proceeding in which to adjudicate his guilt anew, 10 years after conviction, notwithstanding his failure to demonstrate that constitutional error infected his trial. In most circumstances, that question would answer itself in the negative. Our society has a high degree of confidence in its criminal trials, in no small part because the Constitution offers unparalleled protections against convicting the innocent. The question similarly would be answered in the negative today, except for the disturbing nature of the claim before us. Petitioner contends not only that the Constitution's protections "sometimes fail," but that their failure in his case will result in his execution—even though he is factually innocent and has evidence to prove it.

* * *

Nonetheless, the proper disposition of this case is neither difficult nor troubling. No matter what the Court might say about claims of actual innocence today, petitioner could not obtain relief. The record overwhelmingly demonstrates that petitioner deliberately shot and killed Officers Rucker and Carrisalez the night of September 29, 1981; petitioner's new evidence is bereft of credibility. Indeed, despite its stinging criticism of the Court's decision, not even the dissent expresses a belief that petitioner might possibly be actually innocent. Nor could it: The record makes it abundantly clear that petitioner is not somehow the future victim of "simple murder," but instead himself the established perpetrator of two brutal and tragic ones.

* * *

When the police arrested petitioner, they found more than car keys; they also found evidence of the struggle between petitioner and Officer Rucker. Human blood was spattered across the hood, the left front fender, the grill, and the interior of petitioner's car. There were spots of blood on petitioner's jeans; blood had even managed to splash into his wallet. The blood was, like Rucker's and unlike petitioner's, type A. Blood samples also matched Rucker's enzyme profile. Only 6% of the Nation's population shares both Rucker's blood type and his enzyme profile.

But the most compelling piece of evidence was entirely of petitioner's own making. When the police arrested petitioner, he had in his possession a signed letter in which he acknowledged responsibility for the murders; at the end of the letter, petitioner offered to turn himself in:

> I am terribly sorry for those [to whom] I have brought grief.... What happened to Rucker was for a certain reason.... [H]e violated some of [the] laws [of my drug business] and suffered the penalty, like the one you have for me when the time comes.... The other officer [Carrisalez] ... had not [hing] to do [with] this. He was out to do what he had to do, protect, but that's life.... [I]f this is read word for word over the media, I will turn myself in....

There can be no doubt about the letter's meaning. When the police attempted to interrogate petitioner about the killings, he told them "it was all in the letter" and suggested that, if "they wanted to know what happened," they should read it.

* * *

Ultimately, two things about this case are clear. First is what the Court does not hold. Nowhere does the Court state that the Constitution permits the execution of an actually innocent person. Instead, the Court assumes for the sake of argument that a truly persuasive demonstration of actual innocence would render any such execution unconstitutional and that federal habeas relief would be warranted if no state avenue were open to process the claim. Second is what petitioner has not demonstrated. Petitioner has failed to make a persuasive showing of actual innocence. Not one judge — no state court judge, not the District Court Judge, none of the three judges of the Court of Appeals, and none of the Justices of this Court — has expressed doubt about petitioner's guilt. Accordingly, the Court has no reason to pass on, and appropriately reserves, the question whether federal courts may entertain convincing claims of actual innocence. That difficult question remains open. If the Constitution's guarantees of fair procedure and the safeguards of clemency and pardon fulfill their historical mission, it may never require resolution at all.

Justice BLACKMUN, with whom Justice STEVENS and Justice SOUTER join Parts I–IV, dissenting.

Nothing could be more contrary to contemporary standards of decency, see *Ford v. Wainwright*, 477 U.S. 399 (1986), or more shocking to the conscience, see *Rochin v. California*, 342 U.S. 165, 172 (1952), than to execute a person who is actually innocent.

I therefore must disagree with the long and general discussion that precedes the Court's disposition of this case. That discussion, of course, is dictum because the Court assumes, "for the sake of argument in deciding this case, that in a capital case a truly persuasive demonstration of 'actual innocence' made after trial would render the execution of a defendant unconstitutional." Without articulating the standard it is applying, however, the Court then decides that this petitioner has not made a sufficiently persuasive case. Because I believe that in the first instance the District Court should decide whether petitioner is entitled to a hearing and whether he is entitled to relief on the merits of his claim, I would reverse the order of the Court of Appeals and remand this case for further proceedings in the District Court.

The Court's enumeration of the constitutional rights of criminal defendants surely is entirely beside the point. These protections sometimes fail. We really are being asked to decide whether the Constitution forbids the execution of a person who has been validly convicted and sentenced but who, nonetheless, can prove his innocence with newly discovered evidence. Despite the State of Texas' astonishing protestation to the contrary, I do not see how the answer can be anything but "yes."

The Eighth Amendment prohibits "cruel and unusual punishments." This proscription is not static but rather reflects evolving standards of decency. I think it is crystal clear that the execution of an innocent person is "at odds with contemporary standards of fairness and decency." Indeed, it is at odds with any standard of decency that I can imagine.

Execution of the innocent is equally offensive to the Due Process Clause of the Fourteenth Amendment....

Whatever procedures a State might adopt to hear actual-innocence claims, one thing is certain: The possibility of executive clemency is not sufficient to satisfy the requirements of the Eighth and Fourteenth Amendments. The majority correctly points out: "'A pardon is an act of grace.'" The vindication of rights guaranteed by the Constitution has never been made to turn on the unreviewable discretion of an executive official or administrative tribunal.... The possibility of executive clemency "exists in every case in which a defendant challenges his sentence under the Eighth Amendment. Recognition of such a bare possibility would make judicial review under the Eighth Amendment meaningless."

I have voiced disappointment over this Court's obvious eagerness to do away with any restriction on the States' power to execute whomever and however they please. See *Coleman v. Thompson*, 501 U.S. 722 (1991) (dissenting opinion). I have also expressed doubts about whether, in the absence of such restrictions, capital punishment remains constitutional at all. Of one thing, however, I am certain. Just as an execution without adequate safeguards is unacceptable, so too is an execution when the condemned prisoner can prove that he is innocent. The execution of a person who can show that he is innocent comes perilously close to simple murder.

Schlup v. Delo
513 U.S. 298 (1995)

Justice STEVENS delivered the opinion of the Court.

Petitioner Lloyd E. Schlup, Jr., a Missouri prisoner currently under a sentence of death, filed a second federal habeas corpus petition alleging that constitutional error deprived the jury of critical evidence that would have established his innocence. The District Court, without conducting an evidentiary hearing, declined to reach the merits of the petition, holding that petitioner could not satisfy the threshold showing of "actual innocence" required by *Sawyer v. Whitley*, 505 U.S. 333, (1992). Under Sawyer, the petitioner must show "by clear and convincing evidence that, but for a constitutional error, no reasonable juror would have found the petitioner" guilty. The Court of Appeals affirmed. We granted certiorari to consider whether the *Sawyer* standard provides adequate protection against the kind of miscarriage of justice that would result from the execution of a person who is actually innocent.

I

On February 3, 1984, on Walk 1 of the high security area of the Missouri State Penitentiary, a black inmate named Arthur Dade was stabbed to death. Three white inmates from Walk 2, including petitioner, were charged in connection with Dade's murder.

At petitioner's trial in December 1985, the State's evidence consisted principally of the testimony of two corrections officers who had witnessed the killing. On the day of the murder, Sergeant Roger Flowers was on duty on Walk 1 and Walk 2, the two walks on the lower floor of the prison's high security area. Flowers testified that he first released the inmates on Walk 2 for their noon meal and relocked their cells. After unlocking the cells to release the inmates on Walk 1, Flowers noticed an inmate named Rodnie Stewart moving against the flow of traffic carrying a container of steaming liquid. Flowers watched as Stewart threw the liquid in Dade's face. According to Flowers, Schlup then jumped on Dade's back, and Robert O'Neal joined in the attack. Flowers shouted for help, entered the walk, and grabbed Stewart as the two other assailants fled.

Officer John Maylee witnessed the attack from Walk 7, which is three levels and some 40–50 feet above Walks 1 and 2. Maylee first noticed Schlup, Stewart, and O'Neal as they were running from Walk 2 to Walk 1 against the flow of traffic. According to Maylee's testimony, Stewart threw a container of liquid at Dade's face, and then Schlup jumped on Dade's back. O'Neal then stabbed Dade several times in the chest, ran down the walk, and threw the weapon out a window. Maylee did not see what happened to Schlup or Stewart after the stabbing. The State produced no physical evidence connecting Schlup to the killing, and no witness other than Flowers and Maylee testified to Schlup's involvement in the murder.

Schlup's defense was that the State had the wrong man. He relied heavily on a videotape from a camera in the prisoners' dining room. The tape showed that Schlup was the first inmate to walk into the dining room for the noon meal, and that he went through the line and got his food. Approximately 65 seconds after Schlup's entrance, several guards ran out of the dining room in apparent response to a distress call. Twenty-six seconds later, O'Neal ran into the dining room, dripping blood. Shortly thereafter, Schlup and O'Neal were taken into custody.

Schlup contended that the videotape, when considered in conjunction with testimony that he had walked at a normal pace from his cell to the dining room, demonstrated that he could not have participated in the assault. Because the videotape showed conclusively that Schlup was in the dining room 65 seconds before the guards responded to the distress call, a critical element of Schlup's defense was determining when the distress call went out. Had the distress call sounded shortly after the murder, Schlup would not have had time to get from the prison floor to the dining room, and thus he could not have participated in the murder. Conversely, had there been a delay of several minutes between the murder and the distress call, Schlup might have had sufficient time to participate in the murder and still get to the dining room over a minute before the distress call went out.

The prosecutor adduced evidence tending to establish that such a delay had in fact occurred. First, Flowers testified that none of the officers on the prison floor had radios, thus implying that neither he nor any of the other officers on the floor was able to radio for help when the stabbing occurred. Second, Flowers testified that after he shouted for help, it took him "a couple [of] minutes" to subdue Stewart. Flowers then brought Stewart downstairs, encountered Captain James Eberle, and told Eberle that there had been a "disturbance." Eberle testified that he went upstairs to the prison floor, and then radioed for assistance. Eberle estimated that the elapsed time from when he first saw Flowers until he radioed for help was "approximately a minute." The prosecution also offered testimony from a prison investigator who testified that he was able to run from the scene of the crime to the dining room in 33 seconds and to walk the distance at a normal pace in a minute and 37 seconds.

Neither the State nor Schlup was able to present evidence establishing the exact time of Schlup's release from his cell on Walk 2, the exact time of the assault on Walk 1, or the exact time of the radio distress call. Further, there was no evidence suggesting that Schlup had hurried to the dining room.

After deliberating overnight, the jury returned a verdict of guilty. Following the penalty phase, at which the victim of one of Schlup's prior offenses testified extensively about the sordid details of that offense, the jury sentenced Schlup to death. The Missouri Supreme Court affirmed Schlup's conviction and death sentence.

II

On January 5, 1989, after exhausting his state collateral remedies, Schlup filed a pro se petition for a federal writ of habeas corpus, asserting the claim, among others, that his trial counsel was ineffective for failing to interview and to call witnesses who could establish Schlup's innocence. The District Court concluded that Schlup's ineffectiveness claim was procedurally barred, and it denied relief on that claim without conducting an evidentiary hearing. The Court of Appeals affirmed ...

On March 11, 1992, represented by new counsel, Schlup filed a second federal habeas corpus petition. That petition raised a number of claims, including that (1) Schlup was actually innocent of Dade's murder, and that his execution would therefore violate the Eighth and Fourteenth Amendments, cf. *Herrera v. Collins*, 506 U.S. 390 (1993); (2) trial counsel was ineffective for failing to interview alibi witnesses; and (3) the State had failed to disclose critical exculpatory evidence. The petition was supported by numerous affidavits from inmates attesting to Schlup's innocence.

The State filed a response arguing that various procedural bars precluded the District Court from reaching the merits of Schlup's claims and that the claims were in any event meritless. Attached to the State's response were transcripts of inmate interviews conducted by prison investigators just five days after the murder. One of the transcripts contained an interview with John Green, an inmate who at the time was the clerk for the housing unit. In his interview, Green stated that he had been in his office at the end of the walks when the murder occurred. Green stated that Flowers had told him to call for help, and that Green had notified base of the disturbance shortly after it began.

Schlup immediately filed a traverse arguing that Green's affidavit provided conclusive proof of Schlup's innocence. Schlup contended that Green's statement demonstrated that a call for help had gone out shortly after the incident. Because the videotape showed that Schlup was in the dining room some 65 seconds before the guards received the distress call, Schlup argued that he could not have been involved in Dade's murder. Schlup emphasized that Green's statement was not likely to have been fabricated, because at the time of Green's interview, neither he nor anyone else would have realized the significance of Green's call to base. Schlup tried to buttress his claim of innocence with affidavits from inmates who stated that they had witnessed the event and that Schlup had not been present. Two of those affidavits suggested that Randy Jordan — who occupied the cell between O'Neal and Stewart in Walk 2, and who is shown on the videotape arriving at lunch with O'Neal — was the third assailant.

III

As a preliminary matter, it is important to explain the difference between Schlup's claim of actual innocence and the claim of actual innocence asserted in Herrera v. Collins. In Herrera, the petitioner advanced his claim of innocence to support a novel substantive constitutional claim, namely, that the execution of an innocent person would violate the Eighth Amendment. Under petitioner's theory in Herrera, even if the proceedings that had resulted in his conviction and sentence were entirely fair and error free, his innocence would render his execution a "constitutionally intolerable event."

Schlup's claim of innocence, on the other hand, is procedural, rather than substantive. His constitutional claims are based not on his innocence, but rather on his contention that the ineffectiveness of his counsel, see Strickland v. Washington, 466 U.S. 668 (1984), and the withholding of evidence by the prosecution, see Brady v. Maryland, 373 U.S. 83 (1963), denied him the full panoply of protections afforded to criminal defendants by the Constitution. Schlup, however, faces procedural obstacles that he must overcome before a federal court may address the merits of those constitutional claims. Because Schlup has been unable to establish "cause and prejudice" sufficient to excuse his failure to present his evidence in support of his first federal petition. Schlup may obtain review of his constitutional claims only if he falls within the "narrow class of cases … implicating a fundamental miscarriage of justice." Schlup's claim of innocence is offered only to bring him within this "narrow class of cases."

Schlup's claim thus differs in at least two important ways from that presented in Herrera. First, Schlup's claim of innocence does not by itself provide a basis for relief. Instead, his claim for relief depends critically on the validity of his Strickland and Brady claims. Schlup's claim of innocence is thus "not itself a constitutional claim, but instead a gateway through which a habeas petitioner must pass to have his otherwise barred constitutional claim considered on the merits." Herrera, 506 U.S., at 404.

More importantly, a court's assumptions about the validity of the proceedings that resulted in conviction are fundamentally different in Schlup's case than in Herrera's. In Herrera, petitioner's claim was evaluated on the assumption that the trial that resulted in his conviction had been error free. In such a case, when a petitioner has been "tried before a jury of his peers, with the full panoply of protections that our Constitution affords criminal defendants," it is appropriate to apply an "'extraordinarily high'" standard of review.

Schlup, in contrast, accompanies his claim of innocence with an assertion of constitutional error at trial. For that reason, Schlup's conviction may not be entitled to the same degree of respect as one, such as Herrera's, that is the product of an error free trial. Without any new evidence of innocence, even the existence of a concededly meritorious constitutional violation is not in itself sufficient to establish a miscarriage of justice that would allow a habeas court to reach the merits of a barred claim. However, if a petitioner such as Schlup presents evidence of innocence so strong that a court cannot have confidence in the outcome of the trial unless the court is also satisfied that the trial was free of nonharmless constitutional error, the petitioner should be allowed to pass through the gateway and argue the merits of his underlying claims.

Consequently, Schlup's evidence of innocence need carry less of a burden. In *Herrera* (on the assumption that petitioner's claim was, in principle, legally well founded), the evidence of innocence would have had to be strong enough to make his execution "constitutionally intolerable" even if his conviction was the product of a fair trial. For Schlup, the evidence must establish sufficient doubt about his guilt to justify the conclusion that his execution would be a miscarriage of justice unless his conviction was the product of a fair trial.

Our rather full statement of the facts illustrates the foregoing distinction between a substantive *Herrera* claim and Schlup's procedural claim. Three items of evidence are particularly relevant: the affidavit of black inmates attesting to the innocence of a white defendant in a racially motivated killing; the affidavit of Green describing his prompt call for assistance; and the affidavit of Lieutenant Faherty describing Schlup's unhurried walk to the dining room. If there were no question about the fairness of the criminal trial, a Herrera-type claim would have to fail unless the federal habeas court is itself convinced that those new facts unquestionably establish Schlup's innocence. On the other hand, if the habeas court were merely convinced that those new facts raised sufficient doubt about Schlup's guilt to undermine confidence in the result of the trial without the assurance that that trial was untainted by constitutional error, Schlup's threshold showing of innocence would justify a review of the merits of the constitutional claims.

IV

As this Court has repeatedly noted, "[a]t common law, res judicata did not attach to a court's denial of habeas relief." Instead, "'a renewed application could be made to every other judge or court in the realm, and each court or judge was bound to consider the question of the prisoner's right to a discharge independently, and not to be influenced by the previous decisions refusing discharge.'"

The Court has explained the early tolerance of successive petitions, in part, by the fact that the writ originally performed only the narrow function of testing either the jurisdiction of the sentencing court or the legality of Executive detention. See *McCleskey*, 499 U.S., at 478. The scope of the writ later expanded beyond its original narrow purview to encompass review of constitutional error that had occurred in the proceedings leading to conviction. That broadening of the scope of the writ created the risk that repetitious filings by individual petitioners might adversely affect the administration of justice in the federal courts. Such filings also posed a threat to the finality of state-court judgments and to principles of comity and federalism.

To alleviate the increasing burdens on the federal courts and to contain the threat to finality and comity, Congress attempted to fashion rules disfavoring claims raised in second and subsequent petitions.... These same concerns resulted in a number of recent decisions from this Court that delineate the circumstances under which a district court may consider claims raised in a second or subsequent habeas petition. In those decisions, the Court held that a habeas court may not ordinarily reach the merits of successive claims or abusive claims, absent a showing of cause and prejudice, see *Wainwright v. Sykes*, 433 U.S. 72 (1977). The application of cause and prejudice to successive and abusive claims conformed to this Court's treatment of procedurally defaulted claims. *Murray v. Carrier*, 477 U.S. 478. The net result of this congressional and judicial action has been the adoption in habeas corpus of a "'qualified application of the doctrine of res judicata.'"

At the same time, the Court has adhered to the principle that habeas corpus is, at its core, an equitable remedy. This Court has consistently relied on the equitable nature of habeas corpus to preclude application of strict rules of res judicata.

To ensure that the fundamental miscarriage of justice exception would remain "rare" and would only be applied in the "extraordinary case," while at the same time ensuring that the exception would extend relief to those who were truly deserving, this Court explicitly tied the miscarriage of justice exception to the petitioner's innocence. In *Kuhlmann*, for example, Justice Powell concluded that a prisoner retains an overriding "interest in obtaining his release from custody if he is innocent of the charge for which he was incarcerated. That interest does not extend, however, to prisoners whose guilt is conceded or plain." Similarly, Justice O'CONNOR wrote in Carrier that "in an extraordinary case, where a constitutional violation has probably resulted in the conviction of one who is actually innocent, a federal habeas court may grant the writ even in the absence of a showing of cause for the procedural default."

The general rule announced in *Kuhlmann*, *Carrier*, and *Smith*, and confirmed in this Court's more recent decisions, rests in part on the fact that habeas corpus petitions that advance a substantial claim of actual innocence are extremely rare. Judge Friendly's observation a quarter of a century ago that "the one thing almost never suggested on collateral attack is that the prisoner was innocent of the crime" remains largely true today. Explicitly tying the miscarriage of justice exception to innocence thus accommodates both the systemic interests in finality, comity, and conservation of judicial resources, and the overriding individual interest in doing justice in the "extraordinary case," *Carrier*, 477 U.S., at 496.

In addition to linking miscarriages of justice to innocence, *Carrier*, and *Kuhlmann* also expressed the standard of proof that should govern consideration of those claims. In Carrier, for example, the Court stated that the petitioner must show that the constitutional error "probably" resulted in the conviction of one who was actually innocent ...

Then, in *Sawyer*, the Court examined the miscarriage of justice exception as applied to a petitioner who claimed he was "actually innocent of the death penalty." In that opinion, the Court struggled to define "actual innocence" in the context of a petitioner's claim that his death sentence was inappropriate. The Court concluded that such actual innocence "must focus on those elements which render a defendant eligible for the death penalty." However, in addition to defining what it means to be "innocent" of the death penalty, the Court departed from Carrier's use of "probably" and adopted a more exacting standard of proof to govern these claims: The Court held that a habeas petitioner "must show by clear and convincing evidence that but for a constitutional error, no reasonable juror would have found the petitioner eligible for the death penalty." No attempt was made in Sawyer to reconcile this stricter standard with Carrier's use of "probably."

V

We conclude that *Carrier*, rather than *Sawyer*, properly strikes that balance when the claimed injustice is that constitutional error has resulted in the conviction of one who is actually innocent of the crime.

Claims of actual innocence pose less of a threat to scarce judicial resources and to principles of finality and comity than do claims that focus solely on the erroneous imposition of the death penalty. Though challenges to the propriety of imposing a sentence of death are routinely asserted in capital cases, experience has taught us that a substantial claim that constitutional error has caused the conviction of an innocent person is extremely rare. To be credible, such a claim requires petitioner to support his allegations of constitutional error with new reliable evidence — whether it be exculpatory scientific evidence, trustworthy eyewitness accounts, or critical physical evidence — that was not presented at trial. Because such evidence is obviously unavailable in the vast majority of cases, claims of actual innocence are rarely successful. Even under the pre-*Sawyer* regime, "in virtually every case, the allegation of actual innocence has been summarily rejected." The threat to judicial resources, finality, and comity posed by claims of actual innocence is thus significantly less than that posed by claims relating only to sentencing.

Of greater importance, the individual interest in avoiding injustice is most compelling in the context of actual innocence. The quintessential miscarriage of justice is the execution of a person who is entirely innocent. Indeed, concern about the injustice that results from the conviction of an innocent person has long been at the core of our criminal justice system. That concern is reflected, for example, in the "fundamental value determination of our society that it is far worse to convict an innocent man than to let a guilty man go free."

Accordingly, we hold that the *Carrier* "probably resulted" standard rather than the more stringent *Sawyer* standard must govern the miscarriage of justice inquiry when a petitioner who has been sentenced to death raises a claim of actual innocence to avoid a procedural bar to the consideration of the merits of his constitutional claims.

VI

The *Carrier* standard requires the habeas petitioner to show that "a constitutional violation has probably resulted in the conviction of one who is actually innocent." To establish the requisite probability, the petitioner must show that it is more likely than not that no reasonable juror would have convicted him in the light of the new evidence. The petitioner thus is required to make a stronger showing than that needed to establish prejudice. At the same time, the showing of "more likely than not" imposes a lower burden of proof than the "clear and convincing" standard required under *Sawyer*. The *Carrier* standard thus ensures that petitioner's case is truly "extraordinary," while still providing petitioner a meaningful avenue by which to avoid a manifest injustice.

Carrier requires a petitioner to show that he is "actually innocent." As used in *Carrier*, actual innocence is closely related to the definition set forth by this Court in *Sawyer*. To satisfy the *Carrier* gateway standard, a petitioner must show that it is more likely than not that no reasonable juror would have found petitioner guilty beyond a reasonable doubt.

Several observations about this standard are in order. The *Carrier* standard is intended to focus the inquiry on actual innocence. In assessing the adequacy of petitioner's showing, therefore, the district court is not bound by the rules of admissibility that would govern at trial. Instead, the emphasis on "actual innocence" allows the reviewing tribunal also to consider the probative force of relevant evidence that was either excluded or unavailable at trial. Indeed, with respect to this aspect of the *Carrier* standard, we believe that Judge Friendly's description of the inquiry is appropriate: The habeas court must make its determination concerning the petitioner's innocence "in light of all the evidence, including that alleged to have been illegally admitted (but with due regard to any unreliability of it) and evidence tenably claimed to have been wrongly excluded or to have become available only after the trial."

* * *

Though the *Carrier* standard requires a substantial showing, it is by no means equivalent to the standard of *Jackson v. Virginia*, 443 U.S. 307 (1979), standard that governs review of claims of insufficient evidence. The *Jackson* standard, which focuses on whether any rational juror could have convicted, looks to whether there is sufficient evidence which, if credited, could support the conviction. The *Jackson* standard thus differs in at least two important ways from the Carrier standard. First, under *Jackson*, the assessment of the credibility of witnesses is generally beyond the scope of review. In contrast, under the gateway standard we describe today, the newly presented evidence may indeed call into question the credibility of the witnesses presented at trial. In such a case, the habeas court may have to make some credibility assessments. Second, and more fundamentally, the focus of the inquiry is different under *Jackson* than under *Carrier*. Under *Jackson*, the use of the word "could" focuses the inquiry on the power of the trier of fact to reach its conclusion. Under *Carrier*, the use of the word "would" focuses the inquiry on the likely behavior of the trier of fact.

Indeed, our adoption of the phrase "more likely than not" reflects this distinction. Under *Jackson*, the question whether the trier of fact has power to make a finding of guilt requires a binary response: Either the trier of fact has power as a matter of law or it does not. Under *Carrier*, in contrast, the habeas court must consider what reasonable triers of fact are likely to do. Under this probabilistic inquiry, it makes sense to have a probabilistic standard such as "more likely than not." Thus, though under *Jackson* the mere existence of sufficient evidence to convict would be determinative of petitioner's claim, that is not true under *Carrier*.

We believe that the Eighth Circuit's erroneous application of the *Sawyer* standard below illustrates this difference. In determining that Schlup had failed to satisfy the *Sawyer* standard, the majority noted that "two prison officials, who were eyewitnesses to the crime, positively identified Mr. Schlup as one of the three perpetrators of the murder. This evidence was clearly admissible and stands unrefuted except to the extent that Mr. Schlup now questions its credibility."

However, Schlup's evidence includes the sworn statements of several eyewitnesses that Schlup was not involved in the crime. Moreover, Schlup has presented statements from Green and Faherty that cast doubt on whether Schlup could have participated in the murder and still arrived at the dining room 65 seconds before the distress call was received. Those new statements may, of course, be unreliable. But if they are true—as the Court of Appeals assumed for the purpose of applying its understanding of the Sawyer standard—it surely cannot be said that a juror, conscientiously following the judge's instructions requiring proof beyond a reasonable doubt, would vote to convict. Under a proper application of either *Sawyer* or *Carrier*, petitioner's showing of innocence is not insufficient solely because the trial record contained sufficient evidence to support the jury's verdict.

Because both the Court of Appeals and the District Court evaluated the record under an improper standard, further proceedings are necessary. The fact-intensive nature of the inquiry, together with the District Court's ability to take testimony from the few key witnesses if it deems that course advisable, convinces us that the most expeditious procedure is to order that the decision of the Court of Appeals be vacated and that the case be remanded to the Court of Appeals with instructions to remand to the District Court for further proceedings consistent with this opinion.

House v. Bell

547 U.S. 518 (2006)[79]

A Tennessee jury convicted petitioner House of Carolyn Muncey's murder and sentenced him to death. The State's case included evidence that FBI testing showing semen consistent (or so it seemed) with House's on Mrs. Muncey's clothing and small bloodstains consistent with her blood but not House's on his jeans. In the sentencing phase, the jury found, inter alia, the aggravating factor that the murder was committed

---

79. Summary modified from Court Reporter's syllabus.

while House was committing, attempting to commit, or fleeing from the commission of rape or kidnaping. In affirming, the State Supreme Court described the evidence as circumstantial but strong. House was denied state postconviction relief. Subsequently, the Federal District Court denied habeas relief, deeming House's claims procedurally defaulted and granting the State summary judgment on most of his claims. It also found, after an evidentiary hearing at which House attacked the blood and semen evidence and presented other evidence, including a putative confession, suggesting that Mr. Muncey committed the crime, that House did not fall within the "actual innocence" exception to procedural default recognized in *Schlup v. Delo*, 513 U.S. 298, and *Sawyer v. Whitley*, 505 U.S. 333. The Sixth Circuit ultimately affirmed.

Facts: The State of Tennessee charged House with capital murder. At House's trial, the State presented testimony by Luttrell, Hensley, Adkins, Lora Muncey, Dr. Carabia, the sheriff, and other law enforcement officials. Through TBI Agents Presnell and Scott, the jury learned of House's false statements. Central to the State's case, however, was what the FBI testing showed—that semen consistent (or so it seemed) with House's was present on Mrs. Muncey's nightgown and panties, and that small bloodstains consistent with Mrs. Muncey's blood but not House's appeared on the jeans belonging to House.

Regarding the semen, FBI Special Agent Paul Bigbee, a serologist, testified that the source was a "secretor," meaning someone who "secrete[s] the ABO blood group substances in other body fluids, such as semen and saliva"—a characteristic shared by 80 percent of the population, including House. Agent Bigbee further testified that the source of semen on the gown was blood-type A, House's own blood type. As to the semen on the panties, Agent Bigbee found only the H blood-group substance, which A and B blood-type secretors secrete along with substances A and B, and which O-type secretors secrete exclusively. Agent Bigbee explained, however—using science an amicus here sharply disputes, see Brief for Innocence Project, Inc., as Amicus Curiae 24–26—that House's A antigens could have "degraded" into H. Agent Bigbee thus concluded that both semen deposits could have come from House, though he acknowledged that the H antigen could have come from Mrs. Muncey herself if she was a secretor—something he "was not able to determine,"—and that, while Mr. Muncey was himself blood-type A (as was his wife), Agent Bigbee was again "not able to determine his secretor status." Agent Bigbee acknowledged on cross-examination that "a saliva sample" would have sufficed to determine whether Mr. Muncey was a secretor; the State did not provide such a sample, though it did provide samples of Mr. Muncey's blood.

As for the blood, Agent Bigbee explained that "spots of blood" appeared "on the left outside leg, the right bottom cuff, on the left thigh and in the right inside pocket and on the lower pocket on the outside." Agent Bigbee determined that the blood's source was type A (the type shared by House, the victim, and Mr. Muncey). He also successfully tested for the enzyme phosphoglucomutase and the blood serum haptoglobin, both of which "are found in all humans" and carry "slight chemical differences" that vary genetically and "can be grouped to differentiate between two individuals if those types are different." Based on these chemical traces and on the A blood type, Agent Bigbee determined that only some 6.75 percent of the population carry similar blood, that the blood was "consistent" with Mrs. Muncey's (as determined by testing autopsy samples), and that it was "impossible" that the blood came from House.

A different FBI expert, Special Agent Chester Blythe, testified about fiber analysis performed on Mrs. Muncey's clothes and on House's pants. Although Agent Blythe found blue jean fibers on Mrs. Muncey's nightgown, brassier, housecoat, and panties, and in fingernail scrapings taken from her body (scrapings that also contained trace, unidentifiable amounts of blood), he acknowledged that, as the prosecutor put it in questioning the witness, "blue jean material is common material," so "this doesn't mean that the fibers that were all over the victim's clothing were necessarily from [House's] pair of blue jeans." On House's pants, though cotton garments both transfer and retain fibers readily, Agent Blythe found neither hair nor fiber consistent with the victim's hair or clothing.

In the defense case House called Hankins, Clinton, and Turner, as well as House's mother, who testified that House had talked to her by telephone around 9:30 p.m. on the night of the murder and that he had not used her car that evening. House also called the victim's brother, Ricky Green, as a witness. Green testified that on July 2, roughly two weeks before the murder, Mrs. Muncey called him and "said her and Little Hube had been into it and she said she was wanting to leave Little Hube, she said she was wanting to get out—out of it, and she was scared." Green recalled that at Christmastime in 1982 he had seen Mr. Muncey strike Mrs. Muncey after returning home drunk.

As Turner informed the jury, House's shoes were found several months after the crime in a field near her home. Turner delivered them to authorities. Though the jury did not learn of this fact (and House's counsel claims he did not either), the State tested the shoes for blood and found none. House's shirt was not found.

The State's closing argument suggested that on the night of her murder, Mrs. Muncey "was deceived.... She had been told [her husband] had had an accident." The prosecutor emphasized the FBI's blood analysis, noting that "after running many, many, many tests," Agent Bigbee:

> was able to tell you that the blood on the defendant's blue jeans was not his own blood, could not be his own blood. He told you that the blood on the blue jeans was consistent with every characteristic in every respect of the deceased's, Carolyn Muncey's, and that ninety-three (93%) percent of the white population would not have that blood type.... He can't tell you one hundred (100%) percent for certain that it was her blood. But folks, he can sure give you a pretty good—a pretty good indication.

In the State's rebuttal, after defense counsel questioned House's motive "to go over and kill a woman that he barely knew[,][w]ho was still dressed, still clad in her clothes," the prosecutor referred obliquely to the semen stains. While explaining that legally "it does not make any difference under God's heaven, what the motive was," the prosecutor told the jury, "you may have an idea why he did it."

[House was convicted and, after a penalty-phase hearing, sentenced to death. His conviction was affirmed on appeal.]

House next sought federal habeas relief, asserting numerous claims of ineffective assistance of counsel and prosecutorial misconduct. The United States District Court for the Eastern District of Tennessee, though deeming House's claims procedurally defaulted and granting summary judgment to the State on the majority of House's claims, held an evidentiary hearing to determine whether House fell within the "actual innocence" exception to procedural default that this Court recognized as to substantive offenses in *Schlup* and as to death sentences in *Sawyer v. Whitley*, 505 U.S. 333 (1992). Presenting evidence we describe in greater detail below, House attacked the semen and blood evidence used at his trial and presented other evidence, including a putative confession, suggesting that Mr. Muncey, not House, committed the murder. The District Court nevertheless denied relief, holding that House had neither demonstrated actual innocence of the murder under *Schlup* nor established that he was ineligible for the death penalty under Sawyer.

[In an opinion written by JUSTICE KENNEDY, the Supreme Court reversed, holding that because House has made the stringent showing required by the actual-innocence exception, his federal habeas action may proceed:

To implement the general principle that] "comity and finality 'must yield to the imperative of correcting a fundamentally unjust incarceration,'" this Court has ruled that prisoners asserting innocence as a gateway to defaulted claims must establish that, in light of new evidence, "it is more likely than not that no reasonable juror would have found petitioner guilty beyond a reasonable doubt." *Schlup*, 513 U. S, at 327. Several features of *Schlup's* standard bear emphasis here. First, while the gateway claim requires "new reliable evidence ... not presented at trial," the habeas court must assess the likely impact of "'all the evidence'" on reasonable jurors. Second, rather than requiring absolute certainty about guilt or innocence, a petitioner's burden at the gateway stage is to demonstrate that more likely than not, in light of the new evidence, no reasonable juror would find him guilty beyond a reasonable doubt. Finally, this standard is "by no means equivalent to the standard of *Jackson v. Virginia*, 443 U.S. 307" which governs insufficient evidence claims. Rather, because a *Schlup* claim involves evidence the trial jury did not have before it, the inquiry requires the federal court to assess how reasonable jurors would react to the overall, newly supplemented record.... In addition, because the standard does not address a "district court's independent judgment as to whether reasonable doubt exists," *Schlup*, supra, at 329, a ruling in House's favor does not require the showing of clear error as to the District Court's specific findings. It is with these principles in mind that the evidence developed in House's federal habeas proceedings should be evaluated.

In direct contradiction of evidence presented at trial, DNA testing has established that semen on Mrs. Muncey's clothing came from her husband, not House. While the State claims that the evidence is immaterial since neither sexual contact nor motive were elements of the offense at the guilt phase, this Court considers the new disclosure of central importance. This case is about who committed the crime, so motive is key, and the prosecution at the guilt phase referred to evidence at the scene suggesting that House committed, or attempted to commit, an indignity on Mrs. Muncey. Apart from proving motive, this was the only forensic evidence at the scene that would link House to the murder. Law and society demand accountability for a sexual offense, so the evidence was also likely a factor in persuading the jury not to let him go free. At sentencing, moreover, the jury concluded that the murder was committed in the course of a rape or kidnaping. A jury acting without the assumption that the semen could have come from House would have found it necessary to establish some different motive, or, if the same motive, an intent far more speculative.

Moreover, the evidentiary disarray surrounding the other forensic evidence, the bloodstains on House's pants, taken together with the testimony of an Assistant Chief Medical Examiner for the State of Tennessee, would prevent reasonable jurors from placing significant reliance on the blood evidence. The medical examiner who testified believes the blood on the jeans must have come from the autopsy samples. In addition, a vial and a quarter of autopsy blood is unaccounted for; the blood was transported to the FBI together with the pants in conditions that could have caused the vials to spill; some blood did spill at least once during the blood's journey from Tennessee authorities through FBI hands to a defense expert; the pants were stored in a plastic bag bearing a large bloodstain and a label from a Tennessee Bureau of Investigation agent; and the box containing the blood samples may have been opened before arriving at the FBI lab. None of this evidence was presented to the trial jury. Whereas the bloodstains seemed strong evidence of House's guilt at trial, the record now raises substantial questions about the blood's origin.

House's petition is further strengthened by evidence implicating an alternative suspect. In the post-trial proceedings, House presented troubling evidence that Mr. Muncey (the victim's husband) could have been the murderer. Two witnesses described a confession by Mr. Muncey; two others described suspicious behavior (a fight between the couple and Mr. Muncey's attempt to construct a false alibi) around the time of the crime; and others described a history of spousal abuse. Considered in isolation, a reasonable jury might well disregard this evidence, but in combination with the challenges to the blood evidence and lack of motive with respect to House, evidence pointing to Mr. Muncey likely would reinforce other doubts as to House's guilt.

The Assistant Chief Medical Examiner further testified that certain injuries discovered on House after the crime likely did not result from involvement in the murder. Certain other evidence—Mrs. Muncey's daughter's recollection of the night of the murder, and the District Court's finding at the habeas proceeding that House was not a credible witness—may favor the State.

While this is not a case of conclusive exoneration, and the issue is close, this is the rare case where—had the jury heard all the conflicting testimony—it is more likely than not that no reasonable juror viewing the record as a whole would lack reasonable doubt.

House has not shown freestanding innocence that would render his imprisonment and planned execution unconstitutional under *Herrera v. Collins*, 506 U.S. 390, in which the Court assumed without deciding that "in a capital case a truly persuasive demonstration of 'actual innocence' made after trial would render the execution of a defendant unconstitutional, and warrant federal habeas relief if there were no state avenue open to process such a claim." The threshold showing for such a right would be extraordinarily high, and House has not satisfied whatever burden a hypothetical freestanding innocence claim would require. He has cast doubt on his guilt sufficient to satisfy *Schlup's* gateway standard for obtaining federal review, but given the closeness of the *Schlup* question here, his showing falls short of the threshold implied in *Herrera*.

In re Troy Anthony Davis
557 U.S. 952 (2009)

Per Curiam.

The motion of NAACP, et al. for leave to file a brief as amici curiae is granted. The motion of Bob Barr, et al. for leave to file a brief as amici curiae is granted. The petition for a writ of habeas corpus is transferred to the United States District Court for the Southern District of Georgia for hearing and determination. The District Court should receive testimony and make findings of fact as to whether evidence that could not have been obtained at the time of trial clearly establishes petitioner's innocence. Justice SOTOMAYOR took no part in the consideration or decision of these motions and this petition.

Justice STEVENS, with whom Justice GINSBURG and Justice BREYER join, concurring.

Justice Scalia's dissent is wrong in two respects. First, he assumes as a matter of fact that petitioner Davis is guilty of the murder of Officer MacPhail. He does this even though seven of the State's key witnesses have recanted their trial testimony; several individuals have implicated the State's principal witness as the shooter; and "no court," state or federal, "has ever conducted a hearing to assess the reliability of the score of [postconviction] affidavits that, if reliable, would satisfy the threshold showing for a truly persuasive demonstration of actual innocence," 565 F.3d 810, 827 (C.A.11 2009) (Barkett, J., dissenting). The substantial risk of putting an innocent man to death clearly provides an adequate justification for holding an evidentiary hearing. Simply put, the case is sufficiently "exceptional" to warrant utilization of this Court's Rule 20.4(a), 28 U.S.C. § 2241(b), and our original habeas jurisdiction.

Second, Justice SCALIA assumes as a matter of law that, "[e]ven if the District Court were to be persuaded by Davis's affidavits, it would have no power to grant relief" in light of 28 U.S.C. § 2254(d)(1). For several reasons, however, this transfer is by no means "a fool's errand." The District Court may conclude that § 2254(d)(1) does not apply, or does not apply with the same rigidity, to an original habeas petition such as this. See *Felker v. Turpin*, 518 U.S. 651, 663 (1996) (expressly leaving open the question whether and to what extent the Antiterrorism and Effective Death Penalty Act of 1996 (AEDPA) applies to original petitions). The court may also find it relevant to the AEDPA analysis that Davis is bringing an "actual innocence" claim. *See, e.g., Triestman v. United States*, 124 F.3d 361, 377–380 (C.A.2 1997) (discussing "serious" constitutional concerns that would arise if AEDPA were interpreted to bar judicial review of certain actual innocence claims); Pet. for Writ of Habeas Corpus 20–22 (arguing that Congress intended actual innocence claims to have special status under AEDPA). Even if the court finds that § 2254(d)(1) applies in full, it is arguably unconstitutional to the extent it bars relief for a death row inmate who has established his innocence. Alternatively, the court may find in such a case that the statute's text is satisfied, because decisions of this Court clearly support the proposition that it "would be an atrocious violation of our Constitution and the principles upon which it is based" to execute an innocent person.

Justice Scalia would pretermit all of these unresolved legal questions on the theory that we must treat even the most robust showing of actual innocence identically on habeas review to an accusation of minor procedural error. Without briefing or argument, he concludes that Congress chose to foreclose relief and that the Constitution permits this. But imagine a petitioner in Davis's situation who possesses new evidence conclusively and definitively proving, beyond any scintilla of doubt, that he is an innocent man. The dissent's reasoning would allow such a petitioner to be put to death nonetheless. The Court correctly refuses to endorse such reasoning.

Justice SCALIA, *with whom Justice* THOMAS *joins, dissenting.*

Today this Court takes the extraordinary step—one not taken in nearly 50 years—of instructing a district court to adjudicate a state prisoner's petition for an original writ of habeas corpus. The Court proceeds down this path even though every judicial and executive body that has examined petitioner's stale claim of innocence has been unpersuaded, and (to make matters worst) even though it would be impossible for the District Court to grant any relief. Far from demonstrating, as this Court's Rule 20.4(a) requires, "exceptional circumstances" that "warrant the exercise of the Court's discretionary powers," petitioner's claim is a sure loser. Transferring his petition to the District Court is a confusing exercise that can serve no purpose except to delay the State's execution of its lawful criminal judgment. I respectfully dissent.

Eighteen years ago, after a trial untainted by constitutional defect, a unanimous jury found petitioner Troy Anthony Davis guilty of the murder of Mark Allen MacPhail. The evidence showed that MacPhail, an off-duty police officer, was shot multiple times after responding to the beating of a homeless man in a restaurant parking lot. Davis admits that he was present during the beating of the homeless man, but he maintains that it was one of his companions who shot Officer MacPhail. It is this claim of "actual innocence"—the same defense Davis raised at trial but now allegedly supported by new corroborating affidavits—that Davis raises as grounds for relief. And (presumably) it is this claim that the Court wants the District Court to adjudicate once the petition is transferred.

Even if the District Court were to be persuaded by Davis's affidavits, it would have no power to grant relief. Federal courts may order the release of convicted state prisoners only in accordance with the restrictions imposed by the Antiterrorism and Effective Death Penalty Act of 1996. See *Felker v. Turpin*, 518 U.S. 651, 662 (1996). Insofar as it applies to the present case, that statute bars the issuance of a writ of habeas corpus "with respect to any claim that was adjudicated on the merits in State court proceedings unless the adjudication of the claim ... resulted in a decision that was contrary to, or involved an unreasonable application of, clearly established Federal law, as determined by the Supreme Court of the United States." 28 U.S.C. § 2254(d)(1).

The Georgia Supreme Court rejected petitioner's "actual-innocence" claim on the merits, denying his extraordinary motion for a new trial. Davis can obtain relief only if that determination was contrary to, or an unreasonable application of, "clearly established Federal law, as determined by the Supreme Court of the United States." It most assuredly was not. This Court has never held that the Constitution forbids the execution of a convicted defendant who has had a full and fair trial but is later able to convince a habeas court that he is "actually" innocent. Quite to the contrary, we have repeatedly left that question unresolved, while expressing considerable doubt that any claim based on alleged "actual innocence" is constitutionally cognizable. See *Herrera v. Collins*, 506 U.S. 390, 400–401, 416–417 (1993); see also *House v. Bell*, 547 U.S. 518, 555 (2006); *District Attorney's Office for Third Judicial Dist. v. Osborne*, 129 S.Ct. 2308, 2321–2322 (2009). A state court cannot possibly have contravened, or even unreasonably applied, "clearly established Federal law, as determined by the Supreme Court of the United States," by rejecting a type of claim that the Supreme Court has not once accepted as valid.

Justice Stevens says that we need not be deterred by the limitations that Congress has placed on federal courts' authority to issue the writ, because we cannot rule out the possibility that the District Court might find those limitations unconstitutional as applied to actual-innocence claims. (This is not a possibility that Davis has raised, but one that Justice Stevens has imagined.) But acknowledging that possibility would make a nullity of § 2254(d)(1). There is no sound basis for distinguishing an actual-innocence claim from any other claim that is alleged to have produced a wrongful conviction. If the District Court here can ignore § 2254(d)(1) on the theory that otherwise Davis's actual-innocence claim would (unconstitutionally) go unaddressed, the same possibility would exist for any claim going beyond "clearly established Federal law."

The existence of that possibility is incompatible with the many cases in which we have reversed lower courts for their failure to apply § 2254(d)(1), with no consideration of constitutional entitlement. *See, e.g., Knowles v. Mirzayance*, 556 U.S. 111, ___, 129 S.Ct. 1411, 1419–1420 (2009); *Wright v. Van Patten*, 552 U.S. 120, ___, 128 S.Ct. 743, 746–747 (2008) (per curiam); *Carey v. Musladin*, 549 U.S. 70, 76–77 (2006). We have done so because the argument that the Constitution requires federal-court screening of all state convictions for constitutional violations is frivolous. For much of our history, federal habeas review was not available even for those state convictions claimed to be in violation of clearly established federal law. See *Stone v. Powell*, 428 U.S. 465, 474–476 (1976); Bator, *Finality in Criminal Law and Federal Habeas Corpus for State Prisoners*, 76 HARV. L. REV. 441, 465–66 (1963). It seems to me improper to grant the extraordinary relief of habeas corpus on the possibility that we have approved—indeed, directed—the disregard of constitutional imperatives in the past. If we have new-found doubts regarding the constitutionality of § 2254(d)(1), we should hear Davis's application and resolve that question (if necessary) ourselves.[80]

Transferring this case to a court that has no power to grant relief is strange enough. It becomes stranger still when one realizes that the allegedly new evidence we shunt off to be examined by the District Court has already been considered (and rejected) multiple times. Davis's postconviction "actual-innocence" claim is not new. Most of the evidence on which it is based is almost a decade old. A State Supreme Court, a State Board of Pardons and Paroles, and a Federal Court of Appeals have all considered the evidence Davis now presents and found it lacking. (I do not rely upon the similar conclusion of the Georgia trial court, since unlike the others that court relied substantially upon Georgia evidentiary rules rather than the unpersuasiveness of the evidence Davis brought forward.)

The Georgia Supreme Court "look[ed] beyond bare legal principles that might otherwise be controlling to the core question of whether a jury presented with Davis's allegedly-new testimony would probably find him not guilty or give him a sentence other than death." *Davis v. State*, 283 Ga. 438, 447 (2008). After analyzing each of Davis's proffered affidavits and comparing them with the evidence adduced at trial, it concluded that it was not probable that they would produce a different result.

When Davis sought clemency before the Georgia Board of Pardons and Paroles, that tribunal stayed his execution and "spent more than a year studying and considering [his] case." It "gave Davis' attorneys an opportunity to present every witness they desired to support their allegation that there is doubt as to Davis' guilt"; it "heard each of these witnesses and questioned them closely." It "studied the voluminous trial transcript, the police investigation report and the initial statements of the witnesses," and "had certain physical evidence retested and Davis interviewed." "After an exhaustive review of all available information regarding the Troy Davis case and after considering all possible reasons for granting clemency, the Board ... determined that clemency is not warranted."

After reviewing the record, the Eleventh Circuit came to a conclusion "wholly consonant with the repeated conclusions of the state courts and the State Board of Pardons and Paroles." 565 F.3d 810, 825 (2009). "When we view all of this evidence as a whole, we cannot honestly say that Davis can establish by clear and convincing evidence that a jury would not have found him guilty of Officer MacPhail's murder."

---

80. Justice Stevens' other arguments as to why § 2254(d)(1) might be inapplicable—that it does not apply to original petitions filed in this Court (even though its text covers all federal habeas petitions), and that it contains an exception (not to be found in its text) for claims of actual innocence—do not warrant response.

Today, without explanation and without any meaningful guidance, this Court sends the District Court for the Southern District of Georgia on a fool's errand. That court is directed to consider evidence of actual innocence which has been reviewed and rejected at least three times, and which, even if adequate to persuade the District Court, cannot (as far as anyone knows) form the basis for any relief. I truly do not see how the District Court can discern what is expected of it. If this Court thinks it possible that capital convictions obtained in full compliance with law can never be final, but are always subject to being set aside by federal courts for the reason of "actual innocence," it should set this case on our own docket so that we can (if necessary) resolve that question. Sending it to a district court that "might" be authorized to provide relief, but then again "might" be reversed if it did so, is not a sensible way to proceed.

McQuiggin v. Perkins
569 U.S. 383 (2013)

Justice GINSBURG delivered the opinion of the Court.

This case concerns the "actual innocence" gateway to federal habeas review applied in *Schlup v. Delo*, 513 U.S. 298 (1995), and further explained in *House v. Bell*, 547 U.S. 518 (2006). In those cases, a convincing showing of actual innocence enabled habeas petitioners to overcome a procedural bar to consideration of the merits of their constitutional claims. Here, the question arises in the context of 28 U.S.C. § 2244(d)(1), the statute of limitations on federal habeas petitions prescribed in the Antiterrorism and Effective Death Penalty Act of 1996. Specifically, if the petitioner does not file her federal habeas petition, at the latest, within one year of "the date on which the factual predicate of the claim or claims presented could have been discovered through the exercise of due diligence," § 2244(d)(1)(D), can the time bar be overcome by a convincing showing that she committed no crime?

We hold that actual innocence, if proved, serves as a gateway through which a petitioner may pass whether the impediment is a procedural bar, as it was in *Schlup* and *House*, or, as in this case, expiration of the statute of limitations. We caution, however, that tenable actual-innocence gateway pleas are rare: "[A] petitioner does not meet the threshold requirement unless he persuades the district court that, in light of the new evidence, no juror, acting reasonably, would have voted to find him guilty beyond a reasonable doubt." *Schlup*, 513 U.S., at 329; see *House*, 547 U.S., at 538 (emphasizing that the *Schlup* standard is "demanding" and seldom met). And in making an assessment of the kind *Schlup* envisioned, "the timing of the [petition]" is a factor bearing on the "reliability of th[e] evidence" purporting to show actual innocence. *Schlup*, 513 U.S., at 332.

In the instant case, the Sixth Circuit acknowledged that habeas petitioner Perkins (respondent here) had filed his petition after the statute of limitations ran out, and had "failed to diligently pursue his rights." Nevertheless, the Court of Appeals reversed the decision of the District Court denying Perkins' petition, and held that Perkins' actual-innocence claim allowed him to pursue his habeas petition as if it had been filed on time. 670 F.3d 665, 670 (2012). The appeals court apparently considered a petitioner's delay irrelevant to appraisal of an actual-innocence claim.

We vacate the Court of Appeals' judgment and remand the case. Our opinion clarifies that a federal habeas court, faced with an actual-innocence gateway claim, should count unjustifiable delay on a habeas petitioner's part, not as an absolute barrier to relief, but as a factor in determining whether actual innocence has been reliably shown.

I

A

On March 4, 1993, respondent Floyd Perkins attended a party in Flint, Michigan, in the company of his friend, Rodney Henderson, and an acquaintance, Damarr Jones. The three men left the party together. Henderson was later discovered on a wooded trail, murdered by stab wounds to his head.

Perkins was charged with the murder of Henderson. At trial, Jones was the key witness for the prosecution. He testified that Perkins alone committed the murder while Jones looked on.

Chauncey Vaughn, a friend of Perkins and Henderson, testified that, prior to the murder, Perkins had told him he would kill Henderson, and that Perkins later called Vaughn, confessing to his commission of the crime. A third witness, Torriano Player, also a friend of both Perkins and Henderson, testified that Perkins told him, had he known how Player felt about Henderson, he would not have killed Henderson.

Perkins, testifying in his own defense, offered a different account of the episode. He testified that he left Henderson and Jones to purchase cigarettes at a convenience store. When he exited the store, Perkins related, Jones and Henderson were gone. Perkins said that he then visited his girlfriend. About an hour later, Perkins recalled, he saw Jones standing under a streetlight with blood on his pants, shoes, and plaid coat.

The jury convicted Perkins of first-degree murder. He was sentenced to life in prison without the possibility of parole on October 27, 1993. The Michigan Court of Appeals affirmed Perkins' conviction and sentence, and the Michigan Supreme Court denied Perkins leave to appeal on January 31, 1997. Perkins' conviction became final on May 5, 1997.

B

Under the Antiterrorism and Effective Death Penalty Act of 1996 (AEDPA), a state prisoner ordinarily has one year to file a federal petition for habeas corpus, starting from "the date on which the judgment became final by the conclusion of direct review or the expiration of the time for seeking such review." 28 U.S.C. § 2244(d)(1)(A). If the petition alleges newly discovered evidence, however, the filing deadline is one year from "the date on which the factual predicate of the claim or claims presented could have been discovered through the exercise of due diligence." § 2244(d)(1)(D).

Perkins filed his federal habeas corpus petition on June 13, 2008, more than 11 years after his conviction became final. He alleged, inter alia, ineffective assistance on the part of his trial attorney, depriving him of his Sixth Amendment right to competent counsel. To overcome AEDPA's time limitations, Perkins asserted newly discovered evidence of actual innocence. He relied on three affidavits, each pointing to Jones, not Perkins, as Henderson's murderer.

The first affidavit, dated January 30, 1997, was submitted by Perkins' sister, Ronda Hudson. Hudson stated that she had heard from a third party, Louis Ford, that Jones bragged about stabbing Henderson and had taken his clothes to the cleaners after the murder. The second affidavit, dated March 16, 1999, was subscribed to by Demond Louis, Chauncey Vaughn's younger brother. Louis stated that, on the night of the murder, Jones confessed to him that he had just killed Henderson. Louis also described the clothes Jones wore that night, bloodstained orange shoes and orange pants, and a colorful shirt. The next day, Louis added, he accompanied Jones, first to a dumpster where Jones disposed of the bloodstained shoes, and then to the cleaners. Finally, Perkins presented the July 16, 2002, affidavit of Linda Fleming, an employee at Pro-Clean Cleaners in 1993. She stated that, on or about March 4, 1993, a man matching Jones's description entered the shop and asked her whether bloodstains could be removed from the pants and a shirt he brought in. The pants were orange, she recalled, and heavily stained with blood, as was the multicolored shirt left for cleaning along with the pants.

The District Court found the affidavits insufficient to entitle Perkins to habeas relief. Characterizing the affidavits as newly discovered evidence was "dubious," the District Court observed, in light of what Perkins knew about the underlying facts at the time of trial. But even assuming qualification of the affidavits as evidence newly discovered, the District Court next explained, "[Perkins'] petition [was] untimely under § 2244(d)(1)(D)." "[If] the statute of limitations began to run as of the date of the latest of th[e] affidavits, July 16, 2002," the District Court noted, then "absent tolling, [Perkins] had until July 16, 2003 in which to file his habeas petition." Perkins, however, did not file until nearly five years later, on June 13, 2008.

Under Sixth Circuit precedent, the District Court stated, "a habeas petitioner who demonstrates a credible claim of actual innocence based on new evidence may, in exceptional circumstances, be entitled to equitable tolling of habeas limitations." But Perkins had not established exceptional circumstances, the District Court determined. In any event, the District Court observed, equitable tolling requires diligence and Perkins "ha[d] failed utterly to demonstrate the necessary diligence in exercising his rights." Alternatively, the District Court found that Perkins had failed to meet the strict standard by which pleas of actual innocence are measured: He had not shown that, taking account of all the evidence, "it is more likely than not that no reasonable juror would have convicted him," or even that the evidence was new.

Perkins appealed the District Court's judgment. Although recognizing that AEDPA's statute of limitations had expired and that Perkins had not diligently pursued his rights, the Sixth Circuit granted a certificate of appealability limited to a single question: Is reasonable diligence a precondition to relying on actual innocence as a gateway to adjudication of a federal habeas petition on the merits?

On consideration of the certified question, the Court of Appeals reversed the District Court's judgment. Adhering to Circuit precedent, *Souter v. Jones*, 395 F.3d 577, 597–602 (2005), the Sixth Circuit held that Perkins' gateway actual-innocence allegations allowed him to present his ineffective-assistance-of-counsel claim as if it were filed on time. On remand, the Court of Appeals instructed, "the [D]istrict [C]ourt [should] fully consider whether Perkins assert[ed] a credible claim of actual innocence."

We granted certiorari to resolve a Circuit conflict on whether AEDPA's statute of limitations can be overcome by a showing of actual innocence....

II

A

In *Holland v. Florida*, 560 U.S. 631 (2010), this Court addressed the circumstances in which a federal habeas petitioner could invoke the doctrine of "equitable tolling." *Holland* held that "a [habeas] petitioner is entitled to equitable tolling only if he shows (1) that he has been pursuing his rights diligently, and (2) that some extraordinary circumstance stood in his way and prevented timely filing." As the courts below comprehended, Perkins does not qualify for equitable tolling. In possession of all three affidavits by July 2002, he waited nearly six years to seek federal postconviction relief. "Such a delay falls far short of demonstrating the ... diligence" required to entitle a petitioner to equitable tolling.

Perkins, however, asserts not an excuse for filing after the statute of limitations has run. Instead, he maintains that a plea of actual innocence can overcome AEDPA's one-year statute of limitations. He thus seeks an equitable exception to § 2244(d)(1), not an extension of the time statutorily prescribed.

Decisions of this Court support Perkins' view of the significance of a convincing actual-innocence claim. We have not resolved whether a prisoner may be entitled to habeas relief based on a freestanding claim of actual innocence. *Herrera v. Collins*, 506 U.S. 390, 404–405 (1993). We have recognized, however, that a prisoner "otherwise subject to defenses of abusive or successive use of the writ [of habeas corpus] may have his federal constitutional claim considered on the merits if he makes a proper showing of actual innocence." *Id.*, at 404. In other words, a credible showing of actual innocence may allow a prisoner to pursue his constitutional claims (here, ineffective assistance of counsel) on the merits notwithstanding the existence of a procedural bar to relief. "This rule, or fundamental miscarriage of justice exception, is grounded in the 'equitable discretion' of habeas courts to see that federal constitutional errors do not result in the incarceration of innocent persons." *Herrera*, 506 U.S., at 404.

We have applied the miscarriage of justice exception to overcome various procedural defaults. These include "successive" petitions asserting previously rejected claims, see *Kuhlmann v. Wilson*, 477 U.S. 436, 454 (1986), "abusive" petitions asserting in a second petition claims that could have been raised in a first petition, see *McCleskey v. Zant*, 499 U.S. 467, 494–495 (1991), failure to develop facts in state court, see *Keeney v. Tamayo-Reyes*, 504 U.S. 1, 11–12 (1992), and failure to observe state procedural rules, including filing deadlines, see *Coleman v. Thompson*, 501 U.S. 722, 750 (1991); *Carrier*, 477 U.S., at 495–496.

The miscarriage of justice exception, our decisions bear out, survived AEDPA's passage. In *Calderon v. Thompson*, 523 U.S. 538 (1998), we applied the exception to hold that a federal court may, consistent with AEDPA, recall its mandate in order to revisit the merits of a decision. In *Bousley v. United States*, 523 U.S. 614, 622 (1998), we held, in the context of §2255, that actual innocence may overcome a prisoner's failure to raise a constitutional objection on direct review. Most recently, in *House*, we reiterated that a prisoner's proof of actual innocence may provide a gateway for federal habeas review of a procedurally defaulted claim of constitutional error. 547 U.S., at 537–538.

These decisions "see[k] to balance the societal interests in finality, comity, and conservation of scarce judicial resources with the individual interest in justice that arises in the extraordinary case." *Schlup*, 513 U.S., at 324. Sensitivity to the injustice of incarcerating an innocent individual should not abate when the impediment is AEDPA's statute of limitations.

As just noted, we have held that the miscarriage of justice exception applies to state procedural rules, including filing deadlines. *Coleman*, 501 U.S., at 750. A federal court may invoke the miscarriage of justice exception to justify consideration of claims defaulted in state court under state timeliness rules. The State's reading of AEDPA's time prescription would thus accord greater force to a federal deadline than to a similarly designed state deadline. It would be passing strange to interpret a statute seeking to promote federalism and comity as requiring stricter enforcement of federal procedural rules than procedural rules established and enforced by the States.

B

The State ties to §2244(d)'s text its insistence that AEDPA's statute of limitations precludes courts from considering late-filed actual-innocence gateway claims. "Section 2244(d)(1)(D)," the State contends, "forecloses any argument that a habeas petitioner has unlimited time to present new evidence in support of a constitutional claim." That is so, the State maintains, because AEDPA prescribes a comprehensive system for determining when its one-year limitations period begins to run. "Included within that system," the State observes, "is a specific trigger for the precise circumstance presented here: a constitutional claim based on new evidence." Section 2244(d)(1)(D) runs the clock from "the date on which the factual predicate of the claim ... could have been discovered through the exercise of due diligence." In light of that provision, the State urges, "there is no need for the courts to act in equity to provide additional time for persons who allege actual innocence as a gateway to their claims of constitutional error." Perkins' request for an equitable exception to the statute of limitations, the State charges, would "rende[r] superfluous this carefully scripted scheme."

The State's argument in this regard bears blinders. AEDPA's time limitations apply to the typical case in which no allegation of actual innocence is made. The miscarriage of justice exception, we underscore, applies to a severely confined category: cases in which new evidence shows "it is more likely than not that no reasonable juror would have convicted [the petitioner]." *Schlup*, 513 U.S., at 329. Section 2244(d)(1)(D) is both modestly more stringent (because it requires diligence) and dramatically less stringent (because it requires no showing of innocence). Many petitions that could not pass through the actual-innocence gateway will be timely or not measured by § 2244(d)(1)(D)'s triggering provision. That provision, in short, will hardly be rendered superfluous by recognition of the miscarriage of justice exception.

III

Having rejected the State's argument that § 2244(d)(1)(D) precludes a court from entertaining an untimely first federal habeas petition raising a convincing claim of actual innocence, we turn to the State's further objection to the Sixth Circuit's opinion. Even if a habeas petitioner asserting a credible claim of actual innocence may overcome AEDPA's statute of limitations, the State argues, the Court of Appeals erred in finding that no threshold diligence requirement at all applies to Perkins' petition.

While formally distinct from its argument that § 2244(d)(1)(D)'s text forecloses a late-filed claim alleging actual innocence, the State's contention makes scant sense. Section 2244(d)(1)(D) requires a habeas petitioner to file a claim within one year of the time in which new evidence "could have been discovered through the exercise of due diligence." It would be bizarre to hold that a habeas petitioner who asserts a convincing claim of actual innocence may overcome the statutory time bar § 2244(d)(1)(D) erects, yet simultaneously encounter a court-fashioned diligence barrier to pursuit of her petition.

While we reject the State's argument that habeas petitioners who assert convincing actual-innocence claims must prove diligence to cross a federal court's threshold, we hold that the Sixth Circuit erred to the extent that it eliminated timing as a factor relevant in evaluating the reliability of a petitioner's proof of innocence. To invoke the miscarriage of justice exception to AEDPA's statute of limitations, we repeat, a petitioner "must show that it is more likely than not that no reasonable juror would have convicted him in the light of the new evidence." *Schlup*, 513 U.S., at 327. Unexplained delay in presenting new evidence bears on the determination whether the petitioner has made the requisite showing. Perkins so acknowledges. See Brief for Respondent 52 (unjustified delay may figure in determining "whether a petitioner has made a sufficient showing of innocence"). As we stated in *Schlup*, "[a] court may consider how the timing of the submission and the likely credibility of [a petitioner's] affiants bear on the probable reliability of ... evidence [of actual innocence]."

IV

We now return to the case at hand. The District Court proceeded properly in first determining that Perkins' claim was filed well beyond AEDPA's limitations period and that equitable tolling was unavailable to Perkins because he could demonstrate neither exceptional circumstances nor diligence. The District Court then found that Perkins' alleged newly discovered evidence, i.e., the information contained in the three affidavits, was "substantially available to [Perkins] at trial." Moreover, the proffered evidence, even if "new," was hardly adequate to show that, had it been presented at trial, no reasonable juror would have convicted Perkins.

The Sixth Circuit granted a certificate of appealability limited to the question whether reasonable diligence is a precondition to reliance on actual innocence as a gateway to adjudication of a federal habeas petition on the merits. We have explained that untimeliness, although not an unyielding ground for dismissal of a petition, does bear on the credibility of evidence proffered to show actual innocence. On remand, the District Court's appraisal of Perkins' petition as insufficient to meet Schlup's actual-innocence standard should be dispositive, absent cause, which we do not currently see, for the Sixth Circuit to upset that evaluation. We stress once again that the Schlup standard is demanding. The gateway should open only when a petition presents "evidence of innocence so strong that a court cannot have confidence in the outcome of the trial unless the court is also satisfied that the trial was free of non-harmless constitutional error." 513 U.S., at 316, 115 S.Ct. 851.

* * *

For the reasons stated, the judgment of the Sixth Circuit is vacated, and the case is remanded for further proceedings consistent with this opinion.

It is so ordered.

Justice SCALIA, *with whom The Chief Justice and Justice* THOMAS *join, and with whom Justice* ALITO *joins as to Parts I, II, and III, dissenting.*

The Antiterrorism and Effective Death Penalty Act of 1996 (AEDPA) provides that a "1-year period of limitation shall apply" to a state prisoner's application for a writ of habeas corpus in federal court. 28 U.S.C. §2244(d)(1). The gaping hole in today's opinion for the Court is its failure to answer the crucial question upon which all else depends: What is the source of the Court's power to fashion what it concedes is an "exception" to this clear statutory command?

That question is unanswered because there is no answer. This Court has no such power, and not one of the cases cited by the opinion says otherwise. The Constitution vests legislative power only in Congress, which never enacted the exception the Court creates today. That inconvenient truth resolves this case.

I

A

"Actual innocence" has, until today, been an exception only to judge-made, prudential barriers to habeas relief, or as a means of channeling judges' statutorily conferred discretion not to apply a procedural bar. Never before have we applied the exception to circumvent a categorical statutory bar to relief. We have not done so because we have no power to do so. Where Congress has erected a constitutionally valid barrier to habeas relief, a court cannot decline to give it effect.

B

Because we have no "equitable" power to discard statutory barriers to habeas relief, we cannot simply extend judge-made exceptions to judge-made barriers into the statutory realm. The Court's insupportable leap from judge-made procedural bars to all procedural bars, including statutory bars, does all the work in its opinion— and there is not a whit of precedential support for it.... Not one of the cases on which the Court relies today supports the extraordinary premise that courts can create out of whole cloth an exception to a statutory bar to relief.

* * *

"It would be marvelously inspiring to be able to boast that we have a criminal-justice system in which a claim of 'actual innocence' will always be heard, no matter how late it is brought forward, and no matter how much the failure to bring it forward at the proper time is the defendant's own fault." *Bousley*, 523 U.S., at 635, 118 S.Ct. 1604 (Scalia, J., dissenting). I suspect it is this vision of perfect justice through abundant procedure that impels the Court today. Of course, "we do not have such a system, and no society unwilling to devote unlimited resources to repetitive criminal litigation ever could." Until today, a district court could dismiss an untimely petition without delving into the underlying facts. From now on, each time an untimely petitioner claims innocence—and how many prisoners asking to be let out of jail do not?— the district court will be obligated to expend limited judicial resources wading into the murky merits of the petitioner's innocence claim. The Court notes "that tenable actual-innocence gateway pleas are rare." That discouraging reality, intended as reassurance, is in truth "the condemnation of the procedure which has encouraged frivolous cases." *Brown*, 344 U.S., at 537 (Jackson, J., concurring in result).

It has now been 60 years since Brown v. Allen, in which we struck the Faustian bargain that traded the simple elegance of the common-law writ of habeas corpus for federal-court power to probe the substantive merits of state-court convictions. Even after AEDPA's pass through the Augean stables, no one in a position to observe the functioning of our byzantine federal-habeas system can believe it an efficient device for separating the truly deserving from the multitude of prisoners pressing false claims. "[F]loods of stale, frivolous and repetitious petitions inundate the docket of the lower courts and swell our own.... It must prejudice the occasional meritorious applicant to be buried in a flood of worthless ones."

The "inundation" that Justice Jackson lamented in 1953 "consisted of 541" federal habeas petitions filed by state prisoners.[81] By 1969, that number had grown to 7,359. In the year ending on September 30, 2012, 15,929 such petitions were filed. Today's decision piles yet more dead weight onto a post-conviction habeas system already creaking at its rusted joints.

I respectfully dissent.

---

81. Henry J. Friendly, *Is Innocence Irrelevant? Collateral Attack on Criminal Judgments*, 38 U. Chi. L. Rev. 142, 143 (1970).

B. Legal Materials, Exercises, and Media

1. *Problem Case:*

Amrine v. Bowersox

128 F.3d 1222 (8th Cir. 1997)

Amrine was convicted of murdering Gary Barber on October 18, 1985, in a recreation room at the Potosi Correction Center in Cole County, Missouri. Barber was stabbed in the back with an ice pick at a punching bag. There were two correctional officers and approximately 45 to 50 inmates in the room at the time. Amrine has always maintained that he did not kill Barber and that he was involved in a poker game in a different area of the room at the time of the stabbing.

Amrine was charged with first degree murder, and the state relied primarily on three witnesses at trial. Inmates Randy Ferguson and Jerry Poe were the only people who claimed to have seen the killing, and they both testified that they saw Amrine stab Barber. A third prisoner, Terry Russell, testified that he had not seen the murder but that there were bad feelings between Amrine and Barber, that Amrine had threatened Barber a week before the killing, and that Amrine admitted his guilt to him afterward. Although he said he had not been in the recreation room at the time of the slaying, Russell had suggested to investigators that Amrine was the killer. Russell also testified that Barber and he had been placed in detention for fighting with each other and that they had been released back into the general population only hours before the stabbing.

Amrine offered testimony to show he could not have been the killer and to suggest that Terry Russell was. Six prisoners who had been in the recreation room testified that Amrine was involved in a poker game in a different part of the room at the time of the stabbing. Five of them saw Barber turn and chase after someone after he was stabbed, before he collapsed and died. Three identified Terry Russell as the person being chased by Barber; none of them named Amrine.

The two correctional officers who had been in the recreation room testified that they first became aware something was wrong when they saw Barber run across the room toward another inmate before he collapsed. Officer John Noble was called by the state and initially testified that he was sure the person Barber had been chasing was Terry Russell and that he had told another officer this shortly after the stabbing. After repeated questioning by the prosecution, Noble indicated he was not certain that Russell was the one being chased by Barber and that Russell and Amrine were similar in size, coloration, and hair style. A third correctional officer stationed outside of the room testified that he saw Russell leave the recreation room before the stabbing, and a fourth said he saw Russell both inside and outside the recreation room after the incident.

The state's case did not rest on physical evidence. Although a small amount of blood was found on Amrine's clothing, there was no evidence as to its age or source. A state serologist testified that he had been unable to determine the blood type because there was too little to provide a sample that could be tested. The jury found Amrine guilty of first degree murder and sentenced him to death.

After the Missouri Supreme Court affirmed his conviction and sentence, Amrine moved for post-conviction relief. The state court held a hearing at which Randy Ferguson and Terry Russell recanted their trial testimony. Ferguson now testified that he had actually been in the bathroom at the time of the stabbing and did not witness it, but that he had been pressured by Missouri officials into falsely testifying at trial that he had seen Amrine stab Barber. Ferguson testified that George Brooks, an investigator for the state prison system, and Richard Lee, an investigator for the Cole County prosecutor's office, had thrown him up against a wall, choked him, and threatened him with a "snitch jacket"[82] if he did not comply. After Ferguson agreed to testify, he was placed in protective custody, and an unrelated charge against him was dismissed. Terry Russell also testified that he had been pressured into giving false testimony against Amrine. He stated that his trial testimony, claiming he had heard Amrine threaten Barber and confess to his killing, had been false and that Brooks and a deputy sheriff from Cole County named John Hemeyer had threatened he would be charged with the murder if he did not give the desired testimony.[83] Investigators Brooks and Lee testified and denied pressuring Ferguson and Russell to implicate Amrine, but they acknowledged that a charge against Ferguson had been dismissed and that he had been placed in protective custody in exchange for his testimony. Although featured in Russell's testimony, deputy sheriff Hemeyer did not appear as a witness.

The state trial court denied Amrine's post conviction motion for relief. The court found that Ferguson's testimony about threats was "unworthy of belief" and designed merely to help a fellow inmate. It also found Russell's testimony not credible, but motivated by the desire to gain the good will of Amrine so that he could be released from protective custody. Amrine appealed, and the Missouri Supreme Court affirmed.

ii.

Amrine then filed the habeas petition now before the court, alleging ... that his rights to due process were violated because there was insufficient evidence to support his conviction, especially in light of the recantations of Ferguson and Russell, and the state court did not set aside the verdict or order a new trial. After Amrine's appeal was filed, counsel located new evidence to support Amrine's actual innocence and filed the pending motion to remand. The major piece of new evidence is an affidavit of Jerry Poe, the only witness who had testified at trial that they had seen Amrine stab Barber who had not recanted his trial testimony. Like Ferguson and Russell, Poe

---

82. A "snitch jacket" refers to the release of an inmate back into the general prison population after word is spread that the inmate has testified against another prisoner.

83. Russell also testified that at the time of Amrine's trial he had been scheduled to be paroled in a few months so he cooperated with Brooks and Hemeyer because he was afraid another charge would prolong his imprisonment. Russell was subsequently released, convicted on new charges, and sentenced to two life sentences, and he testified that he was recanting his trial testimony because he no longer feared being charged with Barber's murder since he was now already serving two life sentences.

now disavows his prior testimony. He swears that he did not see the killing, but that he gave false testimony that he had and that Amrine was the killer because of pressure from George Brooks and John Hemeyer. Brooks had threatened him with a snitch jacket if he would not cooperate, and both officials repeatedly rehearsed the false testimony with him and modified it as the time for trial approached.

Amrine argues he is entitled to a remand so that he may present this new evidence of actual innocence to the district court in order to obtain review under *Schlup* of his otherwise barred constitutional insufficiency of the evidence claim.

Should Amrine's motion be granted? What standard, *Schlup* or *Herrera*, applies to Amrine's claim?

2. Schlup *and Guilty Pleas.* Should a showing of actual innocence permit a defendant who has waived his right to appeal his sentence as a condition of a plea bargain nonetheless to bring an appeal? The federal courts are split on the issue. See *Patel v. United States of America*, 2017 WL 1629326 (U.S.) (Petition for Writ of Certiorari arguing that the circuits are divided in their articulation and interpretation of the circumstances under which a defendant may appeal a federal criminal sentence, notwithstanding a plea-bargained waiver of the right to appeal).

Chapter Fifteen

Appellate and Post-Conviction Review of Innocence: An Assessment

A. Readings

Henry J. Friendly,[*] *Is Innocence Irrelevant? Collateral Attack on Criminal Judgments*

38 U. Chi. L. Rev. 142, 142–144 (1970)

Legal history has many instances where a remedy initially serving a felt need has expanded bit by bit, without much thought being given to any single step, until it has assumed an aspect so different from its origin as to demand reappraisal—agonizing or not. That, in my view, is what has happened with respect to collateral attack on criminal convictions. After trial, conviction, sentence, appeal, affirmance, and denial of certiorari by the Supreme Court, in proceedings where the defendant had the assistance of counsel at every step, the criminal process, in Winston Churchill's phrase, has not reached the end, or even the beginning of the end, but only the end of the beginning.

Any murmur of dissatisfaction with this situation provokes immediate incantation of the Great Writ, with the inevitable initial capitals, often accompanied by a suggestion that the objector is the sort of person who would cheerfully desecrate the Ark of the Covenant. My thesis is that, with a few important exceptions, convictions should be subject to collateral attack only when the prisoner supplements his constitutional plea with a colorable claim of innocence. If there be fear that merely listening to such a proposal may contaminate, let me attempt to establish respectability by quoting two statements of Mr. Justice Black:

> ... the defendant's guilt or innocence is at least one of the vital considerations in determining whether collateral relief should be available to a convicted defendant.

And more strongly:

> In collateral attacks ... I would always require that the convicted defendant raise the kind of constitutional claim that casts some shadow of a doubt on his guilt.

---

[*] Judge, United States Court of Appeals for the Second Circuit.

Incredibly, these statements were made in dissent. Even more incredibly, the two other dissenting Justices expressed qualms about them. I believe, with qualifications I will elaborate, that this position ought to be the law and that legislation can and should make it so. When I speak of legislation, I am thinking mainly of federal habeas corpus for state prisoners and its equivalent for federal prisoners, since no other course seems realistic in light of Supreme Court opinions. In many states it may still be possible to reach the proper result by judicial decision. Although, if past experience is any guide, I am sure I will be accused of proposing to abolish habeas corpus, my aim is rather to restore the Great Writ to its deservedly high estate and rescue it from the disrepute invited by current excesses. Seventeen years ago, in his concurring opinion in *Brown v. Allen*, Mr. Justice Jackson expressed deep concern over the "floods of stale, frivolous and repetitious petitions [for federal habeas corpus by state prisoners which] inundate the docket of the lower courts and swell our own." The inundation consisted of 541 such petitions. In 1969, state prisoners filed 7,359 petitions for habeas corpus in the federal district courts, a 100 per cent increase over 1964. Federal prisoners filed 2,817 petitions challenging convictions or sentences, a 50 per cent increase over 1964. Prisoner petitions, including those attacking the conduct of prison officials, totaled 12,924. These "comprise the largest single element in the civil caseload of the district courts" and "accounted for more than one-sixth of the civil filings." There has been a corresponding increase in the load imposed by post-conviction petitions upon the federal courts of appeals. Despite the safeguard intended to be afforded by the requirement of a certificate of probable cause, there were over twice as many *appeals* by state prisoners in 1969 as there were *petitions* in 1952. A similar explosion of collateral attack has occurred in the courts of many of the states. If 541 annual petitions for federal habeas corpus by state prisoners were an "inundation," what is the right word for 7,500?

Brandon L. Garrett, *Judging Innocence*

108 Colum. L. Rev. 55, 96–116 (2008)

This study examines which constitutional and state claims each exoneree brought.... The table below provides a breakdown of the percentage of exonerees with written decisions who raised certain claims under the U.S. Constitution or state law; the claims raised by the most exonerees are listed first.

The winning claims, namely those for which a new trial was granted and that ruling was upheld on appeal, were as follows: state evidentiary claims (6); ineffective assistance of counsel claims (4); *Brady* claims (3); claims concerning jury instructions (2); *Bruton* unconstitutional joinder claims (2); prosecutorial misconduct claims (2); *Jackson* claims (1); due process and right to counsel claims (1), and a fabrication of evidence claim (1). As Table 15.1 shows, the winning claims were not necessarily the claims raised most often.

The members of the matched comparison group raised similar claims, but at lower rates across the board than the exonerees in the innocence group, though as noted, they challenged the facts underlying their convictions at similar rates. The NCSC

Table 15.1: Criminal Procedure Claims Raised by Exonerees

Claim: U.S. Constitution unless noted	Percentage of the 133 with written decisions who raised each claim (N)	Percentage of those who raised each claim who received reversals (N)
State law evidence claim	60 (80)	8 (6)
Jackson claim	45 (60)	2 (1)
Prosecutorial misconduct	29 (38)	0
Ineffective assistance of counsel	29 (38)	11 (4)
Jury instructions unconstitutional	26 (34)	6 (2)
Suggestive eyewitness identification	22 (29)	0
Brady claim	16 (21)	14 (3)
Destruction of evidence	15 (20)	0
Jury selection	14 (18)	0
Coerced confession	12 (16)	0
State law newly discovered evidence	12 (16)	0
Fourth Amendment claim	12 (16)	0
Right to counsel	8 (11)	9 (1)
Bruton claim	5 (6)	33 (2)
Herrera actual innocence claim	4 (5)	0
Fabrication of evidence claim	2 (3)	33 (1)

study of postconviction proceedings found that the vast majority of claims raised are claims regarding ineffective assistance of trial counsel and Brady claims regarding suppression of exculpatory evidence by police or prosecutors, typically alongside other due process claims. The 1994 NCSC study also concluded that in federal habeas proceedings the type of claim brought has little effect on the low chances, about 1%, that a prisoner will receive any relief. Furthermore, although only convicts with long sentences will pursue lengthy postconviction proceedings, any zealousness is severely limited where states and federal courts have exhaustion, statute of limitation, abuse of the writ, and procedural default rules that prevent premature, late, and repetitive petitions. Routine dismissals for procedural noncompliance accompany efforts to circumvent such rules.

3. Reversals, Retrials, and Vacated Convictions. — This section develops a central finding that appellate or postconviction courts reversed 14% of exonerees' convictions, or 9% if one excludes capital cases.... The reversal rate found here, though high when compared to criminal review in general, may be no higher than the rate during the review of comparable rape or murder convictions. These complex trials thus appear to be more error-prone than the norm.

Table 15.2: Exonerees' Reversal Rates

Number of cases with written decisions (N)	Number of cases receiving reversals	Percentage of cases with written decisions reversed
All Exonerees (133)	18	14
Noncapital cases (121)	11	9
Capital cases (12)	7	58

a. Reversals in the Innocence Group. — Eighteen exonerees of the 133 with written decisions in their cases received reversals, for a 14% reversal rate. Twelve of the exonerees were retried after reversal of the original conviction. Nine percent were tried multiple times because they received multiple reversals and each time were convicted again by new juries (ten had two trials and two had three trials before being freed as result of DNA testing). Furthermore, six more exonerees' convictions were vacated, but they had no retrials because DNA testing was conducted and exonerated them before their scheduled retrials. Thus, eighteen total exonerees had reversals upheld on appeal.

Table 15.2 displays the reversal rates in capital and noncapital cases. As documented in the landmark Liebman study of all capital cases from 1973 through 1995, there are extremely high (68%) reversal rates in all capital cases, both in state and federal postconviction review. In this study, the reversal rate among all exonerees with written decisions is 14%. Removing the capital cases from the analysis, the reversal rate for noncapital cases falls from 14% to 9%. Few exonerees received capital sentences — fourteen out of 200, or 7%. Yet the percentage of exonerees with capital sentences who received reversals was very high; seven out of twelve with written decisions received one or more reversals (58%). The capital attrition rate among exonerees is 58%, which is similar to the 68% capital attrition rate found in the Liebman, Fagan, and West study. Exonerees sentenced to life also accounted for many of the reversals; five received reversals out of fifty sentenced to life in prison, or 10%.

The table below depicts the reversals that exonerees received, broken down by crime of conviction, separating rape, rape-murder, and murder cases.

Rape cases had a lower reversal rate than murder cases. One explanation may be that in almost all rape cases, the victim identified the defendant, albeit incorrectly,

Table 15.3: Reversals for Exonerees by Crime of Conviction

Type of conviction	Total with written decisions	Number reversed	Percentage reversed
Rape	88	6	7
Rape-Murder	34	11	32
Murder	9	1	11

making it more difficult to challenge the factual support for the conviction due to the difficulty of prevailing on a *Manson* claim. However, rape-murder cases had higher reversal rates than murder cases. This is perhaps surprising, because one would expect that rape-murder cases would be more likely to have semen and blood evidence from the perpetrator, and thus be less prone to reversal.

* * *

The 9% noncapital reversal rate is higher than the rate in criminal appeals generally. Studies have shown that approximately 1% of federal postconviction petitioners receive relief, with similar figures (1% to 2%) in state courts. Federal habeas petitioners are disproportionately persons convicted of homicide (23%) and rape or other violent crimes (%). Yet 13% of federal habeas corpus petitions presented by exonerees received reversals. To date, studies of federal habeas corpus have not isolated reversals for particular crimes, nor have they examined reversal rates in murder and rape convictions. Therefore, in the limited set of cases involving murder and rape charges, reversal rates could be much higher than current studies suggest, just as reversal rates are much higher in capital cases.

b. Reversals in the Matched Comparison Group.—If average rape and murder convictions have a similarly high reversal rate, perhaps the 9% rate of noncapital reversals in the innocence group is not higher than the background rate. The matched comparison group permits examination of this question. It allows this study to isolate the 121 noncapital cases with written decisions and then compare each of them to a case located on Westlaw with an appeal brought in the same state, involving the same crimes of conviction, and having a written decision issued in the same year.

In the matched comparison group there was a 10% noncapital reversal rate (twelve reversals out of 121 cases). The claims that received reversals in the matched comparison group mirrored the claims on which exonerees received relief: five state law evidentiary claims, four ineffective assistance of counsel claims (one accompanied by a prosecutorial misconduct claim), a Jackson claim, a right to counsel claim, and a suggestive eyewitness identification claim.

The innocence group had just one fewer reversal, for a 9% rate (eleven reversals out of 121 noncapital cases). This small difference between the reversal rates in the innocence and matched comparison groups is not statistically significant. Thus exonerees fared no better during review proceedings than the matched rape and murder cases.

This similarity in reversal rates could be because serious rape and murder convictions share a background reversal rate of about 9%. Under this explanation, the reversal rates might have nothing to do with judges detecting innocence, but instead arise from higher rates of procedural error in serious cases. The trials and convictions for murder and rape may simply be more error prone than other less serious or less complex criminal trials. After all, serious crimes may demand that the court make more complex criminal procedure rulings, attorneys may better defend their clients against such crimes, and the State may pursue a case with less evidence due to pressure to clear serious cases.

A second and related explanation for the statistically insignificant difference in reversal rates may be that in a subset of the reversed exonerees' cases, judges accurately detected innocence, and, in a similar percentage of the matched comparison group appeals, judges did the same. A similarity in reversal rates between the two groups suggests similarly high levels of reversals based on factual errors among rape and murder convicts. Six of the twelve claims receiving reversals in the matched comparison group involved a ruling that the jury was seriously misled by unreliable or incomplete factual evidence at trial. Thus, half of the error rate had something to do with a perception of innocence, or relatedly, weakness of the evidence of guilt, and not just with a common rate of procedural error across all serious criminal trials. As discussed in the next section, seven out of eleven noncapital reversals in the innocence group were based on factual challenges.

One explanation for the degree to which reversals were based on factual grounds may be that rape and murder cases disproportionately involve equivocal evidence. Justice Department data suggest that reversal rates may be higher in those rape and murder cases that go to trial. According to BJS statistics, in the 8% of rape cases that went to trial, one-fourth resulted in acquittals, and many more had charges dismissed or resulted in misdemeanor convictions. Murder cases also had high numbers of acquittals: 9% of those that went to trial.

Some number of those who received reversals in the matched comparison group may have been actually innocent, but we cannot know how many. While we know that most in the innocence group did not receive reversals despite their innocence, we obviously do not know whether any innocent people in the matched comparison group received reversals, because in that group none received postconviction DNA testing. The incidence of reversals on factual claims in the matched comparison group suggests, however, that in the views of appellate and postconviction judges, substantive error was prevalent in such cases. Furthermore, the similarity in reversal rates is surprising from another perspective. One might have expected there to be even higher reversal rates in the innocence group, which had fewer acquaintance rape cases than the matched comparison group. In acquaintance cases, consent is more often a defense and an identity defense would face great difficulties if raised at trial or postconviction.

c. Cases Where the Innocent Received Reversals. — The cases where persons later exonerated by postconviction DNA testing received reversals deserve further examination, because in these cases courts provided relief without the benefit of that DNA evidence. Within the select group who received reversals, courts often granted claims relating to the facts supporting the convictions. By "a factual claim," as discussed earlier, this study does not mean an assertion about trial facts, but rather a legal contention that seeks to reverse a conviction or sentence based on the unreliability of the evidence that the State presented at trial. In the matched comparison group, half of the reversals involved granting factual claims. In the innocence group, slightly more than half of the reversals, eleven out of eighteen, involved granting factual claims. The other reversals related not to factual but to purely procedural claims, such as faulty jury instructions, ineffectiveness of counsel unrelated to failure to suppress or challenge factual evidence, or to factual evidence of innocence that the jury did not hear during trial. In four additional cases, reversals were not related to the reliability of the State's case at trial, but were innocence related, since they were based on the trial court's suppression of evidence of third party guilt. This bolsters the conclusion that approximately half of the reversals in the innocence and matched comparison groups had to do with postconviction judgments of the possibility of innocence.

Four of the reversals that exonerees received related to challenges to eyewitness identifications. Among the group of eighteen exonerees that received reversals, thirteen had convictions supported by eyewitness identifications, but for none was a reversal granted based on a claim challenging the identification as unconstitutionally suggestive. Nevertheless, in four cases the claims on which a court granted a reversal related to the eyewitness identification (three state law evidence claims and one Brady claim related to a hypnotized victim's statement). Six more reversals were based on challenges that related to forensic evidence introduced at trial, and the last of the eleven reversals related to testimony of a cooperating codefendant.

Though it was infrequent, when judges made a statement that suggested that an exoneree might be innocent, typically by way of describing how the State's case appeared quite weak, they often reversed. A court made such a statement for eight of the eighteen reversals. This was not typically an outright finding of innocence, but rather a strong acknowledgement of the flimsiness of the evidence of guilt adduced at trial. For example, in the Ron Williamson case, his so-called "dream confession" was admitted at trial despite his manifest mental illness. The federal district court vacated his conviction, citing to the "weakness of the case" against him, which relied on evidence the court of appeals later called "largely circumstantial and hardly overwhelming." Likewise, in the Ronald Cotton case, the state court also vacated the conviction, noting that the excluded evidence "tended to show that the same person committed all of the similar crimes in the neighborhood in question on that night and that the person was someone other than the defendant."

Thus, while many exonerees did not pursue factual claims and while very few obtained any relief on any claims, the subset who did receive reversals most often received reversals on claims regarding seriously erroneous or unreliable factual evidence at their trials.

* * *

4. Merits and Procedural Rulings. — This study next tracked the disposition for each claim raised at each stage: direct appeal, postconviction appeal, and federal habeas corpus. All told, 86% of the exonerees with written decisions during their appeals (115) ultimately had their claims denied. Analysis of these decisions sheds light on why this happened.

Courts typically denied relief on the merits, as opposed to denying relief based also or instead on procedural grounds, at least in the claims that they discussed. Certainly, many more procedurally defaulted claims were likely rejected summarily

Table 15.4: Guilt-Based Rulings During Review of Exonerees' Convictions

Type of Appellate or Postconviction Ruling	Percentage of the 133 with written decisions who received ruling (N)
Court referred to exonerees' guilt	50 (67)
Harmless error (total rulings)	32 (43)
Claim had merit, but error was harmless	16 (21)
Claim lacked merit, and error was harmless	14 (18)
Claim lacked merit, and there was no prejudice	13 (17)
Court referred to "overwhelming" evidence of guilt	10 (13)
Claim had merit, but no prejudice	2 (2)

or without any mention. By contrast, a court reached the merits of the case in 132 out of the 133 innocence group cases with reported decisions. Sixty-one exonerees (46%) had a court rule that a claim had merit, though for all but eighteen this ruling was reversed on appeal. In the present study, forty prisoners (30%) had at least one court during their appeals state that it relied on procedural grounds in reaching its decision. The chief reasons cited were procedural default (i.e., a failure to satisfy a procedural requirement in the state courts) and lack of exhaustion of state remedies. Most exonerees did not pursue federal habeas petitions, however, and the high rates of merits rulings may be explained by the fact that most pursued only the first round of direct appeals, in which there is less of a chance to procedurally default claims.

Each instance in which judges dissented during the various criminal appeals was also collected, since dissents indicate disagreement of sufficient strength to preclude a judge from joining the result reached. In the innocence group, thirty-three received dissents (25%). Nineteen of those dissents were dissents from rulings denying relief; these nineteen dissents also commented on the weakness of the prosecution's case. Other dissents commented on the merits of procedural claims, and six exonerees only received dissents from decisions in their favor, some of which commented on their guilt.

5. Guilt and Innocence Rulings. — When they ruled on the merits, the courts that ruled on these exonerees' claims frequently had to rule on the exonerees' perceived guilt or innocence. Over the past several decades, the Supreme Court has increasingly emphasized that our complex system for appeals serves to remedy the egregious miscarriages of justice in which an innocent person might have been wrongly convicted. In so doing, the Court has developed several methods for assessing guilt or innocence during appeals and postconviction proceedings. The innocence cases in this study suggest that the Court's framework may not serve its intended purpose of sorting the guilty from the innocent. The table above summarizes guilt-based rulings by courts in innocence cases; some exonerees received more than one type of ruling.

Starting with the least deferential test, quite a few exonerees who received rulings on the merits during their appeals had courts rule that errors at trial were harmless. Under the Chapman harmless error test, a court denies relief for a constitutional error if the State can show "beyond a reasonable doubt" that the constitutional error did not contribute to the guilty verdict at trial. Often courts did not explain why they deemed error to be harmless. However, when the State's case is strong, an error may be less likely to contribute to the outcome, and conversely, error may be more likely to affect the outcome when the State's case is weak. A harmless error ruling may also involve a judgment that the error would not have impacted the jury given outweighing evidence of guilt, though the Court has expressly cautioned against employing harmless error analysis in that improper fashion. Of exonerees with written decisions, 32% had a court rely on harmless error, and 16% had a court agree that a claim had merit, but nevertheless deny relief due to harmless error (this occurred for twenty-two of the sixty, or about one-third, for whom a court ruled that a claim had merit).

Other tests incorporate a more stringent harmless error standard into the structure of the right itself. The Strickland test provides an example: A trial attorney's provision of constitutionally ineffective assistance is not a constitutional violation if that performance did not "prejudice" the outcome, given the totality of the evidence admitted at trial. The *Brady v. Maryland* test incorporates the same standard, as do other due process claims. For only two defendants did a court rule that a claim with merit would be denied because the error lacked prejudice, though for 13%, lack of prejudice was part of the merits dismissal.

The remaining rows show how often courts referred to the likely guilt of the exoneree (in 50% of cases), typically by describing the reliability of the prosecution's case. The rows also show the subset of those cases in which courts were so sure of guilt that they called the evidence of guilt "overwhelming" (%). Statements regarding guilt provide additional evidence that judges rarely detected innocence. Some cases citing "overwhelming" evidence of guilt or harmless error are particularly instructive (and ironic) in retrospect. An example is the case of Larry Holdren, in which the Fourth Circuit found harmless the State's forensic expert's false hair comparison testimony, even after initial DNA testing excluded Holdren.

In the matched comparison group, fewer received such rulings: 26% had a court rule that error was harmless, 11% had a court rule that a claim had merit but error was harmless, and 9% had a court rule that a claim lacked merit and error was harmless. However, 8% had a court call the evidence of guilt "overwhelming."

In addition to judging evidence of guilt, courts may rule on evidence of innocence. Courts (typically only state courts) ask whether newly discovered evidence of innocence would have changed the outcome at trial. In limited circumstances federal courts also examine new evidence of innocence. Still other hybrid tests have both guilt and innocence prongs; for instance, the Brady test asks whether favorable evidence was suppressed by the State and whether, given other evidence of guilt in the case, that evidence was material. Added to these various constitutional tests, states

Table 15.5: Exonerees and Innocence Claims

Type of Claim	Percentage of 133 with written decisions who raised claim (N)	Percentage with claim granted and upheld on appeal (N)
Brady claim	16 (21)	1 (3)
State law newly discovered evidence	12 (16)	0 (0)
Herrera actual innocence claim	4 (5)	0 (0)
Schlup (habeas only)	0 (0)	0 (0)

have developed state constitutional law and statutory tests regarding relief based on newly discovered evidence of innocence.

Only thirty-three exonerees, or 25% of those with written decisions, raised innocence-related claims (*Brady*, *Schlup*, *Herrera*, or newly discovered evidence claims); several of those exonerees raised more than one innocence-related claim. Of those, three received vacaturs. These results are summarized in the table above.

Not one exoneree was granted a freestanding claim that they should be released based on newly discovered evidence of their innocence; only twenty asserted such innocence claims, or 15% of those with written decisions.

Only three exonerees out of the thirty-three who brought innocence-related claims had reversals granted, all on *Brady* claims. Again, though *Brady* claims do not provide relief expressly on the ground that the petitioner is innocent, they do relate closely to innocence. *Brady* claims require a showing that the prosecutor concealed from the defense material exculpatory evidence and a reasonable probability that suppressing the evidence of innocence prejudiced the outcome at trial. This study does not include a statistic regarding how many exonerees were convicted based in part on prosecutorial or police misconduct involving suppression of exculpatory evidence, because the number of known cases would be at best highly incomplete. The number may be far higher than just those who brought *Brady* claims, because improper concealment of evidence may often avoid detection even after an exoneration.

Directly asserting freestanding innocence claims, sixteen exonerees raised state law claims seeking a new trial based on newly discovered evidence of their innocence. None received relief during proceedings prior to obtaining DNA testing. Typically these claims require a reasonable probability that the newly discovered evidence would have changed the outcome at trial and, moreover, many include short statutes of limitation.

None raised *Schlup*, the "innocence gateway" that excuses procedural defaults of constitutional claims on the basis of newly discovered evidence. Under the *Schlup* standard, a petitioner must show a reasonable probability of innocence to obtain federal review of a constitutional claim in the face of a state procedural default. Prior to DNA testing, most exonerees likely did not have new evidence of their innocence to bring forward, and thus they could not assert a *Schlup* theory or a newly discovered evidence claim.

Five exonerees raised claims under *Herrera v. Collins* that their conviction should be vacated based solely on their actual innocence (4%), and none received relief. This comes as no surprise: No petitioner has ever received relief under a constitutional theory that they were actually innocent. The Supreme Court only hypothetically indicated in *Herrera* that a petitioner might receive relief in a capital case if he or she could provide a "truly persuasive" demonstration of innocence. The Court thus did not reach whether a freestanding actual innocence claim exists under the Constitution. Any actual innocence right remains so conjectural that the five innocent petitioners who raised such claims were denied relief. Only one of the twelve innocent capital petitioners brought, unsuccessfully, a Herrera claim that he was actually innocent.

These exonerees, lacking any means to claim innocence, did assert in large numbers sufficiency of the evidence claims governed by the Court's ruling in *Jackson v. Virginia*. In contrast to the thirty-two who raised innocence claims, sixty exonerees (45%) brought a Jackson claim, based not on allegations of new evidence of innocence, but rather based on a claim that there was not sufficient evidence presented during their trial to convict them. Such sufficiency claims sometimes highlighted unreliable factual evidence at trial, thereby providing a quasi-factual challenge, though one was based on the context of the entire trial record. In bringing a Jackson claim, a petitioner must show that, viewing the evidence in the light most favorable to the prosecution, no rational juror could find beyond a reasonable doubt that the prosecution proved the essential elements of the crime. Perhaps due to this stringent standard (though states have more relaxed sufficiency standards), only one of the exonerees received a reversal upheld on appeal.

Thus, the above shows just how difficult it remains to obtain relief on a claim of innocence, which explains why few of these actually innocent people raised such claims and why none succeeded. In addition to analyzing such claims, this study collected instances where courts made statements in their decisions that referred to the guilt or innocence of the exonerees, even if these statements were not necessarily connected to a particular claim. As noted earlier, sixty-three exonerees had statements referring to their perceived guilt (twelve courts noted "overwhelming" evidence of guilt). In contrast, courts only made statements that in a way correctly perceived the innocence of thirteen. That is, none of the statements directly asserted outright innocence in the way that judges frequently directly asserted outright guilt. Instead, judges found error to be prejudicial, and, in doing so, referred to the weakness of the prosecution's case. For nine of the eighteen who received reversals, a court referred to innocence in that manner. This is most likely because in order to reverse, judges must almost always find prejudice, and can more readily do so if the State's case is weak.

Exonerees did not frequently raise innocence claims, but, as described, legal avenues for claiming innocence remain extremely narrow. Absent a sound legal theory, simply raising a claim of innocence could signal their innocence, but raising a claim that lacked factual or legal support might negatively color judges' perceptions of their other claims. These exonerees may have felt that the claims were futile, which is borne out by the experience of those who raised innocence claims, none of which received any relief. In addition, state statutes of limitations restrict assertion of innocence claims. Moreover, prior to obtaining DNA evidence, most may have lacked any probative new evidence of innocence that could plausibly support an innocence claim; for some such evidence may have been concealed by law enforcement. Again, this group of known DNA exonerations does not include innocent convicts who obtained reversals without DNA testing, perhaps because some had substantial non-DNA evidence of their innocence.

In the matched comparison group, fewer raised innocence claims, just as fewer raised other claims. Nine raised *Brady* claims, or 7%. Two percent raised Herrera claims, state newly discovered evidence claims, and *Schlup* claims. Judges referred to innocence in three of the decisions that granted reversals in the matched comparison group.

6. Ineffective Assistance of Counsel. — Many states and localities have long provided inadequate indigent defense funding, with predictably persistent poor assistance of trial counsel as a result. The Supreme Court ruled in *Strickland v. Washington* that indigent defendants are constitutionally entitled to minimally effective representation. This representation, however, need only fall "within the wide range of reasonable professional assistance." Studies of postconviction filings show that ineffective assistance of counsel is the most commonly raised claim during appeals. The NCSC study found that 41% to 45% raised such claims. Only thirty-eight exonerees (29%) raised ineffective assistance of counsel claims.

The majority of the thirty-eight exonerees in the innocence group who raised ineffective assistance of counsel claims did not raise procedural errors by counsel. Instead, they presented claims based on ineffectiveness of counsel relating to important evidence introduced at trial, including failures to use blood evidence, to present alibi witnesses, and to challenge eyewitness identification or informant testimony. Of the thirty-eight, four received reversals of their convictions due to grossly ineffective representation of trial counsel. Ron Williamson's claim related to failure of trial counsel to develop evidence of his lack of mental competency and to the confession of another man. The other three, Paula Gray, William Rainge, and Dennis Williams, were all represented by the same lawyer, who was later disbarred in an unrelated matter. Rainge and Williams had their convictions reversed for ineffectiveness, including failure to move to suppress central physical evidence, such as hair evidence. Gray's reversal related instead to conflicts created by the joint representation.

To prevail on an ineffectiveness claim, a convict must show that the attorney's ineffectiveness materially prejudiced the outcome at trial, so that "there is a reasonable probability that, but for counsel's unprofessional errors, the result of the proceeding would have been different." In retrospect, however, some courts appear to have improperly conducted that inquiry in cases where ineffectiveness implicated areas of evidence that centrally supported the convictions. For example, the federal district court granted Willie Jackson relief because his trial lawyer failed to hire an expert to challenge the bite mark evidence central to his trial, finding prejudice where Jackson provided a strong showing of innocence, including that his brother confessed to the crime. Yet the Fifth Circuit reversed without an opinion in 1997, and in 2006 Jackson was exonerated when DNA testing excluded him and matched his brother. Ironically, four other exonerees specifically asserted the failure of trial counsel to request then-available DNA testing that would have proved innocence. One of the four, Anthony Hicks, received a reversal, but only after DNA testing had already excluded him.

While most of the ineffective assistance claims related to facts that the trial lawyer failed to develop or challenge, ten instead related to procedural ineffectiveness of counsel, including conflicts of interest and failures to make new trial motions. As noted in the previous section, for only two exonerees did the courts conclude that a claim had merit, but nevertheless denied relief due to lack of prejudice.

[In sum], during the exonerees' criminal appeals and postconviction proceedings, courts not only failed to effectively review factual claims relating to evidence supporting convictions, but also consistently denied relief on innocence claims. In contrast, they often ruled that exonerees appeared guilty. Moreover, exonerees and the rape and murder cases in the matched comparison group received a similar reversal rate of about 9%. Furthermore, the groups had similar rates of reversals based on claims of factual error.

Keith A. Findley, *Innocence Protection in the Appellate Process*
93 MARQ. L. REV. 591, 601–08 (2009)

Multiple explanations exist for the failure of the appellate process to protect innocence. Principal among these is the way that appellate courts are designed to operate in the United States. Appellate courts generally do not directly address fact-bound questions like guilt or innocence, or truth. For the most part, innocence is not a cognizable claim on appeal. Although innocence protection is the primary goal of the process, the system permits appeals to approach innocence protection only indirectly, by assessing whether the trial process, rather than the outcome, was error-free. If appellate courts vindicate actually innocent people on appeal, it is almost always by an indirect path.

Appellate courts pay extreme deference to trial-level fact finders on factual determinations and related questions like credibility. It is axiomatic that appellate courts do not decide facts, and will affirm a trial-level fact finder's factual conclusion if there is essentially any evidence in the record that supports a factual determination. More specifically, appellate courts defer to trial courts almost completely on ultimate factual questions regarding guilt and innocence. The due process standard for evaluating the sufficiency of a conviction under *Jackson v. Virginia* is itself a highly deferential standard. The Jackson standard permits appellate courts to acquit on the basis of legally insufficient evidence only if, taking the evidence in the light most favorable to the prosecution, there is insufficient evidence upon which a rational jury could find guilt. Although the Supreme Court in Jackson cautioned against equating this rule with a "no-evidence" standard, most courts have applied the standard so deferentially that in practice they uphold convictions unless there is essentially no evidence supporting an element of the crime.

Garrett's data on the DNA exoneration cases confirm that the Jackson standard is a weak protection against convicting the innocent. Of the actually innocent defendants in his study, 45% raised Jackson sufficiency-of-the-evidence claims, but only one of these innocent defendants obtained relief that was ultimately upheld on that basis. In every other case, the courts ultimately ruled that the evidence was legally sufficient to convict, even though the defendant was in fact innocent. Deferential fact review by design makes it difficult for an innocent defendant to prevail on a claim of innocence on appeal.

Professor William Stuntz has argued that procedural claims dominate postconviction and appellate practice in the United States because they are easier to litigate than fact-based claims of innocence. The latter require resource-intensive factual investigations, which are often not possible for resource-deprived providers of defense services to indigent criminal defendants. Professor Garrett agrees:

> Locating an alibi witness, obtaining experts to challenge forensic evidence or undermine eyewitness identifications, or presenting evidence of defendants' lack of capacity requires substantial resources and time. Where neither law enforcement nor defense counsel develop crucial facts, perhaps due to underfunding, reviewing courts may be placed in a difficult position, tasked with judging innocence based on an inadequate record.

Doctrine in other respects also makes it difficult to protect innocence on appeal. Appellate courts routinely avoid substantive review of potentially meritorious claims based on the defendant's failure to preserve the issue or make an adequate record.

Moreover, a number of legal doctrines encourage courts to overlook error, even when they find that it exists. Chief among them, of course, is harmless error. As discussed above, even when addressing cases in which the defendant was subsequently proved innocent by DNA testing, courts have frequently found the errors in their trials to be harmless beyond a reasonable doubt. Even more directly, other legal standards, such as the standard for ineffective assistance of counsel and for establishing a Brady violation, encourage courts to ignore possible impediments to accuracy by imposing on the defendant a burden of proving prejudice from the errors of defense counsel or the prosecutor. Again, Garrett's data confirm that doctrine imposes such a high burden that most defendants—even actually innocent defendants—cannot meet the burden. My own review of the data underlying Garrett's article, for example, reveals that 89% of the decisions rejecting ineffective assistance of counsel claims were based at least in part upon a finding that the defendant could not prove prejudice.

Doctrine governing the admissibility of potentially false evidence also contributes to the ineffectual response of appellate courts. For example, social science research has established that the factors the Supreme Court requires courts to consider when evaluating the reliability of eyewitness evidence are not in fact effective predictors of reliability and lead inevitably to the admission of significantly flawed identification evidence. Applying those flawed standards on appeal, courts are bound to reject the claims of actually innocent and misidentified defendants.

Supreme Court doctrine similarly fails to provide meaningful safeguards against false confessions. In *Colorado v. Connelly*,[84] the Supreme Court shifted the analysis under the Fifth Amendment's Self-Incrimination Clause away from any consideration of the reliability of a disputed confession. After Connelly, police coercion is all that matters, and the defendant must prove that police engaged in misconduct that rendered the confession involuntary. Considerations about reliability of the confession play no role in the analysis.

The Supreme Court has made it clear that no special rules govern the admissibility of jailhouse informant testimony, despite widespread recognition that such testimony is especially unreliable. Doctrine simply provides no adequate mechanism for screening against the most common types of false evidence.

Appellate courts are limited in their capacity to recognize evidence of innocence in another way as well: in almost every jurisdiction in the United States, there is no mechanism that ensures litigants a right to introduce new evidence of innocence during the direct appeal process. Appellate courts do not hear new evidence, and limit their review to the evidence in the record—that is, to the evidence introduced in the trial court proceedings. While most states have statutes permitting motions for a new trial based on newly discovered evidence, or permitting challenges to fact-based constitutional claims such as ineffective assistance or Brady claims, those proceedings are almost always collateral proceedings; they are not a part of the direct appeal process. As such, they usually come after the direct appeal, after the defendant has served significant time or even the full sentence in prison, and, most importantly, after the defendant no longer has a right to the assistance of counsel to present those claims. To the extent a claim of innocence requires evidence not already in the record, most appellate systems are not equipped to hear it, at least not as part of the direct appeal.

Innate cognitive distortions or biases add to the difficulty that appellate courts have in recognizing innocence. Confirmation bias, for example, leads people to seek, recall, and interpret information in a way that is consistent with preexisting theories or beliefs. On appeal, confirmation bias is likely to lead reviewing courts—which begin with the knowledge that the defendant has been found guilty beyond a reasonable doubt—to interpret information about the case in a manner that is consistent with that conclusion. In a related way, hindsight bias and outcome bias tend to lead people to believe that the eventual outcome of a situation was more likely, more inevitable, and even more correct than it really appeared at the outset. On appeal in a criminal case, these biases can make it more likely for a court to find harmless error, or a lack of prejudice in an ineffective counsel or Brady violation case, because the defendant's guilt looks more inevitable in hindsight than it might have actually appeared prior to trial. Research has confirmed that, indeed, judges (like all human beings) are susceptible to such biases. These biases are likely reflected in the many

---

84. 479 U.S. 157 (1986).

cases in which appellate courts have expressed confidence that the defendants before them were guilty, or that the evidence of guilt was "overwhelming," even where DNA later proved that the defendants were in fact innocent.

In addition to these innate cognitive distortions, political pressures make it difficult for courts to reverse convictions, especially in serious cases. No court wants to be responsible for releasing a defendant convicted of a serious crime and risk the fallout should the defendant commit another crime. The empirical evidence indicates that pressures to be "tough on crime" do have a significant impact on judges, especially in jurisdictions, like most, where the judges are elected.

Part of the problem with truth and innocence protection on appeal may be that courts simply believe they lack epistemological access to truth about innocence in the criminal justice system. Without epistemic access to truth, or any readily apparent way to apply standards and principles to the case-specific determinations about truth and veracity, appellate courts naturally prefer to defer to those deemed better positioned to make such judgments. Particularly in jury trial cases, it is comforting to defer to the unexplained and secretive jury decision-making process; it permits ascribing almost mystical truth-divining power to the jury. And it permits appellate courts to avoid dealing with slippery, hard-to-grasp questions of historical fact.

In this sense, it ultimately may be that accuracy and protecting against convicting the innocent are not really the paramount objectives of the appellate system. Rather, the ultimate goal may be simply to resolve the matter before the court. That is to say, it may be that, for the appellate process (and indeed the criminal justice system in general), finality, or "repose," is the most important objective. If so, that means that the perception of accuracy, produced by deference to the inaccessible jury deliberation process, is what really matters. Extreme deference to trial-level fact finders may reflect the belief that such deference creates confidence that the system is accurately determining guilt and innocence, regardless of whether it really is.

While this may be a powerful explanation for past deference, it is becoming increasingly less tenable as a justification. The innocence cases of the past two decades, and the DNA exonerations in particular, are piercing the perception of accuracy in the criminal justice system. Given the parade of exonerations generated by the Innocence Movement, the perception of accuracy is becoming increasingly difficult to maintain. The reality of accuracy is becoming more important than the mere perception engendered by extreme deference to trial-level fact finders. Searching inquiries into truth are, and likely will continue to be, increasingly important, not just as a matter of justice to the innocent, but also for protecting confidence in the process.

Todd E. Pettys, *Killing Roger Coleman: Habeas, Finality, and the Innocence Gap*

48 WM. & MARY L. REV. 2313 (2007)

On May 20, 1992, authorities at Virginia's Greensville Correctional Center executed Roger Keith Coleman. Ten years earlier, a Buchanan County jury had found Coleman guilty of raping and murdering Wanda McCoy, Coleman's sister-in-law. In the years between Coleman's conviction and execution, however, Coleman's attorneys and supporters had galvanized the nation by amassing an impressive body of evidence that raised significant doubts about Coleman's guilt. In its issue dated May 18, 1992, Time magazine placed a photograph of Coleman on its cover with the headline, "This Man Might Be Innocent; This Man Is Due To Die." Newsweek and The New Republic, ABC's Nightline and PrimeTime Live, NBC's Today, CNN's Larry King Live, the Donahue show, the Washington Post, the New York Times, USA Today, and numerous other media outlets featured Coleman's story, as well. Pope John Paul II and thousands of Americans urged Virginia's Governor L. Douglas Wilder to grant Coleman clemency, but Governor Wilder refused, based in part on Coleman's performance on a lie detector test administered the morning of his execution. As the hour of Coleman's death approached, fifty television cameras and more than a dozen satellite trucks, representing at least six different countries, were stationed outside the prison while the Fuji blimp hovered overhead. Having refused to address the merits of Coleman's federal habeas petition in 1991 because of a minor filing error Coleman's attorneys committed, the U.S. Supreme Court declined Coleman's request for a last-minute stay of execution. After Coleman was strapped into the electric chair, he spoke his final words: "An innocent man is going to be murdered tonight. When my innocence is proven, I hope Americans will realize the injustice of the death penalty as all other civilized countries have." Coleman was pronounced dead a few minutes later.

In the years following Coleman's execution, many insisted that Virginia had killed an innocent man. Kathleen Behan, one of Coleman's attorneys, predicted that "Roger's innocence [would] be proven" and that "his case [would] be remembered as 'the Dred Scott of death penalty law.'" Led by James McCloskey, Centurion Ministries worked tirelessly to prove that Coleman had neither raped nor murdered his sister-in-law. John C. Tucker, formerly a criminal defense attorney in Chicago, joined those investigating Coleman's claim of innocence, and in 1997 presented the group's findings in an engaging book titled May God Have Mercy: A True Story of Crime and Punishment. In his book, Tucker presented a painstaking review of the evidence and identified numerous problems with the Commonwealth's case. Following up on rumors that began to circulate even before Coleman was executed, Tucker also presented plausible reasons to suspect that the man responsible for McCoy's death might actually have been one of McCoy's next-door neighbors.

Long after Coleman was killed, Edward Blake — a forensic scientist who worked on Coleman's case — kept small samples of semen taken from McCoy's body following her murder. Blake hoped that DNA technology would one day permit a conclusive determination of Coleman's guilt. Once Blake reported in the summer of 2000 that the necessary technology was available, Coleman's supporters and a variety of media organizations tried to persuade Virginia officials to authorize new DNA tests to determine whether Coleman was wrongly convicted. Four newspapers — the Boston Globe, the Washington Post, the Virginian-Pilot, and the Richmond Times-Dispatch — filed a lawsuit seeking to compel the Commonwealth to approve a new round of DNA testing; but the state courts refused, holding that the media had no legal entitlement to have the tests performed. Those desiring the tests then turned their attention to Virginia's Governor Mark Warner, relentlessly urging him to intervene. Shortly before leaving office in early 2006, Governor Warner arranged for the tests to be performed by a DNA laboratory in Toronto. Coleman's supporters were thrilled, convinced that Coleman finally would be vindicated. Critics of capital punishment were equally elated, believing that conclusive proof of Coleman's wrongful execution would greatly bolster their efforts to abolish the death penalty.

On January 12, 2006, Virginia officials announced the results of the DNA tests: the odds that semen found in McCoy's body came from a man other than Coleman were approximately one in nineteen million. Coleman, in other words, was guilty.

Reactions to the DNA test results were immediate and intense. James McCloskey said that the news felt like "a kick in the stomach" and that he was "'mystified' that Coleman had allowed so many people to believe in his innocence." Tom Scott, one of Coleman's prosecutors, told reporters that he was "euphoric" and "felt like the weight of the entire world had been lifted from [his] shoulders." Peter Neufeld, cofounder of the Innocence Project, urged people to remember that confirmation of Coleman's guilt did not mean that all others facing execution were similarly guilty.

* * *

Trial in Grundy

On March 10, 1981, in Grundy, Virginia, a small coal-mining town on the western slopes of the Appalachian Mountains, Brad McCoy returned home from work at around 11:15 p.m. to find nineteen-year-old Wanda McCoy, his wife, murdered in their home. McCoy's throat had been cut, she had been stabbed twice in the chest, and she had been sexually assaulted. Investigators quickly focused their attention on twenty-two-year-old Roger Coleman, who lived less than two miles away, was married to McCoy's sixteen-year-old sister, and had been convicted of attempted rape several years earlier. Following a month-long investigation during which Coleman served as one of McCoy's pallbearers Coleman was arrested and charged with rape and capital murder. Two local attorneys, neither of whom had ever tried a murder case, were appointed to represent him.

The Commonwealth presented its case at Coleman's trial in the spring of 1982. The medical examiner testified that McCoy died around 10:30 p.m. One of the lead detectives testified that there were no signs of forced entry at McCoy's house, suggesting that the attacker was one of only a handful of men whom McCoy knew and would have allowed into her home late at night. Elmer Gist, Jr., a forensic scientist, testified that hairs found on McCoy's body were consistent with hairs taken from Coleman. Gist further testified that Coleman was a secretor with Type B blood, placing him in a small segment of the male population capable of producing the semen found at the scene. Gist also stated that small amounts of blood had been found on the pants Coleman was wearing the night of the murder, and that the blood was Type O, the same as McCoy's blood. Investigators told the jury that Coleman's pants had gotten wet on the bottom ten to twelve inches of each leg that night and that Slate Creek, near McCoy's home, measured approximately ten to twelve inches deep the following morning, suggesting that perhaps Coleman waded across the creek when approaching or fleeing McCoy's house. Other witnesses' testimony indicated that, on the night McCoy was killed, there was a period of more than half an hour, beginning at about 10:30 p.m., when Coleman had not been seen by others. The prosecution closed with the testimony of Roger Matney, a convicted felon who had been incarcerated with Coleman in the county jail. Matney testified that Coleman had told him that Coleman and another man sexually assaulted McCoy, and that the other man killed her.

Coleman testified in his own defense. In an effort to show that he did not have time to rape and murder his sister-in-law, he described his activities the night the crimes occurred. On Coleman's account, he went to a store at about 9:00 p.m., drove to work at a local coal mine, discovered that his shift had been canceled, talked with co-workers and then with a friend until 10:30 p.m., picked up an audio tape at another friend's house at 10:45 p.m. (a claim inconsistent with the testimony of the friend, who placed Coleman's brief visit at 10:20 p.m.), took a shower at 10:50 p.m. at a local bathhouse frequently used by coal miners, and then arrived home at 11:05 p.m. Coleman testified that he did not know why blood had been found on his pants, but speculated that it might have come from someone who had gotten cut while working with him at the coal mine or from someone who had been scratched by his cat. He said that his pants had probably gotten wet that night when he went to the bathhouse and put his clothes on the floor of the shower. He denied confessing his guilt to Matney.

It did not take the jury long to reach its verdict. After only three-and-a-half hours of deliberation, the jury declared Coleman guilty of rape and murder.

At the sentencing proceedings the following day, the prosecution worked to establish that Coleman was eligible for the death penalty both because he posed a continuing threat to society and because his crimes had been "outrageously or wantonly vile." With respect to the continuing threat that Coleman posed, a woman named Brenda Rife testified that Coleman attempted to rape her in April 1977; Rife's accusations had led to Coleman's conviction in July 1977 and Coleman had been sentenced to three years in prison. Coleman called two ministers to testify on his behalf, though neither man knew Coleman well. Coleman himself took the stand and said that his fate was now "up to the Lord." On March 19, less than twenty-four hours after finding Coleman guilty of the underlying charges, the jury returned with a recommendation that Coleman be executed. The trial judge accepted the jury's recommendation the following month. On direct appeal, the Supreme Court of Virginia affirmed Coleman's conviction and sentence.

Questioning the Evidence, Closing the Courts

The mere fact that Coleman insisted he was innocent certainly did not make his case unique. American prisons are full of individuals who claim they had nothing to do with the crimes of which they were convicted. Some of those individuals undoubtedly are telling the truth, but few of them win the same degree of national — indeed, international — attention that Coleman drew in the months leading up to his 1992 execution, and that he continued to draw in the years after his death.

Apart from the unflagging energies of those convinced of Coleman's innocence, two sets of forces helped to make Coleman's case so compelling. First, the facts underlying Coleman's claim of innocence were difficult to ignore. Second, many believed that the U.S. Supreme Court's rationale for refusing to hear the merits of Coleman's constitutional claims in 1991 represented an astonishingly inhumane departure from the norms that had animated the Court's habeas jurisprudence in earlier years.

A. The Case for Coleman's Innocence

Coleman's supporters based their belief in Coleman's innocence on several key pieces of evidence. First, even on the Commonwealth's own theory of the case, Coleman had less than forty-five minutes to visit a friend, drive to the McCoys' house, gain access to the home, rape and kill his sister-in-law, and then flee the scene before Brad McCoy arrived home after his shift ended a short distance away. As James McCloskey would remark after release of the damning DNA test results in January 2006, Coleman "had to be a ninja to do it."

Second, Coleman's ability to commit those crimes within such a narrow timeframe seemed even more unlikely once the pathologist who performed McCoy's autopsy revealed that McCoy had been subjected to both vaginal and anal intercourse, with semen found in both locations. It seemed probable that two men, rather than one, were responsible for McCoy's rape and murder. The Commonwealth, however, never presented any evidence that Coleman acted with another man. The two-assailant theory gained even more credence when DNA tests performed in 1990 — using DNA technology that was more sophisticated than the technology available at the time of Coleman's trial, but less sophisticated than the technology available today — indicated that sperm from two different men had been present in McCoy's body. Although the Commonwealth would later suggest that McCoy's husband was the second source, Coleman's supporters argued that it had been established earlier that Brad and Wanda had not had sexual relations in the days prior to her death. In the eyes of Coleman's advocates, the most plausible theory was that McCoy had been attacked by two men, not one.

Third, in the estimation of the trial judge, the evidence that had the most powerful effect on the jurors was Elmer Gist's testimony about the similarities between hairs found on McCoy and hairs taken from Coleman's body. Jurors had "exchanged glances and settled back in their seats" after Gist stated that it was "possible, but unlikely" that the hairs came from someone other than Coleman. Yet Coleman's attorneys failed to tell the jury about scientific studies indicating that such hair analyses were far from precise.

Fourth, with respect to Roger Matney's account of Coleman's alleged jailhouse confession, Matney's mother-in-law told Coleman's investigators that she had asked Matney about his testimony in Coleman's case. Matney reportedly replied by saying, "[i]f you use your head for something more than a hat rack, you can avoid a lot of jail time." When she asked Matney whether Coleman really had confessed to him, Matney reportedly stated that Coleman had not.

Fifth, Coleman's supporters made much of the fact that, in a report detailing his examination of the crime scene, the Commonwealth's lead detective indicated that he saw a "pry mark" on the molding around the house's front door. This was significant because it suggested that, contrary to the prosecution's theory, McCoy might not have known her attacker (or attackers). The detective later said that the mark easily could have been caused by something other than a man trying to force his way into the house. But if it was indeed a "pry mark," as the detective initially said that it was, this would help to undercut one of the Commonwealth's theories for focusing the investigation on Coleman in the first place—namely, that Coleman was one of the few men whom McCoy knew and would have welcomed into her home.

Finally, numerous pieces of evidence suggested that the man responsible for McCoy's rape and murder might have been Donald Ramey, who lived with his brother and parents in the house directly behind the McCoys. A woman named Teresa Horn told Coleman's team that Ramey attempted to sexually assault her in 1987 and that, during the attack, he threatened to "do [her] like he did that girl on Slate Creek." Another woman told investigators that Ramey sexually assaulted her in 1983. Yet another woman said that Ramey threatened her with a knife and tried to sexually assault her in 1982 or 1983. In the weeks prior to Coleman's execution, others told Coleman's investigators that Ramey had confessed to McCoy's murder. The day of Coleman's execution, a woman named Pat Daniels reported that Ramey's mother came to Daniels's hair salon soon after McCoy's death and said that, on the night of the crime, her sons and husband got into a terrible fight—the sons left the house and did not return until midnight, and when they finally came home, "she could feel 'murder in the air.' "

In short, the evidence of Coleman's innocence was far from negligible. Many feared that Virginia had sent an innocent man to his grave—a possibility made even more unpalatable by the reception Coleman received from the federal courts when he filed his first petition for habeas relief.

B. The Consequences of Appealing One Day Late

By any reasonable account, Coleman's inexperienced, court-appointed attorneys did a poor job of representing him at his trial. They did not prepare well for crucial motions; they failed to thoroughly investigate all of the available exculpatory evidence; they presented a remarkably weak opening statement; and their questioning of the witnesses was frequently unfocused and ineffective. The efforts of Coleman's trial attorneys, however, are not what made Coleman's case so notorious. Rather, the attorney-created problem that would draw so much public scrutiny occurred after Coleman began state post-conviction proceedings under the pro bono representation of attorneys from Arnold & Porter, one of the most prestigious firms in the nation.

In the fall of 1984, Coleman's new legal team filed papers in Buchanan County's circuit court, seeking state post-conviction relief on Coleman's behalf. They argued, among other things, that Coleman's trial attorneys failed to provide constitutionally adequate representation, that the Commonwealth breached its constitutional obligation to provide the defense with exculpatory evidence in its possession, and that the trial judge should have granted Coleman a change of venue. In an order signed on September 4, 1986, and formally entered into the court's records on September 9, the court denied Coleman's petition on the merits. The rules of the Supreme Court of Virginia gave Coleman thirty days to file his notice of appeal. Apparently calculating the filing deadline from the date the order was entered, rather than the date the order was signed, Coleman's attorneys placed the notice of appeal in the mail on October 6. The notice was received at the courthouse the following day.

The Commonwealth argued that the period for filing Coleman's notice of appeal began to run on September 4, that the thirtieth day after that date was October 4, a Saturday, and that the notice was thus due the following Monday, October 6. They reasoned that because the notice was not received until October 7, it was one day late. In the view of the Commonwealth's attorneys, Coleman had procedurally defaulted and his appeal had to be dismissed. In an unpublished opinion dated May 19, 1987, apparently agreeing with the Commonwealth's calculations, the Supreme Court of Virginia dismissed Coleman's appeal in a brief, three-paragraph opinion.

Innocuous though it might seem to a casual observer, the fact that Coleman filed his notice of appeal one day late would have tremendous consequences for his efforts to obtain habeas relief from the federal courts. If the federal judiciary had still been operating under the rules laid down by the Warren Court in *Fay v. Noia*,[85] Coleman would have had little to fear. In *Fay*, a New York prisoner convicted of murder claimed that his confession was coerced and that the trial court violated his federal due process rights when it admitted that confession into evidence. Because the prisoner did not file a timely appeal after his trial, however, New York's appellate courts refused to consider his federal constitutional claim. When New York officials argued that the prisoner's procedural default should also bar him from receiving federal habeas relief, the Supreme Court vehemently disagreed. After describing the "extraordinary prestige of the Great Writ" and its importance in British and American history, the Court broadly declared that a federal court's habeas jurisdiction "is not defeated by anything that may occur in the state court proceedings." Justice Brennan, writing for the majority, reasoned that "[s]urely no fair-minded person will contend that those who have been deprived of their liberty without due process of law ought nevertheless to languish in prison" simply because they inadvertently failed to obey a state's procedural rules. The Court explained that a procedural default in state proceedings could have adverse consequences for a federal habeas petitioner only when the petitioner himself or herself, and not merely his or her attorney, knew about the procedural rules' requirements and deliberately decided to ignore them. Even then, the Court held, the decision whether to dismiss the habeas petition would be committed to the discretion of the federal judge.

---

85. 372 U.S. 391 (1963).

Between the time *Fay* was decided in 1963 and the time Roger Coleman sought habeas relief in the late 1980s, the Court slowly chipped away at Fay by increasingly deferring to states' procedural rules.... In *Wainwright v. Sykes*, the Court[86] ... held that, if a prisoner failed to obey a state's contemporaneous-objection rule, which requires that evidentiary objections be made in a timely fashion at trial, then the prisoner ordinarily cannot obtain habeas relief based on that evidence's unlawful admission. While "leav[ing] for another day" the question of whether *Fay* remained good law for untimely appeals, the *Sykes* Court declared that, like the state procedural rule at issue in Francis, a state's "contemporaneous-objection rule ... deserves greater respect than *Fay* gives it, both for the fact that it is employed by a coordinate jurisdiction within the federal system and for the many interests which it serves in its own right."

Coleman's habeas petition required the Court to confront the question it had avoided in *Sykes*—namely, whether *Fay's* forgiving standard would continue to apply to prisoners who failed to file timely appeals during state proceedings. Coleman's habeas petition articulated eleven different claims, four of which Coleman's trial attorneys had properly raised on direct appeal, but seven of which (including, most notably, his claim that he received ineffective assistance of counsel at trial) he raised for the first time in state post-conviction proceedings—proceedings that now were clouded by his pro bono attorneys' failure to file a timely notice of appeal. Both the district court and the United States Court of Appeals for the Fourth Circuit refused to hear the seven claims Coleman raised for the first time in state post-conviction proceedings, holding that *Sykes*, rather than *Fay*, provided the governing law. "Even in a capital case," the Fourth Circuit wrote, "procedural default justifies a federal habeas court's refusal to address the merits of the defaulted claims."

Writing for the Court in *Coleman v. Thompson*,[87] Justice O'Connor opened with a sentence that could not have been more ominous for Coleman: "This is a case about federalism." The Court stated that, although the writ of habeas corpus is an important remedy for unlawful detentions, it also forces the states to incur "significant costs." Hoping to make those costs less onerous, the Court declared that the time had come to overrule *Fay* and adopt a new, overarching standard governing the availability of federal habeas relief in all cases involving procedural defaults in prior state proceedings:

> We now make it explicit: In all cases in which a state prisoner has defaulted his federal claims in state court pursuant to an independent and adequate state procedural rule, federal habeas review of the claims is barred unless the prisoner can demonstrate cause for the default and actual prejudice as a result of the alleged violation of federal law, or demonstrate that failure to consider the claims will result in a fundamental miscarriage of justice. *Fay* was based on a conception of federal/state relations that undervalued the importance of state procedural rules.... We now recognize the important interest in fi-

---

86. 433 U.S. 72 (1977).
87. 501 U.S. 722 (1991).

nality served by state procedural rules, and the significant harm to the States that results from the failure of federal courts to respect them.

The Court stated that an attorney's mistake in state post-conviction litigation — even if that mistake is grossly negligent — is not "cause" sufficient to excuse a procedural default. Even in capital cases, a prisoner is not constitutionally entitled to the assistance of an attorney in state post-conviction proceedings; consequently, the Court concluded, a prisoner seeking state post-conviction relief must personally bear the risk of attorney error. Although it would have been a long shot, Coleman's attorneys could have argued that the thirty-day rule was not an "adequate state procedural rule" because, as applied in Coleman's case — a case where Coleman had filed a document just one day late, under circumstances where calculating the filing deadline was possibly confusing and where the document was of a nature that the Court itself described as "purely ministerial" — the rule did not serve legitimate state interests. In their petition for certiorari, however, Coleman's attorneys did not question the state interests purportedly served by the rule's application to Coleman. Nor did Coleman's attorneys argue that refusing to hear Coleman's procedurally defaulted claims would result in a "fundamental miscarriage of justice." As a result, the Court held, Coleman was ineligible for habeas relief on each and every one of his seven procedurally defaulted claims.

Coleman's fate was sealed. As the day of his execution drew near, Coleman filed a second habeas petition, in which he argued that he was actually innocent of McCoy's rape and murder and that denying him habeas relief would thus result in a miscarriage of justice. Eight days before Coleman's execution, however, the district court dismissed Coleman's last-minute request, finding that he had not made "even a colorable showing of 'actual innocence.'" Six days later, the Fourth Circuit affirmed in an unpublished, two-paragraph opinion. Just minutes before Coleman was electrocuted, with Chief Justice Rehnquist and Justice Kennedy communicating from a late-night dinner with the President and others at the Canadian embassy, the Supreme Court denied Coleman's request that the Court stay his execution pending review of the Fourth Circuit's ruling.

The Court's dramatic rejection of *Fay*, in a case involving a document filed just one day late by a death-row inmate whom many feared was innocent, certainly did not escape notice. Justices Blackmun, Marshall, and Stevens filed a powerfully worded dissent, accusing their colleagues in the majority of continuing the Court's "crusade to erect petty procedural barriers in the path of any state prisoner seeking review of his federal constitutional claims" and of "creating a Byzantine morass of arbitrary, unnecessary, and unjustifiable impediments to the vindication of federal rights." In blistering editorials, the New York Times and the Boston Globe agreed. The Times called the ruling "bizarre," saying that it had "produced a terrible injustice" and was based on "a cramped distortion of federalism's scheme of justice under the Constitution." The Globe described the decision as "perverse[]," "cavalier[]," and "moral[ly] bankrupt[]"; it condemned the Court for "penaliz[ing Coleman] for a mistake of his lawyers"; and it concluded that "[t]he role of the federal courts as a last recourse in the nation's judicial system is contorted and diminished by the ruling." In its cover story two days before Coleman's execution, Time magazine stated that "the courts have so far failed Coleman miserably," that Coleman was "the victim of a justice system so bent on streamlining procedures and clearing dockets that the question of whether or not he actually murdered Wanda McCoy has become a subsidiary consideration," and that "the Supreme Court seems more concerned with finality than fairness."

The Court's actions also drew the attention of John Tucker. It was the Coleman decision that inspired him to investigate Coleman's claim of innocence and write the book that eventually would help persuade Virginia's Governor Warner to order new DNA tests in January 2006—tests that, to the astonishment of Coleman's advocates and the relief of Virginia officials, would confirm that Coleman had indeed raped and murdered Wanda McCoy twenty-five years earlier.

The Illusion of Finality in Cases of Suspected Innocence

A. The New Emphasis on Finality

When Roger Coleman's federal habeas petition prompted the Supreme Court to declare that it "now recognize[d] the important interest in finality served by state procedural rules," those who closely followed the Court's habeas rulings could not have been surprised. The writings of two men—Professor Paul M. Bator, of the Harvard Law School, and Judge Henry M. Friendly, of the United States Court of Appeals for the Second Circuit—had already begun to push the Court toward imposing new restrictions on the availability of federal habeas relief, with the aim of helping the states more rapidly achieve finality in their criminal cases.

In a 1963 article in the Harvard Law Review, Bator urged the Court to place the need for finality at the very heart of its habeas jurisprudence by sharply limiting prisoners' ability to relitigate issues that they were given a full and fair opportunity to litigate in prior state proceedings. Seven years later, in an article "draw[ing] heavily" from Bator's work, Friendly reemphasized the importance of finality and argued that, with only limited exceptions, the Court should restrict habeas relief to those prisoners who—in addition to raising meritorious constitutional claims—could make a "colorable claim of innocence." Believing that state prisoners were finding it too easy to drag the states through frivolous and repetitious federal habeas litigation, Bator and Friendly identified numerous reasons that federal courts should be reluctant to allow habeas petitioners to challenge their convictions or sentences after the completion of direct review. Achieving finality in criminal cases is necessary, they argued, in order to conserve scarce judicial resources; preserve the morale of state judges by assuring them that their decisions will not be second-guessed routinely by their federal counterparts; reinforce the deterrent function of the law by making it clear that violators will face prompt and certain punishment; bolster the rehabilitative function of incarceration by helping prisoners shift their focus from winning release to improving their own lives and conduct; ensure that a case's relevant facts are adjudicated at a time when events are still vivid in witnesses' memories; and permit citizens eventually to enjoy a sense of "[r]epose" in each criminal case prosecuted in their names—a sense "that we have tried hard enough and thus may take it that justice has been done."

* * *

When the Court declared in Coleman that it intended to show greater respect for states' procedural requirements and the desire for finality that animates those requirements, therefore, the Court was clearly in pursuit of an overarching, finality-driven reform agenda. The Court determined that Virginia's thirty-day deadline for filing notices of appeal was intended "to set a definite point of time when litigation should be at an end, unless within that time the prescribed [notice of appeal] has been made; and if it has not been, to advise prospective appellees that they are freed of the appellant's demands." If a prisoner could not show good cause for his failure to abide by the Commonwealth's rule, and if he could not demonstrate that failing to consider the merits of his constitutional claims would result in a fundamental miscarriage of justice, then the Court concluded that it should help the Commonwealth achieve finality by foreclosing the possibility of federal habeas relief.

Bator's and Friendly's arguments bore fruit in other cases as well, both in the same Term that the Court decided Coleman and in the years immediately thereafter.... In its 1993 ruling in *Herrera v. Collins*, the Court stated that "the need for finality in capital cases" should make the federal courts exceedingly reluctant to adjudicate a death row inmate's freestanding claim of actual innocence.

B. The Innocence Gap

1. The Elusiveness of Finality

No one can dispute that finality is a value that both the Court and Congress ought to consider when determining the conditions under which federal habeas relief will be available. Judicial resources are indeed scarce; the morale of state judges should not be needlessly undermined; the law's deterrent and rehabilitative functions are important; facts are optimally determined when the evidence is freshest; and the system serves a repose-seeking citizenry well when it gives citizens good cause to believe that the actors in a criminal case have done their best to do justice, and that the time has come to move on. For those cases in which the public believes it has reason to suspect the Court has convicted a prisoner of a crime he or she did not commit, however, the Court has done a poor job of shaping its habeas jurisprudence in a manner that will effectively secure finality and its benefits.

The Justices appear to believe that achieving finality in any given case is the almost inevitable consequence of foreclosing the possibility of federal habeas relief, and that one's only task when shaping habeas law is thus to determine how the need for finality stacks up against objectives that weigh in favor of making habeas relief available. If the Court believes that finality outweighs the competing values in a particular case, then it closes the doors of the federal courthouse; if it believes finality must give way to other concerns, then it leaves the doors open. In either case, the Court treats finality as the predictable result of refusing to consider the merits of a prisoner's federal habeas petition.

As the twenty-five-year story of Roger Coleman's case poignantly demonstrates, however, the Court has significantly overestimated the extent to which a rapid denial of habeas relief on procedural grounds can assure a state and its citizens of finality when there is reason to suspect that the prisoner might be innocent. When citizens have cause to question a prisoner's guilt, notwithstanding the prisoner's prior conviction by a jury of his or her peers, a genuine sense of repose is far more elusive than the Court has acknowledged, the deterrent and rehabilitative functions of the law are not easily advanced, and the state's financial and judicial resources may be repeatedly spent on litigation brought by organizations and individuals who are determined to come to the prisoner's aid. Indeed, far from securing finality and reinforcing a state's legal regime, the perceived moral authority of the criminal justice system is compromised, and the public's confidence in the courts tested, when judges refuse to consider a prisoner's legal claims notwithstanding the prisoner's presentation of significant evidence that he or she might actually be innocent.

In the final eight days of Coleman's life, both the district court and the Fourth Circuit quickly processed Coleman's final habeas petition, and the Supreme Court rejected his last-minute request for a stay of execution. Both the district court and the Supreme Court began their analyses by disparagingly noting that Coleman had already petitioned the courts for relief twelve times before. The courts' rapid-fire efforts to terminate Coleman's judicial proceedings, however, did little to bring a sense of closure to Coleman's case. If anything, the speed with which the courts disposed of Coleman's final arguments, and the courts' continued refusal to consider the merits of his claims, only fed the perception that a man whose constitutional rights may have been violated, and whose guilt remained in question, was being pushed relentlessly toward the electric chair, and the federal courts were refusing to do anything about it, based on his attorneys' minor filing error. The courts surely would have achieved a much greater sense of finality if they had simply agreed to adjudicate the merits of Coleman's constitutional claims. Federal adjudication of those claims would not have resolved the public's doubts about Coleman's guilt, but it would have addressed the public's fear that one of the chief reasons Coleman was on death row in the first place was that the Commonwealth of Virginia had violated his constitutional rights.

Not even Coleman's execution brought the sense of finality that the Court said it coveted on the Commonwealth's behalf. "Repose," in the sense that Bator and Friendly used the term, is hardly the word one would choose to describe the state of affairs as the hour of Coleman's electrocution drew near. To the contrary, the international media scrutiny of Coleman's conviction and execution, the investigations that for many years fueled fears that Virginia may have executed an innocent man, and the litigation and public appeals that eventually culminated in Governor Warner's decision to order a final round of DNA tests — twenty-five years after Wanda McCoy's death — all powerfully demonstrate that finality is exceptionally difficult to achieve in the face of reasonable suspicions of innocence. Genuine finality was not achieved in Coleman's case until January 2006, when new DNA tests showed that there was only a one-in-nineteen-million chance that semen recovered from the scene of McCoy's murder came from a man other than Roger Coleman, and the "weight of the entire world" was finally lifted from the shoulders of Coleman's prosecutors. If a conscientious forensic scientist had not insisted on keeping DNA samples long after the courts tried to put the case to rest, Grundy would continue to be the focus of rumors and suspicions today.

2. The Poorly Calibrated Miscarriage-of-Justice Exception

One might expect to find the tension between finality and suspected innocence resolved by the Court's repeated assurances that, when refusing to adjudicate a habeas petitioner's constitutional claims would result in a "fundamental miscarriage of justice," the Court will make an exception to its tough stance against prisoners' procedural failings. If properly framed and calibrated, the miscarriage-of-justice exception could ensure that procedural mistakes would not foreclose a merits-focused adjudication of a prisoner's constitutional claims when dismissing the prisoner's petition on procedural grounds would do little to advance the cause of finality. As it has taken shape over the past twenty years, however—first at the hands of the Court, and then more recently at the hands of Congress—the miscarriage-of-justice exception has become woefully inadequate to ensure that, when doubts about a prisoner's guilt will thwart finality, the federal courts will consider the merits of the prisoner's procedurally flawed habeas petition. In short, there is a sizable "innocence gap" today—a gap between the amount of exculpatory evidence sufficient to undermine finality and the amount sufficient to trigger the federal courts' willingness to forgive a prisoner's procedural mistakes and address the merits of his or her constitutional claims.

a. The Court's Original Formulation

In his influential 1970 article, Judge Friendly proposed that the Court restrict habeas relief to those prisoners who are able to make a "colorable claim of innocence." Elaborating only briefly on what he meant by that phrase, Friendly argued that, with limited exceptions, a habeas petitioner should be required to

> show a fair probability that, in light of all the evidence, including that alleged to have been illegally admitted (but with due regard to any unreliability of it) and evidence tenably claimed to have been wrongly excluded or to have become available only after the trial, the trier of the facts would have entertained a reasonable doubt of his guilt.

Friendly's proposal found its first stirrings of life in two decisions handed down by the Supreme Court on the same day in 1986. In *Kuhlmann v. Wilson*,[88] a plurality of the Court endorsed using Friendly's standard to identify those instances in which a prisoner would be permitted to bring a successive habeas petition seeking to relitigate a constitutional claim that had been adjudicated and rejected in prior federal habeas proceedings. The plurality believed that, in those circumstances, Friendly's standard would strike the appropriate balance between the state's interest in finality and the

---

88. 477 U.S. 436 (1986) (plurality opinion).

prisoner's interest in achieving "the ends of justice." In *Murray v. Carrier*, after focusing primarily on what might constitute "cause" sufficient to excuse a habeas petitioner's procedural default, the Court noted in dictum that there might be occasions in which it would agree to adjudicate a prisoner's procedurally defaulted claims even if the prisoner failed to justify his or her violation of the state's procedural rules. "[W]e think," the Court wrote, "that in an extraordinary case, where a constitutional violation has probably resulted in the conviction of one who is actually innocent, a federal habeas court may grant the writ even in the absence of a showing of cause for the procedural default." Friendly's formulation of the standard of proof, endorsed by the *Kuhlmann* plurality, appeared less demanding than the standard articulated in *Carrier*: Friendly spoke of a "colorable claim" and of a "fair probability," while *Carrier* spoke of an outright probability. Despite those differences, however, both *Kuhlmann* and *Carrier* signaled the Court's inclination to respond sensibly when confronted with doubts about a prisoner's guilt.

* * *

In *Schlup*, the Court explained that the miscarriage-of-justice exception should be cast in a manner that recognizes the states' strong interest in finality, while still ensuring that habeas relief remains available for those who are "truly deserving." The Court concluded that, although Sawyer would continue to apply to prisoners who claimed they were ineligible for the death penalty, "a somewhat less exacting standard of proof" would apply to prisoners who claimed they were innocent of any crime. Returning to the Court's dictum in *Carrier*, the Court held that, when a habeas petitioner seeks to avoid a procedural bar by claiming actual innocence, he or she must show that, in light of all the available evidence, "it is more likely than not that no reasonable juror would have found [the] petitioner guilty beyond a reasonable doubt."

* * *

To one who worries about the execution or incarceration of innocent people, the *Schlup* standard initially looks fairly appealing, especially when viewed against the backdrop of the far more stringent standard applied in *Sawyer*. Even under *Schlup*, however, there is a significant gap between the amount of exculpatory evidence sufficient to generate a profound sense of public discomfort with a prisoner's punishment and the amount sufficient to trigger the Court's willingness to forgive a prisoner's procedural failings and adjudicate the merits of his or her constitutional claims.

Consider, once again, the case of Roger Coleman. When presented with Coleman's second habeas petition just days before his scheduled execution, the district court was asked to determine whether Coleman qualified for an exception to the general ban on successive petitions. At that point, of course, neither *Sawyer* nor *Schlup* had been decided. After reviewing the opinions in *Kuhlmann* and *Carrier*, however, the district court concluded that Coleman was required to make "a colorable showing of 'actual innocence.'" The court did not say precisely what it understood that standard to require, but it is clear that the court was unimpressed by Coleman's evidence. The exculpatory evidence gathered by that point consisted primarily of Teresa Horn's claim that Donald Ramey had confessed to Wanda McCoy's murder; evidence that Roger Matney had lied when he testified regarding Coleman's alleged jailhouse confession; affidavits of experts raising questions regarding recent DNA tests and the second source of sperm found at the murder scene; and the pry mark that the lead detective originally reported seeing on the McCoys' door frame during his investigation. The court determined that "[a]ll of Coleman's evidence which he claims is new and shows his 'actual innocence' does nothing more than attack the credibility of witnesses and evidence at the original trial." The most that could be said about Coleman's evidence, the court concluded, was that if it had been presented at trial, the jury might have — but need not have — rendered a different verdict. The court declared itself "satisfied that no 'fundamental miscarriage of justice' is occurring." The Fourth Circuit summarily affirmed. While Coleman spent his final moments waiting to be placed into the electric chair, the Supreme Court refused to intervene.

Let us suppose that the district court would have reached precisely the same conclusion if it had had the benefit of the Supreme Court's clarifying ruling in *Schlup* — after all, if the district court believed Coleman's evidence was inadequate to make "a colorable showing of actual innocence," it surely would not have found the evidence sufficient to establish that it was "more likely than not that no reasonable juror would have found [Coleman] guilty beyond a reasonable doubt." The defects in the *Schlup* standard are revealed by the fact that the district court's refusal to consider Coleman's constitutional claims did precious little to advance the cause of finality. The media firestorm that accompanied Coleman's execution, the investigations that continued to stir up fears that Virginia had executed an innocent man, and the litigation and public appeals preceding Governor Warner's decision to authorize new DNA tests, all make it plain that the federal courts' procedure-focused handling of Coleman's case did not bring the desired sense of closure. Even in January 2006, doubts about Coleman's guilt and public discomfort with the way Coleman's case had been handled remained sufficiently strong to persuade Governor Warner to conduct a final round of tests in order, as he put it, to "follow the available facts to a more complete picture of guilt or innocence."

The miscarriage-of-justice exception's failure to help the courts achieve finality in Coleman's case should hardly be surprising. Suppose that the best a death row prisoner can show with new evidence is that there is a fifty-fifty chance that no reasonable juror would have convicted him. A federal court applying the *Schlup* standard would refuse to forgive any procedural defects that had saddled the prisoner's efforts to secure habeas relief, and would refuse to adjudicate the merits of the prisoner's constitutional claims. Yet a large segment of the public undoubtedly would feel profoundly disquieted if they believed there was a fifty-fifty chance that a person whose constitutional rights may have been violated, and who was about to be executed, was actually innocent of any crime. Indeed, the constitutional requirement that a person's guilt be proven at trial beyond a reasonable doubt is based, in part, on the need to assure the public that those who have been convicted are deserving of punishment:

[U]se of the reasonable-doubt standard is indispensable to command the respect and confidence of the community in applications of the criminal law.
It is critical that the moral force of the criminal law not be diluted by a standard of proof that leaves people in doubt whether innocent men are being
condemned.

The fact that doubts about a person's guilt arise after someone has been convicted
is a matter that, while historically of great significance to the legal profession, should
be expected to have comparatively little significance in the eyes of the public. Judges
have grown accustomed in criminal cases to viewing individuals through two very
different sets of lenses: one set for the pre-conviction period, during which a person
is entitled to a presumption of innocence, and another set for the post-conviction
period, after a person's guilt has been proven beyond a reasonable doubt and he or
she thus stands as guilty in the eyes of the law regardless of any new evidence that
comes to light. So far as the courts are concerned, a criminal trial is "a decisive and
portentous event" and "the paramount event for determining the guilt or innocence
of the defendant." The fact that the courts have found it necessary to compartmentalize
the legal status of individuals in this way, however, certainly does not mean that ordinary citizens are equally prepared to disregard newly discovered evidence that casts
doubt on the accuracy of a verdict. Indeed, when exculpatory evidence comes to light
following a conviction, it is only reasonable to expect the public to desire reassurance
that the prisoner's punishment is just. The author of the Time magazine cover story
published just two days before Coleman's execution surely was not voicing an anom-
alous view when she asked why the courts were in such a rush to terminate Coleman's
judicial proceedings: "[A]dditional time is not too much to ask," she wrote, "if there
is a reasonable doubt that he is guilty." Perhaps the public's discomfort need not
compel the federal courts to go into the business of re-adjudicating the guilt and innocence of state prisoners. But one should not be surprised to find citizens dissatisfied
when newly surfaced evidence creates a troubling measure of uncertainty about a
prisoner's guilt, and the federal courts refuse even to consider the prisoner's claim
that his or her basic constitutional rights were violated.

It is impossible to define the precise point at which exculpatory evidence becomes
sufficiently weighty to undermine the public's sense of finality about a case—though
it seems telling that Time's reporter felt disturbed by evidence that, in her judgment,
raised "a reasonable doubt" about Coleman's guilt. Yet one need not precisely identify
that threshold in order to learn a powerful lesson from Coleman's case: the gap between the amount of exculpatory evidence sufficient to undercut finality and the
amount sufficient to satisfy the Court's formulation of the miscarriage-of-justice exception is too large to permit the exception effectively to serve the purposes for which
it was intended. A miscarriage-of-justice exception that does not account for the public's response to newly discovered exculpatory evidence is poorly calculated to assure
the public that "the ends of justice" have been achieved and that habeas relief has
been extended to those who are "truly deserving." When doubts about a prisoner's
guilt are sufficiently strong to undercut finality, but insufficiently strong to satisfy

the miscarriage-of-justice exception, we will find ourselves confronted with the very kind of spectacle that we witnessed in Coleman's case. Specifically, in cases where doubts about a prisoner's guilt will plainly make finality highly elusive, we will nevertheless see courts blithely citing finality as the principal rationale for refusing to adjudicate the merits of a prisoner's constitutional claims.

* * *

Cases like Roger Coleman's do not come along every day. Few prisoners are able to attract the degree of national and international attention that Coleman drew in the months leading up to his execution, and few executions are second-guessed as persistently as Coleman's was until the results of new DNA tests were announced in January 2006. An unusual convergence of powerful forces made Coleman's case particularly newsworthy: the evidence of Coleman's innocence struck many observers as far from negligible; a young man who lived right next door to the victim was rumored to have confessed to the crime; Coleman eloquently maintained his innocence right until the moment of his electrocution; the Supreme Court used Coleman's case as the occasion for announcing a new level of respect for state procedural rules despite the fact that Coleman's procedural error seemed extraordinarily minor; a forensic scientist stubbornly insisted on preserving physical evidence until DNA technology would permit a conclusive determination of Coleman's guilt; and Coleman had the benefit of attorneys and supporters willing to devote tremendous energy to vindicating his claim of innocence, even long after his death. It is hardly surprising that Coleman's case proved so resistant to closure.

Even if a number of those extraordinary features had been absent, however, finality still would have been very difficult to achieve. Although the rest of the world undoubtedly would have shifted its attention elsewhere long ago, the town of Grundy would have remained the site of rumors and speculations long after Coleman's execution, with some insisting that Coleman was guilty and others insisting that the true murderer had escaped punishment and allowed Coleman to go to the electric chair in his place. Even absent the national spotlight, the dismissal of Coleman's habeas petition on procedural grounds would have sorely tested the Grundy community's confidence in the criminal justice system, and a genuine sense of repose would have arrived in that town only with the passing of many years. For a case to resist finality, one does not need the relentless attention of the national media. All one needs is a community that fears it has been the site of a gross miscarriage of justice. By adjudicating the merits of Coleman's procedurally defaulted constitutional claims, the federal courts admittedly would not have been able to resolve the ultimate question of Coleman's guilt. But merits-focused federal habeas proceedings would have bolstered the public's confidence that the courts had pursued justice the best that they could.

Finality in criminal cases is indisputably a worthy goal — criminal convictions should not be second-guessed without end. Procedural rules, moreover, have an important role to play in ensuring that criminal litigation proceeds steadily toward closure. Indeed, we adopt and enforce procedural rules to ensure that disputes are resolved in a manner that is fair, efficient, and ultimately worthy of respect. But when procedural requirements are so rigorously enforced that the public is given good cause to believe that courts ascribe greater value to procedural impeccability than to substantive justice, citizens justifiably lose confidence in the integrity of the criminal justice system. At that point, it is only the rhetoric—and not the reality—of finality that has triumphed.

B. Legal Materials, Exercises, and Media

1. *Discussion, ABA Prosecution and Defense Function Standards:* In response to the growing awareness of wrongful convictions, the American Bar Association in 2015 created expectations of both prosecutors and defense attorneys when new evidence or law undermines the reliability of a criminal conviction. The amended Prosecution and Defense Function Standards established that "[t]he prosecutor should not defend a conviction if the prosecutor believes the defendant is innocent or was wrongfully convicted, or that a miscarriage of justice associated with the conviction has occurred." Prosecution Standards § 3–8.1. Likewise, the defense attorney "has some duty to act. This duty applies even after counsel's representation is ended." Furthermore, "defense counsel should determine applicable deadlines for the effective use of such evidence or law, including federal habeas corpus deadlines, and timely act to preserve the client's rights." Defense Standards § 4–9.4.

    Are these standards sufficient to not only prompt disclosure to the court of evidence of innocence, but timely disclosure?

2. *Discussion, "Miscarriage of Justice":* Often, multi-factored injustice leads to a wrongful conviction. Newly discovered scientific evidence—such as the change in arson science or microscopic hair analysis—may not be sufficient to overturn a wrongful conviction when coupled with a false confession or mistaken eyewitness identification. The standard for a new trial is generally whether the newly discovered evidence alone would have changed the outcome of the trial. What if the standard of review for the court were a holistic review of all evidence and factors? What if the court considered instead whether the totality of the circumstances demonstrates a "miscarriage of justice" worthy of a new trial?

    The Massachusetts Supreme Court adopted "a substantial risk of a miscarriage of justice" standard in *Comm. v. Brescia*, 29 N.E.3d 837 (Mass. 2015). The new standard is discussed by Andrew Cohen in *The Weakest Link Standard: A Massachusetts Case Suggests a Different Way of Judging Evidence*, The Marshall Project (Aug. 8, 2017) https://www.themarshallproject.org/2017/08/08/the-weakest-link-standard.

Chapter Sixteen

Intersections: Race, Gender, Sexual Orientation, and Innocence

A. Readings

1. Race, Mass Incarceration, and Wrongful Convictions

National Registry of Exonerations Report on Race and Wrongful Convictions

(2017)

Drug Crimes

- The best national evidence on drug use shows that African Americans and whites use illegal drugs at about the same rate. Nonetheless, African Americans are about five times as likely to go to prison for drug possession as whites—and judging from exonerations, innocent black people are about 12 times more likely to be convicted of drug crimes than innocent white people.

- In general, very few ordinary, low-level drug convictions result in exoneration, regardless of innocence, because the stakes are too low. In Harris County, Texas, however, there have been 133 exonerations in ordinary drug possession cases in the last few years. These are cases in which defendants pled guilty, and were exonerated after routine lab tests showed they were not carrying illegal drugs. Sixty-two percent of the Harris County drug-crime guilty plea exonerees were African American in a county with 20% black residents.

- The main reason for this racial disproportion in convictions of innocent drug defendants is that police enforce drug laws more vigorously against African Americans than against members of the white majority, despite strong evidence that both groups use drugs at equivalent rates. African Americans are more frequently stopped, searched, arrested, and convicted—including in cases in which they are innocent. The extreme form of this practice is systematic racial profiling in drug-law enforcement.

- Since 1989, more than 1,800 defendants have been cleared in "group exonerations" that followed 15 large-scale police scandals in which officers systematically framed innocent defendants. The great majority were African-American defendants who were framed for drug crimes that never occurred. There are almost certainly many more such cases that remain hidden.

• Why do police officers who conduct these outrageous programs of framing innocent drug defendants concentrate on African Americans? The simple answer: Because that's what they do in *all* aspects of drug-law enforcement. Guilty or innocent, they always focus disproportionately on African Americans. Of the many costs that the War on Drugs inflicts on the black community, the practice of deliberately charging innocent defendants with fabricated crimes may be the most shameful.

* * *

Two of the best-known group exonerations illustrate the range of police behavior that produced these frame-ups:

• *Los Angeles, California, 1999–2000.* In 1999, authorities learned that for several years or longer, a group of officers in the Rampart division of the Los Angeles Police Department had routinely lied in arrest reports and testimony, and framed many innocent defendants by planting drugs or guns on them. On several occasions, they had shot and wounded unarmed suspects, and then planted guns on them. In the aftermath of this scandal, "approximately 156" criminal defendants had their convictions vacated and dismissed by Los Angeles County judges in late 1999 and 2000. The great majority were young Hispanic men who were believed to be gang members. Almost all pled guilty to false felony drug or gun charges.

• *Tulia, Texas, 2003.* In 1999 and 2000, 39 defendants, almost all of them black, were convicted of selling cocaine in Tulia, Texas, on the uncorroborated word of a corrupt undercover narcotics agent named Tom Coleman. In 2003, 35 of them — all who were technically eligible — were pardoned by the governor after a judge investigated the cases and concluded that Coleman had engaged in "blatant perjury" and was "the most devious ... law enforcement witness this court has witnessed. ..." The investigation revealed that Coleman had charged the defendants with selling quantities of highly diluted cocaine that he actually took from a personal drug stash. Two additional defendants were exonerated when their convictions were vacated and dismissed by courts. In 2005, Coleman was convicted of perjury.

Table 16.1 summarizes basic information on the group exonerations we know about. A short description of each of these scandals is included in the Appendix. One of the oldest — from Oaklyn, New Jersey, in 1991 — is an outlier: 155 convictions for driving under the influence of alcohol were dismissed because a single police officer faked the results of breathalyzer tests, and then stole money from the wallets and purses of the suspects he arrested. All of the rest consisted primarily or exclusively of bogus drug cases.

Table 16.1: Group Exonerations, 1995–2017

Place and Date	Number of Exonerated Defendants	Crimes Charged	Racial and Ethnic Identity of Defendants
Washington DC 1990	32	Drugs	Overwhelmingly Black
Oaklyn NJ 1995	155	Drunk driving	Unknown
Philadelphia PA 1995–1998	Approximately 230	Mostly drugs	Overwhelmingly Black
Los Angeles CA 1999–2000	Approximately 156	Mostly drugs & gun possession	Overwhelmingly Hispanic
Los Angeles CA 2001–2002	At least 10	Drugs	Overwhelmingly Black
Dallas TX 2002	6 to 15	Drugs	Overwhelmingly Hispanic
Oakland CA 2003	76	Mostly drugs	Overwhelmingly Black
Tulia TX 2003	37	Drugs	Overwhelmingly Black
Louisville KY 2004	Approximately 50	Mostly drugs	Overwhelmingly Black
Tulsa OK 2009–2012	At least 28	Mostly drugs	Unknown
Benton Harbor MI 2010–2012	At least 69	Mostly drugs	Overwhelmingly Black
Camden NJ 2010–2012	193	Mostly drugs	Overwhelmingly Black
Mansfield OH 2012	20	Drugs	Overwhelmingly Black
Philadelphia PA 2013–2016	812	Mostly Drugs	Overwhelmingly Black
East Cleveland OH 2016–2017	43	Drugs	Overwhelmingly Black
All Cases	At Least 1,840	Primarily Drug Charges	Primarily Black

Ian F. Haney Lopez, *White By Law: The Legal Construction of Race*

111, 118–19 (New York University Press, 1996)

Races are social products. It follows that legal institutions and practices, as essential components of our highly legalized society, have had a hand in the construction of race.

* * *

Almost every state with racially discriminatory legislation also established legal definitions of race. It is no accident that the first legal ban on interracial marriage, a 1705 Virginia act, also constituted the first statutory effort to define who was

Black. Regulating or criminalizing behavior in racial terms required legal definitions of race. Thus, in the years leading up to *Brown,* most states that made racial distinctions in their laws provided statutory racial definitions, almost always focusing on the boundaries of Black identity. Alabama and Arkansas defined anyone with one drop of "Negro" blood as Black; ... Missouri used a one-eighth test, as did Nebraska, North Carolina, and North Dakota; Oklahoma referred to "all persons of African descent," *adding that the "term 'white race' shall include all other persons";* Oregon promulgated a one-fourth rule; South Carolina had a one-eighth standard; Tennessee defined Blacks in terms of "mulattoes, mestizos, and their descendants, having any blood of the African race in their veins"; Texas used an "all persons of mixed blood descended from negro ancestry" standard; Utah law referred to mulattos, quadroons, or octoroons; and Virginia defined Blacks as those in whom there was "ascertainable any Negro blood" with not more than one-sixteenth Native American ancestry.

The very practice of legally defining Black identity demonstrates the social, rather than natural, basis of race. Moreover, these competing definitions demonstrate that the many laws that discriminated on the basis of race more often than not defined, and thus helped to create, the categories they claimed only to elucidate. In defining Black and White, statutory and case law assisted in fashioning the racial significance that by themselves drops of blood, ascertainable amounts, and fractions never could have. In the name of racially regulating behavior, laws *created* racial identities.

David Oshinsky, *Worse Than Slavery: Parchman Farm and the Ordeal of Jim Crow Justice*
56–57, 63, 71 (FREE PRESS, 1996)

When the Civil War ended, Southern officials found their battered jails crowded with convicts who had never been in custody before. The great majority of them, said the Tennessee board of prison directors, were "ignorant" former slaves who had stolen items worth a few dollars or less. They "have no more idea of criminality ... than a dumb beast that helps himself from his master's crib. It is plainly evident that a school of reformation or instruction is much more a fitting place for such uneducated unfortunates than a State Prison."

But the Tennessee legislature thought otherwise. Railroad fever was sweeping the state, and unskilled labor was in short supply. After little debate and much bribery, the legislators turned over the entire prison system to a professional card gambler named Thomas O'Conner for $150,000 on a five-year lease.

By 1871, state convicts were laying track and mining coal from Memphis to Knoxville. Each morning their urine was collected and sold to local tanneries by the barrel. When they died, their unclaimed bodies were purchased by the Medical School at Nashville for the students to practice on.

The advantages of convict labor were quickly perceived. When the Cincinnati Southern Railroad decided to run a trunk line over the Cumberland Mountains to

Chattanooga, it first hired gangs of Irish, Italian, and black workers at wages ranging from $1.25 to $3.50 a day. But free labor proved hard to manage, on and off the job. Some men, homesick and exhausted, wandered away. Others drank and brawled in the brothels and gambling dens that lined the mountain route.

So the railroad turned to convicts. Four hundred of them were leased from O'Conner at a daily rate of one dollar per man. Primitive log stockades were constructed, and local guards, sporting shot-guns, were hired to mete out punishment and prevent escapes. The convicts worked sixteen-hour shifts with a short break for meals. Completed in a single year, the Cumberland line came in well under budget, and the high quality of the work led some to call it the "best railroad yet built in the United States."

Convict leasing spread like wildfire. During the railroad boom of the 1870s and 1880s, convicts laid most of the 3,500 miles of new track in North Carolina. They were "mainly colored," a machinist recalled, and their crimes had been small. They would steal "two or three chickens," a jury would find them guilty, and the judge would sentence them to a few years in prison. Had they been white, he added, the maximum punishment would have been ninety days in the county jail.

* * *

The violent details of convict leasing varied from one location to another, but the larger themes of racial caste and cheap, steady labor were everywhere the same. In Alabama and Arkansas, Texas and Virginia, Florida and Georgia, North and South Carolina, Louisiana and Mississippi, the convict populations were overwhelmingly black. Of South Carolina's 431 state prisoners in 1880, only 25 were white; of Georgia's 1,200 state prisoners in that year, almost 1,100 were Negro. And the figures for Southern county convicts were roughly the same. In *Following the Colour Line,* journalist Ray Stannard Baker described his numerous visits to the local police courts of Georgia. "One thing impressed me especially," he wrote in 1908. "A (black man] brought in ... was punished much more severely than a white man arrested for the same offense. The injustice which the weak everywhere suffer — North and South — is in the South visited upon the negro."

The trends in Georgia mirrored prison changes throughout the South. Between 1870 and 1910, the convict population grew ten times faster than the general one. Prisoners became younger and blacker, and the length of their sentences soared. An investigation of Georgia's state convict population in 1882 showed "coloreds" serving "twice as long as whites for burglary and five times as long for larceny," the two most common crimes. Almost 50 percent of Georgia's convicts were under sentence of ten years or more, "although ten years," reformer George Washington Cable observed, "is the *utmost* length of time that a convict can be expected to remain alive in a Georgia penitentiary."

* * *

In many Florida counties, employers worked hand-in-glove with local officials to keep their camps well stocked with able-bodied blacks.

A journalist in 1907 described an all-too-common arrangement between a local sheriff and a turpentine operator in desperate need of men. "Together," he wrote, "they made up a list of some eighty negroes known to both as good husky fellows, capable of a fair day's work." The sheriff was promised five dollars plus expenses for each negro he "landed." Within three weeks, he had arrested all eighty of them "on various petty charges—gambling, disorderly conduct, assault, and the like. The larger part of the list was gathered with a dragnet at Saturday-night shindigs, and hailed to the local justice, who was in [on] the game."

Bryan Stevenson, *Just Mercy: A Story of Justice and Redemption*
23–24, 58–60 (RANDOM HOUSE, 2014)
http://bryanstevenson.com/see-the-stories/walter-mcmillian/

Walter McMillian was convicted and sentenced to death for the murder of a young white woman who worked as a clerk in a dry cleaning store in Monroeville, Alabama. There was no tangible evidence against Mr. McMillian. He was held on Death Row prior to being convicted and sentenced to death. His trial lasted only a day and a half. Three witnesses testified against Mr. McMillian and the jury ignored multiple alibi witnesses, who were black, who testified that he was at a church fish fry at the time of the crime. The trial judge overrode the jury's sentencing verdict for life without parole and sentenced Mr. McMillian to death.

Bryan Stevenson took on Mr. McMillian's case in post-conviction, where he showed that the State's witnesses had lied on the stand and the prosecution had illegally suppressed exculpatory evidence. Mr. McMillian's conviction was overturned by the Alabama Court of Criminal Appeals in 1993 and prosecutors agreed the case had been mishandled. Walter McMillian was released in March 1993 after spending six years on death row for a crime he did not commit.

* * *

Even though he had lived in Monroe County his whole life, Walter McMillian had never heard of Harper Lee or To Kill a Mockingbird. Monroeville, Alabama, celebrated its native daughter Lee shamelessly after her award-winning book became a national bestseller in the 1960s....

Sentimentality about Lee's story grew even as the harder truths of the book took no root. The story of an innocent black man bravely defended by a white lawyer in the 1930s fascinated millions of readers, despite its uncomfortable exploration of false accusations of rape involving a white woman. Lee's endearing characters, Atticus Finch and his precocious daughter, Scout, captivated readers while confronting them with some of the realities of race and justice in the South. A generation of future lawyers grew up hoping to become the courageous Atticus, who at one point arms himself to protect the defenseless black suspect from an angry mob of white men looking to lynch him.

Today, dozens of legal organizations hand out awards in the fictional lawyer's name to celebrate the model of advocacy described in Lee's novel. What is often overlooked is that the black man falsely accused in the story was not *successfully* defended by Atticus. Tom Robinson, the wrongly accused black defendant, is found guilty. Later he dies when, full of despair, he makes a desperate attempt to escape from prison. He is shot seventeen times in the back by his captors, dying ingloriously but not unlawfully.

* * *

In 1987, all forty elected district attorneys in Alabama were white, even though there are sixteen majority-black counties in the state. When African Americans began to exercise their right to vote in the 1970s, there was deep concern among some prosecutors and judges about how the racial demographics in some counties would complicate their reelections. Legislators had aligned counties to maintain white majorities for judicial circuits that included a majority-black county. Still, Pearson [the prosecutor] had to be more mindful of the concerns of black residents than at the beginning of his career — even if that mindfulness didn't translate into any substantive changes during his tenure.

Like Tate, Pearson had heard from many black residents that they believed Walter McMillian was innocent. But Pearson was confident he could win a guilty verdict despite the suspect testimony of Ralph Myers and Bill Hooks and the strong doubts in the black community. His one lingering concern may have been a recent United States Supreme Court case [*Batson v. Kentucky* (1986)] that threatened a longstanding feature of high-profile criminal trials in the South: the all-white jury.

When a serious felony case went to trial in a county like Monroe County, which was 40 percent black, it was not uncommon for prosecutors to exclude all African Americans from jury service. In fact, twenty years after the civil rights revolution, the jury remained an institution largely unchanged by the legal requirements of racial integration and diversity. As far back as the 1880s, the Supreme Court ruled in *Strauder v. West Virginia* that excluding black people from jury service was unconstitutional, but juries remained all-white for decades afterward. In 1945, the Supreme Court upheld a Texas statute that limited the number of black jurors to exactly one per case. In Deep South states, jury rolls were pulled from voting rolls, which excluded African Americans. After the Voting Rights Act passed, court clerks and judges still kept the jury rolls mostly white through various tactics designed to undermine the law. Local jury commissions used statutory requirements that jurors be "intelligent and upright" to exclude African Americans and women....

So defendants like Walter McMillian, even in counties that were 40 or 50 percent black, frequently found themselves staring at all-white juries, especially in death penalty cases.

L. Song Richardson, *Systemic Triage: Implicit Racial Bias in the Criminal Courtroom*
126 Yale L.J. 862, 882 (2017)

Research demonstrates that many of our decisions result from mental processes that occur without our conscious awareness, intent, and control. These processes help us to cope with all the information that confronts us by making quick, automatic, and unconscious associations in response to a stimulus. For instance, we might automatically and unconsciously associate "nurse" with "compassion" and "hospital." These unconscious associations can influence our perceptions, judgments, and behaviors without our conscious intent.

Implicit racial biases refer to the unconscious stereotypes and attitudes that we associate with racial groups. These biases are pervasive and can influence real world behaviors. For instance, a meta-analysis of 122 implicit bias studies found evidence that implicit racial biases predict racial disparities in employment and healthcare.

There is copious evidence that individuals of all races have implicit racial biases linking blacks with criminality and whites with innocence.

* * *

Implicit racial biases can affect decision making in ways that create and sustain problematic racial disparities. For instance, these biases can cause people to interpret ambiguous information in racially disparate ways. In one study demonstrating this, mock jurors were asked to evaluate evidence that was ambiguous as to guilt or innocence. The results showed that as a result of implicit racial biases, jurors were significantly more likely to conclude that the evidence was probative of guilt when the case involved a dark-skinned perpetrator versus a light-skinned perpetrator. In another study involving an assault, mock jurors were more likely to conclude that the defendant was less aggressive and "more honest and moral" when he was white as opposed to black. These differences in judgment were correlated with implicit bias.

Michelle Alexander, *The New Jim Crow: Mass Incarceration in the Age of Colorblindness*
175–76, 184 (THE NEW PRESS, 2012)

When the system of mass incarceration collapses (and if history is any guide, it will), historians will undoubtedly look back and marvel that such an extraordinarily comprehensive system of racialized social control existed in the United States. How fascinating, they will likely say, that a drug war was waged almost exclusively against poor people of color—people already trapped in ghettos that lacked jobs and decent schools. They were rounded up by the millions, packed away in prisons, and when released, they were stigmatized for life, denied the right to vote, and ushered into a world of discrimination. Legally barred from employment, housing, and welfare benefits—and saddled with thousands of dollars of debt—these people were shamed and condemned for failing to hold together their families. They were chastised for succumbing to depression and anger, and blamed for landing back in prison. Historians will likely wonder how we could describe the new caste system as a system of crime control, when it is difficult to imagine a system better designed to create—rather than prevent—crime.

* * *

The unfortunate reality we must face is that racism manifests itself not only in individual attitudes and stereotypes, but also in the basic structure of society. Academics have developed complicated theories and obscure jargon in an effort to describe what is now referred to as *structural racism,* yet the concept is fairly straightforward. One theorist, Iris Marion Young, relying on a famous "birdcage" metaphor, explains it this way: If one thinks about racism by examining only one wire of the cage, or one form or disadvantage, it is difficult to understand how and why the bird is trapped. Only a large number of wires arranged in a specific way, and connected to one another serve to enclose the bird and to ensure that it cannot escape.

What is particularly important to keep in mind is that any given wire of the cage may or may not be specifically developed for the purpose of trapping the bird, yet it still operates (together with the other wires) to restrict its freedom. By the same token, not every aspect of a racial caste system needs to be developed for the specific purpose of controlling black people in order for it to operate (together with other laws, institutions, and practices) to trap them at the bottom of a racial hierarchy. In the system of mass incarceration, a wide variety of laws, institutions, and practices—ranging from racial profiling to biased sentencing policies, political disenfranchisement, and legalized employment discrimination—trap African Americans in a virtual (and literal) cage.

Fortunately, as Marilyn Frye has noted, every birdcage has a door, and every birdcage can be broken and can corrode.

Figure 16.1

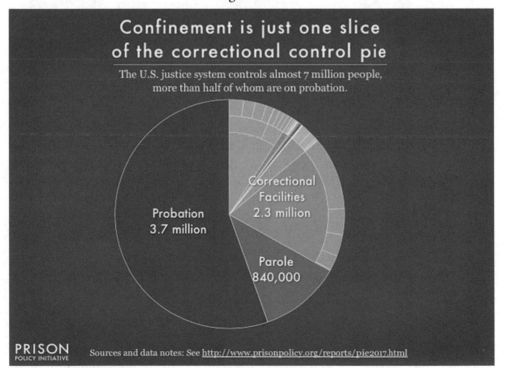

Source: The Prison Policy Initiative

Figure 16.2

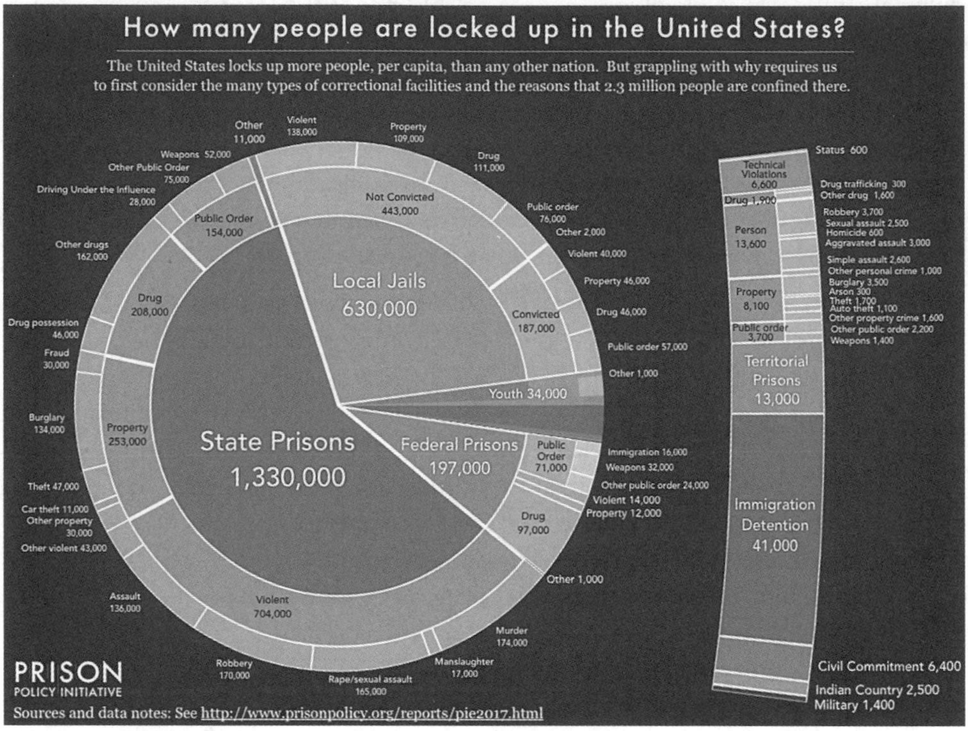

Source: The Prison Policy Initiative

2. Sexual Orientation and the Criminal Justice System

Trial of Kerry Max Cook, Prosecutor's Closing Argument:

> You people have no right to even submit prison guards to the kind of risk that man poses. Think about it. Do you want to give this pervert this butcher knife back? Now, we must look upon it as putting a sick animal to sleep. Kerry Max Cook has forfeited his right to walk among us. He no longer has rights. So let's let all the freaks and perverts and murderous homosexuals of the world know what we do with them in a court of justice. That we take their lives.

Excerpt from *The Exonerated*, a play by Jessica Blank and Erik Jensen 42 (Faber & Faber, 2004).

Joey Mogul, Andrea Ritchie, and Kay Whitlock, *Queer (In)Justice: The Criminalization of LGBT People in the United States*
69–70, xi, xii, (BEACON PRESS, 2012)

"Crime" as a Social Construction

Laws typically define crime in ways that many people take to be neutral, unambiguous, and reflective of widespread social consensus.... The very definition of crime is socially constructed, the result of inherently political processes that reflect consensus only among those who control or wield significant influence.... In reality, crime is never evenhandedly policed and punished. In the United States, as Angela Y. Davis observes, "race has always played a central role in constructing presumptions of criminality." Laws surrounding the abolition of slavery illuminate the ways in which penal provisions purportedly enacted to provide for public safety were no more than thinly veiled efforts to designate particular groups of people as presumptively criminal. In the 1860s, immediately following the abolition of slavery, former slaveholding states produced new sets of laws, known collectively as the Black Codes, which criminalized Black people for engaging in a host of ordinary actions that were legal for white people. Upon conviction, thousands of African-descended people were imprisoned and required to perform forced labor for white business owners.... [T]he rape of a Black woman was not a crime under most slave codes, or common law. Conversely, the rape of a white woman by a Black man could be punishable by castration or death, while commission of the same crime by a white man could lead to incarceration for ten to twenty years, a whipping, or both.

As Salish sociologist Luana Ross argues, the construction of crime was also a tool of colonization and control of Native American peoples. For example, a mid-nineteenth-century California law provided that any Indian who loitered or "strolled about" could be arrested on the complaint of any white citizen. Within twenty-four hours the court was required to hire out those arrested to the highest bidder for a period of up to four months, providing free labor to private interests. In 1883, an extensive listing of offenses by the U.S. Commissioner of Indian Affairs criminalized the practices of traditional medicine people and Native dances that might stir "the warlike passions of the young members of the tribes."

* * *

Mass incarceration is neither a reflection of violence run amok, nor an indication that certain populations are naturally prone to crime. It is deeply rooted in the history and maintenance of racial power relations, and its racially disproportionate impacts are profound.... More than 60 percent of prisoners, and two-thirds of people serving life sentences, are people of color. Women are now being incarcerated at almost twice the rate of men; Black and Latina women are approximately three times more likely to be incarcerated than white women. Native women also experience disproportionate rates of incarceration: for example, in Montana in 2008, Native women made up slightly more than 27 percent of women incarcerated in state prison, but only 7 percent of the population. Poverty also plays a critical role in determining access to justice.

Although there is currently no data on incarcerated LGBT people, what information is available suggests that transgender and gender nonconforming people are disproportionately ensnared in the criminal legal system....

* * *

In May 1988, Rene Chinea, a fifty-year-old gay Cuban immigrant, was murdered in Chicago, Illinois. His throat was slashed, his penis and hands cut off, and his legs partially severed. His decomposing and dismembered body was found in a garbage bag inside his closet. The Chicago police detectives who investigated the homicide determined Chinea was the victim of a "homosexual murder." In so doing, they were not suggesting that Chinea was the victim of violence motivated by his sexual orientation, that is, a hate crime. Rather, they believed that this grisly murder must have been committed by another "homosexual." This belief was based on the premise that gay men who are lovers or roommates are "particularly violent" when they fight, often engaging in "gruesome-type, serious cuttings," and it shaped the investigation from the moment police responded to the scene.

Eight months later, Miguel Castillo, a thirty-seven-year-old Cuban immigrant, was charged with Chinea's murder. Despite overwhelming evidence of his innocence—most notably the fact that he was in jail at the time the crime was committed—Castillo was nevertheless convicted on the basis of an alleged "confession" that appears to have been manufactured in its entirety by three Chicago police officers to support their theory. Castillo was sentenced to forty-eight years in prison. He spent eleven and a half years behind bars before he was exonerated on the basis of innocence, and later successfully sued the Chicago Police Department for wrongful conviction.

Castillo's case demonstrates how far police perceptions, informed by queer criminal archetypes, can drive investigations and prosecutions. In this instance, controlling images of queers—and particularly queers of color—as emotionally stunted, mentally unstable, and prone to commit acts of violence, permeated the case throughout.

* * *

A Spanish conquistador throws dozens of Indigenous people accused of engaging in sodomy to his hunting dogs. Almost five centuries later, a South Asian migrant worker is convicted of engaging in sodomy with a white man, who goes free. In 2006, seven Black lesbian friends, walking home one night through a well-known "gayborhood," are assaulted by a man who threatens to rape one of them "straight." They defend themselves, only to be characterized by the media as a "lesbian wolf pack" and sentenced to up to eleven years in prison. An innocent Latino man spends eleven years behind bars for what police describe as a "homosexual murder" in 1988. Ten years later a Latina woman ends up on death row after the prosecutor argues she is a "hardcore lesbian." At the turn of the twenty-first century, a white gay man is put to death after a prosecutor urges a jury to consider that they are sitting in judgment of an "avowed homosexual." A Black gay man who is repeatedly raped in prison is denied protection from prison officials because he is thought to enjoy it. A club frequented primarily by African American LGBT people is raided; 350 people are handcuffed and detained for up to twelve hours, only to be charged with "loitering inside a building." In 2008, a Black transgender woman is profiled as engaging in sex work, arrested, called "faggot" and "he/she," and savagely beaten by police officers in a public booking area, in full view of a video camera. Her subsequent murder remains unsolved. These are but a few of the many faces of queer injustice in the United States.

Jordan Blair Woods, *LGBT Identity and Crime*
105 Cal. L. Rev. 667, 674, 681, 684 (2017)

Until the mid-nineteenth century, homosexuality was viewed as a series of abominable acts, as opposed to a feature of individual identity. As historian Jonathan Katz explains, the words "heterosexual" and "homosexual" did not even exist in the United States until 1892. The view that homosexuality was a feature of individual identity gained force during the second half of the nineteenth century. As Michel Foucault described, the homosexual "became a personage, a past, a case-history, and a childhood."

[Thus] [a]t the time when our earliest scientific and empirical theories of crime were advanced, homosexuality was not simply viewed as a series of deviant acts; rather, homosexuals were a distinct class of offenders defined by their perceived deviant sexual pathology....

Until the mid-1970s — before which same-sex sodomy was criminalized in almost every U.S. state — there was little space to view LGBT people in the criminal justice system other than as deviant sexual offenders. A wave of sodomy decriminalization in the mid-1970s opened a narrow window for scholars, advocates, and policymakers in the 1980s and 1990s to use anti-discrimination principles to move discussions about LGBT identity and crime away from viewing LGBT people as deviant sexual offenders towards viewing them as innocent and non-deviant hate crime victims.

Queer Criminal Archetypes,
excerpt from *Queer (In)Justice*
at 23–24, 12, 73

The specter of criminality moves ceaselessly through the lives of LGBT people in the United States. It is the enduring product of persistent melding of homosexuality and gender nonconformity with concepts of *danger, degeneracy, disorder, deception, disease, contagion, sexual predation, depravity, subversion, encroachment, treachery,* and *violence....*

Over time, within broader notions of criminality informed by race, class, and gender, a number of closely related and mutually reinforcing "queer criminal archetypes" have evolved that directly influence the many manifestations and locations of policing and punishment of people identified as queer or living outside of "appropriately gendered" heterosexual norms. These archetypes serve to establish compelling, ultimately controlling, narratives, or predetermined story lines that shape how a person's appearance and behavior will be interpreted — regardless of individual circumstances or realities. Written and rewritten across time, space, and the evolution of queer identities, these archetypal narratives may be best understood as means to criminalize queerness. Based on these established criminalizing narratives or scripts, queer people are targeted for policing and punishment regardless of whether they have actually committed any crime or done any harm. Queer criminal archetypes rarely operate in isolation, frequently intersecting and overlapping with other controlling narratives that frame people of color, immigrants, and poor people as inherently criminal.

* * *

Close scrutiny of the nation's courts reveals a judicial system rife with anti-LGBT bias. Within it, discriminatory laws are enforced, queers are often treated with derision, if not outright contempt, and queer criminalizing archetypes are deployed in full force. . . .

Sumptuary and vagrancy laws served to criminalize people who transgressed gender norms. The law in Chicago, Illinois, forbade "appear[ing] in a public place in a state of nudity, or in a dress not belonging to his or her sex," while a Toledo, Ohio, law made it illegal for any "perverted person" to appear in clothing belonging to "the opposite" sex. In New York, an appeals court upheld Mauricio Archibald's conviction in 1968 for being a "vagrant" "who ... [had] his face painted, discolored, covered or concealed, or being otherwise disguised, in a manner calculated to prevent his being identified." After appearing in a subway station wearing a white evening dress, high-heeled shoes, a blond wig, women's undergarments, and facial makeup, Archibald was found guilty, despite being neither unemployed nor homeless. The court found the crime to be one of "conceal[ing] his [sic] true gender," although Archibald's true transgression may have been winking at the officer. As another court declared, "cross-dressing" must be punished because "the desire of concealment of a change of sex by the transsexual is outweighed by the public interest for protection against fraud."

According to sexuality scholar Katherine Franke, "Butch lesbians experienced the weight of these rules every day during the 1950s when police would arrest them if they could not prove that they were wearing at least three pieces of women's clothing." As Leslie Feinberg, author of *Stone Butch Blues,* put it, "The reality of why I was arrested was as cold as the cell's cement floor: I am considered a masculine female. That's a *gender* violation." Poet and activist Audre Lorde reported her own experience in New York City in that era: "There were always rumors of plainclothes women circulating among us, looking for gay-girls with fewer than three pieces of female attire." Such practices continued into the 1960s and 1970s. . . .

Carrie L. Buist and Emily Lenning, *Queer Criminology: New Directions in Critical Criminology*
76–77 (Routledge, Taylor & Francis Group, 2016)

The biases and discrimination that Queer people face in larger society follow them into the courtroom, especially if they are facing charges for sexual offenses. Queer sex offenders are often overcharged and consequently, accept unfair plea deals. Prosecutorial discretion is especially problematic for Queer youth who find themselves charged with statutory rape because they are not extended the "Romeo and Juliet" exception afforded to heterosexual youth by most states.

The "Romeo and Juliet" exception is when the defendant and the victim are close in age, engaged in clearly consensual sex, and are perceived to be committed to one another—some states actually define a range of age differences that would be deemed acceptable in this sort of situation. The problem is that prosecutors are less likely to perceive Queer youth to be in "appropriate" committed relationships, and the legally defined age ranges often exclude same-sex encounters. Texas, Alabama, and California all have age range exceptions for statutory rape, but all of them explicitly apply to heterosexual youth only, meaning that Queer youth face harsher punishment for engaging in the same behaviors as their heterosexual peers....

A striking example of this is the Kansas case involving Matthew Limon, a developmentally disabled 18-year-old. While attending a residential school for the developmentally disabled, Limon had consensual oral sex with a young man who was 15—just over three years younger than him. In Kansas, the Roman and Juliet law can reduce the severity of punishment in cases of consensual sex where the victim is between 14 and 16 years old, the offender is under the age of 19, the victim and offender have no more than a four year age gap, and the victim and offender "are members of the opposite sex." Because the Romeo and Juliet law didn't apply to Limon's case solely because of the "opposite sex" distinction, he was convicted of sodomy and sentenced to 17 years and two months in prison and ordered to register as a sex offender. Had he engaged in heterosexual sex and thus able to use the Romeo and Juliet law, Limon would have served approximately 15 months for his crime and would have avoided the stigma of registering as a sex offender altogether.

Affidavit of Professor of Law and University Distinguished Professor Ruthann Robson

Robson's affidavit was submitted in the post-conviction habeas hearing of Leigh Stubbs and Tami Vance, two lesbians convicted in Brookhaven Mississippi of aggravated assault on another woman. The woman overdosed and was taken to a hospital, where forensic odontologist Michael West said he identified bite marks on her body. The convictions of Stubbs and Vance were reversed in 2012 when exculpatory reports from the FBI were discovered—and which had never been disclosed by the prosecutor.

I, RUTHANN ROBSON, declare under penalty of perjury that the following is true and correct:

1. My name is Ruthann Robson. I am a Professor of Law and University Distinguished Professor at the City University of New York School of Law and a member of the Florida Bar. My legal training and experience consists of a J.D. degree, a LL.M. degree, a clerkship with the Honorable William J. Castagna, United States District Court for the Middle District of Florida, a clerkship with

the Honorable Peter T. Fay, United States Court of Appeals Judge for the Eleventh Circuit, and a practice with Florida Rural Legal Services. I have been teaching at the City University of New York School of Law since 1990 in the areas of constitutional law, criminal procedure, and sexuality and the law ...

5. The materials I have read regarding the convictions of Vikki Leigh Stubbs and Tammy Vance convince me that their convictions were colored in some significant measure by their portrayals as lesbians. In a circumstantial case, such as this one, the role of bias in a trial is especially insidious.

6. Bias against lesbians and other sexual minorities is well documented. For example, the American Enterprise Institute (AEI) for Public Policy Research reports that in 1973, when the National Opinion Research Center at the University of Chicago first polled people about sexual relations between persons of the same sex, 73% characterized such an event as "always wrong." According to AEI's own polls in the years 1996, 1998, and 2000, the percentage of persons judging sexual relations between persons of the same sex as "always wrong" was reported at 60%, 58%, and 59%, respectively.

Members of juries are composed from this population of those who disapprove of homosexuality. Thus, it is not surprising that a disproportionate number of potential jurors admit to being biased against lesbian and gay defendants in the criminal context. As reported in The Chicago Sun-Times in 1998, potential jurors were "more than three times as likely to think they could not be fair or impartial toward a gay or lesbian defendant as toward a defendant from other minority groups, such as blacks, Hispanics, or Asian Americans." This finding, based on the Juror Outlook Survey conducted by the National Law Journal and Decision Quest, a national trial consulting and legal communications company, is especially striking given that "more than 40 percent of those polled and more than 70 percent of blacks polled believe that minorities are treated less fairly than others" in the criminal justice system, meaning that sexual minorities are treated even less fairly. *A study published in the Journal of Homosexuality in the year that Stubbs and Vance were indicted demonstrated that sexual orientation was three times more likely than racial identity to be a cause of bias against a defendant.*

Given the statistics supporting jury bias, it is not surprising that a study published in Criminal Justice and Behavior and one of the very few empirical studies to address the specific issue of discrimination against lesbians in the criminal justice system concludes that lesbians are more likely to be convicted than heterosexual women.

In this case there seems to have been absolutely no attempt to ameliorate bias. The subject of potential prejudice was not addressed in voir dire.

7. [H]ere there seems to me to be no relevance to the sexual identity of the defendants in this criminal trial other than to prejudice the jurors against them. ...

8. Moreover, it is not simply the sexual orientation of the defendants that was introduced at trial. Responding to a question from the prosecutor, Dr. West, a dentist, gave his "expert opinion" that "bite marks" were common—almost "expected"—in a "homosexual rape case." Also responding to questioning by the prosecutor, Dr. Rodrigo Galvez, a forensic pathologist, rendered his "expert opinion" that biting was consistent with a "lesbian rape." Galvez continued that in his opinion, "homosexual crimes" are very sadistic, because sexual minorities "do what we call the overkill" and the crimes are "more gory" and "more repulsive."

9. The prosecutor capitalized upon such testimony in his closing arguments, stressing the bite marks, using the word "torture," and connecting both to the sexuality of the defendants. The prosecutor argued that bites indicate a "homosexual assault." Indeed, the prosecutor admitted that the state relied upon the defendants' "lifestyle" to support an attack on the victim that would otherwise seem to be "for no reason."

10. The judge specifically recalled the testimony of Dr. Galvez about the "violence of homosexual people" during the sentencing. The judge specifically stated that he would "adopt" Dr. Galvez's "testimony as part of my opinion" and imposed the maximum sentence.

11. Neither Dr. West nor Dr. Galvez were experts in sex, sexuality, lesbianism, or criminal behavior. Based upon my knowledge, including 30 years of research into lesbians and crime, there is <u>absolutely no empirical evidence</u> to support a statement that lesbians are more likely than other people, including other women, to be violent or commit violent crimes or to be especially brutal when committing crimes. Additionally, there is also <u>absolutely no empirical evidence</u> to support a statement that lesbians are more likely than other people, including other women, to "bite" during an assault or during sexual activity.

12. While it is not based upon any empirical evidence, the notion that lesbians are especially brutal is believable because it is a frequent negative stereotype of lesbians in popular culture. While the situation in 2012 is improved, the stereotype of the "killer lesbian" endures. According to a Report from GLAAD, the Gay and Lesbian Alliance Against Defamation, the depiction of lesbians on television and movies is "almost uniformly negative," citing as an example that in 1991 "out of a total of the four lesbians appearing on series television last season, two were portrayed as murderers, and one as a murder victim in which the other lesbians are under suspicion for the murder." The Report concludes that in summary, "lesbian images in film and television depict us as man-hating, society-destroying, sex-driven or sexless creatures who have no hearts, homes, families, values, or reasons to live." ...

13. The convictions and harsh sentencing of the defendants are based upon the logical structure advanced by the prosecutor and supported by the opinions advanced by non-experts: all lesbians are sadistic, brutal, and sexually violent;

the defendants are lesbians; therefore the defendants are guilty of the brutal attack on the victim.

What is not based in logic or empirical evidence is the premise that all lesbians are sadistic, brutal, and sexually violent. Instead, it is based on mere prejudice....

16. Doctors, attorneys, jurors and even judges can be biased and unthinkingly accept outdated stereotypes that lesbians are brutal sexual torturers with a propensity to bite. But courts can also act to remedy such prejudice.

Ruthann Robson

Professor of Law & University Distinguished Professor

City University of New York (CUNY) School of Law

65 21 Main Street Flushing, NY 11367 USA

Sworn to me this 27th of February, 2012

Heteronormativity, excerpt from *Queer (In)Justice*

at 24

It is important to recognize that queer criminalizing scripts have never focused exclusively on the policing and punishment of LGBT people. As political scientist Cathy J. Cohen points out in her groundbreaking essay *Punks, Bulldaggers, and Welfare Queens,* gender conforming heterosexuals can also be policed and punished for exhibiting behavior or indulging sexual desires that run contrary to the vast array of punitive rules, norms, practices, and institutions that "legitimize and privilege heterosexuality." Cohen uses the phrase "heteronormativity" to describe this system of framing heterosexuality — constrained within a nuclear family structure and shaped by race, class, and rigidly dichotomous constructions of gender — as fundamental to society, and as the only "natural" and accepted form of sexual and gender expression. Thus women who may be heterosexual, but not heteronormative, are also subject to sex and gender policing.

Bennett Capers, *Cross Dressing and the Criminal*

20 Yale J.L. & Human. 1, 8–10, 18–19, 21 (2008)

Between 1850 and 1870, just as the abolitionist movement, then the Civil War, and then Reconstruction were disrupting the subordinate/superordinate balance between blacks and whites, just as middle class white women were demanding social and economic equality, agitating for the right to vote, and quite literally asserting their right to wear pants, and just as lesbian and gay subcultures were emerging in large cities, jurisdictions began passing sumptuary legislation which had the effect of reifying sex and gender distinctions. Many ordinances explicitly prohibited cross dressing.... Other jurisdictions passed ordinances that were less explicit in language in prohibiting cross dressing, but nonetheless explicit in effect. New York's law prohibited individuals from assembling "disguised" in public places; California passed a law that prohibited an individual from "masquerading" in another person's attire for unlawful purposes. Both laws were used to target cross dressers ... in just one year, 1977, Houston police arrested and charged fifty-three people with dressing to disguise their sex.

Cross dressing prohibitions did not just impact cross dressers, or even "butch" women or "effeminate" men. The prohibitions signaled to everyone what dress, and what behavior, was appropriate. It was not enough that in every government form, in every government census, an answer was demanded: male or female. One had to act and appear it too....

* * *

[T]he imprint of our entire history of sumptuary laws still seems to be with us. Moreover, this imprint implicates troubling issues of class, race, sex, and sexuality. Consider the criminal arena. In too many jurisdictions, a black man driving a BMW or Lexus—that ultimate luxury item, that ultimate accessory, that ultimate item of conspicuous consumption—still seems to raise reasonable suspicion, justifying a stop, justifying questions. Ditto for a black kid dressed in baggy pants and a hoodie, or a group of Hispanics with an expensive camcorder. A woman not dressed "like a lady" still seems to justify reasonable doubt in rape prosecutions. A man not dressed "like a man" can still, in too many jurisdictions, be assaulted with impunity, especially if he is a man of color. And notwithstanding official admonishments that law enforcement witnesses are entitled to no more weight than the testimony of lay witnesses, we still tend to take officers in blue at their word, take their word as truth, even when there is evidence to the contrary.

* * *

But this is what I want to suggest: It is not only the transvestite who signals this category crisis [by cross-dressing], and in doing so problematizes the usefulness of the categories at issue. Rather, anyone who crosses in the broader sense, i.e., by adopting an appearance that crosses socio-cultural boundaries, can also signal a category crisis, and in doing so destabilize hierarchical assumptions. Thus, when Cheryl Harris, in her seminal article "Whiteness as Property," describes her grandmother's daily transformation from black (at home) to white (at the department store where, in order to get a job, she passed as white), or law professor Judy Scales-Trent describes her own repeated crossings as a black woman who looks white, these crossings problematize the very usefulness of the categories black and white. When Paulette Caldwell describes the different reactions occasioned by her hairstyle, depending on whether her hair is braided, in an "Angela Davis" afro, or pulled back in a ponytail, it problematizes her status as a black woman professor. When Kenji Yoshino describes adopting preppy clothes in order to "cover" as American at his New England prep school, "outprep[ping] the preps, dressing out of catalogues that featured no racial minorities," it calls into question the valence of the terms Asian-American and American. When Margaret Montoya describes donning Catholic school uniforms as a "disguise which concealed" her working class status, and then later as an adult, using "dress to fade into the ideological, political cultural background rather than proclaim my difference," it throws into question the usefulness of class categories....

What happens when we disrupt gender assumptions by dressing a male in women's clothing and make-up, or a female in men's clothing? What happens when we disrupt gender/race/status assumptions by dressing a waitress as a social worker, or a police officer in civilian clothes, or a wealthy person in the clothes of a poor person, or a white person in "black" clothes or a black person in "white" clothes? For that matter, what happens when we transpose white and black, male and female, straight and gay, the police and the policed? These questions seem particularly important at this time in the criminal arena, when racial profiling remains a fact of life, when class profiling has been documented, when even judges have been shown to engage in race-based and sex-based discriminatory sentencing, when the law enforcement resources allocated to investigating crime often turn on the race, gender, and status of the victim, and when whether a defendant is facing the death penalty still turns on the race and gender of his victim.

3. Gender and Wrongful Convictions

Andrea L. Lewis and Sara L. Sommervold, *Death, But Is It Murder? The Role of Stereotypes and Cultural Perceptions in the Wrongful Convictions of Women*
78 Alb. L. Rev. 1035, 1035 (2015)

Six days after her three-year-old son died in a house fire, Kristine Bunch was arrested for starting the fire and intentionally killing him. Bunch spent seventeen years in prison after being convicted of murder and arson under the theory she locked the child in a bedroom and lit the room on fire. Tragically, evidence eventually showed there was no arson and Bunch was innocent. After Sabrina Butler spent more than five years on death row in Mississippi, she also was found innocent of killing her son, who actually died from a genetic medical condition. Before she was exonerated in 2008, Audrey Edmunds spent eleven years in prison after the death of a seven-month-old baby in her care. Edmunds's case was one of the first to be reversed based on the arguably questionable science behind shaken baby syndrome, after experts testified that no evidence supported the State's theory that she shook the baby.

As with many wrongfully convicted women these women became suspects because they were mothers or caregivers. Also, like most wrongfully convicted women, these women were traumatized and lost years of their lives over "crimes" which, evidence has shown, did not occur. Consider that sixty-four percent of exonerated women were wrongfully convicted even though no crime had occurred. In contrast, 23.2% of exonerated men were wrongfully convicted for crimes that never happened. That disparity is a clear indication that something different happens in the wrongful convictions of women than when men are wrongfully convicted.

Elizabeth Webster and Jody Miller, *Gendering and Racing Wrongful Conviction: Intersectionality, "Normal Crimes," and Women's Experiences of Miscarriage of Justice*

78 ALB. L. REV. 973, 1000–1007, 1030–31 (2015)

One reason for the large number of white women in the [National Registry of Exonerations] dataset is their overrepresentation among wrongful convictions in the child sexual abuse (CSA) hysteria cases of the 1980s and early 1990s. These cases represented nearly a quarter of the white women in the NRE (20 of 82, or 24.4%). However, even when these cases were excluded, white women still made up the majority of female exonerees. They were 59% of exonerations exclusive of CSA "hysteria" cases (62 of 105), while African American women were 31.4% and other women of color were 9.5% of these cases.

Domestic Crime Scenarios

The wrongful conviction of Nicole Harris was one of forty-five women's cases in the NRE that fit what we have conceptualized as "domestic crime scenarios." What these cases have in common is that the identified crime took (or was believed to have taken) place in the context of women's familial relationships and/or caretaking roles (i.e., the gendered private sphere that is culturally recognized as women's domain of responsibility as wives, mothers, and daughters). Domestic caretaking — of children, intimate partners, and elderly parents — is still considered a defining feature of women's lives, with "contemporary women across racial and ethnic groups ... considered accountable to care for ... [and] presumed responsible for self, for others, for kin, for community, and for controlling the behaviors of men." The contemporary ideal of "motherhood," for example, embodies selfless sacrifice directed toward caring for, nurturing, and protecting one's children, with women held accountable for falling short of this ideal. [T]his was narrated explicitly in Nicole Harris's case — she was called a "monster" by the polygraph examiner and described to jurors by the prosecutor as "not the mother the defense wants to present to you."

Harris's case clearly typifies several of the case processing factors that have been identified as contributing to wrongful convictions across gender: official misconduct, a false confession, and inadequate legal defense. Yet, the process by which her son came to be misidentified as a homicide victim — and she his killer — was also clearly influenced by criminal justice actors' cultural assumptions about gender and race, in particular the ways in which ideas about proper mothering facilitated the "tunnel vision" that occurred in her case.

1. Children as the Victims of Women's "Crimes"

Cases involving child victims predominated domestic crime scenario cases across race and across crime type. In all, there were twenty-seven such cases in the NRE, representing a quarter (25.7%) of all women's wrongful convictions, exclusive of CSA hysteria cases. Fifteen of these cases were for murder, along with one manslaughter, one assault, five child abuse, and five sexual abuse cases. In many of these cases, criminal justice officials' "escalating commitments" to an interpretation of these events as both *crimes* and crimes perpetrated by *mothers* or other female *caregivers* appear to draw closely from cultural interpretations of "bad" mothering, which are utilized in constructing a "compelling narrative" of the crime....

[W]omen's wrongful convictions were imbued with gendered motives that provided a crime narrative placing the women directly at odds with the ideal of motherhood as selfless sacrifice for one's children. Eighteen-year-old Sabrina Butler's attempts at CPR were interpreted as fatal abuse; like Nicole Harris, many hours of questioning immediately following her infant's death led to a false confession that she had punched the baby because he would not stop crying. Seventeen-year-old Michelle Murphy, who also falsely confessed after her eighteen-month-old son was stabbed to death, was accused at trial of being motivated to "get rid of" her infant son so that her estranged husband, who "suspected that he was not [the baby's] father," would reconcile with her. Julie Rea, whose son was murdered by the serial killer Tommy Lynn Sells, was presumed to have taken her son's life due to a "bitter" custody dispute with the boy's father. Kimberly Mawson, whose former boyfriend testified against her but later admitted to causing the injuries that killed her young daughter, was described as "frustrated" by her childcare responsibilities. And Margaret Earle, whose live-in boyfriend at the time later confessed to perpetrating the violence that killed her young daughter and was sentenced to life in prison, was co-convicted of the murder in a separate trial and also given a life sentence for "failing to promptly seek medical treatment," despite evidence that she had done so.

2. Mothers Held Responsible for Others' Crimes

What is particularly striking about these cases is how readily criminal justice officials' tunnel vision narrows in on mothers in attributing blame when a child is harmed or killed, even, as in Earle's case, when the actual perpetrator has confessed. Three cases that are not in the NRE—Tabitha Pollock, Molly Bowers, and Raquel Nelson—provide additional evidence of the power and extremes of mother blaming in women's wrongful convictions. These cases do not meet the definitional criteria for inclusion in the NRE, and in fact appear to be the tip of the iceberg in miscarriages of justice against mothers resulting from the gendered usage of failure-to-protect laws. Though designed as a mechanism to respond to child abuse, "the application of [these] laws is anything but gender-neutral: Defendants charged and convicted with failure to protect are almost exclusively female." Indeed, gender disparities in failure-to-protect prosecutions are so extreme that they cannot simply be explained by women's greater likelihood to be primary caregivers.

Molly Bowers was convicted in 2007 of reckless child abuse resulting in death and sentenced to sixteen years in a Colorado state prison for the death of her ten-week-old son, Jason. The prosecution's case was that Bowers had failed to seek out timely medical care, which resulted in the baby's death, and not that she had abused the infant herself. Instead, her husband at the time, who spent more time at home with the baby, was charged with the actual abuse. Prosecutors have been criticized for using gendered arguments in attempting to show that Bowers was poorly bonded to her son. For example, during a hearing regarding her appeal these attorneys cited the fact that, during her pregnancy, Bowers had engaged in social events outside of the home before the baby's nursery was fully decorated. They also questioned her practice of doing yoga videos in her home after Jason was born. At the trial, the prosecutor argued: "If she didn't know [of the infant's injuries], why didn't she know?... Mothers can read the different cries of their babies. They know everything about their baby.... She has shown no remorse for her inaction. Not once has she stood up and said, 'I should have done something.'"

As striking with regard to Bowers's case, a year after her conviction her husband, Alex Midyette, was found guilty of the lesser charge of criminally negligent abuse when jurors split over the charge of reckless child abuse. Midyette's defense presented expert witnesses who countered the prosecution's theory of abuse by suggesting that the infant had died of a rare metabolic disorder. In addition, defense attorneys argued that there was no outward sign of trauma to the baby, who died with more than thirty broken bones and a skull fracture. Several of the jurors in Midyette's trial were swayed by these arguments, though Bowers herself did not benefit from them. Ironically, her conviction rested on the assumption that she had neglected to seek help when her husband abused the baby—though the basis for this assumption was never proven in court. Midyette was never convicted of physically harming Jason, only of neglecting him.

The tunnel vision that led prosecutors to pursue their case against Bowers, even in the absence of a conviction for Midyette, is equally evident in the wrongful conviction of Tabitha Pollock. When Pollock's boyfriend, Scott English, killed her three-year-old daughter, Pollock was convicted and sentenced to thirty-six years in prison based on the assumption that she "should have known" English was a threat. As for English, he immediately became a suspect based on his self-incriminating statements; nevertheless, officials continued to focus on Pollock. The cause of the child's death was never seriously under investigation, as it was in the Bowers case, and neither was the identity of the perpetrator. Scott English was tried by jury, found guilty of first degree murder and aggravated battery, and sentenced to life in prison. At Pollock's 1996 trial, the State argued that "[s]he should have known. She should have done something.... [S]he's as guilty as Scott English of murder and aggravated battery of a child." The prosecution sought life in prison for Pollock, but the judge would not allow it. Pollock served seven years of her sentence before the Illinois Supreme Court unanimously overturned her conviction. Shortly thereafter, a commentator pondered "whether some judges, prosecutors and communities ask too much of mothers and are prepared to punish them, even at the expense of the surviving family." Indeed, during Pollock's incarceration she was separated from her remaining children, one of whom was adopted by another family.

* * *

Criminal justice actors' attribution processes likely draw less from routine or typical knowledge of crime scenarios and more from cultural ideologies or stereotypes of events and the people presumed to be involved. Thus, we have *monstrous mothers*; *desperate, spoiled*, and *manipulative housewives*; *femme fatales*; *selfish daughters*; women who declare *open season* on (violent) men; and—especially for African American women convicted in street crime scenarios—*cold-blooded killers* who could ruthlessly kill someone as easily as *taking a drink of water*, and where involvement in any illicit activities (like sex work or drug use) is evidence of the capacity to commit murder. It is by drawing on gendered and raced cultural ideologies that the crime narratives constructed by criminal justice actors become "highly credible," with erroneously convicted women held criminally accountable for accidental and natural deaths, crimes committed by others, and their efforts to protect themselves from serious harm.

* * *

We also discovered additional gendered processes relevant for understanding women's wrongful convictions. Most notably, mothers' self-blame and grief, along with their concern about their children's well-being, were sometimes manipulated for securing false confessions; women's experiences of sexual harassment at the hands of criminal justice actors, and others with a stake in their cases, were overlooked as meaningful factors contributing to case outcomes; and emotional displays not in keeping with criminal justice actors' expectations were read as evidence of guilt.

B. Legal Materials, Exercises, and Media

Race and Mass Incarceration

1. *Exercise, Review Questions:* Ian Lopez notes that race is a social product. Although court cases mainly treat race as "extralegal," legal rules fashion races. Lopez quotes James Baldwin: "No one was white before he/she came to America. It took generations, and a vast amount of coercion, before this became a white country."

    A. Ian Lopez identifies law as both a system of behavioral control and an ideology. What does he mean?

    B. How does the legal system influence or create ideas about race? Does the law reflect identities or create identities?(See the excerpt in 2. below for an additional example.)

    C. What role do legal actors play?

2. *How the Legal System Creates Racial Identities:* In a brief example, Ian Lopez answers "how law transforms ideas about race into differences in rights and wealth, which then confirm racial ideas:"

    > Armenians, whose origins lay in what was geographically western Asia, were initially classified by federal authorities as "Asiatics." In 1909, however, a federal court ruled that Armenians were "white persons." This changed status allowed Armenian immigrants to buy agricultural land in California, where as "Asiatics" they would have been barred from doing so by the state's alien land law....

This difference [between being Caucasian and "Asiatic"] was established, and made especially pronounced, by law. Before their immigration here, Armenians were not part of the evolving racial schema of U.S. society. They had not yet been "raced," that is, assigned a racial identity. However, upon their arrival, and despite some initial confusion, they were pronounced legally White. This pronouncement allowed them a prosperous and privileged position in American society. This prosperity then confirmed the common knowledge of their Whiteness, which in turn served to justify the judicial treatment of Armenians as White persons. The opposite occurred with the Japanese. Again, their position in the U.S. racial schema was initially far from certain: some had been naturalized as "white persons," but others had been excluded from citizenship. Partly under court authority, however, the non-Whiteness of Japanese immigrants emerged as common knowledge. As non-Whites, the Japanese were subject to discriminatory treatment that ensured a lack of economic opportunities, and consequently poverty. These legally engineered conditions of social misery then justified the common knowledge that Japanese were not White. In California's Central Valley during the 1930s, the cooperation of law and social beliefs had created a situation in which Armenians were clearly and correctly White and entitled (literally, in being able to hold title to land), while Japanese were obviously non-White and dispossessed. Law easily precipitated the transformation of highly unstable ideas about race — are Armenians and Japanese "Asiatic" or "white"? — into entrenched differences in social status, legal rights, and wealth. The contingency of these relative positions and the role of law in creating them was lost to sight; the role of law in reifying racial distinctions was invisible.

Ian Lopez, *White By Law: The Legal Construction of Race* 130–132.

3. *Reflective Essay:* In the opening chapter of this Reader, you considered Hannah Arendt's question of the Nazis: is evil-doing possible from a lack of thought? Now, consider this excerpt from Ta-Nehisi Coates' book on race in America, *Between the World and Me:*

> "We would prefer to say such people cannot exist, that there aren't any," writes Solzhenitsyn. "To do evil a human being must first of all believe that what he's doing is good, or else that it's a well-considered act in conformity with natural law." This is the foundation of the Dream — its adherents must not just believe in it but believe that it is just, believe that their possession of the Dream is the natural result of grit, honor, and good works.... The mettle that it takes to look away from the horror of our prison system, from police forces transformed into armies, from the long war against the black body, is not forged overnight. This is the practiced habit of jabbing out one's eyes and forgetting the work of one's hands.

Are Arendt and Coates saying the same thing? Why or why not? Explain your answer in a one-page reflective essay.

4. *Group Exonerations, Recommended Viewing:* In the *National Registry of Exonerations Report on Race and Wrongful Convictions*, you learned about group arrests that overwhelming impact innocent African-Americans. In "Tulia, Texas," CBS News investigated and documented the story of one of these group arrests. Part I discusses the background of the arrests, while Part II interviews jurors, discusses racial bias, and reveals how the wrongful convictions were exposed.

   Part I: https://www.youtube.com/watch?v=b8zGIakh2QU (5 minutes)

   Part II: https://www.youtube.com/watch?v=EzyCjlRSc4Y (8 minutes)

5. *Exercise, Read, and Answer:* The judges of the United States District Court for the Western District of Washington have created a video for prospective jurors on unconscious bias, as well as criminal jury instructions on unconscious bias. Read the jury instructions at the Western District of Washington webpage: http://www.wawd.uscourts.gov/jury/unconscious-bias. The video is also available at this webpage.

   When are these instructions given to the jury? Do you think the timing of the jury instructions matters?

6. *Exercise, Read, and Reflect:* In the American Bar Association (ABA) Achieving an Impartial Jury Toolbox, Professor Cynthia Lee is cited for her race-switching jury instruction:

   > It is natural to make assumptions about the parties and witnesses based on stereotypes. Stereotypes constitute well-learned sets of associations or expectations correlating particular traits with members of a particular social group. You should try not to make assumptions about the parties and witnesses based on their membership in a particular racial group. If you are unsure about whether you have made any unfair assessments based on racial stereotypes, you may engage in a race-switching exercise to test whether stereotypes have colored your evaluation of the case before you.

   > Race-switching involves imagining the same events, the same circumstances, the same people, but switching the races of the parties. For example, if the defendant is White and the victim is Latino, you would imagine a Latino defendant and a White victim. If your evaluation of the case before you is different after engaging in race-switching, this suggests a subconscious reliance on stereotypes. You may then wish to reevaluate the case from a neutral, unbiased perspective.

   The entire Impartial Jury Toolbox is available here: https://www.americanbar.org/content/dam/aba/publications/criminaljustice/voirdire_toolchest.authcheckdam.pdf.

   In 2012, African-American teenager Trayvon Martin lost his life when a neighborhood watch volunteer, George Zimmerman, pursued him, inaccurately concluding that Martin was a criminal who did not belong in that gated community. In 2013, Zimmerman was tried before a jury for second-degree murder and acquitted.

Figure 16.3

Source: The Impartial Jury Toolbox

The photos above are race-switched images of Trayvon Martin and George Zimmerman. Do you think a race-switching instruction like the one above can impact a jury? Why or why not?

7. *Shooter Bias Studies:* Studies have shown that African-American faces and bodies can trigger thoughts of crime, and thinking of crime can trigger thoughts of African-American people. Not surprisingly then, unarmed African-American men face a greater threat of being shot than unarmed white men. Similarly, African-American police officers face a greater risk of being shot than white police officers. Shooter bias studies explore the impact of implicit race bias on a person's decision to shoot. The studies generally use simulations similar to video games; the simulations show individuals of different races in many backgrounds where they are carrying either a gun or a harmless item like a cell phone or wallet. Participants are asked to shoot anyone who is armed and not to shoot anyone who is unarmed. *Id.* at 43. The results are that "[p]articipants are faster and more accurate when shooting an armed black man than an armed white man, and faster and more accurate when responding 'don't shoot' to an unarmed white man than an unarmed black man." Joshua Correll et al., *Across the Thin Blue Line: Police Officers and Racial Bias in the Decision to Shoot*, 92 J. Personality & Soc. Psychol. 1006, 1007 (2007). More than twenty studies reveal that both white and African-American subjects are more likely to shoot an unarmed African-American man than an unarmed white man.

8. *Race and Juries:* Bryan Stevenson's excerpt mentions *Batson v. Kentucky*, the 1986 Supreme Court case ruling prosecutors and defense attorneys cannot strike jurors

from the jury simply because of their race. In 2017, the Supreme Court revisited racial bias and the jury in *Pena-Rodriguez v. Colorado*, ruling jury deliberations can be examined if clear evidence exists of racial bias in the jury's decision, bias that may have denied the defendant his right to a fair trial.

9. *Recommended Listening, Race, Power, and Criminal Justice:* Malcolm Gladwell exposes the unseen and pervasive impact of social power in discussing the case of *State of Georgia v. Nathaniel Johnson* with Vernon Jordan on his podcast, *Revisionist History,* "State v. Johnson," Season 2, Episode 7: http://revisionisthistory.com/episodes/17-state-v-johnson (33 minutes). Gladwell further discusses systemic racism in the criminal justice system in his episode, "Mr. Hollowell Didn't Like That," Season 2, Episode 8: http://revisionisthistory.com/episodes/18-mr-hollowell-didnt-like-that (9–12 background; 20–24:30 systemic racism).

10. *Race and Mass Incarceration, Recommended Viewing:* These three short videos discuss and document United States history from slavery through mass incarceration, and the role of race and mass incarceration:

    Slavery to Mass Incarceration, Equal Justice Initiative: https://www.youtube.com/watch?v=r4e_djVSag4 (5:50).

    The Racism of Mass Incarceration, Visualized/An Interview With Bruce Western, The Atlantic: https://www.theatlantic.com/video/index/404890/prison-inherited-trait/ (2:27).

    Mass Incarceration in the US, Vlog Brothers: https://www.youtube.com/watch?v=NaPBcUUqbew (3:40).

11. *Recommended Reading:* For a short and informative blogpost on juvenile wrongful convictions and race, read Edwin Grimsley's piece:

    Lessons about Black Youth and Wrongful Convictions: Three Things You Should Know, https://www.innocenceproject.org/lessons-about-black-youth-and-wrongful-convictions-three-things-you-should-know-2/.

Gender and Sexual Orientation

1. *Recommended Viewing: Southwest of Salem: The Story of the San Antonio Four* documents the wrongful convictions of four Latina lesbians in San Antonio, Texas, and their struggle against homophobia and sexism to prove their innocence. www.southwestofsalem.com (91 minutes). You can also listen to an interview with the San Antonio Four at *Unheard but Unafraid: The Story of the San Antonio 4*, NPR (Aug. 12, 2016): https://www.npr.org/2016/08/12/489822624/unheard-but-unafraid-the-story-of-the-san-antonio-4 (21:18).

2. *Recommended Listening, Criminalizing Behavior:* Before the 1969 Stonewall Uprising in New York City, hundreds of gay men were arrested for holding a New Year's Day Mardis Gras Ball in San Francisco in 1965. Evander Smith and Herb Donaldson were two attorneys who not only organized the Ball, they protested the police shutting it down. They were arrested, faced public scorn, Evander lost his job and both were concerned about losing their law licenses. Listen to their stories,

Figure 16.4: Lifetime Likelihood of Incarceration by Race and Gender

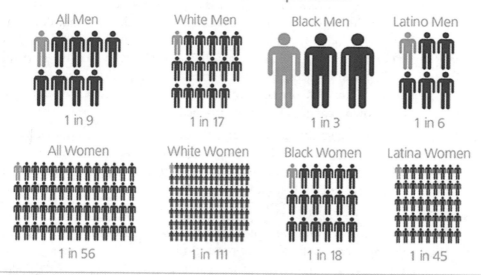

Source: The Sentencing Project

Figure 16.5: Incarceration Rate of Women 1910–2014

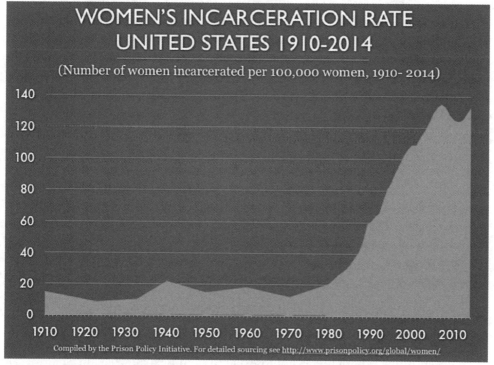

Source: The Prison Policy Initiative

and read more, at Making Gay History, "Evander Smith & Herb Donaldson," http://makinggayhistory.com/podcast/episode-19-donaldson-smith/ (0:00–11:40).

3. *Reflective Exercise and Essay, Implicit Bias:* Implicit bias is unintentional bias arising from "attitudes or stereotypes that affect our understanding, decision-making, and behavior, without our even realizing it." Jerry Kang et al., *Implicit Bias in the Courtroom*, 59 U.C.L.A. L. Rev. 1124, 1126 (2012). Take the Harvard Project Implicit Test at https://implicit.harvard.edu/implicit/takeatest.html — choose any test (Race IAT, Sexuality IAT, Weight IAT, etc.). In a few sentences, what was your own experience with the Implicit Association Test?

4. *Expert Testimony:* Leigh Stubbs and Tami Vance were wrongly convicted based on "expert" testimony about bitemarks and homosexuals. Read the testimony below — what would you have done as a defense attorney representing Leigh or Tami to combat this expert testimony, particularly from your own expert?

Dr. Michael West, State Expert:

> Q. Dr. West, how common are bit marks in — or what kinds of cases — let me ask it this way. Are bite marks more prevalent in?
>
> A. Child abuse, rape, and what we call overkill. They're common in sexual assaults.
>
> Q. Have you investigated homosexual type assaults?
>
> A. Yes, sir.
>
> Q. Are they any more or less prevalent in a homosexual assault than a hetero-sexual rape case?
>
> A. In male homosexuality, in those cases of violence, there seems to be a much greater propensity of bite marks. In female homosexual activity, I haven't had enough experience or read anything in the literature, but it's documented that male homosexual activity is much greater in bite marks.
>
> Q. So, in a rape case or a homosexual rape case, you would expect to find bite marks, it would not be unusual at all to find bite marks on the skin?
>
> A. No, it wouldn't be unusual.
>
> Q. In fact, it would almost be expected?
>
> A. Almost.

Dr. Galvez, Defense Expert:

> Q. Yes, sir. Would you expect to find biting or would biting be consistent with a lesbian rape type situation?
>
> A. I didn't get your question, please.
>
> Q. In a homosexual rape?
>
> A. Yes.
>
> Q. Would you expect to find bite marks, would they be consistent in a situation like that?
>
> A. In homosexual crimes, all they are, they are very sadistic. More violent times I seen in my experience as homosexual to homosexual. They do what we call the over kill. They do tremendous damage, tremendous damage.

Q. Tremendous damage?

A. Pardon me.

Q. Tremendous damage?

A. Tremendous, yes.

Q. They are brutal assaults?

A. Yes, sir. Yes, sir, they are—they're more gory, the more repulsive crimes I've ever seen were homosexual to homosexual.

Prosecutor Closing Argument:

[Dr. Moak] had never seen a woman with these kinds of injuries to her private parts. Never. He said it was brutal. Dr. Galvez says that a homosexual assault, that he has seen homosexual assaults, and in his opinion, a homosexual assault is the most brutal, involves torture. It's the most senseless kind of assault that he sees. He's using both his psychiatric expertise and his pathological expertise to give this jury the information that, if you believe Dr. Moak when he described the brutality of it, then you would look to see if there is evidence that it is a homosexual rape...

You can tell for yourself that that is, in fact, a bite mark. The bites are important because it indicates a homosexual assault. It indicates a sexual assault. It precludes the possibility that it could be self-inflicted. It precludes that, bite marks to the breasts, bite marks to the side, bite marks to the vagina, preclude the fact that it could be self-inflicted. You heard Dr. West's testimony and his highest level of certainty is that it is, in fact, a bite mark...

When you look at all the evidence, you'll realize that while it's a circumstantial evidence case, these two women who were living together, were lovers, whether because of the drugs or the alcohol or their lifestyle, viciously attacked Kimberly Williams for no reason and tried to cover it up.

For a detailed review of the testimony in Leigh and Tami's case, see Jennifer Oliva and Valena Beety, Regulating Bite Mark Evidence: *Lesbian Vampires and Other Myths of Forensic Odontology,* 94 WASH. L. REV. ___ (2019).

5. *Reflective Essay, Voir Dire Questions on Gender and Sexual Orientation*: In *The Gay Panic Defense*, 42 U.C. DAVIS L. REV. 471 (2008), Professor Cynthia Lee suggests questions to ask when selecting a jury:

This trial involves a gay male victim. How might this affect your reactions to the trial? Do you have any biases or prejudices that might prevent you from judging this case fairly given that it involves a gay victim? In your opinion, should the sexual orientation of the defendant influence the treatment he receives in the legal system?

Do you think these kinds of *voir dire* questions are effective? In one page, describe why or why not.

6. *Hear the Voices of Female Exonerees:* Listen to female exonerees speak out about their own experiences at the 2016 Innocence Network Conference: https://www.youtube.com/watch?v=GiSoZsY4Drw (21:00) Professor Zieva Konvisser organized

the panel of female exonerees, and has interviewed female exonerees about "the unique qualities and needs faced by wrongfully convicted women during their arrest, trial, conviction, imprisonment, release, and post-release." Zieva Dauber Konvisser, *What Happened to Me Can Happen to Anybody—Women Exonerees Speak Out*, 3 Tex. A&M L. Rev. 303 (2015).

7. *Women and False Confessions:* In "Why Do Innocent Women Confess to Crimes They Did Not Commit?" exoneree Amanda Knox examines whether women are more likely to falsely confess than men:

> Women are raised under a different social incentive structure than men, where attitudes of compliance and deference to authority are more encouraged. This finds its most damning realization in the interrogation room, a situation designed to amplify the absolute control and authority of investigators—an experience I know only too well.

https://broadly.vice.com/en_us/article/9k9wep/amanda-knox-why-do-innocent-women-confess-to-crimes-they-didnt-commit.

8. *Discussion, the "Usual Suspects":* Who gets wrongfully convicted and why? What features make outsiders convenient suspects? Michel Foucault, a 20th century philosopher, concluded that whoever determines what can be talked about, also determines what can be known. How does the power to create labels, and to reinforce them, justify the treatment of "others" and suspicions of outsiders?

Figure 16.6: Disproportionate Incarceration of Trans People

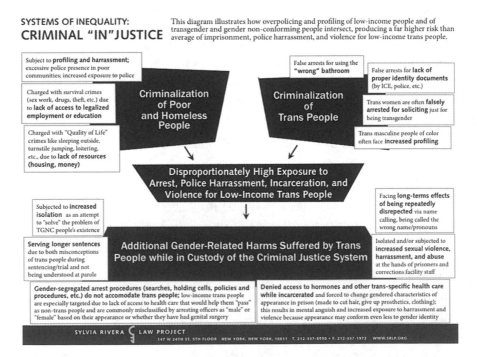

Source: The Sylvia Rivera Law Project

Chapter Seventeen

Reconsidering Innocence: Rethinking Causes and Addressing Consequences

A. Readings

1. Reconsidering Innocence

Abbe Smith, *In Praise of the Guilty Project: A Criminal Defense Lawyer's Growing Anxiety About Innocence Projects*

13 U. PA. J.L. & SOC. CHANGE 315, 323–26 (2010)

[T]here is ... an arrogance to the "innocentrism" of the innocence movement. They are the righteous ones, the virtuous ones. Unlike criminal defense lawyers, who are ethically bound to pursue their clients' interests (even if that client is guilty), the innocence advocate looks after everyone in the system. As one commentator notes:

> In the criminal justice system, neither side wins when an innocent person is convicted. The victim is denied justice because the real culprit remains unpunished. Police and prosecutorial resources are squandered. Public confidence in the system is undermined if and when the mistake is revealed. And, of course, the innocent person who is convicted suffers most of all.

Innocence movement lawyers and their compatriots see this and trumpet it. They are saving the wrongfully convicted and the entire system.

* * *

There is no question that our criminal justice system is in need of reform. Although the number of wrongful convictions cannot accurately be tallied—DNA is available in only a tiny fraction of criminal cases, and the problems underlying the 250-plus DNA exonerations are not unique to those cases—it is fair to say that serious problems plague our system.

* * *

At their best, innocence stories include important, related stories about the state of criminal justice in this country: stories about the ever-present problems of mistaken identification, police and prosecutorial misconduct, defense lawyer incompetence, and so on. But, too often, the stories are regarded as isolated, individual tragedies that are ultimately uncovered and fixed by the system.

The dominance of the rhetoric of innocence also comes at the expense of the not-quite-so-innocent but equally unfairly treated. Examples of the not-quite-so-innocent run the gamut. There are criminal defendants who are guilty of something but not the worst thing they are charged with. There are defendants who are guilty of something other than what they are charged with. There are defendants who committed the crime charged but with significant mitigating or extenuating circumstances. There are defendants who committed the crime but they had never done anything like this before, they lost control in a trying situation. There are defendants who committed the crime and it is no wonder in view of how they came into the world and what they endured after. There are defendants who committed the crime and have no excuse whatsoever but, as death penalty lawyer Bryan Stevenson says, "[e]ach of us is more than the worst thing we ever did." For every crime there is a story. Good lawyers find the story.

But the defendant with the factual innocence story throws every other defendant under the bus.

These not-quite-innocents—the ones whose lawyer too often had no file, had hardly met them, conducted no investigation, and could barely try a shoplifting case much less a capital murder—have no story unless they are also innocent. If they are not factually innocent, it does not matter whether they were coerced into confessing by a ruthless detective, prosecuted by an unscrupulous DA, or represented by a public defender carrying 900 cases.

Compared to a story of factual innocence, these other stories will evoke a "cry me a river" eye-roll by prosecutors, judges, and the general public. The innocent will become the enemy of everyone else at every stage: pretrial, trial, sentencing, post-conviction, and parole.

Factual, DNA-proven innocence poses a threat to the fundamental legal principles underlying our system of justice, in particular to the presumption of innocence. The more we focus on those who can actually be proved innocent, the more we undercut the right of everyone to be presumed innocent unless the state proves otherwise. Our system of justice emphasizes proof, not truth, because of the value we place on individual liberty and our abiding skepticism of state power. To check that power we give the benefit of every reasonable doubt to the accused even if he or she did it. Thus, if proof is lacking, a factually guilty person may nonetheless be legally not guilty. A single-minded focus on factual innocence threatens this important safeguard, this check on the hubris of power.

A focus on factual, DNA-proven innocence also threatens to change the discourse about wrongful convictions. Convictions are wrongful even if the convicted person is guilty when there is demonstrable unfairness. Imprisonment is wrongful if the person in prison is serving a sentence disproportionate to the circumstances of the crime or who the person is or has become. Factual innocence has never been the gravamen of a wrongful conviction, and should not be.

We are only a few years away from the fiftieth anniversary of the Gideon decision and we have still not begun to fulfill its promise. We continue to be a country in which there is rich man's justice and poor man's justice. A focus on innocence alone will not breathe life into the right to counsel for the poor accused or convicted.

I worry, too, about what will happen when the DNA-exonerations dry up—as they one day will—and all the testing is on the front end. Will people say we do not need to look at these so-called systemic problems anymore because there are no innocent people in prison?

And then there is the question of prison. If we get all the innocent people out, does that mean prisons are no longer the brutal, dehumanizing places we know them to be? Does it mean that the other-than-innocent people left in these institutions deserve to be there, and are unworthy of further concern? Perhaps, too, with the innocent out, we do not have to think about either the conditions of confinement or the circumstances that lead some to prison and others to college. Innocence has been important currency in criminal justice reform, but it cannot be the only one. Too much of a focus on innocence can lead to de-emphasizing and devaluing other significant systemic problems.

Carol S. Steiker and Jordan M. Steiker, *The Seduction of Innocence: The Attraction and Limitations of the Focus on Innocence in Capital Punishment Law and Advocacy*
95 J. Crim. L. & Criminology 587, 619–21 (2005)

Our concerns are not focused on the application of existing ethical rules to this new form of representation; rather, we are worried that the proliferation of such limited representational relationships—especially if they outlast the DNA revolution—will create problematic (even if "ethical") attorney-client relationships that may undermine trust in criminal defense relationships more generally.

The most problematic aspects of the relationships forged by the innocence projects are their limited and conditional nature. Many projects take on only those legal claims predicated on the claimant's total innocence of the crime charged and terminate the relationship if it is determined that the claimant has no colorable innocence claim. Thus, actual or potential clients whose claims turn out to be only partial or purely legal defenses (that might establish that the grade of their convicted offense was too high or might mitigate their punishment or might undermine only the legal rather than the factual basis for their conviction), if they are not initially screened out by an innocence project, may have their non-innocence claims ignored or abandoned mid-stream. As Suni points out, innocence projects can avoid or ameliorate ethical issues posed by such limited representation by not taking on formal representation of a client at all or by delaying formal representation until the case is sufficiently screened for innocence and ensuring that their clients are well-informed of the limits of the representational relationship.[89] But from the perspective of the client, however,

---

89. Ellen Yankiver Suni, *Ethical Issues for Innocence Projects: An Initial Primer*, 70 UMKC L. Rev. 921 (2002).

no matter how delayed the formal representation or how informed the consent, there is bound to be some misunderstanding, disappointment, and sense of betrayal—especially given that the vast majority of potential "innocence" clients will be indigent and unsophisticated inmates seeking post-conviction relief without many other possible avenues of legal representation.

As innocence projects become an established feature of the post-conviction inmate assistance landscape, individual inmate experiences of being screened out by such projects will multiply (whether the screening is immediate or, more problematically, after a period of investigation and/or representation). And, as the use of DNA evidence becomes more a part of the pre-trial rather than the post-conviction world, the screening of post-conviction cases for "innocence" will become more difficult, time-consuming, and subjective, with fewer clear victories. We worry that, in such a world, relationships between indigent defendants and their un-chosen representatives at all stages of the criminal process will become more problematic than they already are. The lack of trust that already exists between many indigent defendants and their appointed representatives will be exacerbated. Moreover, many defendants may feel compelled, or more compelled than they already do, to present themselves as factually innocent to their attorneys, neglecting or refusing to provide information that might support powerful legal defenses.

The growth of the innocence project as institution may have repercussions not only for the attitudes of criminal defendants and inmates, but also for public defenders as well. Former defenders who now run legal clinics in law schools have written compellingly of the need that public defenders have for sustenance in their roles. This need arises in large part from hostile questioning by members of the public—including other lawyers—about how defenders justify their zealous defense of the guilty:

> Criminal lawyers cannot escape the scorn heaped upon our clients. Some see us as indistinguishable from those we represent.... Unfortunately, it is not just our parents' friends at random social gatherings who think this way—it is our friends. It is the people with whom we have grown up, gone to college, and even gone to law school—a sad sign of the values being taught in the legal academy.... There is seldom admiration. More and more, when they come to understand that we represent our clients proudly and zealously, no matter the accusation, there is contempt.

The hostility and incomprehension that public defenders face will necessarily be exacerbated by the growth of special-duty public defenders who represent exclusively innocent clients. As one leader of a traditional public defense clinic wryly commented on the creation of an innocence project at his law school, "What should we put over our door—'Guilty Project'?" Given the criminal justice system's desperate need to recruit and retain lawyers willing to take on traditional indigent criminal defense, a need especially acute in death penalty cases, we should be aware and concerned about the impact that innocence projects might have on such recruitment and retention.

David Feige,[*] *The Dark Side of Innocence*

THE NEW YORK TIMES MAGAZINE (June 15, 2003)

Michael Mercer was released in May after serving more than a decade in prison for a rape he did not commit. He is the most recent of at least 128 people to be set free by DNA evidence.

A steady stream of exonerations is shedding new light on just how fallible the criminal justice system is. From eyewitness identifications to false confessions, criminal convictions are being re-examined with an ever more sophisticated eye. There is more talk, too, about what we can do to protect the innocent. The issue comes up not only among the criminal defense bar but also at cocktail parties and in Congress. Innocence projects are springing up all over the country, and two states (Illinois and Maryland) have experimented with a moratorium on the death penalty for fear of executing the innocent. An entire innocence movement is afoot.

There is something a little scary about this, though, especially for those most interested in protecting and defending the rights of the accused. The obsessive focus on innocence runs the risk of eclipsing what should be the central issue of the criminal justice system—protecting the rights of everyone. The more that we highlight the rare cases in which innocence can actually be proved, the less we focus on the right of all to the presumption of innocence. So while criminal-defense attorneys may be gleefully reaping the rewards of DNA exonerations now, the long-term impact may be more pernicious than they anticipate.

The reason everyone is talking about protecting the innocent is simple. It is one of the only things in the criminal justice system that everyone can agree on—Republicans and Democrats, prosecutors and public defenders. And it is because everyone can finally agree on something that the rhetoric of innocence has become the dominant discourse within and about the criminal justice system.

The media has also jumped in. Month after month, newspapers and magazines run stories featuring the faces of the falsely accused. Movie stars like Richard Dreyfuss, Mia Farrow and Jeff Goldblum have lined up to perform in "The Exonerated 2/3" a play that recounts the tragic stories of wrongly convicted death-row inmates. Several groups are already lobbying legislatures in an attempt to compensate the exonerated for the lost years of their lives.

All this attention has had some wonderful effects. Not only are the innocent exonerated, but a healthy skepticism has also begun to take hold in the criminal justice system. Jurors are learning that despite prosecutors' claims to the contrary, a confession or eyewitness identification may not be a perfect predictor of guilt.

But while DNA evidence has given us a definitive look at a certain segment of criminal cases in which biological evidence is deposited, recovered and preserved, these clear cases are few and far between. The reality is that most criminal cases are muddled, confusing affairs, rife with conflicting testimony, jumbled loyalties, complex

---

[*] David Feige is a public defender in the Bronx, New York.

motivations and equivocal evidence. In the vast majority of cases, proof of innocence simply can't be established. Because of this reality, the criminal justice system has developed an arcane but workable system for approximating a truth that is, in all but the most exceptional cases, unknowable. It is a system that relies on fundamental rights afforded anyone accused of a crime: proof beyond a reasonable doubt, conviction by 12 unanimous jurors and, perhaps most important, the presumption of innocence.

As anyone who has served on a jury or watched a legal TV show knows, our standard of proof does not even contemplate innocence. Juries across the country render a verdict of guilty or not guilty (short for "not guilty beyond a reasonable doubt"). Innocent isn't a choice. The danger is that the rhetoric of innocence will function like a Trojan horse, an easy way for conservatives to hijack criminal justice legislation and decision-making, rolling back what they view as the reviled rights of criminals, in favor of protecting a tiny number of demonstrably innocent citizens.

Last month, a coalition of advocates for the exonerated initiated a program to help wrongly convicted inmates recently released from prison deal with the stresses of re-entry to the world. The group offered psychological evaluations and an assessment of needs related to housing, health care and jobs. It sounds fantastic. But it is limited to the exonerated. Prison is a brutal, dehumanizing place. And guilty or innocent, ex-inmates emerge into a world ill-suited to receive them, generally without the skills they need to adapt and prosper. More than two million people are currently behind bars. Almost all of them will re-enter society, and almost all of them could benefit from the kinds of resources the program currently seeks only for those like Michael Mercer.

Eager for public support that has long been denied, even defenders of the criminally accused are beginning to fall for the widespread embrace of innocence. Some public-defender offices have even begun creating their own in-house innocence projects. Each of these moves could fundamentally alter the way the legal system conceives of rights, upending notions that we all take for granted now, like the burden of proof—which does and should lie with the prosecution, rather than with the defense—and the presumption of innocence, rather than the proof of it.

The best way to ensure the integrity of the system is to insist ever more stridently on protecting these notions and ensuring the rights of all. There is, in this, a good lesson for all those riding the wave of innocence: Beware the hubris of certainty.

Daniel S. Medwed, *Innocentrism*
2008 U. Ill. L. Rev. 1549, 1566–70 (2008)

The defense norms that have evolved over time tend to highlight constitutional rights and procedural protections—to buttress the supposition that defendants may be not guilty even if not factually innocent. Accordingly, the ambivalence with which some criminal defense attorneys and criminal law scholars have responded to the innocence movement is hardly surprising. What criticisms from the left occasionally appear to lack is an appreciation for innocentrism as a corollary to—not a replacement for—traditional defense theories; innocentrism simply provides another powerful tool in the strategic woodshed.

First, defendants will not inherently be disadvantaged by having jurors who have been exposed to tales of wrongful convictions. That is, defense lawyers normally must make a choice early on in a case, prior to trial, regarding whether to pursue one of several theories: (1) a "he didn't do it" defense (e.g., mistaken identification or alibi), (2) a "he did it, but it was justified or excused" argument (e.g., self-defense or insanity), or (3) "the prosecution can't prove he did it" (e.g., the evidence is legally insufficient or there is room for reasonable doubt). Sometimes two of these theories can be paired as alternative options, but theories 1 and 2 are usually logically inconsistent and therefore incompatible. If a defense lawyer chooses to present theory 2, then, to be sure, that lawyer might be legitimately wary of jurors for whom factual innocence is the benchmark for a not guilty verdict. And this is exactly what voir dire during jury selection could achieve: allow that lawyer to clarify to all potential jurors that factual innocence is not a sine qua non for an acquittal and, in the process, seek to exclude those who believe otherwise. Social phenomena and "issues of the day" often influence potential jurors and compel lawyers to tailor their voir dire questioning to minimize the prejudicial impact of those events. Indeed, the innocence movement should be no more problematic for defense lawyers pursuing a justification or excuse strategy to overcome during jury selection than many other situations that attorneys face—say, prosecutors grappling with the "CSI Effect" in cases lacking biological evidence, namely, the erroneous impression purportedly created by recent television programs that suggest science is always available to solve crimes.

Moreover, for defense lawyers who opt for theories 1 or 3 or, as is often the case, both of those theories in tandem, the spate of wrongful convictions and the attendant publicity is almost surely a strategic boon. Stories of wrongful convictions in the news would serve to reinforce in the hearts and minds of jurors that such cases do in fact happen and could happen here. A major obstacle to theories 1 and/or 3—the notion that the system accurately filters out innocent suspects early on—has been annihilated by the innocence movement, clearing the path (at least in theory) toward convincing jurors of the merits of a defendant's theory of the case more readily than in the past.

Second, a good number of the legislative reforms advocated by innocence projects would benefit both the factually guilty and the factually innocent. For instance, all criminal defendants stand to gain from calls to boost the funding available to indigent defense counsel as well as to increase training requirements and add greater monitoring of defender performance. Similarly, proposals aimed at curbing police and prosecutorial misconduct would advance the interests of the guilty and innocent alike, as would efforts to limit the misuse of jailhouse informants at trial. That being said, some of the reforms heralded by the innocence movement—typically, those focused solely on improving accuracy—might be less than advantageous for the guilty. By way of examples, augmenting the resources of state crime laboratories would probably accelerate the testing of crime scene evidence and incriminate a larger number of suspects in a shorter period of time and videotaping police interrogations, a reform that seeks to detect and prevent false confessions, might add potent, visual fodder to a case against an accused where the defendant has already made a compelling confession on video.

I acknowledge that legislation directed at increasing the accuracy of the criminal investigatory and adjudicatory processes may hurt factually guilty defendants—an outcome that is not necessarily undesirable. As evidence linking a particular defendant to a crime increases, so too does the hurdle for raising plausible defense arguments under above-mentioned theory 3 ("the prosecution can't prove he did it"), much less theory 1 ("he didn't do it"). Yet implementing procedural safeguards to those reforms designed mainly to bolster accuracy could alleviate some defender fears. To elaborate, greater resources for state crime laboratories would likely produce additional paperwork and methodologies for defenders to scrutinize (and criticize) if provided with thorough access during discovery, and fashioning stringent guidelines to govern the airing of videotaped interrogations to jurors could ensure that guilty defendants are not penalized too severely for inculpatory statements captured on tape. Even more, reforms that enhance factual accuracy by pinpointing the actual culprit and excluding the innocent suspect also improve the legitimacy of the criminal justice system as a whole. Criminal defendants who opt for trial might be given a greater benefit of the doubt by judges and jurors because presumably—in a world with a more accurate system— only the strongest defense cases would proceed to that stage and forego plea bargains.

Third, the contention that innocence is a "distraction" that conceptually weakens other critiques of the criminal justice system formulated by defenders neglects to account for the ability of innocentrism to complement, rather than supplant, those other arguments. As virtually every member of an innocence project would agree, constitutional violations and procedural unfairness are larger "problems" (in the sense of their frequency) than wrongful convictions. Few scholars would deny that dubious Fourth Amendment searches, seizures, and stops occur repeatedly across the country or that the Fifth and Sixth Amendment rights to effective assistance of counsel often seem hortatory in light of cases finding defense lawyers' performances sufficient even where they slept or were inebriated throughout trial.

In my view, though, challenges to the unfortunate prevalence of constitutional violations and procedural unfairness are not at odds with innocentric arguments, whether raised to legislators or judges. This conclusion rests on a very simple premise: that innocence cases are often genuinely "different" from those hinging upon rights. That is, constitutional and procedural rights protect values beyond those of safeguarding the factually innocent; they reflect deeply rooted concerns with government overreaching, the dignity of the individual, and the need to defend the private citizen from the potentially overwhelming force of the state. Accordingly, political calls for greater enforcement of "rights" may not clash explicitly with innocence-themed lobbying tactics, as the former principally (but not exclusively) revolve around fairness and the latter around accuracy.

With respect to constructing arguments in court, again, innocence cases are unique. In such cases the underlying facts take on monumental importance, from pretrial motion practice through post-conviction briefing, and errors of law may soon fade into the background as secondary, even tertiary arguments. Conversely, in cases involving criminal defendants for whom "not guilty" rather than innocent is the most viable defense, legal errors often become the axis upon which the litigation revolves. The focal point of a case resting chiefly on constitutional violations and procedural issues also normally lies in pretrial suppression motions and hearings as well as post-trial filings (new trial motions, appellate briefs, collateral remedies), which are events far removed from jurors' eyes and ears.

At a fundamental level, innocentrism and classic systemic critiques of criminal law relating to constitutional violations and procedural unfairness are not irreconcilable; on the contrary, they are complementary and useful arguments in the halls of legislatures and in courtrooms. While these arguments may serve somewhat different purposes, they enjoy a symbiotic relationship—fairness and accuracy are not mutually exclusive. Constitutional and procedural protections help to guard against the conviction of the innocent and legislation focused on aiding the innocent, in turn, reinforces many of the values—individual dignity, minimizing the power of the state, and so forth—that animate the emphasis on constitutional and procedural rights in the criminal justice system.

2. Systemic Constraints and Solutions

William C. Thompson, *Beyond Bad Apples: Analyzing the Role of Forensic Science in Wrongful Convictions*
37 Sw. L. Rev. 1027, 1028–30 (2008)

Public discourse ... has construed forensic science foul-ups as the product of individual intellectual and moral failure. According to the standard account, the problem is limited to "a few bad apples," and the solution follows from that analysis—the bad apples need to be identified and either re-trained or replaced. In this context, bad apples come in three flavors: careless, incompetent, and malicious.

The problem with the bad apples metaphor is that it lacks explanatory power. Saying that bad forensic science is the product of bad forensic scientists is a bit like saying that crime is caused by criminals—the statement is undeniably true but does little to advance understanding of the underlying problem. Individualistic explanations channel our thinking toward individualistic solutions (replacing the bad apples) and divert attention from broader institutional, structural, and cultural factors that may contribute to laboratory foul-ups. We tend to think that replacing the bad apples solves the underlying problem without considering why we have so many bad apples in the first place, why we find more bad apples in some environments than others, and why the apples repeatedly seem to go bad in the same familiar ways.

The most sophisticated analyses of crime laboratory failure have looked beyond individual examiners and focused on laboratory managers. For example, the reports of Michael Bromwich and his colleagues on problems in the FBI laboratory's explosives unit in the 1990s and the Houston Police Department Crime Laboratory, have assigned the underlying cause to "management failure." But the analysis of managers falls into the familiar "bad apple" motif. There is little discussion of institutional or social factors that might foster "management failure" or explain the particular forms that such failures repeatedly take. The focus instead is on "solving" the problem by simply replacing or rehabilitating the bad managerial apples.

I ... argue that crime laboratory failures can be examined more productively through the lens of organizational theory. A useful model is provided by sociologists, such as Charles Perrow and Diane Vaughan, who have analyzed the failure of major technical systems, such as the Three Mile Island nuclear accident and the crash of the space shuttle Challenger. Their work focuses on institutional, social and cultural factors that shape human behavior and on the organizational environment in which it occurs. They treat individual errors, misjudgments, and even misconduct as expected, "normal" events likely to occur in any organization. They focus instead on factors that make these events more common and on the institutional and organizational circumstances under which such ordinary human behaviors may result in catastrophe.

The merits of such a systemic analysis are most easily illustrated with an example. Suppose we want to address the problem of fatal automobile accidents. If we take the "bad apple" approach we will wait until accidents occur, identify the "bad drivers" who caused the accidents (through carelessness, incompetence, or misbehavior) and seek to eliminate those bad drivers by either revoking their driver's licenses or forcing them to undergo retraining. But this individualistic approach has obvious limitations. We would do better to take it as given that people will occasionally drive in a careless or even dangerous manner and focus instead on systemic ways to make those behaviors less likely to occur and less likely to lead to serious consequences when they do occur. Safe highway design, systems to discourage dangerous driving, safe automobile design, safety measures like seat belts and airbags, and adequate emergency services are likely to do far more to reduce the frequency of fatal accidents than a system that focuses solely on eliminating "bad" drivers.

* * *

Let us begin by introducing some terminology of organizational theory and applying it to the criminal justice system. The word system is used to refer to a complex organization composed of constituent elements often called sub-systems, which in turn are composed of smaller elements called parts or units. So we might say that the American criminal justice system is composed of sub-systems—the police, the district attorney's office, defense lawyers, the courts, the department of corrections. Government forensic laboratories are typically parts of the police sub-system, although in some jurisdictions they are parts of the district attorney's office. Forensic laboratories are in turn composed of units or sections, such as a DNA/Serology unit or a latent print section.

Things that go wrong within a particular unit are called incidents. I will use that term to refer to undesirable events. In a forensic laboratory incidents can be unintentional mistakes, such as accidental cross-contamination of samples, mislabeling of samples, or misinterpretation of test results; incidents can also be intentional actions, such as choosing to ignore failed controls, failing to report inconvenient results, or overstating findings. I will use the term unit failure to refer to situations in which the output of a unit is false or seriously misleading. If a forensic laboratory issues a report falsely linking a suspect to a crime, there has been a unit failure of the lab. Although incidents are undesirable and create a potential for further problems, they do not necessarily lead to unit failure in every case. Correspondingly, while unit failure is usually precipitated by one or more incidents, it could conceivably occur without incidents, as when a laboratory report is wrong even though everyone in the laboratory performed in the expected manner.

The terms incident and unit failure can also be applied to other units of the criminal justice system. Consider the unit of the police department responsible for conducting line-ups for identification of suspects. If the police inappropriately suggested that the eyewitness focus on a particular person it would be an incident. If the eyewitness identified the wrong person it would be a unit failure. Here, also, an incident can occur without a unit failure, and vice-versa, although incidents may make unit failure more likely and unit failure is often precipitated by an incident.

The term system failure is reserved for situations in which the system as a whole fails with catastrophic results. For present purposes, I will treat a wrongful conviction as a system failure. System failure usually requires the failure of one or more units, although failure of any single unit will not necessarily lead to system failure because the criminal justice system, like most complex systems, has what organizational theorists call redundancy. There are many component parts to the system and in most cases the separate parts are thought to be loosely-coupled—i.e., largely independent of one another, such that the failure of one unit will not necessarily lead to failure of the entire system. Suppose, for example, that an incident in a forensic laboratory, let us say misinterpretation of a DNA test result, leads to a unit failure—the laboratory issues a report that mistakenly links a particular suspect to a crime. This unit failure will not necessarily lead to system failure (a false conviction) because, if the system is working properly, there are many opportunities for the error to be caught or corrected. The police or prosecutors may realize that it was impossible for the accused to have committed the crime; the defense lawyer may hire an expert who discovers the mistake; the jury may be unconvinced of the guilt of the accused due to a strong alibi, good character evidence, or the absence of other incriminating evidence. Even after conviction there may be opportunities to catch and correct such a system failure.

With so much redundancy, one might argue (as many have) that in the American system of criminal justice false convictions are virtually impossible. A false conviction should only occur if there are failures on multiple levels all in the same case, which should be extremely unlikely if the system is operating as intended. Organizational theorists generally agree in principle that system failure should be extraordinarily rare in a well-designed and loosely-coupled system. But these theorists are quick to point out flaws in the argument that redundancy necessarily equals safety. There are many instances in which large technical systems carefully designed to be "fail-safe" have nevertheless failed with disastrous consequences. Sometimes the problem is that the supposedly redundant components of the system are not really redundant. An unexpected event might cause several components to fail simultaneously, a situation often called "common mode failure." In other instances the various components of a complex system interact in unexpected and unintended ways, such that the failure of one component changes the operation of the others, creating a cascade of further problems. Components that were thought to be loosely-coupled (independent) turn out instead to be tightly-coupled (linked) in ways that precipitate simultaneous failure and lead to a system failure. As Charles Perrow explained the process:

> The argument is basically very simple. We start with a plant, airplane, ship, biology laboratory, or other setting with lots of components (parts, procedures, operators). Then we need two or more failures among components that interact in some unexpected way. No one dreamed that when X failed Y would also be out of order and the two failures would interact so as to both start a fire and silence the fire alarm. Furthermore, no one can figure out the interaction at the time and thus know what to do. The problem is just something that never occurred to the designers.

Perrow calls such events system accidents. Because he sees them as inevitable features of complex systems, he also calls them normal accidents.

Although the potential for such accidents always exists, their frequency can be minimized, organizational theorists argue, by intelligent analysis of systems. It is crucial to understand the systemic factors that lead to failures. The analysis must get beyond blaming "bad apples" and consider the operation of the system as a whole. What incidents might cause the failure of units? What measures might be put in place to minimize such incidents, or reduce the chances that they will lead to unit failure, or catch the unit failures when they occur? How can the independence of different units be maintained in order to reduce the likelihood of "common mode failures" and system accidents? These questions are more likely to lead to improvements than questions about which particular individuals in the system are the "bad apples."

* * *

One important hypothesis generated by this analysis is that the quality of forensic science in a given jurisdiction is intimately connected to the quality of the legal system. Specifically, I posit that bad forensic science will be more common in jurisdictions in which forensic work receives little scrutiny in the legal process. This analysis suggests that forensic science can be improved by measures designed to expose it to greater external scrutiny. More liberal discovery rules, more generous funding of experts, an independent process for appointment of defense counsel, and adequate funding of defense counsel, may do far more to avoid repetition of the Houston scandal than replacement of crime laboratory staff.

* * *

Although some theorists have suggested that the American system of criminal justice is "loosely-coupled," [a careful analysis of how wrongful convictions occur] illustrates how seemingly independent elements (eyewitness identification and DNA testing) can interact, such that a failure in one may precipitate, or at least reinforce, a failure in another. Organizational theorists have long noted the importance of maintaining the independence of organizational units in order to avoid the "common mode failure" or "system failure" that can lead to catastrophe. In the criminal justice system this may well mean taking steps to isolate actors in different units. There is no need for the DNA analyst to know (before completing the analysis and issuing a report) what the eyewitness said; and there is no need for the eyewitness (before testifying) to know the results of the DNA test. Cross-talk between different elements of the justice system undoubtedly occurs routinely without anyone giving it much thought. Effective communication within the system is generally seen as positive rather than negative. The analysis presented here, however, suggests that too much communication of the wrong types can contribute to system failures. In my view, that is an interesting hypothesis and one that is far more likely to lead to productive research and ultimately to useful reforms than the typical crabbed rhetoric of "bad apples."

James M. Doyle, *Orwell's Elephant and the Etiology of Wrongful Convictions*
79 ALB. L. REV. 895, 897–98 (2016)

Miscarriages of justice can never be fully explained by the failures of a single component or a lone operator. The right answer to the question "Who was responsible for this wrongful conviction?" is usually "Everyone involved, to one degree or another," either by making an error or by failing to anticipate or intercept someone else's error. In this view "everyone" includes actors far from the scene of the event who set the budgets, did the hiring, wrote the laws, developed the jurisprudence, and designed the incentives for the apparent culprits on the frontlines. "Everyone" includes those who created the environment in which the sharp-end actors operated. "Everyone" even takes account of the contributions of individuals who stood by inattentively while the frontline environment was shaped by others.

The hardest case for this approach is presented by the recurrent situation in which the miscarriage of justice seems to have resulted from a moral failure—often a spectacular one—on the part of an individual criminal justice actor. Even people who accept the organizational accident explanation as a general theory resist applying it to those events.

For example, when a prosecutor hides exculpatory *Brady* material, that act is a proximate cause of a miscarriage of justice even if it is not the sole cause, and there is little interest in widening the lens to account for other factors. Disciplining the individual actor seems to be both a sufficient response and an emergency. To give attention to other considerations in these cases seems, to many, to threaten to introduce complication and ambiguity where stark moral clarity is demanded: to generate bogus extenuation where all that is required is a plain statement of culpability.

The assumption, "Good man, good result," once formed the basis of medicine's attitude towards its own tragic failures. Even now it characterizes much of the commentary on wrongful convictions. A similar dependence on good men, and therefore on reform strategies focused on the discovery, denunciation, and excision of the bad men, characterizes criminal justice reform discourse.

But if wrongful convictions are "organizational accidents," can disciplining and punishing an individual be enough to reduce future risk? Can we punish our way to safe verdicts? Is there a way to balance accountability for misconduct and the non-blaming, "forward-looking accountability" we need in order to minimize future risk? Should we be searching for a new practice rather than a new structure? Can we develop a vehicle for holding the data-rich statistical findings and the complex individual narratives in permanent productive tension?

A famous essay of George Orwell's, "Shooting an Elephant," focuses on an individual's moral failure: on the bad choice of an actor who zigged when he should have zagged, and who fully understood that he was doing the wrong thing as he acted. Orwell's narrative might illuminate an issue implicit in the organizational accident etiology of error: is the challenge presented by wrongful convictions one best approached as protecting a presumptively safe system from amoral and incompetent people, or one of repairing an inherently vulnerable system that necessarily relies on ordinary human beings?

* * *

In 1922, at the age of nineteen, at loose ends after leaving Eton, and unlikely to obtain a university scholarship, Orwell passed the necessary examinations and followed his father into imperial service: in Orwell's case, into the Burma Police. Reflecting on that experience he produced "Shooting an Elephant," first published in *New Writing* in 1936.

* * *

By the time of the incident he describes, Orwell had "made up [his] mind that imperialism was an evil thing and the sooner [he quit his] job ... the better...." But that didn't mean Orwell's immediate situation was simple. As he explains in the essay:

> All I knew was that I was stuck between my hatred of the empire I served and my rage against the evil-spirited little beasts who tried to make my job impossible.

In this state of mind Orwell is called out to deal with a rampaging elephant: a working animal that has been maddened by "must" (heat), broken its chain, and eluded its keeper. Arming himself and arriving in the quarter where the elephant had been destroying everything within reach, Orwell "failed to get any definite information.... [I]n the East; a story always sounds clear enough at a distance, but the nearer you get to the scene of events the vaguer it becomes." But soon he is told that the elephant has trampled an Indian coolie to death, and he is shown the corpse. Followed by a growing crowd of Burmese, Orwell tracks the animal down.

> As soon as I saw the elephant I knew with perfect certainty that I ought not to shoot him. It is a serious matter to shoot a working elephant—it is com-

parable to destroying a huge and costly piece of machinery—and obviously one ought not to do it if it can possibly be avoided. And at that distance, peacefully eating, the elephant looked no more dangerous than a cow.... Moreover, I did not in the least want to shoot him.

But at that moment Orwell looks around at the Burmese who had followed him: a crowd of "two thousand" people and "growing," all—according to Orwell—"happy and excited over this bit of fun, all certain that the elephant was going to be shot." This was a turning point: "And suddenly I realized that I should have to shoot the elephant after all. The people expected it of me and I had got to do it; I could feel their two thousand wills pressing me forward, irresistibly."

In Orwell's recounting, he zigged when he knew he should have zagged because his role required it:

A sahib has got to act like a sahib;[90] he has got to appear resolute, to know his own mind and do definite things. To come all that way, rifle in hand, with two thousand people marching at my heels, and then to trail feebly away, having done nothing—no, that was impossible. The crowd would laugh at me. And my whole life, every white man's life in the East, was one long struggle not to be laughed at.

Orwell shoots the elephant. Unable to endure the sight of the animal's agonized death throes, Orwell leaves the scene while the elephant is still alive. Later he learns that its body has been stripped to the bone, and that:

Among the Europeans opinion was divided. The older men said I was right, the younger men said it was a damn shame to shoot an elephant for killing a coolie, because an elephant was worth more than any damn Coringhee coolie. And afterwards I was very glad that the coolie had been killed; it put me legally in the right and it gave me a sufficient pretext for shooting the elephant. I often wondered whether any of the others grasped that I had done it solely to avoid looking a fool.

In the end, the opinions of the Europeans, back in the Club, were what mattered to young Orwell.

John Thompson was convicted of murder in New Orleans in 1985. After a trial where he opted not to testify, Thompson was sentenced to death and spent the next eighteen years in prison, fourteen of them on death row. A few weeks before Thompson's scheduled execution in 1999, a defense investigator learned that a cancer-stricken member of the prosecution team had confessed on his deathbed to having withheld crime lab results from the defense, as well as removing a blood sample from the evidence room. In addition, Thompson's defense learned that the New Orleans district attorney's office had failed to disclose that Thompson had been implicated in the murder by a person who received a reward from the victim's family, and that an eye-

---

90. "Sahib" is a Hindu "term of respect used, especially during the colonial period, when addressing or referring to a European."

witness identification did not match Thompson. Thompson's conviction was overturned on appeal. On retrial, a jury exonerated Thompson in thirty-five minutes.

Reviewing Thompson's experience with Orwell's in mind suggests that the problem we face is neither people, nor systems, but, rather, people in systems.

The rule that prosecutors must turn over exculpatory evidence material to guilt or punishment to defense counsel is a "best practice" that the Supreme Court held in *Brady v. Maryland* is also a minimum requirement of the Constitution. As Thompson indicates, it is a "best practice" that is not reliably followed. According to at least one noted federal judge, violations of the Brady rule are "epidemic."

We tend to think of the *Brady* violation cases as uncomplicated events: a prosecutor, driven by an excess of the All-American will to win, is encouraged to go too far by the apparently total absence of accountability, and conceals exculpatory evidence. As Marvin Schechter, chairman of the criminal justice section of the New York State Bar Association and a defense attorney put it: "Prosecutors engage in misconduct because they know they can get away with it."

Introducing the credible threat of punishment seems to be the simple answer to this simple problem. But the *Brady* (and other misconduct) cases are, like the episode in Shooting an Elephant, more complicated. Even if we put aside for the moment the fact that a wrongful conviction requires not only a *Brady* violation but also an upstream failure by the early police investigators to identify the true culprit and a downstream failure by the defenders to uncover the *Brady* violation or to compensate for its impact, much remains to be explained about the prosecutors' actions.

What if the *Brady* cases involve a problematic—but not abnormal—prosecutor who makes a faulty decision while playing, under intense pressure, the hand he has been dealt by others? What if the problem is not the will to win, but the fear of losing and exposure; not the absence of accountability, but the distorting power of a peculiarly intense, all-embracing, and acutely local accountability that eclipses well-known general constitutional norms?

Safety experts in aviation, medicine, and other high risk fields find that these questions indicate that we should pivot from our focus on writing new rules—and punishing the violations of old ones—to a new focus on developing a culture of safety that has reducing future risk through continuous, collaborative, quality improvement as its goal.

No system can survive without sanctions for its conscious rule breakers, and advocates for "non-blaming" approaches to accountability must keep that reality in mind. Still, it ought to be possible to see the young Orwells in the criminal system as potential resources, not exclusively as dangerous toxins. The most productive question could be not why prosecutors believe they can get away with cheating, but why they feel any desire to cheat in the first place.

The question that the Thompson narrative raises is not whether the choices of either the District Attorney's office as an agency or the individual frontline prosecutors who hid the evidence were wrong. Of course those choices were wrong. The real question is why did the mistaken choices seem to the agency and to the individuals to be good choices at the time? Or, at least, why did the mistaken choices seem from their perspectives to be the only, or "least bad" choices available. Exculpatory evidence has to be turned over. Why didn't the prosecutors know this? (In fact, as the deathbed confession indicates, at least one did know it.) Why, knowing that withholding the evidence was wrong (as fully as Orwell knew shooting his elephant was wrong) did they decide not to act as the *Brady* rule required?

Safety experts reviewing "operator error" events believe that the operators' choices may have been mistaken, may have violated rules—may even have been immoral—but they were locally rational. They promised to solve, at least for a moment, a pressing local problem, and the same choices will seem rational to the operators who next face the same problems unless their circumstances are changed.

To understand why this can happen in a *Brady* exoneration case it is not enough to go "down and in" to find the broken procedural component or the rogue Assistant District Attorney. The problem cannot be fully encompassed within the character of any individual prosecutor. That prosecutor is reacting to the conventional demands within his office. And his office is reacting to pressures from the larger society.

What we see in the *Brady* exoneration cases are choices typical of organizations and individuals reacting to the compelling pressure to provide outputs under conditions of resource scarcity. It may be disappointing but it should not be shocking that prosecutors in the wrongful conviction cases, like workers in many production processes, adopted a "covert work system." They decided to evade well-known formal disclosure requirements and buried alternative narratives because they believed sharing the exculpatory facts would interfere with achieving the "real" production goals assigned to them by people to whom they were accountable, namely, superiors who demand "outputs" in the form of convictions, and, therefore, to the unpredictable lay jurors, who will require persuasion before those "outputs" can be generated.

Were the prosecutors so starved of resources by the city or state that they felt they could not successfully prosecute guilty violent offenders by following the rules? Had their caseloads crept up to a level where competent, thorough practice seemed impossible? Did they feel that they were so swamped that they needed to bluff Thompson into a guilty plea by withholding the evidence that might have demonstrated his innocence? Did supervisory oversight slacken for the same reasons? Did tunnel vision and other cognitive biases set in? Did the prosecutors feel acutely vulnerable to irresponsible media or political pressure? Or did the prosecutors believe that the police department was so under-resourced or ill-managed that no prosecutors could ever convict anyone, no matter how guilty, if they dutifully played the woeful cards the police dealt them? Were they right about that? Did the see-no-evil attitude of local trial judges and the vulnerability of overwhelmed appointed defenders encourage them? Had the prosecutors moved by small increments down the inculpatory-to-exculpatory spectrum over the years, withholding progressively more exculpatory material but seeing no negative local impacts (such as exonerations) from doing so? Did they learn to tolerate ever-widening margins of error in making guilt/innocence judgments? Had deviation from the *Brady* rule been "normalized"?

It is common to speak of the prosecutors' offices as "black boxes," a reference to their characteristic absence of transparency. But it is important to remember that within that black box local norms are well-known and conveyed with great force. Young prosecutors learn very early their local version of "[a] sahib has got to act like a sahib."

The prosecutors who figured in the high profile Brady-driven exoneration cases are not lone wolf outcasts in their offices; typically, they are the rising local stars who had successfully managed the conflicts between the formal legal rules and their office culture and have been rewarded with progressively more visible and important case assignments. The prosecutors feel intensely accountable to the role requirements imposed by the culture within their office.

Inevitably, some prosecutors will do what workers in other fields do when confronted by the end-of-process inspections. (In this case, the inspection is provided by adversary trials.) They will develop "workarounds" that allow them to get on with their "real" job, no matter what the formal rules instituted by the Supreme Court at 30,000 feet (or the Board of Bar Overseers at 10,000) require. As Barbara O'Brien has demonstrated, these prosecutors, driven by criteria of outputs (not processes) and persuasion (not comprehension) find themselves in a cognitive position that degrades not only their willingness to turn over Brady material, but their ability to recognize it. A Brady violation seen from this perspective is a mundane workaround; a well-traveled shortcut through a thicket of rules that if meticulously followed would frustrate the attainment of "higher" goals. In fact, within the prosecutors' "black box" familiarity with these workarounds begins to seem to be the essence of veteran workmanship and professionalism. Impose an improved rule without changing either the internal culture or the external demands on that culture and that new rule will be under immediate attack from its environment: new workarounds will be generated very quickly.

Encapsulation in a local black box dilutes the deterrent efficacy of punitive gestures applied to other prosecutors outside the local world. The disciplining of a prosecutor in Texas will have limited impact on the conduct of prosecutors in Philadelphia. The informal sanctions for violating the local "covert work rules" and then losing a trial as a consequence are immediate, personal, and public: enforced by the people in the next office. Any official sanction for withholding Brady material is — and will remain even if some novel enthusiasm for disciplining prosecutors gradually takes hold in scattered jurisdictions — theoretical. Punishment is necessarily contingent on your concealment being discovered by an actually innocent defendant who insisted on a trial, an eventual official finding that the particular defendant really was innocent, that the withheld evidence was "material," and that your violation was knowing. For all of the reasons that disciplinary actions against prosecutors have not become normal (to put it mildly) up until now, some skepticism about the likelihood of their multiplying any time soon is in order.

Jon B. Gould, Julia Carrano, Richard A. Leo, and Katie Hail-Jares, *Predicting Erroneous Convictions*

99 Iowa L. Rev. 471, 475–77 (2014)

Wrongful convictions ... have become representative of the failure of the justice system to perform its most fundamental duty—to sort the innocent from the guilty. Yet the focus on exonerations has obscured the cases the criminal justice system "gets right": those cases where the innocent defendants ... are identified and released before conviction. What explains the different outcomes in these two scenarios? Why are some innocent defendants convicted and spend years in prison before exoneration ("erroneous convictions"), while others are released before trial or are acquitted on the basis of their factual innocence ("near misses")? Are there factors that could have predicted these dramatically divergent outcomes? Despite substantial scholarly research on high-profile DNA and non-DNA wrongful conviction and exoneration cases, these questions remain largely unanswered.

Advanced statistical and comparative social science methodologies, however, present an opportunity to begin answering these questions. Traditionally, most research on wrongful convictions has relied upon narrative methodologies and case studies. This type of research has revealed a number of factors common among wrongful convictions, such as faulty eyewitness identification, false incriminating statements/confessions, perjured jailhouse informant testimony, and forensic error. Case study research also has deepened our understanding of how wrongful convictions occur, and it has influenced public perceptions and policy debates. However, case study research does not allow scholars to conclusively establish what factors differentiate a wrongful conviction from any other case outcome, including a "near miss"—that is, when an innocent defendant is arrested, indicted, and/or prosecuted, but his case is either dismissed prior to trial or he is acquitted at trial. As a result, we know what problems wrongful convictions share, but not what sets them apart.

[W]e break new ground by analyzing this unanswered question. We report the results from a large-scale empirical research project that compares 260 wrongful convictions to 200 near misses in violent felony cases from across the United States. Drawing on both quantitative and qualitative methods, we examine the factors that statistically explain why an innocent defendant, once indicted, ends up erroneously convicted rather than released. We conclude that a number of variables can predict case outcome, including the age and criminal history of the defendant, the punitiveness of the state, Brady violations, forensic error, weak defense and prosecution cases, non-intentional misidentification, and lying by a non-eyewitness. Moreover, we argue that these individual factors are connected and exacerbated by tunnel vision, which prevents the system from self-correcting once an error is made and leads to general system failure. Interestingly, other factors traditionally suggested as causes of erroneous convictions, including criminal-justice official error, false incriminating statements/confessions, and race effects, appear in statistically similar rates in both sets of cases; although they may increase the chance that an innocent suspect will be indicted, they do not necessarily increase the likelihood that the indictment will result in a conviction.

Our results inform how the legal community can improve its ability to justly adjudicate cases of innocent defendants in the future, in particular by actively working to combat tunnel vision and establishing procedures and policies to learn from past mistakes.

* * *

With the advent of forensic DNA testing and the exoneration of hundreds of innocent prisoners in the last two decades, there has come a boom in research on wrongful convictions. Surprisingly, despite the shift in magnitude, there has been little effort to change the method of studying these cases. Most of the scholarship occurs in law reviews rather than criminology or other social science journals, and, while increasingly systematic, still follows Borchard's classic template.

As a result, the literature continues to focus primarily on identifying the isolated legal causes and consequences of wrongful convictions, as well as proposing legal and policy reforms designed to reduce their occurrence.

Such studies have been important in establishing at least eight major sources of wrongful convictions: (1) mistaken eyewitness identification; (2) false incriminating statements or confessions; (3) tunnel vision; (4) perjured informant testimony; (5) forensic error; (6) police error; (7) prosecutorial error; and (8) inadequate defense representation.

In addition, the research literature discusses the potential effects of race, age, and geographic region on the fate of innocent defendants. The most recent comprehensive compilation of exonerations in the United States confirms that the majority of cases involved at least one, but often several, of the above factors.

However, labeling these factors as "causes" of erroneous convictions can be misleading. As noted above, much of the research to date has been conducted by traditional legal scholars and journalists, who have tended to view wrongful convictions through law's straightforward model of cause and effect: "a wrongful conviction occurred, a cause is presumed, and the trigger is sought in order to prevent its harmful effects in the future." In reality, however, causation is a much more complex phenomenon, and to study it in the social and political world generally requires a control or comparison group to ensure that what is being observed is not merely a correlate. Thus, to accurately assess the cause(s) of erroneous convictions, the researcher requires a comparison group. Without one, we cannot state for certain whether the frequent errors found in erroneous convictions are actually the "causes" of these miscarriages of justice because we do not know to what extent these errors are present in cases that did not result in an erroneous conviction.

In fact, there is evidence that these errors do occur in other cases. Several scholars have documented and analyzed cases in which mistakes led to an erroneous indictment of an innocent person, but the defendant was not convicted.... Although these accounts cite the reason for the defendant's dismissal (such as a new autopsy report or DNA testing), they do not explain how the cases they document differ from other cases in which an innocent defendant was erroneously convicted.... [O]ur research question directly examines how the criminal justice system can and does "get it right" when faced with an innocent defendant.

* * *

Our findings indicate that several of the traditional "causes" of erroneous convictions—including forensic error and quality of defense—do indeed separate erroneous convictions from near misses, while others—such as criminal-justice-official error and false incriminating statements/confessions—appear in statistically non-differentiable rates in both sets of cases. Therefore, only the former factors can be considered statistical predictors of erroneous convictions once an innocent defendant has been indicted. However, this does not mean that the latter issues do not contribute to erroneous convictions. While our statistical analysis indicates that the non-significant factors are insufficient in themselves to statistically predict that an innocent defendant will be convicted, their very numbers in both sets of cases indicate that they do play a role, and it is clear that some types of erroneous evidence—such as false incriminating statements/confessions—create a very high (and statistically significant) risk of erroneous conviction if the case is not dismissed but instead proceeds to plea bargaining or trial.

* * *

Many of the near misses and erroneous convictions started in a similar way—most frequently a misidentification or false incriminating statement/confession, but sometimes an official error or anonymous tip—that led to an indictment. That is, regardless of the ultimate resolution of a case, an innocent individual entered the criminal justice system because, for example, a witness falsely implicated him, a prosecutor or police officer made an error, or he was induced to confess. But an initial error need not necessarily lead to an erroneous conviction. Our near misses show that many erroneous indictments result in a dismissal or acquittal instead.

Thus, the divergent outcomes rest upon mitigating factors—our statistically significant variables—that intervene in the investigation and prosecution of a crime and subsequently influence the likelihood of a mistaken conviction. Some of the factors are environmental or static (and therefore largely uncontrollable), such as the defendant's age, his number of prior offenses, and the state's level of punitiveness. Others, namely the strength of the prosecution and defense and whether there is error in forensic testing, are dynamic and therefore directly dependent on the actions of the people involved in the adversarial system. A summary of the pathways leading to divergent case outcome is illustrated in Table 17.1.

Lest there be any misunderstandings, our results do not suggest that these variables are unrelated to either erroneous convictions or near misses. In fact, although their rates were so similar that they do not statistically account for divergent case outcomes in the bivariate analysis, factors such as eyewitness misidentification and false incriminating statements/confessions occurred regularly in both sets of cases.... [T]hese errors may lead to the arrest and indictment of an innocent defendant. But, once a

Table 17.1 Potentially Important Factors That Were Not Statistically Significant

Variable	Erroneous Convictions Total % (N)	Near Misses Total % (N)
Eyewitness Identification[†]	82 (260)	75 (200)
Incriminating Statement	22 (259)	29 (200)
Lying by Snitch	11 (260)	7 (200)
Similar Criminal History[††]	17 (132)	25 (65)
Police Error	16 (259) [Alleged: 14]	11 (198) [Alleged: 15]
Prosecutor Error	9 (260) [Alleged: 7]	6 (199) [Alleged: 6]
Police Misconduct	8 (259) [Alleged: 9]	12 (199) [Alleged: 15]
Prosecutor Misconduct	4 (260) [Alleged: 5]	3 (200) [Alleged: 4]

[†] Most of the other variables concerning eyewitness identification (such as type of identification procedure or time between crime and identification) were also statistically indistinguishable between erroneous convictions and near misses. The important exception is whether the misidentification was intentional; this was statistically significant and is discussed in greater detail in the text.

[††] Percentage excluding cases where the defendant had no criminal history.

factually innocent defendant enters the criminal justice system, the findings here indicate that conviction will not statistically turn on differences in those factors.

* * *

Our conclusion is that erroneous convictions are more about system failure than individual causes. Erroneous convictions represent complex breakdowns in the adversarial process, which occur when errors are compounded rather than rectified, often as a result of tunnel vision. Most of our cases involved more than one error, sometimes as many as four or five. This was particularly evident with the erroneous convictions. For example, false testimony alone was rarely the direct cause of an erroneous conviction. The larger story often involved a prosecutor who had serious doubts about a witness's story but did not share these with a superior or the defense, and a defense attorney who did not have the time or energy to investigate the witness's story. Just as a jetliner may crash when a multitude of problems arises and distracts the crew's attention from the task at hand, erroneous convictions result from a combination of errors within the criminal justice system.

By contrast, among the near misses, the original errors were corrected in a variety of ways. These corrections included: better or complete forensic testing, an active defense attorney who tracked down and documented an alibi, or a follow-up investigation in which the victim or witness recanted the identification. Crucially, these interventions, regardless of their actual scope, broke the momentum within the escalation of commitment. The cases illustrate that a well-functioning criminal justice system is not one in which there are no errors, but rather one in which one part of the system can correct another.

Table 17.2 Factors That Influence the Likelihood of an Erroneous Conviction

Concept	Variable	Coef.	(Std. Err.)
Location Effect	Death Penalty Culture	172.848**	(57.809)
	Crime Consistency	1.086	(0.792)
	Female Victim	0.601	(0.463)
	High Profile Case	-0.715	(0.486)
Nature of the Defendant	Age	-0.055**	(0.027)
	Black Defendant	0.213	(0.383)
	High School Grad	-0.309	(0.483)
	Prior Criminal History	0.850***	(0.296)
Nature of the Facts	Strength of Pros. Case	-1.091**	(0.490)
	Forensic Error	0.956**	(0.467)
	Non-Eyewitness Testimony/Evidence	0.333	(0.461)
	Testimony Discrepancy	0.422	(0.472)
	Unique Perpetrator Description	0.270	(0.480)
	Intentional MisID	-0.890**	(0.448)
Quality of Work by CJ System	Pros. Withheld Evidence	1.655***	(0.557)
	Lying Non-Eyewitness	1.159**	(0.574)
	Time from Arrest to Indict.	0.241	(0.493)
Quality of Defense	Strength of Defense Case	-1.043**	(0.470)
	Physical Alibi	-0.716	(0.489)
	Other Suspect	-0.693	(0.534)
	Evidence of Misconduct	-0.989*	(0.488)
	Family Witness	0.887***	(0.290)
Controls	Illinois Cases	0.953**	(0.419)
	Post-DNA	-1.213***	(0.347)
	Murder Cases	-0.674*	(0.364)
	Constant	-0.131	(2.111)

*** $p < 0.01$, ** $p < 0.05$, * $p < 0.10$

Of course, it is important to prevent errors in the first place, and we applaud much of the previous research that has suggested reforms to address individual problems such as false incriminating statements/confessions, eyewitness errors, and the like. But because ensuring perfect evidence is not realistic, it is equally as important to consider what practices and policies can break the escalation of commitment and improve the system's ability to self-correct when flawed evidence does arise.

Paul Cassell, *Can We Protect the Innocent without Freeing the Guilty? Thoughts on Innocence Reforms That Avoid Harmful Tradeoffs*

In Wrongful Convictions and the DNA Revolution:
Twenty-Five Years of Freeing the Innocent, 264–241 (Medwed, D. Ed.)
(Cambridge University Press, 2017)

Comparing and Quantifying the Risk of Wrongful Conviction to the Risk of Victimization

Two Kinds of Tragedies

In considering the issue of wrongful convictions, some broader perspective is useful. To be sure, the conviction of even a single factually-innocent person is a tragedy. A grave and serious injustice has been done whenever the criminal justice system wrongfully convicts and imprisons someone for a crime he has not committed. But, sadly, this is not the only kind of tragedy that the criminal justice system must be concerned about. A properly-functioning criminal justice system has to consider not only the suffering of those who have been wrongfully convicted, but also those who have become (or will become) the victims of crimes.

* * *

How to assess these competing risks is exceedingly complex. Fortunately other thoughtful observers have already done important spadework on this issue. An extremely helpful discussion of the convicting-the-guilty-while-sparing-the-innocent tradeoff is found in Professor Ronald J. Allen and Investigator Larry Laudan's article *Deadly Dilemmas*.[91] They explain that "[w]hile the prospect of convicting or executing a truly innocent person is horrifying, this type of mistake occurs within a highly complicated matrix of relationships where other equally horrifying mistakes go unnoticed in the conventional discourse." Allen and Laudan recognize that some public policy reform measures that reduce the risk of convicting an innocent person may simultaneously increase the risk that a guilty criminal will escape conviction and go on to commit additional violent crimes.

I will join Allen and Laudan in focusing on this possible tradeoff—specifically, the risk that putting in place measures to protect against convicting innocent persons will allow guilty criminals to escape conviction.

* * *

[R]ather than embark on what would be a complicated effort to precisely quantify tradeoffs for particular reforms, I would like to search for reforms that help protect the innocent without freeing the guilty—reforms that ought to be relatively uncontroversial, at least for those (including many of the authors in this book) who prioritize

---

91. Ronald J. Allen & Larry Laudan, *Deadly Dilemmas*, 41 Texas Tech. L. Rev. 65 (2008). *See also* Larry Laudan & Ronald J. Allen, *Deadly Dilemmas II: Bail and Crime*, 85 Chi.-Kent L. Rev. 23 (2010); Ronald J. Allen & Larry Laudan, *Deadly Dilemmas III: Some Kind Words for Preventive Detention,* 101 J. Crim. L. & Criminology 781 (2011).

innocence issues over other values in the criminal justice system. I agree with those who argue that the risk our criminal justice system poses to the innocent is not trivial. But ... neither is the risk to crime victims, who bear the brunt of any failures of the system to apprehend or prosecute dangerous criminals....

Protecting the Innocent While Simultaneously Convicting the Guilty

In light of the risk of potential tradeoffs between convicting the guilty while protecting the innocent, the reforms that are most likely to be justified on cost-benefit analysis will be those that do not present any significant risk of increasing crime victimization rates....

More Research on the Frequency and Causes of Wrongful Convictions

At the top of my list of measures to address the problem of wrongful convictions of the innocent is further research on the extent and causes of the problem.... For public policy purposes, we need more information—information about, for example, wrongful convictions through guilty pleas (a key part of the Allen and Laudan estimate) and solid information about the incidence of wrongful convictions outside the areas of homicide and rape.

The additional research needs to focus on the frequency of false confessions. Professor Samuel Gross has aptly observed that "[t]he most important question about false convictions is also the most basic: How frequently are innocent people convicted of crimes?"[92] To be sure, on the twenty-fifth anniversary of the first DNA exonerations, we now have far more information about wrongful convictions than in the past. But even disregarding the questions about how "innocence" is determined in some of this research, a more fundamental problem is the fact that a collection of alleged miscarriages based on DNA or any other factor may not be representative of the processing of cases in the American criminal justice system.

To avoid this problem, researchers could take a random sample of a large number of felony criminal violent crime cases (1,000 seems like a good number) and then track them through the system to see what happens. While it might not be possible to follow all 1,000 cases carefully, it would seem likely that the cases where a defendant might plausibly be innocent would shrink the numbers down fairly rapidly. Researchers could focus on this subset of cases and try to come up with an initial, plausible number of cases in which a wrongful conviction was even a possibility, and then perhaps press even further to try and get to the bedrock truth in this subset of cases. This methodology has already been employed in other countries in the false confessions area. It should be tried on the broader subject of wrongful convictions. Research of this type might be very valuable for revealing both the scope of the wrongful conviction problem and particular areas where wrongful convictions are prevalent. This would permit a targeted response to the problem, perhaps more narrowly addressing the risk to the innocent without freeing the guilty.

---

92. Samuel Gross, *Convicting the Innocent*, 4 ANN. REV. L. SOC. SCI. 173, 176 (2008).

Refocus Post-Conviction Relief on Claims of Factual Innocence

One of the great problems for the innocence movement is trying to find the needles in a large haystack—that is, trying to identify innocent persons in a criminal justice system that processes mostly guilty defendants. Some commentators have made a frontal assault on this problem by proposing that we limit access to some forms of judicial review to those who are making claims of actual innocence. For example, two distinguished legal scholars—Joseph Hoffmann and Nancy King—proposed that federal habeas corpus review of noncapital state court convictions and sentences should, with narrow exceptions, be abolished except for those who couple a constitutional claim with "clear and convincing proof of actual innocence."[93] Relying on a comprehensive study of federal habeas corpus filings,[94] they found that only seven of the 2,384 noncapital habeas filings in the study (0.29%) resulted in a grant of habeas relief, and one of those seven was later reversed on appeal. Hoffmann and King argued that habeas review of such claims "currently squanders resources while failing to remedy defense-attorney deficiencies. Those resources should be redeployed where they have a more meaningful chance of preventing the deficiencies in the first place." They propose moving resources to indigent defense representation instead of largely pointless habeas litigation.

Hoffmann and King's proposal is similar to others that have tried to focus habeas corpus on protecting the innocent. Most famously, Judge Henry Friendly argued that federal habeas relief for most constitutional errors should be conditioned on a showing of innocence.[95] Interestingly, he also proposed that a sufficient demonstration of innocence should itself be a basis for habeas relief, an issue that has bedeviled the Supreme Court in recent years. Similarly, Professors John Jeffries, Jr. and William Stuntz have suggested allowing defaulted federal claims to be raised in federal habeas where those claims raise a reasonable probability that the defaulted claims resulted in an erroneous conviction.[96] Professor Samuel Gross has argued for giving defendant claiming innocence the option for an "investigative trial," in which the defendant would be able to argue his innocence, provided he waived important rights—in exchange, the defendant (if convicted) would be given greater freedom to raise post-conviction claims of innocence.[97] And most recently, in this book, Professor Stephanie Hartung has argued for a post-conviction "innocence track" in federal habeas, under

---

93. Joseph L. Hoffmann & Nancy J. King, *Rethinking the Federal Role in State Criminal Justice*, 84 N.Y.U. L. REV. 791, 820 (2009).

94. NANCY J. KING ET AL., FINAL TECHNICAL REPORT: HABEAS LITIGATION IN U.S. DISTRICT COURTS (2007), available at http://www.ncjrs.gov/pdffiles1/nij/grants/219559.pdf.

95. See Henry J. Friendly, *Is Innocence Irrelevant? Collateral Attack on Criminal Judgments*, 38 U. CHI L. REV. 143 (1970).

96. John C. Jeffries, Jr. & William J. Stuntz, *Ineffective Assistance and Procedural Default in Federal Habeas Corpus*, 57 U. CHI. L. REV. 679 (1990).

97. Samuel R. Gross, *Pretrial Incentives, Post-Conviction Review, and Sorting Criminal Prosecutions by Guilt or Innocence*, 56 N.Y.L. SCH. L. REV. 1009 (2011).

which any prisoner who establishes innocence by a preponderance of the evidence would be entitled to a blanket exemption from procedural bars.[98]

One of the interesting things about post-conviction review is that, by definition, it cannot interfere with the process of convicting the guilty at trial. Accordingly, post-conviction review offers a particularly promising approach for escaping the tradeoffs highlighted earlier.

One proposal worth serious exploration combines aspects of the Hoffmann and King proposal, along with Judge Friendly's insight that federal habeas should focus on innocence and Professor Hartung's idea for an innocence track. We could restrict federal habeas to those who have a colorable claim of factual innocence. Those prisoners could then be required to establish factual innocence by a preponderance of the evidence and, if they did so, they would have a blanket exemption from any procedural bars to raising claims for relief in federal court. I would also add to Hartung's innocence track the idea that if a prisoner who had proven he was innocent did not receive federal habeas relief, the federal courts could at least remand the case back to the prisoner's State Supreme Court for further inquiry as to whether state relief might be available.

Professor Hartung (and others) may wonder about why the innocence track needs to be coupled with the abolition of federal habeas for those who are raising claims unrelated to innocence. The answer is straightforward: time, energy, and resources are limited. Given Hoffmann and King's finding that federal habeas relief for procedural violations is essentially an impossibility, it make no sense to allow those claims to continue to be pressed before federal courts. Restructuring federal habeas so that it *only* concerns prisoners alleging factual innocence would help federal courts reconceptualize their mission to the benefit of wrongfully convicted prisoners—precisely the sort of change that helps the innocent without freeing the guilty. It seems almost irrefutable that the innocent will benefit from a system concentrating on them—that is, that we can find needles more effectively in smaller haystacks.

Increasing Resources for Indigent Defense Counsel and Prosecutors to Focus on Issues Relating to Actual Innocence

On the issue of wrongful convictions, the elephant in the room is little discussed but obvious: money. The root cause of wrongful convictions is almost certainly insufficient resources devoted to the criminal justice system. Whatever individual causes might be pinpointed in particular cases, more resources would often have enabled defense counsel (or police and prosecuting agencies) to locate persuasive evidence of innocence. If this diagnosis is correct, then an important part of the true solution to the wrongful conviction problem may be devoting additional resources to the criminal justice system.

---

98. Stephanie Roberts Hartung, *Postconviction Procedure: The Next Frontier in Innocence Reform*, WRONGFUL CONVICTIONS AND THE DNA REVOLUTION: REFLECTIONS ON TWENTY-FIVE YEARS OF FREEING THE INNOCENT (Cambridge University Press, 2016).

Given the fiscal realities of the world we live in, however, it may be an academic proposal to call for significant new funding for defense attorneys, for example.[99] At a macro level, the funds devoted to the criminal justice system are probably roughly fixed and not much is likely to change in the near term.[100] What is needed, then, is to prioritize innocence over other criminal justice expenditures. Fortunately, for those who truly believe in "innocentrism," there are ways to do this—as I discuss in the next several sections.

Abolishing the Fourth Amendment Exclusionary Rule, and Consequently Shifting Defense Resources Away from Litigating Purely Procedural Claims

If we want the criminal justice system to prioritize the issue of innocence and devote more resources to it, then a good start would be to consider abolishing the Fourth Amendment exclusionary rule. Abolition of the rule and replacing it with a system of civil damage remedies has been advocated by such distinguished legal figures as Chief Justice Warren Burger,[101] Dallin Oaks,[102] Akhil Amar,[103] Bill Pizzi,[104] and Paul Robinson.[105] The classic argument for abolishing the exclusionary rule is that the rule sets criminals free because the constable has blundered.[106] But there is a more subtle, and in many ways more pernicious, defect to the exclusionary rule. Under a regime that allows the "deliberate exclusion of truth from the fact-finding process,"[107] defense efforts will move toward issues involving the validity of evidence collection rather than toward assessing the quality of the evidence itself. Professor William Stuntz perhaps most famously made this point in his writings, explaining how a system with limited resources that emphasizes procedure over substance will give short shrift to factual claims of innocence.[108] Stuntz is cautious in his argument. As he explains, the current system does not simply involve a direct tradeoff, but rather "places substantial pressure on [defense] counsel to opt for the procedural claim rather than the (potential) substantive one." But Stuntz's bottom-line conclusion seems unassailable: there is some tradeoff in the current regime favoring procedural claims over substantive ones.

---

99. See Mary Sue Backus & Paul Marcus, *The Right to Counsel in Criminal Cases, a National Crisis,* 57 HASTINGS L.J. 1031, 1059 (2006); Paul Cassell & Nancy Gertner, *Public Defenders Fall to the Sequester,* WALL ST. J., Aug. 20, 2013 (urging that federal public defender funds not be sequestered).

100. See Erik Lillquist, *Improving Accuracy in Criminal Cases,* 41 U. RICH. L. REV. 897 (2007) (noting a common assumption that there are fixed resources devoted to criminal justice).

101. See Stone v. Powell, 428 U.S. 465, 500–01 (1976) (Burger, C.J., concurring).

102. See Dallin H. Oaks, *Studying the Exclusionary Rule in Search and Seizure,* 37 U. CHI. L. REV. 665, 739–40 (1970).

103. See AKHIL REED AMAR, THE CONSTITUTION AND CRIMINAL PROCEDURE 40–45 (1997).

104. See WILLIAM T. PIZZI, TRIALS WITHOUT TRUTH: WHY OUR SYSTEM OF CRIMINAL TRIALS HAS BECOME AN EXPENSIVE FAILURE AND WHAT WE NEED TO DO TO REBUILD IT (1999).

105. PAUL H. ROBINSON & MICHAEL T. CAHILL, LAW WITHOUT JUSTICE: WHY CRIMINAL LAW DOESN'T GIVE PEOPLE WHAT THEY DESERVE (2006).

106. People v. Defore, 150 N.E. 585, 587 (N.Y.1926).

107. Stone v. Powell, 428 U.S. 465, 496 (Burger, C.J., concurring).

108. William Stuntz, *The Uneasy Relationship Between Criminal Procedure and Criminal Justice,* 107 YALE L.J. 1, 37–40 (1997).

In addition to these kinds of tradeoffs, the exclusionary rule creates a perverse screening at trial. Jurors deciding cases may believe that a weak prosecution case actually is the result of the exclusion of evidence. Because of facts such as these, it seems difficult to contest that "actually guilty defendants are most likely to benefit from the exclusionary rule."

Given these tradeoffs, those with an innocentric view of the world should be the first to jump on the replace-the-exclusionary-rule-with-civil-damages bandwagon. Surely the experience of the rest of the world suggests that the exclusionary rule is not the only way to restrain police abuses. There is good reason to think that we can craft a damages regime for protecting Fourth Amendment rights that will fully preserve them, just as we rely on a damages regime to protect other civil liberties, such as our First Amendment rights.

Once procedural issues regarding the legality of searches are diverted to the civil justice system, the criminal justice system would gain substantial new resources to devote to innocence issues. While the percentage of cases in which the exclusionary rule results in guilty criminals going free is disputed, it does not appear to be disputed that the exclusionary rule results in "tens of thousands of contested suppression motions each year."[109] Instead of filing and litigating these motions that have nothing to do with innocence, defense counsel could turn their attention to substantive issues about who committed the crime. Prioritizing substantive issues of guilt and innocence over procedural issues of the reasonableness of searches is exactly the way the system should be structured — and a way the *both* increases the chance of convicting the guilty while reducing the chance of convicting the innocent.

Replacing the Miranda *Regime with the Videotaping of Custodial Interrogations*

The problem of procedure over substance is not confined solely to Fourth Amendment jurisprudence. The same flaw has developed in confession law. Here again, those who are most concerned about innocence should be skeptical of the law's current structure, which relies largely on *Miranda* warnings and waivers to protect against coercive interrogations. As a practical matter, this approach does little to help the innocent and prioritizes litigation about *Miranda* compliance over litigation about the accuracy of confessions. The result has been a regime that is not particularly well-suited to address "false confession" issues[110] — i.e., is not well-suited to protecting the innocent. Today *Miranda* "serves mainly to distract lawyers, scholars, and judges from considering the real problem of interrogation, which is how to convict the guilty while protecting the innocent."[111]

---

109. McDonald v. City of Chicago, 561 U.S. 742, 785 (2010) (quoting William Stuntz, *The Virtues and Vices of the Exclusionary Rule*, 20 Harv. J.L. & Pub. Pol'y 443, 444 (1997)).

110. See generally Paul G. Cassell, *Protecting the Innocent from Lost Confessions and False Confessions — And from* Miranda, 88 J. Crim. L. & Criminology 497 (1998).

111. Steven B. Duke, *Does* Miranda *Protect the Innocent or the Guilty?*, 10 Chap. L. Rev. 551, 566–67 (2007); see also Ronald J. Allen, Miranda's *Hollow Core*, 100 NW. U. L. Rev. 71 (2006).

The "central problem with *Miranda* is that it was not crafted specifically to prevent false confessions, but rather to regulate interrogations more generally." The problem starts with the probability that innocent defendants are most likely to waive their *Miranda* protections. Innocent persons have nothing to hide from the police, and so they almost invariably waive their *Miranda* rights. Once they waive their rights, the *Miranda* procedures do little (if anything) to restrain police questioning techniques, a point that seems to be generally accepted.

Miranda's procedural requirements, like those of the Fourth Amendment exclusionary rule, also shift defense attorney time and attention away from claims of innocence. The *Miranda* procedures have spawned considerable litigation about whether a suspect was in "custody," whether a suspect "waived" his rights, or whether a suspect "invoked" his right to counsel. These issues generally have little to do with the reliability of any confession that police might obtain through questioning. Thus, like the Fourth Amendment exclusionary rule, these issues tend to draw defense attorney attention toward raising claims about process rather than about substance.

Miranda has also turned the attention of trial judges away from questions of the reliability of confessions and toward questions about police compliance with the *Miranda* rules. As Professor Welsh White has observed, before *Miranda*, reliability "played an important role in our constitutional jurisprudence.... [Since *Miranda*], however, courts and legal commentators have largely ignored issues relating to untrustworthy confessions."[112] To be sure, as a matter of black letter law, the *Miranda* procedural requirements were piled on top of traditional voluntariness requirements. But as a practical matter, judicial attention is a scarce resource. *Miranda* has created a triumph of formalism. Prioritizing one set of claims (*Miranda* compliance) has inevitably reduced scrutiny of the others—to the disadvantage of innocent defendants. As Professor Steven Duke has explained, not only is *Miranda* "virtually useless", but it "replaced a vibrant and developing voluntariness inquiry that took into account the vulnerabilities of the particular suspect as well as the inducement and conditions of the interrogation." The bottom line is that "not only has *Miranda* allowed the police to disregard actual voluntariness, it has enabled the courts to be equally unconcerned with actual innocence."

One last injury to the innocent defendants is worth noting. Good reasons exist for believing that *Miranda* has significantly hampered the ability of police officers to obtain confessions from guilty criminals. This has not only harmed law enforcement's ability to convict guilty criminals but also the opportunity of innocent individuals to use those confessions to exonerate themselves. For example, Professor Gross has noted that the number of exonerations when the actual criminal confessed declined sometime between the mid-1950s and the early 1970s.[113] Gross cites among the possible causes the *Miranda* decision, which "may result in some reduction in the number of

---

112. Welsh S. White, *False Confessions and the Constitution: Safeguards Against Unworthy Confessions*, 17 Harv. C.R.-C.L. L. Rev. 105, 156 (1997).

113. Samuel R. Gross, *Loss of Innocence: Eyewitness Identification and Proof of Guilt*, 16 J. Legal Stud. 395, 430–31 (1987).

confessions." Thus, by impairing the system's ability to get to the truth in cases, *Miranda* has caused the innocent to suffer.

A system that respects the constitutional right against self-incrimination, while at the same time providing greater protection for innocent suspects, could be easily designed. There appears to be wide agreement that video recording interrogations would offer far greater protection for innocent suspects than does the current *Miranda* regime. I made a proposal long ago for substituting video recording of police questioning as a substitute for *Miranda*, based in part in the need to protect the innocence.[114] Other commentators have proposed that recording should supplement *Miranda*.[115] A fair number of jurisdictions are moving forward with requiring video recording of at least some interrogations, although recording is often left to the discretion of police officers or mandated only for very serious crimes. The "Innocence Movement" could speed the adoption of this important reform if they would highlight the extent to which *Miranda* does not offer effective protection to the innocent and suggest that, instead, we should use video recording.

Moving in this direction has the great advantage of not interfering with the conviction of the guilty. It appears that video recording does not greatly interfere with the ability of law enforcement to obtain confessions and, of course, if the *Miranda* rules were relaxed or replaced by video recording, there would be an unambiguous boost to prosecution efforts. As a result, this kind of reform would not only avoid the tradeoffs discussed above, but would indeed be a true "win-win": more convictions of the guilty, while fewer convictions of the innocent.

Requiring All Defense Attorneys to Directly Ask Their Clients, "Did You Commit the Crime?" and Aggressively Investigate Claims of Actual Innocence

A critical resource in the efforts to prevent wrongful convictions is defense attorneys. Yet the great bulk of innocence literature seems to focus attention on prosecutors as the source of the problems.[116] For example, ... Professor George Thomas calls prosecutors "the thin last line protecting the innocent."[117] And he is surely right that prosecutors have critical steps they can take to reduce wrongful convictions, such as by fully discharging their *Brady* obligations to produce exculpatory evidence (a point I have pressed elsewhere).

But the Innocence Movement has largely overlooked what may be an even more important bulwark against false convictions: defense attorneys. Unfortunately, the mindset of the defense bar toward the question of whether their clients are in fact guilty has been aptly described as one of "staggering indifference."[118] Indeed, it is sometimes even

---

114. See Cassell, Miranda's *Social Costs*, at 486–92.

115. See, e.g., Lisa Lewis, *Rethinking* Miranda: *Truth, Lies, and Videotape*, 43 Gonz. L. Rev. 199 (2007); Lisa C. Oliver, *Mandatory Recording of Custodial Interrogations Nationwide: Recommending a New Model Code*, 39 Suffolk U. L. Rev. 263 (2005).

116. See, e.g., Dana Carver Boehm, *The New Prosecutor's Dilemma: Prosecutorial Ethics and the Evaluation of Actual Innocence*, 2014 Utah L. Rev. 613 (2014).

117. George Thomas, *Prosecutors: The Thin Last Line Protecting the Innocent*, *infra*.

118. Barbara Allen Babcock, *Defending the Guilty*, 32 Clev. St. L. Rev. 175, 180 (1983).

argued that it is inconsistent with ethical obligations for defense counsel to focus on innocence.[119] Defense attorneys simply cannot consider whether their clients are guilty, it is argued, because doing so would impair the quality of the representation they provide.[120] And, more broadly it is argued, focusing on innocence issues may distract society from dealing with mass incarceration and other issues associated with the guilty.

I am unconvinced. Innocent persons ensnared in the criminal justice system have a stronger claim to our attention than do the guilty. If we want to structure an "innocentric" criminal justice system that gives highest priority to preventing the conviction of the innocent, defense attorneys must be involved. In fact, defense attorneys — who (unlike prosecutors) have constant and direct access to defendants — may be uniquely positioned to identify a miscarriage of justice before it happens and take steps to prevent it. They are also well-poised to increase the "diagnosticity" of the system, by helping to flag the relatively small percentage of cases in the system genuinely involving factual innocence claims.[121]

Here is one example of how we might think about reorienting defense counsel toward innocence issues. Many defense attorneys do not directly ask their clients whether they are guilty of the crime charged. This ignorance may permit defense attorneys to perhaps raise defenses that might otherwise be barred by rules of legal ethics. But why should we give defense counsel such freedom if we are trying to structure a criminal justice system that focuses on innocence? It is hard to see what larger societal interest is served by allowing counsel to move forward in ignorance of this important fact. It may be true, as some defense advocates have argued, that a defense attorney can never be sure whether her client is telling the truth when a defendant claims to be innocent. But requiring defense attorneys to at least ask that basic question would serve the valuable function of putting this issue squarely out in the open, helping innocent defendants. And the only "cost" is that defense counsel for some guilty defendants might be limited in the kinds of arguments that can be advanced at trial — a cost that society surely ought to be willing to bear to have a system that more accurately sorts the innocent from the guilty.

Simply requiring the defense attorney to ask this straightforward question probably would not make much of a change in the current system. Part of the current criminal justice game seems to be for defendants to deny their involvement in a crime — at least at the start of a case. For example, Professor Robert Mosteller reports that, when he was a defense attorney, virtually all of his clients claimed to be innocent until he recited the advantages of a specific plea offer; at that point, they conceded their guilt.

---

119. Robert Mosteller, *Why Defense Attorneys Cannot, But Do, Care About Innocence*, 50 Santa Clara L. Rev. 1 (2010).

120. See id.; see also Margaret Raymond, *The Problem with Innocence*, 49 Clev. St. L. Rev. 449 (2001). Abbe Smith, *In Praise of the Guilty Project: A Criminal Defense Lawyer's Growing Anxiety About Innocence Projects*, 13 U. Pa. J.L. & Soc. Change 315, 329 (2010).

121. *Cf.* W. Tucker Carrington, *"A House Divided": A Response to Professor Abbe Smith's In Practice of the Guilty Project: A Criminal Defense Lawyer's Growing Anxiety About Innocence Projects*, 15 U. Pa. J.L. & Soc. Change. 1, 23 (2011).

In light of this fact, maybe defense attorneys should be required not only to ask their clients if they committed the crime but to also explore more thoroughly whether a defendant is truly guilty or innocent. This requirement could be enforced by a rule that only if a defendant admits he is guilty would a defense attorney be permitted to explore a standard plea bargain. Such a requirement might promote more frank and open discussion between defense attorneys and their clients about whether they were involved in the crime.

Forcing defense attorneys to truly attempt to learn whether their clients are guilty or innocent would create a real advantage: it would give the criminal justice system one more opportunity to begin sorting innocent defendants from guilty ones through the one person who has the best access to important information—the defendant. Professor Mosteller may properly complain about how defense attorneys have difficulties obtaining access to witnesses and other forms of evidence, but the barriers to information are not all one-sided. Prosecutors are usually precluded from talking to defendants once legal counsel enters the scene. But defendants are obviously in a unique position to provide information that can sort the guilty from the innocent. If defendants can be induced to provide more thorough information to their attorneys about whether they are innocent or guilty, then the system can more effectively protect against wrongful conviction.

With the innocence issue directly on the table for discussion, how should defense counsel proceed when her client reports that he is innocent? Professor Mosteller rightly bristles at the suggestion that there should be some sort of "second-class treatment" of defendants who state clearly that they are guilty. He explains quite nicely that defense counsel have important duties to perform in the criminal justice system, even when performing the far more common duty of defending those who have in fact committed the crimes charged against them. But he interestingly goes on to discuss the idea that perhaps individual defense attorneys—or the criminal justice system more broadly—should try to devote additional resources to cases in which a defendant has a good claim of actual innocence. Of course, defense attorneys— and the system—are not well-positioned to do this if the defendant is not even asked whether he is in fact innocent.

If a defendant claims to be innocent, as a first step defense counsel obviously ought to adequately investigate the claim. Presumably adequate defense investigation happens in many cases, regardless of whether a defendant claims to be innocent or guilty. But if some defense attorneys are not squarely raising the innocence issue because they think ignorance is tactically useful, they may end up missing a chance to discover exculpatory evidence that could set a defendant free.[122]

Following such an investigation, defense counsel should obviously rely on the procedures available in our criminal justice system for presenting a defense. Within our

---

122. See Abbe Smith, *Defending the Innocent*, 32 CONN. L. REV. 485, 510 (2000) (reporting an example of a seemingly delusional defendant blaming thefts on a "chicken man"; defense investigation discovers that man in a chicken suit perpetrated the crimes).

traditional structure, defense attorneys have many tools that they can employ in the defense of innocent clients.

But in reviewing cases of wrongful conviction over the years, one omission from the defense repertoire has always puzzled me. I have always wondered why, in a rare case where a defense attorney believes she is representing a truly innocent client, she almost invariably fails to bring the prosecutor into the discussion. The wrongful conviction literature suggests it is unusual for a defense attorney to communicate her specific concerns directly to a prosecutor. Perhaps this is part of a larger culture of distrust between prosecutors and defense attorneys that appears to afflict at least some jurisdictions. But direct communication on this issue needs to be strongly encouraged.

It would, of course, be naive to think that defense counsel reports to prosecutors could prevent every wrongful conviction of an innocent defendant. But I am surprised to discover that defense counsel so rarely employ this approach. Perhaps an unfortunate reason is that defense attorneys behave in the way that Mosteller suggests: they simply do not view their job as having much to do with guilt or innocence. If defense attorneys proceed in this way, they never learn whether they have an innocent defendant for a client as opposed to a guilty one. This agnostic approach may help to avoid burnout on the job or allow for an increased feeling of self-worth, as some have argued in justification. But this strikes me as a something of a cop-out, leading the Innocence Movement to point fingers first at errant prosecutors and rogue police officers while too often ignoring the role of ignorant defense attorneys. If we wish to leave no stone unturned in our efforts to prevent conviction of the innocent, it is time to broaden our perspective to include defense attorneys as those who have special responsibility — and special abilities — to prevent wrongful convictions.

Conclusion

Preventing wrongful conviction of the innocent is a fundamental priority of our criminal justice system. But it is obviously not the system's only goal. Efforts to prevent conviction of the innocent should avoid interfering with other objectives, most prominently the need to convict the guilty and prevent the suffering of future crime victims. Comparing even rough estimates of the risk of a person being wrongfully sent to prison for committing a violent crime with the risk of becoming a violent crime victim suggests that the current tradeoffs between the two may incline dramatically toward increasing victimization.

But there are some kinds of reforms that can avoid debate about these tradeoffs — true "win-win" measures that simultaneously reduce the number of innocents wrongfully convicted while increasing (or least not decreasing) the number of violent criminals sent to prison.... If we are truly committed to protecting the innocent, we can and should take such specific steps. We can reduce the risk of wrongfully convicting the innocent without setting free the guilty.

3. Compensation, Access to DNA Testing, and Parole Considerations for the Innocent

Michael Leo Owens and Elizabeth Griffiths,
Uneven Reparations for Wrongful Convictions: Examining the State Politics of Statutory Compensation Legislation
75 Alb. L. Rev. 1283, 1283–1305 (2012)

One of the fascinating findings from interviews with the wrongly convicted is that they harbor little or no anger — or more accurately, that "joy overrides the anger" — towards the State following their release from imprisonment. At the same time, they imagine and wish for compensation for their wrongful convictions, especially when it resulted in their incarceration and particularly when they faced the death penalty. Too often, however, recompense remains a mirage. In an age when state governments willingly spend tens and hundreds of millions of dollars to try to positively reintegrate the justly convicted back into society, the unjustly convicted must scrape, toil, and fight for arguably paltry portions of state dollars to positively reintegrate them. As Alan Northrop put it after he served seventeen years in a Washington state prison for a rape he did not commit, "I got no apology, no nothing, no offer of any kind of financial aid." He is not alone.

* * *

A. Legal Hodgepodge: The Means of Compensating the Wrongly Convicted

For nearly a century advocates have called on states to enact compensation statutes. They call for systematic provision of some degree of financial restitution to the wrongly convicted. In 1913, California and Wisconsin became the first states to enact statutes for compensating citizens for wrongful convictions. Two decades later legal scholars advocated for more states to adopt uniform institutions to compensate the wrongly convicted. Their calls followed the recognition that state governments had discretion to compensate the wrongly convicted, that most states chose to not adopt any compensation statutes, and that the statutes that existed typically included provisions that erected barriers to compensation. At the time, Borchard reasoned that state governments would recognize the debt owed to the wrongly convicted and act to reduce it. "It may be hoped," he averred, "that within measurable time remedial legislation may recognize the social obligation to compensate the innocent victims of an unjust conviction." Unfortunately, "over a half-century of exposés about wrongful convictions, from 1930 to 1990, stimulated very little policy activity." During that time and since then, the victims of unjust convictions have traveled hard policy roads through the states towards statutory compensation by their governments.

In many states, the roads toward justice the wrongfully convicted, including the exonerated, trod lead to nowhere. For example, in 2011 the Washington state legislature failed to pass a compensation law that would have established a system for providing wrongly convicted individuals with $20,000 for each year of their imprisonment. As one advocate recalled, "[w]e got lots of support philosophically, from both sides of the aisle. But then people said, 'How are you going to pay for it?'" In lieu of statutory compensation for the wrongfully convicted, civil litigation or private legislation are means by which the unjustly convicted may seek recompense from state governments. Neither means guarantees them compensation.

Civil litigation requires the wrongly convicted to bring suits against the state, as well as criminal justice institutions, such as prosecutors' offices and police departments. Allegations against the state may include false arrest or imprisonment, malicious and/or retaliatory prosecution, fabrication or suppression of evidence, and coercion of and ineffective assistance of counsel for defendants. As many legal scholars note, however, suits against the state, when permissible under state law, may not result in compensation. One reason is that compensation is impossible if the courts cannot attribute the conviction to identifiable wrongdoing by an agent of the criminal justice system. Proving intentional wrongdoing by the state is nearly impossible. "It is hard to overstate," as Michael Avery contends, "the legal and practical difficulties of these cases." Furthermore, inequities influence the use and outcomes of civil litigation, ranging from the variation across the states in the right of the wrongly convicted to sue to differences in access to and competence of legal counsel. One thing we know, however, about civil litigation as a means of recompense for the wrongly convicted: "Thus far, litigation has yielded mixed results."

Borchard argued in Convicting the Innocent that "the least that the State can do to vindicate itself and make restitution to the innocent victim is to grant him an indemnity, not as a matter of grace and favor but as a matter of right." Private legislation, however, trades in "grace and favor" as it requires lobbying by or on behalf of the wrongly convicted to obtain a legislative sponsor and broad legislative support for a bill that will provide restitution. "But such action is spasmodic only, and not all persons have the necessary influence to bring about legislation in their behalf." Beyond the unpredictable nature and outcomes of private legislation, there is variation in legislative access and success by the wrongly convicted. While the wrongly convicted often have ambivalent social constructions and low political resources, policymakers and the public may view some of the wrongly convicted more positively and some of the wrongly convicted have considerably more access to civic support than others, which they can covert to political capital and leverage in legislatures.

Additionally, some states contain provisions in their state constitutions that may disallow private legislation. According to the National Conference of State Legislatures, forty states have constitutional provisions against the introduction and passage of private bills. Even when private legislation is permissible, it is problematic because of legislative discretion. Although scholars and advocates focus attention on legislative influence over amounts of compensation, private legislation may also manifest paternalism towards and regulate the wrongly convicted. For instance, during the 2009 legislative session in Georgia the legislature passed a resolution to award $500,000 over twenty years to John Jerome White, who was wrongly convicted of the burglary, rape, beating, and robbery of an elderly woman. The state chose to compensate him for "loss of liberty, personal injury, lost wages, injury to reputation, emotional distress, and other damages as a result of his 28 years of incarceration and expenses in trying to prove his innocence totaling $3 million...." Compensation of Mr. White came with post-exoneration scrutiny and regulation: The legislation mandated that Mr. White submit to random drug tests, remain in the labor force (i.e., employed or seeking employment), and/or volunteer with a nonprofit organization during his twenty years of compensation.

Beyond the possibility of private legislation being a tool of paternalism and regulation, it is often among the slowest forms of legislation to pass. For example, it took twenty years, and the introduction of four bills (1979, 1980, 1990, and 1998), for the Florida legislature to pass legislation acknowledging the "entitlement to equitable relief" of two wrongly convicted men, Freddie Lee Pitts and Wilbert Lee.

Given the difficulties associated with accessing recompense through civil litigation and private legislation, legal scholars and advocates reason that state governments must enact statutory compensation for the wrongly convicted. "Compensation statutes are necessary," as Professor Bernhard argues, "because individuals convicted and incarcerated for crimes they did not commit are generally precluded from recovering damages by the inflexibility of tort law and civil rights doctrine, despite later exoneration." In a small majority of states such statutes exist, offering the wrongly convicted degrees of triumph at the end of their roads to justice. By the end of 2011, fifty-four percent of all states—twenty-seven of fifty (and the District of Columbia and the federal government)—had compensation laws (with some providing useful revisions to the laws) on their books.

Statutory compensation removes "grace and favor" from the calculus of compensation, privileging right, entitlement, and reason. "Generally, claimants need only establish innocence and prove that they served time in prison as a result of the wrongful conviction." Recently, for instance, after a two-year campaign by and for the wrongly convicted in Utah, the state legislature passed an "exoneration and innocence assistance" bill in 2008 to award approximately $34,000 to those bearing "factual innocence" for each year of incarceration following their wrongful conviction, up to a maximum of fifteen years. Even better, indeed the best, is Texas where in 2009 the legislature increased the annual recompense available to its wrongly convicted citizens to $80,000, which is $30,000 above both the amount the federal government provides for wrongful convictions and the amount the Innocence Project lobbies for in state legislatures.

We must recognize, however, that the statutory victories in some states to compensate the wrongly convicted are more hollow than they are solid, given that the laws include weak provisions for the amount and quality of compensation. The compensation statute in Montana, for example, makes no provision for direct financial compensation while offering indirect financial assistance in the forms of fee waivers, educational scholarships, and tuition payments for higher education. In some jurisdictions, compensation awards may be taxable as income. Overall, eighty-one percent of those exonerated by the courts who have received compensation due to a wrongful conviction compensation statute received less than the federal standard of a maximum of $50,000 for each year of unjust imprisonment. Furthermore, statutory compensation yields inequities in terms of access to compensation (i.e., eligibility and restrictions) and the amount of compensation. Nonetheless, for the advocates of the wrongly convicted, statutory compensation is the favored means of compensation because it reduces the degree to which discretion dominates the process of recompense for wrongful convictions.

The Politics of Reparation and Compensation After Wrongful Conviction

There is a longstanding norm among nations that the wrongly convicted warrant reparation and compensation. International organizations and treaties establish and promote the norm, seeking full compliance by nation states. Key conventions include the International Covenant on Civil and Political Rights of the United Nations and the Convention for the Protection of Human Rights and Fundamental Freedoms of the Council of Europe. "Almost every country," according to Jason Costa, "recognizes the right to compensation in the case of wrongful conviction as a matter of domestic or international human rights law." However, despite being a party to the convention, the United States "recognizes no national right to compensation for wrongful conviction." Moreover, the absence of statutory compensation in twenty-three states suggests that intra-national disagreements exist over the right to compensation for wrongful conviction. This is puzzling.

As early as 1914, Borchard argued that governments of the United States should compensate those burdened by "errors of justice." In his advocacy for a federal compensation law, Professor Borchard posed an enduring rhetorical question, "when the facts subsequently show that [government] has convicted and imprisoned an innocent man, does not the state owe that man compensation for the special sacrifice he has been compelled to make in the interest of the community?" Two decades later, he answered his own question, asserting, "when it is discovered after conviction that the wrong man was condemned, the least the State can do to right this essentially irreparable injury is to reimburse the innocent victim, by an appropriate indemnity, for the loss and damage suffered." Approximately seventy years later Bernhard reprised Borchard's assertion: "The state whose actions have put individuals in prison for crimes they did not commit owes a debt to those who through no fault of their own have lost years and opportunity. The debt should be recognized and paid." This is the consensus of the legal scholarship, and it generally concludes that states should repair the lives of the unjustly convicted as much as possible and do it in part by adopting statutory compensation. Yet this consensus is echoed neither in state legislatures nor the federal legislature.

Nevertheless, the payment of a civic debt to the wrongly convicted for the "taking of [their] liberty for the public use," either automatically or after judicial and bureaucratic processes, is intended to repair and compensate for as much of the damage wrought by miscarriages of justice as possible. This reparation has three beneficiaries. The first beneficiary of reparation is the wrongly convicted individual. The intent of payment for their unjust conviction is to make amends for the miscarriage of justice, to allow the victims of it to recoup financial losses, to reduce the economic vulnerability of the victims, and to increase self-sufficiency upon release. A second beneficiary of reparation is government. Payment to the wrongly convicted is a down payment for repairing damage to the State. By pairing subsequent acknowledgments of miscarriages of justice by government with reparation of the wrongly convicted, governments burnish their public legitimacy and retain (or regain) public respect for its criminal justice institutions and the rule of law. The monetary costs to states compensating the wrongly convicted may also reduce the likelihood of further miscarriages of justice, improving the moral performance of the courts and other institutions of criminal justice. The third beneficiary of reparation is the public. As the observer of miscarriages of justice performed in its name, reparation of the wrongly convicted likewise restores public confidence in the ability of judicial, correctional, and legislative institutions to exercise good judgment and fairness.

Given the diversity of beneficiaries of reparation, one might assume that it—at least as it is possible through forms of financial compensation—would be automatic, generous, and speedy. It is not and it perhaps never will be because the adoption of a wrongful conviction reparation system and the mechanisms for its implementation involve policy design, and politics will influence it. Policy design is the political craft of establishing the sets of institutions (i.e., the formal and informal rules) that bound and bestow the benefits and burdens, credits and costs, and prizes and penalties of distributive politics. Policy design determines "who gets what, when, how." Group conflicts and power dynamics influence the targets, benefits, timing, and process for allocating values—positive and negative—to groups via policy design, often irrespective of the merits of justice, morality, ethics, science, or rationality. Accordingly, we should always anticipate reparation to involve a political process, one that does not necessarily follow a linear path from "good" argument to "good" choices to "good" results. Democratic institutions, buffeted by cross-pressures of equity and efficiency, will influence the breadth, degree, and duration of governmental assistance and benefits for the wrongly convicted, even the extent to which governments take responsibility and/or accept blame for wrongful convictions. Decisions of legislatures, bureaucracies, courts, and voting booths ultimately shape the forms and set the lengths of reparation and compensation for the wrongly convicted. Consequently, democratic politics affects the scale and character of reparation as much as it does the scale and character of punishment in America.

Generally, democratic politics involves conflicts and contests over public respect and regard, representation, and/or the allocation of public resources. If governments are to respond to the preferences, values, and interests of the wrongly convicted, the wrongly convicted and their allies, like other interest groups, must navigate and influence elite and public perceptions of their civic worth for regard, representation, and resources; they must convince policymakers and voters that they are deserving of attention, benefits, and compassion.

In many states, however, the wrongly convicted have a hard time distinguishing themselves from the justly convicted. Like the latter, the former bear the mark of felony conviction and the stigma of imprisonment. This is intentional. "Criminal stigma," as Frederick Lawrence reminds us, "is not an accidental byproduct of the criminal justice system. It is precisely what the criminal justice system is supposed to provide." Consequently, in many instances, democratic institutions, civil society, and neighbors view and treat the wrongly convicted as discredited and scorned citizens. This happens for at least four reasons. First, the initial branding of the innocent by the state as violent felons, often for alleged rape, robbery, and murder, coupled with negative media from their court cases, weakens (but does not preclude) the mutability of their status as "criminal" within a polity. This results in negative consequences for the wrongly convicted, ranging from depression to unemployment. Second, public faith in the judicial system is relatively high, driven at the individual-level by personal experience with the courts, perceptions of procedural justice (e.g., judicial fairness), general trust in governmental institutions, and race. Moreover, public knowledge and acceptance of the causes and biases in wrongfully convicting the innocent is relatively low. Third, the legalities and science of innocence, which are complex and contested, may hinder the general public from forming sure opinions and sustain certain support for the convicted who claim unjust conviction and imprisonment. Fourth, even in the face of "structural injustice," members of the public, including families and friends of the unjustly convicted, may apply what political theorist Iris Marion Young called the "liability model of responsibility," whereby blame for the errors of justice shift from the courts to the convicted person. When that happens, as Saundra Westervelt and Kimberly Cook explain, the unjustly convicted are judged to have contributed to the error of justice, either through their surreptitious involvement in the crime or their failure to adequately defend themselves against the criminal charges. Taken together, these factors begin to suggest why the "mobilization of bias" on behalf of the wrongly convicted is difficult.

At the same time, the wrongly convicted may lack positive social constructions (or possess ambivalent or unsympathetic ones) as citizens and they tend to have a low degree of political resources to influence positive governmental and nongovernmental action, as well as civic regard, on their behalf. That is to say, the quantity and quality of their human, economic, and social capital is inadequate to trouble policymakers and the public, for the "wrongfully convicted are a small and unsympathetic constituency." They are few in number across the United States. As of 2011, for instance, the ranks of the wrongfully convicted cleared through DNA evidence remains fewer than 300. Additionally, "those affected by wrongful arrest or conviction are a weak social group, whose voice is almost unheard," reducing the political incentives of elected policymakers (i.e., legislators, governors, and prosecutors) to respond to the interests and preferences of the unjustly convicted.

In the end, the intersection of their negative social construction and low political resources relegates the wrongly convicted to a "deviant" category of polity membership, one where members are "undeserving" of assistance, benefits, and compassion in the absence of clearing high standards of innocence. Yet even when innocence is established, political institutions may remain unresponsive because of the limited political resources of the wrongly convicted. The membership of the wrongly convicted in the "deviant" category allows other categories of polity members to relegate them to a lower plane of group position, categorizing their claims as illegitimate, neglecting their needs, and signaling that the polity perceives them to be of low civic and political worth.

The Innocence Project:
Access to Post-Conviction DNA Testing[123]

Today every state has enacted a post-conviction DNA statute because the traditional appeals process was often insufficient for proving a wrongful conviction. Prior to the passage of post-conviction DNA laws, it was not uncommon for an innocent person to exhaust all possible appeals without being allowed access to the DNA evidence in his case.

Do all states have post-conviction DNA access statutes?

Although all 50 states have post-conviction DNA testing access statutes, many of these testing laws are limited in scope and substance.

What are the common shortcomings of existing DNA access laws?

- Some laws present insurmountable hurdles to the individual seeking access, putting the burden on the wrongfully convicted person to effectively solve the crime and prove that the DNA evidence promises to implicate another individual.

- Despite the fact that approximately 11% of the nation's more than 350 wrongful convictions proven by DNA involved a guilty plea, certain laws still do not permit access to DNA when the defendant originally pled guilty.

- Many laws fail to include adequate safeguards for the preservation of DNA evidence.

- Several laws do not allow people to appeal denied petitions for testing.

- Several laws prevent people who are no longer incarcerated to seek testing.

What key elements should be included in a DNA access law?

The Innocence Project recommends the following elements be contained in existing statutes in need of amending:

- Include a reasonable standard to establish proof of innocence at the stage where an individual is petitioning for post-conviction DNA testing;

- Allow access to post-conviction DNA testing wherever it can establish innocence, even if the petitioner is no longer incarcerated, and including cases where the petitioner pled guilty or provided a confession or admission to the crime;

- Exclude "sunset provisions," or absolute deadlines, for when access to post-conviction DNA evidence will expire;

---

123. *Access to Post-Conviction DNA Testing*, THE INNOCENCE PROJECT (2017) available at https://www.innocenceproject.org/access-post-conviction-dna-testing/.

- Enable judges to order comparisons of crime scene evidence against national and state-level criminal justice databases, including CODIS and IAFIS;

- Require state officials to properly preserve and catalogue biological evidence for as long as an individual is incarcerated or otherwise experiences any consequences of a potential wrongful conviction (e.g. probation, parole, civil commitment or mandatory registration as a sex offender), as well as to account for evidence in their custody;

- Disallow procedural hurdles that stymie DNA testing petitions and proceedings that govern other forms of post-conviction relief;

- Allow convicted persons to appeal from orders denying DNA testing;

- Require a full, fair and prompt response to DNA testing petitions, including the avoidance of debate around whether currently available DNA technology was available at the time of the trial;

- Avoid unfunded mandates by providing funding to DNA testing statutes; and

- Provide flexibility in where, and how, DNA testing is conducted.

Case in Point: Pennsylvania Man Originally Denied Access to DNA

In May of 1987, Bruce Godschalk was convicted of rape and burglary in Pennsylvania. The conviction was based primarily on eyewitness identification and a confession later proven to be false. Forensics techniques available at the time of the trial and used to test the semen from the crimes could not exclude Mr. Godschalk as the perpetrator.

Following his conviction, Mr. Godschalk petitioned for access to DNA testing and was denied. After contacting the Innocence Project in 1995, which sought testing on his behalf, the District Attorney refused to allow access to the DNA evidence. It was not until November of 2000 that a Federal District Court granted access to the DNA testing.

Delays in setting a testing protocol and delivering the evidence, in addition to some legal hurdles, deferred testing of the evidence until January of 2002. Mr. Godschalk was eventually excluded as the donor of the semen in the crimes and released from prison. Mr. Godschalk had spent seven of his fifteen years of incarceration fighting for access to DNA evidence. As a result of Mr. Godschalk's case, Pennsylvania introduced and later passed a law creating access to DNA evidence.

Justin Brooks and Alexander Simpson, *Blood Sugar Sex Magik: A Review of Postconviction DNA Testing Statutes and Legislative Recommendations*
59 DRAKE L. REV. 799, 804–24 (2011)

Even with all of its benefits to the forensic community, the Supreme Court determined in 2009 that inmates have no substantive due process right to DNA evidence that could prove their innocence. In the Alaska case of District Attorney v. Osborne, Chief Justice John Roberts wrote that those convicted have only limited rights to due process, particularly in regard to postconviction relief. The right to DNA testing—even when testing could conclusively determine the perpetrator—is not automatically part of those due process rights. Thus, the holding in Osborne means the ability of an inmate to gain access to DNA testing as a right depends almost entirely on state legislatures and state courts.

Forty-eight states, the District of Columbia, and the federal government have adopted some form of post-conviction DNA testing law. Some significant challenges arise when these laws are applied to cases like Richards, which do not involve rape kits but rather require a broader view of how DNA testing can prove innocence. Furthermore, the laws are not uniform, and in the politically charged atmosphere of criminal lawmaking, some of the laws are poorly thought out.

* * *

A majority of the jurisdictions that currently have some type of post-conviction DNA testing statute limit the testing to specific crimes or classes of crimes. The most stringent state is Kentucky, which limits the ability to make a motion for post-conviction DNA testing to individuals convicted of a capital offense and sentenced to death. Alabama is a close second; an actual death sentence is not required, but a right to post-conviction DNA testing is limited to capital offense convictions. Indiana, Kansas, Maryland, and Nevada statutes mandate a conviction for murder, certain categories of felonies, or both.

In addition to limiting the types of convictions, Oregon's statute on eligibility to file a post-conviction motion for DNA testing adds a distinction between those individuals who are in custody and those who are not. If an individual is institutionalized, the underlying conviction must have been for aggravated murder or a "person felony." If the applicant is not in custody, the conviction must be for aggravated murder, murder, or a sex crime.

A number of jurisdictions have somewhat less stringent statutes, yet still restrict application to a certain subset of convictions. For example, the District of Columbia's post-conviction DNA statute only limits application to those convicted of "a crime of violence." With similar restrictions, Georgia's statute allows application by those convicted of "a serious violent felony." South Carolina has an even broader statute, which contains twenty-four qualifying offenses. Vermont's statute lists fourteen qualifying crimes, but it also allows application when there is a conviction for any felony not enumerated in the list of qualifying crimes. Tennessee's statute parallels the statute in Vermont in that it lists certain offenses but provides discretion to the trial judge to grant a post-conviction DNA testing motion for any other offense that may contain biological evidence.

What Standards Must Be Met for Postconviction Testing?
The One-Step, Two-Step, Three-Step Dance

In order to obtain postconviction DNA testing in California, the Penal Code requires that a petitioner makes a prima facie showing "the evidence sought to be tested is material to the issue of the convicted person's identity as the perpetrator of, or accomplice to, the crime, special circumstance, or enhancement allegation that resulted in the conviction or sentence" and "the requested DNA testing results would raise a reasonable probability that, in light of all the evidence, the convicted person's verdict or sentence would have been more favorable if the results of DNA testing had been available at the time of conviction."

Section 1405 of the California Penal Code was enacted in 2000. Since then, the courts have had great difficulty in interpreting what "reasonable probability" means and to what the standard should be specifically applied. Some judges have interpreted this provision as requiring the court to first, without having the testing conducted, decide whether there is a reasonable probability the testing will result in exculpatory evidence. Further, these same judges have rules allowing the defendant to be entitled to this exculpatory evidence, which is separate from the question of whether there is "a reasonable probability that, in light of all the evidence," the verdict or sentence should be different.

For example, in the case of *People v. McFadden*, a California molestation case, the California Innocence Project sought to have the victim's underwear tested. Investigators confirmed the presence of semen on the underwear, but they were never previously tested for DNA. The victim positively identified McFadden at trial as the one who committed the molestation. In denying McFadden's motion for DNA testing, the court stated:

> Well, I heard this trial. And I remember the evidence that was presented in this case.... The Court does not conclude that there's a reasonable probability that a different result would have been obtained if testing had been available and performed at the time of the trial.

In the *McFadden* case, the court never considered the question of whether the evidence could be potentially exculpatory because the judge predetermined the outcome of the DNA testing. This "two-step" approach makes it very difficult to win a post-conviction testing motion when there has already been a determination by a judge or jury that the defendant was guilty beyond a reasonable doubt. Thus, it becomes difficult for the judge to conclude it is likely the test results will be exculpatory.

In other words, in *In re Richards*, Richards was convicted based upon all of the evidence presented by the parties—the possible bite mark, the blue thread under Pamela's nail, the blood spatters, and everything else the jury considered in convicting Richards. Under the two-step approach, the judge would have to be confident, without conducting any testing, that the jury got it wrong. Otherwise, how could the judge conclude there was a reasonable probability the testing would be exculpatory?

Compounding the futility of this approach is the fact the statute allows the trial court to rule on a written motion for DNA testing. This is presumably due to the trial court's familiarity with the case, which makes it better able to determine whether, "in light of all the evidence" presented at trial, DNA evidence results would raise a "reasonable probability" that would have favorably affected the outcome at trial. Under the two-step approach, therefore, the judge who actually presided over the case must determine, without first ordering the testing, whether there is a reasonable probability the testing would be exculpatory—in effect, whether it is likely the judge presided over a wrongful conviction. Consequently, under the two-step analysis, the only inmates who would be able to meet the requirement would be those inmates who do not need post-conviction DNA testing; testing would be limited to those cases where the judge is already convinced of innocence regardless of the testing.

The only way the statute can be interpreted without frustrating its purpose is to take a "one-step" approach. The court should determine whether the result of a favorable DNA test could produce evidence that, even when considering all the evidence produced at trial, creates a reasonable probability the convicted person's verdict or sentence would have been more favorable if the results of the DNA testing had been available at the time of trial. If the court fails to make the presumption of a favorable DNA testing result, the statute can never achieve its purpose.

In California, this issue was resolved only after extensive litigation. In *Richardson v. Superior Court of Tulare County*, decided a full eight years after California's DNA statute was enacted, the California Supreme Court explained the proper posture for a superior court's analysis: to presume favorable results when evaluating whether a defendant has met his or her burden under the statute.

The potential ambiguity in California's statute regarding the "reasonable probability" interpretation is also present in the post-conviction DNA testing statutes of the District of Columbia, Georgia, and Iowa.

The fairly recently enacted Hawaii statute was drafted almost identically to the statute in California. In addition, however, the Hawaii statute states the court shall order the testing if it finds, among other things, "[a] reasonable probability exists that the defendant would not have been prosecuted or convicted if exculpatory results had been obtained through DNA analysis, even if the defendant later pled guilty or no contest."

By inserting "exculpatory" before the word "results," Hawaii made the reasonable probability requirement unambiguous. Hawaii's statute thus leaves little room for misinterpretation by requiring the assumption the results will be favorable.

The Arizona statute is similar to Hawaii in that it uses the "reasonable probability" standard, though it requires the court to order the testing if it finds, among other things, "a reasonable probability exists that the petitioner would not have been prosecuted or convicted if exculpatory results had been obtained through deoxyribonucleic acid testing."

The Texas statute permits the court to order the testing if it finds, among other things, "the person would not have been convicted if exculpatory results had been obtained through DNA testing."

The language of the Hawaii, Arizona, and Texas statutes removes the judicial determination of whether the test result would be exculpatory by requiring the court to base its analysis on a presumably exculpatory result of the testing. The post-conviction DNA testing statutes in Colorado, Connecticut, Indiana, Kentucky, Missouri,

Nevada, New Mexico, Pennsylvania, Rhode Island, Tennessee, Wisconsin, and Wyoming all assume test results will be favorable to the defendant. Confusingly, Wyoming's statute assumes exculpatory results but does not mandate testing, merely providing that the court "may order testing" if the defendant meets the requirements of the statute. Thus, Wyoming's statute adds an additional caveat: even in cases in which favorable results would lead to a reversal, testing is ordered only at the court's discretion. This means a court in Wyoming could deny testing even when all parties agree the testing could not only exonerate a defendant, but find the real perpetrator.

The statutes of fifteen additional states and the federal government are written to require the judge to take two steps in determining whether the standard is met.

The statutes of nine states require three steps to be met before a judge can grant a post-conviction DNA testing motion. In these states, courts must determine whether the results would be favorable, whether favorable results would have made a difference in the verdict, and finally, whether the DNA results would have been merely cumulative to the evidence already presented at trial. Only if a defendant proves all three steps is she then entitled to relief.

Only three states have statutes requiring a single step in determining whether or not the standard is met. Two states, Maine and Michigan, create their own variation of the problem explained above by providing that the courts consider only the first step when making their decisions. In determining whether the defendant's motion should be granted, courts in Maine are required to decide whether the applicant preserves prima facie evidence that the results of testing are "material to the issue of whether the [defendant] is the perpetrator of, or accomplice to, the crime that resulted in the conviction." The related statutes do not discuss how "materiality" is defined under the section, but presumably this means the courts must determine whether DNA testing results would be favorable. If, as discussed above, the court believes the evidence used to convict was sufficient, it will likely conclude the DNA testing results will not be favorable, and the testing will not be ordered.

Finally, South Dakota's statute provides for relief if the defendant can "identif[y] a theory of defense that: (a) Is consistent with an affirmative defense presented at trial; or (b) Would establish the actual innocence of the [defendant] of the felony offense." There have been no cases interpreting this seemingly cryptic language, so the defendant's burden under the statute is altogether unclear. Presumably this language means the defendant must show the results of DNA testing would be in line with a third-party culpability defense that had previously been presented at the trial or that the requested results would test favorable to the defendant. If so, this would mean the South Dakota statute runs afoul of the same problems outlined above.

As has been demonstrated in hundreds of DNA exonerations across the country, reliance on a two-step approach to determining whether testing should be ordered will often preclude testing from being performed when, in fact, it should be completed. A study of the first 225 cases of DNA exonerations performed by the New York-based Innocence Project shows 77% involved eyewitness misidentification, 52% involved improper forensics, 16% involved informants and snitches, and 23% — almost one in four — involved false confessions or admissions.

This last statistic regarding false confessions or admissions is particularly telling and demonstrative of why a two-step approach does not work. Courts employing a two-step analysis would logically and invariably conclude further DNA testing would produce inculpatory, not exculpatory, results in cases in which the inmate has confessed to the crime. Yet, in almost a quarter of the first 225 exonerations, courts reaching this conclusion would have prevented testing and consequently failed to overturn a wrongful conviction.

A one-step analysis should be required by a post-conviction DNA testing statute. Given what is known about DNA exonerations, the alternative is simply untenable.

The Identity Issue

A common, and generally misguided, worry is post-conviction DNA laws might "open the floodgate" of inmate litigation. States have generally addressed this concern by only considering post-conviction motions in cases in which the identity of the perpetrator was at issue at trial. A similar or identical limitation is in the post-conviction DNA testing statutes of the federal government and the following states: Alabama, Alaska, Arkansas, Delaware, Florida, Georgia, Hawaii, Idaho, Illinois, Iowa, Maine, Michigan, Minnesota, Missouri, New Jersey, New Mexico, North Dakota, Ohio, Pennsylvania, South Dakota, and Texas.

California employs a similar, albeit somewhat less restrictive, standard. California courts will only consider cases in which "[t]he identity of the perpetrator of the crime was, or should have been, a significant issue in the case." Defense attorneys refer to the defense in these cases as TODDI — "The Other Dude Did It."

Notably, the California statute does not require a showing that the defendant knows or suspects the identity of the actual perpetrator of the crime. The statute merely requires the identity of the perpetrator be "at issue," meaning, at the time of trial, there was a genuine prima facie dispute between the parties as to who committed the crime. Further, the statute also allows for situations in which the identity of the perpetrator "should have been [] a significant issue in the case." Thus, even if the defense's argument at the original trial did not involve the issue of identity, the statute can still be used to secure post-conviction DNA testing if identity should have been argued but was not.

For example, suppose a defendant is charged with murder, and there are no witnesses to the crime. Assume the defendant is developmentally disabled, cannot remember the events because of intoxication, or is otherwise unable to assist the attorney in forming a defense. At trial, the defense pursues a self-defense argument, believing it to be the best opportunity for acquittal. By arguing self-defense, the identity of the defendant no longer remains an issue. However, if evidence later shows the defendant was not involved in the crime, he or she may be prohibited from pursuing post-conviction DNA testing unless a post-conviction DNA statute allows testing where identity was or should have been an issue.

* * *

Montana, West Virginia, South Carolina, New Hampshire, and Oregon impose the same limitation California does. However, the majority of post-conviction DNA testing statutes are silent on the issue of identity. The post-conviction DNA statutes of the following states have no such requirement: Arizona, Colorado, Connecticut, District of Columbia, Indiana, Kansas, Kentucky, Louisiana, Maryland, Mississippi, Nebraska, Nevada, New York, North Carolina, Rhode Island, Tennessee, Utah, Vermont, Virginia, Washington, Wisconsin, and Wyoming.

Given the examples above, it is clear legislatures addressing the identity issue have struggled to balance the goals of exclusion and inclusion. On one hand, there are valid interests in limiting testing in which identity is not an issue because DNA is ultimately a tool for confirming or excluding a suspect. However, the purpose of any DNA statute is to ensure individuals have access to testing when the results of testing would be dispositive of their guilt or innocence, which means they should be broadly construed to prevent innocent inmates from falling through the cracks.

Statutes incorporating the "should have been" language seem to better balance these interests; however, in cases in which identity was not, or should not have been, an issue, statutes should grant courts the discretion to order testing in the interest of justice. This allows even those individuals who may have argued consent or self-defense to be granted testing if the court determines there is merit to testing.

* * *

Should Postconviction DNA Testing Be Granted to Those Inmates Who Plead Guilty or Confess to Their Crime?

One thing we have learned from the hundreds of DNA exonerations over the past two decades is sometimes people confess or plead guilty to crimes they have not committed. This happens for a number of reasons. In the area of confessions, it is sometimes due to the fact police training on interrogations is focused on getting a suspect to confirm the officers' suspicions, not necessarily getting the truth. In the area of plea-bargaining, sometimes innocent people do not want to roll the dice in the criminal justice casino and instead plead guilty to a lesser crime to avoid more jail time. The fact that many people confess or plead guilty to crimes they have not committed almost mandates these people should not be closed off from relief under a post-conviction DNA testing statute.

Four states' statutes either eliminate or impose restrictions on an inmate's ability to access post-conviction DNA testing if the inmate pleaded guilty or nolo contendere. Some statutes state or suggest a plea of guilty does not matter. In one state, Pennsylvania, subsequent case law has barred inmates who plead guilty from requesting testing unless the inmate also claims that the plea was involuntary. Some statutes provide or suggest a plea of guilty does not matter. However, the majority of statutes, including the federal statute, do not address the issue.

Daniel S. Medwed, *The Innocent Prisoner's Dilemma: Consequences of Failing to Admit Guilt at Parole Hearings*
93 IOWA L. REV. 491, 493–541 (2008)

The granting of parole in the criminal justice system is often viewed as an act of grace: the dispensation of mercy by the government to an individual prisoner deemed worthy of conditional release prior to the expiration of his sentence. Yet the criteria upon which state parole boards base these acts of grace remain something of a mystery. Denials of parole are largely unreviewable, and courts have held that due process imposes only a minimal burden upon parole boards to reveal the rationales for their decisions. Nevertheless, surveying state parole release decisions demonstrates that a prisoner's willingness to "own up" to his misdeeds—to acknowledge culpability and express remorse for the crime for which he is currently incarcerated—is a vital part of the parole decision-making calculus. That is, admitting guilt increases the likelihood of a favorable parole outcome for an inmate whereas proclaiming innocence serves to diminish the chance for release. [But is] this practice … wise[?] Should a prisoner's assertions of innocence be held against him in the parole process?

On the one hand, several arguments suggest that parole boards are correct in disregarding an aspiring parolee's claim of innocence and, in fact, holding it against him. The primary argument in support of the current practice relates to the issue of institutional competence. Factual questions of guilt or innocence ordinarily stand outside the scope of parole commissioners' delegated duties and, rather, fall within the province of juries and judges. Moreover, without the resources to conduct extensive field investigations, parole boards simply lack the capacity to verify a prisoner's claim of innocence. Thus, parole boards normally presume the guilt of the inmates seeking release before them and leave it to the post-conviction litigation process to conclude otherwise. The second major justification for the existing norm lies in the parole board's understandable desire to minimize the risk of discharging individuals who are likely to re-offend. Prevailing psychological doctrine maintains that taking responsibility for one's actions is crucial to mental health. According to many psychologists, upon whom parole boards frequently rely, refusing to acknowledge one's guilt signals mental instability or immaturity. These attributes, in turn, may reflect that the inmate has not been rehabilitated during his incarceration and may also portend recidivism, the reduction of which is a central goal and measure of success for parole.

On the other hand, the slew of post-conviction exonerations of innocent prisoners in recent years proves that juries and judges do not always effectively sort the guilty from the innocent at the trial level and indicates that perhaps parole boards can (and should) fill this void to facilitate the release of the innocent. Over the past nineteen years, prisoners have been exonerated through post-conviction DNA testing, their innocence proven to a scientific certainty, and states have freed over 300 other inmates on grounds consistent with innocence during that period. As I have argued elsewhere, these cases represent the proverbial tip of the innocence iceberg in light of (1) the scarcity of biological evidence suitable for DNA testing in criminal cases; (2) the be-wildering array of obstacles to relief contained in most state post-conviction procedures in regard to non-DNA cases; and (3) the waning availability of federal habeas corpus. Furthermore, with all due respect to psychological theory, inmate expressions of re-morse in applying for parole may not reflect genuine acknowledgment and acceptance of the criminal act—a true coming to terms, if you will. The prison grapevine has presumably informed the parole hearing-bound population that remorse is essentially a quid pro quo for release, casting doubt on the sincerity of many pleas of repentance before the board, however contrite they may seem. In reality, considering the profound disincentive to claim innocence at parole hearings, logic suggests those assertions should be taken quite seriously.

* * *

To put it bluntly, innocent inmates currently face a true "prisoner's dilemma" when encountering parole boards. Choice A consists of proclaiming innocence and con-sequently hindering the possibility of parole; Choice B involves taking responsibility for a crime the prospective parolee did not commit and bolstering the chance for re-lease, albeit with dire effects for any post-conviction litigation involving the underlying innocence claim. This type of choice is one that no actually innocent prisoner should be forced to make. Ultimately, parole boards should be mindful of the possible le-gitimacy of some innocence claims and, at the very least, not reflexively hold those assertions against the prisoner in the release decision.

* * *

In light of parole's roots in the rehabilitative ideal of punishment, it should come as no surprise that words and acts associated with rehabilitation—acceptance of re-sponsibility, remorse, and repentance—linger as fixtures in the contemporary parole evaluation process. After all, if discretionary parole is the upshot for the prisoner "cured" of the propensity toward criminal transgression, then how else are board members to divine whether an inmate is healthy if not partially through proof of emotional maturity in the form of verbal admissions of one's past mistakes? At the very core of American rehabilitative theory lies this commingling of acceptance and renunciation, be it a member of Alcoholics Anonymous who must first admit "I am an alcoholic" or a prisoner seeking a pardon or clemency. Moreover, inmate partic-ipation in the rehabilitative endeavor (ideally in an active, honest, and palpable man-ner) has always been a centerpiece of the American conception of parole; ... the leaders of the Elmira Reformatory, the first prison to use parole in the United States, declared in 1876 that the inmate's "cure is always facilitated by his cooperation, and often impossible without it." It may not be too farfetched to suggest that, in their modern incarnation, parole boards view sincere admissions of guilt at a hearing as evidence of that inmate's cooperation in his own rehabilitation and, thus, indicia of having been cured. Mea culpa meets medical restoration, so to speak.

The available quantitative and qualitative data support the assertion that a pris-oner's acceptance of responsibility proves vital to his prospects for an affirmative

parole decision. Specifically, empirical findings from Great Britain, as well as anecdotal accounts throughout the United States, confirm (1) that parole boards attach
great importance to inmate statements taking responsibility for the crime underlying
their current conviction and (2) that the refusal to admit guilt decreases the likelihood
of receiving parole. Parole officials seldom deny that inmate acceptance of responsibility is a critical variable in the release decision and, instead, are often overt in
showing their dependence on this factor. For instance, the preprinted "Rationale
Sheet" that the Utah Board of Pardons and Parole uses in explaining its decision
after each parole hearing expressly designates complete acceptance of responsibility
as a mitigating factor and denial or minimization as an aggravating one.

Generally speaking, an incentive exists for all prisoners facing parole boards to
admit guilt and apologize for the crime in order to maximize their chances for release,
irrespective of their true feelings and culpability. To gain release from prison — the
penitentiary — inmates must essentially display evidence of their repentance. Some
inmates who accept responsibility and express remorse for the crime at parole hearings
are surely both factually guilty and genuinely apologetic; others are factually guilty
yet truly unrepentant; and still others may be factually innocent and motivated solely
by the desire for liberty in choosing to "admit" guilt. It is this last group that troubles
me deeply.

My concern about the pressures confronting actually innocent prisoners when appearing before parole boards originated during my tenure from 2001 to 2004 as assistant director of the Second Look Program at Brooklyn Law School. During that
period, students and faculty in the Second Look Program worked together to investigate and litigate post-conviction claims of innocence by New York state prisoners.
As my students and I struggled, usually to no avail, to help free prisoners whom we
thought to be innocent based on extensive preliminary investigations, it became evident that parole might be the only viable alternative to incarceration in many situations, save for completing a sentence.

Procedural obstacles embedded in most state post-conviction procedures — obstacles relating to statutes of limitations, burdens of proof, and appellate review,
among other things — hinder the ability of wrongfully convicted prisoners to prove
their innocence through litigation in each and every case, especially in those cases
lacking biological evidence suitable for DNA testing. Frequent instances of prosecutorial opposition to inmates' claims of innocence, coupled with the decline of federal
habeas corpus as an effective collateral remedy, further reduce the likelihood of exonerating innocent prisoners by means of the court system. Accordingly, one can
safely conclude that factually innocent prisoners in the United States, however many
there may be, do not always find recourse in the post-conviction arena. For such inmates, addressing the parole board assumes enormous significance as the most realistic
opportunity for freedom and gives rise to the following predicament: what should
the inmate say about guilt or innocence at the parole hearing?

* * *

The reality of innocent prisoners "admitting" guilt during the parole process should be a matter of grave concern. Granted, this form of deception is understandable in light of current norms at parole release hearings. Deception by innocent prisoners at parole hearings arguably acts as a form of "self-defense," a necessary maneuver in the battle for survival. For the innocent inmate facing the parole board, false cries of remorse and responsibility are also justified on basic utilitarian grounds given that the direct results of lying (possible liberty) largely trump those of telling the truth (continued incarceration). Parole hearing officers themselves may suffer limited tangible harm from these fabrications, as prisoners' admissions of guilt reinforce and validate the institutional presumption that the individuals appearing before parole boards are factually guilty.

Even so, the effects of such deception by innocent inmates are not entirely neutral, let alone positive. In order for expressions of remorse and acceptance of responsibility by an injurer to have the greatest constructive impact on the injured, those statements should be genuine. Where a crime victim is deluded into thinking an innocent person was the wrongdoer, any benefits achieved by fraudulent statements of remorse and responsibility would be dashed in the event the actual perpetrator is ever apprehended. Additionally, while the incentive to admit guilt before parole boards may lead to exchanges at release hearings that confirm the belief that all inmates are guilty, such a belief is erroneous, as indicated by the hundreds of post-conviction exonerations of inmates since 1989. Improperly certifying this view therefore provides a disservice to all involved. The pursuit of "truth" is a normative value in and of itself, and one that ought to be fostered, where possible, throughout the criminal justice system.

B. Legal Materials, Exercises, and Media

DNA Access Laws

1. *U.S. Supreme Court: Post-Conviction Access to DNA Testing:*

    a. Dist. Attorney's Office for Third Judicial Dist. v. Osborne, 557 U.S. 52 (2009) (holding that, in light of the existence of a state statute regulating access to post-conviction DNA testing, there is no freestanding substantive due process right to DNA evidence).

    b. Skinner v. Switzer, 562 U.S. 521 (2011) (holding that convicted state prisoners seeking DNA testing of crime-scene evidence may assert that claim in a civil rights action under 42 U.S.C. § 1983 and are not limited to pursuit of such claims by way of petition for a writ of habeas corpus under 28 U.S.C. § 2254).

2. *Discussion, State DNA Testing, and Evidence Preservation Statutes*: Look up your state statute providing defendants with access to DNA evidence. What benefits and limitations does your state DNA Access Law have?

    Does your state have a statute to preserve DNA evidence after trial? Why are DNA preservation statutes important in post-conviction litigation?

Parole

3. *Parole Hearings for the Innocent*: Fernando Bermudez spent 18 years prison after being convicted of murder in 1991, before being found innocent. Read his reflection on parole hearings for the wrongfully convicted in his New York Times Op-Ed, *I Feared I'd Die in Prison for Maintaining My Innocence*, November 13, 2014:

> Imagine yourself happy, on the verge of a career, promotion or meaningful relationship, then suddenly trapped in prison, fighting for freedom and your sanity over a crime you did not commit.
>
> In 1991 I never imagined this would happen to me when I was arrested, convicted and incarcerated for murder. My wrongful conviction stole over 18 years of happiness for my family and I until Justice John Cataldo of State Supreme Court in Manhattan dismissed the charges and declared me actually innocent in 2009. He ruled that the police and prosecutors had used perjured testimony and illegal identification.
>
> *After 18 years, with my parole dilemma looming, a judge finally declared I'd been wrongly convicted and freed me.*
>
> I wrestled with many fears during my incarceration, surrounded by violence. But my greatest fear was that I could die in prison maintaining my innocence. Year after year, I witnessed the parole board deny release to inmates who maintained their innocence, like one friend who died in prison after being denied parole every two years. Others used drugs to numb the painful reality of being trapped while innocent.
>
> If I had stayed in prison, I would have been eligible for an appearance before the board this year. How would I have passed through the eye of that legal needle? I often thought. Exonerating evidence had long been accumulating since 1992. As an innocent man I would have poured my heart out to them with the truth that I was willing to die for. Daily, I was mentally and physically tortured with thoughts that a parole board would consider me in denial and reject my freedom.
>
> Luckily, after years of fighting, with the help of pro bono lawyers, I won my case, which prosecutors never appealed. But the horrible, looming dilemma I faced still pains me.

4. *Reflective Essay, Advising Innocent Clients on Parole*: What advice would you give to Mr. Bermudez if he were facing the parole board? How should he address his innocence? Would your advice change depending on the type of crime, or how frequently he could be considered for parole? In 1–2 pages write your advice to Mr. Bermudez as he prepares for an upcoming parole hearing.

5. *Parole In-Class Exercise*: You are representing your client before the state parole board. In 5 minutes, make your most compelling case for your client to be granted parole, and make a strategic decision about how and whether to discuss her innocence.

6. *Recommended Listening, Parole and Innocence:* Michael VonAllmen was wrongfully convicted of rape and lived on parole as a registered sex offender for 18 years until he was exonerated by the Kentucky Innocence Project. In *Love Matters* on "The Moth Podcast," Michael discusses his attempt to obtain parole—and ultimate freedom—for his friend in prison, Ted Conover: https://themoth.org/stories/love-matters (15:12).

Exoneree Compensation and Expungement

7. *Recommended Listening, CIUs and Exoneree Compensation:* Marissa Boyers Bluestine, Legal Director and then Executive Director of the Pennsylvania Innocence Project from 2009–2019, discusses Conviction Integrity Units and exoneree compensation on the Criminal (In)Justice Podcast with David Harris, Episode 50, *Establishing Innocence After a Guilty Verdict* http://www.criminalinjustice podcast.com/episodes/ (34:25–40:00).

8. *Recommended Listening, "Exonerated and Broke":* Rebecca Brown, Policy Director at the Innocence Project, and exoneree Alan Newton discuss exoneree compensation. "Alan Newton served more than 20 years in prison for a crime he didn't commit before DNA analysis proved him innocent and he was exonerated. Now, had this occurred in Alabama, he would have received $50,000 for every year of wrongful imprisonment. Instead, Newton was convicted in the state of New York, where exonerees receive nothing, and are instead forced to sue the government for compensation." Hear this conversation (set to music and beat by Silent Knight) on Newsbeat, "Exonerated and Broke," Sept. 18, 2017: https://www.usnewsbeat. com/2017/09/18/exonerated-and-broke/.

9. *Recommended Viewing, from Crime Victims to Exonerees:* The National Institute of Justice produced a documentary, *Just Wrong: The Aftermath of Wrongful Convictions, From Crime Victims to Exonerees,* featuring three exonerees and three crime victims or survivors whose lives were impacted by a wrongful conviction. Watch the documentary and learn more about the lives of these crime victims and exonerees after the convictions were reversed: https://www.nij.gov/multimedia/Pages/video-just-wrong.aspx (19:40).

10. *Exonerees and Criminal Records:* After an exoneration, expunging an exoneree's criminal record may take months or years. Evan Mandery and Amy Shlosberg studied 118 exonerees only to find that 1/3 of them still had their criminal records, even up to ten years after the conviction was reversed. The process for expungement varies state to state. You can read more in this article by Jack Healy, *Wrongfully Convicted Often Find Their Record, Unexpunged, Haunts Them.* THE NEW YORK TIMES, May 5, 2013: http://www.nytimes.com/2013/05/06/us/wrongfully-convicted-find-their-record-haunts-them.html.

Appendix: Wrongful Convictions Podcasts

Below is a short list of podcasts on wrongful convictions. Please note the extensive list of films and books available at: http://forejustice.org/biblio/bibliography.htm.

West Memphis Three, Arkansas:
True Crime Garage (2016):
https://truecrimegarage.podbean.com/e/west-memphis-3-part-1-40/

California:
The CIP Podcast, California Innocence Project:
https://californiainnocenceproject.org/cip-podcast/

Florida:
Murder on the Spacecoast, Season One and Two, Florida Today (2016, 2017):
https://soundcloud.com/murderonthespacecoast

Justin Chapman, Tex McIver, Georgia:
Breakdown, Season 1 and Season 5, Atlanta Journal-Constitution (2015, 2018):
https://www.myajc.com/voices/breakdown/

Quad Cities, Iowa:
Suspect Convictions, Season One and Season Two, NPR/WVIK (2017, 2018):
http://www.suspectconvictions.com/

Robert Jones, New Orleans, Louisiana:
Robert Jones, Free at Last?, BBC (2015):
https://www.bbc.co.uk/programmes/p03bmp0b

Adnan Syed, Baltimore, Maryland:
Serial, Season One (2014):
https://serialpodcast.org/season-one

John Ortiz-Kehoe, Michigan:
Creating a Cannibal (2017):
https://player.fm/series/creating-a-cannibal-a-podcast

Curtis Flowers, Mississippi:
In the Dark, Season Two, APM Reports (2018):
https://www.apmreports.org/in-the-dark/season-two

Kansas City, Missouri:
Reveal, the Centre for Investigative Reporting:
https://dts.podtrac.com/redirect.mp3/media.blubrry.com/reveal/cdn-
       reveal.prx.org/wp-content/uploads/Fire-and-Justice_128.mp3

Calvin Buari, Bronx, New York:
Empire on Blood, Panoply (2018):
https://empireonblood.panoply.fm

Ricky Jackson, Cleveland, Ohio:
StoryCorps 521: Rickey and Eddie, StoryCorps (January 10, 2018) (13:21):
https://storycorps.org/podcast/storycorps-521-rickey-and-eddie/

Bob Young, Cincinnati, Ohio:
Accused, Season One and Two, Cincinnati Enquirer (2016-2017):
https://www.cincinnati.com/series/accused/

Eugene Clawson, West Virginia:
Mared & Karen: The WVU Coed Murders, Kromatic Media (2017-2018)
http://kromatic.media/#mared-karen-the-wvu-coed-murders

NATIONAL:

Actual Innocence (2016-2018):
https://www.borrowedequipmentpods.com/actual-innocence

Crime in Color (2018-present):
https://player.fm/series/crime-in-color

Exonerated and Broke, Newsbeat (2017):
https://www.usnewsbeat.com/2017/09/18/exonerated-and-broke/

Medill Justice Project, Northwestern University (2016-2017) (SBS):
http://apple.co/2abBR90

Undisclosed (2015 – present):
http://undisclosed-podcast.com

Wrongful Conviction with Jason Flom (2016 – present):
https://art19.com/shows/wrongful-conviction-with-jason-flom

INTERNATIONAL:

Australia:
Wrongful: Stories of Justice Denied and Redeemed, Earshot (2017-present):
http://www.abc.net.au/radionational/programs/earshot/features/wrongful-stories-of-
       justice-denied-and-redeemed/

Guy Paul Morin, Toronto, Canada:
The exoneration of Guy Paul Morin (2018):
http://1995podcast.libsyn.com/the-exoneration-of-guy-paul-morin-part-1

Index